Hidden Architectures of Information Literacy Programs

Structures, Practices, and Contexts

edited by Carolyn Caffrey Gardner, Elizabeth Galoozis, and Rebecca Halpern

Association of College and Research Libraries
A division of the American Library Association
Chicago, Illinois 2020

The paper used in this publication meets the minimum requirements of American National Standard for Information Sciences–Permanence of Paper for Printed Library Materials, ANSI Z39.48-1992. ∞

Library of Congress Control Number: 2020939252

Copyright ©2020 by the Association of College and Research Libraries.

All rights reserved except those which may be granted by Sections 107 and 108 of the Copyright Revision Act of 1976.

Printed in the United States of America.

24 23 22 21 20 5 4 3 2 1

Table of Contents

TEACHING TEAM MODEL

Describes IL programs where the instruction work is conducted by a team, unit, or department dedicated to teaching

SUBJECT LIAISON MODEL

Describes IL programs where the instruction work is distributed through dedicated subject liaison teams

COMBINATION OF TEACHING TEAM AND SUBJECT LIAISON MODELS

Describes IL programs where the instruction work is conducted by some kind of combination of a dedicated teaching team and a liaison model

SOLO LIBRARIAN MODEL

Describes IL programs led by one individual

FOCUSED ON A FOR-CREDIT COURSE

Describes IL programs where a for-credit course is a core element of the IL program

Foreword

Suchi Mohanty

When Carolyn, Elizabeth, and Rebecca approached me to write this foreword, I was intrigued. I am usually drawn toward publications that lean to the practical rather than the theoretical, publications that I can apply immediately to my work. I am happy to say that this book didn't disappoint. The editors have assembled a set of profiles of diverse institutions that highlight the day-to-day work of running and coordinating information literacy programs and the soft skills necessary for success in the coordinator role. The included authors reflect thoughtfully on the strengths of their programs and areas for growth. They discuss the institutional context into which their work fits and the many varied duties that they balance. When I was a new information literacy coordinator many years ago, this kind of resource would have been invaluable. I would have been reassured to know that my professional experiences were no different from those of my peers and to learn from the experiences of other librarians. Any reader will find something to improve their practice in these pages.

My experiences were no different from those of many new instruction librarians, and every position has its own challenges. I began my professional career at the same institution where I earned my master's in library science degree. The University of North Carolina at Chapel Hill—both then and now—has a decentralized information literacy initiative. The information literacy program for the First Year Writing program is coordinated by staff from the R. B. House Undergraduate Library, part of the University Libraries. All first-year students are required to take a writing class in this program, and all classes are required to have a research component. An information literacy workshop is required, although attendance is not tracked or enforced, by writing program administrators. Subject librarians in the main, special collections, and branch libraries manage their own activities for upper-level undergraduate and graduate information literacy instruction and sometimes provide information literacy instruction for the First Year Writing program. In addition to librarian instructors, graduate students from UNC's School of Information and Library Science are employed by the library as graduate assistants. They conduct information literacy sessions under the guidance of a librarian supervisor.

My first professional position was to coordinate information literacy instruction for the First Year Writing program. Descriptive of nothing, my title was Reference and Instruction Librarian. As with many of the contributing authors, among my "coordinator" duties were to provide outreach to the First Year Writing instructors (who were mainly graduate students), market available library resources, handle all the logistics of requested instruction (scheduling an instruction lab, assigning a library instructor, connecting faculty member and library staff), train and mentor graduate student library instructors, coordinate the libraries' participation in summer orientation and fall welcome events, and serve as a resource to colleagues who wanted to learn more about first-year students. While I taught a large number of sessions myself, I also relied on goodwill and buy-in from other library instructors to meet the demand for in-person information literacy sessions.

Coordinating seasoned professionals and new professionals was certainly a challenge—one that several authors touch on in their profiles. The only staff I directly supervised were graduate student employees, some of whom I had been in class with just months before. They looked to me as the expert, even though I was still finding my own professional footing. It was relatively easy for us to come together as a team with a common instructional philosophy. On the other hand, I was also asking full-time librarians who did not report to me to participate in first-year instruction—librarians who had varying information literacy philosophies of their own. Adding another layer of complexity, most of those librarians had been my supervisors when I was a graduate student employee in the campus library system. I learned quickly that diplomacy and quiet influence were the most effective ways to shape information literacy offerings and to advocate for our first-year students.

As I read through the book, it was exciting to see the common themes woven through each chapter and to relate them back to my earlier experiences as an information literacy coordinator. Many program coordinators I've worked with struggle to balance instructional demands with limited resources, to explain to faculty why their support is crucial to help student development, and to weave a cohesive information literacy program among teaching colleagues throughout a library organization. Authors from the Auraria Library explore how to execute the duties inherent in coordinator roles, such as handling the logistics of an active teaching program, scaffolding information literacy content, marketing instruction and research services, assessing student learning, designing professional development opportunities for librarians *and* faculty instructors, and mentoring peer librarians. Contributors from Ozarks Technical Community College explore how to deliver high-quality instruction within the constraints of their human and financial resources. The author from UNC Greensboro explores the soft skills of influence needed to successfully lead and coordinate an information literacy program—diplomacy, advocacy, and cooperation. The author from Lafayette College notes the important role of networking in building support for an information literacy program—no matter how large or small the institution; helping campus partners understand the role of information literacy in student success is key to the success of any instruction program.

If you have been managing an information program, the main question you might be asking yourself is "Why should I read this work?" In short, there is something in this work to inspire anyone who provides information literacy instruction—frontline instructors, new instruction coordinators, and veteran program administrators. The authors provide plain talk about the challenges and opportunities in coordinating an information literacy program and honest reflection on their work and their institutions. They offer practical advice on how they balance the competing demands on their time and how to effectively collaborate with colleagues. This work will help us think beyond the confines of our daily work to learn from others about how we can most effectively accomplish our goals with the limited resources most of us face. Whether you are at a community college or a research-intensive university, I am hopeful that you will be able to find something valuable to help you take your work a step further.

Suchi Mohanty
Head, R. B. House Undergraduate Library
University of North Carolina at Chapel Hill

Introduction

Carolyn Caffrey Gardner, Elizabeth Galoozis, and Rebecca Halpern

Why We Wrote This

Why this book? When I (Carolyn here) got my first job out of library school I was working as an instruction librarian at the University of Wisconsin - Superior (UWS). I was thrilled! I came directly from graduate school at Indiana University Bloomington, a huge, research-intensive university with multiple libraries, where I had been one of many on an instruction team. At UWS I was one of three librarians total, and the "coordinator" of instruction by default as the only librarian who taught. I was ready! I wouldn't call what I stepped into a full-fledged program, but I was excited to build one. Being a new, enthusiastic professional, I started looking for general guidance and information on how to build an information literacy (IL) program. While I could find tons of information on pedagogy, individual lesson plans, instruction statistics, and at the time, the ACRL *Information Literacy Competency Standards for Higher Education*, I couldn't find much on holistic program development.[1] I searched for a workbook. I wanted a step-by-step list of what to do. And while I had taken coursework in information literacy instruction, those courses did not include anything on program development. I eventually found the ACRL *Characteristics of Programs of Information Literacy that Illustrate Best Practices*,[2] but I didn't see my one-person program reflected in the 2012 version. It seemed impossible for a one-person program to meet the best practices in the staffing section or have formalized articulation in the curriculum as laid out in the document.

Around the same time, I met my friend, Jamie White-Farnham, a writing program administrator at UWS. Like all good friends, Jamie helped me grow as a person, but uniquely she also helped me grow as a scholar. She introduced me to the world of writing program administrator literature and scholarship—authors such as Barry Maid, Barbara D'Angelo, and Elizabeth Wardle and Linda Adler-Kassner, and organizations like Council of Writing Program Administrators.[3] Years later, Jamie and I have been connected again through "scholarship as a conversation." I read her collection coedited with Bryna Siegel Finer, *Writing Program Architecture: Thirty Cases for Reference and Research* and was awestruck![4] This conversation, which they so expertly facilitated for writing programs, is exactly the type of conversation we need to be having in libraries. Their work exposes the contextual bureaucracies that shape and develop writing programs. It is useful for program administrators and participants alike in understanding how individual activities and actions come together to form a cohesive program.

Hidden Architectures of Information Literacy Programs is indebted to their scholarship, and all of the contributors in their book as a model for this one you're now reading. Much like the happenstance of friendship that led to reading a book on writing programs, Carolyn and Elizabeth initially met at ACRL Immersion Program Track in 2012. Years later, we all, including Rebecca, worked at University of Southern California Libraries, and our passion for instruction resulted in us staying in touch and relying on each other as a community of practice even as job opportunities led us elsewhere. Carolyn proposed the book idea after a late-night information literacy coordinator rant text chain, and Rebecca and Elizabeth graciously were on board. Much of the impetus for this book came from these informal networks that get built over time to provide support, ask questions, and bounce ideas around. In particular, we want to acknowledge and thank Sofia Leung for the creation of a private Slack channel for information literacy coordinators in April 2017. This channel has been a great source of inspiration and sharing program documents not necessarily accessible on a public-facing web page. This book would not have fully materialized without the channel revealing the need to us to bring this conversation out fully in our publications.

Hidden Architectures of Information Literacy Programs is an attempt to capture some of the tacit knowledge information literacy coordinators accumulate through trial and error and informal conversations with professional networks. It's still not the step-by-step manual I craved as a new professional, because now I know that kind of rigid how-to instruction wouldn't work for the diversity of the programs and institutions that can and do exist. This book attempts to capture the conversations that don't typically make it into our scholarly literature. It details practices of IL programs that aren't just "innovative" but are the core functions of our jobs day in and day out. This book is for the late-night Slack conversations with coordinators on how you respond to a difficult professor over email. This book is for the conference hallway question about if you're read that article about the demise of the one-shot and how would that even work at your library. Our goal is to expose the mechanics of what makes a program in its entirety, including the invisible inner workings. While this book may be most useful for those who coordinate or lead instruction programs in all their forms, we think it also plays an important role in making all information literacy program labor visible, raising its importance, and encouraging more scholarship on what might seem like the "boring" parts of program development—with a critical eye to why program development hasn't been a focus of scholarship. We hope that these program descriptions help to provide inspiration or affirmation for your own instruction program.

Our Process

Because this book is all about uncovering the hidden work and underlying structures of information literacy programs, it seems only fair that we uncover the work of putting a book like this one together. As participants in ACRL's Immersion Program, we were familiar with, and appreciative of the need for, uncovering our own assumptions about information literacy programs. We began by explicitly stating our assumptions about what makes an information program strategic, successful, and good. One of Elizabeth's was "The people who lead them are usually doing so without explicit authority or supervisory responsibilities." As you will read, this assumption was based on individual experience and that situation is far from common to all institutions. Carolyn, on the other hand, described her assumption that all successful IL programs require similar amounts of enthusiasm and pedagogical knowledge from all librarians. Rebecca noted her assumption that a good IL program should have complete buy-in from campus constituents. We attempted, in the chapter template, to challenge our own assumptions and make room for every kind of program, including for instruction activities that may not be considered a "program" by the librarians involved. We did this because we had a hunch that our assumptions about what makes a program "good" might be commonly shared and that we could use some of those assumptions as the basis of what we'd want our authors to discuss. We also used challenges to our own assumptions to make sure that we created a call for proposals that resonated with all instruction programs, not just those that fit into our preconceived notions.

Individually, we each wrote abstracts for our book-to-be to help us navigate a shared vision. We made connections, looked for commonalities, and sorted out differences to combine our voices into a single abstract. With a clear understanding of the kind of book we wanted to write, we could start building a structure of how each case study would look. Because *Writing Program Architecture* was our original source of inspiration, we borrowed heavily from, and adapted the structure of, those case studies. We drafted descriptions of each chapter section based on what was revealed in our assumption-hunting exercises and in the kinds of conversations our network of program coordinators have. We had a purpose! We had a structure! And, with purpose and structure, we had the foundation for a call for proposals (CFP).

Once the proposal was submitted and accepted, the real work began. We cleaned up our CFP and distributed it as widely as we could via email discussion lists and personal requests from our networks of colleagues. Using the CFP as a guideline, we developed a rubric to help us assess the proposals we received; the rubric included criteria of clarity, completeness, and broad appeal. We evaluated each proposal individually, then came together to as a team to review our evaluations and reach consensus. This sounds easier than it was—we couldn't do this in a single meeting, and choosing proposals based not only on their own merit but also on how each one would fit into the whole of the book was the most difficult part of the entire process. We were extremely pleased to get seventy submissions for the book, 54 percent of which we accepted. We chose the chapters you see here to represent a range of program and institution types. These chapters represent snapshots in time from a specific group of people—in a few cases, authors changed institutions during the writing process. Some initiatives described are at their very beginning; some authors are dealing with very recent reorganizations. This variety captures the changeable and complicated nature of all programs, and we're so grateful to our authors, who showed vulnerability in talking about all parts of their programs, not just the parts that run smoothly or serve as exemplars. Some authors needed to drop out of the book because of concerns about internal politics. We can imagine that potential authors didn't even submit proposals for the same reason. We want to acknowledge that writing honestly about all parts of the program, including its imperfections, is hard, and not possible for everyone.

After we selected the chapters, we collaboratively drafted emails to inform all submitters of our decisions. In order for the process to be as organized and painless as possible for those that were accepted, we consulted with our ACRL editor (more than once) to ensure that we were fully aware of the timeline and process so that we could communicate that to our authors. We had to establish the workflow of how to get chapters to us, for how we would edit them, for how we would ensure as much transparency as possible.

Google Docs was the cornerstone of this process. We had the chapter authors draft their chapters in Google Docs. Each chapter manuscript was placed in a shared folder that all three editors had access to, but not the authors of other chapters. We assigned each author a primary editor so that they would have a single point of contact. Each chapter underwent three revisions. Each chapter was reviewed by its primary editor and a second editor. We rotated the second editor on subsequent drafts so all three editors read every chapter at least once. Within the editing team, we used Slack to avoid endless email threads and inbox glut.

We would like to thank Ray Pun for giving us invaluable advice in the proposal process and Erin Nevius for being an excellent guide in the writing and editing of this collection.

What We Asked

To frame our proposal and structure our chapter template, we wanted the answers to the questions we had when we were just starting out and the ones we have as we move into the future. As we stated in our call for proposals, we were "looking for the realities of coordinating a program in its entirety and not just best practices or one shiny project."

Specifically we asked authors to respond to the following:

- *Population served:* What kind of institution do you work at? Who are the students there? How does this shape what your program does?
- *Program scope:* First year, all undergrads, capstone/thesis, something else? What types of instruction do you do? Workshops? Tutorials? Online or in-person?
- *Operations:* What is the staffing of your program like?
- *Marketing:* Are you actively recruiting one-shot instruction? How?
- *Collaboration:* Do you lead workshops on information literacy on your campus? Who are your biggest allies on campus, and how do you work together?
- *Assessment:* How does your program navigate campus assessment processes? Do you have formal assessment or review of your program? How do you assess student learning?
- *Role of the one-shot:* How does program relate to the one-shot? Is it an uneasy tension, your bread and butter, or something in between?
- *Pedagogical highlights:* What do you teach in your program? How do you create a community of practice around teaching? What is the role of IL inside and outside of the curriculum?
- *Administrative highlights:* Is there a way you administer your program that you're particularly proud of? A sweet calendaring system? A jazzy mission statement?
- *Information literacy coordinator profile:* How did you come to coordinate the teaching activities at your library? Is this role formal or informal? Is it in title or practice only?
- *What you wish people knew:* What about coordinating your program surprised you? Is there advice you would give to others? What kind of hidden labor keeps your program running? Are there skills that you had to develop that you didn't necessarily think you would need?

Not every chapter has responded to every set of questions, so while you will see similar headings across chapters, you may not see every heading in every chapter.

Themes in Chapters

These chapters are about what programs really look like. They are filled with making compromises, acknowledging limitations, and doing a lot with a little. Most importantly, they are deeply contextual. Each program is connected to the cultures of its institutions and libraries and to the particular needs of its communities. In the first round of editing, we often found ourselves curious about a term or acronym so ingrained in the author's culture that it seemed obvious and without need for explanation. Like the assumptions we made as editors, authors made assumptions too, and looking at the breadth of chapters and perspectives let us know that we really could not take anything for granted on the part of readers. It was really interesting for us to read about the ways in which local contexts and priorities intersected with pedagogy, best practices, and guiding documents like the ACRL *Framework for Information Literacy for Higher Education*.[5]

Michael LaMagna, for example, discusses a close alignment with college learning goals at Delaware County Community College, while Don LaPlant connects IL programming with the applied nature of curricula at SUNY Cobleskill. Discussing Wheaton College, Joshua M. Avery and Cathy Troupos detail the process of aligning with a new general education curriculum. And David Vrooman describes a collaboration common to many other chapters, with introductory composition classes, at Eastern Connecticut State University.

Many of these chapters speak to the delicate balancing act of labor distribution. Some coordinators wrote about not placing undue burdens on the librarians they rely on to teach. Jennifer Beach at Longwood University, for example, talks about piloting new approaches and teaching for high-demand departments herself before asking fellow librarians to join in. Sarah H. Mabee and Sarah E. Fancher at Ozarks Technical Community College describe the parameters they have developed for accepting library instruction requests in order to avoid burnout in a small staff and make instruction meaningful. And Veronica Arellano Douglas at the University of Houston describes the clout she has as a coordinator to negotiate with course instructors on behalf of the librarians she supervises. Several chapters, especially those discussing programs with a small number of librarians, describe standardizing or sharing instructional materials to make teaching and learning consistent, but also to reduce individual librarians' instructional planning time. There is a particular emphasis on this in the chapters about the University of Northern Colorado by Lyda Fontes McCartin, Georgia State University by Karen Doster-Greenleaf, Saint Mary's College of California by Gina Kessler Lee and Conrad Woxland, and the University of Nevada, Reno, by Rosalind Bucy, Elsa De Jong, Tati Mesfin, and Rayla E. Tokarz.

Other authors deal with minimal or absent positional authority paired with needing to make decisions and ask people to do things, mentioned earlier by Elizabeth. For some highlighted descriptions of this phenomenon, check out the chapters on the University of New Hampshire by Kathrine C. Aydelott, UNC Greensboro by Jenny Dale, and the University of Maryland, Baltimore County, by Joanna Gadsby and Katy Sullivan.

Finally, a common theme for our authors was that of emotional labor and other "soft" or interpersonal skills required to successfully coordinate a program. Kaitlin Springmier at

Sonoma State University discusses the need to manage staff, student, and faculty emotions; generate buy-in for programmatic goals and approaches; and maintain positive relationships throughout the organization. Liza Harrington, Tim Dolan, and Claire Lobdell of Greenfield Community College discuss how the process for creating programmatic documents can be more beneficial for creating a shared vision than the documents themselves. Other chapters that discuss the hidden, and often taxing, requirements for emotional intelligence and emotion work are Lafayette College by Lijuan Xu and University of California, Riverside by Dani Brecher Cook.

Who Is This Book For?

This book is for you, new graduate student, learning about information literacy programs, maybe even doing that dreaded observe-a-teaching-librarian assignment where you're seeing the tiniest bit of a program. It's for you, administrator, who maybe have never taught an information literacy session. It's for you, instruction librarian, to understand the breadth and depth of a program that you're a part of. It's for you, non-librarian educator or administrator, to see what is out there in the world of IL programming. We hope that all of these audiences will find something of value in this book.

Alternative Organization of the Book

We want this book to be as useful and accessible as possible but realize that knowing how to compare your program to another's can be fraught and complicated. When trying to decide how to organize our book, we could see the merits in organizing by program type—so, say, for instance, if you have a solo-librarian program, you can see examples of how others in your situation manage things—and by type of institution—so you can see how, for instance, liberal arts colleges run a program. We ultimately couldn't decide, so we chose both. Because this is a practical guide, our primary organization is by program type. But you'll see below that we provide an alternative organization structure by type of institution according to broad Carnegie Classifications—the best of both options. We developed the program type categories after reading through all the chapters and consulting with the authors; each category is then organized alphabetically by institution name. Teaching team models are IL programs where the instruction work is conducted by a team of individuals (formal or informal), unit, or department dedicated to instruction. A subject liaison model describes IL programs where instruction work is distributed primarily through a dedicated subject liaison team. The combination of a teaching team and liaison model describes IL programs where the instruction work is organized by some kind of mix of both options. The programs in the solo librarian model option are IL programs organized and executed by one librarian. Finally, we also have some programs that are organized primarily around a credit-bearing course. We encourage you to pick out and read the ones that speak to you!

Community College

- Delaware County Community College (Public)—chapter 14
- Greenfield Community College (Public)—chapter 4
- Ozarks Technical Community College (Public)—chapter 33
- Saddleback College (Public)—chapter 9

Liberal Arts College

- Augustana College (Private)—chapter 22
- Eastern Connecticut State University (Public)—chapter 24
- Lafayette College (Private)—chapter 5
- Paul Smith's College (Private)—chapter 34
- Sonoma State University (Public)—chapter 17
- Wheaton College (Private - Religious)—chapter 31

Research-Intensive Doctoral Granting

- Michigan State University (Public)—chapter 6
- UNC Greensboro (Public)—chapter 25
- University of California, Riverside (Public)—chapter 10
- University of Houston (Public)—chapter 27
- University of Maryland, Baltimore County (Public)—chapter 39
- University of Nevada, Las Vegas (Public)—chapter 28
- University of Nevada, Reno (Public)—chapter 11
- University of New Hampshire (Public)—chapter 19
- University of Southern California (Private)—chapter 20
- Utah State University (Public)—chapter 12
- Washington University in St. Louis (Private)—chapter 21

Master's Comprehensive

- California State University, Dominguez Hills (Public)—chapter 13
- California State University San Marcos (Public)—chapter 2
- Longwood University (Public)—chapter 15
- Northern Kentucky University (Public)—chapter 7
- Saint Mary's College of California (Private—Religious)—chapter 16
- State University of New York at Plattsburgh (Public)—chapter 37
- University of Dubuque (Private—Religious)—chapter 26
- University of Minnesota Duluth (Public)—chapter 18
- University of Northern Colorado (Public)—chapter 38
- University of Portland (Private)—chapter 29
- Worcester State University (Public)—chapter 32

Consortial Libraries

- Auraria Library (Public)—chapter 1
- The Claremont Colleges Library (Private)—chapter 23

- Georgia State University (Public)—chapter 3
- University of Washington Bothell/Cascadia College (Public)—chapter 30

Specialized

- Mary Baldwin University (Private)—chapter 36
- Oxford College of Emory University (Private)—chapter 8
- State University of New York College of Agriculture and Technology at Cobleskill (Public)—chapter 35

Notes

1. Association of College and Research Libraries, *Information Literacy Competency Standards for Higher Education* (Chicago: Association of College and Research Libraries, 2000).
2. Association of College and Research Libraries, *Characteristics of Programs of Information Literacy That Illustrate Best Practices* (Chicago: Association of College and Research Libraries, June 2003, rev. January 2012).
3. Barry Maid and Barbara D'Angelo, "The WPA Outcomes, Information Literacy, and Challenges of Outcomes-Based Curricular Design," in *Teaching and Assessing Writing: A Twenty-Fifth Anniversary Celebration*, ed. Norbert Elliot and Les Perelman (New York: Hampton Press, 2012), 99–112; Linda Adler-Kassner and Elizabeth Wardle, eds., *Naming What We Know* (Logan: Utah State University Press, 2015); Council of Writing Program Administrators home page, accessed May 8, 2019, http://wpacouncil.org.
4. Bryna Siegel Finer and Jamie White-Farnham, eds., *Writing Program Architecture* (Logan: Utah State University Press, 2017).
5. Association of College and Research Libraries, *Framework for Information Literacy for Higher Education* (Chicago: Association of College and Research Libraries, 2016), http://www.ala.org/acrl/standards/ilframework.

Bibliography

Adler-Kassner, Linda, and Elizabeth Wardle, eds. *Naming What We Know: Threshold Concepts of Writing Studies*. Salt Lake City: Utah State University Press, 2015.

Association of College and Research Libraries. *Characteristics of Programs of Information Literacy That Illustrate Best Practices: A Guideline*. Chicago: Association of College and Research Libraries, June 2003, rev. January 2012.

———. *Framework for Information Literacy for Higher Education*. Chicago: Association of College and Research Libraries, 2016. http://www.ala.org/acrl/standards/ilframework.

———. *Information Literacy Competency Standards for Higher Education*. Chicago: Association of College and Research Libraries, 2000.

Council of Writing Program Administrators home page. Accessed May 8, 2019. http://wpacouncil.org.

Finer, Bryna Siegel, and Jamie White-Farnham, eds. *Writing Program Architecture: Thirty Cases for Reference and Research* (Logan: Utah State University Press, 2017).

Maid, Barry, and Barbara D'Angelo. "The WPA Outcomes, Information Literacy, and Challenges of Outcomes-Based Curricular Design." In *Teaching and Assessing Writing: A Twenty-Fifth Anniversary Celebration*. Edited by Norbert Elliot and Les Perelman, 99–112. New York: Hampton Press, 2012.

Chapter 1

Auraria Library
Team Approach at a Tri-institutional Library

Andrea Falcone

Population Served

In spring 2015, I stepped into a newly designed role at the Auraria Library, Department Head for Education and Outreach Services. We are employed by the University of Colorado Denver; however, the Auraria Library serves three separate institutions: the Community College of Denver, Metropolitan State University of Denver, and the University of Colorado Denver. Because of the wide-reaching academic programs and our location in the heart of downtown Denver, we have quite a diverse campus. One illustration of our diversity is the fact that the Community College of Denver and Metropolitan State University of Denver both hold the distinction of being Hispanic-Serving Institutions. My position was charged with evolving an ad hoc instruction program into a strategic and sustainable one serving over 42,000 students with a broad spectrum of curricular needs ranging from general education credits to doctoral programs. Since our 150-acre commuter campus is quite complex (think three administrations, three composition departments, three learning management systems, three writing centers, etc.), it was important to establish our new department as consistent with our mission and to have a proactive philosophy about our work.

Program Scope

To be transparent, the library instruction program is overcoming a somewhat disreputable past. Roughly five years prior, the library, for a variety of reasons, retracted from teaching one-shot information literacy sessions for foundational courses, such as composition and public speaking, and instead relied on customized vendor tutorials to satisfy most instructional needs. This change was also coupled, perhaps coincidentally, with some staff retirements. While I cannot be certain how those changes transpired, I did witness the long-term effects. To name a few: the librarians felt undervalued, there was a lack of communication with academic departments about their information literacy needs, the online content was outdated, the purpose or scope for the department was unclear, and the department no longer had ownership over its physical classroom spaces. The ambition of the library leadership was to create a nationally recognized instruction program, and I also felt a responsibility to the department to reinvigorate their sense of value. Of course, I also knew we needed to successfully contribute to students' learning experiences. To achieve all this, we needed to reenvision our instruction program. After I gained some initial understanding of my new work environment and culture, we began our evolution. That work, in a general sense, encompassed establishing program-level student learning outcomes, embracing shared information literacy curricula and assessments, rebalancing faculty workloads, resuming ownership of newly remodeled teaching spaces, formalizing a peer teaching observation program, and developing two new positions (a Pedagogy and Assessment Lead Librarian and a Graduate Teaching and Learning Librarian). I also formalized our partnerships with campus support offices, which led to a consistent library presence at campus events and trainings. Over the course of a few years, we rebranded ourselves, both within the library and on campus, to focus on student learning outcomes (and assessment) and as the experienced educators I believe us to be.

Our new instruction program primarily consists of one-shot sessions, which are all seventy-five minutes on our campus. We teach approximately 500 sessions per year, and most of the sessions are with undergraduate courses. Given the population we serve, this approach aligns with our campus focus. Most of our programmatic instruction is scaffolded within the curriculum and particular majors, and we have a heavy presence in introductory courses in composition, communications, business, chemistry, and environmental science, to name a few. Much of the programmatic instruction is developed in consultation with program directors or coordinators in order to generate buy-in and full participation from all sections of the same course, likely taught by a multitude of faculty members. These programmatic initiatives are identified by curriculum maps created by our librarians, so we can be assured we are putting our efforts and resources in the right places.

We also receive instruction requests through our online instruction request form. Ideally these are for upper-division courses or electives, but often we receive requests from new faculty members teaching introductory courses who believe students need to know that the library exists. We tactfully steer those faculty members to our self-guided library tour option or try to collaborate on creating a substantial research component for the course, if appropriate. This helps us manage our workload and focus on developing scaffolded experiences. The other area of growth in is graduate offerings, so we hired a dedicated Graduate Teaching and Learning Librarian to lead our initiatives for approximately 5,000 graduate students.

In just a few years, we have proven that we can sustain those (newly revived) partnerships with foundational courses and expand to meet the needs of upper-division and graduate courses.

Operations

We moved away from the subject liaison model and created a dedicated teaching team in 2015. The Education and Outreach Services department has eleven faculty librarians, one staff member, and five to seven graduate assistants, who may or may not be enrolled in a library and information science program. As the department head, I supervise all faculty librarians and rely heavily on two program lead positions; these faculty roles are responsible for overarching functions of the department. The Teaching and Learning Program Lead Librarian focuses on developing online teaching initiatives, reporting statistics, and overseeing the physical classrooms. The Pedagogy and Assessment Program Lead Librarian facilitates our peer teaching observation program and coordinates our student learning assessment projects. We have a few specialized positions (First-Year Teaching and Learning Librarian and Graduate Teaching and Learning Librarian) that take the lead on establishing initiatives for their respective target populations, but most of the other faculty members hold general Teaching and Learning Librarian positions. Each person has a few leadership areas in which to take initiative, for example, special academic program and support offices, including the Honors Program, Veteran Affairs, Summer Bridge, and athletics. The intent is to give librarians flexibility to build their résumés and have some autonomy.

We try to be transparent about these operations and the inner workings of the department to the rest of the library. For example, two years ago we hosted an open house with interactive stations so that library staff could get a better sense of our work and team approach. We also regularly report on our instruction statistics, student learning assessment projects, and curriculum maps during library-wide meetings and provide updates on activities that might impact other library departments in our library's internal newsletter. Reporting on continued progress of the team created its own challenges. As we became successful, colleagues outside the department wanted to be a participate in our department's activities. These interdepartmental tensions necessitated a clearer delineation of roles and responsibilities.

Marketing

This might seem counterintuitive for a campus of our size, but we actively promote one-shots; however, it's done strategically through curriculum mapping. With three institutions, we have to be purposeful in the partnerships we create, which means looking at the overall distribution of instruction sessions and redirecting classes that lack research components to alternatives, such as self-guided library tours and tutorials. We often approach program directors or department chairs rather than individual teaching faculty to promote one-shots. Campus staffing has a significant amount of turnover, so we try to invest our time wisely and talk with individuals who have more political capital and impact on a program. Our approach is to be over-prepared for those discussions by looking at a curriculum map, the course catalog descriptions, and our internal instruction statistics. We bring information about our program-level student learning outcomes, a sample lesson plan or activity, and endorsements from faculty who have been participating in our program. Much of the time is spent listening to the challenges faculty have with information literacy, the library, and their own staffing and time constraints. In most cases, we leave with a commitment to develop a pilot program that we prioritize, teach, assess, and then revisit with those collaborators. We should all be knowledgeable about why we are working with a particular program. It is not happenstance, and it does not rely on personal relationships with individual faculty. It is about strategically scaffolding information literacy into the program's curriculum in a sustainable way.

Collaboration

Drop-in workshops could unintentionally support equity gaps for those students who cannot attend them. Therefore, tying sessions to the curriculum and meeting the students in their classrooms during those designated times is the mindful approach and signals that information literacy is integral to student learning and success. Periodically, we work with support offices to provide workshops that fit within their unique programs. The library also addresses equity concerns by providing supplementary services at the point of need.

Assessment

Assessment was discussed frequently when I first joined the department, but after I reviewed some reports, it became clear that we were indirectly measuring student learning through the perceptions of the faculty. While something is better than nothing, I knew we could evolve in this area. As a department, we established the following program-level student learning outcomes that meld the spirit of the *Framework for Information Literacy for Higher Education* and the former *Information Literacy Competency Standards for Higher Education*,[1] keeping in mind that this was in 2015.

As a result of our instruction, students will be able to:

1. Evaluate information and information sources.
2. Develop a search strategy.
3. Recognize information sources relevant to context or discipline.
4. Identify authoritative information.
5. Recognize that scholarship is an exchange amongst peers.

We develop session-level outcomes that align with the overarching program-level outcomes listed above. We focus on embedding assessments (online worksheets) within the one-shots of the various class sections so that the shared curriculum can be revised for the greatest impact. Everyone (truly everyone) in the department examines that student output, usually with rubrics, and discusses how we can focus on continuous improvement. (One of the first revelations was that we were not challenging students.) This information is shared with the teaching team, the department chairs or program directors, library leadership, and the University of Colorado's Assessment Committee. The reports are also intended to be used for program reviews and accreditation. To continue building upon this good work, I dedicated the Pedagogy and Assessment Lead Librarian position to assessment and the continued evolution of our teaching practices.

Pedagogical Highlights

Since we were rebuilding a program, we created a mission statement that focused on information literacy and program-level learning outcomes (included above), as well as individual teaching philosophies. The creation of this content allowed me to better understand the faculty member's individual perspectives and began unifying us as a team. We also initiated biweekly internal professional development sessions and a peer teaching observation program. Both actions allowed the team to have dedicated time to reflect on teaching and learn more about one another as educators.

Administrative Highlights

To move away from an ad hoc style program that was extremely time-intensive, we developed shared curriculum (and assessments) for multi-section foundational courses (for example, Composition II). One of the Teaching and Learning Librarians distributes these sessions among the teaching team as evenly as possible. When we teach multiple sections of an upper-division course, we designate a lead curriculum designer from our department who works with a smaller team to teach the shared curriculum. Many instruction programs unintentionally overload individual liaison librarians as the library does not determine enrollment growth or course popularity. Our team approach helps equalize workload and allows individuals to gain expertise in as many subject areas as possible. We also employ block scheduling, which means, for example, that we teach all sections of Composition II during designated weeks of the semester. Because the department is staffed for a campus of 15,000 but serves 42,000, we need to be creative in how we approach our instruction workload. Block scheduling greatly reduces time needed for scheduling and instructor preparation: for example, we know that we'll be focusing on all sections of foundational chemistry at Metropolitan State University in week 4 and then University of Colorado Denver Composition II courses in weeks 5 and 6.

Information Literacy Coordinator Profile

My passion for librarianship stems from my love of teaching. I first began teaching composition courses as an English master's student at an urban institution in Toledo, Ohio. Thirteen years later, with a master's in library science and a couple of years of full-time librarianship experience, I found myself leading a department of extraordinary librarians and educators at the University of Northern Colorado. Its program is an exemplary one, consisting of one-shots for foundational courses and a wide range of credit-bearing courses. From there I moved to the University of Colorado Denver to serve as the Department Head for Education and Outreach Services, a newly formed and much larger department. (This was one of two newly designed formal department head roles in 2015, the other being in Researcher Support Services.) In this role, I lead the vision for and development of our teaching activities. I'm not involved in the day-to-day assigning of sessions or communicating with individual faculty about their sessions. Unless there is a concern, our scheduler follows defined processes, and because of the team and programmatic approach, the processes operates fairly smoothly. My focus is on helping our faculty determine priorities, conducting teaching observations, initiating conversations with program directors about developing programmatic instruction pilots, reviewing assessments, and sharing our success stories all over campus.

What I Wish People Knew

When I first joined the department, the librarians wanted to be valued and respected across campus, and unfortunately, in many cases we had a negative reputation to overturn. As challenging as it was, I met with department chairs and program directors to honestly discuss the concerns they had about our instruction, including learning outcomes, the scheduling process, clear and timely communication between instructors, and any concerns with individual librarians. Doing so enabled me to understand the breadth of cultural baggage so that I could begin mending relationships. I don't think most of my colleagues knew how challenging those conversations were and how much pressure there was for us to meet a new set of expectations, ultimately transforming our information literacy program. I spent a lot of time "talking up" our team and emphasizing their individual strengths as educators. Meanwhile, I needed them to prove these statements true by consistently following our procedures and delivering effective sessions. There were many moments where the librarians questioned our approach and resisted doing the work needed, likely because there was no guarantee this challenging evolution would be successful. Every once in a while, skepticism was bluntly expressed in our monthly department meeting, and other times, in quiet dissent, someone fell back on a past process that undermined our team approach. Those were moments of frustration for me and others in the department who were committed to moving forward. However, that's part of change, and quite frankly, human behavior. Since I truly believed in our team's ability to succeed and our approach, the challenge was providing team members with the right support at just the right times. Support came in many forms. Those that were more apparent to the team included development of the team's web page, the peer observation program, biweekly internal professional development sessions, team curriculum development, and successful requests for more personnel resources from library administration. Much of the hidden support was in the form of one-on-one conversations with librarians, encouraging them to believe that their skeptical peers would come around, or with teaching faculty who thought they were better equipped to teach about information literacy (or, in their words, demonstrate the databases) than our librarians. Because I have tremendous respect for my fellow teaching librarians, I never imagined that I would have to convince others of our value. This important work is ongoing, but I feel that we have come a long way toward becoming a team that focuses on student learning, respects one another, and serves as a model for other instruction programs struggling with similar issues.

Note

1. Association of College and Research Libraries, *Framework for Information Literacy for Higher Education* (Chicago: Association of College and Research Libraries, 2016), http://www.ala.org/acrl/sites/ala.org.acrl/files/content/issues/infolit/Framework_ILHE.pdf;Association of College and Research Libraries, *Information Literacy Competency Standards for Higher Education* (Chicago: Association of College and Research Libraries, 2016), https://alair.ala.org/bitstream/handle/11213/7668/ACRL Information Literacy Competency Standards for Higher Education.pdf?sequence=1&isAllowed=y.

Bibliography

Association of College and Research Libraries. *Framework for Information Literacy for Higher Education*. Chicago: Association of College and Research Libraries, 2016. http://www.ala.org/acrl/sites/ala.org.acrl/files/content/issues/infolit/Framework_ILHE.pdf.

———. *Information Literacy Competency Standards for Higher Education*. Chicago: Association of College and Research Libraries, 2000. https://alair.ala.org/bitstream/handle/11213/7668/ACRL Information Literacy Competency Standards for Higher Education.pdf?sequence=1&isAllowed=y.

Chapter 2

California State University San Marcos

Building an Inclusive Team through Collaborative Reflection

Allison Carr, Denise Kane, Talitha Matlin, Yvonne Nalani Meulemans, Lalitha Nataraj, and Judith Opdahl

Population Served

California State University San Marcos (CSUSM) is a comprehensive, rapidly growing four-year public university with 15,000 students. As one of twenty-three campuses of the California State University system, CSUSM serves the students of a specific region, which includes the areas of North County San Diego and Southwest Riverside County. The student body is more diverse than at comparable institutions: significant numbers of students are first-generation college students, veterans, of ethnic backgrounds that are historically under-represented, or have aged out of the foster care system. CSUSM is a designated Hispanic-Serving Institution and an Asian American and Native American Pacific Islander-Serving Institution. Our demographics drive the teaching strategies used in our program and on our campus, including critical and inclusive pedagogies, with an eye toward social justice.

Program Scope

CSUSM's mission and values state a commitment to social justice and to engaging all students in inquiry and research. The Teaching and Learning (TAL) Unit in the CSUSM University Library is a learning laboratory that helps the university achieve this goal. We believe the contemporary academic library can be a place where students learn to be scholars, just as scientists learn in laboratories. TAL library faculty focus on scholarly inquiry and students' development of field-specific expertise so that students can be engaged members of their academic and scholarly communities. We also develop students' abilities in being informed and engaged members of their respective communities.

Information literacy instruction experiences start in the first year through extensive involvement in a credit-bearing, general education, first-year seminar course. Library faculty present a series of lessons where students first develop their Student-Scholar Identity (SSI) that cultivates students' identities as knowledge creators and not just information consumers.[1] This provides a personal, internalized foundation for learning scholarly research skills. Information literacy instruction is also delivered in first-year writing and speech courses, thus providing a holistic foundation for first-year CSUSM students.

Beyond the first year, all TAL library faculty are assigned a portfolio of majors and minors. In this role, library faculty work closely with the college faculty and students to continue the development of students' engagement in research and inquiry. We use a "life span" approach instead of an ad hoc approach to working with programs. This means we consider students' entire experience within a major (and as graduate students) in order to identify appropriate interventions given where students are in the curriculum and what they are being asked to do. By using curriculum mapping, TAL library faculty strategically combine learning experiences (e.g., in-class instruction, online modules, research consultations, etc.) over an entire program rather than in individual courses, ensuring comprehensive coverage of information literacy-related student learning outcomes. Sometimes, close faculty relationships are the way we develop a holistic understanding of academic programs. TAL librarians also work collectively to ensure just-in-time reference and research help for the campus community. This work includes the University Library's physical and virtual Research Help Desk. A focus of this effort is ensuring students have a variety of access points and easy access to librarian expertise.

A guiding principle for TAL faculty is to engage in reflective teaching in order to facilitate student learning, engagement, and development.[2] This is achieved by working collaboratively and inclusively. Few aspects of our work are done solely by individuals. In such an environment, the unit relies on explicitly stated norms and logistics that are practiced daily in the way meetings are conducted, how evaluative practices and policies are written and upheld, and in faculty governance decision-making.

Though in-person class sessions comprise the vast majority of first-year learner instruction, TAL library faculty use flipped teaching and online tutorials to enhance learning and elevate critical discussions in the classroom. We are embedded in several online courses. We effectively deliver learning objects, including instructional videos, library research guides, and tutorials, to both fully online and the more traditional on-campus (or hybrid) courses: around thirteen courses, at last count. Within one major, a librarian monitors discussions in three online courses to answer students' questions about research. These discussion forums also serve as a repository of answers to common challenges facing students to which they can refer back as they progress through their courses.

Essential to this work is our research into the scholarship of teaching and learning, which is considered part of TAL's program scope. TAL library faculty are currently investigating the threshold concept framework, validation theory, relational-cultural theory, and reflective and critical pedagogies, with the ultimate goal of improving student engagement and learning in the unique context in which librarians engage with students. While it is not a stated requirement in their assignments of responsibility, librarians with the rank of lecturer in TAL have also developed research agendas and collaborate with tenure-track and tenured colleagues on presentations and articles.

Operations

TAL consists almost entirely of library faculty. While indeed we are librarians, we make a conscious effort to refer to ourselves as library faculty among ourselves, with college faculty colleagues, and when communicating beyond our campus. We do this in part to make explicit that as faculty, we are partners in facilitating the teaching and learning endeavor of the university. While this practice may appear relatively small, we have as a group found that it can aid in becoming more comfortable and prepared to discuss librarian work within and beyond the University Library. It is a regular occurrence for us to explain the details and reasons for our work, and this focus on language to describe ourselves aids us greatly in making our operations (and therefore, impact on the university) more understood.

As of 2019, the unit has seven tenure-track library faculty, three lecturer library faculty (with renewable contracts), and two staff (one staffer is part-time). As with many academic libraries, our hiring has not kept pace with campus growth. The TAL unit is the sole department responsible for the educational mission of the University Library. In addition to classroom instruction, TAL manages and staffs the reference arm of the University Library, which takes the form of a Research Help Desk (RHD). The RHD is staffed by students who refer specific types of questions to librarians. TAL library faculty are also the subject specialists and are responsible for instruction, research help, and collection development for all programs and majors at CSUSM.

TAL has focused on creating documentation and materials that make explicit our day-to-day operations and long-term vision, with the aim of making transparent to ourselves, the University Library, and the university how we can connect with campus initiatives and efforts. The primary driver for these efforts were and are the unit's, the library's, and the university's rapid growth. After numerous instances in which necessary information either was not communicated or "lived" within an individual's email account or personal memory, the entire department began what is still an ongoing effort to articulate and document our values, vision, and operations.

From the early years of CSUSM, information literacy has been a strong component of the curriculum, but it is strongest in the general education (GE) curriculum. Virtually every GE course, both lower- and upper-division, is required to have disciplinary-appropriate information literacy student learning outcomes. Library faculty can collaborate with college faculty on GE course proposals, as well as participating in the review process. Program-level learning outcomes often have explicitly stated information literacy or inquiry- or research-related outcomes that translate into a formal pathway for library faculty and college faculty collaboration.

Marketing

The work of the TAL department is highly integrated into the curriculum, through long-standing faculty partnerships, and connections to the major and general education curricula. The marketing of library services, writ large, does not fall in within the purview of the TAL unit. We do not view ourselves as a unit offering a service,[3] so we do not approach our work through a marketing lens. Instead, we partner with faculty (and staff when appropriate) to develop and provide learning experiences and opportunities for students. We have found that marketing our expertise can lead to a perception among the campus community that we are service providers who can fulfill requests. We believe strongly that students learn best when librarians and college faculty are partners and collaborators in teaching and learning. While this may seem a simple argument in semantics, we have found it to be imperative in considering our identity and positionality on campus, and as faculty.

Collaboration

As mentioned in the previous section, our success as librarians depends on the collaborations and partnerships we build and maintain. In addition to our work with disciplinary faculty, we also have strong partnerships with various groups on campus, including all of the first-year experience courses, the Faculty Center, and specialized programs such as the Equal Opportunity Program, the Veteran's Center, ACE Scholars Services (former foster youth), a Transfer Student Success Course, and the Writing Center.

While we have a strong philosophy about partnering rather than serving, we are hyper-aware that the only way we can be successful in educating students is through relationships with faculty. Without general workshops, or credit information literacy courses, we rely fully on establishing, developing, and maintaining relationships with the ultimate goal of college faculty understanding of how we can successfully work with them to assist our students in their journey to becoming student-scholars and engaged citizens.

Our most robust curricular partnership is with our first-year courses. First-year students are required to complete General Education Oral Communication (GEO), General Education Writing (GEW), and General Education Lifelong Learning (GEL) within their first year. These courses (affectionately referred to as GEOWL) account for a large portion of the shared work within TAL. All library faculty in TAL are responsible for teaching a portion of the total information literacy curriculum of the GEOWL courses each semester. The TAL curriculum is shared, and thus consistent across all library sessions. Up until recently, the course coordinators and librarians did not collaborate on any part of the curriculum. The Academic Transitions Librarian position was created to coordinate the library instruction for these courses, as well as meetings between the various course coordinators. This allowed TAL library faculty to map curriculum across the course and also coordinate assessment. While we don't know which semester students take each course, we can rely on the fact that all first-year students will take all three courses in their first year. Our strong relationship with these programs has ensured that first-year students attend at least three library sessions within their first year, which provides them a solid foundation upon which to build and develop their student-scholar identity. Content is not scaffolded, as students can take courses in any order, but there are distinct learning outcomes for each session.

Working with the CSUSM Faculty Center provides our first contact with new CSUSM faculty, who have most likely moved from a more traditional research-focused library at their doctoral university to the much more teaching- and learning-focused CSUSM Library. Each year, during the weeklong orientation for new faculty, TAL librarians meet new faculty in an informal meet-and-greet, as well as providing a more formal presentation on how TAL works with faculty and students. From these interactions with new faculty, we have built partnerships that will support our students for years to come.

In the Transfer Student Success course, the instructional components are not assignment-driven, but instead help transfer students understand the difference between the type of research assignments they completed at their community college and what they will do while at CSUSM. For example, some of our community college students haven't used many peer-reviewed journal articles to support their arguments in a paper. Other students may not have had experience collecting articles for a literature review to contextualize original research. Providing general library orientation to these groups has proven useful both in the practical sense of conveying understanding of how to use the library and library tools, and also in helping new transfer students feel supported as members of the CSUSM community.

As with many libraries, TAL's collaboration with the Writing Center is a natural fit. This relationship has grown over the years to include a much more robust collaboration to best support students writing research papers. Most recently, Writing Center tutors have started attending instructional sessions for first-year writing courses that help students understand how to use databases to find scholarly articles. Their attendance serves two purposes: It shows visible support of the Writing Center of first-year students, and the tutors have a broader perspective on the assignments students are completing. Behind the scenes, the Writing Center Director has been integral in developing shared pedagogical approaches to engaging students in research and inquiry.

Assessment

At CSUSM, every degree-granting department must submit documentation regarding its assessment activities. Although TAL is exempt from this requirement, assessment activities take place in several ways. Each year, we conduct assessment that focuses on the first-year curriculum. This can range from including a question related to information literacy in the first-year student survey conducted by the campus assessment office to a concerted effort to collect all student work from a particular in-class activity that we then evaluate as a group to determine whether the activity is helping students achieve stated learning outcomes.

In addition, librarians with liaison responsibilities to specific departments are expected to engage in appropriate assessment activities in light of the scope and nature of each individual librarian's work done with their programs. For example, an individual librarian might work with a disciplinary faculty member to work through common issues exhibited in research assignments to develop a more robust and guided assignment.

Most important, though, is the value placed on reflective teaching by the TAL librarians. Reflective teaching, critical pedagogy, and related theories serve as frameworks that are commonly employed in the unit. Some library faculty engage in formal peer observations, while in other situations, readings and discussion among TAL faculty are done to address identified areas of struggle (e.g., considering diverse and inclusive approaches to motivating learning) and potential solutions.

It is also necessary to note we are active in campus assessment efforts, which include working on the university's Assessment Council, aiding in general education assessment, and leading the curriculum mapping of information literacy components of the first-year general education courses. This particular activity inspired more collaborative efforts among the coordinators of these three courses.

Role of the One-Shot

The "one-shot" has its place, but we have found it is often the "first shot" of many we have with students, and as a result, we can use different instructional approaches as we interact with students multiple times. Working in a collaborative manner with faculty, TAL library faculty determine and develop information literacy instructional approaches and, where relevant, learning objects and activities that deliver meaningful information literacy instruction to CSUSM students. In-class instruction is almost always paired with pre-homework, labs, or flipped or online components.

Due to the high level of integration and the infusion of information literacy across the curriculum, TAL library faculty see the role of the one-shot instructional model as an opening statement to a larger conversation. This "conversation" has been with individual faculty, with entire departments, or through curriculum mapping. A typical one-shot often results in the beginning of a relationship with a faculty member in which library faculty can demonstrate their expertise in both information literacy and student learning. In recent years, library faculty have become more proactive in collaborating with faculty to create other ways for students to develop information literacy, inquiry, and critical thinking skills. One example is working closely with faculty to develop courses in community-engaged research that allow students to develop inquiry skills that don't result in formal papers. Furthermore, as part of their reflective practice, TAL librarians regularly seek out feedback from both students and faculty on their experiences with a librarian. Having honest and constructive dialogue on improvements to pedagogical approaches has afforded TAL expanded access into courses and more impactful instruction activities and approaches, even within a one-shot setting.

Pedagogical Highlights

Within our instructional roles, TAL library faculty work to cultivate student-scholars who are able to navigate an increasingly complex information landscape as information creators who will have an appreciation of being and an ability to be engaged, contributing members of their communities. All library faculty in TAL contribute to cultivating student-scholars in our work with first-year students as well as those in general education courses and within their majors or graduate programs. We believe that an understanding of these different levels of the intellectual experience is necessary to identify and create impactful, transformative learning opportunities.

As library faculty, we approach our teaching intentionally and view all aspects of our work through an instructor lens. Even when we are not working directly with students in a classroom, we bring our identities as teachers to all of our work, whether it be collection development, web design and user experience, space planning, or university shared governance. This shared perspective in which we prioritize our roles as instructors helps to maintain a community of practice in which we discuss, challenge, and reflect upon our theoretical and philosophical approaches to teaching. In interdepartmental meetings with other librarian colleagues and in university meetings outside of the library, we use this perspective to communicate and establish the library's mission to facilitate learning and not just provide information.

Library faculty use a number of learning theories in their work, including threshold concepts framework, constructivist learning theories, validation theory, relational-cultural theory, and critical pedagogy. Further, we have created our own theoretical foundations that include the student-scholar identity (mentioned above) and the research process framework. These have been built into the TAL student learning outcomes, which are used to drive our work with students and faculty.

Administrative Highlights

TAL's intentional, inclusive, and collaborative practices are the cornerstones of our success. One specific way in which inclusivity and collaboration manifest in the unit is in how we run our weekly meetings. These standing meetings are held during the academic year and are a means to make decisions as a unit, assign work to individuals and work groups, and provide an opportunity for information sharing. In January 2012, the unit developed and agreed upon shared meeting logistics and norms, which are quoted verbatim below:

Logistics:

- Participate—Come prepared (even if absent)
- Realistic agenda—Start/end on time
- Stay focused—Discussion ok, don't meander or derail
- Purpose is clear—Info item? Discussion item? Decision-making? Advisory?
- Consensus process for important decisions—Understand what we're deciding on, understand conditions driving decision, accept and support decisions as best possible, have opportunity to discuss view ("groan zone")

Norms:

- Safe environment—All voices solicited, all voices listened to and valued

- No voice of judgment—Consider all ideas before dismissing, separate idea from person proposing idea
- Shared leadership—We all reinforce the norms, all are responsible for productive meetings
- Civilized disagreement—Disagree respectfully and professionally, work toward better understanding, don't avoid conflict
- Self-assessment—Self-check your behavior, team will regularly assess and adjust
- Sense of humor—Laugh! Have fun! Work towards our common goals

This shared approach to running our meetings allows us to discuss difficult topics, ask critical questions, and solicit potential solutions. It brings the unit together, and the meeting is never a wasted hour. An added benefit has been that TAL librarians have been trained in this way of facilitating productive meetings, a skill that has served us well as we chair committees across the university and in our professional associations.

Another highlight in how TAL approaches its administrative work is through its intentional inclusion of lecturer faculty. Lecturer librarians are given full teaching assignments and temporary subject assignments as the need arises. However, beyond the day-to-day work, lecturer faculty are relied upon as valuable members of the unit and are expected to fully participate in unit decisions. It is this intentional inclusion in all aspects of our work (ranging from instruction to research) that creates an environment in which lecturer faculty are integrated into the work of the unit. This helps to prepare lecturers for tenure-track positions within and outside of the university.

Information Literacy Coordinator Profile

The TAL head is a formal role, filled by a library faculty member as a permanent position. This role provides leadership and guidance to the unit's faculty and staff in all aspects of their instructional efforts but does not supervise any library faculty in the unit. Even though the head does provide leadership and management to the unit, few initiatives or efforts are developed solely by the head. Instead, ideas typically come from anyone within the unit. When there is work that the head (or anyone else) brings to the group, there is always discussion as to how (if at all) to approach and complete the work.

One driver for this approach is that the TAL head does not have formal authority. All library faculty report to the library dean, and library staff report to the associate dean. This lack of formal authority then requires a genuinely team-based approach. Individuals can technically choose other courses of action with the approval of the library dean (and have done so in particular situations). Even in such situations, the unit is aware and given a rationale. In virtually every other unit effort, the group works hard to determine a course of action in which everyone can ideally participate and that everyone can support, or at least appreciate the reasons for pursuing the project. Questions and dissent are welcomed and expected; the unit has become accustomed to successfully navigating these aspects of collaboration. Lastly, while the TAL head pays particular attention to ensuring the norms and logistics that allow for this degree of teamwork, an explicitly stated norm is that everyone is responsible for maintaining an atmosphere in which frank and open work can occur.

Much of the TAL head's work is coordinating projects and ensuring that librarians and staff have the resources and support needed to be successful in these projects. A fundamental principle within the unit is that the TAL head contributes an equal amount of instruction and reference work. In some instances, the TAL head will "pinch-hit" if someone is unable to teach a class or do an on-call reference shift, but generally speaking, these situations are covered by anyone who is willing and available. The core idea is that everyone already has a full-time job and no one is more (or less) important. One concern often voiced with this approach is how to address situations when work appears to be inequitably distributed. The unit has tracked instruction and reference for twelve years, and we see that work is indeed equitably distributed, and in those instances when it is not, explicit rationales are provided to the group.

What We Wish People Knew

The TAL library faculty wish that people knew that coordinating, leading, and participating in a program like ours requires hidden architectures to be easily viewable and understood by the entire team.

TAL is a highly collaborative and inclusive unit of library faculty and staff. In order to genuinely practice this, we consistently make explicit and remind ourselves of foundational principles, values, norms, and logistics. As necessary, we check these foundations to ensure we are indeed acting upon them as intended in order to keep student learning and engagement central to our work. This is not always easy, as it requires everyone to be conscious and mindful of their positionality in the unit, the University Library, and the university. In our work, we sometimes find it necessary to surface, explicitly, how our positionality may inform our perspective on something; for example, what might be a minor issue for one person may be a major issue for another and needs to be addressed in order to determine next steps.

We take seriously our role and rank as faculty in the university. Librarian work is often misunderstood or hidden from college faculty work, so establishing and growing partnerships beyond the library can be challenging. We often lean on each other in order to navigate such situations. An ethos of shared agency with college faculty for the curriculum and the teaching and learning endeavor is foundational to our professional practice. To this end, we also support each other in our research activities through collaborating, providing feedback, and serving as informal editors.

All of this does not happen without equal (and sometimes more) attention and effort being directed to considering atmosphere and group culture, listening closely, and responding to resource needs as to actually working with our students and faculty. We have found the that substance of our work is minimized and reduced if we are not paying attention to the experience of those doing the work. That is, *caring for those doing the work* is foundational to having a positive impact on student learning.

Notes

1. Yvonne Nalani Meulemans, Allison Carr, and Torie Quiñonez, "The Student-Scholar Identity: Using Students' Reflective Work to Develop Student Scholars, Address Liminality, and Design Curriculum," in *Threshold Concepts on the Edge*, ed. Julie Timmermans and Ray Land (New Milford, CT: Sense Publishers, forthcoming).
2. This reflective approach is more fully described in the Assessment and One-Shot sections.
3. Yvonne Nalani Meulemans and Allison Carr, "Not at Your Service: Building Genuine Librarian-Faculty Partnerships," *Reference Services Review* 41, no. 1 (2013): 81, https://doi.org/10.1108/00907321311300893.

Bibliography

Meulemans, Yvonne Nalani, and Allison Carr. "Not at Your Service: Building Genuine Librarian-Faculty Partnerships." *Reference Services Review* 41, no. 1 (2013): 80–90. https://doi.org/10.1108/00907321311300893.

Meulemans, Yvonne Nalani, Allison Carr, and Torie Quiñonez. "The Student-Scholar Identity: Using Students' Reflective Work to Develop Student Scholars, Address Liminality, and Design Curriculum." In *Threshold Concepts on the Edge*. Edited by Julie Timmermans and Ray Land. New Milford, CT: Sense Publishers, forthcoming.

Chapter 3

Georgia State University

Student Success Equals Our Success

Karen Doster-Greenleaf

Population Served

Georgia State University (GSU) is a public university comprised of the Robinson College of Business, College of Arts and Sciences, College of Education and Human Development, College of the Arts, Young School of Policy Studies, College of Law, Lewis College of Nursing and Health Professions, Honors College, Perimeter College, School of Public Health, and Institute of Biomedical Studies.[1] The university offers over 250 degree programs in 100 fields of study, including AA and AS degrees through Perimeter College.

One of the largest universities in the University System of Georgia, GSU serves over 45,000 undergraduate and 5,000 graduate students.[2] It has a diverse student population and is a national leader in graduation rate performance for first-generation and black students. Making up 22 percent of the student population, first-year students are the largest group of students served, with over half of them enrolled in Perimeter College. Students enrolled in the Perimeter College have the option to complete an AA or AS , or they can transition to the downtown campus pursue a bachelor's degree after completing thirty or more credits with at least a 2.0 GPA.[3]

Perimeter College plays a unique role in the structure of the university and the library. It is the open access two-year branch of the university, meaning there are no standardized test requirements for admittance. Once admitted to the college, however, students are required to complete a placement test if their high school GPA is below a 2.49.[4] Along with separate admittance requirements, the college also has separate strategic goals, missions, degrees, and faculty structure. It serves over 20,000 first- and second-year students. While there is one downtown campus location for the bachelor's and graduate programs, there are five Perimeter campuses (Alpharetta, Clarkston, Decatur, Dunwoody, and Newton). Many of the Perimeter students "float," taking classes at two or more GSU-Perimeter College campuses.

Organization

Led by the Dean of Libraries, the University Library is comprised of six campus libraries, located in Atlanta, Alpharetta, Clarkston, Decatur, Dunwoody, and Newton County. While all librarians are dedicated to providing assistance and service to students at every campus, library instruction services are split into two groups. These two groups are the Department of Research and Engagement and the Department of Perimeter College Library Services. This chapter will focus on the structure and instructional efforts of the Perimeter College Library Services.

The Department of Research and Engagement (R&E) works largely with upper-level and graduate students at the Atlanta campus. The R&E department has a subject liaison librarian–driven model and is made up of fourteen subject librarians who are supervised by either the Arts and Humanities or Research Data Services team lead. The leads are managed by the Department Head of Research and Engagement, who then reports to the Associate Dean of Public Services for the Atlanta campus library. The team lead provides leadership for library initiatives and serves as the point person for instruction-related activities. Subject librarians are responsible for providing instruction, research assistance, and collection development for their specific disciplines. Instruction and teaching load varies for the subject librarians depending on the needs of their areas.

Perimeter College Library Services is led by a department head who reports directly to the dean. The department head is responsible for the strategic direction of the department and supervises the associate department heads for the Perimeter College libraries. The majority of first- and second-year instruction at GSU is provided by Perimeter College Library Services' instruction program, which is comprised of ten full-time instruction librarians across five campuses, though the number of librarians at each campus differs. While the primary load of instruction falls to the instruction librarians at their home campus, part-time reference specialists and associate department heads assist as needed.

In addition to the R & E team and the Perimeter College instruction team, three integral positions provide collaborative library-wide support and leadership for various aspects of the library's instruction efforts: the Online Learning Librarian, the Assessment & User Services Librarian, and the Student Success Librarian. The Online Learning Librarian plans, supports, and designs online instruction for programs across all campuses and reports to the department head for Research and Engagement. The Assessment & User Services Librarian's primary role is to improve the experience of library users and assess the impact of the library, including working with the Student Success Librarian in the development and implementation of assessment tools regarding student learning and instructional impact. The Assessment & User Services Librarian reports directly to the library dean.

Reporting to the department head of Perimeter College Library Services, the Student Success Librarian (SSL) leads the strategic development of the library's instruction program. This person is responsible for devising an information literacy program that reaches the undergraduate student population across all six campuses with a specific emphasis on targeting first- and second-year students. The SSL's duties include

- building a library information literacy brand through consistent learning outcomes and assessment in consultation with librarians, department heads, and the dean,
- evaluating the impact of instruction on student success, teaching performance of instructor librarians, and faculty feedback, and
- leading new initiatives through collaborative partnerships with faculty, academic department heads, Office of Institutional Effectiveness, and key members of the university's Student Success Program.

While this position does not directly supervise any librarian, it does provide leadership and appropriate training for instruction librarians to grow and expand their instruction skill sets. This training has consisted of facilitated discussion groups (Instruction Talks), peer review and observation opportunities, and teaching simulations (Instructor Boot Camp). These opportunities serve to enhance and cultivate a positive peer environment that allows instructors to learn and grow from their interactions with each other.

Program Scope

The instruction program leads the library in providing pedagogical best practices to deliver scalable information, data, and technology instruction that is integrated into the curriculum across the university to promote information literacy and continuous learning. Aligning with the university's goal to provide outstanding academic support to produce academic success for diverse populations, our team works with faculty to promote critical thinking and foster our students' ability to become effective and empowered consumers, producers, and creators of information.

In the academic year 2018–19, as a strategic initiative the library instituted a standard library instruction plan for first- and second-year students. Focusing on these two groups helped establish a strong information literacy foundation for all students to build upon in their upper-level courses. First- and second-year students make up the largest percentage of the university's student population, providing the library the greatest impact possible. Furthermore, the students benefit from a unified curriculum that ensures all students receive the same level of information literacy instruction regardless of the campus they are on.

To assist in these efforts, in 2016 a working group was charged with establishing learning outcomes and identifying core classes that align with the program's mission. The core classes that were identified are English Composition I and II (ENGL 1101 and ENGL 1102) and Perimeter College Orientation (PCO 1020). These courses were selected because

1. they fulfill requirements for the university's core curriculum (written communication and institutional foundations respectively),
2. their learning objectives align with program learning outcomes,
3. they make up the highest number of sections of any first- or second-year class offered,
4. the majority of existing information literacy sessions taught are either for ENGL 1101 (34%) or PCO 1020 (24%), and
5. further collaboration is already supported by existing relationships between course faculty and the library.

The six learning outcomes generated cover aspects of ACRL's *Framework for Information Literacy for Higher Education* but draw heavily on the *Information Literacy Competency Standards for Higher Education.*[5] Coverage and assessment of the learning outcomes are dependent upon the course and assignment.

Instruction Program Learning Outcomes

1. The learner will be able to develop a research idea.
   - Define academic context of information seeking
   - Acknowledge and participate in research as a conversation

2. The learner will be able to identify tools and materials that are both relevant to information need and appropriate for academic research.
   - Scholarly vs. Popular
   - Primary vs. Secondary

3. The learner will be able to formulate effective search strategies.
   - Identify multiple search terms
   - Refine search

4. The learner will be able to evaluate information and sources critically.
   - Evaluate based on authority, accuracy, content, currency, and audience
   - Identify purposes of types of sources

5. The learner will be able to use information ethically.
   - Avoid plagiarism
   - Learn and use citations

6. The learner will be able to seek assistance from the library.

As part of this initiative, Perimeter College Library Services is in the process of implementing a standard lesson plan and assessment tool for ENGL 1101 that covers two of the program's learning outcomes. These outcomes focus on students' ability to determine and articulate their information need and develop basic search strategies by identifying relevant search terms. While elements of the other learning outcomes may be touched upon during instruction, only the two mentioned will be assessed using a performance-based assessment tool and rubric, discussed in further detail in the Assessment section of this chapter.

These efforts are all centered on the goal of establishing a strong foundation of research skills during the students' first and second years to help students transition and meet advanced research expectations in their upper-level classes. The Research and Engagement department supports these advanced research needs though in-person instruction, tutorials, and workshops. Given the Perimeter College Library Services' core audience, most instruction focuses on discipline-specific research needs and research data services. Research areas and topics covered in research data services have included workshops and course-based instruction sessions on nVivo, Tableau, SPSS, oral histories, citation management software, and many more.[6]

Assessment

The University Library is cultivating a culture of assessment, particularly in regard to library instruction. While there is no library-wide formalized assessment of student learning, we utilize an evaluation survey to assess instruction sessions. The survey focuses on the students' affective reaction to instruction and relies heavily on students' existing knowledge of what they should and should not already know regarding the library and research (see figure 3.1).

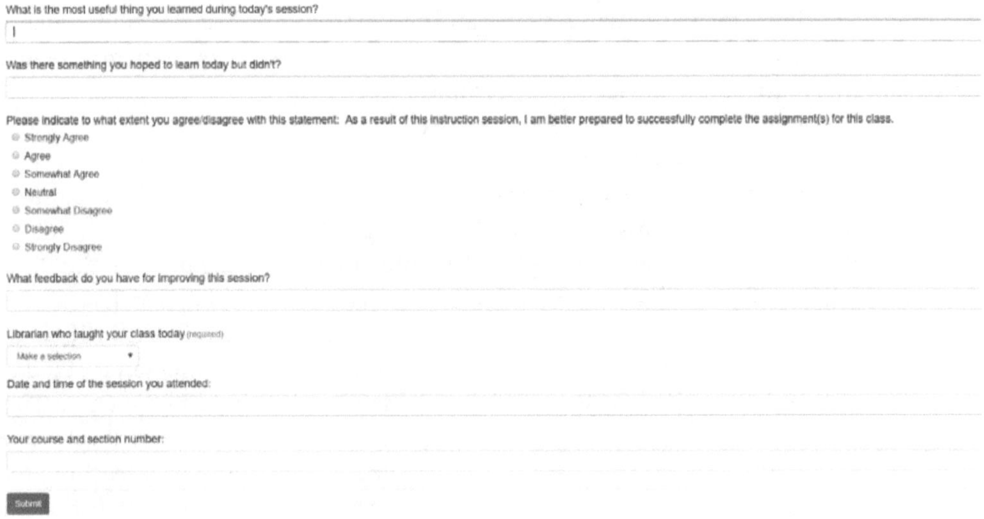
What is the most useful thing you learned during today's session?

Was there something you hoped to learn today but didn't?

Please indicate to what extent you agree/disagree with this statement: As a result of this instruction session, I am better prepared to successfully complete the assignment(s) for this class.
- Strongly Agree
- Agree
- Somewhat Agree
- Neutral
- Somewhat Disagree
- Disagree
- Strongly Disagree

What feedback do you have for improving this session?

Librarian who taught your class today (required)
Make a selection

Date and time of the session you attended:

Your course and section number:

Submit

Figure 3.1
Library instruction evaluation survey

While this tool does provide assessment data on students' perceptions about the instruction session, it does not effectively demonstrate what students have or have not learned or the impact attending a library instruction session. To address this lack, the Perimeter College Library Services (PCLS) team is piloting a formal assessment project tied to student attendance and institutional effectiveness data. Over the next couple of years, the Student Success Librarian plans to analyze the collected data to identify potential correlations between two groups of factors: library instruction and student success measurements. These factors can be broken down into the following variables:

Library Instruction

- student attendance at library instruction

- the number of times they've received library instruction
- the specific classes they received instruction for

Student Success Measurements

- class grades
- semester-to-semester retention
- transition to the Atlanta campus and/or graduation rates

This information will be used to help gauge and enhance the instruction program's overall efforts and impact.

To better understand student learning of information literacy frameworks, PCLS is also in the beta stage of a standardized lesson and performance-based assessment project for English Composition I (ENGL 1101) classes. This course was selected for several reasons. As stated previously, ENGL 1101 is one of the instruction program's core courses and provides a large student sample size. The course also serves as most students' first experience writing a formal research paper and presents an ideal scenario in which to introduce students to the research process. The lesson is designed to cover an introductory understanding of the following learning outcomes:

- The learner will be able to develop a research idea.
- The learner will be able to formulate effective search strategies.

In an effort to better assess and determine students' understanding of these concepts during a one-shot session, an assessment tool was designed to determine students' ability to identify their information need through a structured brainstorming process, the development of a defined focused research topic, and identification of potential search terms (see figure 3.2). Each ENGL 1101 classes is taught using the same standard lesson plan and assessment artifact, a worksheet. The worksheet serves the dual purpose of a teaching tool to support scaffolded instruction and an assessment. After each instruction section, the worksheets are collected and assessed using a normed rubric (see table 3.1). The intent for this pilot, through a unified instruction effort, is to determine the level of students' understanding and ability to put into practice the parts of the research process covered during the class. It should be noted that instructors with assignments that do not align with the learning outcomes of the standardized lesson plan are considered outliers and not counted in the pilot.

Name

Research Map Handout

TOPIC

Who	
What	
When	
Where	
Why	

Focused Research Idea:

Search Terms:

Recommended Information Resources

__ Discover　　__ News and Newspaper

__ Opposing Viewpoints　　__ Google

__ Blooms Literary Sources　　__ CINAHL

Karen Doster-Greenleaf
University Library, Georgia State University

CC BY NC

Figure 3.2
Research map assessment tool

Table 3.1
Research map assessment tool rubric

	Exemplary (5 pts)	**Average (3 pts)**	**Poor (0 pts)**
Exploration	Detailed evidence of exploration that supports a complete research idea (When or Where may be exempt if unrelated to topic).	Some evidence of exploration—partial completion (When or Where may be exempt if unrelated to topic).	No responses or unrelated content provided.
Topic Development	Develops a specific well-defined research idea that articulates the information need as related to the assignment (or approved by instructor).	Identifies a research idea, but may be too broad or not concrete in scope or undefined for the assignment, and needs to be developed further.	Research idea is too broad and does not effectively articulate the information need. **OR** No research idea is provided.
Search Terms	Constructs and implements effectively designed search strategies by identifying key concepts, along with similar and related search terms.	Identifies only key concepts, but no related or similar search terms.	No search terms are identified.

Role of the One-Shot

One-shot instruction sessions are the program's bread and butter and many instructors' comfort zone. Others struggle with the time limitations and faculty expectations the one-shot presents. Many want to explore more integrated or overarching instruction opportunities but find it difficult to identify where to begin. One significant hurdle is the importance of faculty buy-in. Faculty are often unfamiliar with the range of instructional offerings and collaborative support librarians can provide, or even fail to understand how information literacy fits into their curriculum. Disconnect occurs when faculty struggle to envision what nontraditional library instruction looks like and librarians wrestle when creating a nontraditional approach without faculty input. Faculty support, interest, and input in information literacy in the curriculum are essential at Georgia State University because elements of these concepts are implied in the university's core learning outcomes but not explicitly expressed.[7] For this reason, librarians are encouraged to explore best practices in instruction and pedagogy through professional development opportunities, forge relationships with faculty, and advocate for the importance of collaborative development for the critical thinking skills of students. Building this foundation helps establish an equal understanding of higher education pedagogy with our faculty peers.

Librarians experiment and expand the instruction offerings through embedded librarianship, flipped classrooms, badging, tutorials and modules, and emerging instructional trends. Several librarians have had success with embedded librarianship using the university's learning management system and self-directed online tutorials using software like LibWizard. For example, in lieu of face-to-face instruction, an online research tutorial was created for the dental hygiene program (see figure 3.3). Due to the curriculum's tight schedule, this format is ideal as it allows flexibility for the faculty and students on when to assign it and when to complete it. It ties research foundations such as information source types and source evaluation to the subject-specific needs of the dental hygiene field. Since the tutorial is first completed by the student cohorts in the fall semester and again in the spring, the online format also provides the library an opportunity to assess students' learning and retention. There have also been some minor successes expanding one-shot sessions into multiple interactions through assigned research consultations or scheduled guided research days.

Figure 3.3
LibWizard dental hygiene tutorial—web evaluation slide

Collaboration

Workshops are a growing part of the GSU University Library instruction program. An established suite of workshops focused on data analysis tools and methods, in addition to advanced research methods and practices, are offered by the Data Services team librarians (a subdepartment within the R&E department). These workshops are only offered at the downtown campus. However, there are plans to offer the workshops online and at Perimeter College locations in the future.

At the Perimeter College campuses, workshops are not as consistently offered or established as the series provided by R&E. To improve this situation and support the university's quality enhancement plan, Perimeter College Library Services are producing workshops to support student success skills and promote lifelong learning.

An example is a nine-week student success workshop series targeted to first- or second-semester students that was launched in the fall of 2018. The workshops were designed to provide supplemental instruction to the curriculum provided through the college's first-year experience course, PCO 1020. The workshop topics include campus resources, student technology, library resources, personal finance, career-ready resources, self-care and stress management, web research, advanced library research skills, and citations and plagiarism.

The success of these workshops was closely linked to the library's growing relationships with student supports services across Perimeter College, including the Center for Excellence in Teaching and Learning (CETL), TRIO student support services (a federally funded outreach and student services program designed for students from disadvantaged backgrounds), and Student Life.[8] Along with providing promotional support, the Perimeter College CETL—Learning Technology department and TRIO provided instructional support for the student technology and career services workshops.

Marketing

The marketing and promotion of instruction is an evolving component of the program. The two largest Perimeter College Library Services campuses, Clarkston and Dunwoody, bring in one-shot instruction through liaison-driven faculty outreach. This model has been effective at these campuses as a result of the larger staff's ability to provide a direct line of communication and promotion of library and instruction services. Each liaison is responsible for designing marketing materials and strategies that are tailored for their specific liaison subject areas. Marketing strategies have included repacking instruction offerings and promotional materials for email communication, creating custom candy bar wrappers with attached business cards, and hosting faculty mix-and-mingles. Librarians are also encouraged to reach out to faculty individually, rather than send out department-wide emails. Using this approach offers a personal touch to our correspondence in a culture where our faculty are inundated with emails to their whole department. While other variables are involved, using these approaches has resulted in a significant increase in requests for one-shot instruction and faculty-librarian collaboration.

Establishing a structured liaison model has proven unsuitable when the staff consists of only one or two librarians. At the smaller campuses (Alpharetta, Newton, and Decatur), outreach has been minimal and instruction relies heavily on existing faculty relationships and word-of-mouth endorsements. Faculty endorsements are an invaluable marketing asset for the entire program, as they help grow the program and provide feedback on the program's effectiveness. While these smaller campuses have not actively sought out new instruction opportunities, they provide one-shot instruction for a wide array of classes outside the program's core, including environmental science, US history, business, and political science.

Lessons Learned

It has been crucial to learn more about the instruction team's individual teaching styles. As the Student Success Librarian, I've conducted instruction observations and one-on-one meetings and have learned that to maintain consistency, specific learning outcomes are expected to be addressed, but intellectual and instructional creativity is necessary to foster ownership of standardized instructional norms. This in turn creates collegiality within the team. Creative control allows librarians to cultivate their unique teaching identity, which is important in both lesson development and building faculty relationships. From a leadership position, acknowledging and respecting the librarians' individual perspectives supports my goal in making the program stronger.

The span of student college readiness and meeting students at their level requires a unified and structured approach to information literacy instruction. Building this type of program doesn't happen overnight. The library continues to lay the groundwork to establish a strong foundation on which to build a nuanced program curriculum, campus relationships, faculty collaboration, and administrative support. Looking forward, our plan is to use this foundation to generate a multitiered program that fosters breadth and depth of students' skills in preparation for their roles in the workforce.

Notes

1. "Degrees and Majors," Georgia State University, accessed January 14, 2019, https://www.gsu.edu/program-cards.
2. Georgia State University, "IPORT Fall 2018 Enrollment by Student Class," report, accessed October 20, 2018, https://dssapex.gsu.edu/pls/apex/f?p=114:146:::NO:::.
3. "Transition Students," Undergraduate Admissions—Bachelor's Degrees, Georgia State University, accessed January 14, 2019, https://admissions.gsu.edu/bachelors-degree/apply/transition.
4. "Admissions Process and Requirements," Traditional Freshman, Perimeter College, Georgia State University, accessed January 14, 2019, https://perimeter.gsu.edu/admissions/freshman-2.
5. Association of College and Research Libraries, *Framework for Information Literacy for Higher Education* (Chicago: Association of College and Research Libraries, 2016), http://www.ala.org/acrl/standards/ilframework; Association of College and Research Libraries, *Information Literacy Competency Standards for Higher Education* (Chicago: Association of College and Research Libraries, 2000), https://alair.ala.org/handle/11213/7668.
6. "Library Workshops and Events—Upcoming Events," Georgia State University Library, accessed March 29, 2019, https://rooms.library.gsu.edu/calendar/workshops/?cid=2352&t=d&d=0000-00-00&cal=2352.
7. "Consolidated GSU Core Curriculum Learning Outcomes," Georgia State University, last updated October 9, 2015, https://oie.gsu.edu/assessment-and-review-academic-and-adminstrative/academic-assessment-and-review/consolidated-assessment-of-the-core-curriculum/consolidated-gsu-core-curriculum-learning-outcomes.
8. "Federal TRIO Programs—Home Page," Office of Postsecondary Education, US Department of Education, last modified February 7, 2019, https://www2.ed.gov/about/offices/list/ope/trio/index.html.

Bibliography

Association of College and Research Libraries. *Framework for Information Literacy for Higher Education.* Chicago: Association of College and Research Libraries, 2016. http://www.ala.org/acrl/standards/ilframework.

———. *Information Literacy Competency Standards for Higher Education.* Chicago: Association of College and Research Libraries, 2000. https://alair.ala.org/handle/11213/7668.

Georgia State University. "Admissions Process and Requirements." Traditional Freshman, Perimeter College. Accessed January 14, 2019. https://perimeter.gsu.edu/admissions/freshman-2.

———. "Consolidated GSU Core Curriculum Learning Outcomes." Last updated October 9, 2015. https://oie.gsu.edu/assessment-and-review-academic-and-adminstrative/academic-assessment-and-review/consolidated-assessment-of-the-core-curriculum/consolidated-gsu-core-curriculum-learning-outcomes.

———. "Degrees and Majors." Accessed January 14, 2019. https://www.gsu.edu/program-cards.

———. "IPORT Fall 2018 Enrollment by Student Class." Report. Accessed October 20, 2018. https://dssapex.gsu.edu/pls/apex/f?p=114:146:::NO:::.

———. "Transition Students." Undergraduate Admissions—Bachelor's Degrees. Accessed January 14, 2010. https://admissions.gsu.edu/bachelors-degree/apply/transition.

Georgia State University Library. "Library Workshops & Events—Upcoming Events." Accessed March 29, 2019. https://rooms.library.gsu.edu/calendar/workshops/?cid=2352&t=d&d=0000-00-00&cal=2352.

US Department of Education. "Federal TRIO Programs—Home Page." Office of Postsecondary Education. Last modified February 7, 2019. https://www2.ed.gov/about/offices/list/ope/trio/index.html.

Chapter 4

Greenfield Community College

Finding Value in the Process

Liza Harrington, Tim Dolan, and Claire Lobdell

Population Served

Located in the rural western half of Massachusetts, Greenfield Community College (GCC) is one of the smallest public colleges in the state. We have an annual for-credit FTE of approximately 1,300,[1] and the entire college consists of three buildings. While we are small, we serve a large swath of territory in three states, encompassing several postindustrial town centers as well as a number of small, isolated communities. Many towns in our service area have no access to broadband internet or public transportation.

The student body at any community college is likely to be diverse, but this diversity manifests itself in particular ways on a rural campus. While only 21 percent of our students identify as people of color, our position as the only public institution of higher learning in the area makes us the go-to college for students regardless of age, income level, previous education, or career trajectory.[2] Approximately 55 percent of incoming students enroll in developmental level reading, writing, or math classes.[3] Many of our students complete degrees by taking a class or two at a time rather than matriculating as full-time students. We also serve both senior citizens who take classes for personal enrichment and dual-enrolled high school students.

All of this means that the students in any given classroom have vastly different goals, needs, backgrounds, and levels of digital and information literacy. The diverse needs of our students can be difficult for the college to accommodate with a small staff and limited resources. As an institution, GCC addresses this challenge by offering transferable liberal arts degrees with concentrations in specific fields rather than more focused majors, as well as with a variety of professional and job training programs.

Program Scope

The GCC library offers flexible information literacy instruction for all disciplines, face-to-face and online, and we work at every level of the college's curriculum, including developmental and college success classes. The traditional one-shot is still the predominant way that we deliver this instruction, but very little of our instruction is canned; we make a point to tailor each individual session to a faculty member's learning outcomes and to an assignment that is immediately relevant to students. Because each instructor on campus makes curricular choices independently, we end up working with some very intensively but never see others. In particular, our integration into the core English composition curriculum is inconsistent.

Though most of our teaching takes place in the context of a one-shot, our institution is so small that we frequently see the same students in multiple classes during their time here. Many of our students know us by name and vice versa, so even when we see a student only once in a course, it rarely feels like our only opportunity to interact with that student.

We have made strides in recent years working with faculty to create course-level information literacy outcomes, as well as scaffolding information literacy instruction across programs. The most striking example of this is in our biology and nursing departments: a student who both takes the prerequisites for the nursing program and completes an associate's degree in nursing at GCC will see librarians in their classes no fewer than seven times over the course of three to four years and will experience a scaffolded curriculum focused on evidence-based practice.

Additionally, one of the authors of this chapter, Claire, created and administers a "Don't Cancel That Class" program, which allows faculty to invite substitute instructors from a variety of campus departments when they plan to be absent for a class.[4] Through this program, the library offers workshops on campus technology, data visualization, media literacy, online privacy, citation practice, and critical reading, as well as sessions tied to specific research assignments. In addition to the library, other offices on campus, including the wellness center, advising center, and financial aid office, also have Don't Cancel That Class offerings.

Operations

Our classroom instruction team consists of three librarians—the authors of this chapter—who are also the only professional librarians on staff aside from the director. Three library assistants (two full-time and one part-time) as well as a half dozen or so student workers round out the library staff. This arrangement means that, in addition to teaching, the instruction team also have shifts on the reference desk, supervise student workers, plan events, and manage other public service tasks. While our jobs are broadly similar, Liza coordinates the information literacy program (see the Information Literacy Coordinator Profile section below), Tim coordinates open educational resources (OER) for the campus, and Claire manages the college archives and works with distance education classes. We plan the direction of information literacy instruction collectively at semiannual retreats and monthly meetings. We map all of our lesson plans to the learning outcomes in the "GCC Statement on Information Literacy" (more on this below);[5] keep all lesson plans, activities, and materials on a shared drive; and participate in regular peer observations, both of each other and by stakeholders outside of the library. In this way, we share good ideas and approach challenges together while still preserving our autonomy.

Information literacy instruction is the primary task that library staff pursue, and is also an ongoing, campus-wide initiative that we lead. As a result, everyone who works in the library teaches in some capacity. This includes paraprofessionals, who teach library-related skills one-on-one at our shared reference and circulation desk, and student workers, several of whom are trained to troubleshoot technology issues and work with students who lack basic technology skills.

While we as a library focus the bulk of our attention on information literacy, we do not believe that it is a skill set belonging solely to the library. In fact, information literacy is listed as one of the ten general education abilities for the college.[6] We enlist faculty in our efforts by sharing lesson plans in advance of sessions, complete with learning outcomes linked to their assignments, as well as offering professional development around information literacy and helping to design research assignments. We advocate for ourselves to administrators and regularly report on our value, most recently in the form of a data-heavy report to our new college president.

Pedagogical Highlights

In the fall of 2017, GCC adopted the library's "Statement on Information Literacy" as an official part of the college curriculum.[7] This document includes a set of twenty-seven learning outcomes built on the ACRL *Framework for Information Literacy for Higher Education* and refined to suit the needs of our students.[8] We initially drafted this document by reflecting on our own teaching as a group, and then workshopped the draft by visiting departmental meetings and soliciting feedback from campus committees. Later drafts worked their way through four levels of college governance, which allowed us to gather yet more feedback and do further revisions. The process took more than a year to complete, but the final product represents, to the greatest extent possible, a broad campus consensus about what information literacy is and which specific skills it entails, while also setting baseline expectations for programmatic assessment. The final document also connects the ACRL *Framework* with GCC's general education abilities and principles of education, our regional accrediting body's standards, and the Association of American Colleges and Universities "Information Literacy VALUE Rubric."[9]

The "Statement on Information Literacy" is part of an ongoing transformation in our program, which has led us to broaden our definition of information literacy and extend into new teaching modalities, all while moving away from training centered around databases and other library-specific tools and instead toward the kinds of transferable information skills and competencies that students will need throughout their lives. For example, the Statement explicitly foregrounds the role of the student as an information creator, asking students to "share an original idea or creation in an appropriate format, with attention to both audience and convention" and "recognize that their speech, writing, and research influence their own authority." This emphasis in turn has given us permission to spend more time encouraging students to do original, primary research, and we now sponsor an annual student research symposium.[10] Partly due to this expansion in scope, library instruction numbers have grown every year for the past five years, from 84 sessions in FY 2013 to 140 sessions in FY 2018, despite declining enrollments at the college.[11]

As the Statement was working its way through the governance structure, our library experienced significant changes: one established colleague moved on to another institution, and all the members of the current team found themselves in new roles and encountering periodic challenges with workload. We took this opportunity to reevaluate the program and create a structure for ourselves grounded in both our shared conceptions of good teaching and the pragmatic realities of our limited staffing. Our three-member team started with a one-day information literacy retreat at which we discussed the strengths and weaknesses of the existing information literacy program. On the same day, we set in motion the process of creating a shared teaching philosophy and a programmatic assessment plan (outlined in the Assessment section below), both of which work in tandem with the Statement, which had by then become an official curriculum document.[12]

While the Statement documents the content that we teach and the shared teaching philosophy describes the principles that guide our instruction, we all remain free to choose individual teaching methods that suit our strengths as teachers. These principles include the centrality of collaborative partnerships with faculty, the high expectations that we set for our students, our efforts at continual improvement, and our emphasis on the social, cultural, and emotional experience of the research process. We also use the philosophy document to set boundaries, limiting ourselves to no more than two unique lesson plans or seven-and-one-half hours in the classroom in a given week, which ensures that we have the time necessary to do our best work.

We have been using the outcomes, teaching philosophy, and assessment plan for a year and have all felt how useful it is to have this architecture. It has guided our teaching, facilitated better discussions with faculty and our college's new president, and even helped us redesign our teaching space.

Marketing

We strategically reach out to all new GCC employees, including new faculty, in a number of ways. A library staff member attends every new employee orientation session to give a short spiel, and there is also a blurb about the library in the faculty handbook.[13] We individually email all new faculty, offering to set them up with library cards, outlining various services we offer to them and their students (course reserves, OER course support, citation help, etc.), and sharing examples of the information literacy instruction we have done in their discipline in the past. One of our closest collaborations came out of just this sort of new faculty contact: we started communicating by email with a new history professor before she started in her position, met with her in person once she was here, and now teach in all of her classes twice per semester.

We also periodically promote new instruction by reviewing the course catalog for any course descriptions that mention research and contacting those faculty. Claire, our distance education librarian, contacts faculty who teach online with examples of the ways she has worked with other online classes. Likewise, if we see a flurry of student activity in the library around a research assignment for a class in which we're not already involved, we will contact the professor and offer our services. Some of our program expansion is clearly the result of word-of-mouth marketing; a professor will tell a colleague about the work we did in one class and that colleague will get in touch with us, or a new adjunct will be strongly encouraged by departmental colleagues to schedule a one-shot.

Collaboration

Collaboration is key to everything that we do, and the theme appears prominently in both our "Statement on Information Literacy" and our shared teaching philosophy.[14] For example, the teaching philosophy states that we "seek to cultivate meaningful, collaborative teaching partnerships with GCC faculty" and that our instruction "emerges from our relationships with faculty members." The Statement elaborates on these themes, specifying that we "help design assignments, co-teach information literacy components of your course, or assist in assessing students' information literacy skills in a single class, a full course, or a program."

All three of us have found that collaboration outside of the classroom—whether on governance committees, on hiring committees, in the union, or as part of the accreditation process—is one of the biggest drivers of instructional collaboration. The small size of our campus allows us to be involved in events, initiatives, and committees outside of the library, and we also make a point to show up at, participate in, and lead cocurricular programming. A great deal of our faculty collaboration has grown out of the relationships we've developed in these other spaces; people recognize us as folks who show up and care. Through these other projects, we've built a level of trust that translates to the classroom.

Since 2016, the library has run an annual three-day professional development workshop for GCC faculty, co-facilitated by a librarian and faculty member, called Research across the Curriculum (RAC).[15] As part of this workshop, participants create or modify a research-based assignment, design information literacy–infused curricula, and develop methods for grading and feedback. Because this workshop runs in early summer when our faculty are off-contract, the college uses professional development funds to provide participants with stipends of $300. To date, twenty-six faculty members have participated in the program, and past RAC participants have become some of our biggest allies on campus.

We have also recently extended our reach beyond the campus and are in the beginning phases of collaborating with librarians at other area institutions. Specifically, in recent years the college has seen increasing numbers of dual-enrolled high school students, and we realized that some of these students might be conducting research for GCC assignments at their high school libraries. In the fall of 2017, we reached out to the high school librarians in surrounding communities and hosted a meeting at which we learned what information literacy instruction looks like at their schools and discussed how best to share resources and support dual-enrolled students. We also recently met with librarians at the University of Massachusetts at Amherst, which enrolls more GCC transfer students than any other college or university, to discuss ways to support transfer students and align our information literacy programs.

Assessment

The "Statement on Information Literacy" has quickly become the core of our program: it not only codifies what we teach, but also provides clear and consistent expectations that we're able to assess at the lesson, course, program, and college levels.[16] We designed the set of outcomes in the Statement to apply in all disciplines and at all levels of instruction (though some are more appropriate in particular contexts) and set an explicit standard that every student graduating with an associate's degree should be able to demonstrate proficiency in at least one outcome from each frame of the *Framework*.[17] The Statement represents a major change in the way that we assess information literacy, and it facilitated the creation of our first comprehensive assessment plan, which we're currently carrying out in the 2018/2019 academic year.[18] Liza, one of the authors of this chapter and our coordinator, participated in ACRL's Assessment in Action program in 2013–2014[19] and currently cochairs the college's accreditation self-study, so her experience greatly assisted us in creating this plan.

Our assessment plan details the following practices:

- We collectively track the student learning outcomes that we teach in courses, orientations, and cocurricular programs in a Google form.
- We assess outcomes at the session level by using exit tickets, minute papers, mind maps, worksheets, and forum posts and by examining artifacts that students create during the session.
- We assess outcomes at the course level using surveys, focus groups, entrance and exit quizzes, test questions, and rubric scoring of larger projects.
- We assess learning for graduating students by examining artifacts from 200-level classes with a rubric, looking for evidence of at least one learning outcome achieved in each frame identified by the department.
- As noted above, we regularly observe one another's teaching and offer feedback, and bring in observers from other campus departments at least once a year to offer an outside perspective.

Each librarian favors different classroom assessment methods and different approaches for reflecting on the results, and we embrace these differences. At the same time, we occasionally convene to look for trends in session-level data: for example, during the spring semester of 2018, we used a short, standardized exit survey in every class session, which allowed us to draw some general conclusions about student satisfaction. On a larger scale, this past year we collaborated with our institutional research officer on a survey of graduating students. In addition to general questions about the college experience, this survey included a section focusing on students' library use, as well as how they felt about the library and library instruction. We also have plans in motion to work with the institutional research office to track the academic paths of students who do not receive library instruction as part of their curriculum, with the hope of using that data as a tool in targeted faculty outreach.

Administrative Highlights

We schedule all library instruction in our shared library calendar. Given our small staff and multitude of non-instruction-related duties, we need to see everything happening in the library in order to schedule classes. All library staff can schedule sessions for faculty, although most requests come directly to the three instruction librarians. We have a web form for instruction requests but do not require its use.[20] We try to ensure that all classes are assigned to librarians at least two weeks in advance so that we know our upcoming workload and have time to prepare.

As the coordinator, Liza keeps an eye on the number of requests for the full semester and ensures that the teaching load for each librarian is manageable, while flagging busy weeks in our calendar so that nothing additional is scheduled once we reach our agreed-upon limits (two unique lesson plans or seven-and-one-half hours of instruction per week). We sometimes break this rule, but are usually able to negotiate with faculty to make things work for everyone. We used to have very busy instruction weeks (everyone wants instruction on the third week of classes!), and this change has allowed us to maintain a steadier pace with our teaching loads.

We track instruction sessions with a Google form. Each librarian fills out the form after they teach, indicating the course number, faculty member, information literacy learning outcomes taught, when and where the class took place, and number of students present. Having all of this data in one place facilitates assessment, including these questions: Which learning outcomes do we teach the most and least? Does this align with what we hope we're doing? In which programs are students receiving library instruction, and where do we see gaps? Which learning outcomes do departments favor? This system also allows us to easily generate end-of-year statistics and report what we do.[21]

Information Literacy Coordinator Profile

The vision and work of the information literacy program is shared evenly among the instruction team, and we all play equal roles in teaching, assessing, marketing, and collaborating on information literacy. Liza has been at GCC the longest and takes the lead on the administrative details that make the program run smoothly, including keeping the calendar, ensuring everyone has a manageable workload, scheduling internal and external teaching observations, creating agendas for meetings and retreats, keeping assessment tasks on track based on the information literacy assessment plan, and serving as the liaison between the instruction team and campus partners on major projects. She holds the title of Coordinator of Library Services, a change in rank frequently given in a librarian's tenure year that indicates seniority rather than a major change in duties. As professional staff, we are all part of the Massachusetts Community College Council union,[22] and our contract dictates that union members cannot supervise other union members.

What We Wish People Knew

While we find it very useful to have a guiding architecture of learning outcomes, a teaching philosophy, and an assessment plan, we have found the greatest value in the process of developing these documents, not in the documents themselves. The process of creating these foundational documents necessitated many conversations within and outside of the library and has led us to better understand our faculty, our students, and one another. If you see and seek value in the process itself, it is easier to manage the frustration of a long process to achieve campus-wide buy-in. Any steps you take to build your architecture—or change it, if what you have isn't working—are steps in the right direction.

It is equally important to not let these documents sit static after they are created. Any teaching philosophy or set of learning outcomes should be living, breathing things that change over time. The process should be iterative, never finished, and any architecture should be revisited regularly to ensure it is still working for all stakeholders. If and when our instruction team grows or changes here at GCC, we will revisit all of our foundational documents with new team members.

Every institution will eventually need an architecture for its information literacy program. Our library had been operating without one for decades, but as the size and complexity of our program grew, it became necessary to formalize what we teach and how we teach it—for ourselves in the library and for our campus as a whole. Both the process and the final documents had to be grounded in who we are as librarian-teachers and in the very specific context of Greenfield Community College. We encourage you to begin with your own contexts and, gathering inspiration from us and from others in this book, create or change the information literacy architecture at your institutions.

Notes

1. "Fast Facts: Fall 2017 Enrollment Data," Greenfield Community College, September 2017, https://www.gcc.mass.edu/about/files/2018/08/Fall-2017-Fast-Facts-FINAL.pdf.
2. "Fast Facts."
3. Marie Breheny, "Institutional Effectiveness Indicators and Data" (internal document, Greenfield Community College, 2018).
4. "Don't Cancel That Class!" Faculty and Staff Resources, Greenfield Community College, accessed January 11, 2019, https://www.gcc.mass.edu/staff/dont-cancel-that-class.
5. "GCC Statement on Information Literacy," Nahman-Watson Library, Greenfield Community College, October 2017, https://www.gcc.mass.edu/library/gcc-statement-on-information-literacy.
6. "About GCC: General Education Abilities," Greenfield Community College, May 2, 2011, https://www.gcc.mass.edu/about/principles-of-education/general-education-abilities.
7. "GCC Statement on Information Literacy."
8. Association of College and Research Libraries, *Framework for Information Literacy for Higher Education* (Chicago: Association of College and Research Libraries, 2016), http://www.ala.org/acrl/standards/ilframework.
9. "About GCC: Principles of Education," Greenfield Community College, accessed January 17, 2019, https://www.gcc.mass.edu/about/principles-of-education; New England Commission of Higher Education (NECHE) home page, accessed March 22, 2019, https://www.neche.org; "Information Literacy VALUE Rubric," American Association of Colleges and Universities, accessed January 17, 2019, https://www.aacu.org/value/rubrics/information-literacy.
10. "GCC Research Symposium," Nahman-Watson Library, Greenfield Community College, accessed March 21, 2019, http://www.gcc.mass.edu/library/gcc-research-symposium.
11. "Annual Reports," Nahman-Watson Library, Greenfield Community College, accessed January 25, 2019, http://www.gcc.mass.edu/library/annual-reports.
12. "Our Library Teaching Philosophy," Nahman-Watson Library, Greenfield Community College, 2018, https://www.gcc.mass.edu/library/our-library-teaching-philosophy; "Nahman-Watson Library Information Literacy Assessment Plan," Nahman-Watson Library, Greenfield Community College, 2018, https://www.gcc.mass.edu/library/files/2019/01/Information-Literacy-Assessment-Plan-FY-2018.pdf.
13. *A Handbook of Policies, Procedures, and Resources for Faculty 2018–2019* (Greenfield, MA: Greenfield Community College, 2018), 31–32, https://www.gcc.mass.edu/webdocs/student-and-academic-affairs/Faculty-Handbook.pdf (2018–19 version removed from web page).
14. "GCC Statement on Information Literacy"; "Our Library Teaching Philosophy."
15. "Summer Faculty Workshop: Research across the Curriculum," Nahman-Watson Library, Greenfield Community College, accessed January 18, 2019, https://www.gcc.mass.edu/library/summer-faculty-workshop-research-across-the-curriculum.

16. "GCC Statement on Information Literacy."
17. Association of College and Research Libraries, *Framework for Information Literacy*.
18. "Nahman-Watson Library Information Literacy Assessment Plan."
19. "Assessment in Action," Nahman-Watson Library, Greenfield Community College, 2014, https://www.gcc.mass.edu/library/aia.
20. "Librarian Instruction Requests," Nahman-Watson Library, Greenfield Community College, accessed January 25, 2019, http://www.gcc.mass.edu/library/help/faculty-request.
21. "Annual Reports."
22. Massachusetts Community College Council home page, accessed March 18, 2019, https://mccc-union.org.

Bibliography

American Association of Colleges and Universities. "Information Literacy VALUE Rubric." Last updated July 2013. https://www.aacu.org/value/rubrics/information-literacy.

Association of College and Research Libraries. *Framework for Information Literacy for Higher Education.* Chicago: Association of College and Research Libraries, 2016. http://www.ala.org/acrl/standards/ilframework.

Breheny, Marie. "Institutional Effectiveness Indicators and Data." 2018. Internal document, Greenfield Community College.

Greenfield Community College. "About GCC: General Education Abilities." May 2, 2011. https://www.gcc.mass.edu/about/principles-of-education/general-education-abilities.

———. "About GCC: Principles of Education." Accessed January 17, 2019. https://www.gcc.mass.edu/about/principles-of-education.

———. "Annual Reports." Nahman-Watson Library. Accessed January 25, 2019. http://www.gcc.mass.edu/library/annual-reports.

———. "Assessment in Action." Nahman-Watson Library. Accessed November 20, 2019. https://www.gcc.mass.edu/library/aia.

———. "Don't Cancel That Class!" Faculty and Staff Resources. Accessed January 11, 2019. https://www.gcc.mass.edu/staff/dont-cancel-that-class.

———. "Fast Facts: Fall 2017 Enrollment Data." September 2017. https://www.gcc.mass.edu/about/files/2018/08/Fall-2017-Fast-Facts-FINAL.pdf.

———. "GCC Research Symposium." Nahman-Watson Library. Accessed March 21, 2019. http://www.gcc.mass.edu/library/gcc-research-symposium.

———. "GCC Statement on Information Literacy." Nahman-Watson Library. October 2017. https://www.gcc.mass.edu/library/gcc-statement-on-information-literacy.

———. *A Handbook of Policies, Procedures, and Resources for Faculty 2018–2019*. Greenfield, MA: Greenfield Community College, 2018. https://www.gcc.mass.edu/webdocs/student-and-academic-affairs/Faculty-Handbook.pdf (2018 version removed from web page).

———. "Librarian Instruction Requests." Nahman-Watson Library. Accessed January 25, 2019. http://www.gcc.mass.edu/library/help/faculty-request.

———. "Nahman-Watson Library Information Literacy Assessment Plan." 2018. https://www.gcc.mass.edu/library/files/2019/01/Information-Literacy-Assessment-Plan-FY-2018.pdf.

———. "Our Library Teaching Philosophy." Nahman-Watson Library. 2018. https://www.gcc.mass.edu/library/our-library-teaching-philosophy.

———. "Summer Faculty Workshop: Research across the Curriculum." Nahman-Watson Library. Accessed January 18, 2019. https://www.gcc.mass.edu/library/summer-faculty-workshop-research-across-the-curriculum.

Massachusetts Community College Council home page. Accessed March 18, 2019. https://mccc-union.org.

New England Commission of Higher Education (NECHE) home page. Accessed March 22, 2019. https://www.neche.org.

Chapter 5

Lafayette College

A Non-Liaison-Based Information Literacy Program

Lijuan Xu

Population Served

Lafayette College is a private, liberal arts residential college located in Easton, Pennsylvania. Founded in 1826, the college offers bachelor of arts degrees in thirty-seven fields and bachelor of science degrees in fourteen fields, including four in engineering. It has 2,642 undergraduates and 239 faculty members.[1] Ninety-nine percent of the students are full-time and traditional college age. Students represent fifty-three countries. Among domestic students, the majority come from Pennsylvania, the mid-Atlantic region, and New England. In keeping with the college's teaching-centered mission and its commitment to face-to-face interactions with students, the library's information literacy (IL) program focuses on in-class teaching, along with research consultations at the research help desk and in individual librarians' offices.

Program Scope

The IL program contributes to the college's mission and curriculum primarily through course-integrated library instruction classes. Librarians collaborate with faculty members to tailor each class to students' needs and offer assistance in developing and designing assignments. When time permits, librarians embed in classes or co-teach the course with the instructor.

The program has two core levels: basic and advanced. The basic level includes first-year seminars (FYSes) and 100-level courses. Through the FYSes that incoming first-year students (not including transfer students) take during the fall semester of their first year, students are introduced to library resources and services and how to conduct college-level research.[2] The goals for 100-level classes build upon the general library research skills that students have developed through their FYSes. They include developing effective search strategies, defining research questions, and understanding the research process. At the advanced level, students are immersed in specialized resources in a field of study and gain advanced understanding of the scholarly communication process.[3]

IL has been an integral part of the FYS program since 1992. Each FYS, capped at sixteen students, has a designated librarian and includes at least two library sessions on library research and information evaluation. Other courses, unlike the FYSes, have no campus-wide IL mandate. To encourage faculty members to integrate IL into 200-level and above courses, each spring since 2002, the library and the provost's office offer two to four grants ($1,500 each) to faculty members who are interested in incorporating IL into their upper-level courses throughout an entire spring semester. Grant recipients are expected to partner closely with a research and instruction (R&I) librarian and incorporate IL projects that would help students do at least one of the following:

- Discover that the information they use exists within a framework developed to record, store, and access it and that research allows them to tap into an ongoing conversation among scholars
- Critically examine the research process
- Explore the economic, social, legal, and ethical issues surrounding information in today's society[4]

Since 2002, librarians have worked with forty-four grant-funded courses, including capstones. A list of grant recipients, along with the courses for which they received a grant, their proposed IL projects, and librarian partner, is available on the library's website.[5]

Librarians' work with FYSes and grant courses has resulted in some curriculum changes at the college level. In May 2011, when the college revised its core curriculum, faculty members voted to formally adopt four IL outcomes that are based on the ACRL *Information Literacy Competency Standards for Higher Education*:[6]

- IL1. Identify and articulate the need for information relevant to a specific purpose or goal.
- IL2. Select the most appropriate investigative methods for different information needs and develop and employ effective search strategies to locate useful information.
- IL3. Evaluate information and its sources critically and incorporate selected information into personal knowledge bases and value systems.

- IL4. Understand the economic, legal, and social issues surrounding the use of information and access, and use information ethically, wisely, and legally.[7]

During the college's outcome implementation process, IL3 was absorbed by the writing outcomes.[8] IL1, 2, and 4 are currently assessed in the FYS program.

In addition to course-integrated instruction classes, librarians teach several citation management workshops each year and lead the Digital Humanities Summer Scholarship program (DHSS). Drawing participations from all R&I librarians and other library colleagues, such as the GIS librarian, DHSS is a six-week-long program during which six to eight students work as scholars on a project of their own design that incorporates research and digital methodology.[9] Student scholars are selected based on their application essays and research plans. DHSS combines class meetings, readings, and discussions as well as time for students to engage in their own project and share their research with the campus community and at the Bucknell University Digital Scholarship Conference.

During the second and third weeks of the fall semester, librarians offer orientation tours to first-year students. They also provide instruction at the research help desk and in their offices with individual students or student groups. Students, including those who work closely and collaboratively with faculty members on research projects, can sign up for thirty-to-sixty-minute personalized research assistance (PRA) appointments with a librarian. Postcards featuring popular movie titles and librarians have been created every semester since 2001 to advertise the PRA service. The full PRA postcard gallery can be found on the library's website.[10] A similar service is available to thesis students, whom the library contacts via email several times a year after they register for theses, highlighting available resources and services and encouraging them to meet with a librarian. Due to the popularity of PRA, PRA Express service was added to accommodate shorter appointments and to promote the visibility of the research help desk. Unlike regular PRAs, PRA Expresses are arranged at the request of a faculty member. Students from a class can use their course management site to schedule a twenty-minute meeting with a librarian who is on duty at the research help desk.

Operations

The library has five departments and sixteen librarians (see figure 5.1). All librarians have the same rank. They receive annual performance reviews without tenure and promotion. Librarians' job titles evolve over time to reflect the changes in their responsibilities. On the R&I team are the director and associate director of the department, the head of electronic resources, the Kirby librarian, and an R&I librarian.[11] In addition to these five R&I librarians who are dedicated to teaching, the director of access and outreach services, the special collections librarian, the associate college archivist, and the rare books cataloger all teach and participate in the FYS program. The technical services librarian and the director of access and outreach services also work at the research help desk. R&I librarians are all generalists. They can choose to partner with faculty members from any department.[12]

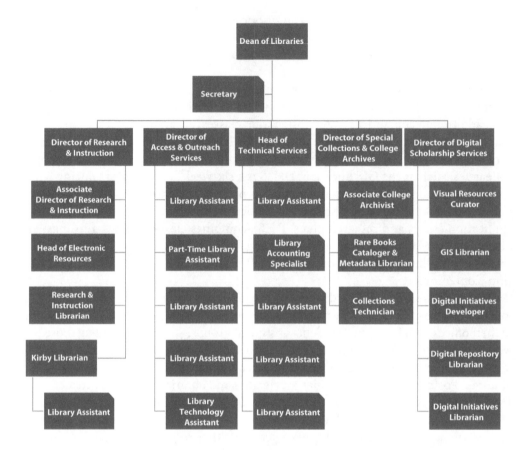

Figure 5.1
Library organization chart

FYSes and grant courses are assigned according to librarians' interests and prior work-ing relationships with faculty members. Each May, the author of the chapter, the associate director of the R&I department, distributes the following fall's FYS list to those who are on the teaching team and asks for their work preferences. These preferences are taken into consideration when FYSes are assigned. For grant courses, after the author meets with potential applicants each fall about their ideas and plans, she discusses with other librarians in the department and asks for their availability and interest in working with a particular course. Beyond FYSes and grant courses, R&I librarians can reach out to and work with any faculty member.

The team-based non-disciplinary approach was implemented in the early 1990s in order to devote more resources to teaching and to give R&I librarians "some choice in what they wanted to do and how they would do it."[13] This decentralized approach offers librarians the freedom to cultivate relationships with faculty members of their own choosing. It has led to meaningful librarian-faculty partnerships, including librarians becoming partners in assignment design and co-teachers.[14] It has also enabled librarians to pursue their own interests and participate in other campus and library initiatives.

One such initiative was the digital humanities initiative. When the library received a $700,000 Mellon Foundation grant in 2013 to foster more participation by faculty members and students in digital humanities (DH), R&I librarians served on the grant's steering committee. They joined colleagues from other library departments such as Digital Scholarship Services (DSS) on a "DH in the Classroom" initiative to teach sessions when faculty members wanted to incorporate DH methods into a course project. The Digital Humanities Summer Scholarship program (DHSS), originally developed by a Council on Library and Information Resources (CLIR) postdoctoral fellow in DSS, is now run by R&I librarians. The Open Educational Resources textbook initiative currently underway is led by librarians in collaboration with instructional technology services. Librarians have also played important roles in national projects such as the Ithaka S+R study of Asian studies scholars in 2017 and the Digging Deeper Reaching Further (DDRF) project, an initiative funded by a grant from the Institute of Museum and Library Services (IMLS).[15] Utilizing what they have learned from their work on the DDRF project, librarians have co-taught with faculty members introductory text-mining workshops at the college to help other library and faculty colleagues develop basic digital methodological expertise. They are extending IL work to include text mining and have teamed up with faculty members to explore the application of computational tools such as Voyant in teaching and student assignments.

All these efforts add dimensions and vibrancy to the IL program and raise librarians' profiles on campus. Librarians have received the college's highest teaching award, the Marquis Distinguished Teaching Award. Reviewed and selected by a faculty committee, the award recognizes four faculty members each year for their exemplary teaching. As librarians gain recognition as important resources and teachers, the number of classes they teach continues to increase every year. The team-based approach and the participation of all librarians in teaching have thus far helped sustain the IL program. The hours that the technical services librarian and the director of access and outreach services cover at the research help desk also free up R&I librarians to teach. However, as the college expands to enroll more students and hire more faculty members, librarians' workload will become a pressing issue, especially during the fall semester when demand for FYSes is at its peak.

Assessment

Since librarians work with a wide range of courses and the emphasis in each course is different, a one-size-fits-all review of the program is not the most appropriate. Librarians instead rely on informal evidence, including faculty members' support for IL (in the form of class requests and IL curriculum adoption) and conversations and interviews with faculty members, to assess the IL program as a whole. Information gathered through these venues is then used to improve librarians' teaching, revise IL assignments, and inform outreach strategies as well as the direction of the IL program, for example, what role R&I librarians can play in data and visual literacy and text mining.

The assessment of student IL learning in each course varies. For FYSes, the college currently assesses all three IL outcomes once every three years: identifying and locating information relevant to a specific purpose or goal, using information critically and effectively to accomplish a specific purpose or goal, and using information ethically and legally. The FYS instructor and librarian assessment team is chaired by the chapter author and the FYS program coordinator. All FYS instructors are expected to submit students' papers from a project that they think best embodies the IL outcomes to the assessment team. From these papers, the assessment team randomly selects 10 percent to assess, using a rubric that was developed by an R&I librarian and an English professor. Since fall 2014, there have been two rounds of assessment, with a faculty compliance rate of 65 and 50 percent, respectively. Following each cycle, the assessment team holds an open meeting to share with faculty members its findings and recommendations and sends a full report to the provost's office. The assessment results have sparked conversations among faculty members about how student IL skills should be further developed in majors and programs. Librarians are also making a more concerted effort to reach out to all faculty members who teach capstones and find out how they could better support students in these courses.

While there is college-wide assessment of students' IL skills in the FYS program, the assessment of student learning in other courses is up to the individual librarian. It varies from no assessment to grading students' papers and providing feedback. When IL is fully integrated in a course, librarians rely on IL-related discussions, projects, presentations, and reflections to gauge students' progress.[16] For grant courses, further evidence is collected through faculty members' presentations on their IL experiences and post-grant interviews with recipients.[17] Grant recipients participate in a lunchtime panel presentation to discuss their grant experiences with the campus community, including what worked in their courses, what challenges they encountered, and if the students achieved the desired learning outcomes. In fall 2008, the library also started to feature an interview article with a grant recipient for the library's biannual newsletter and website.[18] These regular, continuous conversations with faculty members, along with librarians' participation in class or grading student projects, help gauge student learning, improve IL content and pedagogy, and assess the success of the IL grant program.

Collaboration

Since there is no campus-wide IL curriculum mandate, the success of the IL program depends on the support of faculty members. Librarians therefore spend a lot of time building and sustaining relationships with faculty members. The small size of the college, along with librarians' faculty status and their participation in the college's self-governance, offer librarians many opportunities to interact with faculty members. The non-liaison-based approach that the library adopted in the 1990s encourages librarians to take advantage of those opportunities and to foster relationships with faculty members naturally. The freedom that this non-liaison-based approach offers has allowed librarians to connect with faculty members at both personal and professional levels and develop long-lasting and meaningful partnerships. These partnerships have in turn made it possible for librarians to expand their work from one course such as an FYS or a grant course to other courses, experiment with new ideas (e.g., PRA Express appointments and text mining), become more involved in assignment and syllabus design, and embed in or co-teach courses.

The grant program, in particular, relies on close faculty-librarian collaborations. Due to faculty members' positive experience, the collaborative efforts in grant courses have led to closer and more frequent collaborations. Grant recipients have also become IL advocates and "their advocacy has helped generate more awareness and interest among other faculty members in the grant program, and in working with librarians to improve their courses."[19]

As a result, faculty members regard the integration of IL as a pedagogical innovation and seek out librarians to work with their courses with or without a grant.

In addition to partnering with individual faculty members to build IL into their courses, librarians have established strong ties with the Center for the Integration of Teaching, Learning, and Scholarship (CITLS) and the College Writing Program (CWP). The three units co-organize a number of lunchtime presentations each year, all of which feature faculty members. For example, the IL lunchtime presentation each fall, now part of new faculty orientation organized by CITLS, showcases the previous spring's grant recipients and their experiences. Assignment panels such as "What's Your Favorite Writing Assignment?" highlight faculty members' assignments, how and why they develop these assignments, and what revisions they have made over the years. Programs are added as needs arise. In fall 2018, for example, a panel on literature review assignment design was put in place at the request of a professor. The CITLS director has been in conversations with librarians about how IL could be part of the summer teaching institute that she envisions for the center. Librarians have served and serve on CITLS and FYS advisory committees and participate in the summer workshop that the FYS program coordinator organizes for new FYS instructors. All of these faculty development–centered programs expand librarians' involvement in faculty pedagogy, elevate librarians' teaching role, and lead to more collaborations with faculty members. Through librarians' collaboration with faculty members, the library has become an integral and a vital component of the undergraduate experience.

Pedagogical Highlights

The broad IL program goals mentioned earlier guide how librarians generally approach instruction classes. All librarians employ active learning techniques in their teaching. However, each class is tailored to students' needs. What librarians teach in each class and how they teach varies according to the expectations of the course instructor, the course assignments, and the extent of the librarian's involvement. This is true even with the FYS sessions on library research and source evaluation. When these sessions take place and what exercises students will engage in during class differ in each FYS. There is no written script or canned approach to any class. Librarians are free to experiment with different approaches and different classes.

In addition to working with course instructors to determine the appropriate time and content of library sessions, librarians frequently discuss their ideas and plans with their library colleagues and seek their input and suggestions. They also share their experiences as well as readings and tools that they come across that could be helpful to others. Through these informal conversations as well as monthly reference meetings and end-of-the-semester instruction meetings, librarians share their ideas, teaching experiences, and exercises, all of which help create and solidify a team with shared values and practices. At the monthly meetings, discussions about reference questions and traffic often end up instruction-related. For example, librarians might discuss the PRA Express appointments they had at the research help desk, and based on the research challenges that they witness in PRA Express and other students whom they have worked with, decide what could be further emphasized or clarified in a future library instruction session. Lunchtime faculty IL and assignment presentations offer additional venues to learn about team members' teaching experiences and practices. Most of the librarians have attended the ACRL Immersion Program so that they are well grounded in learning theories and pedagogy. New members of the R&I team spend their first semester observing other librarians' classes and co-teaching with more seasoned librarians.

Administrative Highlights

Librarians use a shared room-booking system to schedule classes in the library. As described earlier, FYSes and grant courses are assigned based on librarians' interest or prior working relationship with faculty members. Beyond FYSes and grant courses, class requests often go directly to the librarians with whom faculty members have previously collaborated. Very rarely do they go to the R&I team leaders, the director and associate director of the R&I department, to be distributed. When there is a schedule conflict or another person might be a better fit, librarians forward the requests to those who might be available and interested. The decentralized approach to instruction helps avoid boredom on the librarians' part and injects energy and excitement in the program. Librarians are motivated to partner with faculty members and explore pedagogy out of personal interests and professional growth.

The self-management of librarians frees the R&I team leaders from managing daily operations. It allows them to focus on the bigger picture and strategic direction of the program, whether it is expanding librarians' role in assignment design, embarking on new initiatives such as extending IL to include text mining, or partnering with academic units such as CITLS and CWP on faculty development programs. Although some of the cosponsored programs, including the faculty research forum series (with CITLS and the faculty academic research committee) and the irregular lunch programs (with CITLS and the provost's office), do not have an explicit IL component, all these efforts increase librarians' own knowledge and further enhance the library's role in research and teaching. As one professor recently remarked, faculty members are victims of their own discipline. They lack librarians' breadth of knowledge and appreciate that librarians can make connections for them and help them build methodological expertise outside their discipline. Librarians' work with faculty members across disciplines and open communications among librarians have indeed turned the library into a collective knowledge center for faculty research and teaching. It has allowed librarians to connect faculty with librarians and other faculty members and to "identify and cultivate new collaborative opportunities."[20]

What I Wish People Knew

The library's IL program depends largely on librarians' relationships with faculty members, which take interpersonal skills and time to cultivate. To have a successful and vibrant program, librarians need to be proactive in reaching out to faculty members to learn about their research and teaching. Faculty members often welcome opportunities to discuss what they do. During the conversation, it might become apparent how the library can better support faculty members' teaching and research. For example, faculty members might mention a particular journal or database that is essential to their research or express their frustrations at assigning a research project such as a literature review.

In addition, it is important to pay attention to happenings on campus, such as the lectures given or organized by faculty members. Even though these events might not be directly related to librarians' work and librarians have many projects that demand their attention, it is beneficial to attend some of the events and regard them as professional development opportunities. Going to lectures, serving on faculty committees, or having one-on-one conversations with faculty members can all be learning opportunities. They increase librarians' visibility as well as their familiarity with the institution, along with its culture and curriculum. They also generate goodwill and equip librarians with new knowledge and vocabulary, which librarians can use to initiate and engage in dialogues with faculty members.

It is also worth pausing to consider what kind of teaching role librarians want to play and how they might get there. Librarians can start with one course and one faculty member and expand their work to other courses and other faculty members. Since librarians interact with students in the classroom and through research consultations, they often experience firsthand a wide range of research assignments. Librarians can further develop that knowledge by learning from faculty members, including those that they collaborate with and those at the writing center. Such expertise allows librarians to better assist other faculty members with assignment design and make IL work more meaningful. Using and developing librarians' knowledge of assignment design not only expands but also reaffirms librarians' role in implementing, innovating, and improving the curriculum.

Notes

1. "Common Data Set 2018–2019," Office of Institutional Research, Lafayette College, accessed December 2, 2018, https://oir.lafayette.edu/wp-content/uploads/sites/196/2018/11/CDS2018-2019.pdf.
2. About ten students transfer to the college each year. These students are not part of the first-year cohort. They enter into the sophomore class or above.
3. "Library Instruction: Mission Statement and Goals," Lafayette College Library, last modified July 5, 2017, https://library.lafayette.edu/services-help/services/instruction-and-information-literacy/library-instruction-mission-statement-and-goals.
4. "Information Literacy Grants," Lafayette College Library, last modified January 8, 2018, https://library.lafayette.edu/services-help/services/instruction-and-information-literacy/information-literacy-grants.
5. "Information Literacy Grant Recipients," Lafayette College Library, last modified January 7, 2019, https://library.lafayette.edu/services-help/services/instruction-and-information-literacy/information-literacy-grant-recipients.
6. Association of College and Research Libraries, *Information Literacy Competency Standards for Higher Education* (Chicago: Association of College and Research Libraries, 2000).
7. "First Year Seminar Library Instruction," Lafayette College Library, accessed September 12, 2018, https://library.lafayette.edu/services-help/services/instruction-and-information-literacy/first-year-seminar-library-instruction.
8. The writing outcomes are designated for the writing courses in the core curriculum. When the curriculum was revised, many outcomes, including those for IL and writing, were developed and implemented.
9. Sarah Morris, "The Digital Humanities Summer Scholarship: A Model for Library-Led Undergraduate Digital Scholarship," *College and Undergraduate Libraries* 24, no. 2–4 (2017): 533–35, https://doi.org/10.1080/10691316.2017.1338978.
10. "PRA Gallery," Lafayette College, last modified September 12, 2018, https://library.lafayette.edu/request-a-personalized-research-assistance-pra-session/pra-gallery.
11. The Kirby librarian is historically affiliated with the Kirby government and law department.

12. Lijuan Xu and Benjamin Jahre, "From Service Providers to Collaborators and Partners: A Nondiscipline-Based Approach at a Liberal Arts College," *New Review of Academic Librarianship* 24, no. 3–4 (2018): 422, https://doi.org/10.1080/13614533.2018.1498795.
13. Xu and Jahre, "From Service Providers," 422.
14. Xu and Jahre, "From Service Providers," 423; Lijuan Xu and Nestor Gil, "Librarians as Co-teachers and Curators: Integrating Information Literacy in a Studio Art Course at a Liberal Arts College," *Art Documentation* 36, no. 1 (Spring 2017): 128, https://doi.org/10.1086/691376.
15. Danielle Cooper and Katherine Daniel, *Supporting the Changing Research Practices of Asian Studies Scholars* (New York: Ithaka S+R, June 21, 2018), https://doi.org/10.18665/sr.307642; "HTRC Digging Deeper, Reaching Further: Libraries Empowering Users to Mine the HathiTrust Digital Library Resources," HathiTrust Research Center, University of Illinois, accessed September 27, 2018, https://teach.htrc.illinois.edu.
16. Lijuan Xu, "Establishing a Vibrant Information Literacy Program in the Absence of Curriculum Mandate: A Case Study," *International Journal of Librarianship* 2, no. 2 (2017): 88, https://doi.org/10.23974/ijol.2017.vol2.2.36; Xu and Gil, "Librarians as Co-teachers," 131.
17. "Information Literacy Grant Recipients."
18. "Information Literacy Interviews," Lafayette College, last modified May 10, 2018, https://library.lafayette.edu/services-help/services/instruction-and-information-literacy/information-literacy-interviews.
19. Xu, "Establishing a Vibrant Information Literacy Program," 89.
20. Xu and Jahre, "From Service Providers," 426.

Bibliography

Association of College and Research Libraries. *Information Literacy Competency Standards for Higher Education*. Chicago: Association of College and Research Libraries, 2000.

Cooper, Danielle, and Katherine Daniel. *Supporting the Changing Research Practices of Asian Studies Scholars*. Research report. New York: Ithaka S+R, June 21, 2018. https://doi.org/10.18665/sr.307642.

HathiTrust Research Center. "HTRC Digging Deeper, Reaching Further: Libraries Empowering Users to Mine the HathiTrust Digital Library Resources." University of Illinois. Accessed September 27, 2018. https://teach.htrc.illinois.edu.

Lafayette College. "Common Data Set 2018–2019." Office of Institutional Research. Accessed December 2, 2018. https://oir.lafayette.edu/wp-content/uploads/sites/196/2018/11/CDS2018-2019.pdf.

Lafayette College Library. "First Year Seminar Library Instruction." Accessed September 12, 2018. https://library.lafayette.edu/services-help/services/instruction-and-information-literacy/first-year-seminar-library-instruction.

———. "Information Literacy Grant Recipients." Last modified January 7, 2019. https://library.lafayette.edu/services-help/services/instruction-and-information-literacy/information-literacy-grant-recipients.

———. "Information Literacy Grants." Last modified January 8, 2018. https://library.lafayette.edu/services-help/services/instruction-and-information-literacy/information-literacy-grants.

———. "Information Literacy Interviews." Last modified May 10, 2018. https://library.lafayette.edu/services-help/services/instruction-and-information-literacy/information-literacy-interviews.

———. "Library Instruction: Mission Statement and Goals." Last modified July 5, 2017. https://library.lafayette.edu/services-help/services/instruction-and-information-literacy/library-instruction-mission-statement-and-goals.

———. "PRA Gallery." Last modified September 12, 2018. https://library.lafayette.edu/request-a-personalized-research-assistance-pra-session/pra-gallery.

Morris, Sarah. "The Digital Humanities Summer Scholarship: A Model for Library-Led Undergraduate Digital Scholarship." *College and Undergraduate Libraries* 24, no. 2–4 (2017): 532–44. https://doi.org/10.1080/10691316.2017.1338978.

Xu, Lijuan. "Establishing a Vibrant Information Literacy Program in the Absence of Curriculum Mandate: A Case Study." *International Journal of Librarianship* 2, no. 2 (2017): 84–91. https://doi.org/10.23974/ijol.2017.vol2.2.36.

Xu, Lijuan, and Nestor Gil. "Librarians as Co-teachers and Curators: Integrating Information Literacy in a Studio Art Course at a Liberal Arts College." *Art Documentation* 36, no. 1 (Spring 2017): 122–36. https://doi.org/10.1086/691376.

Xu, Lijuan, and Benjamin Jahre. "From Service Providers to Collaborators and Partners: A Nondiscipline-Based Approach at a Liberal Arts College." *New Review of Academic Librarianship* 24, no. 3–4 (2018): 418–29. https://doi.org/10.1080/13614533.2018.1498795.

Chapter 6

Michigan State University
Focusing on First Year Writing

Benjamin Oberdick and Elizabeth A. Webster

Population Served

Michigan State University (MSU) is a large land-grant research university. Our students represent all fifty states and Washington, DC, as well as 141 other nations; 51.9 percent are women; 20.6 percent are students of color; and 12.5 percent are international students. As of fall 2018, the student population was 39,423 undergraduates and 10,928 graduate and professional students for a total student population of 50,351.[1]

Of that total, about 8,250 are first-year students, and the vast majority of them take the required first year writing (FYW) class offered by the Department of Writing, Rhetoric, and American Cultures (WRAC). MSU students who are a part of one of the three MSU residential colleges (James Madison College, Lyman Briggs College, and the Residential College of Arts and Humanities) do not take the WRAC FYW class because they have their own FYW course within their college. During the matriculation process, incoming MSU freshmen who are not joining one of the MSU residential colleges are placed in one of two WRAC FYW classes: WRA 101: Writing as Inquiry or WRA 1004: Preparation for College Writing. If students are placed in WRA 1004, they must pass this course and then subsequently pass WRA 101. In a typical fall semester, there are around sixteen sections of WRA 1004 and 120 sections of WRA 101. WRA 1004 classes are generally smaller in size—twenty-four students versus the twenty-seven that are typically seen in WRA 101—and the student population is more often dominated by international students. Because of the sheer size of the WRAC FYW program, we teach mainly one-shot sessions as they are an effective way to have face-to-face interactions with a large number of students.

Program Scope

The Teaching and Learning Unit of the library is responsible for teaching information literacy classes for students in FYW classes, whether that is in the WRAC department or a residential college. We also teach other populations, such as visiting scholars or study abroad programs, as well as some general education classes. We teach primarily in-person one-shot sessions that are one hour and fifty minutes in length. We do not have a set curriculum that must be followed for each one-shot; however, all classes are targeted to the specific assignment, and those are usually similar across the WRAC FYW classes. The one-shots usually include a tour of the library, which is always popular and memorable and serves to introduce students to our vast physical space. We encourage faculty to bring students to the library once they have an assignment necessitating library research. Teaching librarians have the freedom to design their classes, and we all hold to the principles of student-centered active learning. Additionally, we also offer information literacy–focused instruction modules should the instructor not have time in the course schedule for an in-person session: for example, for online-only classes or hybrid classes that meet in person once per week. Teaching one-shot information literacy sessions for first-year writing classes accounts for roughly 90 percent of unit instructional time, but in addition to these classes, we also conduct tours and teach workshops and orientation sessions for other groups. These vary from year to year, but usually include some campus-wide student success and bridge programs such as MAGIC (Maximizing Academic Growth in College) and TRIO Student Support Services, orientation sessions for new MSU faculty and graduate students, and on-demand tours for visiting international faculty through programs such as VIPP (Visiting International Professionals Program) and for other outside groups such as K–12 groups coming to visit MSU.

Operations

The Teaching and Learning Unit, housed within the Public Services Division, has a twofold mission: teaching information literacy sessions for students in FYW classes and assisting in the development of MSU librarians in the area of teaching and learning. The Teaching and Learning Unit is comprised of five librarians plus the head of the unit, all of whom teach information literacy classes for FYW classes. The five librarians also have another specialization or focus in the unit:

- One unit member takes the lead in creating and updating our online information literacy–focused instructional modules and also focuses on accessibility issues.
- Another is the liaison to a residential college—the James Madison College (public affairs and public policy)—and teaches its FYW classes in the spring semester.
- Another works with multiple MSU integrative studies groups to incorporate information literacy into their curricula.
- Two members work with our Digital Information Services and the Digital Scholarship Lab, a partnership between the College of Arts and Letters and the libraries, housed in the libraries, for scholars from all disciplines and departments to explore and collaborate using specialized technology.

Librarians at MSU have a primary (75%) and secondary (25%) work assignment. Librarians report to their primary supervisor. Of the five librarians in the Teaching and Learning Unit, four have a primary assignment in Teaching and Learning and report directly to the Head of Teaching and Learning, and one has a secondary assignment. Of the four librarians who have primary Teaching and Learning assignments, three have a secondary assignment in Reference Services, and one has a secondary assignment in the Digital Scholarship Lab—both within the Public Services division.

Other units within Public Services include Outreach, User Experience, and Distance Learning Services. The Head of Teaching and Learning reports to the Assistant University Librarian (AUL) for Public Services, and all requests for monetary support come though this line. There is no dedicated budget line for the Teaching and Learning Unit, but the head can request funding from the AUL for Public Services. Examples include funds for class materials such as worksheets and informational handouts.

Role of the One-Shot

Our program is made up almost entirely of one-shot instruction sessions. We do have some faculty who we work with on double (or even triple) shots, but the vast majority of our classes are of the one-shot variety. We are lucky to get 110 minutes in ours, so it is already much longer than a traditional fifty-minute one-shot, but since there are around 7,000 students who take the FYW class each year, we could not see every class with our current staffing level, even if it were possible for each section to come to the library. We do offer a series of online instructional videos and modules as well, so some FYW faculty who do not bring their classes to the library for a library instruction session use those with their classes. Topics of the videos include searching with a purpose, evaluating online information, embracing uncertainty in the research process, and citation help.

Pedagogical Highlights

The Teaching and Learning Unit has a shared learning outcome for our instruction with FYW classes: as a result of this class, students will be able to identify, locate, and analyze different types of information in order to stimulate inquiry and use the information effectively in their assignment. Librarians in the unit have the freedom and independence to approach their instruction in a way that is authentic and works for them, but unit members share a common philosophy and focus with instruction that it is inquiry-based, active, and student-centered. We believe in engaging students in the class, and we all use some combination of hands-on activities, group work, and giving students time to put the information into action in our classes. A typical class has students engaged in asking questions about sources and working to figure out how to best use and understand a source, and we stay far away from the checklist approach of labeling sources as "good" or "bad." One of the unit librarians runs a popular community of practice around teaching. It is open to any librarian and recently has included staff who have teaching as part of their duties (such as workshops). Some of the topics the community of practice has covered are active learning pedagogy, reflective teaching, backwards design, threshold concepts and the ACRL *Framework for Information Literacy for Higher Education*, and information literacy in the disciplines.[2]

Collaboration

In addition to our course-integrated information literacy instruction, we also teach a series of general library introductory orientations in the fall targeted to new graduate students and faculty. These one-hour sessions, held over the lunch hour, are a basic overview and introduction to the MSU Libraries and are intended to be a first contact point with these populations. As well as teaching the various types of sessions, unit members also work with faculty on assignment design, research projects, and the integration of information literacy into the curriculum. One Teaching and Learning librarian is the liaison to the MSU Integrative Studies units, and she has been able to work with them to integrate information literacy concepts into their curricula.

We often work with some of the campus programs for new students, underserved populations, K–12 groups, and other community outreach efforts. Our closest allies are WRAC, since that department is responsible for teaching the majority of the FYW classes on campus, and the James Madison College. We need strong relationships with these two programs as the bulk of our teaching occurs in their classes. James Madison College underwent a curriculum change in its FYW class, and the liaison worked with the college to ensure that library workshops remained a component. New faculty were recruited to teach the FYW, most of whom the librarian had not worked with previously. She did a significant amount of outreach (individual meetings and group presentations) and relied on word of mouth from faculty she had previously worked with. Ultimately, all the faculty teaching that FYW class scheduled instruction for the semester, which demonstrates that outreach and collaboration are essential to maintaining levels of service. We also work closely with the MSU Hub (a group focused on facilitating projects around innovative approaches to teaching and learning), the Academic Advancement Network (a group focused on faculty and organizational development), the Writing Center, the Social Science Help Rooms (a place in the library where students can receive free and unlimited tutoring for selected social science courses), and other academic units to support campus student success initiatives.

Marketing

The Teaching and Learning Unit has been responsible for working with the Department of Writing, Rhetoric and American Cultures (WRAC) FYW classes for more than twenty-five years. WRAC FYW faculty are not required to bring their classes to the library for an information literacy session, so one of the responsibilities of the Teaching and Learning Unit, especially the Head of Teaching of Learning, is to liaise with WRAC and maintain good relations so that FYW faculty are aware of what the librarians can do for their students. The primary method of making WRAC faculty aware of our services is a presentation at the new FYW teacher orientation given by the department. At the orientation, we present an overview of what we do, demonstrate what our information literacy sessions look like in the classroom, and lay out the logistics and procedures for scheduling an information literacy session with one of the librarians in the Teaching and Learning Unit. Our approach to information literacy sessions for FYW classes is inquiry-based and directly connected to the research assignment students are completing for their FYW class. We give the new WRAC FYW faculty a sense of this approach by having them search and use tools that are similar to those their students will use when they are in our library session.

In terms of connecting with WRAC FYW faculty from semester to semester, we also rely on word of mouth and repeat customers. It is a Sisyphean task as there are many graduate students who teach the WRAC FYW classes for only one or two semesters, so we are constantly reaching out and connecting with the new instructors who are being brought in to teach. Additionally, some members of the unit have connections outside of the library and they use those to bring in other classes as well. The librarian who works with the James Madison College actively recruits professors to schedule sessions by attending faculty meetings, giving presentations about the library, and maintaining relationships with faculty who taught FYW.

Administrative Highlights

We ask FYW faculty to submit a library instruction request using an online form that asks for first, second, and third date and time choices for the class, as well as the topic focus. The form is sent to our shared instruction mailbox, which is managed by one Teaching and Learning librarian. As the requests come in, the librarian in charge of the mailbox fields them. If a specific librarian is requested in the form, the request is forwarded only to the requested librarian. If no librarian is requested, then the request is sent to all the Teaching and Learning librarians. Everyone checks their schedules and then chimes in if they can take the class. Once the request is claimed, the librarian contacts the instructor to confirm and to request a copy of the assignment so that the session can be specifically tailored to the requirements. The process, from the initial request email to the confirmation email by the librarian, is usually completed within a day or two. Each librarian keeps track of the number of classes they teach, and we share the teaching load equally. Because there are six librarians that teach these classes, we can usually accommodate an instructor's requested class time. It is rare for us to have to ask instructors for alternative times beyond the third choice. Toward the beginning of the semester, there is a flurry of emails as the requests are coming in, but we are aware of this and make a point to remain vigilant!

Assessment

Our unit has taken part in campus assessment processes by contributing data to different campus programs and projects, including an ACRL Assessment in Action (AiA) project considering student success. The AiA project was carried out by a librarian in the Teaching and Learning Unit in collaboration with a MSUL User Experience Librarian and attempted to correlate data retrieved from library service points with student success data at the campus level. The authors found different degrees of impact based on student level and human engagement with the library (people services versus book/space services), but did not have sufficient data to make further generalizations.[3]

The Teaching and Learning Unit provides an annual summary of unit work over the past year to the AUL for Public Services, but there is not an annual formal assessment of the program. The unit works together each year to decide on the goals and objectives for the year and what to focus on during that year. Classroom assessment uses a Google form at the end of class to assess student learning. Students are asked how confident they feel using the library, identifying different types of information and their uses, using the search tools used in class, and trying new ways to look for materials. Unit members review the questions asked annually and make any necessary changes. In the past, students were asked about which parts of a library workshop were helpful to them, and the number-one response chosen was always the tour, so the importance of the tour was continually reinforced and it remains a part of the class. Occasionally faculty want to eliminate the tour in favor of more work in the databases, and we use this data to point out that the tour is highly valued by the students.

Information Literacy Coordinator Profile

The current Head of Teaching and Learning worked in the unit as an Instruction/Information Literacy Librarian for six years before an opportunity arose to move into the head of unit position. He was the most senior member of the unit (besides the former head of the unit), and the only internal candidate to express interest in the position, so it was an easy and quick move. The Head of Teaching and Learning position at MSUL is a formal one where the person functions as the head of a unit and supervises the librarians in the unit. The head is responsible for completing an annual evaluation for each member of the unit. The head reports directly to the Assistant University Librarian (AUL) for Public Services and serves on the Public Services Department Head Council.

What We Wish People Knew

This is the first professional leadership position Ben ever held, and he had a lot to learn about leading a unit and supervising other professionals when he became the Head of Teaching and Learning in July 2014. He would advise new coordinators to spend a lot of time working to hire the best teaching librarians you can, and once they join the library, to spend a lot of time working closely with them to help them understand the unit's mission, work, and purpose. This time spent helping onboard new librarians to the unit will make the transition easier for the entire unit and will help to ensure that everyone continues to "row the boat" in the same direction. Our unit maintains web pages where we document these philosophies, share our annual unit goals and objectives, and provide some data about our teaching.

He believes strongly in the powers of observation, and he strongly suggests that coordinators promote a culture of observation for their classes. This includes observing the librarians you supervise and also encouraging them to observe each other and you. We open almost all of the classes we teach for observation by any librarian at the library. It is a great way not only to help orient new unit members, but also to help show new librarians in other departments what we do and how we approach our instruction, which also hopefully gives them a starting place and some ideas for their own teaching practice. In line with this, he would also strongly suggest that new coordinators keep a foot in the classroom and continue to teach. It's important to maintain your teaching skills and to not let your administrative duties overwhelm everything else.

If being a supervisor is a new role for you, he would encourage you to take part in some professional development programs to acquire some skills that may be important when issues arise. He took advantage of some programs offered by MSU's human resources around topics such as crucial accountability, how to have difficult conversations, and how to lead a productive and positive unit. He found these programs to be extremely helpful in building my confidence in leading a unit, and they also assisted me in gaining some of the skills and knowledge necessary when dealing with various personnel situations. He would also suggest looking for additional leadership-related higher education and library-specific professional development programs, which you can find easily online.

Lastly, he would stress the importance of really listening to the people you supervise and doing everything possible to support them in their work. It is the coordinator's job to be a champion for their people, which includes saying no for them at times and helping them maintain a balance in their work. He strives each day to help the librarians in his unit be successful and to create an environment where they can be successful.

Notes

1. "MSU Facts," Michigan State University, accessed February 13, 2019, https://msu.edu/about/thisismsu/facts.php.
2. Association of College and Research Libraries, *Framework for Information Literacy for Higher Education* (Chicago: Association of College and Research Libraries, 2016).
3. Magnus, E. & B. Oberdick. "Investigating the Impact of a Peer Research Service at Michigan State University." Poster, ACRL Assessment in Action (AIA) program. American Library Association Annual Conference. San Francisco, CA. June 27, 2015.

Bibliography

Association of College and Research Libraries. *Framework for Information Literacy for Higher Education.* Chicago: Association of College and Research Libraries, 2016.
Michigan State University. "MSU Facts." Accessed February 13, 2019. https://msu.edu/about/thisismsu/facts.php.

Chapter 7

Northern Kentucky University

Strategic Instruction through Connected One-Shots

Andrea Brooks and Jane Hammons

Population Served

Northern Kentucky University (NKU) is a four-year public university near the Cincinnati metropolitan area and serves more than 14,000 students, including approximately 1,500 graduate students. NKU offers ninety bachelor's degrees, with key majors including organizational leadership, nursing, and social work. Graduate and professional programs include a master of social work, a doctor of education in educational leadership, and a doctor of nursing practice.[1] In addition to on-campus programs, NKU offers several fully online undergraduate and graduate degrees in both traditional and accelerated formats.[2]

The majority of NKU's students come from surrounding counties in the immediate region, and nearly half of the student population is first-generation college students.[3] In recognition of the needs of these students, the information literacy program does provide support in introductory 100-level courses. In recent years, however, the emphasis of the program has shifted to focus more on instruction within the disciplines.

Program Scope

The mission of the library's information literacy (IL) program is to develop and enhance the information behaviors of students by strategically integrating information literacy across the curriculum. The Association of College and Research Libraries' *Framework for Information Literacy for Higher Education* influences the focus of the program, as information literacy librarians emphasize not only research skills, but also the need for students to develop broader conceptual understandings related to information creation, access, and use.[4] After the publication of the *Framework*, IL librarians developed revised information literacy learning outcomes, identifying foundational and advanced outcomes for instruction sessions.

In order to achieve strategic IL integration, the information literacy program consists of a connected one-shot approach that spans a student's academic career. Librarians have selected key first-year courses to engage students with foundational information literacy concepts. These courses include UNV 101 (Orientation to College and Beyond), ENG 101 (College Writing), and ENG 102 (Advanced College Writing), which are traditionally taken by the majority of first-year students. Information literacy librarians also collaborate with disciplinary faculty to identify targeted upper-level courses within each academic program where information literacy should be integrated. Most often, the disciplinary courses targeted for instruction are research methods or capstone courses in the major. Ideally, undergraduate students attend a series of one-shot sessions during their academic career that are connected, but scaffolded, creating relevant and meaningful instruction for each discipline. In taking this approach, IL program librarians hope to teach higher-level concepts to students in the disciplinary courses and to avoid the problem of repetition that often comes when students attend disconnected one-shot sessions.

Information literacy instruction is delivered on campus and online. Online modules, which consist of a mix of videos, text, and searching activities, have been created for several targeted courses, at both foundational and advanced levels. These modules are created in Canvas (NKU's learning management system) and exported to the university's Canvas Commons, where they are available for upload. All instructors are notified if a module is available for their course. The learning outcomes for targeted courses remain consistent whether the instruction is delivered online or on campus.

IL program librarians also provide instruction for graduate students. Graduate-level instruction is mainly targeted at introductory graduate courses. A growing number of graduate programs are offered online, and librarians have developed numerous online modules for these courses.

In December 2017, information literacy was chosen as the topic for NKU's next quality enhancement plan (QEP). The QEP, a requirement for institutions accredited by the Commission on Colleges of the Southern Association of Colleges and Schools, is a multiyear initiative focused on enhancing student learning. NKU's information literacy QEP kicked off in fall 2018 and focuses on formalizing and assessing disciplinary information literacy learning outcomes. As faculty and students engage with information literacy across campus, the library's information literacy program will invariably change, and hopefully grow to incorporate deeper, more lasting collaborations.

Operations

The information literacy program is a separate department within a broader Research and Instruction (RI) division in the library. The RI division includes four liaison librarians, who provide one-on-one research consultations to students in their liaison areas, and three public services librarians, who provide drop-in assistance at the reference desk, in addition to the information literacy program team.

While the activities of each group within the division are intended to support the information literacy development of NKU students, and there is some overlap in duties, the development and delivery of formal, course-integrated information literacy instruction is the primary responsibility of the three information literacy librarians: the Information Literacy Coordinator, an Instructional Services Librarian, and a First-Year Experience (FYE) Librarian. These three librarians write student learning outcomes, develop curriculum, teach IL instruction sessions on campus, and create online instructional materials. The workload is split among the three librarians, with the FYE librarian focused solely on first-year courses. The other two librarians focus on disciplinary integration, reaching out to disciplinary faculty to identify appropriate courses and developing the information literacy curriculum in selected programs. As described in more detail below, these two librarians each maintain responsibility for a certain number of disciplines, identifying the courses within those disciplines to be targeted for instruction.

The lines between each of the three groups within the RI division are not rigid and have in fact shifted several times in recent years. For example, the FYE librarian is also one of the public services librarians, providing research assistance at the reference desk. And, while the three IL program librarians teach most of the library's instruction sessions, both for targeted and nontargeted courses, liaison librarians, on occasion, provide instruction for courses within their departments. Most requests for instruction come through an online scheduling system and are handled by the IL team. However, liaison librarians sometimes receive instruction requests directly from instructors in their departments. When these requests do occur, the liaison librarian is encouraged (but not required) to consult with a member of the IL program team so that the two can work together to decide who should teach the session. Generally, the decision is made together and based on the instructor's goals for the session.

While this structure allows for flexibility when needed, it can also create uncertainty regarding the responsibilities of librarians within each group, especially in regard to instruction requests that come directly to the liaison librarian. To mitigate this, the information literacy librarians, liaison librarians, and public service librarians meet a few times each semester to address joint concerns and build connections between the units.

Additionally, the library houses a Library Informatics (LIN) department, which administers an undergraduate LIN degree. One of the LIN courses is a three-credit information literacy course (LIN 175), which may be taken for general education credit. The LIN department is separate from the information literacy program, but IL librarians have frequently taught the LIN 175 course as adjunct instructors. Teaching this course has allowed IL program librarians the opportunity to gain a better understanding of students' knowledge related to IL, and librarians have been able to incorporate these insights into one-shot instruction sessions.

Marketing

Information literacy librarians actively seek to integrate information literacy instruction within pre-identified, targeted classes. In order to do this, announcements go out via email to the instructors teaching selected courses prior to the semester start, allowing targeted faculty first choice in scheduling classes. These emails indicate that, due to the nature of the course, it has been identified as one in which information literacy instruction will be especially relevant. Since taking this approach in 2015, the bulk of instruction is now directed at targeted courses. For example, in the 2014–15 academic year, 25 percent of instruction sessions were provided to nontargeted courses. In the 2018/19 academic year, nontargeted classes made up only 15 percent of the workload.

While information literacy instruction is promoted through email only to targeted courses, , the instruction calendar is posted online and open to anyone. Instruction requests are not turned away, although there are times when nontargeted instruction requests are passed on to the liaison librarians.

Collaboration

Information literacy librarians have collaborated with disciplinary faculty in many programs to integrate IL learning outcomes and relevant instructional resources into the curriculum. While much of this development remains in flux, some efforts have been formalized to provide consistent and purposeful instruction. One of the most successful collaborations has been with a doctorate of nursing program (DNP) on campus. After many conversations, information literacy is now part of the nurse anesthesia program and included in the syllabus. DNP-anesthesia students are required to attend an information literacy seminar in the library and complete an online module. Additionally, students write a reflective narrative at the beginning, middle, and end of the program to self-assess their strengths and weaknesses regarding research and scholarship. IL librarians grade the reflections and provide a summary of major themes that emerge from the reflections to the course instructors and program coordinator. The relationship with this DNP has extended to other campus DNPs including those offered online, and similar information literacy efforts are taking shape.

More broadly, a successful collaboration with NKU's Office of Graduate Education led to the creation of an annual Graduate Student Research Symposium. The event brings librarians and disciplinary faculty together to guide students in the transition to graduate-level research practices and habits. While the focus is on students, the event also creates connections between librarians and graduate faculty, and the symposium is now organized by a campus-wide committee. Further details of the symposium have been published in a *Kentucky Libraries* article.[5]

At a foundational level, the FYE librarian developed a partnership with the Office of First-Year Programs to deliver a consistent introductory experience to new students taking UNV 101, a freshman seminar course. The instruction combines online modules with a hands-on learning experience in the library. IL program librarians have also forged successful relationships with the English department, and while information literacy is not yet a formal outcome of introductory English courses, the majority of students taking

ENG 101 or 102 courses are exposed to information literacy instruction through either a face-to-face one-shot or an online module.

Finally, information literacy librarians have worked with disciplinary faculty from multiple departments on campus to create targeted information literacy instruction for students. However, factors like turnover, multiple sections of one course, and a lack of formal information literacy learning outcomes within the course sometimes result in one-time collaborations rather than lasting partnerships. The selection of information literacy as the QEP is creating opportunities that should lead to deeper collaborations. A major component of the QEP relies on recruiting ambassadors from all departments on campus. Ambassadors participate in a summer institute to develop their understanding of information literacy and then use that knowledge to integrate IL learning outcomes into their courses. Information literacy librarians work with ambassadors to facilitate this integration through the development of instructional resources and assessment. The first summer institute was held in June 2018 with ten participants representing nine disciplines.

Assessment

In order to ensure that one-shot sessions build upon earlier sessions, the information literacy team developed broad program outcomes using the ACRL *Framework* as a guide.[6] Foundational and advanced learning outcomes stem from these broad outcomes and are assigned to either first-year or disciplinary courses respectively. At the advanced disciplinary level, general outcomes are often revised slightly to suit the needs of a specific course. After developing learning outcomes, instruction librarians created a strategic assessment plan that outlines instruction program goals and identifies assessment methods to measure those goals.[7]

Information literacy librarians do not attempt to assess student learning in all courses that attend instruction. Instead, prior to the start of the academic year, IL librarians identify one specific assessment question and include formal assessment in only those courses that will provide data relevant to the selected questions. For example, in 2017–18, IL librarians were interested in learning more about the effectiveness of online modules, both on their own merits and also in comparison with face-to-face instruction. Librarians developed specific assessment questions that were included at the end of all online instructional modules. These questions measured students' feedback about the format of the instruction and their perceptions regarding their own learning. In addition, for certain courses in which one section attended a face-to-face session and another section completed an online module, students in both sections were asked to complete the same pretest and posttest. Students in both online and face-to-face classes demonstrated improvement from the pre- to the posttest, but as far as which group (online or face-to-face) improved more, the results varied by course.

Assessment data is mostly used internally to make changes to instructional methods or curriculum. For example, one assessment project focused on students in ENG 102 and involved the collection and analysis (using a rubric) of student research papers. Results from this assessment project were used to make revisions to the information literacy learning outcomes addressed during the one-shot session. The coordinator also submits an annual report to the library dean showcasing major accomplishments, sharing results of assessment projects, and reporting instruction statistics.

Role of the One-Shot

Our goal is to provide scaffolded instruction by focusing on foundational skills in specific general education courses and then progressing to more advanced information literacy concepts in upper-level courses that are relevant to students in their field of study. Librarians believe this goal can be accomplished through a series of one-shot sessions as long as those one-shot sessions are part of the course curriculum. In other words, librarians advocate to integrate information literacy learning outcomes within the course so that teaching faculty are reinforcing IL concepts in the classroom and through assignments. The *Framework for Information Literacy* asserts that a single one-shot will not develop information-literate learners, but one-shot sessions that are integrated purposefully within the curriculum, at the appropriate level, can have an impact. "Over the course of a student's academic program, one-shot sessions that address a particular need at a particular time, systematically integrated into the curriculum, can play a significant role in an information literacy program."[8]

A connected, integrated one-shot approach is the goal for NKU information literacy librarians, and targeting specific classes for instruction has been somewhat successful in establishing a scaffolded connection between the one-shots. However, the formal integration of information literacy outcomes into the curriculum continues to be a challenge. IL outcomes, more often, are explicitly addressed only during the one-shot session, rather than integrated as a course outcome. This means that IL outcomes are not assessed in the broader context of the student's course. Although efforts have been made to better collaborate with teaching faculty, as noted with the DNP example above and the integration of the information literacy QEP, many students likely view information literacy instruction as a series of disconnected one-shots. Since most sessions do include at least some focus on database searching, students may struggle to see differences between what they learned in previous sessions. In order to overcome this, librarians explain to students during a one-shot that the specific instruction session they are attending is part of a broader instruction program and that students should expect to attend multiple sessions during their time at NKU.

Pedagogical Highlights

Our program emphasizes that information literacy is more than database search skills. While database instruction is usually included in most sessions, this is often the shortest component of a one-shot. For us, information literacy instruction should focus less on the tools and services at a library and more intently on broad understandings about research and scholarship in a student's discipline. For example, it is important for students majoring in business to be aware of the Business Source Premier database, but it is more important that they understand how and why they are searching a database in the first place. Upon graduation, student access to information resources will vary. Being able to seek, retrieve, analyze, build upon, and ethically use information from a multitude of resources is of great importance to future graduates.

To achieve our learning goals, we embrace an active and collaborative learning environment that allows students to learn from us and from each other. For example, one activity, related to the Scholarship as Conversation frame, has students discuss multiple true/false statements about the purpose of a literature review. The goal is to help students recognize that a literature review is necessary to understand the conversation that scholars have been having related to their topic and how this conversation should influence their own research. Another activity, related to both the Scholarship as Conversation frame and the Information Has Value frame, asks students to review an article from which all the references have been removed. Students discuss what the lack of references means for their understanding and the value of the article.

Administrative Highlights

To support instruction at the disciplinary level, the instructional services librarian and the IL coordinator split the disciplinary instruction workload in half, with each holding responsibilities for specific programs. These responsibilities include determining which courses are appropriate to target for instruction, communicating with program faculty, identifying course-specific IL learning outcomes, and developing instructional resources (such as online videos and tutorials) for the targeted courses.

Depending on scheduling, either of the two librarians may be responsible for providing instruction to any targeted course. To ensure some consistency of instruction, the two librarians developed instruction support forms for each targeted course in their areas. These forms are derived from course support forms created at Portland Community College and help librarians work with teaching faculty to "consider how best to situate the IL learning experiences and concepts" within a discipline.[9] Each instruction support form follows a similar template, including a course description, the learning outcomes that have been identified for the course, and recommended learning activities. The forms are kept in a Google Drive folder and available for access by any of the information literacy librarians. Although the initial development of the instruction support forms can be time-consuming, once created, they significantly reduce the necessary prep time, especially if a librarian is tasked with providing instruction for a course outside of her primary area of responsibility. With the forms, a librarian is able to quickly identify the targeted learning outcomes for the course and to locate any resources (such as online videos) that have already been created. In addition to the course-specific instruction support forms, each librarian also maintains a document for each program in their area. These forms indicate all of the targeted courses in that program, the learning outcomes and resources for these courses, and methods for assessment.

The collaborative nature of Google Drive has enabled us to easily work together. All program documents and corresponding instruction plans are stored in Drive for easy sharing and updating. We also use Drive to store assessment summaries, pre- and posttests, and surveys related to instruction. Additionally, we use LibCal, a Springshare product, to automate our instruction scheduling. LibCal allows us some flexibility in scheduling so that we can use both of our classrooms at the same time, as needed. The system also easily generates statistics.

Information Literacy Coordinator Profile

Early in my graduate studies, I (Andrea Brooks) wanted to be an instruction librarian, but didn't give a lot of thought to coordinating an instruction program until later in my career. I was fortunate to have a graduate assistantship at NKU where I shadowed and worked with instruction and reference librarians. I went on to manage a library at a small for-profit college and provided a lot of instruction, among other duties. I returned to NKU a few years later as an instruction librarian, and after a few years, the opportunity to coordinate the information literacy program presented itself after some reorganization and after the prior coordinator took on a new role within the library. The opportunity came along a little earlier than I might have expected in my career, but I didn't want to pass it up.

The coordinator position is a tenure-track position at NKU, while the FYE and instructional service librarians are non-tenure-track lines. The coordinator position is a formal position, but with only three librarians in the IL program, the integration of information literacy has very much been a collaborative effort, as evidenced in the coauthorship of this chapter! While the coordinator provides broad oversight on overall direction, including the scaffolding of instruction from the first-year experience to the disciplinary level, all information literacy program librarians manage the development of curriculum.

What We Wish People Knew

As I (Andrea Brooks) stepped into the coordinator role, I was surprised that a significant amount of time is spent educating colleagues, both within and outside of the library, on information literacy. Because the *Framework*, which we used to develop our learning outcomes, is a relatively new document, most faculty do not have a conceptual understanding of information literacy. As a result, some are resistant to information literacy instruction that emphasizes discussion surrounding information creation, value, and analysis, while deemphasizing an orientation to all the library databases. It is important that we, as librarians, can explain the value of information literacy as something that will help students beyond completing a research paper. I recommend writing a teaching philosophy that describes your understanding of information literacy and the approach you take to teach IL concepts, skills, or dispositions. Then, simplify your philosophy to write an elevator speech that reflects why information literacy matters and reuse for various contexts.

Additionally, the abundance and coordination of data present a challenge. Librarians have access to a significant amount of student data, but it is challenging to collect and organize the data in a meaningful way. Learning how to ask the right questions and focusing efforts to collect data that will reflect impact and student learning are a constant struggle. I have found additional coursework in research methods very valuable for learning statistical tests and recognizing when information is statistically meaningful. Training in qualitative research has also helped in text analysis and deciphering themes from mounds of data.

Despite challenges, information literacy is highly on valued on our campus, as evidenced by the recent QEP selection. We expect the library's information literacy program to continue growing and having a positive impact on student learning.

Notes

1. "At a Glance," Northern Kentucky University, accessed December 11, 2018, https://www.nku.edu/about/at-a-glance.html.
2. "Online Degree Programs," Northern Kentucky University, accessed December 11, 2018, https://www.nku.edu/admissions/adult/online.html.
3. "Student Data," Northern Kentucky University, accessed December 12, 2018, https://inside.nku.edu/ir/StudentData.html.
4. Association of College and Research Libraries, *Framework for Information Literacy for Higher Education* (Chicago: Association of College and Research Libraries, 2016), http://www.ala.org/acrl/standards/ilframework.
5. Jane Hammons, "Reaching Out to a 'Hard to Reach' Population," *Kentucky Libraries* 82, no. 1 (2018): 4–9.
6. "Information Literacy Framework Outcomes," Steely Library, Northern Kentucky University, last modified October 20, 2018, https://docs.google.com/document/d/1KnPAvzqNDVUBB0eveF3kMAU6udRQV0v8PTEEZ0_51OU/edit?usp=sharing.
7. "Steely Library Information Literacy Program: Outcomes and Assessment Plan," Steely Library, Northern Kentucky University, last modified August 7, 2018, https://docs.google.com/document/d/1qX2_wtD_hD3CRUqBlcZOH-dM4xmzdd_1lhG0RmAVwHE/edit?usp=sharing.
8. "Appendix 1: Implementing the Framework," Framework for Information Literacy Appendices, Association of College and Research Libraries, January 11, 2016, http://www.ala.org/acrl/standards/ilframeworkapps.
9. Pamela Kessinger, "Integrated Instruction Framework for Information Literacy," *Journal of Information Literacy* 7, no. 2 (2013): 40, https://doi.org/10.11645/7.2.1807.

Bibliography

Association of College and Research Libraries. Framework for Information Literacy Appendices. January 11, 2016. http://www.ala.org/acrl/standards/ilframeworkapps.
———. *Framework for Information Literacy for Higher Education*. Chicago: Association of College and Research Libraries, 2016. http://www.ala.org/acrl/standards/ilframework.
Hammons, Jane. "Reaching Out to a 'Hard to Reach' Population." *Kentucky Libraries* 82, no. 1 (2018): 4–9.
Kessinger, Pamela. "Integrated Instruction Framework for Information Literacy." *Journal of Information Literacy* 7, no. 2 (2013): 33–59. https://doi.org/10.11645/7.2.1807.
Northern Kentucky University. "At a Glance." Accessed December 11, 2018. https://www.nku.edu/about/at-a-glance.html.
———. "Online Degree Programs." Accessed December 11, 2018. https://www.nku.edu/admissions/adult/online.html.
———. "Student Data." Accessed December 12, 2018. https://inside.nku.edu/ir/StudentData.html.
Northern Kentucky University, Steely Library. "Information Literacy Framework Outcomes." Last modified October 20, 2018. https://docs.google.com/document/d/1KnPAvzqNDVUBB0eveF3kMAU6udRQV0v8PTEEZ0_51OU/edit?usp=sharing.
———. "Steely Library Information Literacy Program: Outcomes and Assessment Plan." Last modified August 7, 2018. https://docs.google.com/document/d/1qX2_wtD_hD3CRUqBlcZOH-dM4xmzdd_1lhG0RmAVwHE/edit?usp=sharing.

Chapter 8

Oxford College of Emory University

A Team-Based Approach to Teaching Information Literacy to First-Year and Second-Year Students

Courtney Baron, Kitty McNeill, Ellen Neufeld, and Jessica Robinson

Population Served

Emory University offers academic degrees and programs through nine schools, including more than seventy undergraduate majors and dozens of graduate and professional specialties. Four schools collaborate in undergraduate education—Emory College of Arts and Sciences, Oxford College, Goizueta Business School, and the Nell Hodgson Woodruff School of Nursing. Undergraduates have two options when they apply to Emory—Emory College of Arts and Sciences, the four-year liberal arts division, or Oxford College, where students complete the first two years of the Emory bachelor's degree in a distinctive small-campus setting. Upon completion of their second year, students from both divisions have the option to continue and pursue a liberal arts degree in Emory College, or they may apply to enter Emory's nursing and business schools.

As a liberal arts college connected to a prestigious research (R1) university, Oxford College is unique. The college is located in Oxford, Georgia, where Emory College was founded in the early nineteenth century. In 1919, Emory College moved to a new campus in Atlanta; however, Oxford College continued and became known for its focus on the undergraduate liberal arts experience. Today, all Oxford College students are in either their first or second year of college, live on campus, and automatically matriculate to their third and fourth years at the Atlanta campus after completing Oxford's inquiry-driven general education requirements. Oxford offers an unusually intensive focus on the liberal arts, leadership, and service, as well as the close attention of committed and outstanding faculty and staff.

Oxford's population of almost 1,000 students is an extremely diverse cross section of students from over thirty countries and forty states. The current student body represents a demographic shift from the early years of Emory University as a predominantly white and southern institution and has shaped the focus of the library's resources and services. Our information literacy program must respond to the needs of a culturally and ethnically diverse group of faculty and students. All of our instruction classes are specifically tailored to the request of a faculty member and to the needs of the student population. For example, all sections of first-year English classes have individual syllabi developed by the teaching faculty. Depending on the faculty member, the focus of these courses ranges from literature to special topics to writing. Students are required to take English 185 (or English 186 for multilingual speakers), but many students place out of introductory courses due to advanced placement credit. This means there is no one-size-fits-all information literacy class because each professor has different assignments, information needs, and student learning outcomes.

Program Scope

In 1998, the library initiated our Research Practices instruction program that in five years, evolved into a successful multipronged approach including[1]
- collaborating with faculty to design library instruction
- course-specific web-based research guides
- fifty-minute library instruction sessions with hands-on active learning activities
- individual research consultations

At that time, two librarians taught twenty-nine library instruction sessions for the entire academic year. The librarians found that successful library instruction could not be done in isolation, and in a foreshadowing of the future ACRL *Framework for Information Literacy for Higher Education*, acknowledged that librarians must enter in to a conversation about teaching and learning with faculty, as documented by Oxford College librarians McNeill and Haines.[2]

Nearly fifteen years later, in 2018, four librarians conducted 192 instruction sessions at Oxford College. This annual incremental increase in instruction sessions leveled off in the 2015–16 academic year, and the number of instructions sessions has held steady just shy of 200 for three years. Part of this increase can be attributed to standing relationships the librarians have built with faculty. For example, as described in an article by Jacob and

Heisel, our relationship with the biology department developed with a goal to provide critical thinking and information literacy skills to students as they experience scientific laboratory work.[3]

But the biggest change that contributed to library instruction growth has been the inclusion of information literacy as a stated goal in the college's general education curriculum. In 2016, Oxford College adopted a new strategic plan and general education program. One of the key components of the program is the Discovery Seminar. Students enroll in a Discovery Seminar of their choice in their first semester. The Discovery Seminars are intensive, discipline-specific courses taught by faculty who also serve as their students' advisor during their two years at Oxford. Since information literacy is one of the three outcomes of the Discovery Seminars, librarians are assigned to each course as teaching partners with the faculty. Our hope is to build a shared foundation in information literacy for all first-year students at Oxford College while partnering with faculty to teach any discipline-specific research skills required for the course. At full implementation of the Discovery Seminars, thirty seminars will be taught each fall. Therefore, we anticipate another large jump in our instruction numbers. Further, students will complete their Oxford College general education requirements with the new Milestone experience in their last semester. This project requires students to reflect upon their time at Oxford College and create digital portfolios to document coursework, experiential learning opportunities, cocurricular experiences, and leadership endeavors to express how the Oxford experience has shaped them and influenced their future plans. Librarians have a role in supporting faculty and helping students create their digital portfolios for the Milestone.

The instruction program leverages strong librarian-faculty partnerships to design information literacy learning opportunities tailored to specific course objectives. In addition to the Discovery Seminars and the Milestone, librarians teach several one-shot and scaffolded sessions in all subject areas and have a long history of teaching multiple sessions throughout the semester in biology and English courses. Each library session is tailored specifically to each course's research assignment. These learning opportunities may be a combination of individual or multiple in-class sessions led by a librarian with hands-on, small-group, active-learning exercises; individual research consultations; online modules based on the ACRL *Framework for Information Literacy*; or customized subject research guides.[4]

Operations

The Oxford College Library is a teaching library, and all librarians are expected to teach and participate as members of our Research Practices team. The library is team-based rather than a departmental, hierarchical organization. The Head of Library Teaching and Outreach Services coordinates the instruction program and leads the Research Practices team. All teaching librarians, along with a few staff members with specific subject expertise and advanced graduate coursework, participate as integral members of the team. The team reaches over 3,500 students each year, including some students in more than one class. In Oxford College's approach, unlike the traditional subject liaison approach, all Oxford College librarians are generalists and teach in a variety of disciplines.

Most notably, the Dean of the Library considers the Research Practices program as the top priority for the library, and the program has the full support of the Dean of the College and the Dean of Academic Affairs. The college and the library invest significant human and financial resources in the information literacy instructional program. Specifically, two additional teaching librarians were hired in spring 2019, bringing the total number of librarians to seven, to support the library's teaching efforts and in particular to staff the information literacy component of the Discovery Seminars.

The University Librarian, who oversees all Emory Libraries including Oxford, recognized Oxford College's Research Practices instructional program as a model for the Emory Libraries' goal to improve the undergraduate experience across Emory. In June 2018, librarians presented a session for the other Emory librarians on Oxford's Research Practices instructional program, the connections to the college general education program, and best practices and resources to help other librarians develop information literacy teaching and learning opportunities for undergraduates.

Marketing

Due to our small campus size, it is easier for librarians to develop close relationships with various campus constituents. Librarians serve on committees at the college level and build partnerships with faculty through various events, such as new faculty orientation, faculty retreats, and the annual Institute for Pedagogy in the Liberal Arts, as described below.

Additionally, each faculty member is assigned a personal librarian by the Dean of the Library. Since we do not have subject liaisons, the library instituted a personal librarian program so that faculty members would feel the library staff was accessible and approachable and that they would have an automatic contact regardless of the type of help needed. New faculty are introduced to their personal librarian at the library's portion of new faculty orientation and receive an individualized letter from the Dean of the Library in a packet with a list of library services, a bookmark with their personal librarian's photo and contact information, and library swag.

At the beginning of the academic year, returning faculty are sent a letter with their librarian's contact information and a reminder list of the types of services the library offers, including strategies for plagiarism prevention, specialized research assistance, and training on citation software like Zotero. Further, faculty are reminded that librarians can provide library instruction sessions or research consultations for students outside of class. In collaboration with Oxford's Center for Academic Excellence (CAE), the library staff offers lunch-and-learn sessions to faculty and staff. Past topics have included the ACRL *Framework for Information Literacy* and how the six threshold concepts have been integrated into the instruction program, along with testimonials from faculty who have used the library's teaching services. All of these efforts broaden the library's reach into the college curriculum.

Our participation in the Oxford College Institute for Pedagogy in the Liberal Arts (IPLA) has resulted in positive marketing for the library. This annual summer conference was designed and is supported by the CAE and invites teachers and scholars from across the country to participate. IPLA morphed into an internal opportunity for our faculty to learn and share strategies to inspire creativity and foster effective teaching in the liberal arts. Librarians were invited to present sessions at IPLA and used this opportunity to share directly with our faculty information about common misconceptions about students' information literacy abilities and feedback from a focus group with Oxford first-year students. The librarians again explained the ACRL *Framework for Information Literacy*, provided potential assignment ideas, shared learning outcomes, and introduced online learning modules based on the information literacy threshold concepts. The development of these modules is an ongoing project in partnership with the Emory University Libraries.

Collaboration

Collaboration with faculty, other departments, and programs is key to the library's success. Built over many years, strong librarian-faculty partnerships in disciplines such as English, biology, and religion serve as the foundation of the library's information literacy program. Further, librarians serve on college groups, including the Writing Support and Signature Outcomes Assessment Committees, and work closely with the Writing Program and the CAE. As a result of these robust collaborative efforts, in 2016 librarians participated in the development of the college's strategic plan, "Forging Pathways of Excellence."[5] The Dean of the Library served on the Curriculum Group that developed the new general education program (GEP) requirements outlined in the strategic plan, including the required Discovery Seminar. Also, the Dean of the Library served on a committee that developed another key GEP component, the Milestone Project, mentioned in the Program Scope section.

Librarians serve a crucial role at the college as new programs are developed and implemented. They design and lead workshops for faculty on topics such as incorporating information literacy into Discovery Seminars and developing undergraduate research projects that enable students to develop and apply inquiry and research skills. Also, librarians work closely with the CAE to provide workshops to support faculty teaching and research.

Assessment

Oxford College Library uses a team-based approach to assessment through the Research Practices program. Librarians assess student learning of library and information skills, faculty satisfaction with our teaching program and library services, and librarian teaching skills. With assistance from a faculty member, the team completed a curriculum mapping project to track research skills across the disciplines at the college as outlined in Moser and colleagues' conference paper.[6]

Librarians use a variety of assessment methodologies, customized to individual classes and based on the Emory Libraries' development of a *Framework*-based list of student learning outcomes, to evaluate student learning. These methodologies include the use of LibWizard forms, Kahoot! quizzes, classroom assessment techniques such as one-minute papers and muddiest points, and analysis of end products including bibliographies. The Research Practices instruction team works to identify new ways to assess student learning by participating in workshops, attending webinars, and staying abreast of current assessment literature. Self-evaluation of teaching and presentation skills, as well as peer observations, help librarians improve and maintain their pedagogical skills.

To evaluate faculty and student satisfaction with library services and resources, the library forms annual faculty and student focus groups to obtain feedback about our instructional program. This feedback is used to make changes as necessary to ensure the highest level of service for Oxford faculty and students. For formal assessment, the library participates in a biennial implementation of the HEDS Research Practices Survey and, most recently, the MISO (Measuring Information Service Outcomes) Survey. The MISO Survey, designed by Bryn Mawr College, analyzes perceptions of library and IT services. The library adds locally developed questions to the MISO Survey designed to assess student research abilities. In the annual graduation survey administered by the Oxford College Office of Institutional Research, students were asked about their perception of their research abilities. In the last iteration of the survey, students self-rated library research skills as the top area of improvement during their time at Oxford.

The librarians at Oxford College collaborate with faculty, administration, and Institutional Research to maintain an assessment plan for the college curriculum. Librarians serve on the college's Signature Outcomes Assessment Committee. Librarians serve on the Emory Libraries' Assessment Integration Group and submit a biennial assessment report to the university. Currently, the library is forming a new team to coordinate all assessment efforts and document the overall impact of our Research Practices program on achievement of the college's student learning outcomes.

Role of the One-Shot

While the Research Practices program was built upon the one-shot library instruction session, it has grown to include multiple sessions in some courses and even an embedded librarian model in others. In addition to teaching one-shots in a variety of subject areas, they work extensively with biology and art courses and will be fully embedded in the new Discovery Seminars.

For example, librarians have a longstanding relationship with the biology faculty and are fully embedded in the Biology 141 and 142 classes. In collaboration with the biology faculty, librarians visit Biology 141 classes three times during the semester to teach information literacy skills and attend research symposia. Biology faculty and students feel supported by librarians and value librarians' expertise from the start of the research process to the final student presentations. To supplement in-class instruction, students are encouraged to schedule research consultations individually or as a group with librarians for additional help.

Recently, the library piloted a fully embedded model for library instruction in Art 213, a survey course in Egyptian art history. The assigned librarian attended every class period, taught twelve sessions, and met with all students for one-on-one research assistance. The librarian accompanied the class on a trip to the Michael C. Carlos Museum at Emory's Atlanta campus. Students' feedback was overwhelmingly positive; they appreciated having a class librarian who could help them navigate the challenging research concepts and resources required to be successful in the course.

Pedagogical Highlights

The library's Research Practices information literacy program is based on the ACRL *Framework for Information Literacy*, which complements the college's inquiry-based liberal arts curriculum. For example, the Research as Inquiry frame fits nicely with the college's inquiry program, which emphasizes critical thinking skills across the liberal arts. Librarians use the *Framework* to teach information literacy threshold concepts through active learning strategies and collaborative group activities in the classroom. Since the *Framework* is deliberately conceptual and can present challenges for librarians teaching research instruction classes to undergraduates, an Information Literacy Framework Task Force was formed to create shared learning outcomes for all undergraduate divisions at Emory University. The Head of Library Teaching and Outreach Services represents Oxford College Library on this group, which produced a document with learning outcomes for each information literacy frame.[7]

After the *Framework* was officially adopted in January 2016, the Research Practices team read and discussed *Teaching Information Literacy Threshold Concepts: Lesson Plans for Librarians* to prepare for teaching the information literacy concepts.[8] Each team member led chapter discussions and group activities to brainstorm lesson plans to teach each threshold concept. The lesson plans created during this time formed an internal instruction tool kit, a collection of instruction planning materials including learning outcomes, lesson plans for each frame, assessment techniques, and handouts.

Librarians use backward design techniques to create lesson plans for classes. Working closely with the faculty for each course, librarians identify learning outcomes, plan class activities to reinforce research concepts, and determine appropriate assessment techniques to evaluate student learning. The active learning techniques include think/pair/share, concept mapping, student-led demonstrations or mini-presentations, collaborative group work using instructional tools such as Padlet, and citation formatting games.

The Research Practices team functions as Oxford College Library's internal community of practice around teaching. Librarians share the "guide on the side" teaching philosophy, introduced by Alison King's influential 1993 article in *College Teaching*, where the goal is to facilitate a learning experience for students.[9] Critical library pedagogy scholarship informs how to create a welcoming classroom that aligns with diversity and inclusivity efforts on campus. Further, librarians also participate in the Emory Libraries' Instructor Development Community of Practice, which emphasizes continuous learning through journal clubs and instructional technology show-and-tells. The Head of Library Teaching and Outreach Services collaborates with other Emory librarians to steer the group that builds partnerships around teaching information literacy across the Emory Libraries.

Administrative Highlights

True collaboration among the teaching librarians is key to the success of the library's information literacy program. Often, librarians share in lesson planning with faculty and co-teach instruction sessions, especially when there are multiple sections of a course. The team has an established practice of sharing lesson plans with each other in case of an emergency and the need for another librarian to step in at the last minute and teach a class.

The Research Practices team meets bimonthly to review a shared teaching calendar, assign teaching responsibilities, share successes and challenges in the classroom, and collaborate on teaching projects and other special initiatives. In addition to these meetings, the team meets biannually to review team accomplishments, discuss challenges, and set new goals to guide the direction of the program.

Information Literacy Coordinator Profile

The Head of Library Teaching and Outreach Services started out as a Teaching and Learning Librarian but was promoted as more teaching librarians were hired. The head formally coordinates the instruction program and leads the Research Practices team. The head has two direct librarian reports, while other team members report to other individuals in the organization, so the head's authority as a team leader is based on the ability to facilitate a shared vision and develop team goals. The person in this position works with the other teaching librarians to assess student learning in the classroom, but also focuses on the overall impact of the program by collecting statistics, such as number of classes taught, number of students reached, number of research consultations, and minutes librarians spent in research consultations. This data is necessary to demonstrate the continued impact and value of the program. The Dean of the Library has used this data to get support from stakeholders and administration, including approval to add more teaching librarians.

The Head of Library Teaching and Outreach Services assists librarians with collaborative efforts, including working with disciplinary faculty through the personal librarian program. In addition, the head looks at the big picture of how the program can support faculty and students, searches for new opportunities to map our programmatic learning outcomes with the curriculum, and determines the scalability of these efforts. Along with fellow librarians, the person in this position shares information about research and learning at the new faculty and student orientations. Since the library's instruction program is so team-based, the Head of Library Teaching and Outreach Services determined that the best approach for guiding the program is to use facilitation techniques as outlined in *Facilitator's Guide to Participatory Decision-Making* by Kaner and colleagues.[10] The Dean of the Library provides generous funding for professional development and learning opportunities for all librarians, including attendance at the ACRL Immersion Information Literacy Program. Due to this support, the Head of Library Teaching and Outreach Services encourages librarians to engage in the profession by contributing to the scholarly conversation, such writing as a book chapter in the recent publication *Disciplinary Applications of Threshold Concepts*;[11] presenting at conferences; attending workshops and webinars; and reading the latest literature in the field as a team.

What We Wish People Knew

Oxford College Library is proud of its team-based approach to teaching, which fosters a supportive and collaborative environment. Oxford College faculty and students place a heavy demand on library teaching services and resources, so it's critical for all librarians to participate in the Research Practices program to manage the heavy teaching load. In fact, all librarians are hired with the expectation that they will teach in our instructional program.

Teaching is very time-intensive! It takes a considerable amount of time to prepare a lesson plan, brainstorm activities, and create an assessment strategy. Oxford librarians always design their lessons to the specific course and assignment. Working with faculty, librarians carefully prepare the lesson plan they think will best deliver effective instruction and motivate students to learn and engage in the research process. The Head of Library Teaching and Outreach Services shares these tools with all teaching librarians, which results in a programmatic and cohesive approach to our teaching. This is a great benefit to librarians who have other responsibilities besides instruction. The head functions as the coordinator of the Research Practices instructional program, a key role as defined in the recent workbook for new instruction librarians by Banjes-Small and Miller.[12] Coordinators of library instruction programs must support their team and ensure they have the tools and support to succeed. Coordinators have to think about the bigger picture and how the program comes together, not just the individual classes they teach.

Notes

1. Kitty McNeill and Beth Haines, "Scholarship of Teaching and Librarians: Building Successful Partnerships with Faculty," *Georgia Library Quarterly 39*, no. 4 (Winter 2003): 4–8.
2. Association of College and Research Libraries, *Framework for Information Literacy for Higher Education* (Chicago: Association of College and Research Libraries, 2016), http://www.ala.org/acrl/standards/ilframework; McNeill and Haines, "Scholarship of Teaching."
3. Nitya Jacob and Andrea P. Heisel, "A Faculty-Librarian Partnership for Investigative Learning in the Introductory Biology Laboratory," *Journal of College Science Teaching 34*, no. 4 (March/April 2008): 54–59.
4. Association of College and Research Libraries, *Framework*.
5. "Oxford's 2020 Vision: Forging Pathways of Excellence" (strategic plan), November 15, 2016.
6. Mary T. Moser et al., "A More Perfect Union: Campus Collaborations for Curriculum Mapping Information Literacy Outcomes" (presentation, Association of College and Research Libraries, Philadelphia, Pennsylvania, March 30–April 2, 2011).
7. Oxford College Library, "Student Learning Outcomes," accessed March 25, 2019, http://oxford.library.emory.edu/research-learning/instruction-classes/learning-outcomes.html (page discontinued).
8. Patricia Bravender, Hazel Anne McClure, and Gayle Schaub, *Teaching Information Literacy Threshold Concepts* (Chicago: Association of College and Research Libraries, 2015).
9. Alison King, "From Sage on the Stage to Guide on the Side," *College Teaching 41*, no. 1 (Winter 1993): 30–35.
10. Sam Kaner et al., *Facilitator's Guide to Participatory Decision-Making*, 3rd ed. (San Francisco: Jossey-Bass, 2014).
11. Courtney Baron et al., "Images Have Value: Changing Student Perceptions of Using Images in Art History," in *Disciplinary Applications of Threshold Concepts*, ed. Samantha Godbey, Susan Beth Wainscott, and Xan Goodman (Chicago: Association of College and Research Libraries, 2017), 135–47.
12. Candice M. Benjes-Small and Rebecca K. Miller, *The New Instruction Librarian* (Chicago: Association of College and Research Libraries, 2017), 143–60.

Bibliography

Association of College and Research Libraries. *Framework for Information Literacy for Higher Education.* Chicago: Association of College and Research Libraries, 2016. http://www.ala.org/acrl/standards/ilframework.

Baron, Courtney L., Christopher Bishop, Ellen Neufeld, and Jessica Robinson. "Images Have Value: Changing Student Perceptions of Using Images in Art History." In *Disciplinary Applications of Threshold Concepts.* Edited by Samantha Godbey, Susan Beth Wainscott, and Xan Goodman, 135–47. Chicago: Association of College and Research Libraries, 2017.

Benjes-Small, Candice M., and Rebecca K. Miller. *The New Instruction Librarian: A Workbook for Trainers and Learners.* Chicago: American Library Association, 2017.

Bravender, Patricia, Hazel Anne McClure, and Gayle Schaub. *Teaching Information Literacy Threshold Concepts: Lesson Plans for Librarians.* Chicago: Association of College and Research Libraries, 2015.

Jacob, Nitya, and Andrea P. Heisel. "A Faculty-Librarian Partnership for Investigative Learning in the Introductory Biology Laboratory." *Journal of College Science Teaching* 34, no. 4 (March/April; 2008): 54–59.

Kaner, Sam, with Lenny Lind, Catherine Toldi, Sarah Fisk, and Duane Berger. *Facilitator's Guide to Participatory Decision-Making*, 3rd ed. San Francisco: Jossey-Bass, 2014.

King, Alison. "From Sage on the Stage to Guide on the Side." *College Teaching* 41, no. 1 (Winter 1993): 30–35.

McNeill, Kitty, and Beth Haines. "Scholarship of Teaching and Librarians: Building Successful Partnerships with Faculty." *Georgia Library Quarterly* 39, no. 4 (Winter 2003): 4–8.

Moser, Mary T., Andrea P. Heisel, Nitya Jacob, and Kitty McNeill. "A More Perfect Union: Campus Collaborations for Curriculum Mapping Information Literacy Outcomes." Presentation Association of College and Research Libraries conference, Philadelphia, PA, March 30–April 2, 2011.

Oxford College of Emory University. "Oxford's 2020 Vision: Forging Pathways of Excellence." Strategic plan. November 15, 2016.

Oxford College Library. "Student Learning Outcomes." Accessed March 25, 2019. http://oxford.library.emory.edu/research-learning/instruction-classes/learning-outcomes.html (page discontinued).

Chapter 9

Saddleback College

Embracing Growth with a Small but Mighty Team

Carolyn Seaman

Population Served

Saddleback College is a community college in southern California serving about 25,000 students, with enrollments of 7,000 full-time equivalent students. Our student population is primarily comprised of recent high school graduates but includes a wonderful mix of veterans, working parents, and everything in between. The library's mission is to assist students, faculty, staff, administrators, and community members in achieving their educational and personal goals for independent lifelong learning. Our library provides a wide range of resources and services to meet the needs of all programs and learning goals, from career technical education to associate's degrees, including offering credit courses that articulate with the University of California and California State University systems for our transfer-oriented students.

Given our type of institution, our program is not one-size-fits-all and has to meet a wide range of information literacy needs. It is important to scaffold our instruction for our students who require basic skills instruction while retaining enough rigor and flexibility to meet the needs of our university-bound students fulfilling transfer level credits.

Program Scope

Ever since a 1998 white paper on information competency from the Academic Senate for California Community Colleges formalized suggestions on how colleges should implement information competency requirements[1]—either distribute the information competency skills

81

across the curriculum in all subject areas or focus information competency skills in a specific class all students must complete—Saddleback has opted for a distributed model. Our students can choose from a number of classes to fulfill their information competency requirements, including our two online credit courses: LIB 100, a one-unit basic information competency course, and LIB 2H, a three-unit, transferable honors research course. This means that our program must also include many different instructional formats to supplement information competency instruction across the curriculum, such as scheduled drop-in workshops, asynchronous online workshops through our college's learning management system (LMS), in-class instruction sessions by instructor request, and one-on-one research consultations.

When I first began at Saddleback College, I was new to the community college system and wanted to learn what the information competency instruction trends were over the 114 different colleges in California in order to make informed decisions about our instructional program. In 2016, we were lucky enough to have a San José State University library and information science intern who was tasked with mapping out the different types of instruction offered by each college's library based on information provided on its website. What we learned was that out of the 105 California community colleges she investigated, no two libraries were addressing information competency instruction in exactly the same way. The prescheduled drop-in workshop model, which our library relied on heavily for information competency instruction before I came on board, was being offered by only twenty-eight community colleges, a little over a quarter of those represented in our intern's analysis.[2] Our own in-person workshop attendance rates dropped each semester, giving us further data to support the transition away from our old model of providing library instruction primarily with prescheduled workshops. No longer offering drop-in workshops has given us more availability to fulfill individual instruction requests and the flexibility to meet the information literacy needs of specific assignments.

The format of our instruction has also transitioned over time to match the way our student population is changing. Our campus offers a large number of online classes for a traditional community college, so we want to meet the needs of our students where they require information competency support for their courses. As of fall 2018, about 24 percent of all the college's classes are offered online (see figure 9.1).

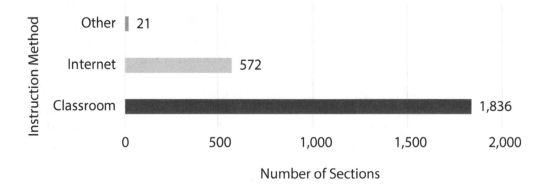

Figure 9.1
Section offerings by instruction method, fall 2018

Our online workshops are housed within the college's LMS, which was Blackboard until December 2018. The Distance Learning Librarian created two hour-long online workshops—Finding Articles and Avoiding Plagiarism—using a video and quiz format for Blackboard, but opened only Finding Articles to all classes, while Avoiding Plagiarism was offered to one specific class. In 2014, we opened Avoiding Plagiarism to all students to better meet our online students' information competency needs. Since fall 2015, Avoiding Plagiarism is the most assigned and completed online workshop. At the end of the 2017–18 academic year, 1,473 students had completed Avoiding Plagiarism, which is over half of all completed online workshops for the year.

Operations

At Saddleback, the library department is situated in the Online Education and Learning Resources division, along with the Tutoring Center, the Faculty Center for Student Success, Online Education, and Honors. We currently have four full-time librarians and two part-time librarians who contribute to our instruction program; our other four part-time librarians provide only reference services. As our department is fairly small and most of our annual budget is already spoken for with database renewals and collection development needs, the instruction program does not have its own budget. Support for marketing initiatives, new software, or extra hours for part-time librarians is usually requested on a case-by-case basis. This funding has come from specific grants, allocation of additional funding by the dean, and our Friends of the Library organization.

Most in-class research instruction and all research consultations are handled by the full-time librarians, and our two credit courses and in-person workshops have been taught by a couple of full-time and part-time librarians for the past several semesters. Recently, some additional funding was allocated to have part-time librarians teach some of our in-class instruction sessions so that we could offer evening instruction that the full-time schedules could not provide. We have just started this "on-call" support model with some moderate success, but we will need to expand our part-time instructional pool in the future to continue to accommodate these types of requests.

We have always tried to align our instruction program with the educational initiatives happening across campus, but recent statewide initiatives, such as California Assembly Bill (AB) 705 and the California Guided Pathways Project, have helped to focus our efforts.[3] As a result, we were part of a grant headed by the Liberal Arts division to provide embedded information competency instruction for students in corequisite English classes specifically developed to provide extra support mandated by AB 705. The 2017 bill requires California community colleges to increase students' ability to complete transfer-level courses in English and math. Guided Pathways is a reform of how California community colleges map and sequence their programs to minimize the time students take to complete credentials and has provided all colleges with a campus-wide platform to promote information competency initiatives. We now have a seat at the table in conversations about how to move forward as a college in addressing and meeting information competency requirements.

Marketing

We actively market our online workshops to students during our one-shot instruction sessions. I also partner with faculty members who value what we offer and use their department meetings and professional development opportunities to tout our services, such as presenting business-specific library resources at the business department's spring retreat. From these opportunities, I usually have new faculty recruits who did not know about our program previously and start to assign our online workshops to their students or request in-class instruction. Word of mouth from one faculty member to another has also helped market our instruction services, especially with part-time instructors who are sometimes not aware of what libraries offer from one college to another.

Past attempts at marketing have included a combined brochure with our tutoring department, which highlighted our entire instruction program, including our credit courses, for our campus outreach department to distribute at different high school recruiting events. Serving on the college's Curriculum and General Education committees has also been an opportunity for marketing, as I was able to get our three-unit transferable credit course to be included in more competency areas of our local general education pattern for an AA degree. As we don't have a specific budget for marketing, leveraging any available opportunity to share what we do with colleagues across campus has been instrumental in getting the word out about our program.

Collaboration

Some of our biggest supporters, other than the English department, are the faculty from the sciences. The nursing, environmental sciences, and food and nutrition departments not only assign our workshops as mandatory but also ask us for instruction visits every semester. During the past summer, nutrition faculty invited me to collaborate on how to best use the library's resources as they were updating their research assignment to better meet their student learning outcomes (SLOs). This provided me with an opportunity to let them know how our resources could realistically support the changes they wanted to adopt, but also allowed them a forum to give feedback on how we could revise some of our instruction to better serve their specific students.

As mentioned previously in the Operations section, the dean of the Liberal Arts division invited the library to be part of a grant directed toward AB 705 that aimed to help students entering transfer-level English classes better utilize support services. Being able to collaborate with English faculty on embedding librarians, information competency, and library instruction in their courses has helped us to understand how we can best leverage our staffing and technological resources and how to enhance these resources in the future for our instruction program.

We have also had success collaborating with colleagues other than teaching faculty. For example, we partnered with the Tutoring Center to revise our MLA and APA citation guides using feedback from tutors on what students found most helpful. This project led to more opportunities to work with the Tutoring Center, allowing us to make sure that tutors were delivering information consistent with library standards and that tutors had a solid understanding of our resources and services in order to better refer students.

Another great opportunity was when I was invited as a guest speaker at the Career and Reentry Center during its Digital Fluency workshops, as I was able to share researching and evaluating skills with students we typically are not able to reach.

Assessment

An assessment of the library instruction program is included in the formal Administration Unit Review of the library department, which happens every three years. The process includes analyzing our credit course data as well as looking at our completion numbers for workshops, along with attendance numbers for in-class instruction and research consultations. The credit courses are assessed using the metrics the college uses for all courses: enrollment, completion, persistence, retention, and success. We also assess SLOs in our credit courses, but because we are not part of a degree or certificate program at the college, it can be difficult to determine what the metrics might mean for our students' overall success. However, survey feedback from students who take our LIB 2H course in online searching indicates that the class is very helpful, and many students say they wished they had taken the research class before any of their other courses. Assessing student learning outside of the credit courses can be challenging, but we try to incorporate student surveys, instructor feedback, and graded quizzes from our online workshops.

For an assessment project dedicated to our online workshops, we partnered with the Office of Planning, Research, and Accreditation on campus to examine if any data linked library workshop attendance to the different metrics used on campus to measure student success. In spring 2016, we looked at data from the fall 2015 semester for students who took one, two, or three library workshops. Although the conclusion was that we would need to examine future semesters of students to effectively gauge any trends in academic performance, there were some positive links between academic success and students who took three library workshops. Students who took three workshops had a considerably higher rate of persistence than students who took only one or two workshops. Students in this category also saw an increase in average GPA, which was rewarding to see even though the reasons are likely multifactoral.[4] We plan to duplicate this analysis for the fall 2018 semester to see if we can find any repeating trends or new areas where we can optimize our program.

Role of the One-Shot

Although our program continues to grow embedded instruction and one-shot offerings, our online workshops consistently reach more students each semester (see figure 9.2). As important as I believe it is for students to have an in-person encounter with a librarian and the physical library, our online workshops offer information competency instruction to a much broader audience. Many instructors I have never met or who teach online classes assign their students our online workshops, allowing us to reach a large group of students we might not reach with traditional in-person instruction. For the faculty members who utilize our one-shot offerings and assign students a workshop, I find this optimizes the role of our one-shots as the workshops can provide additional support through a flipped classroom option or as follow-up instruction. While they have a much smaller reach, our two credit courses and our one-on-one research consultations give us alternatives in how we offer information competency instruction to the diverse student population at our college.

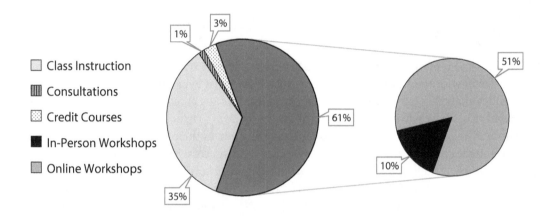

- Class Instruction
- Consultations
- Credit Courses
- In-Person Workshops
- Online Workshops

Figure 9.2
Library instruction by modality and percentage of students reached, 2014–2018

Pedagogical Highlights

Although we still incorporate the older Association of College and Research Libraries (ACRL) *Information Literacy Competency Standards* in our instruction, mainly because some community college students still require an introduction to the basic skills that are outlined in the performance outcomes, it was also important to look at the instruction we were offering through the new lens of the ACRL *Framework for Information Literacy for Higher Education* to see if what we were teaching was still relevant and useful to the curriculum across campus.[5] One of my first priorities when I joined the team was to revise the lesson plans of the library workshops to incorporate the *Framework*'s knowledge practices, particularly ensuring that the objectives and outcomes of the workshops were built on the new proficiencies. The *Framework* has also helped guide us to revise our SLOs in our credit courses and helped us to create fresh instruction content to better meet the current information needs of our students.

Whether we were visiting a class for a brief demonstration or creating a new workshop, our team's teaching philosophy is to incorporate evaluation and analysis of the resources and information students are looking at or gathering. In addition to catalog and database navigation, we try to highlight deeper information competency concepts where appropriate. Our LIB 2H course focuses on the evaluation and analytical skills students must acquire when working with information, so I like to think of our one-shots and workshops as smaller components of the semester-long class. Even with our instruction, students will tend to fall back to their comfort zone and rely on searching the open internet for their sources, so having evaluation and analytical skills as the foundation of our instruction will help regardless of the searching tool they decide to use.

For a period of five years, our campus was also part of the Advancement via Individual Achievement (AVID) for Higher Education (AHE) grant,[6] and there was a big push to train instructors in the high engagement and collaborative learning teaching styles of AVID. I attended a four-class practicum in order to learn new ways of engaging students with active learning opportunities, as well as understanding the pedagogical foundations that many instructors were incorporating into their courses. I have found that it is easier to insert these types of active learning opportunities when teaching our credit courses, where I can develop the content and curriculum; however, there have been a few one-shot instruction sessions where I was able to develop more engaging lessons with the help of the AVID training. For example, I have incorporated a lesson into counseling classes where students use our website to create their own library brochure highlighting our services and resources instead of the typical orientation and have tried a human APA citation activity, assigning each student a citation element and having them line up in correct order, which worked well with a psychology faculty member's class. Some of the ideas from AVID have also been helpful for online instruction, and I try to let these principles guide the development of new online workshops and instruction content that students access from our website.

Administrative Highlights

In spring 2014, I created an online workshop focused on how to find books and articles using our newly adopted catalog, WorldCat Discovery. I wanted to employ more interactive and self-grading features into the online workshop, so I created it using Articulate Storyline software, knowing that its data tracking abilities would integrate nicely with Blackboard. Currently, we have just finished migrating to the Canvas LMS as a district, and I have found that Articulate's active learning features that I used effectively with Blackboard do not work as well with Canvas nor are they all ADA compliant. Moving forward, this means our new workshops will go back to our original video and quiz format until we find a new solution.

Library instruction data was not collected systematically at the beginning of fall 2014, so I introduced a formal process for data collection for all instruction efforts, including individual classroom visits and in-office consultations. This additional data helps give our program substance and forms the basis for our decision-making during our Administrative Unit Review and goal setting. Until August 2014, there was also no organized structure to process instruction requests from instructors or one-on-one research requests from students. I employed a free web form service by SurveyMonkey, Wufoo, to set up online request forms that are automatically emailed to me when submitted. This has also made marketing one-on-one research consultations easier while simultaneously increasing the demand for the service.

There is a lot of communication back and forth among the requesting instructors, the other librarians, and myself in order to schedule instruction during the semester. This can be a challenge if a request must be fulfilled quickly or if one instructor must be scheduled for multiple classes. Recently, we were able to create a shared instruction-specific

Outlook account, and although I do not see this decreasing the need for the back-and-forth communication, I hope it will alleviate some of the tracking inefficiencies.

Information Literacy Coordinator Profile

I was hired in fall 2014 specifically to focus on coordinating our information competency program. The coordination aspect of my role fluctuates and changes focus depending on the time of year, but it can take a good chunk of time. My expected instruction workload has never been communicated; however, I often try to take double the number of sessions that I give to the other librarians. I feel inclined to take on more sessions than I schedule for others due to our availability, new content that I am delivering and want to pilot myself first, or because *instruction* is in my job title. I not only take care of the day-to-day scheduling and act as the point person for faculty communication, but I also often create the lesson plans or outlines for the commonly visited classes. Tracking students' attendance at our workshops and sending the information to faculty also falls under my domain. As students complete our workshops, I generate lists to send to the faculty who assign the workshops to instructors when they request a report. Students do not always list their instructors when they complete the workshops, so communication with both faculty and students is key to making sure that all students are accounted for accurately. Other administrative duties, such as cleanup of the data in our reporting system can also take up time that I have allocated for other projects.

What I Wish People Knew

At a community college, we faculty members wear a lot of hats, so scheduling the time to coordinate instruction can be a bit of a challenge. As small details can be a significant portion of the day-to-day work, time management is a must in order to get to big-picture projects, campus committee work, or preparation for your own instruction sessions. Keeping track of multiple people, visiting multiple places on campus, and juggling cancellations or rescheduled visits is not something that comes naturally to me, so relying on multiple tracking systems helps to keep me organized and on top of the instruction calendar.

As we all tend to work in silos on campus, it can be difficult to think outside the box and understand where our allies and partnerships across the college can be most influential. Our role outside of the library should include making positive connections with colleagues who see us as experts in our field and beneficial to their own area's student success goals. Beginning and sustaining those positive, campus-wide connections is key to expanding the instruction program outside the classroom. Sometimes turnover in staffing at different centers or with different part-time faculty can be challenging when you have invested time in building partnerships, but satisfied colleagues will generally pass along library contact information to new faculty or staff.

My advice to anyone who finds themselves in an instruction coordinator position is to try anything new pertaining to instruction and technology at least once, even if it may not be a fully formed or vetted idea. It is helpful to understand that what may have been a great solution one semester may have to be rethought, modified, or completely scrapped the next. Surprise success is an uplifting experience, but failures are a great learning opportunity, and sometimes they are the only way to gain insight about student preferences, learning habits, and where our efforts will best support student success. Saying yes to any faculty request or new idea, within reason, will create positive and lasting relationships for the program. If you know that a faculty member's idea might not be the most realistic or effective use of resources, saying yes can serve as an invitation to collaborate and revise future classes. Willingness to be open and flexible will guarantee repeat customers and ensure future conversations about what you can realistically provide for effective instruction. Embracing the faculty who value the library and the instruction program will lead to positive word-of-mouth marketing to faculty who never thought of the library before as a resource for collaboration.

Notes

1. Academic Senate for California Community Colleges, *Information Competency in the California Community Colleges* (Sacramento: Academic Senate for California Community Colleges, Spring 1998), https://www.asccc.org/sites/default/files/publications/InfoComp_0.pdf.
2. Marie Ingram, "Analysis of Information Competency Requirements at California Community Colleges" (unpublished manuscript, last modified May 14, 2016), PDF file.
3. "What is AB 705?" California Community Colleges, 2018, https://assessment.cccco.edu/ab-705-implementation; California Guided Pathways home page, 2018, https://www.caguidedpathways.org.
4. Shouka Torabi, "Analysis of the Library Workshops (Fall 2015)" (unpublished manuscript, last modified August 8, 2016), PDF file.
5. Association of College and Research Libraries, *Information Literacy Competency Standards for Higher Education* (Chicago: Association of College and Research Libraries, 2000); Association of College and Research Libraries, *Framework for Information Literacy for Higher Education* (Chicago: Association of College and Research Libraries, 2016), http://www.ala.org/acrl/standards/ilframework.
6. "AVID for Higher Education (AHE)," 2018, https://www.avid.org/highered.

Bibliography

Academic Senate for California Community Colleges. *Information Competency in the California Community Colleges*. Sacramento: Academic Senate for California Community Colleges, Spring 1998. https://www.asccc.org/sites/default/files/publications/InfoComp_0.pdf.

Association of College and Research Libraries. *Framework for Information Literacy for Higher Education*. Chicago: Association of College and Research Libraries, 2016. http://www.ala.org/acrl/standards/ilframework.

———. *Information Literacy Competency Standards for Higher Education*. Chicago: Association of College and Research Libraries, 2000.

AVID. "AVID for Higher Education." 2018. https://www.avid.org/highered.

California Community Colleges. "What is AB 705?" 2018. https://assessment.cccco.edu/ab-705-implementation.

California Guided Pathways home page. 2018. https://www.caguidedpathways.org.

Ingram, Marie. "Analysis of Information Competency Requirements at California Community Colleges." Unpublished manuscript. Last modified May 14, 2016. PDF file.

Torabi, Shouka. "Analysis of the Library Workshops (Fall 2015)." Unpublished manuscript. Last modified August 8, 2016. PDF file.

Chapter 10

University of California, Riverside

Positioning Librarians as Co-educators

Dani Brecher Cook

Population Served

The University of California, Riverside (UCR), is a public research university with R1 status located in the Inland Empire region of Southern California. UCR enrolls approximately 23,000 students (of those, about 20,000 are undergraduates) and retains 1,100 faculty. It is both a Hispanic-Serving Institution (HSI) and an Asian American and Native American Pacific Islander-Serving Institution (AANAPISI). A 2018 national analysis showed that UCR enrolls and graduates more Pell Grant recipients than any other research university in the US, and 58 percent of undergraduates are first-generation college students.[1] There is a significant population of commuter students, and a growing number of transfer, veteran, international, and nontraditional-age undergraduate students. All of these factors influence the architecture of UCR's information literacy program, which must meet the needs of students with vastly different life experiences, who have varying amounts of time that they can spend on school-related activities, across fifty-five different undergraduate majors, at scale.

Program Scope

The Department of Teaching and Learning is responsible for the vision and execution of the UCR Library's information literacy program. The majority of the department's attention is focused on the undergraduate experience, from the moment that students arrive on campus for orientation to completing capstone projects and papers. Most support for graduate students comes from our Research Services Department. The major exception to this is the initial graduate student orientation, which is a collaborative effort between departments. Other interactions between Teaching and Learning and upper-level graduate students and faculty tend to be around the pedagogy of information literacy (IL) for undergraduate courses, rather than information literacy for those populations themselves.

The varying nature of our student body, as well as the lack of a single pathway (or even just a few) through the undergraduate experience means that our information literacy program cannot take for granted previous research or library experience and also needs to provide differentiated experiences for those students who have either worked with the UCR Library previously or who enter college with more familiarity or fluency with IL concepts.

Developing a baseline understanding of library services on an R1 campus is key for our unit, given the large percentage of our student body who are the first in their family to access higher education. To this end, the largest portion of the department's time is spent in providing information literacy instruction for three very large introductory courses: an introductory writing course that is taught across three quarters (ENGL 1A-B-C), an introductory chemistry course (CHEM 001A), and an introductory biology laboratory course (BIOL 005LA). Across these three courses, we reach several thousand students each quarter, with the intention that most matriculating students will encounter a library session at least once in their undergraduate careers. Two key challenges are to differentiate the information literacy content of each course and to make it relevant to the goals of the individual course and discipline.

Our information literacy program also conducts workshops with upper-level courses across every academic unit, with each session individually tailored to course goals. We employ a less programmatic approach to these courses, working with individual instructors on an opt-in basis, but anticipate working with departments to sequence skills in the near future.

Almost all of our instruction is conducted in person, but we recently piloted opt-in online instruction for the BIOL 005LA courses, with the intention of offering more asynchronous options for students, especially for library workshops that do not meet at the normal class time. These pilots were incredibly popular with students, filling up quickly. Interestingly, we found that some students preferred the online option even when they were on campus or in the library(!) at the same time.

We are also in the early stages of developing a suite of online learning modules that will be used for addressing library orientation–type learning goals (e.g., How do I find the library's hours?). The goal of this project is to provide a uniform learning experience for all incoming students for information that otherwise has previously been addressed only in first-year writing classes where instructors opt in to library instruction (and some students test out of the sequence). An online learning object of this type, used as part of orientation, will also allow us to spend the limited in-person time that we have with students to actively facilitate more complex concepts related to their courses, including ideas from the ACRL *Framework for Information Literacy for Higher Education*.[2]

Operations

Historically at UCR, information literacy instruction was divided between traditional reference librarians in the humanities/social science library and the science library. This led to a bifurcated approach to information literacy and limited the potential for developing a teaching community of practice across disciplinary lines. As part of a larger reorganization process in 2017, the Department of Teaching and Learning was created to centralize teaching efforts in one library department and to focus both the work and the professional development of librarians in that department on teaching without dividing attention between the traditional trio of high-level reference, teaching, and collection development.

This new unit is staffed by six librarians, one staff coordinator, and the department director. Each teaching librarian has a specific disciplinary alignment or user population for which they focus on developing additional skills and training; in addition, all teaching librarians support the large introductory courses in writing and the sciences. The teaching librarian positions are

- *Arts and Humanities Teaching Librarian:* Works with courses in the visual arts, humanities, music, and business. Has specialized knowledge of visual literacy.
- *Social Sciences Teaching Librarian:* Works with courses in the social sciences, education, and gender and ethnic studies. Has specialized knowledge in data literacy.
- *STEM Teaching Librarian:* Works with courses in the sciences, engineering, and mathematics. Has specialized knowledge in science information literacy.
- *Early Experience Teaching Librarian:* Develops approaches and coordinates staffing for the large entryway undergraduate courses, as well as plans orientations for all of our user populations.
- *University Programs Teaching Librarian:* Provides information literacy instruction and support for non-major and non-curricular programs, such as prestigious undergraduate fellowships, the honors program, the undergraduate student journal, and international student programs.
- *Primary Source Literacy Teaching Librarian:* Works primarily with classes that utilize primary source materials from our Special Collections and University Archives. Has specialized knowledge in teaching with archives and unique materials.

The staff coordinator processes requests for instruction from faculty and course instructors, as well as supervises the student-staffed reference service. The director supervises the department, advocates for the department both internally and externally to the library, and provides the structure for ongoing professional development and a teaching community of practice within the department (more in the Pedagogical Highlights section). All of the librarian positions (including the director) contribute to teaching the large undergraduate courses.

One major goal of the department reorganization was to localize all teaching within the unit, so other departments do not participate in the undergraduate teaching program, with a few exceptions when teaching librarians colead classes on specialized topics with research services librarians (such as upper-level classes that need GIS instruction). Orientation events do include librarians from research services and collection strategies, but we do not consider them part of the curriculum-integrated information literacy program.

Teaching and Learning is supported by library administration with a small budget, which is primarily intended for teaching supplies and professional development of librarians in the unit. The director has relatively broad discretion in spending the budget and has used it to purchase whiteboard paint for a classroom space that previously did not have a writing surface, webinar fees for the entire department, and other departmental supplies related to teaching (e.g., whiteboard markers, index cards). The spending of this budget is transparent to the department, and it is updated on any spending at biweekly department meetings. Department members are also asked to submit requests and ideas that require a relatively small amount of resources (> $200), which are then usually discussed as a department. This transparency with the budget was crucial for building trust in our department and helping to establish a feeling of shared ownership over the work of the new unit.

Beyond the fiscal, Teaching and Learning is strongly supported by library administration via advocacy for the unit's work on campus, latitude in designing the unit's approach to information literacy work, and help in including the department in campus-wide conversations about undergraduate education and pedagogy. While there is no other unit on campus that is focused on information literacy support, there are many commonalities in approach and mission with units such as the Division of Undergraduate Education (including the campus instructional design team and the new Center for Teaching and Learning). Library administrators have helped to open doors to these conversations and send a steady stream of referrals to our department.

Marketing

We are not currently promoting one-shot instruction as we are at maximum capacity with honoring historical commitments to introductory courses, but as we transition those courses to less librarian labor–intensive strategies, we intend to meet with departments and advocate for specific moments of information literacy instruction in the major degree pathways, using curriculum maps as a guide. However, despite not currently marketing our services beyond brief mentions at New Faculty Orientation, we have seen about a 50 percent increase in number of course requests in eighteen months, most likely both because of word of mouth and because we have been reaching out directly to course instructors who assign scavenger hunt–type assignments to participate in library instruction rather than send 300+ students to the reference desk.

Collaboration

We work closely with Undergraduate Education (which includes Assessment) to support undergraduate research across the curriculum and determine pathways through majors. The Dean and Assistant Dean of Undergraduate Education are two of our biggest allies on campus and have been crucial in the library being included in conversations about teaching on campus. In 2018, we were included in the campus-wide Celebration of Teaching in May and have an open invitation to host workshops and events in collaboration with the new Center for Teaching and Learning. We cosponsored our first workshop with the center in spring 2018, focused on open educational resources. This event was also cosponsored by our local chapter of CALPIRG (California Public Interest Research Group) and campus IT and included voices from faculty who had transitioned courses to OERs and students who had either benefited from those courses or struggled to afford course materials.

Developing and maintaining relationships with campus partners is critical for the success of our reimagined information literacy program. In fact, it would not be over-stating it to say that, without collaboration, our model would not succeed. One of the core tenets of our program is to develop programs and initiatives only in collaboration with other campus entities and departments so that we have a better chance of having students attend sessions and better understand the context of their needs. In other words, we are no longer offering drop-in IL workshops targeted at undergraduates. At the moment, our most significant curricular focuses are with the Writing Program, chemistry department, and biology department. We are also supporting cocurricular collaborations with the Writing Center, a small number of prestigious undergraduate fellowship programs, and international student programs. As we cement these relationships and solidify our approaches and assessments for these programs, we plan to expand outreach to new programs within those units, as well as approaching new strategic campus partners with (ideally) evidence of past successful collaborations.

Assessment

Historically, our IL program has not had a significant assessment component, so that has been one of the main focuses of our redesigned unit—How can we tell if students are learn-ing in our sessions? At the moment, all of our assessment efforts are being undertaken by the department as a whole—we're designing assessments to use in our large introductory classes that we can then analyze in aggregate. Our first major undertaking was to design, in collaboration with the coordinator of BIOL 005LA, a pre- and post-assessment tightly targeted around the learning goal of learners being able to find an academic journal arti-cle based on popular press coverage. This assessment arose from the (honest) question of whether or not students inherently knew how to find this kind of evidence intuitively. This assessment effort is a test case for the types of assessments we'd like to continue to focus on as a program: deeply collaborative with an academic department, answering a question about student learning that we are genuinely curious about and could influence how and where we teach, tightly focused on evidence of learners' retention and transfer of skills, and IRB-approved from the beginning so that we can share out results with the broader IL community.

We are not yet continuously part of campus assessment and accreditation efforts, but we feel that conducting these types of assessments will be useful for those efforts in the future. While our in-house assessment efforts are still in the early phases, we intend to use them primarily as reflective tools for designing our instruction, with a secondary goal of using any positive results to demonstrate the efficacy of our teaching efforts.

Role of the One-Shot

We do think there's a role for one-shots, especially in upper-level courses, but would like to see them more as the beginning of a conversation than a magic bullet for indoctrinating students in research. To this end, we are banking on a consultative model that allows for IL to be approached multiple times within a course or degree program, rather than on just a single day—while the librarian may work with a course in person only once, they can work with the instructor to help design assignments or syllabi so that the ideas of IL can be incorporated throughout the quarter. We've also designed a number of activities and tools that instructors can take and adapt on their own or with librarian guidance. In all honesty, given the size of our department and current and potential demands for IL instruction, the one-shot has to be our primary mode of operating, but we're thinking of it as part of a constellation of IL instruction throughout the undergraduate experience, rather than a lone event.

Pedagogical Highlights

When we re-formed our department in September 2017, creating a shared set of values about how we would approach our teaching was crucial. For that reason, one of the first things we did was collaboratively create such a list:

- We encourage curiosity and lifelong learning.
- We aim to identify, develop, and teach resources and tools to help learners thrive in their research-focused coursework.
- Our methods are grounded in evidence-based best practices in response to changing learner needs and learning environments.
- We strive to be reflective in our learner-centered pedagogical approaches, and encourage and support creative approaches to teaching information literacy.[3]

This was our first step toward creating a library community of practice around teaching, helping us to identify the factors that we cared about most (evidence-based practice, empathy, context awareness) so that we could grow in those areas together.

Within the first month of the department, we began meeting every other week for forty-five minutes to begin exploring these issues together. For the first quarter of the year, each session would ask department members to either read a brief article or write a short reflection on a theme related to "How do people learn, and what is learning?" For example, one week, we read and discussed "Do Learners Really Know Best? Urban Legends in Education" by Paul Kirschner and Jeroen van Merriënboer to examine our assumptions about our learners.[4] Another week, we engaged in a reflective exercise borrowed from *The Courage to Teach*, writing down "a moment when things were going so well that you knew you were born to teach and a moment when things were going so poorly that you wished that you had never been born."[5] In our third quarter, we focused on instructional design principles, including a daylong retreat facilitated by an outside instructional designer. Setting aside time and space for us to intentionally think and talk about our teaching practices, as a group, has been the most important part of developing our teaching community within the department.

Even less formally, we have standing thirty-minute meetings each week where people can come and share things that went well for them in teaching that week, or that went poorly, and ask for feedback from one another on both. People aren't expected to attend every week, but the whole department almost always attends. It's a low-stakes way to maintain our connection to one another as teachers and learn.

Continuous learning and developing as teachers is deeply important for us as a department, as we try to position ourselves as equal educators to our faculty colleagues. If we have a department that is solely about teaching and learning, then we *have* to be knowledgeable about what we are doing. So having this kind of dedicated time and space is nonnegotiable, and it's been critical to have administrative support for doing so.

Administrative Highlights

In addition to having a set of core values that are externally facing, we wrote a set of values for how we want to work together in the department:

- A success for one member of the team is a success for us all. We also celebrate individual successes, and appreciate and value the labor of our colleagues.
- As challenges arise, we work together to create a solution.
- We strive to embody a community of respect, within our team and the greater campus community.
- We practice an ethic of care for one another, as we believe this leads us to understand, improve, and nurture our environment, as well as ourselves.

This list led to us creating a clear-cut set of expectations for each other, both as teammates and in the managerial relationship, which we keep on our internal wiki. It includes items such as meeting structures and agenda deadlines, expectations for answering emails (including not at night or on weekends), asking for help when needed, and "You don't have to be perfect, you do have to try, reflect on your experiences, and grow." This has been helpful for working together as colleagues, specifically with regard to the balance of labor, time to plan and learn, and thinking about how best to support one another. As we are tempted to bite off more than we can chew, we can return to these two sets of values to help set boundaries, as well as prioritizing.

Information Literacy Coordinator Profile

I was an information literacy coordinator at my previous institution; in that role, I was frustrated in feeling that it always felt as if teaching was taking a back seat to other duties in terms of time and attention. A major reason that I was interested in this position is that it is explicitly managerial—on par with other department heads, and similarly resourced. Rather than spending my time arguing for why we should spend time and resources on teaching, I can focus on how we spend that time and resources.

I spend the majority of my time managing the department—meeting one-on-one with librarians, planning team professional development, leading team meetings, representing the unit on the library's leadership team, writing reviews, meeting with campus partners. That said, I still teach about 10 percent of our one-shots, as I think it's important for me to continue to understand the work by doing it. But I'm fortunate in that it's my decision to do that, and I'm not expected to teach *more* than everyone else (which was how I felt as a coordinator).

The formality of the role, with dedicated staffing, has been a game changer for me in terms of what I think we can accomplish. Pedagogical growth isn't something we are trying to shoehorn in, but rather central to the roles of each person in our department. My coordinator experience definitely helped me to define what I wanted from the role of director and how I thought a department focused on IL could and should operate.

What I Wish People Knew

One of the most challenging parts of the coordination role has been feeling empowered to say no and helping others in my department to say no. But since we have a clearly defined number of people and amount of time, we have to decline participation in some courses or ask to be included next time when we can devote the attention required to do a good job. That's been one of the hardest things to learn: that when you say yes to everything, it means you can't do things as well. So one hard-won lesson has been to learn to say no in a productive way that leaves the door open to future collaborations.

Notes

1. Wesley Whistle and Tamara Heller, "The Pell Divide: How Four-Year Institutions Are Failing to Graduate Low- and Moderate-Income Students," Third Way, May 1, 2018, https://www.thirdway.org/report/the-pell-divide-how-four-year-institutions-are-failing-to-graduate-low-and-moderate-income-students; University of California Riverside, "First Generation," accessed September 27, 2018, http://firstgen.ucr.edu.
2. Association of College and Research Libraries, *Framework for Information Literacy for Higher Education* (Chicago: Association of College and Research Libraries, 2016), http://www.ala.org/acrl/standards/ilframework.
3. UCR Library, "Instructional Support," accessed October 30, 2018, http://library.ucr.edu/instructional-support.
4. Paul A. Kirschner and Jeroen JG van Merriënboer, "Do Learners Really Know Best? Urban Legends in Education," *Educational Psychologist* 48, no. 3 (2013): 169–83.
5. Parker J. Palmer, *The Courage to Teach* (San Francisco: John Wiley & Sons, 2007), 103.

Bibliography

Association of College and Research Libraries. *Framework for Information Literacy for Higher Education*. Chicago: Association of College and Research Libraries, 2016. http://www.ala.org/acrl/standards/ilframework.

Kirschner, Paul A., and Jeroen JG van Merriënboer. "Do Learners Really Know Best? Urban Legends in Education." *Educational Psychologist* 48, no. 3 (2013): 169–83.

Palmer, Parker J. *The Courage to Teach: Exploring the Inner Landscape of a Teacher's Life*. San Francisco: John Wiley & Sons, 2007.

UCR Library. "Instructional Support." Accessed October 30, 2018. https://library.ucr.edu/instructional-support.

University of California Riverside. "First Generation." Accessed September 27, 2018. https://firstgen.ucr.edu.

Whistle, Wesley, and Tamara Heller. "The Pell Divide: How Four-Year Institutions Are Failing to Graduate Low- and Moderate-Income Students." Third Way, May 1, 2018. https://www.thirdway.org/report/the-pell-divide-how-four-year-institutions-are-failing-to-graduate-low-and-moderate-income-students.

Chapter 11

University of Nevada, Reno
Tackling English Composition as a Team

Rosalind Bucy, Elsa De Jong, Tati Mesfin, and Rayla E. Tokarz

Population Served

We work at the Mathewson-IGT Knowledge Center at the University of Nevada, Reno (UNR), a research land-grant institution located in northern Nevada. The region is known for its mining, ranching, and casino industries. In recent years, companies such as Tesla and Apple have contributed to a technology boom that has influenced the community and surrounding areas. Both the university and its community are experiencing fast-paced growth and change, which have created a growing need for education and research support. Over the last ten years, the university has enjoyed a steadily growing freshman class. In fall 2018, total undergraduate student enrollment for at UNR was close to 18,000. The university also has just under 300 medical students and almost 3,000 graduate students. The top majors in fall 2018 were community health sciences, engineering, business, biology, and psychology.[1] First-generation students make up 40 percent of undergraduates. Nevadans make up 72 percent of undergraduates, many from rural areas. Rural students need extra help adjusting to college and a new classroom environment.[2] Just under 25 percent of incoming students are transfer students.[3] The presence of these traditionally underserved students along with the growing student population has increased the need for information literacy instruction.

Program Scope

Most information literacy (IL) instruction at UNR resides within the Research and Instructional Services Department (RIS), whose mission is to "[assist] students, faculty, and community members with the discovery, evaluation, and use of information."[4] Eight RIS tenure-track librarians serve as liaisons to a variety of disciplines on campus and provide IL instruction for lower-division, upper-division, and graduate courses. RIS and other liaison librarians work directly with their disciplines and coordinate with faculty individually to schedule instruction sessions. At this time, the only programmatic IL instruction at UNR occurs in conjunction with the English (ENG) department's Core Writing Program, which provides freshman-level composition classes to incoming students.

Within RIS, a dedicated Core Writing Team works directly with the Core Writing Program to provide foundational IL instruction for these students. The Core Writing Program (CWP) refers to the English department's core composition curriculum. The Core Writing Team (CWT) is the team of librarians who provide IL instruction for Core Writing. Our vision is to reach every student enrolled in ENG 102 (Composition II). ENG 102 explicitly addresses the university's Core Objective 3: Critical Analysis and Use of Information, making it an ideal course for IL instruction.[5] Although ENG 102 has long been the focus of our instruction efforts, the CWT provides instruction for other CWP courses as well, from remedial composition classes to composition for English language learners.

Operations

As of fall 2018, the CWT comprised four liaison librarians holding MLS degrees and two library instructors. The liaison librarian for English is the CWT lead, coordinating instruction as an informal but agreed-upon responsibility. The liaison librarians involved with the CWT also support IL in their respective departments. In contrast, the library instructors on the CWT focus solely on supporting CWP classes. For simplicity, we refer to all CWT members as librarians, except where functional distinctions are necessary to highlight.

Instruction requests are assigned to librarians by the CWT lead based on several factors, including librarian availability and job responsibilities (see Administrative Highlights). The reality is that each of us has a different capacity to teach CWP classes in any given semester. As a result, an effort is made to distribute the number of classes taught by each librarian equitably, not equally. What is equitable is not a precise measure. However, the team lead considers factors such as full-time or part-time status as well as primary job responsibilities and competing projects when assigning classes. The unequal (but hopefully equitable) distribution of classes for the fall 2018 semester can be seen in table 11.1.

Table 11.1
Distribution of CWP classes across CWT members (fall 2018)

Team Member	LL* 1	LL2	LL3	LL4	LI† (24% FTE)	LI (80% FTE)	Total
Sessions Taught	16	23	19	12	11	34	115
* LL = Liaison Librarian † LI = Library Instructor							

In addition to liaison librarians and library instructors, the RIS department employs Peer Research Consultants (PRCs), undergraduate students trained in reference services who provide drop-in research help at the Research Help desk. PRCs also provide occasional assistance with IL instruction for the CWP, offering individual research assistance for students during sessions.

Costs associated with IL instruction for the CWP are minimal, and the CWT does not manage its own budget. Rather, the CWT is supported through the RIS department, which funds ongoing instruction costs including

- teaching materials (e.g., dry-erase markers, whiteboards, Play-Doh, Koosh balls, etc.)
- class incentives (e.g., candy, mini-highlighters, flash drives, etc.)
- professional development (e.g., online courses, books, workshops, etc.)

Marketing

Over the years, marketing IL instruction to the CWP has evolved with changes to the CWT and the CWP. A failed past marketing technique was the provision of warming sessions, in which librarians would drop by classrooms to give a brief presentation of library resources and distribute bookmarks. The goal of these sessions was to gently introduce students to the library and to encourage instructors to schedule a follow-up instruction session. The low return on investment made these warming sessions unfeasible.

Our current promotion strategy is tied closely to the academic year as well as to the activities within the CWP. We use a marketing plan with a strong focus on outreach activities at the start of the fall semester. Here's an outline of our fall 2018 marketing plan:

- *Summer:* Design Core Writing newsletter using Canva.com; host new CWP instructors for a library tour and information session during their orientation.
- *Faculty Reporting Week* (the week before the start of the semester): Librarian visits CWP faculty meeting to show instructors how to request session through the library website.
- *Week 1 of the semester:* Obtain a list of CWP instructors from the CWP office.
- *Week 2:* Email informational newsletter to instructors and distribute print copies in mailboxes.
- *Week 4:* Send personalized email check-ins to all CWP instructors who have not yet requested a session.

The current marketing plan focuses on fostering relationships with individual CWP instructors (through personalized emails) and highlighting differentiated IL instruction for ENG 101 and ENG 102 (as outlined in Pedagogical Highlights). As we review our instruction statistics at the end of the semester, we reflect on our outreach efforts and adjust our marketing plan accordingly.

Collaboration

The cornerstone of our collaboration with the CWP is the librarian-instructor relationship. This occurs on both the program level and the individual level. To facilitate communication and foster collaborative relationships, each instructor requesting a session is assigned one librarian to work with for all their CWP classes that semester. The librarian and instructor then discuss the goals for the instruction session and begin to develop a plan together.

We have also attempted collaboration at a more programmatic level. For example, our CWT meets annually with the directors and assistant directors of the CWP. These meetings are especially important for sustaining collaboration as they allow us to reassess and realign IL instruction with the broader CWP objectives. Changes in program leadership and priorities underscore the importance of continual communication. In addition to communicating with the CWP leadership, we have reached out to Graduate Writing Program Administrators and participated in CWP subcommittees such as the Pedagogy Committee, the Publicity Committee, and the Assessment Committee.[6] Outcomes of these collaborations have included sharing IL activities for instructors to include in the classroom and providing assistance with program assessment projects.

Role of the One-Shot

One-shots are the primary mode of IL instruction, with a few instructors each semester opting for a follow-up session. Our team recognizes the disadvantages associated with one-shot sessions, and we are constantly seeking strategies for making the best of these sessions. We frequently discuss concerns about one-shot sessions, which range from limitations on building effective learning environments for students to identifying which IL concepts to teach during a one-hour session. Whatever its drawbacks, the one-shot is here to stay at UNR.

Our team addresses the challenges of the one-shot by using active learning strategies (see Pedagogical Highlights) and rapport-building techniques in the classroom to engage students. In both cases, librarians develop their unique style for engaging students in meaningful ways. For example, some instructors use storytelling techniques, while others share a few personal details (such as a picture of a beloved cat). We have observed that these techniques increase student involvement in our sessions. We have also tried to extend the impact of one-shots through online tutorials that can be assigned to students outside of class for a flipped classroom. These tutorials are optional, and usage has remained low. As more courses move to online and hybrid formats, however, we are seeking to embed online IL tutorials in more classes.

Pedagogical Highlights

As discussed above (see Program Scope), our IL instruction model was built on the assumption that ENG 102 was the gravitational center of our instruction efforts. The crowning assignment in ENG 102, the research paper, lent itself well to this assumption. As a result, we tried to reach as many ENG 102 classes as possible, with the other CWP courses forming a minority of our instruction load. Recent trends have required us to reexamine those assumptions. We have seen an increasing number of ENG 101 sections and a decline in the number of ENG 102 sections in the spring semester. What accounts for the shifting focus on IL, and what should we do about it? Table 11.2 includes all CWP classes served by the library.

Table 11.2

CWP courses

Course Number	Course Name	Course Catalog Description
ENG 98	Preparatory Composition	The writing process including paragraph development, sentence structure, usage, and grammar.
ENG 100j	Composition Studio	Writing the expository essay; emphasis on revising and editing for development, coherence, style, and correctness. Enhanced instruction in critical reading and extended workshop time.
ENG 101	Composition I	Writing the expository essay; emphasis on revising and editing for development, coherence, style, and correctness.
ENG 102	Composition II	Exploration of essay forms with particular attention to interpretation and argument; emphasis on analytical reading and writing, critical thinking, and research methodologies.
ENG 113	Composition I for International Students	Satisfies the ENG 101 requirement for non-native English speakers.
ENG 114	Composition II for International Students	Satisfies the ENG 102 requirement for non-native English speakers.

In examining these questions, we identified a primary problem: we had not differentiated IL learning objectives for ENG 101 and ENG 102. Not only was this problematic from a pedagogical perspective, but it was also indefensible in the face of student complaints that they had already had an IL session (in ENG 101) and that another one would be redundant. We therefore undertook a curriculum mapping project. The goals of the project were to bring some uniformity to our teaching and to differentiate instruction while leaving the responsibility and space for creative lesson planning to individual librarians.

The joint effort of creating an activity bank has helped build our community of practice while realigning our teaching with the current goals of the CWP. Working in teams and using recent ENG 101 and ENG 102 syllabi as our starting point, we identified course learning outcomes with IL components. From the course outcomes, we wrote IL learning outcomes that were tied to the ACRL *Framework for Information Literacy for Higher Education* and identified or developed activities for each IL learning outcome (see table 11.3).[7] This process fostered a shared teaching philosophy across the CWT. Prior to the launch of our new lesson plans in fall 2018, we hosted an activity show and tell in which each librarian demonstrated an IL activity for ENG 101 or ENG 102. Experiencing the activities firsthand prepared the CWT to teach new activities, forcing us to become more adventurous and flexible teachers. Our community of practice around these shared lesson plans comes full circle as we all provide written evaluations of activities tried and we participate in regular peer teaching observations.

Table 11.3

Sample learning outcomes and activities for ENG 101 and ENG 102

Course	ACRL Frame	Learning Outcome (Students will be able to . . .)	Activity Option 1	Activity Option 2
ENG 101	Research as Inquiry	Recognize different steps of the research process	Mapping the Research Process	Draw These Characters
ENG 102	Searching as Strategic Exploration	Select appropriate library databases and search tools for different information needs	Database Evaluation	Pass the Paper

Administrative Highlights

Administrative responsibilities consist of scheduling and communication. While everyone contributes to developing our communications strategy, the CWT lead is the primary communicator with the CWP.

Scheduling is primarily handled by the team lead. Core Writing instructors complete an online instruction request form, which is received by the team lead and one other librarian. We schedule the request within one business day of receiving it. This requires aligning a person, a place, and a time (easier said than done!). Instructors indicate their first and second (and sometimes third) choices of a date. The team lead uses Outlook to determine librarians' availability at the requested times. If more than one class section is requested by the instructor, every attempt is made to assign all their classes to the same librarian. Once the availability of a librarian at the requested times is confirmed, one of three library computer labs is reserved. The team lead checks class enrollment against the room capacity of available labs. If an appropriate lab is not located, an alternate date is considered and the process restarts.

Once a date, place, and librarian are aligned, the class information is entered into the RIS department's shared instruction calendar. The team lead then forwards the original instruction request to the assigned librarian, along with the room reservation details. At this stage, assigning classes is approached with regard for the librarian tasked with teaching the IL instruction session. The assignment of a session is always posed as a question—"Can you take this class?"—and refusals (though rare) are respected.

Once the librarian has confirmed the class, the team lead tracks the number of classes each librarian teaches on a whiteboard. This helps the team lead to track progress toward meeting our teaching goals and to monitor the instruction load. This informs scheduling decisions since maintaining an equitable teaching load (as outlined in Operations) is as important as librarian availability.

Tracking IL instruction sessions as they are scheduled allows for continuous assessment of our instruction impact and instruction load. We measure instruction impact in the number of unique class sections taught, collectively. Instruction load is measured in the total number of class sessions taught, both collectively and individually. At the start of the semester, we set goals for instruction impact (e.g., 55% of CWP classes will receive IL instruction). As classes are scheduled, the team lead can see how close we are to meeting our goal and determine whether more outreach is required. (Because the whiteboard tracks sessions and not sections, instruction impact is merely approximated until the end of the semester when instruction data from LibInsight is reviewed.[8]) Similarly, the team lead consults with individual librarians at the start of the semester to set targets for instruction load. As IL sessions are assigned, the team lead can see how close a librarian is to reaching their target instruction load.

From the moment the librarian accepts an instruction session, they assume all communication, scheduling, and planning responsibilities. If the requesting instructor wants to reschedule or add a follow-up session, it's up to the librarian to handle. This way, the instructor communicates with only one librarian.

What We Wish People Knew

As the team lead for Core Writing, I (Rosalind) was surprised by how uncomfortable I would be with assigning instruction sessions to other librarians. As a liaison librarian, the decision to accept a request for instruction from one of my departments has always been my own. I appreciate having such control over my schedule, particularly because a blank space on a calendar does not always indicate availability. We all have job and life responsibilities that are unscheduled but are nevertheless real work. Since I did not like the idea of someone else controlling my instruction calendar, I was uncomfortable with assigning instruction to other librarians, especially because I do not supervise any of the Core Writing librarians. They are my peers, and leading a team of peers requires cultivating a great deal of goodwill. With respect to scheduling, it helps to have a discussion about what a reasonable instruction load looks like for each individual. Knowing that one of my Core Writing librarians is teaching a semester-long class, another has a young child at home, another has demanding liaison departments, and another has limited hours allows me to be more sensitive to the hidden demands on their time. Then, when I do schedule an instruction session for a Core Writing librarian, I know that I have given them and their valuable time due consideration.

Beyond the hidden labor of scheduling is the logistics of scheduling. We all know that scheduling can be a challenge, but it never ceases to impress me just how intractable a problem it is, particularly those midsemester, last-minute requests that come during peak instruction when rooms and people are already booked. Then, finding a workable solution is headache-inducing. Having a clear system for tracking requests and schedules helps, as does being flexible and accepting that sometimes not everything aligns. It's okay to adjust your expectations as well as those of the requesting instructor. If computer labs aren't available, be open to going to the regular classroom to teach. If the instructor's preferred date doesn't work, offer to schedule their second- or third-choice date or propose an alternative date.

Aligning the library's IL instruction with the goals of the CWP in a systematic way can also be challenging. CWP administrators, tenure-track faculty, adjuncts, and teaching assistants all have their own perspectives and concerns that influence their approaches to teaching. Often, each individual instructor is executing the stated goals of the CWP, but interpreting them differently. This can make building a cohesive IL program a challenge. Nevertheless, stepping back and finding common ground is important. With the larger goals of the CWP in focus, librarians can depend a little less on individual instructors to set goals for IL instruction sessions. Rather, we can teach IL in the best way we know how, grounded in the goals of the program.

As team lead, I attempt to foster a sense of community of practice through shared lesson plans and activities, as well as peer teaching observations and group active learning demonstrations. These activities further the cohesiveness of our IL instruction, providing for shared values as well as shared tips. From my own experiences and the experience of my team, I have gathered some practical advice for fellow coordinators to share: be prepared with a lesson plan, but be prepared to abandon that plan. Be flexible and ready when unexpected situations arise. Whether it's a technical interruption (such as a power outage, slow or no internet connection, or authentication issue) or a digression from your original lesson plan (such as low attendance or a last-minute request from the instructor to change your airtight lesson plan), minor preparations made ahead of time can save you in a pinch.

Here's what has helped us when the unexpected happened:

- *Save important pages offline.* If there is a website you frequently show students, save an offline version and bookmark it. If the library website is down or if the internet is disconnected, you can still direct students to helpful resources they can use following the session. For instance, we have saved and bookmarked the library home page, English Composition Library Guide, and research help page. Showing students library resources from an offline page can buy you some time while you wait for the internet connection to return.
- *Keep it low-tech.* It's a good idea to have a few pen and paper activities on hand in the event of a power outage or tech failure. Simple, low-tech activities can still engage students.
- *Know your classroom support or IT.* Whom do you contact if the equipment in the classroom isn't working? Is it the same contact for every room in the building? On campus? If your institution has a classroom support or IT department to assist with classroom technology, keep its contact information in your phone so you can contact it quickly.

Coordinating an information literacy program brings with it many surprises and challenges. Success does not depend on one person alone, but on a team of dedicated librarians. An instruction coordinator can foster a professional learning community by demonstrating a willingness to share ideas and take risks, to listen and be flexible.

Notes

1. University of Nevada, Reno, "Student Headcount by College and Degree Program," Institutional Analysis, accessed January 17, 2019, https://www.unr.edu/ia/census-date.
2. Elissa Nadworny and Jon Marcus, "'Going to Office Hours Is Terrifying' and Other Tales of Rural Students in College," NPR, December 12, 2018, https://www.npr.org/2018/12/12/668530699/-going-to-office-hours-is-terrifying-and-other-hurdles-for-rural-students-in-col.
3. Shannon Ellis, "Academic Affairs and Student Service" (presentation, New Faculty Orientation, University of Nevada, Reno, August 2018).
4. University of Nevada, Reno, "Research and Instructional Services," University Libraries, accessed March 12, 2019, https://library.unr.edu/ResearchServices (page discontinued).
5. University of Nevada, Reno, "Core Objective #3: Critical Analysis and Use of Information," Office of the Provost, accessed January 17, 2019, https://www.unr.edu/provost/academic-resources/

curriculum-central/silver-core-general-education-requirements/silver-core-objectives/core-objective-3.

6. Graduate Writing Program Administrators are graduate students who help administer the Writing Program. This is a common practice in the field, and the Council of Writing Program Administrators has a dedicated Graduate Organization (the WPA-GO): see "WPA-GO," Council of Writing Program Administrators website, accessed November 25, 2019, http://wpacouncil.org/wpa-go.

7. Association of College and Research Libraries, *Framework for Information Literacy for Higher Education* (Chicago: Association of College and Research Libraries, 2016).

8. A single section of a class may schedule multiple sessions. This increases the instruction load but does not change the instruction impact.

Bibliography

Association of College and Research Libraries. *Framework for Information Literacy for Higher Education.* Chicago: Association of College and Research Libraries, 2016.

Ellis, Shannon. "Academic Affairs and Student Service." Presentation, New Faculty Orientation, University of Nevada, Reno, August 2018.

Nadworny, Elissa, and Jon Marcus. "'Going to Office Hours Is Terrifying' and Other Tales of Rural Students In College." NPR, December 12, 2018. https://www.npr.org/2018/12/12/668530699/-going-to-office-hours-is-terrifying-and-other-hurdles-for-rural-students-in-col.

University of Nevada, Reno. "Core Objective #3: Critical Analysis and Use of Information." Office of the Provost. Accessed January 17, 2019. https://www.unr.edu/provost/academic-resources/curriculum-central/silver-core-general-education-requirements/silver-core-objectives/core-objective-3.

———. "Research and Instructional Services." University Libraries. Accessed March 12, 2019. https://library.unr.edu/ResearchServices (page discontinued).

———. "Student Headcount by College and Degree Program." Institutional Analysis. Accessed January 17, 2019. https://www.unr.edu/ia/census-date.

Chapter 12

Utah State University

English Composition Library Instruction Program—A Program within Programs

Katie Strand, Dory Rosenberg, and McKenzie Hyde

Population Served

Utah State University (USU) is our state's only land-grant institution, which supports both strong undergraduate and graduate programs. The students on our main campus are primarily traditional students. However, we also serve a large online and regional campus student population with many students who are classified as nontraditional. Given the various mediums of instruction at our school, our library provides information literacy through face-to-face and online courses, as well as courses that use interactive videoconferencing technology (i.e., broadcast classes). Total enrollment is approximately 27,700, of which 18,000 attend the main Logan Campus. Approximately 89 percent of our student population is made up of undergraduates.[1]

Program Scope

This case study will describe our English Composition Library Instruction Program (ECLIP), which is a program within our library-wide instruction efforts and a collaborative partner with USU's Writing Program, housed within the English department. Our library does not offer a for-credit information literacy course, and instead, library instruction is integrated at all course levels. Moreover, to allow you to better understand ECLIP, it is important to describe the current state of our library's broader instruction program, which includes (1) ECLIP, an in-depth integration through first- and second-year writing courses; (2) instruction in the majors by liaison librarians assigned to academic departments; (3) digital literacy instruction provided by our Digital Initiatives unit; (4) primary source analysis and use of materials directed by our Special Collections and Archives unit, and (5) research assignment design workshops coordinated and facilitated by librarians for university faculty. These efforts span library divisions, and historically these areas of instruction have predominantly worked independently of each other with little interaction in relation to assessment or planning. As of 2014, a formal Coordinator of Instruction was appointed with the idea of offering support across these varied instructional efforts. However, in practice, that position has worked most closely in supporting the instruction efforts of our liaison librarians and ECLIP. With the goal of unifying assessment and breaking down the silos of instruction within the areas described above, a new library-wide Instruction Committee was formed in 2018. This new committee includes representatives from across the library, and the group is chaired by the Coordinator of Instruction. Currently, this committee is working to redefine the structure and goals of a library-wide information literacy program and to clarify how smaller programs, such as ECLIP, connect to larger library-wide assessment and planning.

ECLIP currently consists of an integration with our Writing Program's English 1010 and English 2010 courses. Both of these courses have their own separate objectives and learning outcomes, and the overall goal is that once students finish (or test out of) both courses, they will have developed foundational research and writing skills related to rhetorical argumentation. With this goal in mind, English 1010 is seen as a stepping stone to English 2010. Librarians are available to meet with students one-on-one for both English 1010 and 2010 courses. However, our integration with English 1010 is online only, while we offer in-person library sessions for English 2010. In addition to the interactive tutorials and videos embedded in English 1010 courses, lessons targeting course-specific information literacy needs are taught by course instructors in their classroom. For our regional campus and online students, librarians offer support through Canvas (our learning management system), broadcast classes, or consultations via email or phone. Our goal in describing our ECLIP program is to showcase an example of an internal structure that falls under a larger umbrella of information literacy goals and expectations library-wide.

Operations

Our Coordinator of Instruction also currently serves as the unit head of Learning and Engagement Services (LES), which is part of our library's Instruction, Collections, and Patron Services division. Prior to 2017, the work of coordinating ECLIP was part of the coordinator's responsibilities. However, due to concerns about sustainability and workload, ECLIP was separated, and in 2017 an ECLIP Coordinator role was created and is now held by a librarian in LES.

The ECLIP Coordinator leads a core team of two teaching assistants and oversees instruction related to English 1010 and English 2010, while the LES unit head oversees all other unit work. Each semester, LES librarians are assigned multiple sections of English 1010 and English 2010. On average each librarian will partner with five to seven courses, and our two teaching assistants will partner with twelve to fifteen courses. At a minimum, librarians are expected to communicate and collaborate with instructors in regard to library-developed materials and serve as a direct library resource for students. On average, English 2010 students will attend two to three information literacy instruction classes led by their assigned librarians. Currently, our strongest integration is with face-to-face courses at our main campus.

One major operational challenge we experience with face-to-face integration is balancing librarian workloads. LES librarians hold many other roles, including liaison assignments, that impact how much time we can ask in support of ECLIP. One strategy we've used in navigating this challenge is applying a targeted approach when creating librarian/instructor partnerships. For example, graduate instructors who teach English 2010 are required to bring their classes to the library three times for specific lessons; however, some lecturers and adjunct instructors come to the library for fewer than three sessions. Based on a librarian's workload, the ECLIP Coordinator and two teaching assistants pair librarians with instructors whose course load and library content will match the librarians' availability. This partnering approach is a time-intensive endeavor that involves at least two to three meetings toward the end of each semester at which the ECLIP Coordinator and two teaching assistants look at the current partnerships and tentatively plan for any changes that might need to be made due to workload shifts, librarian sabbaticals, number of composition sections to be offered, or changes in instructors' class assignments. Taking this in-depth approach to partnerships allows us to work around librarians' shifting workloads, so we can better respond to the needs of librarians individually and the unit at large.

An example of a related operational challenge connects to reserving rooms for our English 2010 library sessions. As of fall 2018, the ECLIP Coordinator and two teaching assistants collaborated with Writing Program administration to preschedule all library days for English 2010 courses taught by a graduate instructor. Prior to this change, librarians scheduled their own library days and were in charge of making sure a library room was available for their session. The response to this prescheduling has been overwhelmingly positive from librarians who teach these composition sessions. However, this change has added to the workload of the ECLIP Coordinator and teaching assistants, and also brings up a question of access. With the prescheduling, ECLIP has most, if not all, of our library instruction rooms booked for six days each semester. If other instruction efforts across the library need an instruction room during one of our prescheduled days, how do we effectively share the space? Likewise, how can ECLIP be as efficient as possible when rooms often need to be reserved before the English department finalizes class schedules?

Another operational challenge is maintaining consistency in library services provided at our main campus, and regional locations, and in online courses. A specific example of this challenge is evident in our integration with English 1010. Given that research demands in English 1010 are typically much less than English 2010 and that our program strives to maintain sustainable workloads for librarians, our current integration with English 1010 is online only. However, instructors at our regional campuses often have more autonomy over their curriculum, and the result is that some English 1010 classes teach more research elements than others. While students will receive a more in-depth library integration when they later take English 2010, the concern is still there that students, and especially incoming freshmen, are being missed at their time of need. One of the top priorities of our program is to ensure that the services we provide to our online and regional students are equivalent to what students receive in face-to-face Logan campus–based courses. How we will develop in this area moving forward is heavily reliant on the Writing Program itself, which is currently in a process of transition following the retirement of the previous program director.

Marketing

A need for marketing support has been identified in our library. However, we do not currently have a set position that directs this work. In order to market library instruction services more broadly, LES created an instruction services area on our library's website that includes a teaching philosophy, available online tutorials, and scheduling information.[2] This section of the library website is currently "owned" by LES and primarily targets instruction for discipline-specific classes. However, as our new Instruction Committee moves forward, this ownership and online presence might evolve.

ECLIP, as a smaller program, has an ultimate goal to make sure all of our composition instructors, including lecturers, adjuncts, and graduate instructors, either bring their classes to the library for information literacy instruction or integrate our online materials into their courses. In tackling this goal, we've found that we often need to market library materials and lessons differently based on our instructor group. For example, graduate instructors are currently required by Writing Program administration to teach a set curriculum. While graduate instructors can still modify content to fit their teaching style, ECLIP is able to target marketing based on the common curriculum they teach. As an example of what this looks like in practice, the ECLIP Coordinator drafts emails at the beginning of each semester that librarians then send to their partnered graduate instructors before each online integration or prescheduled library day. Librarians are welcome to add their own voice to the message, but the end result is that the same programmatic message is being sent to graduate instructors.

The ECLIP Coordinator also drafts language that librarians can send to their partnered lecturers and adjunct instructors. However, this instructor population is granted a higher level of autonomy by the Writing Program, and as a result, we market our library support in broader terms when working with these instructors. For example, instead of listing the prescheduled library lessons and content as we do with graduate instructors, our message more heavily encourages lecturers and adjunct instructors to work with their partnered librarians to develop library content that aligns with their course goals and assignments. Ultimately, our end goal is to ensure students are receiving equitable library instruction in all classes, and to be successful in this endeavor we must shape our communication and marketing of library resources based on our respective stakeholder groups.

Collaboration

The Writing Program is one of the library's biggest allies on campus. Its leadership structure consists of a Writing Program director (a faculty member), an associate director of English 2010 (a lecturer), and two associate directors of English 1010 (graduate instructors). In spring 2018, both ECLIP and the Writing Program acquired new leadership. Given this change, new relationships had to be built and mutual trust had to be established before successful collaboration could take place. Numerous face-to-face meetings and inclusive email chains successfully laid the foundation for collaborative working relationships between both teams and their leadership.

A recent example of our collaborative efforts was the development of library content designed to match a new curriculum that Writing Program administration released in fall 2018. This redesign provided us with an opportunity to have library materials and resources automatically integrated into the instructor-taught curriculum. In this process, we held face-to-face meetings with all Writing Program administration, the ECLIP Coordinator, and two library teaching assistants to discuss cohesion and growth between the two courses. Likewise, smaller meetings with individual English 1010 or English 2010 leadership were used for lesson development and finalizing integration details. Collaboration at the administrative level has supported the organic nature of our current integration, especially with graduate instructor–led courses.

Even with administrative support, our instruction would have little to no impact without the continued support and cooperation of individual instructors. It is the librarian's responsibility to initiate communication with instructors and demonstrate how our expertise can help their students succeed. Although it is not always possible, we try to keep instructors partnered with the same librarians semester after semester. This allows instructor/librarian relationships to flourish by setting the foundation for deeper collaboration and a better understanding of individual strengths.

Our relationships with our current allies require consistent commitment and open communication. We seek out feedback on our services in both formal and informal settings. For example, in spring 2018, we held focus groups for all English 2010 instructors. The primary goal of the focus groups was to find out how we could improve our current collaboration model. From these focus groups, we learned that several instructors felt a stronger focus on evaluating sources was needed in our English 2010 content. We used this feedback, along with findings from other assessment projects, in the redesign of our materials in fall 2018 and were able to address these concerns by offering a new evaluating sources lesson. Maintaining collaborative relationships with our partnered program, remaining open to change, and actively responding to constructive criticism has allowed us to become more deeply integrated into composition curriculums.

Assessment

We cultivate a culture of assessment in our library by engaging in a cyclical and iterative process that is informed by our unit's instruction mission and course learning outcomes. In relation to ECLIP, each of our developed lesson plans includes an element of formative assessment, whether that be through gathering examples of student work or asking students to contribute to a Canvas discussion board. We also encourage individual librarians to ask students to complete anonymous surveys at the end of their final library session. We create this survey using Qualtrics and include the survey link on the English 2010 LibGuide. Each semester, we receive hundreds of student responses, and individual librarians are able to use that data for promotion and tenure or other professional development needs. Moreover, we were able to use trends gathered from this data to inform the redesign of our library curriculum for fall 2018. When analyzing the data, we learned that the library sessions felt repetitive for students. The combination of the prework materials we asked instructors to share with their students before a library session and the library session's content itself was redundant. As a result, we revised the content for spring 2019 and specifically pared down the prework and used different examples and visuals in the prework materials than those we share in our library session.

Programmatically, we have initiated and completed several larger assessment projects. For example, in fall 2017, a team of LES librarians completed an analysis of seventy-nine English 2010 persuasive research essays, and their study is discussed in a recent article in *Communications in Information Literacy*.[3] In brief, the team used multiple rubrics to identify shifts in student learning and compared the results to findings from a previous study completed by LES librarians. The findings indicated that our instruction was contributing to student improvements in synthesis, topic refinement, and source variety. However, the analysis also informed us that our students are still struggling with evaluating sources, incorporating multiple perspectives, and maintaining their own voice when synthesizing their research. These larger assessment projects have been instrumental in making sure our integration with the Writing Program and the content we teach does not become static.

In order to make sure we are conducting our assessment studies ethically and to be able to use data collected for publication purposes, we submit Institutional Review Board (IRB) protocols for projects that are intended for purposes beyond the internal structure of ECLIP or LES. Much of our assessment work has involved human participants or examples of student work, and according to the requirements of our university's IRB office, we submit protocols even if our study will be categorized as exempt. For example, our most recent focus group study was categorized as exempt, but we still had to have the language and marketing materials we used approved by IRB as our study incorporated human participants. Overall, our university's IRB office is very responsive and supportive of library research, but the process does add extra logistics and work for larger projects. While we still pursue these larger assessment needs, we are continually looking for assessment data for internal use only in improving our program and procedures.

Pedagogical Highlights

We believe that students learn research skills best when those skills are tied to specific, immediate, and class-related needs, and as a result, ECLIP's pedagogical approach is heavily student-centered. Our lessons are carefully scaffolded to ensure that the skills being taught are relevant to course content. For example, in our English 2010 curriculum redesign, we first worked with the Writing Program to design research outcomes for both English 1010 and 2010, and we then applied a backward design approach and used the research outcomes to inform the development of our new lessons. The research outcomes we collaboratively developed are as follows:

English 1010 Research Outcomes:

- Understand the value and characteristics of a variety of sources
- Identify relevant sources in relation to audience and purpose
- Describe the ethical and practical significance of citation

- Reflect on the challenges and strategies of your research process

English 2010 Research Outcomes:

- Identify a research question with a manageable scope
- Evaluate different types of sources in relation to the researcher's information need
- Recognize the value of multiple perspectives
- Organize an argument by synthesizing sources into conversation with each other
- Develop effective searching strategies

All of our face-to-face lessons include some form of active learning, whether that be evaluating case studies or using the library databases in a group activity. Generally, we implement a flipped approach and use online resources to introduce library resources to students and then focus on higher-level skills and active learning practices during class time. However, many lecturers still consistently request database demonstrations rather than specific lessons. While there can be variability in library content depending on the instructor population, we advocate for one-on-one librarian time with students in each of our library sessions. In fact, student surveys continually request more one-on-one time with librarians. Overall, a number of different pedagogical approaches are used in our library sessions. Figure 12.1 represents statistics gathered from fall 2017 through summer 2018 and demonstrates the variety of instruction types utilized in 295 face-to-face English 2010 library sessions. Many library sessions include a combination of instruction types ranging from an orientation to the library to lecture, active learning, or one-on-one interaction.

INSTRUCTION TYPES

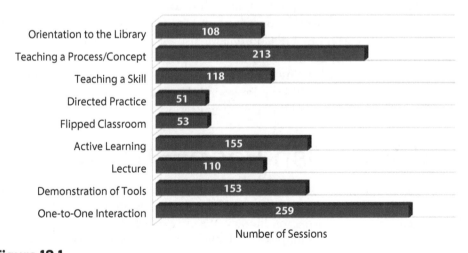

Figure 12.1
Instruction types in face-to-face English 2010 library sessions, fall 2017– summer 2018

Administrative Highlights

We have a strong partnership with the Writing Program, and our instructional efforts continue to evolve based on iterative assessment and data analysis. We collect different kinds of composition-related data, and this data has played a crucial role in showing the impact of ECLIP in advocating for resources and positions and in initiating conversations on best practices within the LES unit. As an example, a teaching assistant recently visualized themes that emerged from our student survey data and created an engaging graphic that integrated student comments. We used this graphic as a way to spark discussion on instruction practices during an LES meeting. Moreover, for many years, LES has created an annual report that details the work of the unit as a whole, and as of 2018 a separate annual report was created for ECLIP. This report will be shared with Writing Program administration at the end of the academic year, as well as with all library staff via our library-wide email list.

Information Literacy Coordinator Profile

As a whole, our library is moving toward the development of a more structured approach to library instruction. The creation of the library-wide Instruction Committee and the creation of the ECLIP Coordinator position reflect this move at both a larger library-wide level and a smaller program-specific level. The ECLIP Coordinator is a formal role held by a faculty librarian and is responsible for ensuring the ECLIP follows established standards, contributes to the Mission and Vision of the Library, and fosters the continued success and growth of the program. The Coordinator of Library Instruction, who previously facilitated this work, and the current ECLIP Coordinator both have second master's degrees in English, and they both have experience in teaching English composition courses. This familiarity with rhetoric and composition, in both theory and practice, has served as a valuable point of connection when establishing and maintaining relationships with the Writing Program. The current ECLIP Coordinator also serves as the liaison librarian for two academic departments, including the English department. This is the first time the library point person for the Writing Program has also been the library liaison for the English department, and as the Writing Program is housed in the English department, this move has served well in streamlining communication.

What We Wish People Knew

The hardest part of being a targeted program within a larger information literacy effort is fostering a library-wide understanding of our specific instruction area and how it fits within a shared vision of information literacy. We are excited about the ways our new Instruction Committee can help address this challenge. Our advice would be if you have a colleague who teaches in a unit that differs from your area, take the initiative to ask questions about how and what they teach. It's easy to describe communication barriers in the context of working with stakeholders outside the library; however, it's the communication that happens (or doesn't happen) in house that has the greatest impact on a program's growth and development.

Notes

1. "Utah State University Quick Facts," Utah State University, accessed March 26, 2019, https://www.usu.edu/about/at-a-glance.
2. "Instruction Services," Utah State University Libraries, accessed March 26, 2019, https://library.usu.edu/instruct.
3. Eastman, T., Lundstrom, K., Strand, K., Davis, E., Martin, P. N., Krebs, A., & Hedrich, A. (2018). Closing the Loop: Engaging in a Sustainable and Continuous Cycle of Authentic Assessment to Improve Library Instruction. *Communications in Information Literacy, 12* (2), 64-85.https://doi.org/10.15760/comminfolit.2018.12.2.2.

Bibliography

Eastman, T., Lundstrom, K., Strand, K., Davis, E., Martin, P. N., Krebs, A., & Hedrich, A. (2018). Closing the Loop: Engaging in a Sustainable and Continuous Cycle of Authentic Assessment to Improve Library Instruction. *Communications in Information Literacy, 12* (2), 64-85.https://doi.org/10.15760/comminfolit.2018.12.2.2.

Utah State University. "Utah State University Quick Facts." Accessed March 26, 2019. https://www.usu.edu/about/at-a-glance.

Utah State University Libraries. "Instruction Services." Accessed March 26, 2019. https://library.usu.edu/instruct.

Chapter 13

California State University, Dominguez Hills

Revitalizing a Program from the Ground Up

Carolyn Caffrey Gardner and Tessa Withorn

Population Served

California State University, Dominguez Hills (CSUDH), is a regional public university located in the South Bay of Los Angeles County. It is one of the twenty-three campuses within the California State University system. In spring 2018, CSUDH had a total enrollment of 14,635 students and a full-time equivalent of 11,325 students. CSUDH offers forty-four undergraduate degrees, twenty-two graduate degrees, and several postgraduate certificates. Popular degree programs are in business administration, psychology, criminal justice, sociology, and health science.[1] Over half of our students are the first in their families to attend college, and many work full-time, transfer from community colleges, and live in LA County.[2] We are a designated Hispanic-Serving Institution, with 61.9 percent of the student population identifying as Hispanic/Latino, 14.1 percent as Black/African American, 11.1 percent Asian, and 9.5 percent White/Caucasian.[3] Originally founded in 1960, CSUDH received its permanent home in Carson as a response to the Watts Rebellion of 1965.[4] The governor selected Carson in response to the lack of educational opportunities for the region and demands from African Americans in the rebellion advocating for access to higher education.[5] Historically, CSUDH has been economically disadvantaged, receiving less state funding than other campuses. Among other disparities, this has resulted in the lowest tenure density (28%) within the CSU system and over half of the classes offered in temporary buildings well past their intended years of use.[6]

This history directly shapes the culture of CSUDH, which we see as an institution passionately committed to social justice, though at times we are resigned to under-resourced conditions. As a direct result of this institutional culture, the information literacy program is actively committed to social justice in its pedagogy. We also have to market the program as necessary to instructors who are already overextended. Despite information literacy being an institutional learning outcome,[7] faculty may perceive it as a superfluous task when working with students who have basic unmet needs (food, housing, etc.) on an under-resourced campus.

Program Scope

The information literacy (IL) program is made up of several components: in-person course-integrated instruction, assignment design, online learning, stand-alone workshops, and a credit-bearing course (to be implemented in the spring 2020 semester). In combination, each component should ideally contribute to a well-rounded information literacy program where students have multiple information literacy touch points throughout their time at CSUDH. In practice, some students receive much more attention than others, and we are still working on finessing the program's reach.

As a result of attrition and hiring freezes during the 2008 recession, the CSUDH library was extremely short-staffed when I (Carolyn) arrived as IL coordinator in 2016. The IL program was dormant, and few classes were taught. The program had to be entirely rebuilt, including a web presence, request form, policies, learning outcomes, assessment plan, and establishing a reputation on campus. Because we were building a program from the ground up, we were not as tied to legacy one-shots and relationships as other programs may be. In consultation with our associate dean, the IL coordinator brainstormed what an ideal program would look like without these long-standing relationship, and agreed there would be a greater emphasis on assignment and curricular design not tied to an in-person one-shot for sustainability reasons. Assignment design is featured prominently on our IL program website via handouts designed by the IL coordinator on designing effective research assignments and alternatives to the research paper genre (see figure 13.1).

Since 2017, CSUDH librarians have engaged in twenty significant assignment design consultations resulting in everything from the revision of course learning outcomes to the adoption of scaffolded research assignments designed by librarians. We see this as a great accomplishment considering that a majority of our library faculty have been with the institution for fewer than three years. As relationships with instructional faculty grow, we have been invited to the table at the start of some entirely new degree programs and courses that are moving online or undergoing curriculum review.

In reviving the program, we focused our initial attention on upper-division course-integrated one-shots. These courses are typically taught by permanent faculty, and we anticipated this would cut down on the typical churn in one-shot relationships as we attempted to reestablish a presence on campus. Upper-division course-integrated information literacy instruction is typically provided upon request from the course instructor through either a web form or personal contact with their liaison librarian. As of fall 2018, over 60 percent of our one-shot instruction sessions are for upper-division or graduate courses.

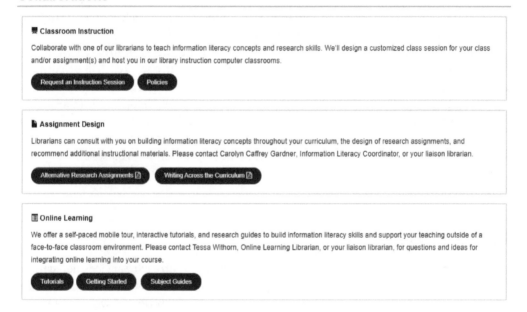

Figure 13.1
Information literacy program website with assignment design featured

Our only systematic information literacy instruction for undergraduates in general education coursework takes place in the summer for early-start English composition courses. These composition courses reach more than half of incoming freshmen.[8] In the coming years we hope to engage intentionally with the general education curriculum now that our reputation as information literacy experts is established.

The library offers a handful of stand-alone workshops each semester that are often linked to other programming within the library or with campus partners. For example, the library participates in a student affairs workshops series where students select from several workshops on academic success and receive a certification of completion. Our reference services coordinator has offered several workshops in this series focused on becoming a Google pro with filetype and site searching. Other workshops have been part of our Open Access Week celebrations and centered on editing Wikipedia or finding open access resources after graduation.

Digital learning objects (DLOs) are integrated into the library's website through a Getting Started with Library Research guide and Tutorials page,[9] as well as frequently asked questions and research guides where needed. We use DLOs as stand-alone, self-paced resources, but also as a way to extend a one-shot session by either preparing students for an in-person library session as a pre-assignment, or as a follow-up to concepts that were not fully addressed in the session. As of fall 2019, we have piloted three course-integrated tutorials using Springshare's LibWizard platform. This approach mirrors our upper-division in-person instruction in an attempt to provide a more holistic online learning experience that connects DLOs to a specific assignment (e.g., citation tracking for a literature review) or disciplinary resources (e.g., primary research, evidence-based practice). As more courses move to fully online or hybrid modalities, we anticipate partnering with instructors to adapt what was once an in-person session into a course-integrated tutorial, making stand-alone, self-paced tutorials readily accessible to students, and consulting with instructors on assignment and module design.

Finally, in spring 2020, the CSUDH Library will be launching a three-credit course, Fundamentals of Information Literacy. Once offered, the course will reach approximately thirty students each semester and meet a general education requirement in the category of lifelong learning. The course was developed by library faculty in order to create a space for librarians to have deep learning opportunities with students and to focus on concepts that can be a challenge for one-shot instruction to address. Specifically, the course will dive into how we evaluate information including the role algorithmic biases and cognitive biases play and contemporary information issues such as privacy and commercial content moderation.

Operations

All librarians are part of the Reference, Instruction, and Outreach Services department (RIOS), including the IL coordinator. As of the time of this writing, there are eight tenured or tenure-track faculty librarians who participate in the IL program who have both a functional role (i.e., information literacy coordinator, collections coordinator, reference coordinator, user services) and subject liaison responsibilities. We also have two temporary positions dedicated to reference and instruction. The IL coordinator assesses the program, communicates with librarians about their teaching, provides instruction professional development, advocates for IL on campus-wide committees, communicates with faculty, and schedules our instruction rooms. The online learning librarian is primarily responsible for creating and marketing tutorials, but collaborates with the IL coordinator and other librarians on creating DLOs for specific courses in their liaison area and for a general audience.

Instruction requests within a liaison area are assigned to the designated librarian when available, but in an effort to keep one-shot instruction equitable, the IL coordinator assigns general education (GE) instruction based on current instructional load. Since the temporary lecturer positions have different responsibilities from the tenure-track librarians, they have been teaching the bulk of GE instruction sessions, but when they are unavailable the request moves on to the librarian with the fewest sessions scheduled. In 2016, I (Carolyn) called a meeting with all librarians, and we discussed how we would distribute classes equitably. This was a productive strategy for having all librarians feel invested in our instruction program and not dismissing GE sessions as an extra burden or unimportant. The IL coordinator tries to not schedule anyone for more than three sessions in one day, with three being the exception rather than an expected number, in order to set boundaries and expectations with course instructors. It can be a challenge to enforce a sustainable workload with our faculty partners when many of them are lecturer faculty themselves who often teach five or more sessions in one day at CSUDH and also teach at other college campuses in the region. We strive to balance our own needs with the expectations of faculty who may themselves be teaching five 75-minute classes back-to-back. For instructors teaching multiple sections, the request is typically shared by two librarians who design the lesson plan together and then divide up the sections as evenly as possible. Distributing our work this way also leads to an increase in lesson plan sharing and collaborative teaching experiences for librarians.

While the IL program does not have its own dedicated budget, library administration is very supportive of the IL program's financial needs. For example, librarians have received funding to attend ACRL's Immersion Program, to purchase requested software such as Articulate Storyline and LibWizard, and to update equipment in library classrooms. Library administration also supports the IL program in other meaningful ways. Our library dean is a former IL coordinator and therefore centers the teaching work we do in the library's mission and strategic goals as well as campus-wide conversations with which she is involved.[10]

Marketing

Because we are a department of librarians who are relatively new to the institution, forming relationships and mutual respect with course instructors is essential to the maturation of our IL program. At the beginning of each semester, liaison librarians send newsletters and emails to their colleges and departments. For example, the sociology liaison librarian emails all of the faculty teaching the research methods course with a sample lesson plan and an explanation of how this course is a key place to teach information literacy concepts required of all sociology majors. This approach helps the liaison teach multiple sections of the same course rather than just those that may have sought out instruction. Assignment design and online learning opportunities usually spring from conversations between liaison librarians and instructors while preparing for a one-shot or discussing the needs of courses undergoing modification.

Many of our librarians are also invited to department meetings and use this time as an opportunity to highlight current collaborations and start a conversation around curricular needs, rather than just present on what the library can do for individual students and instructors. While we are actively engaging in promotional conversations about the IL program, we are not seeking additional one-shot instruction sessions for the sake of increasing their quantity. We are now trying to engage faculty in conversations about strategic places where we can partner in the curriculum. The campus-wide committees librarians serve on are essential for being thought of as institutional partners. For example, our librarians have served on committees that have allowed them to position the library as expert collaborators in assessment for program review and accreditation.

While relationship building and personal connections have been the most effective way to meaningfully engage instructional faculty, we also use our web presence to reinforce how integral information literacy is to the institution. In a recent redesign of the IL program page, we created buttons to encourage users to explore and act (e.g., request instruction, modify assignment language, browse tutorials) rather than scan information and created graphics to show how learning outcomes are built from a foundation of orientation to GE to disciplinary concepts in the major (see figure 13.1).[11] By using language like "partner," "collaborate," and "outcomes" in person and online, we market ourselves as an academic program rather than a service.

Collaboration

Our strongest instructional collaborations have been with individual programs and colleges through the liaison model; however, we also have significant partnerships with our Faculty Development Center (FDC), our Supplemental Instruction program, and the Toro Learning and Testing Center (TLTC). The FDC regularly asks us to contribute professional development workshops on designing effective research assignments and teaching students how to evaluate information, which are well attended. The conversations we are able to have in these environments promote a shared understanding of information literacy with faculty. The IL program has an active role in the early-start Summer Bridge program where many of our first-year students come to campus for a week before their first fall semester to take English composition and math courses for credit. We provide one-shot instruction for all summer early-start composition courses, which include supplemental instructors (SIs). SIs are undergraduate and graduate peer educators employed by the English department who are embedded into introductory courses and lead their own workshops in addition to tutoring. We also participate in ongoing training for English SIs and in their annual professional development conference. For example, we were recently asked to present on plagiarism. We interpreted that request through our learning outcomes and chose to focus on how SIs can effectively teach the why behind citation, ways to discuss plagiarism with students that are not punitive, and a vigorous debate on the ethics of Turnitin.com.[12] The SIs who participated in the session responded positively in a feedback form and in personal conversations to being addressed as fellow educators and found the tools we provided useful for their own instruction. This approach has been especially effective in moving our instructional load away from dozens of one-shot sessions while still reaching undergraduate students in first-year writing courses through assignment design and consultations.

Historically, the CSUDH library has tended to seek collaboration primarily to forward our own goals of increased utilization of our resources, but now, we are actively seeking to equalize one-sided relationships by offering support and communicating shared goals. Relationship building with other campus partners with similar educational missions can initially require compromise, setting boundaries, and establishing trust. For example, we were approached by TLTC to collaborate on a drop-in workshop series for students writing research papers after TLTC had already developed IL content for evaluating sources. Instead of micromanaging the ways TLTC would teach these concepts, we decided not to overly critique its approach with how we would address the same subjects. For example, TLTC wanted to use a web evaluation checklist that would not be a typical element of our teaching practice. In order to create a sustainable partnership, we had to compromise and aim for a shared understanding of IL. Over time, our approaches to teaching have grown closer together through mutual respect and focusing on our shared goal for student learning, which might not have happened if we had focused our energy on TLTC's content.

Assessment

We assess information literacy in multiple ways both within class sessions and programmatically. After each one-shot session, library faculty ask students to take a brief survey that measures satisfaction and perceptions about library instruction. This kind of "perceived teaching" evaluation is required for all faculty in our retention, tenure, and promotion process, serving a perfunctory role even if we don't gather meaningful information on student learning from them. However, we have used the student comments to advocate for additional time and resources, such as lobbying library administration to provide funds to update slow computers or asking instructors for the entire class period to be devoted to IL instruction. Library faculty also typically use active learning strategies in their classrooms that include formative classroom assessment techniques built in such as interactive polling (Kahoot!), digital worksheets, one-minute papers, gallery walks, and discussion. Library faculty individually make use of the assessment data from classroom activities to reflect on and modify their pedagogy. In a previous academic year the IL coordinator asked each librarian to respond to the question "How have you used formative assessment to modify your instruction?" and included the answers in a year-end report.

Currently, the campus assessment committee's charge is limited to degree-granting programs. However, the library has submitted an annual IL report in the assessment management software, Campus Labs Planning, in order to take part in ongoing campus conversations on learning outcomes. While assessment is not mandated for the library, we do see the value of programmatic assessment for continuous improvement. To achieve that goal, we've partnered with other instructional faculty to assist in programmatically assessing information literacy student learning outcomes in their degree programs. Our biggest collaborations to date have been with biology and psychology senior capstone courses to assess mastery of programmatic learning goals. Approximately 100 to 250 students are in the psychology course with varying instructors each semester. Together as a department and with the psychology faculty, we created a rubric to score final research papers that was inspired by the Claremont Colleges' Information Literacy in Student Work rubric.[13] After several norming sessions, two librarians scored each final student paper in the areas of attribution, sources selected, and source integration. Based on assessment of student work over several semesters, the library successfully recommended changes to the curriculum of this course and the sequencing of information literacy across the psychology major, creating an online tool kit comprising assignment design recommendations developed by librarians for psychology instructors.[14] Both biology and psychology include IL as part of their annual assessment for their mandated reports. Lastly, our IL coordinator compiled data on institutional learning outcomes linked to information literacy to contribute evidence of information literacy assessment for a recent campus-wide reaccreditation through the Western Association of Schools and Colleges (WASC).[15] Our library dean also led the committee that looked at the WASC core competency for information literacy.

Pedagogical Highlights

Our liaison and instruction librarians are dedicated to student engagement and embrace IL concepts from the Association of College and Research Libraries' *Framework for Information Literacy for Higher Education*.[16] Individual librarians have full control over what and how they teach, but we have a culture of sharing materials that contributes to how we create a community of practice. A shared Google Drive with previous lesson plans and materials has helped us set a consistent tone with faculty and learn from each other, especially considering the lack of institutional memory and a shuffle of liaison responsibilities. Lesson plan documents typically include learning outcomes, a bit of background about the course and communication with the instructor, and a general outline of content and activities. We share slides, handouts, and materials collected from instructors such as assignments and syllabi that often go unchanged. Our drive is organized in nested folders by course, instructor, and semester to make it easier to trace the history of what has been taught for the curriculum. Several of our librarians have contributed to and adapted activities from shared repositories and instruction handbooks, and we rely on shared materials in the profession to generate and inspire new ideas. We continue to foster this community through informal conversations and feedback and occasional co-teaching. The IL coordinator typically leads a more formal professional development workshop once a semester on topics ranging from curriculum mapping to communicating goals with faculty.

A representative example of how we try to infuse a one-shot session with curricular needs, collaboration with instructors, and active learning would be a seventy-five-minute session with an upper-division course in a major. In this scenario, the health sciences librarian met with the faculty member at the beginning of the semester to discuss the syllabus and outcomes. One of the sessions that came out of that meeting focused on a core disciplinary framework, evidence-based health-care management (EBM), in which students would be able to formulate a PICO research question, use subject headings in PubMed, and analyze the methodology of a research study, with an enduring understanding that EBM is an iterative and systematic process for decision-making.[17] As a result of consulting with the instructor, the librarian was able to call back to their textbook and course readings and draw connection between the course outcomes, IL outcomes, and assignment with students throughout the session. Activities included think-pair-shares about students' previous experience with research and specific prompts related to the readings, a highlighter activity to identify methodologies on printed articles with varying levels of evidence, and guided searching. While this level of course integration is not always possible, we strive to increase communication and transparency with faculty through sharing lesson plans in advance and provide learning experiences for students that allow them to actively participate.

Our instruction request form asks, "What would you like students to learn from the session?" but we do get some instruction requests for students to "learn about the library," or requests with no clear indication that students will be preparing for a specific research assignment. We try to use those requests as an opportunity to discuss concepts from the ACRL *Framework* that we wouldn't have time for during a session. For example, we received a request for an English composition courses taught by an instructor we partner with regularly who is enthusiastic about the library, but requires only a few scholarly sources and doesn't stipulate that we cover specific resources or concepts. For this session, one of our librarians used a concept mapping activity, the Information Spectrum, that addresses "Information Creation as a Process" to talk about evaluating source formats and discuss how information is created, accessed, and shared.[18]

In terms of pedagogical approaches for online learning and tutorials, we use tools like LibWizard that allow for directions and text on the side and interactive application of concepts whenever possible. One of our tutorials, for example, focuses on tools in a database, Opposing Viewpoints in Context, but also allows for free responses and individual topic searching. The tutorial asks open-ended and exploratory questions that guide students through using research tools to develop IL concepts such as choosing a topic that interests them and reading source information to identify an author's expertise and their unique contribution to a conversation (see figure 13.2).

Figure 13.2
Page from the Opposing Viewpoints tutorial

While we have a public-facing IL vision statement, our internal guiding vision is "Fake it 'til you make it." This is about not reacting solely to what faculty request from their IL sessions or tutorials and pushing the content where we see it needs to go through intentional conversations with our partners. We strive to be seen as IL experts on campus by outwardly behaving as IL experts even when we don't feel like our most confident selves. We are not waiting around for someone to ask for an IL session on, say, the intersections of scholarly communication and information literacy, but instead proactively seek opportunities in the sessions we do have to show faculty the greater possibilities. As our program has developed, we have found that these interactions do shift the conversations we have with faculty. For example, what started as a request for a library tour has shifted into a librarian-designed nongraded assignment with meaningful information literacy concepts integrated in the course. If we had been content to offer the tour that was requested, we have no doubt that is what we would still be providing for that class.

Administrative Highlights

One administrative highlight of our IL program is the way we gather and report statistics about our instructional activities. Because we hope to further our instructional reach beyond one-shots, we've also begun collecting statistics demonstrating our work and impact outside of the one-shot environment. Specifically, we record in Springshare's LibInsight anytime a librarian collaborates on or creates an ungraded assignment, graded assignment, or other supplemental instructional materials for a course.[19] While these may not be the numbers formally collected by ACRL's "Academic Library Trends and Statistics Survey,"[20] we have made a decision to gather evidence that supports what we value. These statistics are reported out to the rest of the library in a visually engaging infographic-style report each semester.[21]

Information Literacy Coordinator Profile

I (Carolyn) applied to CSUDH because it was advertising for a formal information literacy coordinator position that would not supervise any librarians and would also have subject liaison responsibilities. It can be hard to assign percentages to the work that I do, but in a typical week of the semester I probably spend about 10 percent to 20 percent of my time involved with some aspect of coordinating our program. There are certainly some weeks where it feels like I spend no time doing coordinator work and periods in the summer where I can spend nearly 100 percent of my time planning program development. I don't teach significantly more than any other liaison librarian because I'm a coordinator; however, I may teach more one-shots than some of my colleagues by the nature of my liaison assignment. Our library administration understands that being a coordinator does not necessarily mean teaching all of the one-shot sessions that come in last minute or others don't want to teach (like our 7:00 a.m. classes!), so I do not feel additional pressure to pick up more than my fair share. I see it as my responsibility to spend more of my time on assignment design and IL assessment than other librarians.

What We Wish People Knew

One of the best things I (Carolyn) have done to help manage my administrative workload is to save all the emails I've written that help set appropriate boundaries and expectations with our teaching faculty. I paste them in a Google Doc so that I'm able to quickly find and retrieve effective language that explains tactfully why we don't offer scavenger hunts or database demonstrations. Having language readily available based on past experiences helps ensure that I'm able to respond to faculty quicker and can share some of the tips I've found over the years in negotiating with faculty and my colleagues.

I wish more people knew that the most important parts of your job as an IL coordinator are completely hidden from others. As a coordinator, it is your responsibility to set the tone and expectations within your program, and often this relational work isn't seen as "real work." While it may seem like I'm just chatting with my colleagues, I'm actually purposely working to establish rapport and engage in informal conversations about teaching. Likewise, I have encountered an expectation for me as coordinator to divulge all my knowledge of every university program and its intersection with information literacy. These requests often feel dismissive of this kind of information gathering as not a formal part of my coordinator role. I have fielded comments that imply this is busybody work and yet they would like me to spend significant time reteaching others what I have learned. I view my responsibilities in this position to be our resident expert in the library on the curriculum of the institution. For example, I spend time reading the catalog, following the curriculum announcements on campus, and keeping an eye out for information on campus in part so that not every individual instruction librarian has to. This type of work may not be valued by colleagues or the library as a whole, but without it I would not be able to effectively do my job. At the end of the day, a successful IL program doesn't happen by chance or luck but instead through hard and often invisible work.

Notes

1. "Student Enrollment by Major," California State University, Dominguez Hills, accessed November 20, 2018, https://www.csudh.edu/ir/campusprofile/major.
2. "Student Enrollment Characteristics," California State University, Dominguez Hills, accessed November 20, 2018, https://www.csudh.edu/ir/campusprofile/student.
3. "California State University, Dominguez Hills," Hispanic Association of Colleges and Universities, accessed November 20, 2018, https://www.hacu.net/assnfe/cv.asp?ID=56; "Student Enrollment by Ethnicity," California State University, Dominguez Hills, March 15, 2017, https://www.csudh.edu/Assets/csudh-sites/irap/docs/enrollment/profile/ethnicitycampus5yrs (1).pdf.
4. We have chosen to use the preferred name of this historical event in our community of the Watts Rebellion or Uprising, which denotes political activism as opposed to riots.
5. Carla Rivera, "50 Years On, Cal State Dominguez Hills Renews Effort to Transform Underserved Community," *Los Angeles Times* October 11, 2015, https://www.latimes.com/local/education/la-me-cal-state-watts-20151012-story.html.
6. California Faculty Association, "Tenure Density at CSU Campuses," last modified November 7, 2017, https://www.calfac.org/sites/main/files/file-attachments/tenure_density_2012-16_hc_0.pdf.; "Campus Master Plan 2018," California State University, Dominguez Hills, accessed December 10 2019, https://www.csudh.edu/Assets/csudh-sites/fpcm/docs/campus-master-plan/csudh-initial-study-web.pdf
7. "Assessment of Student Learning," California State University, Dominguez Hills, accessed March 15, 2019, https://www.csudh.edu/academic-affairs/student-learning.
8. Bridget Driscoll, "Student Freshman and Sophomore Retention" (presentation, Academic Senate, California State University, Dominguez Hills, Carson, CA, February 14, 2018), https://www.csudh.edu/Assets/csudh-sites/academic-senate/docs/insidethesenate/academic-senate/presentations/DHFYE-2015-SALO-Infographic-Sophomore021418.pdf
9. "Getting Started with Library Research," California State University, Dominguez Hills, University Library, accessed March 18, 2019, https://libguides.csudh.edu/start; "CSUDH Library Tutorials," California State University, Dominguez Hills, University Library, accessed March 18, 2019, https://libguides.csudh.edu/tutorials.
10. "Mission, Values, and Vision," California State University, Dominguez Hills, University Library, accessed March 18, 2019, https://www.csudh.edu/library/about/mission; "University Library Strategic Goals," California State University, Dominguez Hills, University Library, accessed March 18, 2019, https://www.csudh.edu/library/about/goals.
11. "Information Literacy Program," California State University, Dominguez Hills, University Library, accessed March 18, 2019, http://libguides.csudh.edu/information-literacy.
12. For an example of the nonpunitive approach, see Kevin P. Seeber, "The Failed Pedagogy of Punishment: Moving Discussions of Plagiarism beyond Detection and Discipline," in *Critical Library*

Pedagogy Handbook, vol. 1, ed. Nicole Pagowsky and Kelly McElroy (Chicago: Association of College and Research Libraries, 2016), 131–38.

13. Char Booth, Sara Lowe, and Natalie Tagge, "Information Literacy in Student Work Rubric—Claremont Colleges Library (Version 2013/14)," last modified September 1, 2013, http://libraries.claremont.edu/informationliteracy/documents/CCL_Information_Literacy_Rubric_v2013-2014.pdf.

14. Carolyn Caffrey Gardner and Tessa Withorn, "Psychology 490 Toolkit for Instructors," accessed March 26, 2019, http://libguides.csudh.edu/psy490.

15. Carolyn Caffrey Gardner, "CSU Dominguez Hills and the WASC Senior College and University Commission," Information Literacy Assessment website, last modified April 18, 2018, https://www.informationliteracyassessment.com/?p=1127.

16. Association of College and Research Libraries, *Framework for Information Literacy for Higher Education* (Chicago: Association of College and Research Libraries, 2016), http://www.ala.org/acrl/standards/ilframework.

17. Grant Wiggins and Jay McTighe, *Understanding by Design*, 2nd ed. (Alexandria, VA: Association for Supervision and Curriculum Development, 2005).

18. Tessa Withorn, "The Information Spectrum," CORA (Community of Online Research Assignments) website, May 25, 2018, https://www.projectcora.org/assignment/information-spectrum.

19. Carolyn Caffrey Gardner, "Counting What We Actually Value: Gathering Instruction Statistics outside of the One-Shot Environment" (poster presentation, Association of College and Research Libraries conference, Cleveland, OH, April 12, 2019), https://acrl2019-acrl.ipostersessions.com/default.aspx?s=9E-BE-00-CC-8D-DA-2C-F2-AD-6A-D5-9B-6C-43-1F-BD; "Assignment Design," CSUDH Library LibInsights form, California State University, Dominguez Hills, University Library, accessed December 10, 2018, https://csudh.libinsight.com/assignment.

20. "Academic Library Trends and Statistics Survey," Association of College and Research Libraries, accessed November 20, 2018, https://acrl.countingopinions.com.

21. Carolyn Caffrey Gardner, "CSUDH University Library Fall 2018 Information Literacy Instruction Statistics," last modified December 10, 2018, http://libguides.csudh.edu/ld.php?content_id=46072025.

Bibliography

Association of College and Research Libraries. "Academic Library Trends and Statistics Survey." Accessed November 20, 2018.https://acrl.countingopinions.com.

———. *Framework for Information Literacy for Higher Education*. Chicago: Association of College and Research Libraries, 2016. http://www.ala.org/acrl/standards/ilframework.

Booth, Char, Sara Lowe, and Natalie Tagge. "Information Literacy in Student Work Rubric—Claremont Colleges Library (Version 2013/14)." Last modified September 1, 2013. http://libraries.claremont.edu/informationliteracy/documents/CCL_Information_Literacy_Rubric_v2013-2014.pdf.

California Faculty Association. "Tenure Density at CSU Campuses." Last modified November 7, 2017. https://www.calfac.org/sites/main/files/file-attachments/tenure_density_2012-16_hc_0.pdf.

California State University, Dominguez Hills. "Assessment of Student Learning." Accessed March 15, 2019. https://www.csudh.edu/academic-affairs/student-learning.

———. "Student Enrollment Characteristics." Accessed November 20, 2018. https://www.csudh.edu/ir/campusprofile/student.

———. "Student Enrollment by Ethnicity." March 15, 2017. https://www.csudh.edu/Assets/csudh-sites/irap/docs/enrollment/profile/ethnicitycampus5yrs (1).pdf.

———. "Student Enrollment by Major." Accessed November 20, 2018. https://www.csudh.edu/ir/campusprofile/major.

California State University, Dominguez Hills, University Library. "Assignment Design." CSUDH Library LibInsights form. Accessed December 10, 2018. https://csudh.libinsight.com/assignment.

———. "CSUDH Library Tutorials." Accessed March 18, 2019. https://libguides.csudh.edu/tutorials.

———. "Getting Started with Library Research." Accessed March 18, 2019. https://libguides.csudh.edu/start.

———. "Information Literacy Program." Accessed March 18, 2019. http://libguides.csudh.edu/information-literacy.

———. "Mission, Values, and Vision." Accessed March 18, 2019. https://www.csudh.edu/library/about/mission.

———. "University Library Strategic Goals." Accessed March 18, 2019. https://www.csudh.edu/library/about/goals.

Driscoll, Bridget. "Student Freshman and Sophomore Retention." Presentation, Academic Senate, California State University, Dominguez Hills, Carson, CA, February 14, 2018. https://www.csudh.edu/Assets/csudh-sites/academic-senate/docs/insidethesenate/academic-senate/presentations/DHFYE-2015-SA-LO-Infographic-Sophomore021418.pdf.

Gardner, Carolyn Caffrey. "Counting What We Actually Value: Gathering Instruction Statistics outside of the One-Shot Environment." Poster presentation, Association of College and Research Libraries conference, Cleveland, OH, April 10–13, 2019. https://acrl2019-acrl.ipostersessions.com/default.aspx?s=9E-BE-00-CC-8D-DA-2C-F2-AD-6A-D5-9B-6C-43-1F-BD.

———. "CSU Dominguez Hills and the WASC Senior College and University Commission." Information Literacy Assessment website, April 18, 2018. https://www.informationliteracyassessment.com/?p=1127.

———. "CSUDH University Library Fall 2018 Information Literacy Instruction Statistics." Last modified December 10, 2018. http://libguides.csudh.edu/ld.php?content_id=46072025.

Gardner, Carolyn Caffrey, and Tessa Withorn. "Psychology 490 Toolkit for Instructors." Accessed March 26, 2019. http://libguides.csudh.edu/psy490.

Hispanic Association of Colleges and Universities. "California State University, Dominguez Hills." Accessed November 20, 2018. https://www.hacu.net/assnfe/cv.asp?ID=56.

Rivera, Carla. "50 Years On, Cal State Dominguez Hills Renews Effort to Transform Underserved Community." *Los Angeles Times*, October 11, 2015. https://www.latimes.com/local/education/la-me-cal-state-watts-20151012-story.html.

Seeber, Kevin P. "The Failed Pedagogy of Punishment: Moving Discussions of Plagiarism beyond Detection and Discipline." In *Critical Library Pedagogy Handbook*, vol. 1. Edited by Nicole Pagowsky and Kelly McElroy, 131–38. Chicago: Association of College and Research Libraries, 2016.

Wiggins, Grant, and Jay McTighe. *Understanding by Design*, 2nd ed. Alexandria, VA: Association for Supervision and Curriculum Development, 2005.

Withorn, Tessa. "The Information Spectrum." CORA (Community of Online Research Assignments) website. May 25, 2018. https://www.projectcora.org/assignment/information-spectrum.

Chapter 14

Delaware County Community College

An Information Literacy Program Designed for a Diverse Student Population

Michael LaMagna

Population Served

Founded in 1967, Delaware County Community College (DCCC) is a large suburban community college serving students from a range of socioeconomic and educational backgrounds across two counties, Delaware and Chester, in southeastern Pennsylvania. The college offers courses on eight campus locations in addition to a growing online learning population. In fall 2018, the college enrolled a total of 10,920 students with a full-time equivalent (FTE) of 7,539 students.[1] During the fall 2018 semester, 60 percent of students identified as female and 40 percent of students identified as male.[2] The majority of students enrolled at DCCC identified as Caucasian (52.1%) followed by Black/African American (29.9%), Asian (4.8%), Other (4.3%), two or more races (3.9%), and Hispanic (3.1%).[3] With a college that spans two counties, each campus location has a unique student population demographic that reflects the communities the institution serves. In Delaware County, the college enrolls a total of 8,128 students, with 6,502 of those students completing classes on the Marple Campus.[4] Throughout Chester County, the total enrollment of students is 2,328 students.[5] It is important to note that students have the ability to enroll in courses across multiple campus locations to meet their educational needs. A growing population at DCCC continues to be students enrolling in online courses. During the fall 2018 semester, Online Learning had a total student enrollment of 3,580 students, which reflected an 11 percent increase in enrollment from the previous year.[6]

In thinking about the population DCCC serves, it is important to understand a particularly significant enrollment trend of more students choosing to enroll part-time. In the fall 2016 semester, 31 percent of students were enrolled full-time at the college.[7] This declined to 28 percent for the fall 2018 semester.[8] Along with the increase in the number of students choosing to attend college part-time, students are also enrolling in fewer classes.

Understanding the population the college serves in southeastern Pennsylvania, Library Services, located within the Learning Commons, designed the information literacy (IL) program to meet the educational needs and goals of the students. With an increase in part-time students and students taking longer to complete their degree and certificate programs, the IL program needs to adapt and provide opportunities for updating of research skills.

Program Scope

Library Services at DCCC has an active IL program that grew out of the bibliographic instruction offered in the 1980s and early 1990s. The goal of the bibliographic instruction program during those years was to allow students to become familiar with the physical library and learn how to access the largely physical collection. It was not until 2001 that the library secured a dedicated classroom for instructional purposes.[9] During this transition from a bibliographic instruction model to an IL instruction model, which moved beyond just resource demonstrations toward a more in-depth program designed to teach students to become effective users of information, the library was able to align the learning goals of the IL program with the College Competencies that all degree-seeking students had to meet. In 2014, the college adopted new College Academic Learning Goals (CALG), which all graduating students must meet through their degree programs. Under the new CALG system, IL has its own goal to ensure that "graduates will demonstrate the ability to find, evaluate, and communicate information found in the course of their research."[10] For students completing courses with an IL CALG designation, Library Services has identified specific learning goals that should be met. These IL CALG goals are just part of the larger learning goals of the IL program. They are

- Apply critical thinking skills in performing the stages of the research process
- List, define, and identify appropriate source types and search tools for the information needed
- Describe common characteristics and features of library databases and apply techniques to retrieve relevant results
- Evaluate information for accuracy and credibility
- Summarize the purpose, characteristics, and publication formats (formal and informal) of scholarly communication
- Explain the value and purpose of source attribution and describe common rules and conventions of formal writing styles

- Identify the legal, ethical, economic, and social issues (including privacy, copyright and plagiarism) associated with the use of information[11]

Given the range of academic preparedness of students enrolling at the college, the IL program was designed with specific learning objectives for each level of student academic readiness based on placement test results and academic preparation. The IL program curriculum has an articulated program sequence to ensure all students who graduate from the college meet the IL CALG. Currently, the program sequence is enhanced orientation, developmental learning competencies, college-ready learning competencies, general learning competencies (CALG courses), advanced learning competencies, and discipline-specific learning competencies. When faculty librarians are assigned to teach a one-shot class, they work with the requesting faculty member to determine the learning goals based on the assignment in the class linked to the session. The faculty librarian will discuss the learning goals with the course faculty member and link them to the IL program learning competencies (see table 14.1). The learning competencies are sequenced throughout the program.

Table 14.1
IL program learning competencies

IL Program Learning Competencies	
Enhanced Orientation Learning Competencies	As a result of attending and participating in this information literacy orientation, students will be able to • Describe how the topics and skills introduced during the orientation program are necessary for academic success • Explain differences between academic libraries and high school/public libraries • Navigate the library's physical and virtual presence (through the website and delaGATE) • Identify the different resources and services offered by Library Services • Explain how to receive reference and research assistance from faculty librarians • Demonstrate the ability to use the library's resources to complete a research assignment
Developmental Learning Competencies	As a result of attending and participating in this information literacy session, students will be able to • Describe library services available through the Delaware County Community College Learning Commons and in what contexts they are useful • Differentiate between information source types (books, magazines, scholarly journals, websites) and in what contexts they are useful • Recognize a variety of research tools (library catalog, article database, Summon, web) and understand how they provide access to information sources • Formulate an appropriate search strategy based on the information need • Match resources to the information needed (database versus internet, etc.) • Locate materials within a physical or online library (call #s, etc.) • Interpret parts of a citation and abstract (through a database or library catalog) • Explain how to receive reference and research assistance from faculty librarians

IL Program Learning Competencies	
College-Ready Learning Competencies	As a result of attending and participating in this information literacy session, students will be able to • Define the stages of the research process • Explain how to receive reference and research assistance from faculty librarians • Locate appropriate background information based on information need • Formulate an effective search strategy • Locate appropriate resources from both the library catalog and databases • Describe the different types of information sources • Distinguish between scholarly and popular sources • Evaluate information selected to ensure it is appropriate to the defined research question • Demonstrate the ability to use information in an ethical and legal manner

General Information Literacy Learning Competencies—College Academic Learning Goals

Advanced Learning Competencies	As a result of attending and participating in this information literacy instruction, students will be able to • Define the peer-review process and its role in scholarly publishing • Distinguish between primary and secondary sources • Identify services available through the Learning Commons and on the web, such as ILL and the e-Journal title finder • Distinguish between keywords and controlled vocabulary • Demonstrate the ability to thoroughly evaluate sources and select those most appropriate to the research question and assignment requirements • Demonstrate familiarity with traditional and emerging formats of scholarly communication, including blogs, wikis, data sets, infographics, web conferences, etc. • Demonstrate the ability to generate correctly formatted citations in the appropriate style for all source types and proficient use of style guide handbooks when needed • Implement a research plan that appreciates the role of background research in topic, question, and knowledge development • Demonstrate a disposition for lifelong learning
Discipline-Specific Learning Competencies	As a result of attending and participating in this information literacy instruction, students will be able to • Identify discipline-specific research tools and information sources • Demonstrate backward citation analysis as a technique to identify seminal works on a topic in the discipline • Compare and contrast the core resources in a specific discipline with general resources • Demonstrate familiarity with subject-specific databases and other research tools • Demonstrate proficiency with discipline-specific terminology as it relates to interpreting scholarship within the discipline and the ability to identify and comprehend this terminology • Demonstrate familiarity with discipline-specific research methods and scholarly communication practices • Identify key journals, professional organizations, and other resources for continuing education in a selected discipline

The Library Services IL program offers seven different models of instruction to meet the program's learning goals and in support of the IL CALG: (1) course-integrated instruction, (2) self-paced online tutorials, (3) noncredit research workshops (seminars, webinars, and simulcasts), (4) a credit-bearing course, (5) faculty partnership through course-embedded librarianship, (6) train-the-teacher, and (7) reference and research services.[12] While Library Services offers seven models of instruction through its IL program, the primary modes of instruction are through course-integrated instruction (one-shot model) and noncredit research workshops. Library Services offers approximately 350 course-integrated instruction classes each academic year and approximately 70 noncredit research workshops each semester. The noncredit research workshops include online synchronous webinars, in-person seminars, and occasionally the simulcast of in-person workshops that are streamed online. While these workshops are not required, student can self-select to complete these workshops to enhance their research skills or may be encouraged by faculty members to enroll. Students are able to pursue research workshops either online or in person across two tracks. The Research Fundamentals track requires students to complete three workshops:

- **Getting Started With Research:** Learn to interpret assignment requirements, identify a research topic, gather background information, develop a research question, determine the type of information you need, and develop a research strategy.
- **Finding Relevant Sources:** Learn to identify relevant sources to answer your research question, select useful search tools, search effectively, and evaluate your search results to select the best sources for your assignment.
- **Organizing and Citing Your Research:** Learn about tools and services for saving and citing your sources, integrating your sources into your assignment, and writing in-text and end-of-paper references and citations.[13]

In addition to completing these workshops, students are required by Library Services to complete one additional elective workshop from the Expanding Research Skills track to earn a digital badge or microcredential. Workshops in the Expanding Research Skills track offer students the ability to enhance their research skills, with workshops focused on researching using mobile apps, organizing sources with mobile apps, copyright and intellectual property for students, or privacy in the digital age, as some examples. Students self-select to register and attend these workshops and complete the requirements for each track. Students can earn digital badges or microcredentials if they complete all the necessary requirements for each track.[14] These digital badges are offered by a third-party provider and can be displayed by students in their digital profiles.

In designing the IL program, the dean, coordinator, and librarians viewed reference services as an opportunity to provide one-on-one instruction to students at the reference desk. Whenever a librarian works with a student or group of students at the reference desk, this interaction is viewed through the lens of teaching IL skills. Granted, the discrete transactional nature of reference services means students are not meeting specific set learning goals, but based on the questions being asked, they will meet individual learning goals of the IL program. Moving forward, this area will need to be better assessed by mapping these questions to the learning goals of the program.

Like many academic libraries, DCCC offers a number of self-paced IL tutorials. These include a General Information Literacy Tutorial designed to support faculty members teaching courses designated with the IL CALG. In addition to this more comprehensive tutorial, Library Services developed shorter tutorials designed to instruct students on database searching, evaluation of sources, and citation style and structure.

Because DCCC is a community college, the IL program is designed to ensure that students can receive IL instruction at their point of need when they first start at the college. Moving forward, Library Services will expand its focus on developing enhanced self-paced tutorials to meet the enhanced orientation, developmental learning, and general learning competencies.

Operations

While Library Services at DCCC supports the research and IL instructional needs of a population of 7,539 students FTE, the staffing of this area within the college is modest. Currently, ten librarians, five full-time faculty librarians, and five adjunct faculty librarians teach in the IL program. Each full-time teaching librarian holds faculty rank and status and the title of Reference Librarian. In addition to teaching in the IL program, each librarian is responsible for staffing the reference desk and the virtual chat reference service. Each full-time librarian serves as a liaison to one of the academic divisions at the college. These duties include outreach and collection development. Full-time librarians also focus on a particular specialty area of need within Library Services. These areas can be electronic resources management, collection management, open educational resources, or online learning. While the full-time librarians understand the importance of the IL program as a central service offered to the college community, given the size of the staff, there is often conflict between enhancing the program and other job responsibilities. The part-time librarians have the primary responsibility of teaching in the IL program and providing reference services. With this level of staffing and eight campus locations across two counties, librarians are often required to be flexible with their schedules and campus locations to meet the needs of the faculty members requesting classes and the educational needs of the students.

In 2002, the library administration understood the need to have leadership guiding the IL program at the college and hired a full-time temporary faculty librarian with the title of Information Literacy Librarian. After approximately eight years, the temporary faculty position was converted to a full-time tenure-track position. While the person in this position was responsible for overseeing and developing the IL program, the structure at the college often created roadblocks. Faculty members at DCCC work under a collective bargaining agreement that dictates specific roles and responsibilities. One member of the bargaining unit is unable to supervise other members within the same bargaining unit. This restriction removes the ability of the Information Literacy Librarian to supervise or assign specific tasks. Instead, the process of dividing work related to the IL program is done through a collegial collaborative process. With the arrival of a new dean responsible for Educational Support Services, which the Learning Commons and Library Services fall under, the decision was made to transition the position of Information Literacy Librarian to a title more in line with other faculty members on the campus: Information Literacy Program and Library Services Coordinator. This change allows the Information Literacy Program and Library Services Coordinator to engage in conversations throughout the college that might not have been open to them without the title. Transitioning this role required the librarian in this position to add liaison responsibilities to an academic division to their position, mirroring the other full-time faculty librarians. The responsibility of coordinating the program is compensated through either release time from other responsibilities or through overload payments.

The program includes, in addition to the librarians teaching, a staff member tasked with scheduling all of the one-shot IL classes. This staff member receives the requests from faculty members and, based on a block schedule used to staff Library Services, assigns a specific class to the librarians scheduled to teach at that time. Often, requests will come from a single faculty member for IL one-shot instruction for multiple sections of a course in a given semester. When this occurs, all librarians scheduled to teach during the class times are included on an email confirmation that is sent to the faculty member. Internally, the librarian teaching the first class will contact the faculty member to determine the learning goals of the IL instructional session. While the class request form asks for copies of any relevant assignments and a syllabus, the librarian will request these materials if they were not provided. The librarian teaching the first class will communicate with the librarians teaching future sections for the same faculty member to ensure there is consistency across the multiple sections.

While the IL program does not have a dedicated budget line within the Library Services budget or within the larger Learning Commons budget, any instructional technology, teaching tools, and materials costs are covered through the relevant budget lines. These costs include the web conferencing software that is required to offer online synchronous workshops.

Marketing

Given that the IL program is central to the mission of Library Services at DCCC, librarians actively market course-integrated one-shot classes, the workshop series, and the tutorials through college-wide email announcements, the liaison program, online advertisements on campus computers, and printed material. The course-integrated one-shot classes are often marketed to faculty members through conversations. Having faculty status as librarians affords us the opportunity to build relationships with other faculty members and interact with them on campus committees. Discussions at committee meetings provide opportunities to promote one-shot course-integrated instruction. Librarians will direct interested faculty members to complete the online form to ensure they can schedule the class on the desired day and time.

The marketing of online workshops is more formal. It includes the production of a printed color brochure each semester with a calendar of workshops offered, mirroring the information that is found on the college's Learning Commons website.[15] In addition, workshops are advertised each semester throughout the college via computer screen savers and in the college portal students use to access campus resources and services. Posters are produced each month listing the workshops for that month. That month's poster is hung at the entrance of the Learning Commons on the Marple Campus so that it reaches the large number of students that facility serves daily. In collaboration with the Online Learning Department, each semester an announcement is posted in the college's learning management system by the Director of Online Learning to notify students of upcoming workshops.

Each academic division at the college also receives communications from its liaison librarian. While there is not a standard message, each librarian often promotes the one-shot course-integrated IL classes with a link to the request form online and to the list of upcoming online workshops.

Collaboration

With the introduction of the College Academic Learning Goals in 2014, IL became part of a larger discussion on campus. As of 2018, four courses at the college have received the IL CALG designation. These courses are English Composition I, English Composition II: Writing about Literature, Teaching with Technology (offered through the education department), and Research Methodology (offered through the sociology department). The CALGs provided Library Services with an opportunity to collaborate with those departments and faculty members in designing multiple ways for those courses to meet the CALG. Librarians were able to discuss with English faculty members how to best meet the IL CALG given the large number of students who take the two composition courses. With an understanding of the Library Services staffing levels and the need to provide instruction on eight physical campus locations and online, it was determined that multiple approaches to meet this CALG were necessary. While not all approaches are required to meet the CALG, they are one-shot course-integrated instruction, completion of online synchronous workshops, completion of the General Information Literacy Tutorial, and having the English faculty member teach the IL content.

In addition to working directly with faculty members, Library Services works with the Online Learning Department to enhance and promote the IL program. As faculty members, librarians are also able to offer workshops during scheduled professional development days at the college to promote IL initiatives. While collaborative efforts often can be complicated, as each group has its own needs, these relationships have been positive, as the goal is to meet the needs of the students.

Assessment

Within Library Services, an assessment cycle for the IL program was developed in which the process from assessment to closing the loop takes five years. The assessment of the IL program included a variety of both qualitative and quantitative methods targeting the different components of the program. These include specific performance criteria for the overall quiz scores students receive on the General Information Literacy Tutorial and quizzes and tests that are part of one-shot course-integrated classes and workshops. Student artifacts are also collected for analysis as part of the assessment efforts. This analysis informs improvements to the overall program. In addition, the program tracks other data points from workshops and course-integrated instruction. While Library Services has its own assessment efforts, with the introduction of the CALGs at the college, some assessment was transitioned specifically to the courses meeting the IL CALG. Representatives from the library faculty are on each of the IL CALG course assessment committees to serve as conduits for information.

Role of the One-Shot

Currently, the course-integrated one-shot class model of instruction allows Library Services to reach the largest number of students; however, we understand this approach is unsustainable based on our staffing. With five full-time librarians and five part-time librarians, it is often difficult to meet the needs of the college community during peak times during the semester at all of the college locations. In addition, the faculty librarians understand that pedagogically, this model is not the best method to meet the educational needs of the students. Ultimately, this model of delivery is a primary way for Library Services to offer IL instruction to students, and it is the model that faculty members at the college are familiar with. While staffing this model is difficult at certain times during the semester, the flexibility of those teaching in the program ensures that all requests can be accommodated.

The synchronous online workshops allow librarians to more effectively reach a larger population of students, and we continue to market the Research Fundamentals track as a good alternative to the one-shot model of IL instruction. This track within the workshop program is designed with clear articulation between the learning objectives of each workshop and the Association of College and Research Libraries (ACRL) *Framework for Information Literacy for Higher Education.*[16]

Administrative Highlights

In administering the IL program at DCCC, the Information Literacy Program and Library Services Coordinator's goal is to provide a framework that ensures every faculty librarian at the college has the information they need to be successful. This framework includes ensuring the program has clear learning goals for each sequenced area so that any new librarians teaching in the program can jump right into teaching. New librarians are offered the opportunity to shadow a current librarian in the classroom to better understand the instructional needs of the students. While many of the administrative functions are designed to onboard new librarians, our workshops are scheduled collaboratively to ensure workshops are offered to the greatest number of students.

Information Literacy Coordinator Profile

My first position out of library school was as a reference librarian at a small liberal arts college, which included teaching in the information literacy program. The size of the institution allowed me to build relationships with faculty members across the campus and build specific instructional sessions and assignments based on this collaboration. With a small staff, I had the ability to engage in projects across the library and was promoted to Coordinator of Electronic Resources. While my main responsibility centered on electronic resources and serials, I continued to staff the reference desk and teach in the information literacy program. When the college began offering graduate classes in education at sites in southeastern Pennsylvania, I researched options to offer information literacy instruction through web conferencing. My interest in using educational and instructional technology led me to apply and accept the full-time faculty position of Information Literacy Librarian at DCCC. As my position evolved based on the needs of the Library Services department, I took on new responsibilities, which eventually led to the creation of the Information Literacy Program and Library Services Coordinator position. This role provides the equivalent of three credits of release time each semester to coordinate the IL program. Because I am a librarian, this requires the credit formula to be broken down into hours and provides me with release from one-fifth of my librarian responsibilities. While much of that time is spent working on the information literacy program, I find there is an increasing demand to address larger issues within Library Services and the Learning Commons that fall under the second part of the job title of coordinating library services.

What I Wish People Knew

Coordinating an IL program at a community college offers hidden challenges based on how courses transfer. While the college administration understands the importance of IL, it is often difficult to find places in the curriculum for IL instruction. Being an active member of the faculty and serving in leadership roles on college-wide committees has provided me with a better understanding of how to advocate for IL instruction.

Anyone interested in coordinating an IL program should have a strong understanding of current pedagogical methods, both in a traditional classroom and in a range of virtual environments, but should also have the ability to build personal relationships with those teaching in the program and with faculty members outside the library. With increasing demands on instructional time in the classroom, faculty members are finding it harder than ever to make room for one-shot course-integrated sessions. Having a personal relationship with teaching faculty outside the library will allow those coordinating a program to find solutions to offer information literacy instruction to students regardless of the format.

Notes

1. Institutional Effectiveness Office, *2018 Fall Third Week Credit Enrollment Report* (Media, PA: Delaware County Community College, 2018).
2. Institutional Effectiveness Office, *Fall 2018 Demographic Profile by Campus* (Media, PA: Delaware County Community College, 2018).
3. Institutional Effectiveness Office, *Fall 2018 Demographic.*
4. Institutional Effectiveness Office, *2018 Fall Third Week Credit.*
5. Institutional Effectiveness Office, *2018 Fall Third Week Credit.*
6. Institutional Effectiveness Office, *2018 Fall Third Week Credit.*
7. Institutional Effectiveness Office, *2018 Fall Third Week Credit.*
8. Institutional Effectiveness Office, *2018 Fall Third Week Credit.*

9. Delaware County Community College Library Faculty Librarians, *Delaware County Community College: Information Literacy Plan* (Media, PA: Delaware County Community College, 2004).

10. "College Academic Learning Goals," Delaware County Community College, last modified 2018, https://www.dccc.edu/academics/resources/college-academic-learning-goals.

11. "Information Literacy Program Learning Goals," in "Information Literacy Faculty Toolkit," Learning Commons, Delaware County Community College, last modified 2018, http://libguides.dccc.edu/c.php?g=386844&p=2903065.

12. "Models of Information Literacy Education," in "Information Literacy Faculty Toolkit," Learning Commons, Delaware County Community College, last modified 2018, https://learningcommons.dccc.edu/c.php?g=386844&p=2624134#s-lg-box-8910120

13. "Research Workshop Series," Learning Commons, Delaware County Community College, last modified 2018, http://libguides.dccc.edu/c.php?g=386890&p=4172044.

14. "Digital Badge Offerings," in "Research Workshops," Learning Commons, Delaware County Community College, last modified 2018, http://libguides.dccc.edu/workshops/digitalbadges#s-lg-box-20253401.

15. "Workshops," Learning Commons, Delaware County Community College, last modified 2019, http://libguides.dccc.edu/workshop-schedules.

16. Association of College and Research Libraries, *Framework for Information Literacy for Higher Education* (Chicago: Association of College and Research Libraries, 2016).

Bibliography

Association of College and Research Libraries. *Framework for Information Literacy for Higher Education.* Chicago: Association of College and Research Libraries, 2016.

Delaware County Community College. "College Academic Learning Goals." Last modified 2018. https://www.dccc.edu/academics/resources/college-academic-learning-goals.

———. "Digital Badge Offerings." In "Research Workshops." Learning Commons. Last modified 2018. http://libguides.dccc.edu/workshops/digitalbadges#s-lg-box-20253401.

———. "Information Literacy Faculty Toolkit." Learning Commons. Last modified 2018. http://libguides.dccc.edu/c.php?g=386844&p=2903065.

———. "Models of Information Literacy Education." In "Information Literacy Faculty Toolkit." Learning Commons. Last modified 2018. https://learningcommons.dccc.edu/c.php?g=386844&p=2624134#s-lg-box-8910120.

———. "Research Workshop Series." Learning Commons. Last modified 2018. http://libguides.dccc.edu/c.php?g=386890&p=4172044.

———. "Workshops." Learning Commons. Last modified 2019. http://libguides.dccc.edu/workshop-schedules.

Delaware County Community College Library Faculty Librarians. *Delaware County Community College: Information Literacy Plan.* Media, PA: Delaware County Community College, 2004.

Institutional Effectiveness Office. *Fall 2018 Demographic Profile by Campus.* Media, PA: Delaware County Community College, 2018.

———. *2018 Fall Third Week Credit Enrollment Report.* Media, PA: Delaware County Community College, 2018.

Chapter 15

Longwood University

Communication and Collaboration for Greater Faculty Investment in Information Literacy

Jennifer Beach

Population Served

Longwood University, located in Farmville, Virginia, is a public liberal arts college with a student population of over 4,500 undergraduate and 500 graduate students. We have students from twenty-five states and twenty countries. Our average undergraduate admissions data includes a midrange grade point average (GPA) of 3.08–3.79, midrange SAT of 1010–1160 (based on the new SAT, beginning March 2016), and a midrange ACT of 19–25. Of our students, 39 percent report being first-generation, and 93 percent report receiving some form of financial aid. Twenty-one percent of Longwood's students transfer from other institutions.[1] Many of our students enter Longwood with a rudimentary knowledge of finding trustworthy websites and the formulation of citations; however, the concepts of scholarly research and source evaluation are new. Longwood University's mission includes "the development of citizen leaders who are prepared to make positive contributions to the common good of society."[2] Librarians contribute to the mission, in part, by developing graduates with strong information literacy skills.

After four years of thoughtful and intense work, Longwood University launched a new general education program in fall 2018, the Civitae Core Curriculum (Civitae). In its final form, Civitae is made up of three levels: the Foundations Level, composed of 100- and 200-level courses, including the first-year writing and speaking courses; the Perspectives, comprising multidisciplinary courses at the 300 and 400 levels; and the Symposium on the Common Good, which "is designed to engage students in critical deliberation of citizenship and the issues citizens face in their communities."[3] Throughout Civitae's development, librarians lobbied that information literacy should be an objective equal to critical thinking, writing proficiency, and speaking proficiency, and thus should be explicitly taught, as the other objectives are. The counterargument often posed was that information literacy is implicit in most courses and did not need to be codified in Civitae. In the end, information literacy was set as a mandatory learning outcome for the Perspectives level courses. Students must complete twelve credits at this level, which translates to the successful completion of four courses where information literacy is a required outcome.

Program Scope

In addition to its place in Civitae, information literacy is one of the general educational competencies at Longwood. Our Office of Assessment and Institutional Research (OAIR) explains the competencies thus: "As defined by the Governor's Blue Ribbon Commission on Higher Education in 1999, these are areas of knowledge and skills that cross the bounds of academic discipline, degree major, and institutional mission to comprise basic competencies that should be achieved by all students completing a degree program at a Commonwealth institution of higher education."[4]

As a result, we prioritize information literacy in instruction and then assess and report to the State Council of Higher Education for Virginia (SCHEV). The Research and Instructional Services Librarian, who coordinates library instruction and provides annual faculty development, also serves as the Information Literacy Coordinator for the campus. In this role, she facilitates the university's annual information literacy assessment and consults on information literacy across the campus.

With the inclusion of information literacy as a learning outcome in the new Civitae Core Curriculum, it is now mandatory that information literacy be taught, assigned, and assessed in each Perspectives course. Most disciplines have chosen to propose courses at this level within Civitae, which allows for greater coordination between faculty and librarians on information literacy instruction. The Information Literacy Coordinator represents the information literacy core competency on the Civitae Core Curriculum committee, allowing for conversations about information literacy at the syllabus-planning stage. Her participation on the committee has also increased consistent messaging about the importance of information literacy throughout campus. Assessment for the university's information literacy core competency will flow from the Perspectives level courses, as well.

We strongly target the first-year English and history courses, as few students test out of both of these requirements, thus allowing us the greatest opportunity to teach information literacy to a broad swath of students. Library instruction in the first-year English courses is standardized so that all librarians teach the same material, with the goal that students acquire the same skills, including searching the library's discovery layer, developing strong search techniques, and ethically citing sources. Though we emphasize instruction to our first-year courses, information literacy instruction is not limited to them. Librarians provide instruction in all disciplines and at all levels. Faculty who wish to have information literacy instruction contact their liaison librarian directly to coordinate scheduling and instructional needs. For disciplinary and upper-level courses, liaison librarians design their course instruction to best meet the needs of the faculty and students, including appropriate levels of information literacy.

In addition to traditional in-person one-shot instruction, we have also formalized an embedded librarian option, allowing librarians to provide hybrid and online instruction through our learning management system, Canvas. The goal of embedded instruction is to increase librarian contact opportunities with faculty and students. This could mean multiple visits with a single class, required one-on-one student consultations with the librarians, a librarian-facilitated discussion board on Canvas, or librarian-created instructional modules imported into a course's Canvas shell. The level of librarian involvement is driven by the goals of the instructional faculty. We view our program as a way to enhance student learning while respecting the academic freedom of the instructional faculty and thus do not require a threshold level of involvement. The embedded librarian program has had varied success dependent upon the discipline, faculty involvement, and course level. Embedding seems to work best in online and hybrid courses, as well as upper-level classes in certain disciplines, such as English, nursing, and communication studies. We initiated this program in 2016, and among faculty who have embraced it, it has been highly successful in building stronger relationships between librarians and our instructional colleagues.

We also have information literacy tutorials available on our website, borrowed and adapted, with permission, from the Board of Regents of the University of Wisconsin System. These comprehensive tutorials include videos, instructional text, and a glossary and cover such topics as searching, source evaluation, the Library of Congress system, and citation. We have situated the tutorials on our For Faculty page so that faculty could easily assign them if they could not schedule time for a librarian session.[5]

Operations

Longwood University maintains one campus library, the Janet D. Greenwood Library, which houses all six full-time librarians. Librarians are faculty with rank, eligible for promotion but ineligible for tenure. The Research and Instructional Services Librarian acts as the instruction coordinator, but all librarians maintain instruction responsibilities within their liaison areas, in addition to other duties. With a ratio of roughly one librarian per 750 undergraduates, we are a busy department. At peak times, such as in September and early October, finding a librarian outside of scheduled available reference hours can be difficult, as we are often on the run from class to class. We suffer for our success!

Our information literacy program does not have a defined budget. However, the administration values our efforts on campus, and if we can justify a need for materials or technology, funding requests are generally approved. Such was the case recently when we were introduced to the card game Search&Destroy, created by Mari Kermit-Canfield and Gary Maixner.[6] This game allows students to explore the library's discovery layer in a fun environment that promotes learning. The Dean of the Library enthusiastically endorsed the purchase of enough sets to run two classes concurrently. Students have embraced the game and, unsurprisingly, vastly prefer it to lecture-based instruction.

With such a small staff of librarians, no decisions are made in a vacuum. During the academic year, we discuss instruction ideas and trends at our weekly librarians' meeting.

In the summer, the librarians meet monthly to share ideas, discuss assessment, and develop new instruction plans for the following year. We strive for clear communication with the circulation and technical services staff as well. However, the main work of our six librarians may seem invisible to our other library colleagues. The Greenwood Library transitioned to a single service desk several years ago, eliminating the reference desk and making circulation the first point of contact. Because of this, much of our work happens outside of the sight of our colleagues, whether through research appointments with students or faculty in our offices, through our online or in-class instruction around campus, or through meetings out of the library. This invisible work can lead to misunderstandings of what we do and how we serve our patrons. To improve communication, we will often provide sessions for the staff when we introduce a new instructional program, both so that we may practice our instruction and so that our noninstructional library colleagues will understand and promote our efforts to students and faculty.

Marketing

Communication is an active goal for our department. After noting the confusion of many faculty when we talked about information literacy on campus, librarians at Longwood began a communication campaign in 2016 to promote our definition and to make clear the benefits of partnering with a librarian for information literacy instruction. At Longwood, "information literacy is defined as the ability to recognize the types of information best suited to the argument, and effectively locate, critically evaluate, appropriately use, and ethically cite the information."[7] In a coordinated campaign, librarians shared this message through email and in departmental meetings. We also began clearly stating that we offer "information literacy instruction" instead of "research instruction" to increase clarity. As a direct result of our communication campaign, faculty now rarely ask us to "teach the website," and as the graph in figure 15.1 demonstrates, information literacy instruction requests have doubled, increasing from 130 instruction sessions in 2015–16 to 260 sessions in 2017–18.

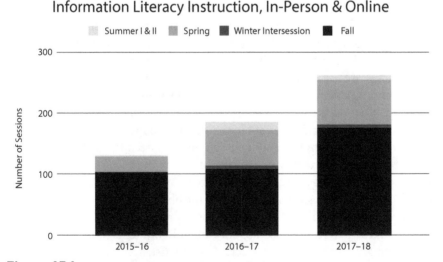

Figure 15.1
Information literacy instruction, in person and online

As ranked faculty without tenure, librarians have a status that is a little different from that of our teaching colleagues. The library is situated within Academic Affairs, but not in a specific college, though librarians maintain relationships with their liaison departments in the colleges. At the beginning of each semester, all librarians send an email to their liaison departments offering information literacy instruction. We also seek out invitations to departmental meetings and capitalize on one-on-one conversations. We try to listen when faculty express frustration with their students' research skills and offer our services. We also have a section of our web page devoted to instruction, allowing faculty to see what information literacy instruction looks like at different levels and how to contact their liaison librarian.

Collaboration

As the Instruction Coordinator and the Information Literacy Faculty Lead, I collaborate annually with our Center for Faculty Enrichment (CAFE) and the Office of Student Research (OSR) to provide a faculty development workshop called Teaching the Research Process, including how to teach information literacy and how to model best practices. I also work directly with OSR to guide students who have received research funding on information literacy best practices. I have presented at Longwood's annual Teaching and Learning Institute, specifically addressing information literacy in the Civitae Core Curriculum. As the liaison to Longwood University's signature Brock Experience, briefly defined as "a growing group of immersive, citizenship-focused courses at sites around the United States,"[8] I also collaborate on information literacy training for Brock fellows as they develop their syllabi for their travel courses.

In general, our department has strong allies in the English and modern languages, history, communication studies, and biological and environmental sciences departments. Faculty in these departments have been open to change and willing to experiment with new pedagogical techniques. At other times, though, information literacy instruction can be a hard sell to faculty. Certain departments have expressed that information literacy is not necessary in their fields and in one instance an instructional faculty member baldly stated the opinion that students who seek outside sources would be plagiarizing. Other faculty have voiced their beliefs either that students have already learned the skills elsewhere or that they themselves model the skills without need for formal instruction from a librarian. The inclusion of information literacy as a learning outcome in the Civitae Core Curriculum has increased faculty understanding of and investment in explicitly teaching information literacy in the classroom, as well as assigning and assessing information literacy within their courses.

The Civitae Core Curriculum has also created opportunities to collaborate with faculty as they develop their syllabi. Within the Perspectives level courses, the required information literacy outcome has allowed for new opportunities for faculty development. During the pilot phase of these courses, participating faculty were required to attend a two-hour workshop on teaching, assigning, assessing, and reinforcing information literacy. They were led through the "backwards design" process, with the goal of combatting the vague, yet pervasive, assumption that information literacy is inherently part of every course. Some faculty took to this more readily than others, finding ways to include intentional information literacy components in their assignments. Others struggled with the misconception that including information literacy must mean including scholarly, peer-reviewed sources, which are not always appropriate for their disciplines. The workshops offered opportunities to clear up misconceptions and for faculty to think creatively about what information literacy means in different disciplines.

In the future, we would like to see standing librarian participation in departmental meetings and intentional inclusion of librarians in departmental curricular planning, thus allowing librarians to quickly address instructional needs to better serve our faculty and students. If we can accomplish this without stepping on faculty toes or impinging on departmental autonomy, I feel that information literacy instruction will grow rapidly across campus. While this may put a greater strain on our limited librarian resources, the benefits to our students will outweigh the costs and may someday lead to an opportunity to add personnel in our department.

Assessment

We formally assess student information literacy skills across the curriculum, as reported annually to SCHEV. However, we do not currently formally assess librarians' specific efforts. The university's annual assessment of information literacy is facilitated between the library and OAIR. In its current iteration, we collect samples of student writing at all levels and assess them based upon a rubric. Our current rubric is modified from the Association of American Colleges and Universities Information Literacy VALUE Rubric,[9] but it is not perfect, and committee assessment of student writing can be subjective, despite efforts to norm the group to the rubric. Additionally, we often receive writing samples that seem to originate in assignments that did not require student research, making them difficult to rate. I facilitate the assessment day, norming the rubric, ensuring each writing sample is assessed by both a librarian and a faculty member, and acting as the third rater in cases where their ratings diverge too greatly. OAIR then evaluates the assessment data and is tasked with sharing the reported data with departments, the library, and SCHEV. We are investigating changing to a test-based assessment in the next few years, which we hope will reach a more representative sample of our students, be less subjective, and create a smaller burden on faculty, including the librarians.

In the past, Longwood's response to information literacy assessment data has been hit-or-miss. Departments either claim to have not been provided the annual information literacy assessment data or have chosen not to act upon it. There is currently no formal mechanism to see what, if any, changes have been made following assessment. With Longwood's move to the new Civitae Core Curriculum, we will collect our data from students in Perspectives level classes. Professional development following our annual assessment will become an intentional part of the process, allowing instructional faculty and librarians to improve our practice. The Civitae committee will facilitate faculty development that specifically addresses areas for student improvement, which will then be implemented in all Perspectives courses. While past assessments have shown little change in students' information literacy skills from year to year, it is our hope that we will start to see real gains in information literacy skills in our students, now that we have a consistent instruction point in Civitae.

On a departmental level, we have begun to assess our first-year English instruction, as that course is taught consistently to most students, excepting some transfer students, and by all librarians. In the 2017–18 academic year, we instituted an online, game-based assessment quiz through Kahoot.com that assessed and reinforced our instruction. Students found the quiz fun and useful, and our data allowed us to adjust our methods. We have frequent discussions on how to improve assessment on more of our instruction efforts, but as yet have not settled on a method. We have plans to coordinate with CAFE to evaluate all librarians' teaching in order to improve our practice. With such a small department, the consensus among librarians is that evaluation would be better received coming from outside the library, so CAFE is the natural choice.

Role of the One-Shot

Most librarian instruction is in one-shot format, as class time is at a premium and we have only six librarians to serve the entire campus. The uneasy tension occurs when we try to advocate for more classroom time. For example, in the 2018–19 academic year, we began pressing for two one-shot sessions in the first-year English course, one to focus on the basics of searching the discovery layer using the instructional card game Search&Destroy, and one for assignment-specific instruction and additional information literacy skills. As expected, we initially received some faculty resistance, given the rigors of their course schedules and the potential for a card game to be perceived as frivolous. However, we were pleasantly surprised at the number of faculty who agreed to the additional instruction day. As student participation and performance seemed to improve based on anecdotal evidence, we anticipate more faculty finding room for a second session in future semesters. With faculty with whom we have built strong relationships, the pushback when we seek to expand in-class instruction is minimal. In all cases, we make every effort to respect the autonomy of the instructional faculty, making clear that we are open to new ideas, but always willing to stick to the one-shot if they prefer.

Pedagogical Highlights

At Longwood, we teach students how to create and revise research topics, how to navigate our discovery layer, how and when to search a discipline-specific database, citation styles, and specific search techniques based upon project or disciplinary needs. We try to stay in touch not only with the needs of our instructional faculty, but also with their perception of the library's place in their classrooms. To that end, we recently created information literacy learning objectives for library instruction at each course level, as laid out in figure 15.2, originally posted to our website.

By creating these objectives, librarians are better able to speak the language of our teaching colleagues and communicate the value of information literacy instruction in all disciplines.

Within our department, I coordinate instruction meetings with the librarians to discuss plans, trends, and practices. I try to lead by example, and thus was the first librarian to become certified to teach in online and hybrid courses. Longwood University restricts online and hybrid course access to faculty who have completed the Longwood Online Technology Institute (LOTI) training, which covers best practices for online teaching based upon the Quality Matters national standards.[10] After I piloted our embedded

Greenwood Library librarians have developed the following student learning objectives to align with course levels.

100 Level Courses

Students will be able to:

- Identify types of resources available from the library
- Define the scope of the investigation with a clear research question
- Identify keywords based on a research question
- Perform a basic keyword search on the library homepage's main search bar
- Recognize the characteristics of authoritative sources
- Understand why citations are ethically important
- Cite information clearly and consistently

200 Level Courses

Students will be able to:

- Perform all of the above, and
- Combine Boolean operators to perform a search in a database.
- Locate and search within subject specific databases
- Consistently draw from relevant, authoritative research sources
- Access enough information to explore research question (multiple sources & varying opinions)

300/400 Level Courses

Students will be able to:

- Perform all of the above, and
- Perform multi-level (multiple keywords, database specific limiters, Boolean, truncation, etc.) searches in discipline specific databases

Figure 15.2
Information literacy learning objectives. Source: "Student Learning Objectives," in "Information Literacy: Instruction," Greenwood Library, Longwood University, accessed October 17, 2018, http://libguides.longwood.edu/c.php?g=540388&p=3700811.

librarian program, my librarian colleagues all became certified through LOTI so that we could all teach within online courses. Participating in LOTI had the added benefit of putting all librarians on equal pedagogical footing and establishing core practices we can use both online and in the classroom. I am also a certified Quality Matters evaluator for campus courses and have increased my pedagogical expertise through the certification process and the practice of evaluation.

Administrative Highlights

I am proud of the growth we have demonstrated since I came to Longwood in 2016. There are many indicators that librarians are providing services of value to our instructional colleagues and our students. We successfully introduced the embedded librarian program, thus expanding our touch points with faculty and students. Our instruction numbers are increasing, a personal goal; feedback from faculty has a positive trend; and the librarians are growing as a team. I am additionally proud of the impact prioritizing communication has had in reducing what had become a combative relationship between faculty and librarians on the place of information literacy in the curriculum. The role of information literacy in the Civitae Core Curriculum will continue this positive trend.

Information Literacy Coordinator Profile

After fifteen years working in public and state libraries, I joined Longwood University as the Research and Instructional Services Librarian. Coordinating information literacy instruction is a formal part of my job description and in large part why I was hired. The coordinator aspect is key, as it is not supervisory, so I am here to lead my colleagues, but have no power over them. My intent is that we grow together as practitioners, but at times it is like herding cats. Each librarian works with designated departments, which often have differing disciplinary standards for research and differing expectations for information literacy instruction. These differences can affect instructional styles and goals for librarians. Additionally, each librarian has other assigned priorities that may influence their instruction, such as student services, marketing, or digital services. With such varied areas of expertise and priorities, it can be challenging to find consensus on pedagogical goals and instructional techniques.

I do have years of supervisory experience, including coordinating groups with diverse interests and priorities. I know how important it is to develop investment from colleagues before rolling out new ideas. Therefore, whenever I want to make a change or spearhead a new idea, I meet with the other librarians and talk it through first. Once the concept is fleshed out, I make sure I pilot the idea first, primarily so that I may reduce the burden on my colleagues as we work out the kinks in the new plan. For example, I went through the LOTI course and then piloted the embedded librarian program the first semester we offered it. As my colleagues came on board in the following semesters, they were able to build on what I learned in our first iteration. Respecting the input of colleagues, as well as practicing the behaviors I hope to see in them, is key to coordination.

Our instructional workload is directly related to our liaison areas, and I liaise with our two heaviest hitters for instruction: the English and Modern Languages Department, and the History, Philosophy, and Political Science Department. As their liaison I teach all of their information literacy instruction sessions, as well as providing collection development and research assistance. These departments fit with my educational background, but I also feel that taking on the two most demanding departments makes coordinating instruction easier. I am not asking my colleagues to shoulder a burden that I myself am not willing to bear.

What I Wish People Knew

We still fight the mentality that bringing a class to the library is busywork where students will get a tour and "learn the website," or worse, that a library day is an opportunity to take attendance and monitor a class while faculty are off campus. The latter happens rarely, but does happen. Communication with faculty using their language is key to changing perceptions. Once we developed our learning objectives, we were able to align them to faculty course outcomes and clearly demonstrate that students will gain skills in our one-shot sessions that will help them succeed in their courses. This conversation made our instruction appear more relatable and valuable for the individual faculty, beyond the intangible goal of growing information-literate students.

The wonderful thing about working in academia is that there are ample opportunities to improve your own knowledge. Since I serve the modern languages department, I am taking advantage of Longwood University's faculty education benefits and auditing courses in French. My goal is full fluency, which will allow me to teach information literacy in French classes, in French, as well as pursuing a second master's degree in French and Francophone studies. I have been surprised by how this desire to improve my own skills has caught the attention of all of our language faculty, demonstrating both an interest in their field and a commitment to reaching their students at the point of need.

My advice is to be active on campus and open to opportunity, whether that means going to receptions, attending events, or auditing classes. Build bridges. Listen when faculty express frustration with student progress or comment on upcoming research projects. Even after three years of determined campus communication, we still encounter faculty who are surprised to learn that information literacy instruction is something we offer. That said, if faculty push back, I remind them that students may always make an appointment with a librarian outside of class, if time for in-class instruction is not an option. I find that respecting faculty's time and demonstrating that our focus is on the student goes a long way. No matter what, keep the communication channels open; faculty investment will follow.

Notes

1. "Longwood University," Institutional Profile, State Council of Higher Education for Virginia, accessed January 20, 2019, http://research.schev.edu/iprofile.asp?UID=232566
2. "Mission," Longwood University, accessed January 20, 2019, http://www.longwood.edu/about/leadership/mission.

3. "Program Overview," Civitae Core Curriculum, Longwood University, accessed March 8, 2019, http://solomon.longwood.edu/civitae/program-overview.
4. "Longwood General Education Competencies," Longwood University, accessed January 25, 2019, http://www.longwood.edu/assessment/assessment-info/longwood-general-education-competencies.
5. "Information Literacy Tutorials," Greenwood Library, Longwood University, accessed January 20, 2019, https://libguides.longwood.edu/c.php?g=540388&p=3712695.
6. "Search&Destroy," Card Games, The Game Crafter, accessed October 19, 2018, https://www.thegame-crafter.com/games/search-destroy.
7. "Information Literacy: Home," Greenwood Library, Longwood University, accessed January 20, 2019, https://libguides.longwood.edu/c.php?g=540388&p=3700806.
8. "Brock Experiences," Longwood University, accessed October 24, 2018, http://www.longwood.edu/academics/brock-experiences.
9. "Information Literacy VALUE Rubric," Association of American Colleges and Universities, last updated July 2013, https://www.aacu.org/value/rubrics/information-literacy.
10. Quality Matters home page, accessed October 29, 2018, https://www.qualitymatters.org.

Bibliography

Association of American Colleges and Universities. "Information Literacy VALUE Rubric." Last updated July 2013. https://www.aacu.org/value/rubrics/information-literacy.

Game Crafter, The. "Search&Destroy." Card Games. Accessed October 19, 2018. https://www.thegame-crafter.com/games/search-destroy.

Greenwood Library. "Information Literacy: Home." Longwood University. Accessed January 20, 2019. https://libguides.longwood.edu/c.php?g=540388&p=3700806.

———. "Information Literacy Tutorials." Longwood University. Accessed January 20, 2019. https://libguides.longwood.edu/c.php?g=540388&p=3712695.

———. "Student Learning Objectives." In "Information Literacy: Instruction." Longwood University. Accessed October 17, 2018. http://libguides.longwood.edu/c.php?g=540388&p=3700811.

Longwood University. "Brock Experiences." Accessed October 24, 2018. http://www.longwood.edu/academics/brock-experiences.

———. "Longwood General Education Competencies." Accessed January 25, 2019. http://www.longwood.edu/assessment/assessment-info/longwood-general-education-competencies.

———. "Mission." Accessed January 20, 2019. http://www.longwood.edu/about/leadership/mission.

———. "Program Overview." Civitae Core Curriculum. Accessed March 8, 2019. http://solomon.longwood.edu/civitae/program-overview.

Quality Matters home page. Accessed October 29, 2018. https://www.qualitymatters.org.

State Council of Higher Education for Virginia. " Longwood University." Institutional Profile. Accessed January 20, 2019. http://research.schev.edu/iprofile.asp?UID=232566.

Chapter 16

Saint Mary's College of California

Tradition and Transparency on a Tight-Knit Campus

Gina Kessler Lee and Conrad M. Woxland

Population Served

Saint Mary's College of California (SMC) is a private Catholic liberal arts college of 2,675 undergraduates and 1,086 graduate students. Located in a suburb of San Francisco, SMC is a Lasallian institution with a number of Christian Brothers teaching and serving on campus, which influences its strong social justice mission.[1]

The college has four schools: the School of Liberal Arts, the School of Economics and Business Administration, the School of Science, and the Kalamanovitz School of Education. SMC offers forty-three majors for undergraduate students, with an average class size of nineteen.[2] The student population is 45 percent white and 47 percent students of color,[3] and the college is a Hispanic-Serving Institution.[4] There are more female students on campus than male students. More than half of undergraduate students live on campus.[5] All students, regardless of major, take Collegiate Seminar, a four-semester series that focuses on student-led discussion surrounding a common syllabus of readings from the Western canon, such as Aristotle's *Nicomachean Ethics*, and others, such as Chinua Achebe's *Things Fall Apart*. Couple these intimate classes with the small campus situated in a semirural environment, and students begin to feel ownership of the college's physical spaces. The library building is often very busy, and students utilize both the silent study areas and group study rooms often. A reference desk shift can be punctuated by students stopping by just to say hello or announcing a grade received on a research paper a librarian assisted with. Library staff are proud of creating a positive culture where students are not shy about asking for help within or outside of a library instruction session. Students at SMC expect to create close relationships with faculty and staff and interact with people casually and without being intimidated.

Program Scope

Librarians teach library sessions for both undergraduate and graduate students, with one-third of instruction hours being devoted to introductory composition courses. Librarians communicate directly with faculty in their liaison departments to coordinate and teach library sessions. Rather than scheduling and delegating library sessions, the information literacy coordinator's (known at SMC as the "Instruction and Outreach Coordinator") role is instead to give direction for the instruction program as a whole.

Information literacy (IL) instruction is typically based around a research assignment, takes place in person, and occurs when a course instructor is willing to collaborate. Librarians can assist faculty and instructors in integrating IL content into the campus course management system, with online web tutorials, and with the development of research assignments. However, most requests from instructors are for in-person bibliographic instruction, and librarians rely on building relationships and trust in order to incorporate more advanced or critical information literacy–related learning objectives. This system can lead to librarians in some cases feeling that they are at the whim of the instructor, and when asked to do minimal instruction feel that is all they are allowed to do. Other times, librarians can be asked to do too much and must tactfully pull back from a department that is saturated. Librarians offer a wide spectrum of instruction, from twenty-minute database showcases in some business courses to a chemistry course where the librarian is embedded, attends every class, and is listed as a co-instructor on the syllabus.

It is difficult for librarians to scaffold instruction in a given department due to variance in instruction requests between classes and instructors, and also because most students progress through the Core Curriculum and their major in an unpredictable order.[6] Each major's Writing in the Disciplines class would be an ideal place to deliver information literacy instruction, but library instruction in these courses is not required, and many of the faculty teaching these courses decline our offers of instruction. Librarians are currently piloting information literacy curriculum mapping for each department to better communicate this situation to faculty.

At the undergraduate level, IL is built into the curriculum as Information Evaluation and Research Practices (IERP) learning outcomes that are part of the "habits of mind" area of the Core Curriculum (see figure 16.1) and are expected to be taught in the composition program and a Writing in the Disciplines course in each of the majors. IL also overlaps heavily with the Core Curriculum's Critical Thinking (CT) learning outcomes (see figure 16.1).

At the graduate level, all students are expected to achieve Scholarly Research and Information Literacy learning outcomes (see figure 16.1), but how, when, and to what extent they are taught these skills varies by program. For example, programs in the School of Education, which require students to complete a research-based thesis, dissertation, or action research project, typically include more information literacy instruction than the graduate programs in the School of Economics and Business Administration or the School of Liberal Arts. In the kinesiology graduate program, students receive library instruction in their sports law class, which includes discussion of primary and secondary legal sources and how to find and access relevant court decisions, statutes, and law reviews in databases such as Nexis Uni.

Undergraduate Learning Outcomes
Information Evaluation and Research Practices

With increasing proficiency, students will

1. Develop search strategies and use library catalogs and databases to find relevant material; and
2. Critically evaluate sources; and
3. Integrate and cite evidence appropriately. In addition, students will
4. Understand the concept of intellectual property and practice academic honesty.

Critical Thinking

With increasing proficiency, students will

1. Identify and understand assumptions and theses that exist in the work of others; and
2. Ask meaningful questions, originate plausible theses, and identify their own underlying assumptions; and
3. Seek and identify confirming and opposing evidence relevant to original and existing theses; and
4. Evaluate and synthesize evidence for the purpose of drawing valid conclusions.

Graduate Learning Outcomes
Scholarly Research and Information Literacy

With increasing proficiency, students will

1. Understand when information or research is needed;
2. Acquire and critically evaluate data, information, and research appropriate for the field;
3. Make appropriate and ethical use of data, information, and research in projects, papers, or performances.

Figure 16.1
Information Evaluation and Research Practices undergraduate learning goals and outcomes, and Scholarly Research and Information Literacy learning outcomes for master's degree programs.

The composition program is comprised of three classes:
- English 3: Practice in Writing (developmental English for students with lower incoming test scores)
- English 4: Composition (required for all students except for those with high incoming test scores or an equivalent course from another institution)
- English 5: Argument and Research (required for all students except for transfer students with an equivalent course from another institution)

Every English 4 and 5 class requires one to three library sessions (depending on the professor's preference, in consultation with their librarian), and most English 3 instructors also opt for a library session. Every English 4 class assigns a small research essay, while every English 5 class assigns an eight-to-twelve-page research essay that requires at least three peer-reviewed, scholarly sources. These sessions are largely taught by the English liaison librarian, who is also the Instruction and Outreach coordinator. A part-time librarian assists the coordinator with the instruction, and some librarians with less intensive instruction commitments help out as needed.

Until 2014, English 4 instruction was divided among all librarians, but with the hiring of a new first-year programs librarian, instruction was consolidated among three librarians for greater consistency and to allow the other librarians to focus on their own liaison departments. At that time, the composition librarians revised the library curriculum to intentionally scaffold research skills between English 3, 4, and 5, with a focus on source evaluation. The scaffolding was developed for the Core Curriculum's IERP and CT learning outcomes as shown in table 16.1.

Table 16.1

General learning outcomes scaffolded between the three composition courses and Writing in the Disciplines classes in the majors. Learning outcomes IERP 4, CT 1, and CT 4 are not directly taught in this scaffolding model.

English 3: Practice in Writing	English 4: Composition	English 5: Argument and Research	Writing in the Disciplines courses
IERP 1: With increasing proficiency, students will develop search strategies and use library catalogs and databases to find relevant material.			
Students are able to find and use basic library services and collections (e.g., get to website, check out books). Students are able to use discovery service to find different types of sources.	Students are able to use some interdisciplinary databases for finding information (e.g., Opposing Viewpoints, discovery service, Credo Literati).	Students are able to use advanced techniques (e.g., Boolean) to search the library catalogs and databases for relevant evidence. Students are able to reflect on their own search strategies.	Students are able to develop search strategies and use library databases appropriate for their discipline.
IERP 2: With increasing proficiency, students will critically evaluate sources.			
Students are able to identify and articulate the differences between different source formats.	Students are able to evaluate sources of information using provided criteria.	Students are able to construct their own criteria for evaluating sources and use them to evaluate an article.	Students are able to critically evaluate scholarly sources according to the conventions of their discipline.
IERP 3: With increasing proficiency, students will integrate and cite evidence appropriately.			
Optional: Students understand how to cite sources and avoid plagiarism.	Students understand how to cite sources and avoid plagiarism.	Students understand why to use and cite sources. Students cite their sources accurately in MLA style.	Students are able to cite their sources according to their discipline's preferred citation style.

English 3: Practice in Writing	English 4: Composition	English 5: Argument and Research	Writing in the Disciplines courses
CT 2: *With increasing proficiency, students will ask meaningful questions, originate plausible theses, and identify their own underlying assumptions.*			
	Optional: Students are able to narrow their topic to an appropriate scope (originate plausible theses). **Optional:** Students are able to analyze the arguments of others and reflect on assumptions and how they relate to the student's own assumptions on the topic.	Students are able to develop a research question of appropriate scope. Students practice letting the research lead them to new ideas (and, eventually, a thesis), rather than trying to fit the research into prior assumptions.	
CT 3: *With increasing proficiency, students will seek and identify confirming and opposing evidence relevant to original and existing theses.*			
Optional: Students are able to find opinion articles expressing different viewpoints on the same topic.	Students are able to seek, identify, and reconcile sources representing different viewpoints in response to their research question.		

The composition librarians created a shared lesson plan to meet these learning outcomes in English 4 and English 5 classes, but the lesson plan can be adapted to the class's particular assignment, the competencies and curiosities of the particular students, and the desires of the faculty member teaching the course.

Outside of credit-bearing disciplinary classes, SMC Library does not generally host optional information literacy workshops for students, due to low attendance in the past. However, the library hosts monthly information literacy–related workshops for faculty and staff on topics such as financial research, new library databases, using the College Archives, research assignment design, and researching ballot measures, which are moderately well attended. While we would love to implement a "teach the teacher" model that empowers faculty to teach their students information literacy skills,[7] on this campus, getting participation from every department and requiring identifiable improvements would require faculty compensation in the form of stipends or course releases, which we don't have the resources to provide at this time.

Operations

The library has one classroom (see figure 16.2), which contains a projector, interactive whiteboard, and twenty-four laptops. The room has five large whiteboards that are used for group work and icebreaker activities. Scheduling for the room is done on a first-come, first-served basis in Google Calendar. Librarians can also reserve a large conference room in the library (with an instructor station and iPads in place of laptops) or, if necessary, a classroom computer lab in another building.

Figure 16.2
Library classroom

Like many midsize libraries, SMC Library is a horizontal organization with only a few supervisory positions (see figure 16.3). This library employs twenty-eight staff members, including fourteen librarians. Some reference and instruction librarians report to the dean, while others report to the Reference Services Coordinator. Organizationally, there are departments for access services, collections, and cataloging; there is no reference or instruction department. Instead, instruction librarians meet every four to six weeks, led by the instruction coordinator, to maintain group communication, set and track progress on goals, and discuss changes or challenges.

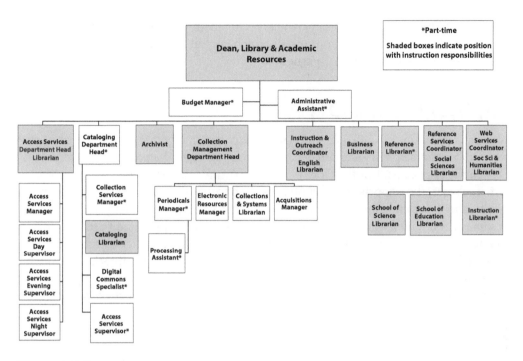

Figure 16.3
SMC Library organizational chart

Most librarians at SMC do instruction, but the amount they do depends on their other responsibilities. For example, some of the instruction librarians head a department, while others are the liaison for an entire school, and others lead a function such as reference or web services. In contrast with larger institutions where librarians may be more specialized, balancing the many different responsibilities can be challenging. For instance, when the instruction coordinator initiated a peer teaching observation program and a monthly pedagogy reading group, not every instruction librarian participated, but about two-thirds of them did. The instruction coordinator is very understanding and has adopted an attitude of "participate where you can," which sustains a positive environment.

Marketing

Library instruction within a course can come about in many ways: some initiatives are programmatic, such as when the education department conducted a program-wide review and requested instruction in response to information literacy gaps it discovered. Other instances occur more serendipitously through instructor word of mouth. While established relationships thrive due to SMC Library's high staff retention, a wave of recent retirements has resulted in a few recent hires, which have sparked additional opportunities through SMC's conversational culture.

Librarians often build upon established instruction patterns (going into similar classes each year) and relationships (working with the same faculty each year). While we are always trying to build new bridges, we also value and regularly try to improve upon long-standing instruction partnerships. Our initiatives to increase library instruction have been successful in a number of departments. Our main goal at this point is not to just increase instruction—many librarians already have full instruction calendars—but to more carefully target focused IL instruction.

Collaboration

We teach approximately 300 one-shots (with the occasional two-shot or three-shot) each year. Our partnerships with certain departments are stronger than others (see figure 16.4). This disparity is a result of the Core Curriculum's information literacy requirements in certain classes, the importance of library research to certain disciplines' curriculum and faculty, and the relationships with faculty that librarians have built over years (or decades in some cases). Often, these relationships are between a librarian and particular faculty members, rather than a librarian and a department. So when faculty members retire or a research-intensive class rotates between different instructors, the librarian usually has to put in effort to establish new relationships, understand professors' differing goals, and work with instructors to negotiate how students will meet the information literacy learning outcomes and how the librarian and instructor will collaborate.

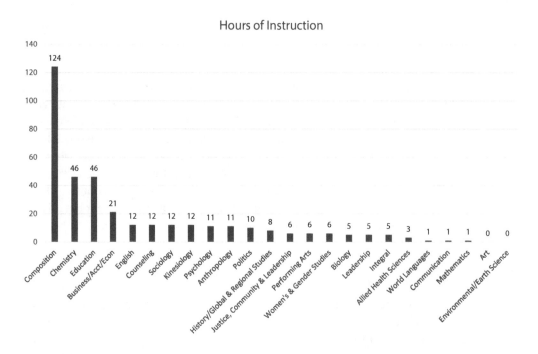

Figure 16.4
Number of hours of library instruction time by department in 2017–18.

The largest portion of our library sessions is for the composition program, which generally collaborates closely with the library, and a librarian serves on the Composition Program Committee. However, the program is led by a rotating directorship, which means the instruction coordinator must build a new relationship every two years. Most of these classes are taught by adjunct faculty, and while they each design their own class themes and research essay requirements, they are generally enthusiastic about library instruction and flexible in partnering with a librarian.

Following English composition, the chemistry department receives the most instruction time, thanks to the science librarian being fully embedded in that major's Writing in the Disciplines class. The education librarian also teaches multiple sections in many courses, resulting in high instruction time for the education program as well.

Outside of academic departments, SMC Library partners with Student Life offices (including New Student and Family Programs, Career and Professional Development Services, the Intercultural Center, and the Center for Writing across the Curriculum). Librarians meet with these offices regularly to discuss shared goals for student success, support each other's programs, and, occasionally, weave information literacy into their programs, such as career workshops or orientation leader trainings.

Assessment

Currently, the instruction coordinator encourages assessment of student learning by sharing and discussing classroom assessment techniques (minute papers, using PollEverywhere to check in throughout class, etc.), but ultimately assessment of a session is left up to the librarian, and we have never collated classroom assessment data to look at it holistically.

However, librarians have done some formal and informal assessments of student essays, including a study for ACRL's Assessment in Action project that compared the effect of two different approaches to one-shots on student research essays.[8] Librarians have also been included in carrying out assessments conducted by faculty partners on campus. We hope to organize larger-scale assessments of what information literacy skills SMC students are learning, but planning for this is ongoing.

Librarians, though classified as staff, sit on a variety of faculty curriculum committees tasked with assessment. Academic departments undergo a review every four years, and a portion of these reviews involves the librarian reviewing syllabi and research assignments to recommend additional library instruction and collection materials.

Role of the One-Shot

The one-shot is the instruction program's main source of sustenance. In composition classes, a one-shot is required; in Writing in the Disciplines classes, one is encouraged; and in many others, faculty who assign research projects are offered one or request one. Some classes take more of an embedded-librarian model, and the faculty who regularly teach those courses have become our strongest allies.

In 2016, we ran an analysis of what classes each student had taken during their time at SMC and which of those course sections had library instruction. We found that students were receiving anywhere from one to eleven one-shots at SMC, with an average of 4.4.[9] While we are proud of our instruction program's popularity, we are concerned that undergraduate students are receiving one-shots without scaffolding. Since they receive one-shots in a variety of departments and may not take their major courses in a designated order, we can't assume a common skill set among the students in a class. Students sometimes express that they've "had the library class before," implying that every class is the same. Librarians would like to partner with departments to more carefully scaffold the teaching of research skills within and across classes and also to make room for critical information literacy practices and dispositions that may be unrelated to a particular assignment. We recently began detailed curriculum mapping across the departments to inform our conversations. We are also challenging ourselves to incorporate more differentiated instruction to accommodate students of different skill levels and engage more advanced students in teaching their peers.

Our graduate and professional programs have highly structured curricula, which makes scaffolding easier. In education programs, a librarian is embedded in the key research courses for students completing master's theses and doctoral dissertations. Many other graduate programs, primarily in business, incorporate librarians through one-shots, though with the adoption of new programs and courses, opportunities for collaboration are arising all the time.

Pedagogical Highlights

What we teach is guided by our institutional information literacy learning outcomes (see Program Scope), which were based on the retired *Information Literacy Competency Standards for Higher Education*, but our lessons also incorporate the ideas of the ACRL *Framework for Information Literacy for Higher Education*.[10] For example, we teach a library session for an English 5 class in which students are researching topics related to the personal history of a family or community member. In this class, we teach to and assess the Core Curriculum learning outcome "Students will develop search strategies and use library catalogs and databases to find relevant material," but our framing of the class conversations and activities is shaped by *Framework* knowledge practices such as "define different types of authority, such as subject expertise (e.g., scholarship), societal position (e.g., public office or title), or special experience (e.g., participating in a historic event)."[11] We might do this by examining the question of who gets to write history and the value of considering primary, secondary, and tertiary sources from those in positions of varying power. We might also address the *Framework*'s dispositions, like "Learners . . . persist in the face of search challenges, and know when they have enough information to complete the information task,"[12] acknowledging to our students that research is challenging and requires persistence and knowing when to get help.

Our librarians share a teaching philosophy that strives to meet students where they are and then work to build upon those skills. We tend to use hands-on, active-learning activities in class that allow students to practice the skills they will actually need to succeed on their assignment and to be successful throughout their time at SMC and beyond. In line with SMC's mission, we have committed to incorporating social justice concepts whenever possible. To be effective, librarians must teach compassionately without the benefit of previous rapport with a student and sometimes without exact knowledge of the research assignment. The Instruction and Outreach Coordinator and instruction librarians have made great strides in focusing professional development on teaching skills and classroom management, including starting a pedagogy reading group for librarians and fostering transparent communication around teaching challenges.

Administrative Highlights

Teaching librarians share nearly all lesson plans in a shared folder on Google Drive; this practice helps us learn from each other, preserves institutional knowledge of past teaching practices when there is a new liaison, and serves us in emergencies when a librarian needs a substitute. This practice required some adjustments for librarians who wrote out lesson plans by hand or were uncomfortable with Google Drive, but we have achieved almost complete participation.

Information Literacy Coordinator Profile

At SMC Library, the Instruction and Outreach Coordinator role is a set of responsibilities that are added onto a librarian's existing position. For example, the current Instruction and Outreach Coordinator was already coordinating first-year programs and serving as the librarian for the English department when she was also named Instruction and Outreach Coordinator by the dean. The Instruction and Outreach Coordinator role does not rotate; the coordinator remains in that role indefinitely.

Overall, the coordinator is responsible for managing the instruction team, functioning as a liaison and teaching librarian (with collection development duties), maintaining an active calendar of outreach events, and, with the help of a part-time instruction librarian, doing library instruction for the many composition courses.

What We Wish People Knew

Coordinating instruction is a job of contradictions. Here, as at many other libraries, it involves taking responsibility for a program's quality while having no actual supervisory role.[13] In our library, most librarians do instruction as part of their liaison responsibilities, but they all have additional responsibilities. So while the librarians are impressively committed to teaching, instruction is a higher priority for some of us, and less so for those with a smaller instruction emphasis in their job descriptions. Consequently, the Instruction and Outreach Coordinator must focus on using influence and persuasion to encourage participation in instruction team professional development opportunities.

Similarly, the role requires keeping up on small-scale tasks, like making sure broken things in the library classroom get fixed, but also big-picture thinking, like trying to quantify our impact on the entire undergraduate and graduate student population. It includes very public-facing responsibilities, like representing the library at campus events, but also hidden labor, like nudging the team to accomplish set goals or serving as an ear for fellow librarians' teaching struggles. Being a leader in an academic library while still learning how to teach effectively can lead to impostor syndrome.[14] Veronica Arellano Douglas and

Joanna Gadsby have connected the supportive, relational, and "housework" aspects of coordination to gendered expectations of instruction coordination.[15]

While it is important to be mindful of the stresses and hidden labor that go into coordinating library instruction, the role also involves many rewards. We have a thriving one-shot program that is extremely popular with faculty and reaches almost every single one of our students (often multiple times). Our teaching librarians make up a collegial team that is interested in innovating and committed to effective pedagogy. Long-term librarians bring a wealth of institutional knowledge, while new team members bring best practices and fresh ideas from other institutions. We see the college's Catholic, Lasallian, and liberal arts identities as aligning with the library profession's own values, such as those of social justice, democracy, and lifelong learning. While we progress toward goals involving assessment, scaffolding, and ensuring the sustainability of our teaching efforts, we have a supportive dean and an optimistic, hardworking team. It is an invigorating challenge, filled with small victories and proud moments, sending the team down these paths.

Notes

1. Lasallian schools are based in the mission of John Baptist De La Salle, who founded in France in 1680 the community of teachers that became known as the Brothers of the Christian Schools. Today, the Christian Brothers run 1,000 educational institutions around the world, including six institutions of higher education in the United States, founded in the Lasallian Core Principles of "quality education," "respect for all persons," "inclusive community," "concern for the poor and social justice," and "faith in the presence of God." La Salle RELAN, Christian Brothers Conference, https://www.lasallian.info, accessed January 25, 2019.
2. "Facts & Figures," About SMC, Saint Mary's College of California, last updated March 5, 2019, https://www.stmarys-ca.edu/about-smc/facts-figures.
3. "Fall 2017 Enrollment (Headcount) by Gender and Ethnicity," Office of Institutional Research, Saint Mary's College of California, December 18, 2017, https://www.stmarys-ca.edu/sites/default/files/attachments/files/Factbook 2017-18 Final 17FA Count FTE gender Ethnicity_0.pdf.
4. "HACU Member Hispanic-Serving Institutions (HSIs)," Hispanic Association of Colleges and Universities, accessed January 25, 2019. https://www.hacu.net/assnfe/CompanyDirectory.asp?STYLE=2&COMPANY_TYPE=1%2C5.
5. "Facts & Figures."
6. The core curriculum requires students to take specified numbers of courses that address various "habits of mind" or "pathways to knowledge" or that involve "engaging the world." It also requires students to take classes in composition, including a Writing in the Disciplines class in their major, as well as in SMC's signature programs, January Term and Collegiate Seminar.
7. For example, see Fiona Hunt and Jane Birks. "Best Practices in Information Literacy," *portal: Libraries and the Academy* 4, no. 1 (January 2004): 27–39, https://doi.org/10.1353/pla.2004.0010; Maya Hobscheid, "From Instruction to Instructional Design: Scalable Approaches to Information Literacy," in Conference Proceedings, CARL Conference, San Francisco, CA, April 13–15, 2018, http://conf2018.carl-acrl.org/wp-content/uploads/2018/08/hobscheid_engaging_scalableinfolit.pdf.
8. Elise Y. Wong and Sharon Radcliff, "Evaluation of Sources: A New Sustainable Approach," *Reference Services Review* 43, no. 2 (2015): 231–50, https://doi.org/10.1108/RSR-09-2014-0041; Sharon Radcliff et al., "Assessment in Action Program: Four Perspectives in Its Value to Librarians, Institutions and Students," in Conference Proceedings, CARL Conference, Costa Mesa, CA, March 13–April 2, 2016, http://conf2016.carl-acrl.org/wp-content/uploads/2016/05/radcliffCARLAssessment-in-Action-Program_rev-1-final.pdf.
9. Gina Kessler Lee, "Visualizing Library Instruction across the Curriculum" (lightning talk, ACRL Conference, Baltimore, MD, March 23, 2017).

10. Association of College and Research Libraries, *Framework for Information Literacy for Higher Education* (Chicago: Association of College and Research Libraries, 2016), http://www.ala.org/acrl/sites/ala.org.acrl/files/content/issues/infolit/Framework_ILHE.pdf.
11. Association of College and Research Libraries, *Framework*, 4.
12. Association of College and Research Libraries, *Framework*, 9.
13. Candice M. Benjes-Small and Rebecca K. Miller, *The New Instruction Librarian* (Chicago: ALA Editions, 2017), 144–55.
14. Melanie Clark, Kimberly Vardeman, and Shelley Barba, "Perceived Inadequacy: A Study of the Imposter Phenomenon among College and Research Librarians," *College and Research Libraries* 75, no. 3 (2014): 255–71, https://doi.org/10.5860/crl12-423.
15. Veronica Arellano Douglas and Joanna Gadsby, "Gendered Labor and Library Instruction Coordinators: The Undervaluing of Feminized Work," in *At the Helm: Leading Transformation: ACRL 2017 Conference Proceedings*, ed. Dawn M. Mueller (Chicago: Association of College and Research Libraries, 2016), 266–74, http://www.ala.org/acrl/sites/ala.org.acrl/files/content/conferences/confsandpreconfs/2017/GenderedLaborandLibraryInstructionCoordinators.pdf.

Bibliography

Arellano Douglas, Veronica, and Joanna Gadsby. "Gendered Labor and Library Instruction Coordinators: The Undervaluing of Feminized Work." In *At the Helm: Leading Transformation: ACRL 2017 Conference Proceedings.* Edited by Dawn M. Mueller, 266–74. Chicago: Association of College and Research Libraries, 2017.

Association of College and Research Libraries. *Framework for Information Literacy for Higher Education.* Chicago: Association of College and Research Libraries, 2016. http://www.ala.org/acrl/sites/ala.org.acrl/files/content/issues/infolit/Framework_ILHE.pdf.

Benjes-Small, Candice M., and Rebecca K. Miller. *The New Instruction Librarian: A Workbook for Trainers and Learners.* Chicago: ALA Editions, 2017.

Christian Brothers Conference. La Salle RELAN. Accessed January 25, 2019. https://www.lasallian.info, accessed January 25, 2019.

Clark, Melanie, Kimberly Vardeman, and Shelley Barba. "Perceived Inadequacy: A Study of the Imposter Phenomenon among College and Research Librarians." *College and Research Libraries* 75, no. 3 (2014): 255–71. https://doi.org/10.5860/crl12-423.

Hispanic Association of Colleges and Universities. "HACU Member Hispanic-Serving Institutions (HSIs)." Accessed January 25, 2019. https://www.hacu.net/assnfe/CompanyDirectory.asp?STYLE=2&COMPANY_TYPE=1%2C5.

Hobscheid, Maya. "From Instruction to Instructional Design: Scalable Approaches to Information Literacy." In Conference Proceedings, CARL Conference, San Francisco, CA, April 13–15, 2018. http://conf2018.carl-acrl.org/wp-content/uploads/2018/08/hobscheid_engaging_scalableinfolit.pdf.

Hunt, Fiona, and Jane Birks. "Best Practices in Information Literacy." *portal: Libraries and the Academy* 4, no. 1 (January 2004): 27–39. https://doi.org/10.1353/pla.2004.0010.

Lee, Gina Kessler. "Visualizing Library Instruction across the Curriculum." Lightning talk, ACRL Conference, Baltimore, MD, March 23, 2017.

Radcliff, Sharon, Stephanie Alexander, Gina Kessler Lee, and Sara Davidson Squibb. "Assessment in Action Program: Four Perspectives in Its Value to Librarians, Institutions and Students." In Conference Proceedings, CARL Conference, Costa Mesa, CA, March 31–April 2, 2016. http://conf2016.carl-acrl.org/wp-content/uploads/2016/05/radcliffCARLAssessment-in-Action-Program_rev-1-final.pdf.

Saint Mary's College of California. "Facts & Figures." About SMC. Last updated March 5, 2019. https://www.stmarys-ca.edu/about-smc/facts-figures.

———. "Fall 2017 Enrollment (Headcount) by Gender and Ethnicity." Office of Institutional Research. December 18, 2017. https://www.stmarys-ca.edu/sites/default/files/attachments/files/Factbook 2017-18 Final 17FA Count FTE gender Ethnicity_0.pdf.

Wong, Elise Y., and Sharon Radcliff. "Evaluation of Sources: A New Sustainable Approach." *Reference Services Review* 43, no. 2 (2015): 231–50. https://doi.org/10.1108/RSR-09-2014-0041.

Chapter 17

Sonoma State University
Be Curious; Be Critical; Be a Community

Kaitlin Springmier

Population Served

Sonoma State University (SSU) is a midsize public comprehensive (albeit largely under-graduate) university, part of the twenty-three-campus California State University (CSU) system. Located in Northern California, Sonoma is the only CSU that is also a member of the Council of Public Liberal Arts and Colleges (COPLAC), providing students with a balanced program of liberal arts and sciences and career preparation with selected professional programs in business, nursing, and engineering science.

Sonoma's student demographics are changing. After the appointment of President Judy Sakaki in 2016, Sonoma reaffirmed a commitment to recruit and retain a more diverse student body, including first-generation, underrepresented minority, and Pell-eligible students.[1] In 2017, SSU underscored this commitment by receiving designation as a Hispanic-Serving Institution, which provided funding for new student success programs, notably a resource center for undocumented students.[2] The library has recently undertaken new actions to mirror the university's initiatives, including hiring a new librarian with primary roles in inclusion and outreach, building relationships with student services across campus, and developing new cultural and intersectional lesson plans and programming.

The library's instruction program faces challenges similar to those of many: creating a high-quality, meaningful, and culturally responsive information literacy curriculum that serves students through a structured set of integrated paths that teach skills, knowledge, and dispositions learners need to be successful, both academically and postcollege, while operating almost exclusively with one-shot instruction.

Program Scope

The goal of our program is to, in collaboration with disciplinary faculty, develop and implement holistic information literacy instruction that students encounter throughout their studies at Sonoma State University. Sonoma State prides itself in its liberal arts identity. Faculty have developed curricular practices that are hallmarks of a liberal education, such as first- and second-year experience courses, service learning, and field work experiences, as well as integrative and culminating learning.[3] However, these instructional practices were inconsistently implemented and rarely assessed, making the library involvement within academic programs variable and almost entirely dependent on instructor preference. Most of our library sessions are in-person and are customized to instructors' preferences and students' upcoming research assignment. The personalized model of instruction helps librarians to build relationships and trust with disciplinary faculty. Our reputation across campus is that we are the collaborative, reliable, information literacy experts—a reputation that has allowed librarians to implement shared assignments and assessments in core university courses.[4]

Through liaison work, the library instruction program has seen demonstrated growth in the number of sessions offered (about 20% each year over the past two years). There has been growing concern, however, that the current growth model is unsustainable, as each one-shot is tailored for instructor preference and student skills. Additionally, the model has proved problematic for developing a programmatic information literacy curriculum: some first-year students report a having a librarian visit their classroom six-plus times in their first year, while others receive their first-ever library session in a senior seminar or capstone course.

Operations

Sonoma State University Library has four professional staff, nine faculty librarians, and seventeen classified staff. Each faculty librarian is expected to contribute to the instruction program; however, levels of engagement vary depending on the faculty librarian's desire to teach and their operational role. As structured through the library's Reappointment, Tenure, and Promotion policy, all faculty are responsible in managing a functional area (e.g., systems and metadata, collection development, outreach, reference, special collections, scholarly communication). After a change in leadership, it became expected that faculty, in addition to managing a functional area, would assume academic departmental liaison responsibilities that include collection development and management, information literacy instruction, and outreach. Within this structure, the library has two full-time librarians dedicated to instruction: a library instruction coordinator and a reference and instruction librarian who focuses on first-year programming, and seven librarians who contribute to the program through liaison work. All librarians report directly to the library dean.

Historically, librarians had assumed a liaison role for one of the university's five schools: Arts and Humanities, Business and Economics, Education, Science and Technology, and Social Sciences. However, as the expectation for all librarians to serve as liaison is applied, liaison work is split between schools and departments. Some faculty are a liaison to a school, while others are liaison to selected departments within a school. A librarian's liaison role is determined by librarian election after conversation surrounding gaps in the current program, research background and interests, and the intersection between the faculty members' functional role and departmental connections. This model is relatively new to us, and we continue to learn the benefits and pitfalls to this model through ongoing assessment and conversation.

Administration recognizes the import and need for library instruction through advocating for faculty lines and preserving classroom space; however, there is no allocated budget for the instruction program.

Marketing

Due to the library's organizational structure and the variable nature of Sonoma State's curriculum, the number of library instruction sessions taught in a semester largely depends the liaison's marketing and advocacy for the program. Most promotion occurs through direct email, but can also arise through presentations at department and school meetings.

Part of my job as coordinator is to help liaisons successfully market and engage in conversations with their constituents. As a new instruction coordinator with a relatively new instructional team (the most senior librarian has been at Sonoma for five years), I have found that the most effective way to help is to, within the library, facilitate conversations that create a shared language, understanding, and confidence in teaching library instruction in our library team. I have learned that developing a shared set of goals helps liaisons make sense of their work and enables them to find and market their role within Sonoma's curricula.

Librarians also create opportunities for library instruction through university service. Librarians serve on curricular committees within Sonoma's faculty governance structure. The committees oversee large- and small-scale educational initiatives, including institutional accreditation, general education reform, improving graduation rates while eliminating opportunity and achievement gaps, and reviewing and approving curriculum revisions, including changes to course content and new course proposals. By serving with departmental faculty on governance committees, librarians make new connections while advocating for information literacy in university courses and curricula.

Collaboration

At the heart of Sonoma's library instruction program is collaboration because we believe that our work is only strengthened by partnering with stakeholders across campus. Librarians collaborate with each other to develop library instruction lesson plans; with disciplinary faculty to create successful one-shot instruction and research assignments and to develop new courses; and with student services to grow library services and programming. While collaboration has long been a hallmark of the library instruction program, it has been difficult to sustain partnerships in the face of employee departures and transitions.

For example, in 2011 librarians, in collaboration with the coordinator of the lower-division composition program, implemented a common assignment for lower-division composition classes in order to create consistent assessment of first-year information literacy outcomes.[5] Over the course of three years, librarians worked with the lower-division coordinator and instructors to implement, assess, and refine the common assignment. However, when both the composition coordinator and library instruction coordinator departed Sonoma State, the infrastructure that had been developed to teach, implement, and assess the common assignment fell away.

Similarly, in 2015–16, librarians partnered with Sonoma State's Faculty Center to create professional development training for faculty interested in teaching digital literacies.[6] In a program dubbed Digital-Critical, cohorts of three to four faculty were selected for a $1,500 stipend, which paid for the cohort's attendance at workshops on information and digital literacies. Each faculty member then teamed up with a librarian to create an assignment that required students to use multimedia skills in a capstone course. In one instance, business faculty and the business liaison partnered to teach students how to create digital case studies. When asked about their experience in the classroom, students reported that they felt that learning how to build and present digital content gave them a competitive career edge.[7] Digital-Critical was successful in helping liaison librarians develop close relationships with departmental faculty, explore innovative digital pedagogies, and teach digital literacies. However, while successful in developing faculty-librarian partnerships, the projects developed in the program rarely expanded beyond the participants, and after three years, the program lost support. It lost support for two primary reasons: the instruction coordinator, who also served as the coordinator for Digital-Critical, left Sonoma State; and the funders of Digital-Critical, the Faculty Center and library administration, determined that the program was "boutique" and reallocated the monies to programs that were projected to reach a larger audience.[8]

While the funding and implementation of the program are no longer, remnants of the partnerships remain. Instructors who participated in the aforementioned programs consistently request library instruction and involve the library in curricular conversations. For example, in 2017–18, the library and the English department held train-the-trainer workshops for lecturers in lower-division composition courses. Workshops focused on identifying the relationship between instructors' learning objectives and the library's information literacy program while providing examples of how instructors can teach research skills in their classroom. We see these workshops as a cornerstone to rebuilding partnerships the library once had, with hope that they can lead to again creating and implementing a shared assignment.

Assessment

At Sonoma State, academic programs are inconsistently assessed, with some departments lacking measurable student learning outcomes. The university's most recent accreditation letter includes recommendations that SSU formalize and adhere to consistent assessment practices for program development, as well as student learning.[9] Uneven assessment has adversely affected the development of a comprehensive library instruction program because library faculty cannot predict students' understanding of or skills in information literacy prior to walking into the classroom.

In the library, we perform summative and formative assessment, the results of which we use to measure the type of instruction we do, the reach of our instruction program, and to a smaller extent, the success of our library sessions. Quantitative reports are produced annually and published on the library's website.[10] In addition to being used for internal analysis of the extent and reach of our instruction program, these reports have been used recently to articulate the importance of library classroom space and preserve the library's current teaching space from campus encroachment. Qualitative reports are developed from a "muddiest point" assessment that librarians can choose to distribute at the end of their library instruction session.[11] Data from these reports is de-identified, shared, and discussed among librarians to reflect on and refine our pedagogical practices. These assessments have been formative in helping teaching librarians to reflect on their teaching practices, gain insight on student takeaways, and have productive conversations with faculty on how to extend the effectiveness of library instruction.[12]

Role of the One-Shot

The bread and butter (about 80–90%) of our instruction program is in-person, course-integrated one-shot sessions initiated by a faculty invitation. In these sessions, the librarian typically develops and provides a customized research lesson corresponding to a course assignment.

The one-shot model is not without benefits: it teaches students skills they need to complete their research assignment; it allows librarians to build relationships with faculty across campus; it provides flexibility and variability in instructional content and design. However, as it has been noted, the one-shot model fails in teaching students critical thinking and higher-order information literacy skills because students need time to dissect, ponder, and explore the complexities of the information they encounter.[13]

Consequently, librarians have worked to build relationships with disciplinary faculty to integrate information literacy outcomes more cohesively into core university courses, most prominently Sonoma State University's English 101 and First Year Experience courses. In these courses, library and disciplinary faculty collaborate to develop student learning outcomes, assignments, and instructional content. Best practices and details of the partnership are described in Brasley's "Effective Librarian and Discipline Faculty Collaboration Models for Integrating Information Literacy into the Fabric of the Academic Institution."[14]

The collaborations have, in some instances, led to a librarian being embedded in or co-instructor of a course.[15] In Sonoma's School of Arts and Humanities Second Year Research and Creative Experience (SYRCE) program, a librarian is embedded: they are added to the course site, provide lectures on research, and design breakout research instruction on specialized topics.[16] In the School of Business and Economics' BA and MBA capstone courses, the librarian is a co-instructor. Throughout the students' capstone experience, the liaison provides an information literacy session, feedback on students' work, and research assistance in class meetings or on the students' course site. Because the librarian is a part of the course, they are more able to provide consistent and personalized assistance for the students. This is because the librarian is more familiar with the course content and because students are more familiar with the librarian. Informally, we have found that librarians provide more research consultations (requested by the student) for courses in which they are embedded than for courses in which they have provided a one-shot.

Pedagogical Highlights

Librarians have been working to define the curricular objectives of the library instruction program for a number of years. However, due to disparate functional and liaison areas, it had been difficult to synergize our instructional efforts. In spring 2018, I discovered Nicole Pagowski's *ACRLog* post and was inspired to start a dialogue with my colleagues about developing a shared curriculum philosophy.[17] Over summer, we came together to craft a curriculum philosophy that would guide our practices, not only in teaching, but also in our functional roles. The curriculum philosophy, which was completed in September, now functions as a foundational document for our instructional design, strategic planning, and goal setting.

The curriculum philosophy is based on the premise that we teach not only in the classroom, but also through designing, applying, and developing systems, spaces, programming, and services in the library. It is structured by three directives: be curious, be critical, be brave.[18] Within these directives, librarians designate strategies they can practice in functional or instructional roles at the university.[19]

Developing a curriculum philosophy not only helped us create a shared vision; it is the beginnings of our community of practice. Investing time, effort, and sentiment in a shared document helped us to develop trusting relationships and create shared execution of our work.[20] Moving forward, our community is reinforced through monthly teaching circles: knowledge-sharing sessions in which librarians present ways they are realizing the curriculum philosophy, most particularly in their instruction. The teaching circles can be focused on a learning outcome (e.g., teaching how to develop and refine a research topic), a lesson plan (e.g., demoing a new activity for an upcoming one-shot), or a structured discussion of newly published or discovered research on pedagogy or information literacy. The structure is intentionally informal to encourage librarians to choose topics and lead discussion.

Information Literacy Coordinator Profile

The role of instruction coordinator has been formalized for a number of years at Sonoma. While my title, Instruction and Learning Assessment Librarian, was crafted for a new recruitment in 2017, I stepped into a coordination responsibility that had been formalized by my predecessor.

At Sonoma, coordination of instruction includes scheduling and managing classrooms, convening meetings, and performing assessment. However, because our program is so relational (the liaison librarian, through lasting contacts with departmental faculty, develops, schedules, and executes information literacy instruction), the coordination of instruction takes a very small amount of my time. The largest percent of my workload is teaching, although this is not a formal expectation. In 2018, I taught on average three instruction sessions per week in a fifteen-week semester. Librarians at Sonoma do not have established teaching quotas.

When I am not in the classroom, I am working within and outside of the library, embedding information literacy as an integrative learning component of the university's curriculum and an intrinsic component of the university's assessment of student learning. I do this through serving on curricular committees in faculty governance and developing train-the-trainer workshops on teaching information literacy, as well as crafting shared lesson plans and instructional content for our most prominent instructional requests.

Serving in faculty governance has been crucial for me to bring information literacy into campus-wide conversations. For example, in 2018, Sonoma began work to provide more consistent student learning by tasking faculty to review and revise the general education (GE) program, implementing consistent course content, learning outcomes, and assessments.[21] Because I served as library representative in the governance review of proposed GE revisions, I was able to advocate for the inclusion of an information literacy learning outcome, written by librarians, in the GE program. If approved, this learning outcome would be the first time that information literacy is formally recognized as something that must be taught and assessed in Sonoma's curriculum.

What I Wish People Knew

Prior to accepting this position at Sonoma State, I had worked in a residency librarian position, meant to provide early-career librarians with initial job experience. I had not anticipated that the position would include such a high level of emotional labor. As articulated by Veronica Arellano Douglas and Joanna Gadsby, library instruction coordination is a complex navigation of relationships with other teaching librarians, "especially when 1) the coordinator is no one's boss, 2) colleagues were reluctant to teach, and 3) the coordinator was a more junior member of the library."[22] When hired, I was the most junior member of the library and was tasked with leading a program. I had to develop skills in navigating colleagues' emotions, generating buy-in, and managing relationships, which I had never thought I would have to do. It was difficult, frustrating, and time-intensive, and it was not until I had embarked upon a summer-long project with my team in developing a shared vision that I began to feel heard and respected, but also learned how to listen to my colleagues.

I had had a perception that instruction coordination could be algorithmic, systematic, programmatic—something that could be solved with well-organized systems and processes in isolation of university operations. Since being in this role, I have learned that no library instruction program operates seamlessly, and more importantly, no library instruction program is an island—the structure, functions, and success depend both on the university's investment in teaching as well as teaching effectiveness. Developing a shared curriculum philosophy helped the library bring what seemed to be disparate, uncoordinated efforts together under a shared vision and values. We see the document as a way to guide internal and external communication: in the coming years we hope to communicate our philosophy across campus, generating understanding, buy-in, and a community of advocates for the library. The growth and success of our program will directly correlate our community: how we work with each other, with our colleagues in other departments, and with the leaders of our institution.

Notes

1. Jenny Rogers, "In California's Wine Country, a New President Acts to Move a University Forward," *Chronicle of Higher Education*, October 2, 2016, https://www.chronicle.com/article/In-California-s-Wine/237952.
2. "SSU Attains Eligibility as Hispanic-Serving Institution, Announces New Resource Center for Undocumented Students," *WorkPlace*, Sonoma State University, February 23, 2017, http://web.sonoma.edu/workplace/2017/02/21/hsi.html.
3. Carol Geary Schneider, "Practicing Liberal Education: Formative Themes in the Re-invention of Liberal Learning," *Liberal Education* 90, no. 2 (Spring 2004), https://www.aacu.org/publications-research/periodicals/practicing-liberal-education-formative-themes-re-invention-liberal.
4. Felicia Palsson and Carrie L. McDade, "Factors Affecting the Successful Implementation of a Common Assignment for First-Year Composition Information Literacy," *College and Undergraduate Libraries* 21, no. 2 (2014): 197–98, https://doi.org/10.1080/10691316.2013.829375.
5. Palsson and McDade, "Factors Affecting the Successful Implementation," 198.
6. Nicolas Grizzle, "See What's beyond PowerPoint with Digital-Critical Faculty Presentations," *WorkPlace*, Sonoma State University, February 16, 2016, http://web.sonoma.edu/workplace/2016/02/16/digitalcritical.html.
7. Armand Gilinksy, Jr., and Nicole D. Lawson, "Are You Ready for Digital Case Studies?" *Case Research Journal* 36, no. 1 (Winter 2016): 140, http://nacra.net/pdf/AreYouReadyforDigitalCaseStudies.pdf.
8. The instruction coordinator and coordinator of the program stated that this program "stood apart from liaisons' traditional work in the instruction program," making it difficult to sustain in workforce changes.
9. Jamienne S. Studley, Letter to Dr. Judy Sakaki, President, Sonoma State University, Western Association of Schools and Colleges, March 9, 2018, https://web.sonoma.edu/aa/ap/accred/WASC_Ltr_03.09.18.pdf.
10. "Instruction Program," Sonoma State University Library, March 16, 2018, http://library.sonoma.edu/research/instruction/program.
11. Thomas A. Angelo and K. Patricia Cross, "Muddiest Point," Active Learning in the Classroom: Classroom Assessment Techniques, Blended Learning Toolkit, University of Wisconsin–Madison, September 2016, https://blendedtoolkit.wisc.edu/wp-content/uploads/2016/09/Muddiest-Point.pdf.
12. Kaitlin Springmier, Hilary Smith, and Marjorie Lear, "College Research: Competencies and Challenges for First-Time Freshmen at Sonoma State University" (presentation, Faculty and Graduate Student Scholarship Symposium, Sonoma State University, April 17, 2018), http://sonoma-dspace.calstate.edu/handle/10211.3/207779.
13. Latrice Booker, "Death to the One-Shot: Replacing Individual Information Literacy Sessions to Maximize Learning," *InULA Notes* 27, no. 2 (Fall 2015): 4-6, https://scholarworks.iu.edu/journals/index.php/inula/article/view/20669/26731; Karen Anderson and Frances A. May, "Does the Method of Instruction Matter? An Experimental Examination of Information Literacy Instruction in the Online, Blended, and Face-to-Face Classrooms," *Journal of Academic Librarianship* 36, no. 6 (November 2010): 496, https://doi.org/10.1016/j.acalib.2010.08.005.
14. Stephanie Sterling Brasley, "Effective Librarian and Discipline Faculty Collaboration Models for Integrating Information Literacy into the Fabric of an Academic Institution," *New Directions for Teaching and Learning* 2008, no. 114 (Summer 2008): 78, https://doi.org/10.1002/tl.318.
15. Kathy Drewes and Nadine Hoffman, "Academic Embedded Librarianship: An Introduction," *Public Services Quarterly* 6, no. 2–3 (2010): 76–77, https://doi.org/10.1080/15228959.2010.498773.
16. "SYRCE," School of Arts and Humanities, Sonoma State University, accessed January 16, 2019, http://ah.sonoma.edu/syrce. For more information on the librarians' contribution to the SYRCE program, visit the library's SYRCE research guide at http://libguides.sonoma.edu/SYRCE.
17. Nicole Pagowsky, "One Instructional Philosophy to Unite Them All," *ACRLog* (blog), July 16, 2015, http://acrlog.org/2015/07/16/one-instructional-philosophy-to-unite-them-all/.
18. "Instruction Program."

19. For example, library instruction teaches source evaluation not on provided authority, but on the information need and the context in which the information was produced and will be used. See more strategies in "Curriculum Philosophy," in "Instruction Program," Sonoma State University Library, March 16, 2018, http://library.sonoma.edu/research/instruction/program.
20. Darren Cambridge, Soren Kaplan, and Vicki Suter, "Community of Practice Design Guide: A Step-by-Step Guide for Designing and Cultivating Communities of Practice," Educause, 2005: 1, https://www.educause.edu/ir/library/pdf/NLI0531.pdf.
21. "General Education," Sonoma State University, accessed January 10, 2019, http://ge.sonoma.edu.
22. Veronica Arellano Douglas and Joanna Gadsby, "Gendered Labor and Library Instruction Coordinators: The Undervaluing of Feminized Work," in *At the Helm: Leading Transformation: ACRL 2017 Conference Proceedings*, ed. Dawn M. Mueller (Chicago: Association of College and Research Libraries, 2017), 269, http://www.ala.org/acrl/sites/ala.org.acrl/files/content/conferences/confsand-preconfs/2017/GenderedLaborandLibraryInstructionCoordinators.pdf.

Bibliography

Anderson, Karen, and Francis A. May. "Does the Method of Instruction Matter? An Experimental Examination of Information Literacy Instruction in the Online, Blended, and Face-to-Face Classrooms." *Journal of Academic Librarianship* 36, no. 6 (November 2010): 495–500, https://doi.org/10.1016/j.acalib.2010.08.005.

Angelo, Thomas A., and K. Patricia Cross. "Muddiest Point." Active Learning in the Classroom: Classroom Assessment Techniques. Blended Learning Toolkit. University of Wisconsin–Madison. September 2016. https://blendedtoolkit.wisc.edu/wp-content/uploads/2016/09/Muddiest-Point.pdf.

Arellano Douglas, Veronica, and Joanna Gadsby. "Gendered Labor and Library Instruction Coordinators: The Undervaluing of Feminized Work." In *At the Helm: Leading Transformation: ACRL 2017 Conference Proceedings*. Edited by Dawn M. Mueller, 266–74. Chicago: Association of College and Research Libraries, 2017. http://www.ala.org/acrl/sites/ala.org.acrl/files/content/conferences/confsandpreconfs/2017/GenderedLaborandLibraryInstructionCoordinators.pdf.

Booker, Latrice. "Death to the One-Shot: Replacing Individual Information Literacy Sessions to Maximize Learning." *InULA Notes* 27, no. 2 (Fall 2015): 4–6. https://scholarworks.iu.edu/journals/index.php/inula/article/ view/20669/26731.

Brasley, Stephanie Sterling. "Effective Librarian and Discipline Faculty Collaboration Models for Integrating Information Literacy into the Fabric of an Academic Institution." *New Directions for Teaching and Learning* 2008, no. 114 (Summer 2008): 71–88. https://doi.org/10.1002/tl.318.

Cambridge, Darren, Soren Kaplan, and Vicki Suter. "Community of Practice Design Guide: A Step-by-Step Guide for Designing and Cultivating Communities of Practice." Educause, 2005. https://www.educause.edu/ir/library/pdf/NLI0531.pdf.

Drewes, Kathy, and Nadine Hoffman. "Academic Embedded Librarianship: An Introduction." *Public Services Quarterly* 6, no. 2–3 (2010): 75–82. https://doi.org/10.1080/15228959.2010.498773.

Gilinksy, Armand, Jr., and Nicole D. Lawson. "Are You Ready for Digital Case Studies?" *Case Research Journal* 36, no. 1 (Winter 2016): 129–40. http://nacra.net/pdf/AreYouReadyforDigitalCaseStudies.pdf.

Grizzle, Nicolas. "See What's beyond PowerPoint with Digital-Critical Faculty Presentations." *WorkPlace*, Sonoma State University. February 16, 2016. http://web.sonoma.edu/workplace/2016/02/16/digitalcritical.html.

Pagowsky, Nicole. "One Instructional Philosophy to Unite Them All." *ACRLog* (blog), July 16, 2015. http://acrlog.org/2015/07/16/one-instructional-philosophy-to-unite-them-all.

Palsson, Felicia, and Carrie L. McDade. "Factors Affecting the Successful Implementation of a Common Assignment for First-Year Composition Information Literacy." *College and Undergraduate Libraries* 21, no. 2 (2014): 193–209. https://doi.org/10.1080/10691316.2013.829375.

Rogers, Jenny. "In California's Wine Country, a New President Acts to Move a University Forward." *Chronicle of Higher Education*, October 2, 2016. https://www.chronicle.com/article/In-California-s-Wine/237952.

Schneider, Carol Geary. "Practicing Liberal Education: Formative Themes in the Re-invention of Liberal Learning." *Liberal Education* 90, no. 2 (Spring 2004). https://www.aacu.org/publications-research/periodicals/practicing-liberal-education-formative-themes-re-invention-liberal.

Sonoma State University. "General Education." Accessed January 10, 2019. http://ge.sonoma.edu.

———. "SYRCE." School of Arts and Humanities. Accessed January 16, 2019. http://ah.sonoma.edu/syrce.

———. "SSU Attains Eligibility as Hispanic-Serving Institution, Announces New Resource Center for Undocumented Students." *WorkPlace*, February 23, 2017. http://web.sonoma.edu/workplace/2017/02/21/hsi.html.

Sonoma State University Library. "Instruction Program." March 16, 2018. http://library.sonoma.edu/research/instruction/program.

Springmier, Kaitlin, Hilary Smith, and Marjorie Lear. "College Research: Competencies and Challenges for First-Time Freshmen at Sonoma State University." Presentation, Faculty and Graduate Student Scholarship Symposium, Sonoma State University, April 17, 2018. http://hdl.handle.net/10211.3/208020.

Studley, Jamienne S. Letter to Dr. Judy Sakaki, President, Sonoma State University. Western Association of Schools and Colleges, March 9, 2018. https://web.sonoma.edu/aa/ap/accred/WASC_Ltr_03.09.18.pdf.

Chapter 18

University of Minnesota Duluth

Surfacing Shared Purpose

Kim Pittman

Population Served

The University of Minnesota Duluth (UMD) is a midsize public comprehensive regional university in the University of Minnesota system. As of 2017, the library's instruction program served 9,199 undergraduate and 1,021 graduate students.[1] Our program supports a wide range of subjects, including ninety-plus undergraduate and twenty-plus graduate programs across six colleges and schools.

Unlike the range of programs we support, our student population is quite homogenous. In 2017, 85 percent of our students were from Minnesota, with 72 percent of students hailing from the Duluth and Minneapolis/St. Paul regions.[2] Additionally, 77 percent of the 2017 UMD student body identified as white.[3] Given the high concentration of Minnesotan students, librarians often incorporate topics of local interest, such as statewide access to affordable housing, mining, or local environmental issues, into library instruction. With the predominantly white makeup of our student population in mind, librarians also use social justice–related topics in sessions as a subtle way to encourage students to develop a more inclusive lens. In 2017, 295 international students attended UMD.[4] Our program works closely with courses designated for English language learners in order to support international students in navigating a US academic library environment.

Program Scope

Our instruction program primarily serves undergraduates through in-person course-integrated library sessions. At the core of the program is a partnership with our campus writing program. Students in our required first-year writing course, College Writing, participate in two library sessions and complete three online tutorials. Sessions for College Writing account for approximately 40 percent of each year's instruction, while sessions for required subject-specific advanced writing courses account for roughly 10 percent. In addition to working with the writing program, liaison librarians partner with faculty to reach students at key points in their academic careers by offering sessions in research-intensive courses within disciplines, including capstone and thesis courses. We also offer drop-in workshops on topics like citation management, evaluation of news, and research data management. Online course support is an area in which we are working to grow our program.

Operations

Our program is primarily staffed by eight librarians within the library's Research and Learning Team, representing approximately 29 percent of the total library staff. In addition to this core group, the library director and Research and Learning's archivist and scholarly communications librarian also teach a more limited number of sessions each year. All Research and Learning librarians have teaching responsibilities for College Writing and assigned liaison areas written into their job descriptions, and the archivist is responsible for teaching sessions related to archival research. The library director and scholarly communications librarian opt to teach based on personal interest.

In 2016, a library-wide reorganization generated structural changes for our program, including updates to the instruction coordinator position, the creation of an online learning librarian role, and a revised distribution of subject areas for liaisons. Rather than assigning liaison areas based on interest and expertise after filling positions, the reorganization and a series of retirements allowed us to assign individual librarians to broad subject areas (e.g., humanities and fine arts or science and engineering, rather than unpredictable combinations like engineering and music). This structure streamlines faculty outreach and allows librarians to work with programs that share more similarities than differences. Changes to liaison roles have also made our program's structure more transparent in and outside the library, making it easier for colleagues and campus partners to identify the appropriate liaison for a particular department or major.

Five of the eight Research and Learning librarians have liaison-intensive roles, providing instructional support, research help, and collection development for broad subject areas like humanities or business. The other three librarians in our team have primarily functional roles (Head of Research and Learning, Information Literacy and Assessment Librarian, and Online Learning and Outreach Librarian), but offer College Writing instruction and act as liaisons to smaller programs. In addition to teaching, all of these librarians provide drop-in research help for the campus community.

Despite its small size, our team teaches a high number of sessions each year: we taught 433 sessions in 2017–18, and our total number of sessions has grown in six of the last seven years despite frequent librarian turnover and some years of declining student enrollment. In 2017–18, our team taught more sessions per professional staff member than in any of the eleven institutions UMD identifies as peers based on size, programs, research, and degrees offered, demonstrating the reach and scope of our program as well as our team's commitment to teaching and learning.[5]

While the instruction program does not have its own budget, it receives substantial support from library leadership. Library administration supports the program through the library director's delivery of classroom instruction, participation in trainings related to teaching and learning, sharing of instruction program information with campus partners and leaders, and identification of opportunities for librarians to participate in campus educational initiatives.

Marketing

As instruction coordinator, I promote the library's role in teaching and learning through campus presentations and our web presence. At new faculty orientation each year, I lead a discussion about preconceptions or expectations students might have about academic libraries and research. As we discuss students' perspectives, I draw connections to what we know about students' research experiences from Project Information Literacy and introduce instructors to options for information literacy instruction.[6] I also maintain a library web page where instructors can learn about information literacy, contact their liaison librarian, and request library instruction.[7]

Liaison librarians promote one-shot instruction through outreach to instructors via email, departmental meetings, and working with faculty members who serve as "library liaison" for their department. While liaison librarians vary in their approach to outreach, common strategies include identifying assignments that generate a high volume of research questions, courses where key information literacy skills and understandings can be addressed, or instructors who are interested in information literacy. Our social sciences librarian creates and shares a regular email newsletter with her departments in order to share library updates and publicize her teaching role. Our business librarian checks in each semester with instructors who are teaching research-intensive courses and proactively reaches out to new faculty members in order to establish new relationships.

Because of our team's small size and heavy teaching loads, some liaison librarians are limited in their ability to seek new teaching opportunities. Within our department, we have begun to discuss ways to increase awareness of information literacy on campus while keeping in mind our limited capacity to work with new courses.

Collaboration

We enjoy a long-standing productive relationship with our campus writing program. While information literacy instruction delivered by librarians has been a required component of College Writing, our required first-year writing course, for many years, our relationship has become stronger recently through my participation in our campus Writing Program Committee and collaboration with our writing program administrator on a 2015–16 ACRL Assessment in Action (AiA) project.[8] As a result of this strengthened partnership, we now work more closely with writing instructors to design information literacy instruction, gather student work for assessment, and offer additional optional information literacy instruction for College Writing.

While liaisons have developed positive relationships with faculty in the disciplines, we plan to enhance those collaborations through faculty development. In the near future, we will develop a workshop series in which instructors will partner with librarians to incorporate information literacy into course design.

The library's participation in campus initiatives generates new opportunities to promote information literacy. In 2018, digital literacy was a topic of focus for our campus shared governance. Library staff involvement in these committees enabled librarians to participate in conversations about supporting digital literacy learning at all levels. The library is an active participant in campus-wide student learning assessment efforts, allowing us to build relationships and share strategies with staff members in Student Life and other cocurricular departments. The library's efforts to work collaboratively with campus partners on student outreach and events have strengthened these partnerships. A recent example of a teaching opportunity arising from an existing Student Life partnership occurred in the lead-up to the 2018 midterm elections. Our Vice Chancellor for Student Life assembled a cross-campus team to coordinate campus voter education efforts. As a result of our existing partnership, librarians were invited to offer voter education workshops designed to help attendees evaluate information critically when researching candidates and issues. Our Student Life partners worked hard to publicize these events, leading to higher than typical attendance for drop-in workshops.

Assessment

Assessment is one of our program's strengths. As part of a campus-wide assessment process, we assess and report on one to two student learning outcomes per year on a three-year cycle. Our original student learning assessment plan focused on assessing search skills as demonstrated in one-shot sessions. This plan enabled us to meet campus assessment requirements but rarely generated data that informed our teaching. Following our AiA project that focused on using reflective writing to understand how students respond to challenges in the research process, I created a new assessment plan. Working from this plan, we gather authentic evidence of student learning in first-year and advanced writing courses, helping us better understand information literacy learning over time. Rather than focusing exclusively on discrete research tasks, we analyze reflective writing, allowing us to identify "stuck places" in student learning and understand students' motivations, values, and feelings related to the research process.

Each year's assessment work is completed by an ad hoc working group of librarians. With the exception of my role as instruction coordinator, this group's membership rotates yearly, allowing all interested teaching librarians to participate in assessment. For each outcome, we assess student work from library instruction, including online tutorial quizzes, in-class worksheets, or written reflections. In order to see how students apply what they learn over time, we complete rubric-based assessment of work produced after library sessions, including annotated bibliographies, written reflections, and research topic proposals. We developed our rubrics internally, drawing inspiration from the ACRL *Framework for Information Literacy for Higher Education* and Association of American

Colleges and Universities VALUE rubrics.[9] We partner with writing instructors to gather anonymized student work and discuss results with instructors once the process is complete. This approach helps us understand how students experience the research process and informs the way we design instruction and partner with instructors.

In addition to our ongoing student learning assessment efforts, in 2017, we partnered with our Office of Institutional Research (OIR) to include the "Experiences with Information Literacy" module of the National Survey of Student Engagement (NSSE) in that year's survey delivery. This NSSE module invites first-year students and seniors to identify how frequently their instructors address information literacy in course assignments and activities.[10] Survey results compare UMD students' responses to those from other institutions, allowing us to contextualize our campus information literacy curricular integration. Our survey results indicate that UMD instructors emphasize information literacy less frequently than instructors at other comparably sized public institutions, suggesting the need for additional faculty development in this area. Our campus administers the NSSE every three years and includes only one topical module each time. We see OIR's willingness to include this module as evidence that our institution values information literacy. While we do not plan to administer this NSSE module regularly, we will incorporate results from relevant questions on the standard NSSE survey into our assessment practice.

Role of the One-Shot

The majority of our instruction happens in one-shot sessions; however, librarians have an expanded presence in a growing number of courses at the first-year level. In College Writing, librarians teach a minimum of two library sessions in each section and offer additional sessions at instructor request. Last year, after we added a section on follow-up sessions to our College Writing library instruction scheduling form, requests for these sessions tripled. This means that instead of seeing a College Writing section twice, librarians may work with one section up to five times per semester, allowing librarians to address concepts more fully and develop rapport with students and instructors. Similarly, librarians have a significant presence in first-year developmental writing courses, including courses for English language learners. In the majority of these course sections, librarians teach a multi-session sequence on reading academic journal articles, evaluating sources, and navigating the research process.

In addition to these examples, librarians extend learning beyond the one-shot by creating online tutorials and research guides and promoting research help options. While these approaches support deeper learning and library engagement, they present problems of scale for our program. Because librarians already teach more sessions per staff member than our peer institutions, we have limited potential for growth as we work to integrate instruction more fully into research-intensive courses.

Pedagogical Highlights

The content we teach in our instruction program is guided by a set of *Framework*-inspired learning outcomes. Following ACRL's 2015 filing of the *Framework*, we mapped our existing outcomes to the frames, drafted new outcomes to fill gaps we identified, and revised existing outcomes to reflect the *Framework*'s focus on conceptual understandings, the affective dimension of learning, and students' roles as content creators. Our outcomes consist of one overarching outcome derived from each frame with matching learning outcomes mapped to levels of student development (beginning/undergraduate, major/discipline, and graduate).

Information literacy is not specifically highlighted in our campus student learning outcomes, although many of the outcomes can be linked to information literacy. Our liberal education program includes a writing and information literacy requirement fulfilled by College Writing. Liberal education program requirements also state that liberally educated students "will be prepared to access, evaluate, and make use of information gathered through multiple methodologies."[11]

Within the library, we create a community of practice around teaching by emphasizing teaching and learning in the hiring and training process and providing ongoing training and support for librarians who teach. Candidates for librarian positions with teaching responsibilities complete teaching presentations that are open to all library staff members. This means that non–search committee staff feedback on candidates is primarily based on performance in the teaching presentation. Once hired, new librarians complete a training process designed to introduce them to our instruction program and their role in it. First, they complete a series of meetings with me to discuss our program's structure and goals, tools and resources to support their teaching, and logistics involved in developing and delivering instruction. Second, new librarians observe other librarians in the classroom. Finally, I arrange a time to observe new librarians teaching and offer feedback.

I make regular opportunities for support and discussion available to librarians who teach. During our busiest teaching weeks, I schedule optional, unstructured drop-in teaching prep sessions. Librarians who participate can request feedback on lesson plans, collaboratively design instruction, or work in the company of colleagues. At the beginning of each semester, we hold instruction-focused team meetings to discuss new approaches for teaching College Writing sessions and plan for the semester ahead. Toward the end of each semester, we hold debrief discussions that help us identify successful strategies and areas for improvement. I also make it clear that I am available to consult with librarians on the instructional design of their sessions, and librarians frequently drop by my office or schedule time to discuss lesson plans with me.

Based on librarian requests and changes like the release of the *Framework*, I offer additional training sessions on timely topics. This year, I facilitated a five-part training series on instructional design. In these sessions, librarians discussed learning theories that inform the *Framework* and created instruction plans based on the *Understanding by Design* approach to backward design.[12] I have also facilitated "jigsaw" article discussion sessions in which small groups of librarians read different articles on teaching and learning and share what they've learned with the rest of our team. This focus on ongoing learning and development builds a culture of collaboration and sense of shared purpose among teaching librarians, helping us continuously grow as educators.

Administrative Highlights

I complete detailed annual reports on our program statistics and present highlights from these reports at library all-staff meetings. These reports allow librarians to monitor changes in our programmatic and individual teaching loads, as well as the distribution of instruction by subject, course level, format, and location. These documents make our teaching efforts more visible to library administration and library colleagues outside our department. Beyond the library, our director discusses these reports with the Information Technology and Library Subcommittee of shared campus governance and the Executive Vice Chancellor for Academic Affairs, highlighting the scope of our instructional work for campus partners and leadership. Most importantly, these reports inspire discussion of big questions about our program within our team and with library leadership: How do we ensure that our growth is strategic and sustainable? What is a reasonable teaching load for a librarian? How does our growth impact our capacity for reflective practice as educators and our capacity to meet other job responsibilities?

In order to explore these questions and learn more about librarians' individual experiences beyond statistics, I held recent conversations with each teaching librarian about their teaching load and experiences with instruction. These discussions invited librarians to share how their teaching loads impact their approach to instruction and outreach to faculty. Librarians also reflected on their coverage of key courses in their subject areas and big-picture goals for instruction. These conversations generated valuable, informative feedback that complements the data I track in our annual statistical reports. While I'm proud of our team's enthusiasm for teaching and willingness to grow our program each year, these reports illustrate the challenges of workload and scale that our small team faces. Identifying these challenges has generated productive discussions with library administration about how we can work strategically to ensure that our program is sustainable.

Information Literacy Coordinator Profile

While information literacy has been a longstanding priority for UMD librarians, the instruction coordinator role has evolved over time, resulting in positive changes for me and our program. For many years, a liaison librarian with several competing responsibilities coordinated our program in an informal capacity. In 2009, the library formally defined the role and hired an instruction program coordinator. This position does not rotate. Teaching responsibilities are shared among teaching librarians and are not seen as the primary domain of the instruction coordinator. While not articulated in my job description, early in my career, I was expected to be the first to fill in for absent or unavailable colleagues. These coverage decisions are now made with availability, subject expertise, and teaching workload in mind.

When I was first hired into the position in 2011, instruction coordination was one part of a role that included significant liaison responsibilities. Although my original position description identified "leadership and direction in the planning, implementation, and evaluation of the library's information literacy instruction program" as a responsibility, it was clear that in practice, coordinating logistics for College Writing library instruction was the position's highest priority. After some time in the position, I began to view my role more expansively, understanding that I should seek opportunities to grow our program beyond the first year; guide our teaching practices proactively, rather than primarily coordinating logistics and responding to instructor requests; and support librarians' ongoing growth by facilitating regular learning opportunities.

Unfortunately, this clarity of purpose was not accompanied by time with which to make my goals a reality. While I still found my work rewarding, I felt frustrated by the ways in which my workload limited my capacity to work toward these priorities. As part of our 2016 library reorganization, every library staff member met individually with our library director to discuss our roles, including challenges we faced, what we liked best and least about our positions, and areas of opportunity we felt the library should pursue. This meeting allowed me to articulate how I could provide more support and leadership for our program in a redefined role. In what I think of as a significant turning point in my career, my desire to shift focus from logistics to leadership aligned with our library director's goal of providing more support for teaching and learning. Fortunate timing facilitated the shift of my departmental liaison, student engagement, and outreach responsibilities to new positions created as a result of retirements. My job title and duties were updated, increasing my role's emphasis on information literacy and assessment. In my position description, information literacy and assessment-related duties now account for roughly 60 percent of my responsibilities, increasing from 40 percent in my original position description. In my updated role, I can devote more time to the big-picture work of leading our program, rather than primarily keeping up with what Arellano Douglas and Gadsby characterize as day-to-day "housework" that keeps our program running.[13]

While my position now allows me a greater focus on information literacy, it still includes additional responsibilities like coordinating projects that assess user satisfaction with library services, facilities, and collections. In contrast to my original role, these activities often inform, rather than compete with, my work as instruction coordinator. For example, library website usability testing provides insight into students' approaches to the research process. Similarly, user satisfaction surveys help me understand students' feelings and attitudes about libraries and research, highlighting affective components that impact student engagement in learning experiences. While balancing these different aspects of my role remains challenging, I value the ways in which my responsibilities complement and enrich each other.

What I Wish People Knew

While I most enjoy the big-picture components of my role, many routine tasks are required to keep our program running. Most of my role's hidden labor involves coordinating the information literacy components of College Writing. My goal is to avoid becoming bogged down in logistical details while still completing the behind-the-scenes preparation for our involvement in this course. By taking responsibility for these necessary but mundane tasks, I hope to enable my colleagues to focus on collaborating with course instructors and working with students. Based on instructor requests submitted in an online scheduling form, I create a schedule that factors in librarians' teaching load and schedule preferences and matches librarians and instructors based on personality and teaching style whenever possible. In addition to scheduling, I prepare lesson plans; create templates for presentation slides and emails to instructors; reserve classroom space; design and print worksheets for activities; work with library systems and campus IT staff to resolve technology issues; and troubleshoot problems students encounter when sharing their online tutorial results with instructors. Whenever possible, I have streamlined this work by eliminating unnecessary handouts, altering activities to reduce printing and preparation, and working with library administration to simplify classroom booking.

As a new librarian in my first professional role, I had limited awareness of what this position would require, so in many ways, most of my growth as an instruction coordinator has been a surprise. While I had more teaching experience than many new graduates, I was still uncomfortable in the classroom and lacked confidence in my ability to effectively design instruction. By developing expertise for my individual teaching role, I have strengthened my ability to coordinate our program, collaborate with instructors, and serve as a resource for my colleagues who teach. While these skills and strengths positively impact our program, our success is contingent on our team as a whole. Our collective enthusiasm, willingness to learn together, and commitment to supporting students make our continued progress possible.

Discussing the potential of my role and our program with my library director during our reorganization helped initiate changes to my position. While our reorganization provided a convenient impetus for these conversations, instruction coordinators need not wait for an invitation to provide feedback. Documenting growth in our teaching activities, identifying areas of need based on student learning assessment results, and articulating the importance of alignment with the ACRL *Framework* all helped me make an effective case for change, demonstrating that there are many possible approaches to advocating for your program. Based on my experience, my advice for other instruction coordinators is to seek out opportunities to make your hidden labor visible. Advocate for what you need in order be an effective instruction coordinator and initiate conversations within your library about your program's future. Develop a vision of your program's purpose and potential, and articulate that vision in order to create a sense of shared purpose with your colleagues, library administration, and campus partners.

Notes

1. "Student Profile," University of Minnesota Duluth, accessed November 1, 2018, http://d.umn.edu/about-umd/student-profile.
2. "2017 All Student Profile," University of Minnesota Duluth, Office of Institutional Research, November 2017, http://www.d.umn.edu/vcaa/institutionalresearch/All_Student_Profile_2017.pdf.
3. "2017 All Student Profile."
4. "2017 All Student Profile."
5. "University of Minnesota Duluth Peer Institutions," University of Minnesota Duluth, Office of Institutional Research, accessed March 29, 2019, http://www.d.umn.edu/vcaa/institutionalresearch/OIR_CDB_Peer Institutions.html; "ACRLMetrics," Association of College and Research Libraries, accessed October 30, 2018, https://www.acrlmetrics.com.
6. "Publications," Project Information Literacy, accessed January 3, 2019, http://www.projectinfolit.org/publications.html.
7. "Library Instruction," Kathryn A. Martin Library, University of Minnesota Duluth, accessed October 31, 2018, https://lib.d.umn.edu/research-collections/library-instruction.
8. "University of Minnesota Duluth: Project Description," Assessment in Action, Association of College and Research Libraries, accessed January 9, 2019, https://apply.ala.org/aia/docs/project/13916.
9. Association of College and Research Libraries, *Framework for Information Literacy for Higher Education* (Chicago: Association of College and Research Libraries, 2016), http://www.ala.org/acrl/standards/ilframework; "VALUE Rubrics," Association of American Colleges and Universities, accessed January 9, 2019, https://www.aacu.org/value-rubrics.

10. "Topical Module: Experiences with Information Literacy," National Survey of Student Engagement, accessed November 1, 2018, http://nsse.indiana.edu/pdf/modules/2017/NSSE_2017_Experiences_with_Information_Literacy_Module.pdf.
11. "Liberal Education," University of Minnesota Duluth, accessed October 31, 2018, http://d.umn.edu/catalog/liberal-education.
12. Grant P. Wiggins and Jay McTighe, *Understanding by Design*, 2nd ed. (Alexandria, VA: Association for Supervision and Curriculum Development, 2005).
13. Veronica Arellano Douglas and Joanna Gadsby, "Gendered Labor and Library Instruction Coordinators: The Undervaluing of Feminized Work," in *At the Helm: Leading Transformation: ACRL 2017 Conference Proceedings*, ed. Dawn M. Mueller (Chicago: Association of College and Research Libraries, 2017), 270, http://www.ala.org/acrl/sites/ala.org.acrl/files/content/conferences/confsandpreconfs/2017/GenderedLaborandLibraryInstructionCoordinators.pdf.

Bibliography

Arellano Douglas, Veronica, and Joanna Gadsby. "Gendered Labor and Library Instruction Coordinators: The Undervaluing of Feminized Work." In *At the Helm: Leading Transformation: ACRL 2017 Conference Proceedings*. Edited by Dawn M. Mueller, 266–74. Chicago: Association of College and Research Libraries, 2017. http://www.ala.org/acrl/sites/ala.org.acrl/files/content/conferences/confsandpreconfs/2017/GenderedLaborandLibraryInstructionCoordinators.pdf.

Association of American Colleges and Universities. "VALUE Rubrics." Accessed January 9, 2019. https://www.aacu.org/value-rubrics.

Association of College and Research Libraries. "ACRLMetrics." Accessed October 30, 2018. https://www.acrlmetrics.com.

———. *Framework for Information Literacy for Higher Education*. Chicago: Association of College and Research Libraries, 2016. http://www.ala.org/acrl/standards/ilframework.

———. "University of Minnesota Duluth: Project Description." Assessment in Action. Accessed January 9, 2019. https://apply.ala.org/aia/docs/project/13916.

National Survey of Student Engagement. "Topical Module: Experiences with Information Literacy." Accessed November 1, 2018. http://nsse.indiana.edu/pdf/modules/2017/NSSE_2017_Experiences_with_Information_Literacy_Module.pdf.

Project Information Literacy. "Publications." Accessed January 3, 2019. http://www.projectinfolit.org/publications.html.

University of Minnesota Duluth. "Liberal Education." Accessed October 31, 2018. http://d.umn.edu/catalog/liberal-education.

———. "Library Instruction." Kathryn A. Martin Library. Accessed October 31, 2018. https://lib.d.umn.edu/research-collections/library-instruction.

———. "Student Profile." Accessed November 1, 2018. http://d.umn.edu/about-umd/student-profile.

———. "2017 All Student Profile." Office of Institutional Research. November 2017. http://www.d.umn.edu/vcaa/institutionalresearch/All_Student_Profile_2017.pdf.

———. "University of Minnesota Duluth Peer Institutions." Office of Institutional Research. Accessed March 20, 2019. http://www.d.umn.edu/vcaa/institutionalresearch/OIR_CDB_Peer Institutions.html.

Wiggins, Grant P., and Jay McTighe. *Understanding by Design*, 2nd ed. Alexandria, VA: Association for Supervision and Curriculum Development, 2005.

Chapter 19

University of New Hampshire

Renaissance in Action

Kathrine C. Aydelott

Population Served

The University of New Hampshire (UNH) is a public flagship, land sea and space grant, Carnegie-classed "Research High" institution of about 13,000 undergraduates and 2,400 graduate students in Durham, on the New Hampshire seacoast.[1] UNH students come from all fifty states and seventy countries. About 44 percent are from New Hampshire,[2] and many are first-generation students.[3] Nearly all first-year students and 56 percent of undergraduates live on campus, but much off-campus housing is in Durham, and students walk, skateboard, or moped to class; others take transportation from nearby communities. UNH has fewer than 1,000 international students, and fewer than 2,300 who list an ethnicity other than "White non-Hispanic."[4] In this regard, UNH's population resembles that of many other public institutions in northern New England.

Besides eleven of UNH's thirteen colleges and schools, the Durham campus houses the main Dimond Library and three branch libraries supporting STEM fields. In this chapter, *the library* means the Durham campus libraries collectively.[5] While the library's information literacy (IL) program aspires to address the lifelong learning needs of the community broadly, in practice more emphasis is placed on undergraduate support, specifically for first-year students, and secondarily on those involved in research at all levels.[6]

Program Scope

The history of information literacy at UNH is one of New England self-sufficiency and tradition, best summarized by New Hampshire's state motto, "Live Free or Die." There is no single authority responsible for IL at UNH; the decentralized and independent nature of campus means that IL may be taught in scattered pockets, but it is not codified, directed, or managed. Even the term *information literacy* is to some degree new: departmental faculty may incorporate elements of IL into their courses, but they might call it *research skills* or *critical thinking*; others may not have a specific term for it at all. The university's graduation requirements do not reference information literacy, and the general education curriculum does not have a stated IL outcome.

Although the library has a long history of providing instruction, as late as 2015, teaching was a concern secondary to reference service, with a traditional desk staffed only by librarians and workflows that supported this model. Four reference librarians taught "BI"—bibliographic instruction—which at its foundation consisted of providing support to approximately 120 face-to-face sessions per year in first-year English composition classes. As one-shots, these generally involved lecture-based database, library website, and catalog demonstrations. The rapid-fire pace of moving from interface to interface left each class of twenty-four students more shell-shocked than inspired. Because there was no attempt to catch classes throughout any department's curriculum, there was no scaffolding of skills for upper-level undergraduate or graduate courses; therefore, IL sessions for these students were more or less identical to first-year sessions. Nevertheless, the team taught in approximately 280 classes per year. The library's dedicated instruction room was arranged in fixed traditional rows with laptops tethered to the tables. The librarians had never incorporated the ACRL *Information Literacy Competency Standards for Higher Education.*[7] There was no assessment.

In 2014, I was hired to look at library instruction more programmatically. I quickly learned that change would be incremental as the professional identities of my colleagues were broadly built upon a vision of libraries the way they used to be. Evolution would be difficult without a dramatic cultural shift.

This occurred in 2016, when three of the librarians retired. The library mourned the loss of decades of collections and institutional knowledge, but we found ourselves in the enviable position to look across the IL landscape to collectively observe what others had been doing. I knew we had a lot of ground to make up. We needed a renaissance.

That effort began by hiring subject librarians rather than reference generalists. By adding librarians to specifically support the College of Health and Human Services (CHHS) and the Paul College of Business and Economics (PCBE), for example, we brought in disciplinary expertise and leveraged our new colleagues' teaching and technology skills. We hired a First-Year Instruction (FYI) Librarian dedicated to foundational-level support, including IL for the first-year English classes. And we built instruction capacity internally by breaking down silos that divided departments. Librarians outside of reference, such as the Scholarly Communications Librarian and the Collections Management Librarian, had been shut out from instruction even as they exercised other liaison responsibilities for specific disciplines. We empowered these librarians to expand their liaison work to include reference and IL instruction and supported them in their early teaching. From a team of four, we became a new team of fifteen. We began a phase-out of librarians on the quiet reference desk and moved to a triaged service model with staff and students. Finally, we broke up the traditional rows in the instruction room, untethered the laptops, and moved the tables into pods to create a flexible, adaptable teaching space where group work and hands-on learning could occur. We were now positioned to shift from an inward-facing service institution to an outward-facing campus partner.

In 2019, from my position as Information Literacy Librarian, I can say that our IL program has been reborn. It still largely serves the undergraduate population, and first-year students in particular, but we have expanded our foundational reach beyond English. We have piloted an embedded librarian initiative with CHHS, and librarians have signature roles in PCBE's First-Year Innovation and Research Experience (FIRE) program. The Head of Special Collections teaches hands-on primary source activities to introductory history classes. We have pioneered gamified IL and badging programs.

Beyond our first-year efforts, librarians have begun building partnerships to support more upper-level undergraduate and graduate-level classes. We have incorporated more active learning and developed more online modules and self-paced tools. Our sessions now feature interactive survey games using the online tool Mentimeter, and "jigsaw" small-group work and student presentations. We teach at a distance with the web conferencing tool Zoom, and we partner with library colleagues to teach face-to-face in the disciplines.

Further, we have expanded our IL offerings to include a series of workshops and brown-bag lunchtime discussions each semester that are aimed variously at faculty, staff, and students. Topics have addressed citation management programs, GIS software, financial literacy, data management, open access, OER (open educational resources), and understanding ACRL's *Framework for Information Literacy for Higher Education*.[8] Attendance at these events has been uneven and often low, but feedback from attendees has been positive, and we have a growth mind-set.

Today, the library's IL program remains the only concerted effort on campus, but it is now better positioned than ever to partner with and expand upon the distributed efforts of others at UNH who incorporate information literacy into their teaching and learning initiatives.

Operations

Lean for UNH's size, the library has a dean, associate dean, assistant dean, fifteen librarians, and a staff of about forty-two. The library also relies heavily on student workers to supplement its staffing, and employs nearly eighty per year.

Operating staff report to PAT-level (professional, administrative, technical) staff, but with the exception of Dean's Office staff reporting to the assistant dean, all other staff in what had been nine units ultimately report to five librarians. A 2017 reorganization brought these units under the umbrella of five divisions: Special Collections and Archives; Academic and Community Engagement; Research and Learning Services; Resource Acquisition and Discovery; and Technology, Scholarship and Publishing. The five librarians who supervise were further appointed as division heads, creating a de facto middle-management layer serving as a link among divisions to promote communication, collaboration, and coordination between what had been very siloed units. Division heads also act as links between the divisions and the Dean's Office, "translating strategy and vision into daily operations."[9]

Fourteen of the librarians have full tenure-track faculty status and are unionized with the broader UNH faculty; the FYI Librarian is non-tenure-track and on an extended three-year term position. Currently, seven librarians (50%) are on the tenure track and must master the duties outlined in their position descriptions as well as participating in scholarship and service, including regular project and committee work both internal and external to the library. If they don't already come in with one, a second master's degree is also required before the sixth year in order to qualify for tenure.[10] Librarians report to the dean through an elected faculty chair. Faculty members do not supervise other faculty members; therefore, librarians have broad autonomy over their work to exercise academic freedom and teach as they see fit, based on their knowledge and in collaboration with faculty in academic departments. Several librarians are shouldering responsibilities that normally would be divided into separate positions.

All of the tenure-track librarians have liaison assignments, consisting of reference and IL instruction support, communications, and collection development. As in the case of the Business Librarian, some assignments directly align with the position and expertise for which a librarian was hired. Some librarians have liaison assignments in addition to the more operational or functional work for which they were hired, as is the case of the Head of Cataloging, who must support one or more departments in the midst of her other work. Because the library strives to assign at least one librarian to every college and increasingly to various populations, offices, and schools, we struggle to align departments with librarian expertise and to support all programs equitably. We all wear many hats. In my case, I am Information Literacy Librarian with a broad functional role to oversee instruction and IL initiatives; I am liaison to the English department with all intended communication, collections, and discipline-specific IL instruction responsibilities; I supervise a staff member and oversee reference service; and I am Division Head for Research and Learning Services; I am also in my fifth year on the tenure track.

Given that all librarians are expected to perform instruction, the IL program is distributed throughout the library, but it is concentrated in the division of Research and Learning Services, to which eight librarians and one staff member are assigned. The staff position, the Research and Instructional Services Coordinator (RISC), was created in 2016 to begin to shift legacy workloads in reference and instruction away from faculty. The RISC manages reference service, supervises and trains students, works with the FYI Librarian to coordinate IL support for the English Composition classes, and implements and maintains reference and instruction-related tools, such as those in the Springshare suite.[11] In 2018, I expanded the RISC's position responsibilities to include assisting the FYI Librarian in foundational-level IL instruction.

Within this complex and high-workload environment, IL instruction is broadly unstructured and practice varies among librarians to a large degree. Some of the dedicated liaisons have been extraordinarily successful in building relationships in the short time they have been here; others, particularly those with more functional roles and operational responsibilities, struggle to prioritize liaison and IL work or have yet to find recurring IL partners. Depending upon the success of their individual initiatives, some may teach dozens of classes per semester, and others may not teach all year.

The IL program has no budget, and library funding at UNH generally is tightening. Library administration supports the IL program by urging all librarians, not just subject specialists, to actively seek out suitable partners for embedded instruction and IL assessment. Combine primary professional responsibilities with the tenure-track responsibilities for active engagement in the profession, including publishing, presenting, and service work, and it's understandable that tensions arise between the administration and the library faculty in balancing all of these activities.

Marketing

The face-to-face one-shot support for first-year English classes is a long-standing legacy program that largely runs itself without having to solicit participation; PCBE's FIRE program has its own marketing initiatives. Beyond these two programs, we continue to search for instruction opportunities across the curriculum through our liaison channels. In most cases, an IL opportunity with a new faculty partner is likely to be a one-shot.

Collaboration

Collaboration is essential for furthering our revitalized efforts. I have partnered variously with Academic Technology and the University Writing Program to include IL opportunities in programs sponsored by these offices. UNH's Center for Excellence and Innovation in Teaching and Learning (CEITL) has also been a supportive partner. Last year CEITL formed a steering committee with membership from these aforementioned partners, along with the library, the Graduate School, and the Center for Academic Resources. Together we meet monthly to share information about our initiatives and to better understand the teaching and learning environment across campus. CEITL also began a Certificate of Participation program that has already enrolled more than 140 faculty and graduate students from across campus: participants accrue points toward a certificate that demonstrates "a commitment to promote the highest quality of student learning through implementation of best practices in college teaching."[12] The library's eligible offerings, including brown-bag discussions introducing the ACRL *Framework*, award points in this program. When enrolled in the program, librarians can also earn points for teaching eligible sessions.

The relationship with CEITL not only facilitates increased communication and collaboration, but also allows the library to share in CEITL's extensive and well-established email lists for marketing our events linked to IL, teaching, and learning. We see this partnership as essential for highlighting our IL work, increasing participation in our extracurricular instruction offerings, and elevating our position on campus as a partner in providing educational opportunities. As a result, CEITL is helping to bestow legitimacy on the library's IL efforts after a long period of relative invisibility.

Assessment

Assessment has been one of our biggest challenges, in part because UNH does not yet have a campus-wide culture of assessment. The university is accredited under the New England Commission of Higher Education (NECHE), and most colleges also have their own assessment bodies that dictate standards and practices.[13] As two NECHE standards do reference information literacy,[14] the library did participate on the committee advising UNH on its five-year self-study in 2017, and UNH included the library's instruction numbers as one of the only data points available for demonstrating attention to this area.

Comprehensively assessing our one-shots, particularly at the foundational level, has been challenging. In 2014, an early project to assess English composition students' retention of our IL instruction was derailed: I was told by the program coordinator that library faculty could neither assign "[the English Department] students" homework before our IL sessions nor assess them afterwards. Since that time, efforts have been sporadic. On a campus without broader directives, the librarians' academic freedom has meant having the ability to assess or not based on their own reflective practices. As many of the librarians are still new to their liaison assignments, and no assessment had been done earlier, most have been working to build relationships with departmental faculty with the expectation that further assessment efforts will be initiated as partnerships develop.

I am currently in discussion with CEITL to collaborate under a grant from the Davis Educational Foundation to create an information literacy module in UNH's learning management system, Canvas, that will teach and assess information literacy skills as a way to demonstrate the library's impact on student learning. The grant was awarded funding in December 2018.

Role of the One-Shot

One-shots are still our bread and butter. Today, they are much more geared toward active, participatory learning, but many are still tool-based to some degree, as tool-based demo is still what many UNH faculty think of when they think of the library—a legacy perspective we are eager to amend. We actively negotiate with our departmental colleagues to look for new ways to move beyond the one-shot to more integrated IL instruction. We have one strong, embedded relationship with PCBE's FIRE program; others have been piloted but may or may not continue based on departmental initiatives and faculty interest.

Pedagogical Highlights

UNH's IL program has changed so dramatically in three years that many elements have already been mentioned in this chapter, but two pedagogical highlights stand out. In 2017, and based on the Writing Center model of helping walk-in students with their writing, we began a program of First-Year Research Drop-In Sessions. Scheduled in the instruction room for two hours a day, twice a week, these are sessions where first-year students—and anyone who walks in—can get one-on-one help from a librarian without an appointment. We advertise these sessions widely and specifically to the first-year programs we already work with. Students come as individuals or in groups, stay for a few minutes or hang out for forty-five. The service provides students with agency to get point-of-need assistance, and the open invitation allays some of the anxiety that can come from having to ask for help at a service desk. The program is already successful and is growing in popularity with both students and faculty. The service also has allowed us to begin shifting our face-to-face instruction for English to a less labor-intensive, more sustainable model that will incorporate a variety of modes for this introductory instruction.

The library has also pioneered gamified IL instruction and badging on UNH's campus. Beginning in 2015, librarians were given opportunities to create information-literacy-themed mini-games that were awarded points as part of PCBE's FIRE program. Games have evolved from a web-based "unlock the door"-style IL game designed around finding journal articles and discovering a secret "key" to a game where a badge is awarded automatically to students who complete a series of short information-literacy-themed modules. The FYI Librarian and the Business Librarian investigated badging platforms, designed the games and badges, and worked to incorporate them into the Canvas system. The FIRE badging modules have issued over 500 badges in two years and were broadened in 2018–19 with an additional business-focused module and badge. A first-year English badging module premiered this year and has already issued 150 badges. We believe it's possible to expand this delivery method for IL instruction to other departments and colleges as well.

Information Literacy Coordinator Profile

My position doesn't place me at the top of a hierarchy with direct authority over IL instruction; instead, my role is best described as first among peers. I look at my management style as something akin to what Vineet Nayar described as "more like a racetrack where each [individual] can compete successfully" based on four fundamental ideas:

1. **Overlapping goals.** Goals will have significant overlaps; each individual and each team understands that they are pursuing one collective organizational goal.
2. **Role linkages.** Each individual, team, and function will play a distinct role in the race while also supporting each other's roles. Every individual has to be clear about how the individual, team, and organizational roles are linked.
3. **Constant collaboration.** At the foundation of this model is the fact that no one individual or team can win the race alone. They will win only if they play their roles to perfection and help others that they're linked to.
4. **Continuous reinvention.** Teams will continuously process new data, creating a landscape of learning and realignment across levels.[15]

My colleagues and I work together to identify overlapping goals, many of which have thus far formed around foundational first-year instruction. I work to leverage role linkages, the best example of which is the role the FYI Librarian plays with the Business Librarian to form a bridge between foundational first-year support in FIRE and upper-level IL in the college. We constantly collaborate, with other librarians taking the lead to build tutorials or to share new active-learning approaches. And the program is under continuous reinvention as the library landscape and the campus climate continue to change.

Three years out from the 2016 retirements that relaunched the IL program, the new librarians have found their footing individually, and we are now coming together as a whole to begin developing a community of practice around teaching. We have begun recasting our IL program as less a series of "liaison activities, including instruction" to a curriculum-based program using the ACRL *Framework* to develop learning outcomes for each of our areas, allowing us to rethink what we do as librarians. This work has just begun, but is generating excitement as we work together toward a more holistic approach to IL instruction and contemporary librarianship. Further, I currently hold the role of vice chair of the university committee that oversees and manages UNH's general education program. As the ten-year review of that curriculum nears in 2020, I am advocating through this faculty body for the inclusion of information literacy as a critical element of that program.

What I Wish People Knew

Challenges to our program remain legion. Working outside of a top-down, delta-shaped, hierarchical model, my energies are more outward-facing, toward campus, than inward-facing toward my librarian colleagues. The labor, then, is sometimes seen more by faculty on campus than by my dean. It is difficult to bring about cultural change, and I often wish we in the library were more integrated as an IL body. And yet, we have moved the program significantly forward in a short three years, and in that time, we have already raised IL awareness both in the library and on campus. I am confident that as our renaissance continues we will forge new partnerships that will lead to richer, more robust IL opportunities.

Notes

1. In January 2019, UNH was granted Carnegie Classification R1, "Doctoral Universities—Very high research activity," for the first time.
2. "Facts and Figures," University of New Hampshire, accessed September 28, 2018, https://www.unh.edu/main/facts-figures.
3. UNH doesn't currently track first-generation students specifically.
4. "Common Data Set," Office of Institutional Research, University of New Hampshire, accessed January 15, 2019, https://www.unh.edu/institutional-research/common-data-set.
5. In this chapter, references to UNH and the IL program reflect the Durham campus only. The libraries at UNH-Manchester and UNH Law have their own information literacy programs and initiatives.
6. Besides teaching, research, and clinical faculty, UNH has one of the largest undergraduate research conferences in the US. See "Undergraduate Research Conference," University of New Hampshire, accessed November 25, 2019, https://www.unh.edu/urc.
7. Association of College and Research Libraries, *Information Literacy Competency Standards for Higher Education* (Chicago: Association of College and Research Libraries, 2000), https://alair.ala.org/handle/11213/7668.
8. Association of College and Research Libraries, *Framework for Information Literacy for Higher Education* (Chicago: Association of College and Research Libraries, 2016), http://www.ala.org/acrl/standards/ilframework.
9. Kimberly Sweetman, "Our Charge," Division Heads Group, University of New Hampshire Libraries, Durham, NH, 2017. Division heads were appointed to an initial three-year term, and this work is estimated to amount to 20 percent of their workload.
10. Librarian promotion and tenure documents differ only slightly from those for UNH's departmental faculty and are available here: Library Promotion and Tenure Committee, *Criteria and Procedures for the Promotion and Tenure of Library Faculty*, report (Durham: University of New Hampshire, 2017), https://scholars.unh.edu/library_docs/1.
11. The library has had LibGuides since 2009, but since 2016 has implemented LibCal and LibAnswers, including LibChat, and has relaunched use of RefAnalytics.

12. Center for Excellence and Innovation in Teaching and Learning, "CEITL Participation Certificate Program," University of New Hampshire, 2017, https://www.unh.edu/cetl/ceitl-participation-certificate-program.
13. For example, PCBE is accredited independently under the Association to Advance Collegiate Schools of Business.
14. New England Commission of Higher Education, "Standards for Accreditation," July 1, 2016, https://cihe.neasc.org/standards-policies/standards-accreditation/standards-effective-july-1-2016. See specifically 4.12: Assuring Academic Quality and 4.15: Undergraduate Degree Programs.
15. Vineet Nayar, "Don't Let Outdated Management Structures Kill Your Company," *Harvard Business Review*, February 10, 2016, https://hbr.org/2016/02/dont-let-outdated-management-structures-kill-your-company.

Bibliography

Association of College and Research Libraries. *Framework for Information Literacy for Higher Education.* Chicago: Association of College and Research Libraries, 2016. http://www.ala.org/acrl/standards/ilframework.

———. *Information Literacy Competency Standards for Higher Education.* Chicago: Association of College and Research Libraries, 2000. https://alair.ala.org/handle/11213/7668.

Center for Excellence and Innovation in Teaching and Learning. "CEITL Participation Certificate Program." University of New Hampshire. 2017. https://www.unh.edu/cetl/ceitl-participation-certificate-program.

Library Promotion and Tenure Committee. *Criteria and Procedures for the Promotion and Tenure of Library Faculty.* Report. Durham: University of New Hampshire, 2017. https://scholars.unh.edu/library_docs/1.

Nayar, Vineet. "Don't Let Outdated Management Structures Kill Your Company." *Harvard Business Review*, February 10, 2016. https://hbr.org/2016/02/dont-let-outdated-management-structures-kill-your-company.

New England Commission of Higher Education. "Standards for Accreditation." July 1, 2016. https://cihe.neasc.org/standards-policies/standards-accreditation/standards-effective-july-1-2016.

Sweetman, Kimberly. "Our Charge." Division Heads Group, University of New Hampshire Libraries, Durham, NH. 2017.

University of New Hampshire. "Common Data Set." Office of Institutional Research. Accessed January 15, 2019. https://www.unh.edu/institutional-research/common-data-set.

———. "Facts and Figures." Accessed September 28, 2018. https://www.unh.edu/main/facts-figures.

———. "Undergraduate Research Conference." Accessed November 25, 2019. https://www.unh.edu/urc.

Chapter 20

University of Southern California

Building Consensus over Time

Elizabeth Galoozis

Population Served

The University of Southern California (USC) is a private, doctoral-granting research university located in Los Angeles, California, with 20,000 undergraduate and 27,000 graduate students. Twenty-three percent of students come from countries other than the United States.[1] USC is made up of twenty-two graduate and professional schools, along with the Dornsife College of Letters, Arts, and Sciences (which comprises thirty-six departments and programs). Among the most popular undergraduate majors are business, engineering, international relations, and communication.[2] Online/distance education takes place only within graduate programs, so all of our undergraduate course-related instruction takes place in person. Many of USC's operations—for example, advising and admissions—are situated within individual schools. This can make it challenging to identify common experiences among all students.

Undergraduates' six-year graduation rate has held steady at 92 percent for the four years preceding the writing of this chapter,[3] so for the most part, students progress from introductory to senior-level classes at similar rates. USC admits a high number of transfer students, almost one-third of new undergraduates.[4] Our program needs to adjust to serve transfer students better, because they don't always take the writing class that our undergraduate information literacy instruction focuses on. USC is also admitting an increasingly higher number of first-generation college students, leading to the establishment of First-Generation Success Workshops for both first-year and transfer students.[5] Librarians have been working to tailor programming for these students.

Almost all first-year students live on campus in residential housing; many more students live in the surrounding area. Only about 10 percent of students are commuters.[6] And despite the number of students, the geographical footprint of the (main) University Park Campus is relatively small. Therefore, when we do on-campus programming, we can be relatively sure we are reaching a large percentage of students. We are often asked to participate in information literacy instruction for K–12 schools associated with the university; programs that take place on campus, such as Upward Bound; and students in the Leslie and William McMorrow Neighborhood Academic Initiative, a precollege prep program for students from South and East Los Angeles.[7]

Program Scope

The information literacy (IL) program described in this chapter includes the undergraduate and graduate academic programs on USC's main campus. USC's Health Sciences Campus, which comprises most of the university's faculty and graduate students and is about seven miles away from the main campus, is covered by a different program. Our Special Collections department works intensively with many classes; their work is also not covered in this chapter. Our IL program focuses mostly on foundational courses at both the undergraduate and graduate levels. Instruction at the undergraduate level is guided by a set of information literacy outcomes for undergraduates, built around the six frames of the ACRL *Framework for Information Literacy for Higher Education* and agreed upon by library faculty and staff through a formal process of consensus and a final vote.[8] Foundational undergraduate experiences include courses in the Writing Program, orientation, and lower-level courses across majors, which are discussed below.

At the undergraduate level, USC Libraries has a longstanding relationship with the Writing Program, specifically with two of its courses that teach processes of research and culminate in research-based writing assignments. WRIT 150 (Writing and Critical Reasoning), which students must take by the time they earn sixty credits (typically within their first year), is offered in ten different "thematics," such as Identity and Diversity and Issues in Law and Social Justice, and focuses on rhetorical strategies. WRIT 340 (Advanced Writing), which students can take any time but usually do so in their junior or senior year, focuses on writing in nine disciplinary categories, such as Social Sciences and Visual and Performing Arts. The majority of the undergraduate instruction we do is for WRIT 150 and WRIT 340. We teach sessions for about 65 percent of the roughly 200 WRIT 150 sections offered each academic year, and more avail themselves of IL instructional activities on our website (though we don't have a good mechanism for keeping track of those integrations). We have developed shared IL outcomes for WRIT 150 with the Writing Program and focus on these outcomes in our instruction sessions:

- Develop a strategic search plan
- Demonstrate an understanding of citation style in order to track a scholarly conversation

· Identify the purpose, audience, and context of various information sources[9]

Other courses we focus on in the first year are CORE 112, which students in the
Thematic Option (Honors) program take instead of WRIT 150 (we usually teach 100%
of the fifteen or so sections offered each spring), and the General Education Seminar, a
required first-year course introduced in 2015, which varies widely in topic and is meant
as an introduction to a group of disciplines. The size of all of these classes is limited, and
usually capped at either fifteen or nineteen.

The rest of our course-related instruction is highly dependent on the libraries' liaison
program, which is described in more detail in the Operations section. Our reach into
majors and programs depends on curriculum, liaison relationships, or both. Programs
in social work, for example, are extremely prescribed and have lent themselves to deep
embedding of information literacy. Capstone and thesis work across schools are well
supported through the liaison program. Curriculum mapping and other efforts have tried
to connect better to gateway courses within majors and to General Education–designated
courses. These efforts have been slow to take hold in a truly programmatic way, partly
because of a long-standing culture of individualist approaches by liaison librarians and
partly because of turnover in both the libraries and academic departments, but they are
taking hold.

New student orientation happens mostly in the schools and departments for graduate students and through a university-level orientation program for undergraduates.
The libraries offer optional workshops (focused on library services and resources) for
all new undergraduate and graduate students and staff a table at student services fairs
during orientation, but these efforts are not systematic enough to rely on students having
a consistent base level of knowledge. General library workshops offered at other times of
the year have had very low attendance; successful workshops target either specific skills
or audiences. For example, our Social Sciences Data Librarian and Visualization Specialist offer workshops on data management and mapping, and a group of librarians offers
a very popular series of workshops aimed at international students that explains library
services and resources. Our instruction program also works with cocurricular and partner
programs, such as executive courses in the Marshall School of Business, the American
Language Institute (which prepares students whose primary language is not English), and
affiliated K–12 programs.

While librarians have always made online tutorials individually, the instruction team
has recently taken more ownership and direction over this mode of instruction. In 2018,
spurred by a revision of the libraries' website, we formed a Tutorials Working Group with
several liaison librarians and other staff in order to create best practices, provide software
training for librarians, and create consistent tutorials about information literacy concepts
rather than specific resources.

Operations

USC Libraries have responded to the school-based structure of the university with a traditional liaison program, in addition to a growing number of functional specialists. Liaisons
are attached to a school or program and have responsibilities for reference, instruction,

collection development, and outreach to support those schools. Functional specialists often support multiple schools in areas of need such as data services. All liaison librarians are in the Public Services Division of the libraries and report through various hierarchies to the Associate Dean of Public Services. Most people who participate in instruction are faculty in the libraries, on either a continuing appointment (aka tenure) track or a short-term contract. Some staff, and occasionally interns or fellows, also participate in instruction. Public Services librarians are expected to participate in what is often termed at USC "general" reference, instruction, and orientation outside courses and students in their designated majors and programs. In terms of instruction, this mostly consists of the Writing Program instruction described above.

The instruction team consists of the Head of Information Literacy (the author of this chapter) and the Instructional Design and Assessment Librarian, both of whom report to the Assistant Dean for Instruction, Assessment, and Engagement, who in turn reports to the Associate Dean for Strategic Initiatives. Briefly speaking, I, as the Head of Information Literacy, coordinate the IL program; the Instructional Design and Assessment Librarian heads up teaching development and orientation; and the Assistant Dean for Instruction, Assessment, and Engagement oversees assessment and provides direction for the team. Intermittently, the instruction team is assisted by a part-time student worker who helps with scheduling and statistics. While the two instruction team librarians sometimes take on collection or liaison responsibilities, it is not a focus of our positions.

Since 2016, the small instruction team has been in a completely separate division from Public Services, Programs and Planning, which also includes the libraries' communication, grants, and events staff, along with the university's master's program in library and information science and the Sidney Harman Academy for Polymathic Study, an interdisciplinary research center. The advantages of being in a separate department from most of the librarians we work with include separate funding and administration; in contrast to Public Services, we do not oversee physical library spaces. Another benefit is that many projects and initiatives at the libraries are accomplished through cross-departmental task forces or working groups, so working across departments to implement information literacy instruction is not culturally unusual. For example, there is no head of reference or reference department; policies and schedules are set by a reference task force, on which I serve. One disadvantage is that we are not always included in Public Services information distribution, decision-making, or organizational shifts. Information tends to get to us informally through relationships, rather than formally through the leadership structure. The culture in the libraries is one of independence. Librarians feel very strongly about our status as faculty and the perceived freedom afforded by that status. In a large, distributed system with an independent culture, sometimes outreach and instruction efforts are duplicated.

Most classes that are not WRIT 150, WRIT 340, or GE seminars are arranged between liaison librarians and course instructors. Class requests that are not individually arranged come through a Request a Class form, which goes to a dedicated email account managed by the instruction team. Instructors are asked to allow at least seven business days before the date of their request. Besides logistical questions like time and number of students, instructors are asked "What would you like your students to learn from the session?"; are provided with a link to Undergraduate Information Literacy Learning Outcomes; and can upload documents such as assignments and syllabi.

Working from a spreadsheet of teaching librarians, a student worker schedules the class in the library instruction account's Outlook calendar and invites a librarian. Librarians can accept or reject the request or propose the alternate time indicated in the request. Librarians are periodically polled on availability and preferred thematics for WRIT 150. The spreadsheet also helps to keep track of how many classes librarians are teaching. The two librarians on the instruction team should teach up to ten sections per semester; liaison librarians should teach no more than five. We are constantly trying to improve this system based on feedback from librarians and instructors. The libraries do not at the time of writing have a dedicated library-based classroom, though construction is concluding on two of them. Librarians generally go to the classroom where the course takes place and use our laptops to project, and schedule instruction in library spaces upon request. (More on this in the Administrative Highlights section.)

Marketing

One-shots are actively marketed through
- emailing new GE seminar instructors at the beginning of each semester
- presenting about instruction to the Writing Program faculty meetings at the beginning of each semester
- contributing to the Center for Excellence in Teaching's monthly newsletter (which is a marketing tool for other library resources and services as well)
- using liaison outreach (which varies by liaison)

Some liaisons are more embedded in their departments' curricula than others; in particular, the librarians serving the Marshall School of Business have long-standing embedded relationships with several courses, including the business-themed WRIT 340 class. Instruction of all kinds is informally marketed through conversations at university events. For example, I attended a reception in fall 2018 for new and promoted faculty, chatted with a new instructor in the English department who asked about what I do, and ended up scheduling instruction for her class.

Collaboration

Like other IL programs, our biggest ally on campus is the Writing Program, described earlier in this chapter. We have developed a much closer relationship with USC's Center for Excellence in Teaching (CET) since the introduction in 2018 of a provost-level initiative called Excellence in Teaching, aimed at improving and valuing teaching across the university.[10] As part of this initiative, each school and department, including the libraries, has been charged with developing its own definition of excellence in teaching and with weaving evaluation of teaching into its peer review and promotion processes.[11] (More on this process in the Pedagogical Highlights section.) As part of this initiative, the CET has developed a Faculty Fellow Leadership Institute to train teacher-leaders in each school and department in pedagogical training for the rest of their faculty.[12] The Head of Education and Social Work Library Services and I are both completing a year in the first cohort of this institute in 2018–19, and more library faculty will join the second cohort. This institute has been enormously helpful in promoting understanding of pedagogical issues and in developing a shared language around pedagogy across the university.

The Instructional Design and Assessment Librarian maintains close relationships with both the university's Writing Center and the Office of Orientation Programs. The libraries are involved in campus-wide undergraduate and graduate orientation programming, though our programming—workshops during the week leading up to the first day of class and tabling at student services fairs—is optional for students. The libraries and the Writing Center have worked together on workshops and are currently working on an online tutorial about research topic design. The Instructional Design and Assessment Librarian also worked with the director of the Writing Center to create a research guide, for writing tutors to use, of frequently-used databases in the Writing Program.[13]

Within the libraries, one of our strongest allies is a reference and instruction librarian who focuses on new students, particularly first-generation students, and has strong ties to cultural centers on campus. We work with her to reach these populations through collaborating on instruction and occasional workshops and outreach events. We also collaborate often with the librarians who lead Special Collections' instruction program. For example, we met with them to discuss the ramifications of the *Guidelines for Primary Source Literacy* on our own learning outcomes,[14] and we try to ensure that their department is represented in instructional committees and task forces.

In 2017, my title changed from Information Literacy and Educational Technology Librarian to Head of Information Literacy, which came with additional administrative responsibilities. Though this title change may seem small, I believe it has led to different partnerships. For example, information literacy is a core competency in our accrediting body, the Western Association of Schools and Colleges (WASC). With 2020 accreditation coming up, an administrator from the provost's office emailed me to discuss a collaboration (described in the Assessment Section), which I believe happened in part because of this new title.

Finally, the instruction team, along with other librarians, joined a group of graduate students who formed an Antiracist Pedagogy Collective after the 2016 presidential election to provide resources and venues for discussion of antiracist pedagogical methods and concepts. We created a research guide together,[15] and during the 2018–19 school year, we hosted a series of discussions for any teaching faculty or students interested.[16]

Assessment

Overall, session-based assessment varies according to the librarian teaching and tends to be formative. As part of the Excellence in Teaching initiative described above, librarians who teach will need to include a Teaching Reflection Statement in their annual reviews beginning in January 2020. Formative assessment is meant to inform the content of these statements, so as part of the initiative, I put together a group in spring 2019 to structure and oversee peer teaching observation and feedback.

There are several larger summative assessment projects happening as well. The Assistant Dean for Instruction, Assessment, and Engagement is a primary investigator in a large, multi-institutional study on the effect of library instruction methods on student GPA and is working on a similar study of USC-level data.[17] Also at the time of writing, the instruction team is in the assignment collection phase of an assessment project for the core competency of information literacy as part of the university's accreditation process for 2020. We will be assessing finished student work in order to demonstrate achievement of information literacy as operationalized in a rubric based on undergraduate information literacy outcomes in 2019 and 2020.

We have also undertaken assessment projects specific to the key courses we work with. Each spring, we have asked librarians teaching WRIT 150 to submit artifacts of active learning from their classes; for example, collaborative online spreadsheets where students track search terms. A small rotating group of librarians assesses these artifacts according to a rubric based on the WRIT 150 learning outcomes, and we use this to make adjustments to instructional practice and the scope of our lesson plans. We are planning to change this up in coming years to focus more deeply on one outcome each spring. And finally, I am involved in an assessment project for the CORE 112 class at the time of writing, in which a group of librarians and instructors will score finished papers, along with a pre- and posttest, to gauge growth of learning in information literacy over the semester.

Pedagogical Highlights

One major pedagogical highlight is the Libraries' Information Literacy Course Enhancement Grant Program. This program started as a one-year Dean's Challenge Grant, a USC Libraries grant that aims to encourage innovation in the libraries, and has since been supported financially through the libraries' Department of Programs and Planning. Any faculty member or graduate student teaching a course can apply for "the opportunity for disciplinary faculty to collaborate with librarians, acting as instructional designers, to infuse a course or major assignment sequence with information literacy,"[18] which also comes with a stipend. In 2018, we also added a Primary Source track, in which Special Collections librarians enact the same collaboration using the Society for American Archivists' *Guidelines for Primary Source Literacy* and USC's primary resource collections.[19] Since 2015, we have worked with several courses, including schools and departments as diverse as dance, Spanish, architecture, anthropology, international relations, social work, and history.[20] The grants have helped to attract instructors who have not necessarily seen the value of "library instruction" per se, but are interested in redesigning syllabi and assignments to bolster students' information literacy skills.

Creating a community of practice can be challenging with a large, dispersed group of teaching librarians. In the past, the team has held regular "kickoffs" at the beginning of the year, along with teaching exchanges where librarians share techniques or approaches with their colleagues. After adopting the libraries' Definition of Excellence in Teaching in December 2018 (see appendix), the Instructional Design and Assessment Librarian and I have begun offering a series of highly interactive workshops aimed at different elements of the definition. The two well-attended workshops held so far have been

- "Beginning Learning Assessment," which addresses these elements:
    - Articulates goals and learning outcomes for information literacy instruction, and makes these explicit during the course of instruction
    - Demonstrates effectiveness of instruction through assessment of defined learning outcomes

- Uses assessment of the success and impact of learning experiences to make appropriate adjustments in order to improve student engagement and learning
- "Connecting with Students: Incorporating Learners' Identities into the Teaching Process," which addresses these elements:
  - Includes students' strengths, interests, experiences, and identities in the learning process
  - Encourages student curiosity, exploration, and self-directed learning
  - Engages with students in a non-judgmental manner of mutual regard and respect
  - Respectfully expresses curiosity about the histories and lived experiences of underrepresented cultures and groups
  - Applies multiple techniques and strategies to reach all students using culturally responsive teaching

The Instructional Design and Assessment Librarian also offers a regular series of discussions around principles and methods of evidence-based instructional design, documented in infographics available on the libraries' website.[21] In addition, an instruction librarian in Special Collections and I have coordinated small, opt-in communities of practice called Instructional Learning Communities (ILCs) since 2017. We have experimented with the structure every year, but ILCs always involve coming together regularly over the course of a semester to discuss readings or reflect on instructional strategies.

While lesson plans and activities are not standardized, many librarians draw from an online instructional repository, a shared Google Drive folder of lesson plans, activities, handouts, and readings for common classes. Anyone can contribute to the repository, which is arranged by information literacy outcome, and is an expansion of a smaller set of templates developed by a previous colleague.

Administrative Highlights

One program I am proud of is our team's growing participation in the libraries' annual Research Award. Originally an award for students using USC primary resources in research papers, it has grown as instruction team members were invited by Special Collections' instruction coordinator to expand the scope of submissions (undergraduates can use any library resources or services) and to redesign the rubric used to score submissions. We helped to bolster the number and variety of subjects represented in submissions by soliciting submissions from instructors whose classes had received library instruction. The year 2018 marked a record number of submissions, and the reflective essays required as part of the submission serve as a qualitative assessment of the effect of library instruction and other library services and resources on students' development as researchers.[22]

I'm proud of the way we have shifted from having dedicated library instruction space (that was remodeled and is now used by another campus department) to teaching primarily via laptops in the classrooms where regular class meetings take place. There are advantages to entering a class environment that students are already comfortable with, and it helps to debunk the stereotype of libraries as buildings only.

What I Wish People Knew

This is my second position as a coordinator, and while some issues and responsibilities are similar (like balancing curriculum needs with number of staff), I was surprised at how different the job was in a new context—my previous institution was much smaller and very different, hierarchically and culturally. I wish that I had spent more time listening when I first came to USC. I got caught up in early, easy wins such as standardizing orientation, while there are nuances of culture, relationships, and positions that I'm still learning. I have had to develop skills of diplomacy, tact, and patience, whether in dealing with conflicts between instructors and librarians or in hearing from others that instruction is not a top priority.

Something it's taken me a while to learn is that putting resources out there and trusting that people will take advantage of them, or know how to, assumes a lot. In USC's particular culture, it has been more effective to work one-on-one with people so that they can see how things like active learning or curriculum mapping apply to them in their individual contexts. But I don't feel as if I fully grasped that in my first few years here, though it makes a lot of sense with a large, somewhat isolated workforce and diffused authority. Exercising implicit authority is *really* hard. Getting people to trust you and go along with you depends so much upon openness to change, positions of privilege and power, and what is valued in your library and at your institution.

Appendix 20A

USC Libraries Teaching Excellence Definition

Finalized December 6, 2018

Introduction

The University of Southern California is committed to excellence in teaching through the use of evidence-based, inclusive pedagogies that foster the knowledge, skills, relationships, and values necessary for students to navigate ambiguity and succeed in a rapidly changing world. The faculty of the USC Libraries engage with learners through various modes of instruction (for example, classroom instruction, one-on-one interactions, and asynchronous learning objects such as research guides), partner with faculty and administrators, and incorporate information literacy into disciplinary and interdisciplinary contexts, in order to foster curiosity, critical thinking, and lifelong learning.

Ongoing Pedagogical Engagement

- Demonstrates a commitment to continuous improvement of teaching through openness to implementing new pedagogical practices, exploring new instructional technologies, and applying research-based best practices in information literacy and instructional design (including specialized or discipline-specific practices and standards).
- Analyzes the needs of each teaching/learning setting, environment, or group and employs appropriate pedagogical and classroom management techniques to meet those needs.
- Seeks out and engages teaching partners, remaining open to various ways of collaborating and building mutual respect, trust, and understanding.
- Actively participates in discussions on teaching and learning with colleagues in person, online, and in other forums.

Defining and Assessing Learning

- Articulates goals and learning outcomes for information literacy instruction, and makes these explicit during the course of instruction.
- Creates innovative and engaging lessons with instructional materials that align with learning outcomes, and that are current, rigorous, and informed by theory, research, evidence, and context.
- Demonstrates effectiveness of instruction through assessment of defined learning outcomes.
- Uses assessment of the success and impact of learning experiences to make appropriate adjustments in order to improve student engagement and learning.

Designing Learning Experiences

- Includes students' strengths, interests, experiences, and identities in the learning process.
- Models and fosters critical, analytical, and creative thinking.
- Encourages student curiosity, exploration, and self-directed learning.
- Cultivates in learners a belief that mistakes and failed experiments further knowledge and understanding and fosters a mindset where growth is always possible, and ability is not fixed.
- Engages with students in a non-judgmental manner of mutual regard and respect.
- Uses active learning strategies and deliberative practice to promote development of expertise.
- Fosters situated learning through student use of discipline-specific customs and language.
- Fosters transfer of non-resource-specific learning and problem-solving skills applicable across a broad range of contexts.

Creating Inclusive Environments

- Recognizes the influence of power and privilege on the dynamics of instructional contexts and provides materials, cases, or applications that include underrepresented experiences, perspectives, and/or populations.
- Respectfully expresses curiosity about the histories and lived experiences of underrepresented cultures and groups.
- Applies multiple techniques and strategies to reach all students using culturally responsive teaching.
- Recognizes stereotypes and relates to people as individuals rather than representatives of groups.
- Follows guidelines of Universal Design for Learning, accessibility best practices, and ACRL Diversity Standards.

Notes

1. "Facts and Figures," University of Southern California, accessed April 21, 2019, https://about.usc.edu/facts.
2. "Common Data Set 2017–2018," Office of Institutional Research, University of Southern California, accessed April 21, 2019, http://oir.usc.edu/wp-content/uploads/2018/03/CDS_2017-2018_FINAL_2.pdf.
3. "Facts and Figures."
4. Rosanna Xia, "Most Private Colleges Take Very Few Transfers. At USC, About 1,500 Get a Spot Each Year," *Los Angeles Times*, June 5, 2017, https://www.latimes.com/local/lanow/la-me-usc-transfers-20170605-story.html.
5. Eric Lindberg, "First-Generation Workshops Help Students Settle into College Life," *USC News*, September 10, 2018, https://news.usc.edu/148581/first-generation-workshops-help-students-settle-into-college-life.
6. Karan Nevatia, "To Go the Distance," *Daily Trojan*, 2018, http://dailytrojan.com/projects/sp18/housing/commuter.html.
7. "Leslie and William McMorrow Neighborhood Academic Initiative," Communities, University of Southern California, accessed April 21, 2019, https://communities.usc.edu/college-access/nai.

8. "Information Literacy Outcomes for Undergraduates," USC Libraries, accessed April 21, 2019, https://libraries.usc.edu/research/instructional-services/learning-outcomes; Association of College and Research Libraries, *Framework for Information Literacy for Higher Education* (Chicago: Association of College and Research Libraries, 2016), http://www.ala.org/acrl/standards/ilframework.

9. "Library Instruction for the Writing Program," USC Libraries, accessed April 21, 2019, https://libraries.usc.edu/research/instructional-services/library-instruction-writing-program.

10. Michael Quick and Elizabeth Graddy, "Excellence in Teaching: Message to USC Faculty," Office of the Provost, University of Southern California, March 27, 2018, https://www.provost.usc.edu/excellence-in-teaching.

11. "USC Libraries Teaching Excellence Definition," December 6, 2018, http://bit.ly/2Y0feY5.

12. "Faculty Fellow Leadership Institute," USC Center for Excellence in Teaching, accessed April 21, 2019, http://cet.usc.edu/faculty-fellow-leadership-institute.

13. Kevin Klipfel, "Writing Center Library Database Resources," USC Libraries, last updated October 11, 2018, https://libguides.usc.edu/writingcenter.

14. Society of American Archivists and Association of College and Research Libraries, *Guidelines for Primary Source Literacy* (Chicago: Society of American Archivists and Association of College and Research Libraries, June 2018), https://www2.archivists.org/standards/guidelines-for-primary-source-literacy.

15. "Anti-racist Pedagogy Guide," Research Guides, USC Libraries, May 9, 2018, http://libguides.usc.edu/antiracistpedagogy.

16. More information on the collective and the discussion series can be found at Antiracist Pedagogy Collective website, accessed November 25, 2019, https://sites.google.com/usc.edu/arpc.

17. Greater Western Library Alliance, *The Impact of Information Literacy Instruction on Student Success* (Phoenix, AZ: Greater Western Library Alliance, 2017), https://www.arl.org/wp-content/uploads/2017/10/mm17fall_impact-on-student-success-Bowles-Terry-Winn.pdf.

18. "Information Literacy Course Enhancement Grants," USC Libraries, accessed April 21, 2019, https://libraries.usc.edu/information-literacy-course-enhancement-grants.

19. Society of American Archivists and Association of College and Research Libraries, *Guidelines for Primary Source Literacy*.

20. A full list of grant participants and example course revisions an be found at "Information Literacy Course Enhancement Grants." The grants are also described in the following poster: Elizabeth Galoozis and Carolyn Caffrey Gardner, "New Maps for Familiar Waters: Framework-Inspired Information Literacy Grants for Faculty" (poster presentation at ACRL Conference, Baltimore, MD, March 24, 2017).

21. "Instructional Design," USC Libraries, accessed April 21, 2019, https://libraries.usc.edu/research/instructional-services/instructional-design.

22. More information and a list of winners can be found at "USC Libraries Research Award," in "Research Guides," USC Libraries, accessed November 25, 2019, https://libguides.usc.edu/researchaward.

Bibliography

Antiracist Pedagogy Collective website. Accessed November 25, 2019. https://sites.google.com/usc.edu/arpc.

Association of College and Research Libraries. *Framework for Information Literacy for Higher Education.* Chicago: Association of College and Research Libraries, 2016. http://www.ala.org/acrl/standards/ilframework.

Galoozis, Elizabeth and Carolyn Caffrey Gardner. "New Maps for Familiar Waters: Framework-Inspired Information Literacy Grants for Faculty." Poster presentation, ACRL Conference, Baltimore, MD, March 24, 2017.

Greater Western Library Alliance. *The Impact of Information Literacy Instruction on Student Success: A Multi-institutional Investigation and Analysis.* Phoenix, AZ: Greater Western Library Alliance, 2017. https://www.arl.org/wp-content/uploads/2018/10/The_Impact_of_Information_Literacy_Instruction_on_Student_Success_October_2017.pdf.

Klipfel, Kevin. "Writing Center Library Database Resources." University of Southern California Libraries. Last updated October 11, 2018. https://libguides.usc.edu/writingcenter.

Lindberg, Eric. "First-Generation Workshops Help Students Settle into College Life." *USC News,* September 10, 2018. https://news.usc.edu/148581/first-generation-workshops-help-students-settle-into-college-life.

Nevatia, Karan. "To Go the Distance." *Daily Trojan,* University of Southern California. 2018. http://daily-trojan.com/projects/sp18/housing/commuter.html.

Quick, Michael, and Elizabeth Graddy. "Excellence in Teaching: Message to USC Faculty." Office of the Provost, University of Southern California. March 27, 2018. https://www.provost.usc.edu/excellence-in-teaching.

Society of American Archivists and Association of College and Research Libraries. *Guidelines for Primary Source Literacy*. Chicago: Society of American Archivists and Association of College and Research Libraries, June 2018. https://www2.archivists.org/standards/guidelines-for-primary-source-literacy.

University of Southern California. "Common Data Set 2017–2018." Office of Institutional Research. Accessed April 21, 2019, http://oir.usc.edu/wp-content/uploads/2018/03/CDS_2017-2018_FINAL_2.pdf.

———. "Facts and Figures." Accessed April 21, 2019. https://about.usc.edu/facts.

———. "Leslie and William McMorrow Neighborhood Academic Initiative." Communities. Accessed April 21, 2019. https://communities.usc.edu/college-access/nai.

USC Center for Excellence in Teaching. "Faculty Fellow Leadership Institute." Accessed April 21, 2019. http://cet.usc.edu/faculty-fellow-leadership-institute.

USC Libraries. "Anti-racist Pedagogy Guide." Research Guides. May 9, 2018. http://libguides.usc.edu/antiracistpedagogy.

———. "Information Literacy Course Enhancement Grants." Accessed April 21, 2019. https://libraries.usc.edu/information-literacy-course-enhancement-grants.

———. "Information Literacy Outcomes for Undergraduates." Accessed April 21, 2019. https://libraries.usc.edu/research/instructional-services/learning-outcomes.

———. "Instructional Design." Accessed April 21, 2019. https://libraries.usc.edu/research/instructional-services/instructional-design.

———. "Library Instruction for the Writing Program." Accessed April 21, 2019. https://libraries.usc.edu/research/instructional-services/library-instruction-writing-program.

———. "Research Guides." Accessed November 25, 2019. https://libguides.usc.edu/researchaward

"USC Libraries Teaching Excellence Definition." December 6, 2018. http://bit.ly/2Y0feY5.

Xia, Rosanna. "Most Private Colleges Take Very Few Transfers. At USC, About 1,500 Get a Spot Each Year." *Los Angeles Times,* June 5, 2017. https://www.latimes.com/local/lanow/la-me-usc-transfers-20170605-story.html.

Chapter 21

Washington University in St. Louis

Reorganizing and Reframing an Instruction and Information Literacy Program

Amanda B. Albert

Population Served

Washington University in St. Louis (WashU) is a research-intensive institution. As of fall 2018, there were over 15,900 enrolled students. Sixty percent of Washington University students identify as Caucasian, and 40 percent as nonwhite ethnic or racial groups. Twenty-two percent of enrolled students are international students.[1] According to a 2017 ~~2015~~ *New York Times* report, 84 percent of students attending Washington University came from households of the top 20 percent of income earners, and the median family income of a student from WashU was $272,000.[2] Other reports from the University indicate that the issues of diversity, equity, and inclusion have been on the University's radar for some time, and the University made steps to improve in these areas.[3] For example, the University set a goal to increase its Pell Grant–eligible enrollment from 5 percent to 13 percent by 2020. The university also diligently worked to increase its commitment to diversity and inclusion by establishing a robust Office of Diversity and Inclusion that "supports and advocates for undergraduate, graduate, and professional students from underrepresented and/or marginalized populations, creates collaborative partnerships with campus and community partners, and promotes dialogue and social change among all students."[4] This effort has been felt across the university, including in the classroom with courses such as a first-year course called Identity Literacy, which brings issues of diversity, inclusion, and social justice to the forefront of the student academic and social experience. This course was first piloted in 2015 and is looking to receive approval to become a required course. Academically, the undergraduate population (7,187 residential full-time enrollees) is positioned heavily within the College of Arts and Sciences, while the graduate and professional population (7,377) is more evenly distributed among arts and sciences, business, and professional schools such as medicine and law.[5] Olin Library is the heart of the University Library System on campus, with nine other libraries rounding out the system. The distributed libraries are a strength of the system as they are embedded in the academic buildings, communities, and curriculums in which they serve.

The diversity of the student body sparks quite a bit of discussion among library instructors about how we teach, what we teach, and who we reach out to. For example, we often discuss how to engage students in conversations about power and privilege in regard to information in order to challenge our students and get them to think critically about their place in society. The fact that 84 percent of the student population hails from affluent backgrounds causes librarians to think about ways in which we relate to these students with class discussions, resources we show, and how we talk about the libraries. This came across in our work with the aforementioned Identity Literacy course, where we engaged students on a variety of topics related to power, identity, and information. For example, when talking about citation, we didn't talk about only a particular citation style, but we also discussed reasons why it is important to cite. These reasons include not only attributing ideas to authors, but also demonstrating to readers that the student sought many voices within a conversation and is presenting a diversity of sources in the project.

In addition to this work, for many years we have also been a leader on campus in focusing our outreach to students who are first-generation college students, racial and ethnic minority students, and students who come from low socioeconomic backgrounds. The University Libraries have a Diversity Programs and Policy Department staffed by the Head of Diversity Initiatives and Outreach as well as another librarian who works closely with diversity initiatives on campus, such as the TRiO program, a US Department of Education program that serves first-generation college students, low-income students, and those who have a learning or physical disability.[6] The libraries also sponsor an internship that supports students of color who might be exploring librarianship as a career. The instruction program is expanding ways in which we work with students of diverse backgrounds by exploring open educational resources, inclusive pedagogy, and inclusive instructional spaces.

Program Scope

The focus of our instructional efforts runs the gamut of possibilities and includes first-year students who take a required college writing course as well as graduate students in specific subject areas, including professional schools, and everything in between. The bulk of our instruction is subject liaison–driven. In addition to the twenty-four subject librarians, library staff across a variety of departments teach information literacy or information-literacy-related topics. These topics include data literacy, geographic information systems (GIS), and special collections research. There are a total of forty-two library staff in the University Libraries who teach. Collectively, the type of instruction is as vastly varied as the content. The majority of our teaching is in-class and face-to-face, relying heavily on the one-shot (or two-shot) model, though we are working on revamping our language for this. Using the term *one-shot* feels inappropriate due to the prevalence of gun violence happening in schools. Other instructional models include one-on-one instruction, or the research consultation, and research workshops. During the fall of 2018, we brought back research workshops after a brief hiatus due to the remodeling of our instruction spaces. Library instructors volunteer to teach one workshop two times a semester. The workshops are conducted over the course of two weeks early in the semester and cover a wide range of information literacy, data literacy, and technology topics. Another series, called the Humanities Research Hub, which was previously conducted as a mini-conference, is being piloted at the time of writing to graduate humanities students approaching the dissertation phase of their research. This workshop series covers topics important to graduate student research, writing, and technology that enhance the dissertation process. The final event of the series is a reception meant to build relationships among graduate students and between students and librarians.

As the instruction program evolves, we are expanding our modes of teaching. The campus recently adopted Canvas as its learning management system, and the library is looking to pilot plug-and-play information literacy modules for faculty to use in their courses. This is in its early stages of development, starting with the ever-present question, "What do we want students to know and be able to do?"

Operations

The University Libraries have historically taught information literacy instruction sessions; however, these sessions were not formalized as a program until 2018. As a part of the restructuring of the library organizational chart (see figure 21.1), the instructional activities of the libraries are now housed under the Instruction and Information Literacy Program, which is in the Research and Academic Collaboration Division.[7] This program is staffed by one librarian, the Information Literacy Coordinator. The coordinator's initial job is to identify who teaches, what they teach, who they teach, and how they teach, and to assess the teaching and learning activities of the libraries. This has involved designing a program statement, establishing instructional content, understanding what modes and tools are being utilized in instruction, and understanding what current assessment of instruction is being done. Also falling under the purview of the coordinator are instructional spaces, instructional technology, managing a small budget, and conducting professional development and training. Staffing is a major challenge, as the coordinator is responsible for all aspects of program development, implementation, assessment, instructional development and training, instructional design, marketing, relationship building internally and externally, and logistical aspects such as room management. Goals, or desired deliverables, of the program include curriculum mapping, developing research workshops, developing a plan for holistic assessment (learning assessment, programmatic

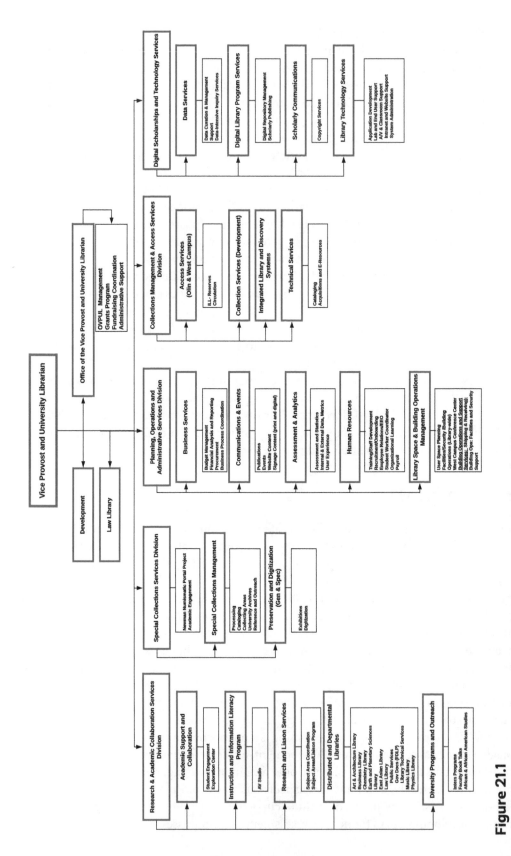

Figure 21.1
Washington University Libraries organizational chart, July 2019

assessment, and assessing for teaching effectiveness), developing online learning objects as part of the libraries' instructional tool kit, and providing instructional development for teaching staff in the libraries.

Individual subject librarians and library staff are responsible for their subject or content areas. They are the Subject Matter Experts (SMEs) and are responsible for instruction that happens within their liaison areas. The Information Literacy (IL) Coordinator is responsible for coordinating instruction and teaching anywhere from ten to fifteen sections for College Writing, providing instructional literacy training for the SMEs, and leading student learning and teaching assessments. Library administration regularly calls on the coordinator to provide updates, and reports, announcements, and information about events are regularly communicated to the coordinator's supervisor (Associate University Librarian for Research and Academic Collaboration), as well as during staff meetings and via staff newsletters. As the IL Coordinator, I created a team of subject librarians, the Instruction and Information Literacy Task Force, that assists with providing a vision and direction for information literacy within the libraries and on campus, as well as instructional development of librarians and staff who teach. The Instruction and Information Literacy Task Force has been instrumental in getting the program off the ground. A program as big and important as this needs more than one coordinator, and I am so proud and grateful for their work and assistance. I recruited each person individually, and we are working together to assess the current landscape of instruction internally and externally, as well as coming up with direction for the program. At this institution, task forces are time-limited, so the work of this group is coming to an end in the spring of 2019.

Marketing

Marketing of library instruction is primarily carried out by subject librarians via established relationships with faculty members in their subject areas, emails to faculty, participation in new faculty orientations, and visits to departmental meetings. The library is also working on a website presence that will allow greater information sharing virtually, including providing information on our instructional services and instruction rooms, and a new instruction request form.[8] A major goal of our one-shot instruction sessions has been to market other library services, mostly librarian expertise and one-on-one consultations. If we can get our foot in the door for a one-shot, some librarians feel their time is better spent in a one-on-one environment with the student. See the Role of the One-Shot section for an explanation of why some of the librarians feel this way.

Role of the One-Shot

The one-shot is seen as a necessary part of our work, but not something some librarians particularly enjoy or find effective. A goal of our instruction is to use the one-shot to get our foot in the door to expand our instruction beyond one class or to discuss other services. Librarians sometimes use one-shots as a marketing tool to talk about librarian expertise and draw in students to see a librarian for consultations. Some librarians prefer to work one-on-one with students because they are better able to discuss the students' research topics and provide more direct guidance in regard to library resources. Librarians experience the students as more engaged in the process, and getting more targeted assistance builds the students' relationship with the librarians. In this way, one-on-one instruction can be viewed as a signature pedagogy of librarianship, as it is a specific way of conveying knowledge to students and has advantages over the one-shot as a way to actively engage students on a more personal level. The one-shot will probably always have its place in our library's instructional repertoire; however, is the goal of the IL Coordinator to encourage movement beyond the one-shot to a two- or three-visit model of instruction or even embedded instruction. Scalability must be considered, though, so this is something that will be in development over the course of the next few semesters.

Administrative Highlights

The Information Literacy Coordinator was asked to create a program statement that encapsulated the instruction program in a succinct manner. What came out of this is a statement that is aspirational and practical:

> The Instruction and Information Literacy Program at Washington University Libraries engages undergraduate and graduate students in disciplinary applications of information literacy skills and behaviors. This Program coordinates and facilitates the deployment of Libraries-wide subject and information expertise to provide instruction in information literacy through various methods, including face-to-face instruction sessions, online learning objects, and assignment design. Grounded in evidence-based teaching, the Program promotes holistic, student-centered instruction where students are engaged in active learning and metacognitive processes, resulting in the mastery of skills (current and life-long) to appropriately use information and become successful scholars in a complex information environment.

The thing that I am most proud of is the support from librarians I have been able to garner in such a short amount of time. Librarians are excited about their teaching, and they just want to share it. They are hungry for information and training on how to become better teachers, and they are eager to share and learn from each other. The way I have been able to build this support and excitement is simply by talking with librarians who teach. I have arranged one-on-one meetings with a variety of librarians who teach, and the Instruction and Information Literacy Task Force conducted a focus group assessment in the summer of 2018. These focus groups asked three main questions with follow-up questions:

1. What does instruction/training look like for you in your role in the library?
   a. What and who do you teach (this could be any content including concepts, skills, or behaviors)?
   b. How do you currently communicate about instruction/training with colleagues in and outside the library?

2. Describe your approach to teaching/training.
   a. What are your main/preferred/most successful teaching methods?
   b. What do you hope your students get out of instruction/training?
3. What instructional/training opportunities could the Libraries provide internally and/or externally?
   a. In what areas do you think we should expand our instruction offerings? OR would you like to expand your instruction experiences?
   b. What type of support do you need in regards to instruction/training?

The responses from this assessment have helped shape the direction of the program, including identifying programmatic needs, such the need for as a common definition of information literacy situated within our institutional context and for training resources in regard to various technology including the campus learning management system, and the goal of developing a more robust instructional literacy professional development program.

Information Literacy Coordinator Profile

The Information Literacy Coordinator role is a formalized role whose scope used to be much smaller. The coordinator was mainly in charge of liaising with the College Writing Program, working with some librarians on their teaching, and working to create online learning objects in collaboration with other library staff. In 2018, the role expanded with the reorganization and creation of the Instruction and Information Literacy Program to include formalizing the program and working collaboratively with all librarians and library staff who teach (in other departments such as Special Collections and Data Services) on their teaching. In terms of the teaching workload, as the coordinator, I take on the bulk of the instruction within the College Writing Program (about 20% of the sections), with the remaining sections taught by twenty librarian and library staff volunteers. Other teaching within the disciplines is left up to the subject librarians. The other parts of my work that take up the most time are assessment, relationship building or networking, and continuing education.

Personally, I received training in graduate school in instruction through formal classes and internships. I like to say I worked to learn both the art and science of teaching; for example, I attended workshops to improve my public speaking skills, and I delved into the literature on instructional design. I specifically sought out this type of work after graduation. I started out as a distance learning librarian, but quickly moved to an instructional services librarian role and then to Information Literacy Coordinator. As one colleague put it, I am a "teacher's teacher." I love the professional development side of the job where I get to talk about teaching and learning with my colleagues, run workshops, and create resources for us.

What I Wish People Knew

The major challenge of running this program is staffing. One person running a program as large as this is a huge task, and most of the work, if not done by the IL Coordinator, is completed by the Instruction and Information Literacy Task Force. This makes developing the program a slow process, as the task force is a time-limited team and members have many other responsibilities outside of this team. The emotional, invisible labor is another challenge. One person is in charge of all aspects of program development, including being the face of information literacy on campus, developing relationships within and outside the libraries, providing pedagogical support to librarians, providing logistical support and occasionally technological support in the library's instruction rooms, and developing a holistic assessment plan. The amount of work and time that goes into this is not small, and I sometimes feel like I'm dropping the ball in one of these areas. Along with these broad, sweeping tasks, I often find myself in charge of the little day-to-day to-dos, in which I sometimes get lost in the details. For example, when coordinating the library's Research Workshops, I am not only making sure we are providing sessions that meet the mission of the instruction program, but also scheduling the rooms, creating the workshop calendar, delegating other tasks to the workshop team (a small group that assists with putting on the workshops), and making sure our marketing and communications staff have the correct information for flyers. I have to think big picture, but I often find myself in the weeds working to get small things off the ground.

Advice I would give to others is to establish a team, even if your library is small, or if you have to go outside your library. Work to find partners you can trust to bounce ideas off and give you straight talk. Get comfortable asking for help, delegating, and in essence creating work for others. This is something that I have really struggled with and continue to work on. It's impossible to run a successful program without involving people who are experts in their subject areas, people who understand how to troubleshoot technology, people who can create a decent instructional video, and so on. Most often, people will enthusiastically support you. Don't *not* ask because you don't want to create work for other people. That's a big lesson I had to learn. People will tell you when their plates are full![9]

Notes

1. "Student Body Diversity," Office of the University Registrar, Washington University in St. Louis, accessed October 31, 2018, https://registrar.wustl.edu/student-information-systems/student-enrollment-and-graduation-statistics/student-body-diversity.
2. Gregor Aisch et al., "Economic Diversity and Student Outcomes at Washington University in St. Louis," *New York Times*, January 18, 2017, https://www.nytimes.com/interactive/projects/college-mobility/washington-university-in-st-louis.
3. "Community Report," (2014), accessed January 14, 2020, https://diversity.wustl.edu/wp-content/uploads/2016/08/MOSAIC-PROJECT-Report-working-group-index2.pdf; "A Report of the Steering Committee for Diversity & Inclusion," (2015), accessed January 14, 2020, https://diversity.wustl.edu/wp-content/uploads/2016/06/Diversity-and-Inclusion-Report-2015-1.pdf; "Executive Summary Report from the Commission on Diversity and Inclusion," (2017), accessed January 14, 2020, https://diversity.wustl.edu/wp-content/uploads/2018/01/Commission-Diversity-Inclusion-Executive-Summary-Report.pdf.
4. "Center for Diversity and Inclusion," Washington University in St. Louis, accessed October 31, 2018, https://diversityinclusion.wustl.edu.

5. "Current Enrollment and Graduation Data," Office of the University Registrar, Washington University in St. Louis, Accessed October 31, 2018, https://registrar.wustl.edu/student-information-systems/student-enrollment-and-graduation-statistics/enrollment-graduation-data.

6. "TRiO Program," Learning Center, Washington University in St. Louis, accessed January 25, 2019, http://learningcenter.wustl.edu/trio.

7. "Organizational Chart," Washington University Libraries, accessed October 31, 2018, https://library.wustl.edu/wp-content/uploads/2018/03/Libraries-Organizational-Chart-3.1.18-functional.pdf.

8. "The Instruction and Information Literacy Program." Accessed January 14, 2020. https://library.wustl.edu/research-instruction/about-library-instruction/.

9. The library is also working on a website presence that will allow greater information sharing virtually, including providing information on our instructional services and instruction rooms, and a new instruction request form. "The Instruction and Information Literacy Program." Accessed January 14, 2020. https://library.wustl.edu/research-instruction/about-library-instruction/.

Other reports from the University indicate that the issues of diversity, equity, and inclusion have been on the University's radar for some time, and the University has made steps to improve in these areas. "Community Report." (2014). Accessed January 14, 2020. https://diversity.wustl.edu/wp-content/uploads/2016/08/MOSAIC-PROJECT-Report-working-group-index2.pdf; "A Report of the Steering Committee for Diversity & Inclusion." (2015). Accessed January 14, 2020. https://diversity.wustl.edu/wp-content/uploads/2016/06/Diversity-and-Inclusion-Report-2015-1.pdf; "Executive Summary Report from the Commission on Diversity and Inclusion." (2017). Accessed January 14, 2020. https://diversity.wustl.edu/wp-content/uploads/2018/01/Commission-Diversity-Inclusion-Executive-Summary-Report.pdf.

Bibliography

Aisch, Gregor, Larry Buchanan, Amanda Cox, and Kevin Quealy. "Economic Diversity and Student Outcomes at Washington University in St. Louis." *New York Times*, January 18, 2017. https://www.nytimes.com/interactive/projects/college-mobility/washington-university-in-st-louis.

Washington University in St. Louis. "Center for Diversity and Inclusion." Accessed October 31, 2018. https://diversityinclusion.wustl.edu.

———. "Community Report." (2014). Accessed January 14, 2020. https://diversity.wustl.edu/wp-content/uploads/2016/08/MOSAIC-PROJECT-Report-working-group-index2.pdf

———. "Current Enrollment and Graduation Data." Office of the University Registrar. Accessed October 31, 2018. https://registrar.wustl.edu/student-information-systems/student-enrollment-and-graduation-statistics/enrollment-graduation-data.

———. "Executive Summary Report from the Commission on Diversity and Inclusion." (2017). Accessed January 14, 2020. https://diversity.wustl.edu/wp-content/uploads/2018/01/Commission-Diversity-Inclusion-Executive-Summary-Report.pdf

———. "Student Body Diversity." Office of the University Registrar. Accessed October 31, 2018. https://registrar.wustl.edu/student-information-systems/student-enrollment-and-graduation-statistics/student-body-diversity.

———. "A Report of the Steering Committee for Diversity & Inclusion." (2015). Accessed January 14, 2020. https://diversity.wustl.edu/wp-content/uploads/2016/06/Diversity-and-Inclusion-Report-2015-1.pdf

———. Washington University in St. Louis. "TRiO Program." Learning Center. Accessed January 25, 2019. http://learningcenter.wustl.edu/trio.

Washington University Libraries. "Organizational Chart." Accessed October 31, 2018. https://library.wustl.edu/wp-content/uploads/2018/03/Libraries-Organizational-Chart-3.1.18-functional.pdf.

———. "The Instruction and Information Literacy Program." Accessed January 14, 2020. https://library.wustl.edu/research-instruction/about-library-instruction/

Chapter 22

Augustana College
Scaffolding to Success

Stefanie R. Bluemle

Population Served

Augustana College, in Rock Island, Illinois, is a private, four-year liberal arts college with a population of about 2,500 students. The college has a long history, going back to its founding in 1860, of serving first-generation college students, who in recent years have made up between one-quarter and one-third of each incoming class. Although Augustana remains a predominantly white institution, its student body is steadily diversifying, especially within the last decade; since the 2007–08 academic year, the proportion of domestic students of color in each incoming class has grown from about 10 percent to more than 25 percent, and the proportion of international students from less than 1 percent to nearly 10 percent.

The library's program of course-integrated information literacy (IL) instruction has been a defined component of Augustana's general education curriculum since 2003–04; many majors also emphasize IL and rely significantly on library instruction. Librarians recognize that entering Augustana students have had a wide array of experiences in secondary school, and the extent and nature of their prior experience with library research varies greatly, as well. Additionally, in the United States, budget cuts and inconsistent levels of political support have both reduced the presence of school librarians and increased pressure on public libraries. As a result of the above, we assume little about what incoming first-years are likely to know; even a concept as seemingly ubiquitous as the Dewey Decimal System can be unfamiliar when a tenth of students are international and many domestic students had no high school library or limited access to public libraries. Our program, therefore, places emphasis on reaching *every* student, especially in the first year, and scaffolding IL skills throughout students' time at the college.

Program Scope and Curriculum Design

As this chapter is being written, in the 2018–19 school year, Augustana approaches a curricular transformation. In spring of 2015, the college faculty voted to move from a trimester system (three ten-week terms) to semesters with a three-and-one-half-week January term. The first school year on semesters will be 2019–20. Unsurprisingly, this curricular restructuring means significant changes to the library's information literacy program. Augustana librarians have approached these changes as an opportunity to strengthen and streamline our program and continue to improve collaborations with faculty. Yet our current trimester-based program is the foundation on which all of these developments will build; therefore, I will describe that program before looking ahead to planned changes under semesters.

Information Literacy on Trimesters

All first-year Augustana students take a year-long sequence: either First Year Inquiry (FYI) or, for a selected subgroup, Honors. Although faculty bring their own content of interest to FYI, the sequence's primary purpose is to teach college-level reading, writing, information literacy, and oral communication skills. Christian Traditions, a 200-level religion requirement arising from the college's affiliation with the Evangelical Lutheran Church in America, must be completed by the end of sophomore year. Majors culminate in a senior inquiry experience, which typically includes a research component. This academic program—structured around inquiry, with several experiences that all students have in common—permits information literacy to be scaffolded throughout the curriculum.

Information literacy, along with reading, writing, and oral communication, has been a defined skill in the FYI skills matrix since the sequence was introduced in 2003. The 2018–19 version of the skills matrix, which has been in use since 2013, focuses on high-level IL skills similar to the frames Authority Is Constructed and Contextual, Research as Inquiry, and Searching as Strategic Exploration in the ACRL *Framework for Information Literacy for Higher Education:*[1] exploratory searching (fall term), evaluating sources (winter term), formulating research questions (spring term), and allowing questions to guide inquiry (fall and spring terms). Students come to the library with their FYI classes four to five times over the course of the year-long sequence, allowing subsequent course-integrated sessions to build on one another. FYI faculty's participation in the library visits is nearly universal, and librarian-faculty collaboration is extensive. Similar IL skills—though at a slightly higher level—and universal faculty participation characterize first-year Honors. Therefore, the librarians work with 100 percent of first-year students repeatedly over the course of the year, introducing progressively more complicated IL skills.

The 200-level Christian Traditions requirement was originally part of FYI and continues to play a role in developing students' college-level writing, reading, and IL skills beyond the first-year sequence. Christian Traditions, therefore, serves as a bridge between the non-disciplinary IL skills of FYI and the disciplinary IL required within majors. Library visits—typically one for each Christian Traditions class—are planned in close collaboration between the religion librarian and faculty and push students beyond their FYI experience to practice skills such as critical reading and high-level analysis of sources, or placing arguments in conversation with one another.

FYI and Christian Traditions form the foundation for disciplinary IL skills. These are integrated differently into each major, depending on the structure and needs of the curriculum. Linear majors—that is, majors in which a number of the required courses must be taken in sequence—such as biology, communication sciences and disorders, and psychology scaffold disciplinary IL skills throughout the curriculum; there are designated places for librarian involvement and other points at which teaching faculty are responsible for IL. Other, less-structured majors still incorporate disciplinary IL at key points, such as required introductory or methods classes, to ensure students have the research capabilities that the major's curriculum requires. At the senior inquiry (SI) level, librarians work closely with students on advanced disciplinary research skills in settings that range from workshops with SI seminars to one-on-one meetings with SI students. Whatever form it ultimately takes, the scaffolding of IL skills within majors occurs in collaboration between departmental faculty and their liaison librarian, who provides instruction and professional consultation.

Information Literacy on Semesters

As the college moves to semesters, a first-year sequence—either FYI or Honors—consisting of two four-credit, semester-long classes will continue to be required. The new FYI curriculum, which the Honors curriculum echoes, was written by a group of eight faculty, including a research and instruction librarian, and approved by the full faculty. In the new FYI, the key information literacy skills are closely tied to the overarching question for each semester. The overarching question for FYI 101 (fall semester) is *How do you know what you think you know, and to what extent can you be certain?* The information literacy component of 101 involves not just basic skills, such as identifying keywords and constructing database searches, but also the ability to research from questions and articulate how new sources of information have changed one's thinking about various topics. The overarching question for FYI 102 (spring semester) is *How is difference constructed, and what differences matter?* Correspondingly, students in 102 will consider source evaluation from the standpoint of both credibility and authority; they should develop a basic understanding of where authority comes from and how it is different from credibility. The IL concepts for both semesters deliberately echo elements of the ACRL *Framework*, particularly Research as Inquiry in 101 and Authority Is Constructed and Contextual in 102.[2] But just as importantly, IL also reinforces the actual content of each semester. Fall semester is about enacting a liberal arts education, and the IL skill offers one way for students to both develop and question their own knowledge. Spring semester turns to diversity and social justice; the corresponding IL skill asks students to consider whose voices are heard and whose are not heard in a given conversation, and how that comes to be.

Augustana's librarians view the new FYI as an opportunity to strengthen and streamline our work with the sequence. Curricular restructuring, combined with the extensive faculty buy-in described above, creates a valuable opportunity to encourage more and more faculty to collaborate with librarians in ways that are most meaningful to student learning. Despite our ongoing efforts, some faculty still equate IL with "searching the databases" or "finding sources at the library." But all faculty must redesign their FYI classes for semesters, and this creates an intervention point for the librarians: specifically, to nudge the more reluctant faculty toward an understanding of IL that is more in line with the *Framework*. The alignment between the overarching question and the IL skills that has been written into the new curriculum is one important step in this direction.

Librarians' longer-term goal is to guide the culture of FYI toward one of weaving IL skills effectively throughout each class so that faculty will become less dependent on librarians for that component of the sequence. Ideas under consideration include the following:

- Developing tutorials faculty can assign to teach basic skills, such as reading Library of Congress call numbers, searching the catalog, or searching popular databases, to enable in-class time to focus on higher-level skills.
- Using existing librarian-faculty relationships to

    - encourage those faculty who have the greatest understanding and comfort level with IL to embed IL skills throughout their classes and reduce the need for sessions with a librarian
    - coach those faculty who value IL but lean on librarians' expertise so they can develop the confidence to teach more IL themselves, again reducing the need for sessions with a librarian

Our hope is to maintain and even strengthen our current relationships with faculty and build on their assumption that librarians are deeply involved in FYI, in order to both improve student learning *and* reduce the instruction burden on the library.

The Christian Traditions requirement will be renamed Reasoned Examination of Faith (REF) as the college moves to semesters. Religion faculty remain committed to REF as an opportunity to further develop students' skills from FYI. The religion librarian, for her part, hopes to create a shift with these classes similar to the one occurring in the first-year sequence. Particular frames from the *Framework* may align with goals and content for REF as they did with the overarching questions for FYI. Beyond that, the religion librarian intends to have conversations with REF faculty about what, exactly, IL should look like within these classes, again with the intention of integrating IL in a way that decreases the reliance on librarian-led instruction.

The component of the IL program that is likely to change least on semesters is liaison librarians' work with departments on discipline-specific information literacy skills. Certainly, liaisons will need to speak to their departments about their new curricula to understand how their work with majors and minors will need to adjust. These conversations will create important opportunities to rethink collaborations that need improvement and to ensure that IL is integrated into each major strategically so that librarian involvement occurs when it is most important.

Operations

In 2012 the Augustana faculty voted to approve nine college-wide student learning outcomes; information literacy is paired with critical thinking as one of them.[3] By this point, nearly a decade since IL became integrated into the general education curriculum, it was enough a part of the campus's vocabulary that the college's assessment committee included it without prompting from the library. These circumstances—wherein the majority of faculty and academic administrators either understand information literacy or hear it spoken of enough to recognize its importance—arise from the library's long-standing vision of itself as a teaching organization, with a mission to "serve Augustana College by making learning the touchstone of all library activities and decisions."[4] In other words, librarians position themselves as educators alongside the teaching faculty.

Cultivation of liaison relationships is one way this positioning has occurred. Augustana has six faculty librarians—four research and instruction librarians, a special collections librarian, and a technical services librarian—a library director, a head of circulation, and five full-time staff. The four research and instruction librarians and the technical services librarian are each liaisons to, and members of, an academic division: natural sciences, social sciences, fine and performing arts, humanities, and business and education.[5] Each division comprises several academic departments, thereby creating natural liaison relationships between librarians and a group of related disciplines. Liaisons are responsible for providing course-integrated information literacy instruction for the departments in their division, collaborating with faculty to integrate IL into their departmental curricula, working with faculty to develop and manage the library's collections in their liaison areas, providing research and other library assistance to students and faculty in their liaison areas, and communicating with their divisions about developments in the library. Attending division meetings as members of the division, in turn, keeps librarians apprised of concerns and issues their liaison departments face on campus and contributes to a sense of community and shared interests among librarians and teaching faculty.

While disciplinary instruction is always the responsibility of the relevant liaison, the four research and instruction librarians teach the bulk of course-integrated IL sessions for the FYI and first-year Honors programs. The instruction coordinator assigns sections of the first-year sequence to librarians based on liaison relationships where possible. If a particular division is heavily represented in FYI in a given term, the instruction coordinator will partner some librarians with non-liaison faculty in order to balance workloads. The instruction coordinator attempts to maintain librarian/faculty partnerships for FYI and Honors from year to year for the sake of consistency. The library director and technical services librarian both work with a small number of FYI sections as well.

Assigning FYI and Honors partnerships is only one component of the instruction coordinator role, which is always held by a research and instruction librarian.[6] The instruction coordinator is responsible for the big picture of the IL program: they develop vision and direction for the program in conversation with the other librarians; plan and implement assessment projects; monitor and participate in curricular developments on campus that are relevant to IL; and, often, act as spokesperson for IL on campus on behalf of the library. For example, in 2013 the instruction coordinator liaised between the library and the college's general education committee as the committee revised the FYI skills matrix. The result was a set of IL outcomes for the sequence that were based on an assessment project recently conducted at the library, which the instruction coordinator had led.

Collaboration

The most important allies on campus of the library's information literacy program are undeniably the teaching faculty. In planning the integration of IL into the college's general education curriculum in 2003–04, librarians worked tirelessly to demonstrate the value of our contributions, and IL more broadly, to student learning. The effort was spearheaded by an instruction coordinator who had a background in sales, which she used to teach her colleagues a needs satisfaction approach—a concept from marketing that involves crafting a message based on the customer's identified needs—to help faculty see the benefits of incorporating IL instruction into their classes.[7] As buy-in to the instruction program became more and more widespread, a culture of valuing information literacy developed on campus. Librarians are currently fortunate to know that, at least to some extent, new members of the faculty enter a climate where IL is already part of the community's vocabulary and experienced faculty will recommend that they work with their division's liaison. Yet we also recognize that we cannot take the culture we have built for granted. Collaboration is just as much a way of building and sustaining relationships as relationships are a gateway to collaboration.

Among the key relationships to maintain are those with the coordinators of the First Year Inquiry program and the chairs of the Honors program. The present (2018–19) faculty leading these programs are among the library's strongest advocates on campus. In the 2017–18 school year, the library's instruction coordinator worked with seven other teaching faculty, including the FYI coordinator at the time, to design the FYI curriculum. As the college approaches its transition to semesters, librarians have collaborated with the FYI coordinators to plan professional development meetings for FYI faculty about teaching IL skills in the new curriculum. Similarly, librarians will collaborate with the Honors chair in the 2018–19 year to determine how IL will be incorporated into its curriculum as it develops.

At the department level, liaisons are contacting department chairs and other interested faculty to have conversations about scaffolding IL in their redesigned semester curricula. In some cases, these discussions may reinforce relationships but not lead to significant changes in how librarians and faculty work together. In others, librarians might collaborate with faculty to rethink how IL fits in a particular major or to develop new delivery methods, such as online tutorials. These conversations are ongoing at the time of this writing.

Whatever their shape, department- and program-level collaborations are enabled and preceded by the work that occurs one-on-one between librarians and faculty. For example, a librarian recently collaborated with the faculty member for an upper-level class on critical theory to revise an assignment from a short research paper to a series of "source analyses," each of which involved a page of careful writing about how the particular source engaged or illuminated the theory in question. The same librarian spent several hours brainstorming with a new faculty member about an assignment for a creative project that can tie the focus of the faculty member's class to local history. In another case, a librarian is engaged in a casual, ongoing conversation with an FYI instructor about how best to guide students to write a simple research question. Collaborations such as these need not always result in IL instruction; their importance lies in bringing IL more fully into the curriculum.

Assessment

With each graduating class, the college conducts a longitudinal assessment of one of the nine college-wide student learning outcomes: disciplinary knowledge, critical thinking/information literacy, quantitative literacy, collaborative leadership, intercultural competency, communication competency, creative thinking, ethical citizenship, or intellectual curiosity.[8] Students take the assessment at the beginning of their first year and again near the end of their senior year. Additionally, each department and program is asked to pose, and collect data to answer, one question about student learning in its major each academic year. But even though information literacy is paired with critical thinking as one of the college-wide outcomes, the library has not formally been drawn into the assessment process. The graduating class for which critical thinking/information literacy was assessed took the "Need for Cognition" scale, which focuses on critical thinking.[9] The library is also not required to submit yearly assessment reports along with other departments and programs, although the college's writing center, which would seem to have a similar relationship to student learning on campus, does submit such reports.

Librarians have considered various possible reasons for these circumstances, particularly our not being asked to submit yearly assessment reports.[10] We have debated whether to simply ask that we be included, a request that would likely be granted. One benefit to our inclusion would be the additional formal recognition of our role as educators. Up to this point, however, the library has chosen to follow the same approximate assessment cycle as other departments and programs—asking and answering a question about student learning each year—but without submitting reports to the college assessment committee. This approach has permitted us flexibility in how we conduct assessment while still giving us information to report as needed.

The library's assessments of IL learning have shifted over the years from a reliance on multiple-choice assessments to performance-based assessments and from mechanical to higher-level skills. In the early days of IL integration into the general education curriculum, the library relied on a homegrown, ten-question, multiple-choice instrument. One year, it administered the HEDS Research Practices Survey.[11] Over time, however, librarians concluded that these assessments were not providing the information we needed to improve our teaching. In the 2011–12 school year, the research and instruction librarians instead conducted a series of performance-based assessments in FYI. We created simple assessment exercises in the form of in-class worksheets that were intended to be authentic and capable of being organically integrated across various sections of the sequence.[12] This project led to a shift in librarians' pedagogy toward higher-level skills and a thorough reworking of the IL outcomes for FYI; these outcomes anticipated the kinds of complex thinking that would later become the focus of the *Framework*. The special collections librarian later adopted performance-based assessment as part of the first cohort for ACRL's Assessment in Action program and published an early example of a study involving direct assessment of student learning in special collections.[13]

At present, librarians have paused direct assessments of information literacy learning until the semester transition; these will likely resume, with a focus on our new outcomes and curricular structure, after the first year on semesters.

What I Wish People Knew: Working with Special Collections

Information literacy programs and special collections instruction often work in isolation from one another, as though their aims and outcomes do not overlap. Yet, while special collections librarians teach numerous literacies—including visual, primary-source, and archival literacy—that information literacy programs address partially or not at all, it is arguable that most of what information literacy encompasses is also being taught in special collections.[14]

At Augustana, we find that aligning special collections and IL instruction results in a stronger library team and a richer IL program. This realization evolved over nearly twenty years, beginning in 2000, when the library hired a special collections librarian whom the director tasked with increasing students' use of the materials. She and a second special collections librarian, hired in 2007, conducted outreach to departments across campus, including not just programs like history and English but also anthropology, art history, education, geography, graphic design, and FYI, among others. The special collections librarians have always been fully integrated within the larger library team.

When a new instruction coordinator, who had worked in the archives as a college student and had a passion for special collections, began leading the IL program in 2012, it seemed natural for these two strong instruction programs to work more closely together. The library now writes all of its IL outcomes with the intention that they can be taught in special collections as well as in IL instruction sessions. As librarians prepare for FYI on semesters, providing faculty with suggestions about how to teach the defined IL skills, we are including options for assignments in special collections. Similarly, when the librarians wrote IL outcomes for the program as a whole in 2015, the special collections librarian was an equal partner in the process; the eight program outcomes, which we mapped to the ACRL *Framework* and the college-wide learning outcomes, are all taught in special collections as well as other IL instruction sessions.

Alignments such as these build on the demonstrated benefits of special collections instruction. A study by Project Information Literacy that surveyed employers about the information skills they need from college graduates suggests that the patience and ability to sift through print materials is still important in today's workplace, where not everything has been digitized.[15] Another recent study by the Brooklyn Historical Society found that conducting research in special collections increases undergraduate students' academic engagement and possibly their course grades;[16] it may even improve retention rates.[17] Close collaboration between IL programs and special collections, therefore, promotes an important aim of information literacy and libraries more broadly: empowering students to be successful both during and after their college educations.

Notes

1. Association of College and Research Libraries, *Framework for Information Literacy for Higher Education* (Chicago: Association of College and Research Libraries, 2016), http://www.ala.org/acrl/standards/ilframework.
2. Association of College and Research Libraries, *Framework*.
3. "Augustana Student Learning Outcomes," Augustana College, accessed October 9, 2018, https://www.augustana.edu/files/2017-01/student_learning_outcomes.pdf.
4. "Strategic Plan for Thomas Tredway Library," Thomas Tredway Library, Augustana College, last modified September 27, 2019, https://www.augustana.edu/library/strategic-plan.
5. Liaison relationships with the departments in a sixth academic division, language and literature, are divided among three of the librarians due to current staff shortages.
6. Each research and instruction librarian coordinates an element of the library's services. The other three coordinator roles are research help coordinator, outreach coordinator, and displays and events coordinator.

7. Jim Blythe, "Need Satisfaction," in *Key Concepts in Marketing* (Los Angeles: SAGE, 2009), 111–14, https://search.credoreference.com/content/entry/sageukmark/need_satisfaction.

8. "Augustana Student Learning Outcomes."

9. Mark Salisbury, "Does Our Students' Interest in Complex Thinking Change over Four Years?" *Delicious Ambiguity* (blog), September 26, 2017, https://markhsalisbury.org/2017/09; John T. Cacioppo, Richard E. Petty, and Chuan Feng Kao, "The Efficient Assessment of Need for Cognition," *Journal of Personality Assessment* 48, no. 3 (1984): 306–7, https://doi.org/10.1207/s15327752jpa4803_13.

10. The focus on critical thinking over IL in the longitudinal assessment was less puzzling, as this was not the first time a component of one of the nine outcomes had been assessed rather than the entire outcome as defined. For example, oral communication was the focus when communication competency was assessed, although the college recognizes that reading, writing, listening, and speaking are all components of this outcome.

11. "Research Practices Survey," Higher Education Data Sharing Consortium, accessed October 17, 2018, https://www.hedsconsortium.org/heds-research-practices-survey.

12. Stefanie R. Bluemle, Amanda Y. Makula, and Margaret W. Rogal, "Learning by Doing: Performance Assessment of Information Literacy across the First-Year Curriculum," *College and Undergraduate Libraries* 20, no. 3–4 (2013): 298–313, https://doi.org/10.1080/10691316.2013.829368.

13. Sarah M. Horowitz et al., "Assessing Hands-On Learning in Special Collections: A Pilot Study" (poster presentation, American Library Association Annual Conference, Las Vegas, NV, June 28, 2014); Sarah M. Horowitz, "Hands-On Learning in Special Collections: A Pilot Assessment Project," *Journal of Archival Organization* 12, no. 3–4 (2014): 216–29, https://doi.org/10.1080/15332748.2015.1118948.

14. See for example, the recent Society of American Archivists and Association of College and Research Libraries *Guidelines for Primary Source Literacy* (Chicago: Society of American Archivists and Association of College and Research Libraries, June 2018) http://www.ala.org/acrl/sites/ala.org.acrl/files/content/standards/Primary Source Literacy2018.pdf. One (then) current and one former Augustana special collections librarian served on the task force that wrote these guidelines.

15. Alison J. Head, *Learning Curve*, research report (Project Information Literacy, October 16, 2012), http://www.projectinfolit.org/uploads/2/7/5/4/27541717/pil_fall2012_workplacestudy_fullreport-1.pdf.

16. Alice Anderson et al., "Our Findings," TeachArchives.org, accessed June 11, 2018, http://www.teacharchives.org/articles/our-findings.

17. Education Development Center, *Students and Faculty in the Archives*, final evaluation report (Waltham, MA: Education Development Center, March 31, 2014), http://www.teacharchives.org/wp-content/uploads/2014/12/Final-FIPSE-Evaluation-Report.pdf.

Bibliography

Anderson, Alice, Julie Golia, Robin M. Katz, and Bill Tally. "Our Findings." TeachArchives.org. Accessed June 11, 2018. http://www.teacharchives.org/articles/our-findings.

Association of College and Research Libraries. *Framework for Information Literacy for Higher Education*. Chicago: Association of College and Research Libraries, 2016. http://www.ala.org/acrl/standards/ilframework.

Augustana College. "Augustana Student Learning Outcomes." Accessed October 9, 2018. https://www.augustana.edu/files/2017-01/student_learning_outcomes.pdf.

Bluemle, Stefanie R., Amanda Y. Makula, and Margaret W. Rogal. "Learning by Doing: Performance Assessment of Information Literacy across the First-Year Curriculum." *College and Undergraduate Libraries* 20, no. 3–4 (2013): 298–313. https://doi.org/10.1080/10691316.2013.829368.

Blythe, Jim. "Need Satisfaction." In *Key Concepts in Marketing*, 111–14. Los Angeles: SAGE, 2009. https://search.credoreference.com/content/entry/sageukmark/need_satisfaction.

Cacioppo, John T., Richard E. Petty, and Chuan Feng Kao. "The Efficient Assessment of Need for Cognition." *Journal of Personality Assessment* 48, no. 3 (1984): 306–7. https://doi.org/10.1207/s15327752jpa4803_13.

Education Development Center. *Students and Faculty in the Archives: A Project of Brooklyn Historical Society*. Final evaluation report. Waltham, MA: Education Development Center, March 31, 2014. http://www.teacharchives.org/wp-content/uploads/2014/12/Final-FIPSE-Evaluation-Report.pdf.

Head, Alison J. *Learning Curve: How College Graduates Solve Information Problems Once They Join the Workplace*. Research report. Project Information Literacy, October 16, 2012. http://www.projectinfolit.org/uploads/2/7/5/4/27541717/pil_fall2012_workplacestudy_fullreport-1.

Higher Education Data Sharing Consortium. "Research Practices Survey." Accessed October 17, 2018. https://www.hedsconsortium.org/heds-research-practices-survey.

Horowitz, Sarah M. "Hands-On Learning in Special Collections: A Pilot Assessment Project." *Journal of Archival Organization* 12, no. 3–4 (2014): 216–29. https://doi.org/10.1080/15332748.2015.1118948.

Horowitz, Sarah M., Stefanie R. Bluemle, Ellen Hay, and Mark Salisbury. "Assessing Hands-On Learning in Special Collections: A Pilot Study." Poster presentation, American Library Association Annual Conference, Las Vegas, NV, June 28, 2014.

Salisbury, Mark. "Does Our Students' Interest in Complex Thinking Change over Four Years?" *Delicious Ambiguity* (blog), September 26, 2017. https://markhsalisbury.org/2017/09.

Society of American Archivists and Association of College and Research Libraries. *Guidelines for Primary Source Literacy*. Chicago: Society of American Archivists and Association of College and Research Libraries, June 2018. http://www.ala.org/acrl/sites/ala.org.acrl/files/content/standards/Primary Source Literacy2018.pdf.

Thomas Tredway Library. "Strategic Plan for Thomas Tredway Library." Augustana College. Last modified September 27, 2019. https://www.augustana.edu/library/strategic-plan.

Chapter 23

The Claremont Colleges Library
Instruction in a Consortium

Rebecca Halpern

Population Served

The Claremont Colleges Library (TCCL) is unusual in that it is a central library that serves seven independent, private liberal arts colleges known collectively as the Claremont Colleges and colloquially as The 7Cs. The 7Cs are composed of five undergraduate colleges (colloquially known as The 5Cs)—Pomona College, Scripps College, Pitzer College, Harvey Mudd College, and Claremont McKenna College—and two graduate institutions—Claremont Graduate University and Keck Graduate Institute. We are located in Claremont, California, approximately thirty miles east of downtown Los Angeles. The colleges physically adjoin each other, totaling about one square mile in size. All 7Cs are private, predominately white institutions. Six of the seven of the colleges are liberal arts colleges, while Keck Graduate Institute is dedicated entirely to applied health sciences. While the colleges operate independently, many student services, such as the health center, are administered consortially under The Claremont Colleges Services (TCCS); TCCL is a member of TCCS. In total, the seven Claremont Colleges serve approximately 7,700 students. The demographic makeup of students across the campuses is fairly similar. Nearly all students live on or near campus. On average, international students make up approximately 10 percent of undergraduate students. There is a small population of transfer students.

Because TCCL serves all 7Cs, the complexity of the organization greatly influences the instruction program. Most curricular programs are independently run through each college, meaning a biology student at Pitzer may have a very different set of course requirements and degree path than a biology student at Pomona. The impact of this is discussed in greater detail below, but in general, the consortial nature of the library requires us to be as strategic and transparent as possible.

237

Program Scope

Instruction at TCCL is generally grouped into two types: first-year instruction and subject-integrated instruction. First-year instruction comprises around 40 percent of all instruction and about 100 sessions a year. Subject-integrated instruction comprises around 50 percent of all instruction and about 150 sessions a year. The remaining 10 percent takes place outside of the primary instruction division, such as special collections instruction or instruction on digital scholarship tools.

TCCL has a shared pedagogical framework called Habits of Mind that we use to guide all instruction sessions.[1] First adopted in 2013, the Habits of Mind provide an overall framework for student learning aimed at preparing students to become confident researchers and critical thinkers who contribute to thriving communities of practice through the lifelong cultivation of information literacy Habits of Mind. The five Habits are inquiry, evaluation, communication, attribution, and insight. When first adopted, each Habit had associated learning outcomes, differentiated by first-year and capstone years. Over the years, the specific outcomes for each Habit have been revised and in 2017 were condensed to no longer be differentiated by year. However, we are now seeing the benefit of that differentiation and working to differentiate those outcomes once again.

Prior to a library session, librarians are strongly encouraged to have a meeting with the faculty member who requested the instruction session to discuss the course, research assignment, Habits of Mind and associated learning outcomes, and the type of collaboration that makes the most sense. We collaborate with faculty in several ways, including teaching a traditional in-class librarian-facilitated workshop, consulting on research assignments to make them more transparent and accessible for students, developing a course guide or other self-paced learning object, or providing information literacy activities that faculty can lead in class throughout the semester.

Because subject-integrated instruction is not administered programmatically—that is, subject librarians have the freedom to decide which classes are the best candidates for information literacy integration and to assign learning outcomes appropriate for those classes—this chapter focuses on our first-year instruction program. Each of the five undergraduate colleges (the 5Cs) requires a first-year seminar of all first-year and transfer students; the seminar is taken either in their first or second semester (the small number of transfer students are required to take a first-year seminar in their first or second semester at the college). While each college has its own course titles, programmatic goals, assignments, and student learning outcomes, all of the first-year seminars serve to introduce students to college-level writing and research. TCCL's instruction program is well integrated into these seminars. In the 2017–18 school year, 87 percent of first-year seminars had at least one information literacy session led by an instruction librarian. Because each college designs these seminars differently, and because individual section instructors can design their research assignment however they like, the instruction program does not have a shared lesson plan or learning outcomes for our information literacy sessions. Instead, we tailor each session to the specific needs and assignments for that course section and align those needs to our Habits of Mind outcomes.

In addition to in-class instruction, TCCL created two asynchronous, self-paced tutorials to orient and introduce students to research: Start Your Research (SYR) and Exploring Academic Integrity (EAI). We often use SYR as a presession activity for students or in lieu of an in-class session when the learning outcomes of the course don't necessitate one, such as when the assignment doesn't require outside sources. EAI is used in similar ways and is required for all incoming students of Claremont McKenna College and as a remediation of academic integrity infractions at Claremont Graduate University. In the 2018–19 academic year, these tutorials will undergo substantial revisions to content and functionality to better align with the Habits of Mind and the changing needs of the colleges.

Operations

The Claremont Colleges Library has, at the time of writing, twenty-six librarians, thirty-one staff, and seventy-two student employees divided among five divisions: User Services and Resource Sharing; Cataloging and Technical Services; Digital Strategies and Scholarship; Special Collections; and Research, Teaching, and Learning Services (RTLS), which is where the instruction program is located.[2] Each division has a director who reports to the Dean of the Library.

All librarians at TCCL are classified as staff and do not have any requirements for publication or research. The Director of RTLS supervises seven subject librarians (three arts and humanities, two STEM, one social science, and one interdisciplinary studies), a Scholarly Communications Coordinator, and the Undergraduate Engagement Team Leader. The Scholarly Communications Coordinator, the director, and I serve as the leadership group for RTLS (within TCCL, coordinator and team leader roles are considered middle management and have leadership or supervisory responsibilities). The leadership group sets strategic priorities, develops professional development opportunities, and plans and facilitates our monthly division meetings. As the Undergraduate Engagement Team Leader, I supervise two Teaching and Outreach Librarians and one administrative support staff position. The Undergraduate Engagement Team (UET) is comprised of the Teaching and Outreach Librarians and one support staff member. The UET oversees the first-year instruction program, cocurricular and extracurricular outreach, and research support services. UET members, including me, teach about 80 percent of all first-year seminar library sessions, with the remaining 20 percent divided among the subject librarians, the Scholarly Communications Coordinator, and the three instruction librarians in the Special Collections division (see more on this in the Administrative Highlights section). All RTLS librarians provide research support in the form of one-on-one research consultation appointments. In addition to subject-integrated instruction, subject librarians are also responsible for collection management and outreach to their academic departments.

Marketing

For the first-year instruction program, I market library instruction through each of the first-year seminar coordinators at the 5Cs. Early in the summer, I reach out to the faculty course leads via email, reminding them of our long-standing partnership and asking if I can make a presentation at their instruction retreats or send along any information about our program. In those presentations, I give an overview of our instruction program, talk about our library's Habits of Mind, facilitate a discussion about challenges of research for first-year students, and give examples of different ways we can collaborate with a course.

Subject librarians market instruction through departmental email discussion lists, attendance at faculty meetings, and existing (and in some cases long-standing) relationships with faculty who then recommend library instruction to their colleagues.

Collaboration

In addition to the first-year seminar faculty, our biggest ally on campus is the Center for Teaching and Learning (CTL), a consortial center for teaching-specific faculty development for all 7Cs. Both I and the director of RTLS serve on CTL's advisory board, where we set priorities for the year. Through our partnership with CTL, I've led several workshops on designing effective research assignments. These hour-long workshops are marketed through representatives from each campus on the board, who communicate what's going on in CTL with our campus communities through email discussion lists and faculty meetings. Our positions on CTL's board also keep us apprised of what's going on at all the campuses, where the teaching priorities are, and any changes to curricula that may impact our program, such as Scripps College revising how to distribute writing classes throughout the curriculum. My being an active participant in our faculty development center helps position librarians as educators and partners in teaching, which affords us credibility we might otherwise not have, not being faculty members ourselves.

Teaching librarians also connect with CTL by attending workshops, participating in CTL's book clubs, and communicating with library staff about CTL events, all of which help maintain this great relationship.

Assessment

From 2012 to 2014, there was active assessment of instruction in various forms.[3] Since then, due to staffing changes and reorganizations, no systematic assessment has been in place, and librarians feel overwhelmed at the prospect of assessing the instruction program as a whole. Since coming into my role in 2016, I've focused on rebuilding a critical culture of assessment, grounded in accountability to our mission, reflection on our teaching practices, and transparency in decision-making. Sometimes using those values-based terms instead of the word *assessment* helps reframe assessment from something that can feel punitive to something that is based in our values as educators.

We focus our assessment efforts on in-class, formative assessment that allows us to reflect on and improve our teaching strategies and move toward building a culture of assessment. To that end, each teaching librarian is required to observe one library session a semester and to be observed at one of their own sessions. The observed and observer meet before the library session to talk about the session goals and if the observed would like special attention to anything in particular. During the session, the observer uses a simple double-narrative observation form that we adapted from CTL to keep track of their observations.[4] A double-narrative form has two columns: observations and reflections intended to help the observer separate observations from reflections and interpretations about those observations. After the session, the pair meets to debrief. The observer can share both the specifics and mechanics of what was observed and offer insight to the instructor about the impact some of those specifics might have on student learning. Our observation program has led to greater reflection on our teaching practices, sharing of successful active learning and critical pedagogy strategies through a Habits of Mind tool kit, and conversations about what and why we teach.

Pedagogical Highlights

As the Undergraduate Engagement Team Leader, I am responsible for developing a community of practice for all teaching librarians in TCCL. I do this through two primary means: monthly professional development meetings and monthly skillshares (note that this term is generic and not connected to the online learning company of the same name).

The professional development meetings are designed around one theme for the entire semester, and the leadership team plans the curriculum. One especially successful semester had us critically interrogating the ACRL *Framework for Information Literacy for Higher Education* to understand how it does and does not work for our instructional goals, and ultimately had us revising our Habits of Mind to better reflect the frames.[5] For example, we modified the language in our Inquiry Habit to better match the language in the Information Has Value frame. Other topics we've covered in these professional development series are microaggressions and inclusive pedagogy and incorporating scholarly communications into information literacy instruction.

Skillshares are an opportunity for all teaching librarians to demonstrate a database, search technique, instruction approach, or new way of thinking for each other. Each semester, I prepare a skillshare calendar where any of the teaching librarians (in RTLS or special collections) can sign up to facilitate a skillshare. While skillshares are informal and are intended to be low-preparation, I do ask that they include specific takeaway, provide cases for when the skill might be needed, and (for pedagogy- or instructional approach–related skillshares) time and resources needed to prepare the technique, possible pitfalls and benefits, and assessment approaches. Generally, skillshares fall into one of two categories: tools and teaching techniques. Some of the tools we've explored are Sage Research Methods Online, Omeka, and NexisUni. For tool-based skillshares, I ask the presenters to share why they chose a specific tool for the class or student population, which Habits of Mind might be reflected through the use of the tool, and any teaching technique that is particularly useful when teaching the tool. Some of the more teaching-specific skillshare topics we've covered are applying Universal Design for Learning principles to our sessions, an introduction to the BEAM model, and how a lesson plan evolves over time.[6] Regardless of topic, I encourage presenters to reflect candidly about what's worked and what hasn't.

Administrative Highlights

The way I administer our first-year program is quite structured. Each semester, I reach out to the coordinators of all five first-year seminars for a list of their section titles and descriptions. I send that list to all teaching librarians—those in RTLS and our three special collections librarians—and ask them to indicate their preferred classes. During the fall semester, which is our heaviest teaching semester, UET members take about twenty sessions each, and I ask non-UET teaching librarians to take four to six sessions. I ask for preferences instead of assigning classes myself because many of the first-year seminar instructors have long-standing relationships with librarians and because the first-year program is an opportunity for subject librarians to do instruction for topics outside of their subject areas. I create a Google Sheet that pairs each seminar with a librarian.

Once that's complete, I send an email to each seminar instructor introducing them to their course librarian. I encourage the instructor-librarian pair to schedule a time to meet and remind the instructors that even if they aren't assigning a traditional research paper, the librarian can help them incorporate information literacy skills into their class and direct them to our instruction page of the website that lists our philosophy and session guidelines.

Librarians are expected to enter basic information into a statistics-gathering platform, Springshare's LibWizard, to keep track of how many classes are taught each year. I use that form to keep track of which seminars have library sessions to be able to identify courses or instructors who may need more encouragement to take advantage of our expertise. For those instructors who don't frequently take advantage of instruction sessions, I will invite them out for coffee or lunch to find out more about their classes and assignments to see if there are other opportunities for collaboration.

Information Literacy Coordinator Profile

When I was hired in 2016, it was as the Teaching and Learning Services Coordinator, a formal instruction and reference coordinator role with no direct reports. At that time, all RTLS librarians were subject librarians who reported to the RTLS Director, and my role was to coordinate our instruction efforts by assigning first-year seminar classes, overseeing research support, and developing teaching-focused professional development activities. Since then, as a response to my feedback that first-year instruction was so time-consuming that other responsibilities such as collection development and outreach were neglected, RTLS was restructured to have a dedicated team responsible for first-year instruction and non-curricular outreach: the Undergraduate Engagement Team. The Teaching and Learning Services Coordinator position morphed into the UET Leader position, which still oversees the first-year program and research support, but now supervises the two Teaching and Outreach Librarians and an administrative staff person. In addition, my role now is also formally charged with developing programmatic outreach to targeted student populations and programs.

What I Wish People Knew

I feel much more effective guiding the direction of an instruction program with formal supervisory responsibilities. Overseeing a program without positional authority was challenging and required fine-tuned interpersonal skills. As a coordinator, I needed skills of emotional intelligence, negotiation, relationship and consensus building, and advocacy. In my new role, those skills have proven invaluable, and I have worked on developing more management- and supervisory-specific skills. One important skill is engaging folks with the processes you develop. It isn't enough to have workflows and structure for getting work done—you also have to help people engage with those structures in order to make them work.

Regardless of supervisory responsibilities, coordinating a program requires unparalleled critical listening skills: you need to be listening to the needs of your students and faculty, to the challenges and opportunities for teaching librarians, and to the direction of information literacy pedagogy at large. Then you have to translate all those needs into a program and get everyone to feel ownership and buy-in—it often feels like an impossible task! Like all near-impossible tasks, asking for help is a must. Who are your allies? Who understands and can help articulate your vision? How can you leverage relationships with those who do have supervisory responsibilities to ensure accountability? It is difficult, emotionally heavy work, but is doable—and even rewarding—with a support network.

Notes

1. "Our Instruction Philosophy," in "Request an Instruction Session," The Claremont Colleges Library, last modified August 2018, https://library.claremont.edu/request-an-instruction-session/#block-2.
2. "Library Divisions," Our Organization, The Claremont Colleges Library, last modified March 2018, https://library.claremont.edu/people.
3. "Assessment," The Claremont Colleges Library, last modified September 24, 2014, http://libraries.claremont.edu/informationliteracy/assessment.asp.
4. "Multi-campus Teaching Observation Program," The Claremont Colleges Center for Teaching and Learning, accessed April 2, 2019, https://teaching.claremont.edu/observation.
5. Association of College and Research Libraries, *Framework for Information Literacy for Higher Education* (Chicago: Association of College and Research Libraries, 2016).
6. Joseph Bizup, "BEAM: A Rhetorical Vocabulary for Teaching Research-Based Writing," *Rhetoric Review* 27, no. 1 (2008): 72–86.

Bibliography

Association of College and Research Libraries. *Framework for Information Literacy for Higher Education*. Chicago: Association of College and Research Libraries, 2016.

Bizup, Joseph. "BEAM: A Rhetorical Vocabulary for Teaching Research-Based Writing." *Rhetoric Review* 27, no. 1 (2008): 72–86.

Claremont Colleges Center for Teaching and Learning, The. "Multi-campus Teaching Observation Program." Accessed April 2, 2019. https://teaching.claremont.edu/observation.

Claremont Colleges Library, The. "Assessment." Last modified September 24, 2014. http://libraries.claremont.edu/informationliteracy/assessment.asp.

———. "Library Divisions." Our Organization. Last modified March 2018. https://library.claremont.edu/people.

———. "Request an Instruction Session." Last modified August 2018. https://library.claremont.edu/request-an-instruction-session.

Chapter 24

Eastern Connecticut State University

One-Shots across First-Year Programs

David Vrooman

Population Served

Eastern Connecticut State University (Eastern) is a four-year, predominantly undergraduate, public liberal arts university and a member of the Council of Public Liberal Arts Colleges (COPLAC).[1] Information literacy is one of four core competencies of the Liberal Arts Core Curriculum, which serves as the general education curriculum. The information literacy program focuses a considerable amount of its efforts on full-time undergraduates to increase student success and retention for the student body, which though mainly residential (81% of first-year students live on campus; 4,063 FTE), also includes a large commuter population, many of whom juggle jobs and families.[2] The university has a smaller population of part-time degree-seeking students, as well as non-degree-seeking students who take courses but who are not matriculated in a degree program.

Eastern is one of four state universities, which are overseen, along with twelve community colleges, by the state's Board of Regents (BOR) for Higher Education. The University of Connecticut is in another system entirely and is not under the auspices of the BOR.

Eastern is academically split into two schools: Arts and Sciences, which houses humanities, arts, social sciences, and sciences; and Education and Professional Studies, which houses business, education, communication, and kinesiology and physical education.

The School of Education and Professional Studies is home to Eastern's graduate programs, including several professional programs. Eastern offers forty undergraduate majors and sixty-five minors.[3] The university web page for the Liberal Arts Core Curriculum explains the program:

> At Eastern, students take their liberal arts core sequentially in three stages, with introductory courses preparing students for more advanced learning. The curriculum is designed in steps that progress logically from the first to the third or fourth year. Eastern students build foundation methods and concepts in the first step, synthesize their learning and apply this knowledge in the second step, then conclude their liberal arts education in the third step with a capstone experience such as a research paper, thesis, performance, or internship. Students develop complex ways of knowing the social and the natural worlds, as well as the arts and literature; this knowledge is combined with action and interaction. Eastern expects its students to apply their learning to real problems to become effective problem-solvers whether they work alone or as part of a team.[4]

Therefore, we have built our information literacy program around the Liberal Arts Core Curriculum as described in the next section. It is the best way to meet the needs of the most students given limited resources.

Scope

Information literacy is taught broadly to first-year students by the Information Literacy Librarian and the Reference and Instruction Librarian as a basis for the specialized sessions students receive from specific liaison librarians within courses later. As information literacy is a core competency, the expectation is that skills and concepts should be embedded throughout the curriculum. There are four formal programs for information literacy run by the library: (1) the library orientation online tutorial, (2) the FYI 100 Information Literacy session, (3) the English 100 or 100P (ENG 100) Introduction to Using Library Resources, and (4) the various sessions created and carried out by librarians as requested by teaching faculty.

The scope of the program largely focuses on first-year students. Most instruction is done in person, although there has been considerable effort to get the library's LibGuides embedded into Blackboard, Eastern's learning management system.

The Library Orientation

The library orientation is an overview of all the resources and services of the library so that when students come for information literacy sessions, they have an idea of what the library has to offer. The current library orientation for first-year students is the culmination of multiple iterations of library orientations developed over several years. Originally, all first-year students were given tours of the library by librarians or library staff. This version proved unwieldy, and a library video tour series was recorded to deliver the same content.

From 2007 to 2016, this video tour series was embedded into a larger PowerPoint presentation and delivered by several librarians to all new students, whether the student was a first-year, transfer, continuing education, or non-degree-seeking student, in their first or second week of classes. In this version, students were required to sign up for a noncredit course called Introduction to the Library and attend one of sixteen presentations (each presentation had seventy to ninety-six students in attendance) held in the library.

The library orientation now exists (starting fall 2017) for first-year students as an online tutorial. They are required to complete the library orientation online tutorial as part of their three-credit FYI 100: First Year Introduction course during their first or second week of classes. The orientation is still an overview of the resources and services the library has to offer, and still includes the video tour series, but now includes a voice-over of the original presentation recorded by a student theater major. The entire tutorial was recorded using Panopto, a lecture capture software embedded within Blackboard Learn. Students take a quiz after viewing the recorded presentation. The completion of the library orientation counts as one point toward a student's final grade for FYI 100, which ensures a much higher completion rate than an ungraded assignment.

Additionally, other versions of the library orientation exist starting in fall 2017 for transfer students as well as other student populations. Transfer students are prompted by the Office of Continuing Studies and Enhanced Learning to complete a self-guided orientation linked to on its website, which at the time of writing this is being redeveloped as the university has recently moved to a new website. The self-guided version, which is different from the FYI 100 orientation, is contained in a LibGuide, although there is no accountability measure currently in place.[5]

International students are given their own library orientation, which includes a physical tour of the library. The international students' setup is different from other students' because they go through a two-day orientation that has different stops on campus scheduled each hour. It is a small program, and it makes more sense for them to come in person than to do an online orientation. The online versions are helpful either for student groups that are too large for a single session or for students who cannot necessarily make it at a scheduled time due to classes, work, and personal schedules.

The FYI 100 Information Literacy Session

All new, full-time students take the three-credit FYI 100 course in their first semester. FYI 100 is the gateway course for first-year students for the university's Liberal Arts Core Curriculum. In addition to the embedded online tutorial, the Information Literacy Librarian has run a program, required of all students, each year for the last three years. The program has included either a required class in the library for approximately forty sections (split with the Reference and Instruction Librarian) or an online WebEx Event. Due to the scheduling for the WebEx Event, students complete this on their own schedules and not by section. These sessions address issues pertaining to information literacy, and topics and activities for this session have included fake news, website evaluation, and source evaluation.

Structurally, the first-year program changes from year to year, and the Information Literacy Librarian and the Reference and Instruction Librarian work with the First Year Program Committee to respond to these changes. However, the current source evaluation lesson plan has appeared effective for scaffolding content to the ENG 100 information literacy session (described below) and received favorable feedback from teaching faculty and so will be likely put in place as the official content. The source evaluation session in ENG 100 has been more helpful for students when it is scheduled later in the semester because at that point students are looking for sources for a particular topic. This lesson plan introduces students to scholarly, peer-reviewed articles and has them compare these articles with articles from online news, newspapers, and magazines. One of the main learning outcomes from this session is that students identify how the reporting of research studies by various forms of media is often watered down or sensationalized and that these formats do not necessarily do justice to what the research is saying. Students get one point toward their final grade in FYI 100 for completing the source evaluation activity in the session.

Teaching faculty in FYI 100 can request an additional information literacy session. One year a scavenger hunt, introduced during the information literacy session, was carried out by the entire first-year class (approximately 1,000 students) as a homework assignment and submitted by students through Blackboard. The scavenger hunt was historically the lesson plan that FYI 100 sections received if they requested a session on their own before the decision was made to have all sections participate in information literacy. The hunt used a template that can be modified to suit the varying topics students are focusing on in the different sections of FYI 100. Some faculty for different courses will request a scavenger hunt, and we use a similar template. The requests for scavenger hunt sessions are infrequent, and the chance of a student repeating a scavenger hunt is low. The year all students in FYI 100 did scavenger hunts included a moratorium on other courses being able to request one.

The English 100 Information Literacy Session

All new full-time students also take either the three-credit ENG 100 or five-credit ENG 100P within their first year. (It does not have to be taken simultaneously with FYI 100 although about half of first-year students do so.) ENG 100P includes additional writing support if students need it. This is the critical writing course for first-year students. The focus of the information literacy session for this course is an introduction to how to access the print and electronic resources of the library. The Information Literacy Librarian works with faculty to modify the ENG 100 session upon request although each session is standardized and covers both concepts and practical skills. The session is treated as if it is required of all faculty; the Coordinator of the First Year Writing Program tells everyone to sign up (though there is no mechanism to prevent faculty from not signing up). The information literacy program has had 100 percent participation of all sections for over three years with a dip in perfect attendance only recently (2018). Faculty teaching in this program ask the library to schedule the session when students are doing assignments where they will need to utilize the library's resources. This way, the session occurs within the context of what students are doing in class and is reinforced by teaching faculty as students continue with their assignment. Currently, the in-class activity students complete is collected and samples of student work are assessed.

The source evaluation lesson plan in FYI 100, scheduled in the second through fourth week of the semester, scaffolds well into the ENG 100 session, which tends to get scheduled after the first month of the semester, when students need sources for research assignments. Supplemental sessions are available upon request. These supplemental sessions have included topics such as evaluating websites, fair use and copyright, and looking for research on the open internet versus in subscription databases.

Information Literacy Sessions by Request

Though the information literacy program is focused on formal programs, we like to maintain the flexibility for teaching faculty to request sessions when they decide it is appropriate for their students. Most requests are for upper-division courses, though some are for lower-division ones. These requests tend to come from teaching faculty with specific needs for their courses, and these faculty tend to request a session each time they teach the course. A request for instruction is handled by the liaison librarian for the faculty member's department.

Several faculty members who teach required courses for the sociology major have made repeated requests over a long period of time. The nature of the sociology requests have been similar, but the lesson plans are varied so that students do not get the same session multiple times. Students get an overview of sociology-specific content and databases in their required course SOC 201: Introduction to the Sociology Major. In SOC 350: Methods of Social Research, students get a more focused session on how to use the databases, most notably SocINDEX with Full Text and Social Sciences Citation Index, along with interlibrary loan (students are given time to create their interlibrary loan accounts in class if they do not have one already), and an assignment where they are given citations and are required to either find the article or explain how they could acquire the article if it is not immediately available. In the culminating course for the sociology major, SOC 400: Senior Seminar, students are given an annotated bibliography on a sociology-related topic and are required to find additional research that adds to and improves the original list. The annotated bibliography they are given is already very specific, so special attention must be paid on the student's part to what the research they are adding to says. This session has the librarian go one-on-one with each student to address any lingering issues that individual students are experiencing.

The requests from sociology do not represent a formal program are but the result of several sociology instructors independently requesting one-shots from the information literacy program. The frequency with which sociology instructors have requested one-shots led to a different approach to what students would do in the various courses. So although this is not a formal program, it has functioned as one.

Operations and Staffing

Eastern has twelve librarians. The nine full-time librarians are split between Public Services and Technical Services and have instruction responsibilities solely within their liaison areas. Librarians under the auspices of Public Services are the Head of Access Services, the Information Literacy Librarian, the Reference and Instruction Librarian, the Head of Archives and Special Collections, and the Head of the Curriculum Center/Education Librarian. The Head of Access Services, the Head of Archives and Special Collections, and the Head of the Curriculum Center/Education Librarian have their own service desks and operate much like their own departments within the library.

All librarians in Public Services used to be overseen by a Head of Public Services, but this position was not given a funding line after the last person in this position retired. Public Services librarians report directly to the Director of Library Services, and the Technical Services librarians report to the Head of Technical Services. There are also three part-time librarians who staff the reference desk.

The Information Literacy Librarian and the Reference and Instruction Librarian teach all information literacy sessions in programs for first-year students. The FYI 100 program is split evenly between the Information Literacy Librarian and the Reference and Instruction Librarian. The ENG 100 program skews toward the Information Literacy Librarian teaching most sections (thirty-seven for 2017–18), but the Reference and Instruction Librarian teaches several each semester (thirteen for 2017–18) at the former's discretion.

Because all (approximately forty) sections of FYI 100 are currently scheduled to have their information literacy session during the second through fourth week of the semester, the Information Literacy Librarian and the Reference and Instruction Librarian each teach twenty sessions in about two weeks. The schedule is decided by the Information Literacy Librarian early on during the summer and given to the First Year Program Coordinator, who oversees FYI 100, to communicate to teaching faculty. Because the schedule is created early in the summer, the library classroom can be booked accordingly and other instruction sessions, if requested, can be scheduled around the FYI 100 program.

The largest instruction programs for upper-division students are run by the Head of Archives and Special Collections, who is liaison to history and biology, and the Information Literacy Librarian, who is liaison to English, environmental earth science, and kinesiology and physical education. The Information Literacy Librarian also handles instruction for several departments including business, sociology, and social work at the upper-division level. The arrangement is due to established relationships with those faculty. The Reference and Instruction Librarian has the most liaison areas and handles a wide variety of instructional needs as well.

Full-time librarians hold faculty status and are evaluated on their portfolios yearly until they go up for promotion and tenure, after which they are evaluated less frequently. Part-time librarians are considered faculty, although they are seasonal employees who receive renewable contracts for set periods of time (i.e., the fall and spring semesters). They do not keep portfolios, nor can they go up for promotion and tenure. Faculty status allows librarians to serve on university standing committees, which has been a boon for the information literacy program. For instance, the Information Literacy Librarian's seat on the First Year Program Committee directly led to the formal information literacy program for FYI 100. Serving on the Liberal Arts Program Committee and the Assessment Committee has allowed the Information Literacy Librarian to tackle assessment of information literacy across the university. Service to the university, rather than formal marketing efforts, has been the overwhelming driver of expanding information literacy in terms of one-shot programs, individual one-shots, and assessment.

Marketing

Faculty outside of ENG 100 and FYI 100 can and do request information literacy sessions for classes, and sometimes discussions on campus lend themselves to a librarian recommending a one-shot session, but one-shot instruction is not actively pursued for individual classes. The Information Literacy Librarian looks to expand information literacy with a focus on one-shot programs such as the FYI 100 and ENG 100 programs. Expanding information literacy instruction, however, is not really viewed as a marketing effort. It is a curricular improvement effort of the information literacy program within the Liberal Arts Core Curriculum, and for expansion to occur, the case needs to be made to a department chair or program coordinator that the student learning outcomes of the information literacy program align with those of a specific course. Faculty in academic departments would also need to buy in.

The current goal for expanding information literacy is to create a one-shot program within HPE 104, the Department of Kinesiology and Physical Education's course that students overwhelmingly take to fulfill the Health and Wellness category requirement of the Liberal Arts Core Curriculum. We plan to focus on evaluating health-related websites if this collaboration moves forward.

Collaboration

Outside the library, the biggest allies on campus for information literacy are the First Year Program Coordinator, who runs FYI 100, and the First Year Writing Program Coordinator, who runs ENG 100. Both help with matters of scheduling in different ways, as the two programs require different approaches.

The program with FYI 100 was the result of the First Year Program Coordinator trying to revamp the series of learning modules that students in each section take. During the summer of 2016, the coordinator asked the Director of Library Services and the Information Literacy Librarian in a meeting if the library would be willing to help. The information literacy program has been on the schedule of learning modules for FYI 100 since that time. Logistical matters pertaining to keeping the program going are decided between the First Year Program Committee Coordinator and the Information Literacy Librarian.

Assessment

The information literacy program is part of a formal effort to teach and assess information literacy. Overarching assessment of information literacy as a core competency of the Liberal Arts Core Curriculum is part of a larger effort led by the University Assessment Committee and the Liberal Arts Program Committee. The Information Literacy Librarian currently serves on both these committees. This formal effort, which is enshrined in the language for the Liberal Arts Core Curriculum, has only recently been carried out. During the 2017–18 academic year, a sample of incoming first-year students and outgoing seniors were given the Information Literacy Test (ILT) developed by James Madison University.[6] The information literacy program would like to know what students arrive at Eastern knowing and what change has occurred over their academic careers. Results from the test showed that students toward the end of their academic careers appear to have a strong understanding of what peer review is, what plagiarism is, how to acquire a source, knowledge of search operators, and evaluating source credibility. One area that the data suggests students might have regressed on from their first year to senior year was distinguishing between source types. The Information Literacy Librarian and the Reference and Instruction Librarian changed the FYI 100 lesson plan to a source evaluation plan for fall 2018, which will hopefully rectify the problem in this area.

Librarians have conducted several in-class assignments and surveys to see what students are learning in individual sessions. The results over time show that students come to their initial library sessions with widely varying knowledge and abilities. As a result, students are given plenty of time to work on their own during sessions, and the librarian teaching walks around addressing questions on an individual level in order to differentiate instruction.

Role of the One-Shot

One-shot programming really is the bread and butter of the program. This is largely due to Eastern's institutional structure and the curriculum. Occasionally, a one-shot session will lead to teaching faculty making a request for a second session. Librarians are largely called upon by faculty to teach students how to find and access resources using the library's databases and discovery layer.

Pedagogical Highlights

The ENG 100 program does not require information literacy sessions; however, in practice we have usually had 100 percent participation of sections each semester. This amounts to about twenty-five requests each semester, depending on the number of sections being run. Having at least a high percentage of freshmen, if not perfect attendance, has been exciting, as the library can feel confident that students have had at least some exposure to the library's resources in the context of doing assignments.

The FYI 100 program also receives 100 percent attendance each year. This works because faculty who teach the class agree to give up a certain amount of class time (15%) to various university initiatives and programs, including the information literacy program.

Information Literacy Coordinator Profile

The role of information literacy coordinator is considered a responsibility of the Information Literacy Librarian position, though the word *coordinator* is not part of the job title. As coordinator, the Information Literacy Librarian decides what is taught with the first-year student programming, schedules other librarians for sessions based on liaison area responsibilities, manages the library's electronic classroom, and occasionally meets with other librarians who teach to discuss what they are teaching. Eastern is a tight-knit community, not overly large, and faculty and staff generally know each other and each other's jobs, so I feel confident that the lack of *coordinator* in the job title does not matter.

What I Wish People Knew

The advice I would give to others is to get involved in the life of your institution if you are able. The hidden labor that helps keep the program running is the number of university standing committees librarians currently serves on, many of which are relevant to information literacy in various ways: the First Year Program Committee, the Liberal Arts Program Committee (which the Information Literacy Librarian currently chairs), and the University Assessment Committee. This has required the Information Literacy Librarian to become very involved in university politics, which has been a learning experience of its own. It has had the side effect of the Information Literacy Librarian establishing a much larger number of working relationships with faculty across the university than he otherwise would have had had he not participated in committee. These working relationships have resulted in requests for information literacy sessions from numerous faculty from academic departments that were not already making requests, such as business, environmental earth science, and math. Additionally, serving on university standing committees has allowed the Information Literacy Librarian to better assess information literacy across the university. Therefore, weaving information literacy into Eastern's curriculum is best done not through marketing efforts, but through visibility on campus and working with teaching faculty in various capacities so that they get to know you as a person and a professional.

Notes

1. COPLAC (Council of Public Liberal Arts Colleges) home page, accessed December 11, 2018, http://coplac.org.
2. "Facts at a Glance," Eastern Connecticut State University, accessed January 15, 2020, https://www.easternct.edu/about-eastern/facts-at-a-glance.html.
3. "Academics," Eastern Connecticut State University, accessed January 15, 2020, https://www.easternct.edu/academics/index.html.
4. "Liberal Arts Core Curriculum," Eastern Connecticut State University, accessed January 15, 2020, https://www.easternct.edu/liberal-arts-program-committee/liberal-arts-core-curriculum.html.
5. "Library Orientation—Continuing Studies: Home," Library Guides, J. Eugene Smith Library, Eastern Connecticut State University, accessed December 11, 2018, http://easternct.libguides.com/c.php?g=678268.
6. "Information Literacy Test," Madison Assessment, accessed December 11, 2018, https://www.madisonassessment.com/assessment-testing/information-literacy-test.

Bibliography

COPLAC (Council of Public Liberal Arts Colleges) home page. Accessed December 11, 2018. http://coplac.org.

Eastern Connecticut State University. "Academics," Eastern Connecticut State University, accessed January 15, 2020, https://www.easternct.edu/academics/index.html.

———. "Facts at a Glance." Accessed January 15, 2020. https://www.easternct.edu/about-eastern/facts-at-a-glance.html.

———. "Liberal Arts Core Curriculum." Accessed January 15, 2020. https://www.easternct.edu/liberal-arts-program-committee/liberal-arts-core-curriculum.html.

J. Eugene Smith Library. "Library Orientation—Continuing Studies: Home." Library Guides, Eastern Connecticut State University. Accessed December 11, 2018. http://easternct.libguides.com/c.php?g=678268.

Madison Assessment. "Information Literacy Test." Accessed December 11, 2018. https://www.madisonassessment.com/assessment-testing/information-literacy-test.

Chapter 25

UNC Greensboro
A Diverse Program for a Diverse Campus

Jenny Dale

Population Served

UNC Greensboro (UNCG) is a public university within the University of North Carolina system. UNCG had just over 20,000 students enrolled in fall 2018.[1] The university "offers 82 undergraduate majors in more than 100 areas of study, 74 masters programs and 32 doctoral programs."[2] Our Carnegie classification is "Doctoral Universities: High research activity," and we also hold a Carnegie classification for community engagement.[3] In practice, this means that the university is committed to both teaching and research, and we have developed many strong community partnerships.

UNCG is classified as a minority-serving institution (MSI). In fall 2018, 49.4 percent of enrolled students identified as belonging to a racial or ethnic minority.[4] Pell eligibility is a key performance indicator for UNCG, and since 2015 more than half of our students have been Pell eligible.[5] Our program serves students from diverse backgrounds, which shapes the way we approach information literacy because our instruction needs to be engaging and accessible to students coming in with varying levels of experience and preparation.

Student success—particularly as shown by retention and graduation rates—has been a major area of focus for the university in recent years. The current university-level strategic plan at the time of writing (*Taking Giant Steps*) highlights three areas of transformation that both reflect and impact the information literacy work of the University Libraries. The first of these areas is student transformation, which "occurs when students acquire knowledge and develop skills and habits of mind necessary to be life-long learners, informed and engaged members of society, and successful in life and work."[6] Our information literacy program strives to align our work with this area, focusing particularly on critical analysis of and engagement with information both within and beyond the academic context. The second is knowledge transformation, which "occurs when understanding is enhanced through research, creative activity, critical analysis, and translation of research to practice."[7] The third, regional transformation, "occurs when local economies are strong and well-aligned with current and future needs, and when equitable access is provided to a reasonable standard of living and quality of life for all."[8] In service of this goal, our program provides information literacy support for external populations (including local high schools) to promote equitable access to resources and support lifelong learning.

Operations

All liaison librarians teach, though teaching loads vary depending on the needs of our liaison areas. While our First-Year Instruction Librarians tend to have particularly heavy loads, our Business Librarian, our Social Science Data Librarian, our department head, and I also each taught at least eighty classes during the 2017–18 academic year. Additionally, there is no central mechanism for distributing instruction sessions. Research, Outreach, and Instruction librarians all promote, schedule, design, teach, assess, and document information literacy sessions in their own areas of responsibility, requesting help from colleagues as needed. We are very much an "all hands on deck" group.

As the Information Literacy Coordinator, I also coordinate with administratively separate departments within the University Libraries beyond the Research, Outreach, and Instruction (ROI) department teaching and learning efforts. Our Special Collections and University Archives (SCUA) department has an active instruction program of its own, and I frequently work with the Instruction and Outreach Archivist to foster collaboration in our work with disciplinary faculty between our two programs. I similarly coordinate with the teaching faculty and staff in the Digital Media Commons (DMC), a department within the libraries that focuses on instruction and support related to multimedia and digital design projects.

The libraries' current liaison structure was put in place in 2013. At that time, we implemented a team structure with subject-specific teams (Humanities, Science, Social Science) and overlapping functional teams (Collection Management, Information Literacy, and Scholarly Communication). When I moved into my current role, I took over leadership of the Information Literacy functional team, which includes representatives from the three subject teams. In the past, this team has primarily been responsible for leading workshops and providing other opportunities for professional development on information literacy–related topics. For example, in summer 2016, we sponsored a "Teaching Tuesdays" series in which team members led short discussions on teaching topics. The functional team structure is currently under review, and we are discussing the possibility of the Information Literacy functional team becoming more of a community of practice. This is largely because my job description includes responsibility for providing professional development programming on teaching-related topics.

Finally, information literacy is the core focus of the libraries' Critical Analysis and Digital Literacy Engagement (CANDLE) initiative, a task force formed in 2017 charged to "expand our existing programs to embrace and implement a broad range of information literacies including primary source literacy, digital literacy, media literacy, visual literacy, health literacy and data literacy."[9] The initiative team includes members of ROI, SCUA, DMC, and the University Libraries' administration unit and consults with disciplinary faculty and other university stakeholders about information literacy within the context of the undergraduate curriculum.

Program Scope

To address the scope of UNCG's information literacy program, I need to first address the program's structure. Organizationally, the program exists in the ROI department of the University Libraries. As the Information Literacy Coordinator, I also serve as a liaison and I report directly to the head of that department, as do seven other librarians who also have a combination of functional and liaison responsibilities. However, I also supervise two First-Year Instruction Librarians who share the primary responsibility for our First-Year Instruction program.[10] One result of this reporting structure, however, is that my colleagues often conflate the boundaries of my supervisory responsibilities and my coordination work, seeing information literacy as primarily the concern of first-year instruction instead having pedagogical and programmatic implications for the whole department.

The First-Year Instruction Librarians target key 100-level general education courses for information literacy instruction, such as English 101 (College Writing I) and Communication Studies 105 (Introduction to Communication Studies). During the 2017–18 academic year, they provided more than 200 face-to-face instruction sessions for these and other first-year courses, reaching an aggregate total of more than 4,300 students. However, because we do not collect student-level data on our instruction sessions (such as student identification numbers), we are not able to take into account students who might come to multiple sessions in a year, making estimations of the percentage of our student body reached by the First-Year Instruction program nearly impossible.

As previously mentioned, in addition to our varied functional roles, all twelve librarians in the ROI department (including the two First-Year Instruction Librarians, myself, and the ROI department head) serve as liaisons to academic departments on campus. Liaisons taught more than 500 sessions in their academic liaison areas, primarily face-to-face, course-integrated, and assignment-driven workshops at all levels of the undergraduate and graduate curricula. Liaison-driven information literacy activities are not under my supervisory purview, but administratively are considered part of the larger information literacy program. According to my position description, my responsibilities include

- Lead instruction initiatives for the liaisons and take a leadership role in information literacy for the University Libraries
- Collaborate with First-Year Instruction team and other liaison librarians on innovative teaching practices and assessment
- Develop and implement an assessment plan for information literacy
- Provide professional development to other liaison librarians on teaching-related topics
- Maintain statistics and create annual reports on library instruction programs and initiatives
- Stay abreast of trends in information literacy and teaching

In other words, many of these responsibilities involve coordinating teaching and assessment activities for librarians who do not report to me. I sometimes feel uncomfortable "coordinating" the colleagues I don't actually supervise. In some cases, I have needed to rely on my department head to ask colleagues to participate in information literacy and assessment initiatives so that the request is seen as having more authority.

While the bulk of the teaching in our information literacy program is face-to-face, an Online Learning Librarian in ROI works with liaisons to facilitate both synchronous and asynchronous instructional materials for an increasing number of online students. I am currently working with the Online Learning Librarian and the ROI department head to develop a new information literacy tutorial, which will be modular and designed around our information literacy learning goals.

Marketing

We take a pretty decentralized approach to marketing information literacy instruction and other collaborative work, especially in the one-shot format. Individual librarians tend to communicate directly with faculty and instructors in their areas of responsibility; most of us continuously promote one-shot instruction, often through direct email communication. Considering the teaching loads mentioned above, I consider us to be at (or beyond) full capacity for one-shot instruction, especially since many of the librarians in ROI pursue more time-intensive forms of course-integrated instruction alongside teaching one-shots. Nine teaching librarians in ROI averaged seventy-eight one-shot sessions last year, with four of those librarians teaching ninety or more sessions. The demand for information literacy instruction from disciplinary faculty has trended upward over the years, though our staffing has not increased at a commensurate rate.

Collaboration

First-Year Instruction Librarians lead workshops for new College Writing program and basic communication course instructors. These programs are also some of our biggest allies and advocates on campus, and we tend to be very well integrated in both. We have also cultivated a core group of information literacy advocates among UNCG faculty by offering Information Literacy Course Development Awards each year. I inherited this program from my predecessor (now the department head), and it continues to be an excellent marketing tool for the information literacy program. Faculty members apply to redesign courses to meaningfully integrate information literacy by partnering with a librarian or archivist. Successful faculty receive $1,000 stipends, funded by the Libraries with the approval of the Dean of the University Libraries. As of fall 2018, we have had fifteen award recipients. Many of these faculty members have continued to integrate information literacy in later semesters, developing or deepening partnerships with libraries' faculty.

We have used information literacy as a tool to extend our collaboration work outside the library with many other campus and community partners. For example, we provide information literacy workshops for federal TRiO programs and Frontier Set programs on our campus, including the McNair Scholars Program, which supports first-generation or underrepresented minority undergraduate students who plan to seek doctoral degrees. Our McNair collaboration is a recent development, but a rich collaboration. Each McNair Scholar has a dedicated librarian mentor in addition to a faculty mentor, and we provide one-on-one research support as well as group instruction on topics such as literature searching and citation management. We have implemented a scaffolded program of support for the Middle College, a public high school that is located on our campus. We work with other high school groups as well, providing information literacy instruction and resource access for a number of high school programs in Greensboro and surrounding counties.

Assessment

One of the responsibilities listed in the Information Literacy Coordinator position description is to "develop and implement an assessment plan for information literacy." This has been a major goal for me since I transitioned into the position in January 2017. ROI librarians have been encouraged to assess information literacy sessions since before I arrived at UNCG; however, that assessment has traditionally been done individually, idiosyncratically, and with inconsistent reporting. When documenting instruction sessions in our statistical software, ROI librarians are required to indicate whether they assessed the session, to describe what type of assessment was used, and to indicate what learning outcomes were assessed. Reporting beyond this basic information has been very inconsistent as we have not had a clear plan for sharing the results of our assessment efforts.

During the 2017–18 academic year, I began work toward developing and implementing an assessment plan for information literacy by setting out to revise our then-current information literacy student learning outcomes, which had last been updated in 2012.[11] At the beginning of the redesign process, I asked library liaisons to submit ideas for understandings and essential questions (based on Wiggins and McTighe's *Understanding by Design*) related to information literacy for learners at different levels.[12] Librarians from ROI and SCUA submitted ideas, and I worked with our First-Year Instruction/Humanities Librarian to code the resulting qualitative data using an iterative process that drew on the work of Hall and colleagues and of Cornish, Gillespie, and Zittoun.[13] Based on the results of this process, I drafted a set of information literacy learning goals for the University Libraries as a whole, then mapped these goals to student learning outcomes at the first-year/general education, disciplinary/major, and graduate levels. I workshopped these goals and outcomes in a series of meetings with liaisons, with representatives from SCUA and the DMC, and with the CANDLE team members and made them available for comment online in July 2018. The final draft was adopted at our liaison retreat on July 26, 2018.[14] I am proud that, because they were developed through a consensus-building process, these goals reflect the University Libraries' values as they relate to information literacy.

When the learning goals and outcomes were approved, our Associate Dean for Public Services brought together an ad hoc group of librarians involved in assessment of information literacy skills (several members of CANDLE and other liaison librarians) and charged us with taking a coordinated approach to assessment. In 2019, we are focusing on gathering assessment data related to the goal "Students will feel empowered to locate, access, and select information sources appropriate to their information needs." The outcomes associated with this goal are

- Students will develop and use effective search terms for their information needs. (First-Year/General Education)
- Students will select appropriate general databases, catalogs, archival resources, and search engines for their information needs. (First-Year/General Education)
- Students will revise search strategies based on search results. (Disciplinary/Major)
- Students will identify appropriate discipline-specific databases and resources for their information needs. (Disciplinary/Major)
- Students will demonstrate expertise in using discipline-specific databases and resources. (Graduate)

We determined that we would collect and report assessment on an annual cycle, focusing on one goal each year. Working with this ad hoc group, I will analyze assessment data from ROI and SCUA instruction sessions (typically in the form of Google Forms surveys or more authentic instruments like worksheets) at the end of each academic year with the goal of drawing some general conclusions about student learning in the category selected for emphasis.

For many years, ROI librarians have been asked to collect data from in-class assessments. For the past three years, we have had a departmental goal related to final product assessment. Each liaison has been asked to assess final products (typically research papers or speeches) in at least one course they support. This assessment initiative has strengthened existing teaching partnerships, as liaisons tend to engage in final product assessment with classes they work with regularly. Anecdotally, liaisons have shared with me that they use final product assessment to inform instructional design when they work with the same or similar courses in subsequent semesters. I have led departmental workshops on final product assessment and authentic assessment in order to facilitate this process and often consult with other librarians at their request about their assessment approaches. I encourage all liaisons to assess these final products based on a rubric (many of them use the AAC&U Information Literacy VALUE Rubric),[15] but I can require only the two librarians that I supervise to complete and submit this assessment.

Information literacy assessment is a major area of focus for me, and I continue to work with my department head and our Associate Dean for Public Services to determine the best ways to collect, store, analyze, and share assessment data in a more systematic way among all of our teaching librarians.

Pedagogical Highlights

As is the case for many academic libraries, most of UNCG's library instruction takes the form of one-shot workshops. The limitation of this format is well documented and familiar to all instruction librarians. However, I am proud of the pedagogical approach we take to the one-shot, which is student-centered and focuses on active learning, inclusive teaching, and authentic assessment. This approach is reflected in our information literacy goals and outcomes, which emphasize the cognitive and affective dimensions of information literacy. While our one-shot-heavy program makes it difficult to engage in deeper teaching collaborations with disciplinary faculty on the same scale, several of our librarians do have opportunities to embed in courses as teaching partners, work with faculty on assignment design and assessment, and act as research mentors for capstone students, graduate students, and McNair Scholars.

One of my job responsibilities (and probably one of my favorites) is to provide professional development to other liaison librarians on teaching-related topics. I enjoy leading workshops for my teaching librarian colleagues on topics ranging from classroom assessment techniques to developing rubrics for authentic assessment to integrating concepts from the ACRL *Framework for Information Literacy for Higher Education* into one-shot sessions.[16] I also try to lead regular reflective teaching workshops to give teaching librarians some time and space to reflect on their practice.

Administrative Highlights

In many ways, our program is a well-oiled machine in terms of basic administrative mechanisms. We use a shared Google calendar for scheduling our instructional spaces and keep our personal calendars updated to show our individual availabilities for meetings and student consultations. However, we have recently reworked our instruction statistics portal to help foster more collaboration with other teaching units. This involved aligning the ROI, SCUA, and DMC instruction forms to collect data on what literacies we are teaching (based on the work of the CANDLE initiative) and which broad categories of learning outcomes were covered (based on our established UNCG Libraries Learning Goals and Outcomes; see figure 25.1). Standardizing our statistics across all of the University Libraries instruction programs will also help us see which disciplinary instructors and courses work with more than one library unit and get a picture of whether and to what extent students are receiving comprehensive instruction on multiple literacies over the course of their educations.

Figure 25.1

Screenshot of LibInsight fields for tracking student learning outcomes categories and literacies addressed in instruction sessions

Another highlight relates to one of our instructional spaces, which reflects our approach to teaching by supporting active learning and peer teaching or group work. Until 2015, we had a single computer instruction lab in Jackson Library, UNCG's main campus library. However, I had the opportunity (as the then–First-Year Instruction Coordinator) to work with the previous Information Literacy Coordinator and the Associate Dean for Public Services to design a second instructional lab with Information Technology Services (ITS). While ITS maintains the lab and all of the technology in it, our program has first priority for scheduling the lab for instruction sessions. Because we were invited into the design process, we were able to contribute ideas that led to a larger instruction lab (40 computers) that is more conducive to collaborative work than our original lab.

Information Literacy Coordinator Profile

I officially became Information Literacy Coordinator and took on supervisory responsibility after serving as the First-Year Instruction Coordinator at UNCG for seven years. While this position was created in 2009, it did not initially have supervisory responsibilities. My predecessor has referred to her work in that position as "leading from the side," a phrase that captures the tension between having coordination responsibilities for a program and having limited official supervisory control over that program. When she was promoted to the department head for ROI, the insight she had into this role based on her experience helped her advocate for some structural changes to this position.

My role is formal, but I have supervisory purview over only the First-Year Instruction program even though significant information literacy work happens in the liaison program. Because, like most teaching librarians, I wear a lot of hats, it is difficult to pinpoint exactly what percentage of my role is coordination. Since librarians primarily promote and schedule their own information literacy sessions, I do not spend much time on the logistics of assigning and scheduling classes. My regular coordination responsibilities are more in the areas of professional development for colleagues, assessment, and maintaining statistics related to the information literacy program.

What I Wish People Knew

One piece of advice I would give to new information literacy program coordinators would be to seek out opportunities to get involved in campus curriculum initiatives. This not only provides insight into the processes that go into curriculum development, but also affords an opportunity to remind faculty colleagues that information literacy has a place in the curriculum and that it is a shared responsibility, not belonging to only the library. I currently serve on the General Education Revision Task Force and my inclusion at the table has given me opportunities to dispel some misconceptions (information literacy is not just about searching the library catalog) and to advocate for thoughtful inclusion of information literacy and critical thinking in the next iteration of our General Education Program.

I transitioned into this role after seven years of teaching 100 to 150 information literacy sessions each year. I was tired, and I saw this as an opportunity to step back and have more time to spend on continuing to develop the information literacy program itself. What I learned is that a reduced teaching load did not magically free up my time to write a flawless assessment plan or to integrate revolutionary pedagogical approaches. I'm not any less tired or less busy with fewer classes to teach, but I do have more time to spend thinking about our program and how to make it the best that it can be for this institution. This involves a lot of trial and error, which is often invisible labor. It also involves staying current in the profession and being aware of trends and developments in pedagogy, which is fun but can also feel daunting and endless. I've learned—and am still learning—that you don't have to be perfect to be a good leader and a good advocate for the program.

Notes

1. "UNCG Enrollment Summary," Office of Institutional Research, UNC Greensboro, accessed November 6, 2018, https://ire.uncg.edu/factbook/enrollment.
2. "UNCG at a Glance," UNC Greensboro, accessed November 7, 2018, https://www.uncg.edu/inside-uncg/inside-glance.php.
3. "University of North Carolina at Greensboro," Carnegie Classification of Institutions of Higher Education, accessed November 6, 2018, http://go.uncg.edu/phslx4.
4. "Fast Facts 2018," UNC Greensboro, accessed November 7, 2018, https://ire.uncg.edu/fastfacts.
5. "UNCG Degree Seeking Undergraduate Students: Percent Pell Eligible," Office of Institutional Research, UNC Greensboro, accessed November 7, 2018, https://ire.uncg.edu/kpi/pell.
6. "Core Elements," Taking Giant Steps: The University of North Carolina at Greensboro Strategic Plan, UNC Greensboro, accessed November 6, 2018, https://strategicplan.uncg.edu/core-elements.
7. "Core Elements."
8. "Core Elements."
9. "Critical Analysis and Digital Literacy Engagement Initiative: Precis," UNC Greensboro University Libraries, accessed November 7, 2018, https://library.uncg.edu/info/candle/precis.aspx.
10. Librarians at UNCG have faculty status and rank.
11. "Learning Outcomes for Information Literacy," UNC Greensboro University Libraries, last updated July 10, 2012, https://library.uncg.edu/info/help/Information_Literacy_learning_outcomes.pdf.
12. Grant P. Wiggins and Jay McTighe, *Understanding by Design*, 2nd ed. (Alexandria, VA: Association for Supervision and Curriculum Development, 2005).
13. Wendy A. Hall et al., "Qualitative Teamwork Issues and Strategies: Coordination through Mutual Adjustment," *Qualitative Health Research* 15, no. 3 (March 2005): 394–410, https://doi.org/10.1177/1049732304272015; Flora Cornish, Alex Gillespie, and Tania Zittoun, "Collaborative Analysis of Qualitative Data," in *The SAGE Handbook of Qualitative Data Analysis*, ed. Ewe Flick (London: SAGE, 2014), 79-93, https://doi.org/10.4135/9781446282243.
14. "UNCG Libraries Learning Goals and Outcomes," UNC Greensboro University Libraries, last updated July 26, 2018, http://go.uncg.edu/libslos.
15. "Information Literacy VALUE Rubric," American Association of Colleges and Universities, last updated July 2013, https://www.aacu.org/value/rubrics/information-literacy.
16. Association of College and Research Libraries, *Framework for Information Literacy for Higher Education* (Chicago: Association of College and Research Libraries, 2016).

Bibliography

American Association of Colleges and Universities. "Information Literacy VALUE Rubric." Last updated July 2013. https://www.aacu.org/value/rubrics/information-literacy.

Association of College and Research Libraries. *Framework for Information Literacy for Higher Education.* Chicago: Association of College and Research Libraries, 2016.

Carnegie Classification of Institutions of Higher Education. "University of North Carolina at Greensboro." Accessed November 6, 2018. http://go.uncg.edu/phslx4.

Cornish, Flora, Alex Gillespie, and Tania Zittoun. "Collaborative Analysis of Qualitative Data." In *The SAGE Handbook of Qualitative Data Analysis.* Edited by Ewe Flick, 79-93. London: SAGE, 2014. https://doi.org/10.4135/9781446282243.

Hall, Wendy A., Bonita Long, Nicole Bermbach, Sharalyn Jordan, and Kathryn Patterson. "Qualitative Teamwork Issues and Strategies: Coordination through Mutual Adjustment." *Qualitative Health Research* 15, no. 3 (March 2005): 394–410. https://doi.org/10.1177/1049732304272015.

UNC Greensboro. "Core Elements." Taking Giant Steps: The University of North Carolina at Greensboro Strategic Plan. Accessed November 6, 2018. https://strategicplan.uncg.edu/core-elements.

———. "Fast Facts 2018." Accessed November 7, 2018. Office of Institutional Research. https://ire.uncg.edu/fastfacts.

———. "UNCG at a Glance." Accessed November 7, 2018. https://www.uncg.edu/inside-uncg/inside-glance.php.

———. "UNCG Degree Seeking Undergraduate Students: Percent Pell Eligible." Office of Institutional Research. Accessed November 7, 2018. https://ire.uncg.edu/kpi/pell.

———. "UNCG Enrollment Summary." Office of Institutional Research. Accessed November 6, 2018. https://ire.uncg.edu/factbook/enrollment.

UNC Greensboro University Libraries. "Critical Analysis and Digital Literacy Engagement Initiative: Precis." Accessed November 7, 2018. https://library.uncg.edu/info/candle/precis.aspx.

———. "Learning Outcomes for Information Literacy." Last updated July 10, 2012. https://library.uncg.edu/info/help/Information_Literacy_learning_outcomes.pdf.

UNC Greensboro University Libraries. "UNCG Libraries Learning Goals and Outcomes." Last updated July 26, 2018. http://go.uncg.edu/libslos.

Wiggins, Grant P., and Jay McTighe. *Understanding by Design*, 2nd ed. Alexandria, VA: Association for Supervision and Curriculum Development, 2005.

Chapter 26

University of Dubuque
Liaison Model with an Embedded Core

Becky Canovan

Population Served

The University of Dubuque is a small private college with professional programs and a liberal arts core; it is affiliated with the Presbyterian Church USA. The information literacy program is rooted within this required liberal arts core but extends into professional programs ranging from flight operations to nursing, sports marketing, and criminal justice, as well as business and accounting. Our population of around 2,200 full-time equivalent (FTE) students drives the direction of our information literacy program. A third of our 1,800 FTE undergraduate students are people of color. In addition, a third of undergraduates come into our university underprepared, and many are also first-generation college students. With a significant number of underprepared and first-generation students, we find that many students lack basic information literacy (IL) skills. The situation also presents less obvious challenges. For example, many students are very career-focused due to circumstances such as family pressure or financial strain, sometimes leading them to focus exclusively on their major classes and see the liberal arts core as nothing more than a checklist to be completed. In comments and session evaluations, students often say they don't or can't see the utility of IL skills, which are primarily taught in these core courses, because in their minds these skills don't explicitly connect to their professional programs. This has caused us to be intentional and explicit in connecting IL skills taught in non-major courses to professional programs to increase buy-in. Beyond the core courses, the professional programs often require rather specialized sources, meaning our staff can find and show students how to use biblical commentaries, Federal Aviation Administration (FAA) data, and the Census Bureau's American FactFinder.

The programs beyond the traditional undergraduate degree offer additional challenges and opportunities. For example, some of our seminary students and undergraduate and graduate students in our adult evening program haven't been in an academic setting in over a decade. We've learned having a second library staff member assist in those IL sessions has been particularly helpful in offering additional one-on-one support. Similarly, our physician assistant and adult evening programs run year-round and have different meeting times requiring differing staffing needs and some IL instruction shifts beyond the previously typical September-to-May calendar and 8:00 a.m. to 5:00 p.m. workdays.

Program Scope

Our IL program is primarily undergraduate-focused, assignment-driven, face-to-face instruction that mostly occurs in sequenced IL sessions in core courses. In 2017–18, we conducted 399 information literacy sessions, 54 percent of which were taught in core classes; the rest cover twenty-one additional academic departments. Over 90 percent of our instruction is directly tied to specific assignments such as research papers, presentations, speeches, posters, multimodal projects, debates, and digital designs. The remaining 10 percent comprise orientations to international, underprepared, transfer, or new students. While the bulk of the information literacy program resides in the undergraduate college, including our adult evening degree program, the library also provides IL instruction in our advanced degrees in management, seminary, MBA, and physician assistant programs. This instruction is delivered almost exclusively face-to-face, with supplemental online learning objects including self-guided tutorials, videos, and other point-of-need resources housed in course-specific LibGuides.

Our instruction program in the liberal arts core includes a combination of required IL sessions in required courses, optional faculty-requested sessions in required courses, and optional faculty-requested sessions in elective courses students take to fulfill a core or major requirement. The required course comprising the bulk of our core instruction is Introduction to Research Writing (RES104), an interdisciplinary course that doesn't belong to a particular department. RES104 is taken any time between a student's second semester and their senior year. One librarian, and sometimes an additional library staff member, is assigned to each section of RES104. The course is divided into research projects in three different disciplines, where librarians lead class five to six times throughout the semester. We take a holistic approach in this course by covering developing research questions, narrowing topics, evaluating sources, finding sources, searching known items, using sources to answer research questions, and reflecting the student's own research process. This course allows us to build a foundation of IL skills that we know all students will see.

We also employ a liaison model in noncore departments, where single and sequenced in-person sessions are both common. Because we know that the foundational IL skills are covered in RES104, we can focus on the discipline, assignment-specific, or advanced skills that the liaison courses require instead of attempting to cram all library skills into one fifty-minute session. This has clear advantages for upper-level classes, but in 100-level classes it gives us the freedom to tell faculty we're going to focus on just the basic skills such as selecting and narrowing a topic and understanding what to do with the sources once the students find them. This also allows us to scaffold skills in departments where we see students in multiple courses.

Operations

The library has ten staff members, five of whom are professional librarians. All aspects of the IL program are coordinated by the Assistant Director of Public Services (henceforth assistant director), including scheduling instruction, coordinating the instruction lab, and assigning librarians to core instruction. All five librarians, including the director and assistant director, teach IL instruction in their assigned liaison departments. The three teaching librarians and the assistant director also evenly divide the IL sessions in core curriculum courses. In addition, two of our five paraprofessional staff members also work directly with classes, helping in approximately twenty to thirty sessions apiece each year. These staff members also staff the reference desk alongside the liaison librarians. Each is assigned to one section of RES104 each semester so that they can see how we teach, what language we use, and how we approach each course to reinforce this student learning at the reference desk. We have explicitly and purposely integrated our IL and reference teams in this way because we see reference as an extension of instruction. The final three library staff members indirectly assist in the IL program as the main library contacts for resources for our distance seminary programs as they handle interlibrary loan and our book mailing programs. Our sports marketing major provides another great example. The primary database we have for that major is not full-text, and an assignment requires students to find an empirical study. I work directly with our interlibrary loan person to warn her when we're teaching that class and when the assignment is due so she can prepare her workflow for that influx. In turn, she notifies me if she's noticed a distinct lack of requests in that subject area so I can prompt the professor to remind the students.

Our IL program is significant to our campus identity. Information literacy is an explicit student learning outcome of our core curriculum and one of the four goals of our library's strategic plan. As with many major decisions and projects in the library, many of the decisions about the IL program are made as a group, including building and updating core instruction materials and assessment measures. The bulk of this planning happens over the summer during our library strategic planning. These goals, objectives, and initiatives are created and shared with the whole library staff so everyone knows what each of us is hoping to accomplish for the year.

Marketing

Well under half of our IL instruction happens in required sessions of required classes. The vast majority of our sessions fall under recommended or optional categories in a variety of courses taken for core requirements and in departmental majors. As a result, we are always recruiting instruction. Our director meets with all new faculty during their orientation, and each liaison librarian reaches out to new instructors in their disciplines via email. Additionally, librarians consistently lead workshops at our campus-wide spring and summer faculty meetings to showcase what IL can look like. These have resulted in numerous IL sessions.

During the semester, if we see multiple students asking questions about the same course or assignment at the reference desk, we reach out to the professor to suggest a short IL session to address the student concerns instead of doing it one-on-one at the reference desk. Some of us have also been known to wander the hallway where our liaison departments have offices with baked goods or use the lure of the coffee shop in the library to start conversations about IL. Beyond simply recruiting an instruction session, it's also our job to continue to cultivate that relationship both with that course and with that instructor. We've been able to turn a one-shot into a consistent session in each section of that course each semester because the faculty member was impressed and told her colleagues. That department has since changed hands in the library without any loss of instruction due to the strong relationships built. Similarly, we rely on IL evangelists among the faculty to convince their colleagues of the benefits of library instruction. A new faculty addition in our sports marketing program has netted us an additional eight sessions a year after hearing his colleague rave about IL instruction.

Collaboration

Because we don't have any credit-bearing IL courses in the undergraduate curriculum and don't lead workshops, we are entirely dependent on collaborations for access to students in classes. Most of the core classes have a separate coordinator, who isn't the department head, to coordinate and steer that course. Our relationships with those faculty are vital. Their interaction with us can change over the years. They dictate whether sessions in classes are required, highly recommended, or optional. How they view the library and IL instruction is especially important, as many sections of our core classes are taught by adjunct instructors. Having a positive relationship with the coordinator can help us build relationships with individual instructors.

However, if these relationships with coordinators change due to new personnel, changing curriculums, or a negative interaction with the library, there can be drastic impacts on the IL program overall. For example, our relationship with the required composition and writing course has shifted. Originally, we had a required multiday unit in the course. Over time, this morphed into a unit the coordinator highly recommended that new adjuncts use at least once. Then we worked with the coordinator to adapt and build a unit that fit the changing curriculum of the course. This unit is currently optional, leaving much of the burden of selling the instruction on the librarians. Each semester the librarians must reestablish that relationship with every instructor for the course.

One very important collaboration we rely on is with the current campus Director of First Year Experience. We have collaborated with her in numerous ways since she started in the Student Activities office ten years ago. When she took over the coordination of New Student Orientation (NSO), she carved out valuable time for the library thanks to our earlier collaborations. Because of this, the library has had an hour of face-to-face time with every entering first-year student since 2012. Students come in groups of twenty-five to thirty at scheduled times over the required three-day orientation. We have used this as an active and engaging introduction to the library and library services, using a scavenger hunt or a pub-style trivia session. While we recognize that NSO is a busy time and students won't retain all the information with which they are presented, our main outcome for that session is that students learn the library exists, has stuff they can use, and has friendly people who don't take themselves too seriously to help them with just about anything. This seemingly simple session lays the groundwork for future IL instruction, freeing up librarians to say no to professors asking for "a basic intro to the library" when no assignment requires it. It also helps us break down negative perceptions about the library and librarians before the students even get to class. It grounds the idea that students will frequently see librarians in class, not just in the library.

Assessment

The IL team uses direct and indirect measures to assess the program's four learning outcomes annually. An assessment conducted in RES104 constitutes the bulk of this assessment. It contains a few multiple-choice questions on simple skill-based outcomes, but it is composed primarily of short-answer responses to assess higher-level application outcomes. Although much more time- and effort-intensive, these short-answer questions provide a much richer picture of our students' IL skills. They also allow us to understand better where along the process our students are getting lost. Previously, the assessment asked only "define" questions, not the "define and apply" questions we ask now. Further measures include a quiz in an introductory-level English course, faculty-provided information regarding rubric outcomes, and student product analysis.

The learning outcomes for the program were developed and adapted from ACRL's *Framework for Information Literacy for Higher Education*.[1] At the university level, we complete the same assessment forms other campus units complete, which include a plan for the upcoming year based on the prior year's results. Additionally, IL is one of the four goals our library's strategic plan, so selected results are also shared with the entire library staff during our strategic planning each summer. The IL team is also currently developing a curriculum map of our student learning outcomes (SLOs) across our instruction as an internal guide to our instruction and an external accreditation tool.

On the IL team level, each summer we sit down to look at all our assessment results to make changes to our approach, instruction instruments, or the assessment tool itself. Like much of the instruction design and decision-making about the program, our assessment creation, scoring, review, and revision process is collaborative rather than top-down. For example, one year we were surprised at low scores on the question dealing with developing appropriate research questions. Upon a discussion with the instruction team, we realized the wording of our assessment favored the way half of our team taught research questions but alienated the methodology of the rest of the team. We tweaked the wording to be more inclusive of everyone's teaching methods and accurately reflect our students' understanding. The following year's results moved as we expected. Similarly, one year results showed that our students understood the importance of evaluating sources but struggled to articulate how to actually do so. As a team, we developed a new module on evaluation and strategies to reinforce these ideas in additional places during the course.

Role of the One-Shot

One-shot isn't a term we use to differentiate instruction. Because we have long-standing guaranteed multi-session instruction in our core, the pressure to cover everything in a single instruction session, as found with traditional one-shots, is not present within our curriculum. Therefore, the *one-shot* term and its connotations don't really apply. Instead, we designate the sessions in our instruction program in terms of core courses and our liaison instruction. Librarians work with faculty to determine what is necessary to accomplish the IL outcomes for their course, whether that be fifteen minutes or multiple class periods. Some of these liaison sessions are multi-session sequences, including a five-session sequence over a five-week period for an archives exhibit project with a history course and a three-session sequence in *Social Research; others are a twenty-minute drop-in in a business or literature course. The same range applies to our required core courses.*

Pedagogical Highlights

Librarians (minus the director) meet weekly to reflect on the current week's instruction, plan and prep for the upcoming week, troubleshoot and brainstorm new instruction or techniques, and generally check in and be supportive of each other. This process is so important because teaching can be very isolating. Bringing everyone together each week grounds the teaching in a supportive community. Sometimes the most important part of that meeting is the opportunity to decompress, vent, and try to fix something that didn't work. We always celebrate the successes in these meetings, even if they are small. Our core class sessions are taught with common SLOs developed collectively as an IL team, but the strategies and specific lesson plans vary by librarian. Because of our schedules, we don't often get to plan lessons together, so checking in about ideas and how similar strategies played with students is particularly helpful. Any large-scale changes in our core instruction or major decisions about the IL program start here so decisions can be made collectively.

Administrative Highlights

One of our administrative triumphs is explicitly connecting our reference and instruction services. Beyond the training and staffing, we've also recently worked on pulling all the relevant materials together in the same space, whether that be physically or digitally. For example, we have a reference LibGuide that includes all our passwords, quick links, and frequent technology problems and fixes. It also contains a tab with assignment specifics, FAQs, and advice for peculiar course or assignment requirements. We have also organized all the physical learning objects into the underused filing cabinets behind the reference desk. These learning objects can range from a set of articles used to develop research questions about an East Asian humanities topic to worksheets about APA citation format to felt buckets used for sorting activities. Some of these are particular to one course; others can be modified for an assortment of activities. Previously, these objects were housed in various librarian offices, meaning no one knew the extent of what existed, and many objects were recreated in very similar forms, wasting time and materials. Putting them in a public, accessible space we all use on a regular basis addressed many problems with one simple solution.

Additionally, I build the reference team schedule on my wall using sticky notes so I can see any conflicts with our core instruction assignments, which are on the wall right next to it. Building the reference schedule after assigning core sections to librarians, and seeing when classes I know we will inevitably work with are, means I can avoid some common issues, such as booking someone so they have no possibility for lunch or scheduling a reference shift during a time I know that person will have class multiple times a semester, necessitating reference swaps. I also color-code the staff members on my wall, in the online reference calendar, and in the online instruction calendar so I can easily see conflicts. I also do my best to take everyone's preferences into account. I am a big believer in the idea that happy employees do great work. I can't always give each person what they want, but I think making sure they understand that I hear them and their concerns is important.

Information Literacy Coordinator Profile

I've been in the role of Assistant Director of Public Services since 2015. Prior to stepping into this role, I coordinated library instruction for core courses for seven years. That entailed prepping core instruction materials, learning objects, and outlines; teaching them to the other librarians; and acting as a point person for all the core instructors, many of whom were adjuncts. I worked with the previous assistant director to build the overall schedule and act as second-in-command of IL coordinating and scheduling of our library instruction lab. When my supervisor left, I stepped into the role and took the core coordinating with me as a natural fit for that position. This position is a formal role that also includes coordinating the reference desk, scheduling the instruction lab, and handling liaison and teaching responsibilities, as well as approximately ten hours of reference desk shifts. Due to turnover in the teaching library staff over the past three years, the amount of teaching expected of this position is currently likely higher than it will eventually be. During the 2017–18 academic year, I taught 126 of the 399 IL sessions we did. However, 66 of those were my liaison sessions. Since taking on the coordinator role, I have transitioned two of my departments to another liaison librarian to lessen my load so I can spend more time on the coordination part of the job.

The timing of my taking over the position coincided with turnover in our teaching librarian positions. I went from being the least seasoned of the teaching team to a mentor to very new and green teaching librarians. What previously had been a position of coordinating schedules for veteran teachers has become much more leading, mentoring, and encouraging new librarians while also coordinating all the schedules and people. This was actually a blessing in disguise. It gave us a chance to really integrate our reference and instruction strategies, training staff for both reference and instruction simultaneously to show the staff how important each is to the other. We also started treating the reference staff as a team rather than a collection of individuals who happen to staff reference.

What I Wish People Knew

Many parts of the coordinator role go unrecognized, but the piece that keeps it running is my understanding that relationships make all the difference. When I'm scheduling librarians to core sections, I try to pair personalities and teaching styles with the instructor. I have instructors who love to interrupt and interject because they're so excited, keeping the students from answering themselves. I avoid scheduling a new librarian to those sections as such an instructor is just one additional person you need to manage, and that can be difficult when you're new and still learning the material you're teaching. I love to try new things, sometimes on the fly in classes, so I purposely don't schedule myself with an instructor who has taught the class the same way for years. Also, cultivating professional relationships all over campus can be fruitful in ways you might not imagine. You never know when someone's role might change, the power may shift, or new opportunities may arise. Vocal advocates and library supporters can be coaches, office managers, or on-campus day-care teachers. You never know who may be at the table when decisions get made.

My advice for IL coordinators is to be an IL advocate wherever and whenever you can. One of the easiest ways to do this is to simply be professionally curious. When a professor complains about student papers or a particular project being problematic, I ask why and what happened. I try to ask leading questions like "Did the students not turn it in?" "Did they not expand on their thesis?" "Did they not use the right kind of sources?" or "What part of the process didn't meet your expectations?" The answer to their problem might not always be IL instruction, but honestly, often it is something the library can help address. We can help them break down their assignment into a scaffolded assignment, help reword it using language we know students have heard in prior research projects, or direct them to the Writing Center for help in guiding students' writing. And sometimes it can be addressed with IL instruction. Even if we can't help that time, they might remember us when something is problematic next time. I sometimes take a more forward approach when a professor is complaining about a student lacking a particular advanced IL skill, asking them where they mastered that skill. More often than not, I hear "graduate school." This is where I gently remind them that the students in front of them are undergraduates, and although we like to think many of these skills are ones students come in knowing nowadays, that's simply not true. I also remind them IL skills are like any other, they take practice, and "learning" them once in RES104 isn't going to be enough if they aren't reinforced and maintained throughout a student's college career.

Note

1. Association of College and Research Libraries, *Framework for Information Literacy for Higher Education* (Chicago: Association of College and Research Libraries, 2016).

Bibliography

Association of College and Research Libraries. *Framework for Information Literacy for Higher Education.* Chicago: Association of College and Research Libraries, 2016.

Chapter 27

University of Houston

Creating a Space for Care and Connection

Veronica Arellano Douglas

Population Served

The University of Houston (UH) is a school deeply rooted in the city of Houston. Our student body of 46,000 reflects the diversity of the city in which it resides. We are a majority minority campus, with 32 percent of students identifying as Latinx, 21 percent Asian American, 10 percent African American, and 8 percent international students.[1] Approximately 80 percent of students live off campus, making UH a primarily commuter campus.[2] Many students also work either part-time or full-time while attending classes. Given their competing priorities, these students are motivated and engaged in their studies and are often very focused on practical application of knowledge and meeting impending deadlines. Our information literacy program attempts to draw on the experiences and knowledge they bring to the classroom. We focus not just on what is applicable for academia, but on the skills and concepts that they can take with them to their jobs and their life after college. Our information literacy class sessions are course-integrated as opposed to add-on workshops so that students can learn and apply concepts and skills within the coursework necessary to complete their degree requirements. This is true for both our undergraduate and graduate information literacy program.

The recent creation of two UH satellite campuses in Houston suburbs (Sugarland and Katy) means that some librarians drive twenty miles to either location to provide in-person information literacy instruction. This situation, along with an increase in the main campus student population without the necessary accompanying classroom space growth, has created a pressing need for more online education. Our information literacy program is growing to support students in those learning environments through online modules, instructional videos, and research guides.

Although undergraduate student success is an important part of the university's mission and goals for the future, there has been a large-scale cultural shift at UH in the last ten years. UH System Chancellor and President Dr. Renu Khator has dramatically increased fundraising and research initiatives at the university. UH is now a Carnegie-designated Tier 1 research university, Currently, efforts are underway to position UH to become a member of the Association of American Universities. These efforts involve a concerted push to increase research output and grant awards by 50 percent in five years.[3] As a result, much of the library's focus has shifted to research support for faculty and graduate students, which has implications for the library's information literacy education program.

Program Scope

The UH Libraries' information literacy education program is based on course-integrated library classes, typically one- or two-shot sessions for undergraduate and graduate students. These primarily take place in a face-to-face library classroom setting, although we are making inroads in online instruction using self-paced learning modules (created with Articulate software). Our Instruction Team includes me (the instruction coordinator), the English liaison librarian, the instruction librarian, and the online learning librarian (position vacant at the time of writing this chapter). The Instruction Team oversees information literacy curricular integration for foundational undergraduate courses and is responsible for teaching those information literacy class sessions. Foundational courses include the freshman rhetoric and composition two-course sequence (ENGL 1303 and 1304), a multi-section engineering technical communication course (ENGI 2304), and introduction to biology laboratory sections. These cornerstone curricular efforts are a result of over a decade of advocacy and collaborative work on the part of the previous instruction coordinators and English liaison librarians. Each course focuses on research, writing, and information evaluation, making them a natural fit for information literacy integration.

ENGI 2304, ENGL 1303 and 1304 each have a two-shot information literacy class sequence that corresponds to major writing assignments and accounts for 48 percent of the course-integrated classes taught within the liaison services department, of which the Instruction Team is a part. Over the past three years, the previous instruction team created a series of learning modules focused on foundational concepts in information literacy such as developing a research question, developing keywords and search strategies, integrating sources into writing, and evaluating information sources. These interactive modules (created using Articulate software) are used by the biology laboratory courses and online ENGL 1303 and 1304 sections in place of face-to-face instruction and supplement face-to-face instruction for traditional and hybrid English composition sections. The continued growth of the university's student population means that we need to continue to explore options for teaching students online in a meaningful way because we will never have the staff to keep pace with face-to-face instructional demands.

Outside of the Instruction Team, liaison librarians are responsible for teaching classes within graduate and undergraduate courses in their assigned disciplines outside of the foundational classes listed above. Many liaison librarians have developed recurring instructional relationships with faculty in multiple departments, and other regularly taught information literacy classes include those for a general business course, psychology research methods, and upper-level biology courses. This split in instruction responsibilities was originally developed to ease the instruction load presented by rhetoric and composition courses on the English liaison librarian, but later the Instruction Team subsumed the responsibilities for planning and implementing the technical communication and intro to biology lab information literacy curriculum. As a relatively new instruction coordinator to this program (at the time of this chapter's writing, I've been in this position for six months), I would like to see the Instruction Team expand its reach beyond these foundational courses into interdisciplinary collaborative teaching efforts.

Although undergraduate education remains the foundation of our information literacy program, there is certainly room to grow the reach of information literacy to connect with faculty and graduate students. Members of the Instruction Team are also working closely with the education liaison librarian and Coordinator for Graduate Student Services to create a series of asynchronous online "Lit Review 101" courses for new graduate students.

We work hard to sustain teaching relationships that carry on from year to year and are built into the fabric of the teaching program of both the library and the university curriculum, yet we are all limited by what we can accomplish given multiple competing job priorities. I anticipate that facilitating professional development for faculty on information literacy integration and expanding our online instruction efforts will help our program grow in scope without necessitating additional teaching librarian lines (that we will likely never receive). The relationship developed between students and their professors is sustained over an entire semester, with librarians appearing as guest lecturers from time to time. If we can teach faculty to incorporate information literacy into their courses, we could be reaching a far greater number of students in a more meaningful, integrated way.

Operations

The operations of our program is where things get complicated! I am the Instruction Coordinator, a mid-level management position within the department of Liaison Services at the UH Libraries. Liaison Services is composed of fifteen librarians and operates on a team structure with one department head and six coordinators. This structure is a microcosm of the functional model of librarianship developed at the University of Guelph.[4] Within Liaison Services, three teams (Research Services, Outreach, and Instruction) of three librarians each are led by coordinators with supervisory responsibilities. The remaining three coordinators (of Open Education Resources, Graduate Studies, and Collections) are in nonsupervisory positions. As Instruction Coordinator, I supervise three librarians: the English Librarian and two Instruction Librarians. This is a unique situation for an Instruction Coordinator, as the individuals in these positions very frequently oversee programs, but not people.[5] It provides an opportunity for me to gain managerial experience in a subfield of librarianship—teaching—that frequently suffers from a lack of upward mobility.[6]

The Instruction Team is responsible for shaping the tenor and philosophy of the UH Libraries' information literacy education program. We provide professional development opportunities for liaison librarians within our department and for librarians in other parts of the library. In addition, we work specifically with liaison librarians to develop meaningful curricular integration of information literacy, which may include course-integrated library classes, assignment creation, or curriculum mapping.

Four science librarians (from Research Services and Outreach Teams) work with the Instruction Team to plan, assess, and teach several sections of an engineering technical communications class. That process is highly democratic, with all instructors offering feedback on the library workshop curriculum every semester. The Instruction Team operates on a similar model to plan and deliver our English composition library curriculum. As mentioned in the previous section, these two courses are part of the foundation for our information literacy program.

To further complicate matters, the Special Collections department also has its own instruction coordinator, and the Research Services Team is delivering a series of open workshops on digital research tools and data management. Although I am in conversation within these individuals, we don't have a shared instructional philosophy or approach. They are invited to any professional development workshops I lead or facilitate but not required to attend. Therefore, my ability to shape an information literacy education program is dependent on my own and my team's efforts to get people on board with our approach to teaching. Our primary goal for 2019 is to develop a shared definition of information literacy for the library and programmatic learning outcomes that will inform all information literacy education efforts.

Marketing

Our instruction program is interested in seeking opportunities for curricular integration and graduate student support. The language that I've encouraged all teaching and liaison librarians to use when talking to faculty about information literacy focuses on meaningful educational partnerships—not instruction, library days, tours, or orientations. Any information literacy classes should be integral to the content of the class and directly related to an assignment or course content. Additionally, in my interactions with faculty I stress that we put time, thought, and energy into planning high-quality learning experiences for students and that we bring pedagogical expertise around information literacy. This tends to shift the conversation away from "teaching the library" to discussions about learning outcomes and hopes for students.

There is no marketing needed for the ENGI 2304 course or introduction to biology laboratories as we have a solid instructional integration. Each semester I set up two information literacy classes for each section with the ENGI 2304 faculty coordinator and work with the biology lab coordinator to incorporate online modules into the learning management system. ENGL 1303 and 1304 instructors are primarily graduate students and are not required to schedule information literacy classes; however, each semester I communicate directly with the graduate students via email, as well as the program coordinator and graduate student supervisors in person, to encourage instructors to schedule information literacy classes.

Outside of these foundational courses, marketing of our instruction program is done primarily by the liaison librarians in their respective departments. My goal is to empower liaisons to advocate for information literacy education at department meetings, in casual conversations, via email, or with any other communication methods that work for them. In an effort to do so, I've led professional development sessions on talking to faculty about information literacy and teaching and held individual consultations with liaison librarians seeking to revive their instructional relationship with their departmental faculty. I think the strongest way to market any information literacy program is to have a group of librarians who feel confident in their teaching ability and knowledge of information literacy. With this kind of expertise they are able to advocate for our teaching program and find ways to expand it throughout the university curriculum.

Role of the One-Shot

Because our information literacy program does not offer any credit-bearing courses, we are, like so many libraries, tied to the one- or two-shot guest lecture model for information literacy education. That said, I think we are strategic about the classes that we teach and are focused on high-impact, meaningful information literacy one- and two-shots rather than simply getting into all the classes that we can. Students don't learn information literacy via osmosis, and simply interacting with or seeing a librarian isn't a key to unlocking college success. Any one-shot classes we teach within our instruction program should supplement or further course learning outcomes around research and information literacy. That said, having only one or two opportunities to teach and work with students in a course is very limiting, and as much as we—the librarian "we"—want to collaborate with faculty to incorporate information literacy throughout an entire semester course, this is not a frequently available opportunity.

I am a part of a research team that is investigating teaching librarian identity, authority, and power in the classroom setting and higher education more broadly.[7] What we continue to find is that much of the stress and strife that impact teaching librarians' self-efficacy is rooted in the problematic one-shot model of information literacy instruction. It is an inherently unequal relationship that makes our ability to teach, as librarians, completely dependent on the instructor of record.[8] A teaching librarian may work for years to be deemed trustworthy enough to teach one class for an instructor's course, placing an inordinate amount of stress on that one educational interaction. Teaching librarians may feel pressured to adhere to the instructor's objectives for the class, and should it go poorly, as classes sometimes do, the librarian may not be invited to teach a second time. As a profession, we are relying on imbalanced power relationships as the foundation for our teaching practice, and it's made our educational effectiveness, as well as our morale, questionable.

I see the impact of this structure on the liaison librarians in my department, who often have to revive dormant teaching relationships with faculty or solicit new ones to do any kind of teaching at all. They feel pressure to deliver a good class to the instructors who take the information literacy bait so that the relationship will continue and, hopefully, grow. When librarians leave, as they inevitably do from all institutions, those teaching relationships leave with them because they are dependent on one-on-one relationships rather than structured programs. As an instruction coordinator I want to give structure to as much of our teaching program as I possibly can. That means replicating processes and relationships such as those that we have with technical communication, introduction to biology lab, and English composition so that information literacy is interwoven into the fabric of the course.

Collaboration

There is an interesting split on this campus between faculty who focus on research and those who focus on student success and teaching. It may not seem unique to those working in large research university libraries, but as someone who worked at a small liberal arts college for a number of years, I found it a cultural adjustment. Many of the individuals teaching lower-division undergraduate courses are graduate students and nontenured faculty who are either full-time lecturers or adjunct instructors. Courses with several sections, such as the English rhetoric and composition courses, technical communication, and introduction to biology, all have what are called "course coordinators" or supervisors. It can be difficult to sustain teaching relationships with individual instructors, who often change from year to year, so I maintain strong ties to the course coordinators and supervisors. They are the people I turn to when I want to revise our lesson plans, implement larger assessment projects, or discuss issues that are impacting our teaching. Graduate students and adjuncts come and go, as is the precarious nature of nontenured academic employment, but these coordinators are sincerely committed to student success and improving teaching and learning within their designated courses and disciplines.

Maintaining strong ties with our Writing Center is also an essential part of our instruction program. We share certain educational relationships in common—technical communication, English composition and rhetoric—and take a similar approach to learning as an iterative process. The ultimate collaborative goal is to coordinate professional development for teaching faculty, librarians, and writing tutors on information literacy, research, and writing. Existing collaborative Writing Center-Library models, such as those at Stetson University and Rollins College, provide a pathway towards integrated information literacy and writing.[9] I think it's important to find like-minded faculty and staff on campus who share a passion for teaching and learning and student success. It's so easy to feel the strains of burnout in our subfield of instruction librarianship. We're teaching the same topics over and over again to the same classes and trying our best to make our educational efforts meaningful. It can often feel like screaming into the void—Information Literacy and Critical Thinking Matter!—but these collaborations with others also focused on teaching and learning can be revitalizing. Earlier this year a portion of the English department, including the rhetoric and composition coordinator, temporarily moved into the liaison services department suite after a series of fires and flooding rendered their office unusable. Chatting with the rhetoric and composition coordinator regularly about the importance of setting a foundation for students to succeed in their college career was a moment of truly being seen. We spoke the same language, were able to validate our commitment to education, and created a space where we could reflect on the challenges and small victories we face daily in the classroom.

Assessment

I've tried to focus our instruction program on formative assessment, specifically, the Alverno College assessment-as-learning model.[10] Liaison librarians are encouraged to make formative assessment practices an integral part of their class planning process by incorporating learning activities that double as assessment. In ENGL 1303 and 1304 and

ENGI 2304, student learning artifacts from in-class activities (worksheets, student work demonstrated on flip charts, concept maps) are used to determine whether or not students grasp the most salient aspects of the class.[11] At the end of each semester, I facilitate a debriefing meeting with the librarians who teach information literacy classes for these courses. Using instructor reflection in conjunction with these student artifacts helps us modify our lesson plans, change activities, or introduce new ways of teaching particular concepts and skills when needed. Most recently the English Librarian and I revised a lesson plan we'd created for ENGL 1303 to help students analyze video advertisements on social media. The small-group activity we'd originally created didn't facilitate critical analysis of the advertisements, which was demonstrated in students' individual responses to video analysis worksheets. The thinking demonstrated was surface level, and we realized we needed to do a better job of modeling—step-by-step, in detail—the process of analysis. So we turned the small-group activity into a large class activity and discussion with multiple video viewings, guided questions, and instructions for students to research specific aspects of the company sponsoring the advertisement. This modeling of tacit knowledge ultimately led to better individual analysis of their own selected video advertisements, which we were able to see in the worksheets they completed in class. This kind of change may seem small, but it shows the power of formative assessment, which is accessible to all of us whenever we teach a class.

Over the summer I facilitated a series of professional development workshops for my teaching librarian colleagues about learner-centered pedagogy and the general student learning assessment cycle. I focused exclusively on formative assessment because I wanted my colleagues to see that assessment is really about care and concern for students, the act of learning, and the instructor, too. As much as our profession has moved toward the rhetoric of value and impact around information literacy instruction and libraries more broadly,[12] the best we can ever do in libraries in terms of that kind of research—because it is research, not assessment—is hope for correlation. The last large-scale information literacy assessment project at the UH Library took place in 2009 and was the result of a larger assessment of student writing in the first year undertaken by the university. This kind of summative assessment is particularly time-consuming and not something easily replicated year after year. What I appreciated about the legacy of this assessment effort was that it wasn't used to show "impact" of the library's teaching program, but rather was used to gather information about student instructional needs and how our instruction program could meet those needs. As I continue to shape and facilitate our library's instruction program, I am constantly trying to center the needs of students and instructors within our assessment efforts to work toward a "critical assessment practice."[13]

Pedagogical Highlights

One thing I appreciate about the UH Libraries liaison services structure is that Instruction Team members, and myself as coordinator, aren't pigeonholed as "the people who teach freshman comp." I think my team and I have worked hard to demonstrate our experience and expertise in information literacy and pedagogy while maintaining a spirit of openness, accessibility, and collaboration. As a result, we really are seen as teaching and learning consultants within our department and the library. Although we maintain oversight of information literacy classes for foundational undergraduate courses, we are able to engage in conversations about pedagogy and information literacy in many different disciplines and with different groups of learners.

For example, we are currently working with the Coordinator of Research Services and the Data Librarian to develop a series of workshops for librarians and graduate students on finding, evaluating, and using data, as well as a curriculum mapping project on integrating data information literacy into the social sciences undergraduate curriculum. This collaborative relationship combines our Instruction Team's pedagogical expertise with our Research Services Team's vast knowledge of data and research trends to create something meaningful to liaison librarians, researchers, and students. It also ensures that members of the Instruction Team aren't simply "teaching robots," but respected, skilled professionals with knowledge and expertise to share and opportunities to work on new and varied teaching projects.

We've collaborated with multiple liaison librarians to rework existing lesson plans and facilitated training for our colleagues and are currently working on a series of point-of-need and information literacy concept instructional videos for online graduate student instruction. We are also getting a new teaching community of practice off the ground within our library, which includes colleagues from Special Collections, Health Sciences, and other parts of the library. As the instruction coordinator, I am trying to create space where a culture of discussing and reflecting on our teaching can take place. This community of practice is a step toward getting our teaching out in the open where we can all learn from one another.

To that end, our Instruction Team is currently working on an information literacy teaching online tool kit, which will connect all UH librarians to shared lesson plans, sample activities, assessment methods, and resources for teaching and information literacy. The more we can make the hidden work of teaching visible—the planning, emotional work, thinking, assessment, and so on—the more it will be honored for the hard work that it is.

Administrative Highlights

I am still very early in my role as instruction coordinator at the UH Libraries, but drawing on my previous experience as a reference and instruction librarian, I am actively attempting to create an instruction program that staves off burnout. Teaching librarianship and burnout often go hand in hand,[14] and as someone who suffered their own bout right around tenure and promotion time, it's something I want to avoid happening to members of the Instruction Team and my liaison colleagues. This desire informs my administration of our information literacy instruction program and creates an atmosphere that I hope empowers librarians as teachers.

We have shared lesson plans for our information literacy sessions for our foundational undergraduate classes to ease the burden of class planning from scratch for members of the Instruction Team. Those lesson plans were collaboratively created with those librarians teaching those classes and allow librarians to make modifications to activities and facilitation based on their own teaching styles. Class requests for ENGI 2304 and English rhetoric and composition courses are all scheduled by me and used to create spreadsheets where librarians can sign up to teach classes. I keep an eye on the distribution of classes and may reassign sessions if I see that one librarian is teaching a much larger number of classes than colleagues. I tend to assign more difficult faculty—those that don't show up to classes or aren't preparing their students adequately—to myself, since I feel that as a person in a managerial position, I have a bit more clout to nip bad behavior in the bud.

Our onboarding process for new liaison and teaching librarians involves a series of class observations, opportunities to team teach, and then, finally, independent teaching. The timeline varies based on the librarian's teaching experience and comfort, but this onboarding process—which existed before I became instruction coordinator—has been a helpful way to ensure comfort in the classroom.

After noticing this fall that so many ENGL 1303 and 1304 instructors failed to share much needed assignments and timing information with us when scheduling their classes for information literacy sessions, my colleague and Instruction Team member, the English Librarian, created an online instruction request form. It outlines our conditions for teaching—two weeks' notice, instructor must be present, class request must be tied to an assignment or class lesson, students must be aware of their assignment—as well as making submitting a syllabus and assignment mandatory for a class request. In spring 2019 we are trialing this form with the English program, but it may be something we expand for use with other courses.

Lastly, I try to focus on the emotional health and well-being of our Instruction Team members and teaching colleagues. Frequent check-ins and fledgling community of practice are ways to incorporate reflection and much needed emotional sharing space for teachers. We can exchange and learn from one another's experiences.

Information Literacy Coordinator Profile

I've been the instruction coordinator at the UH Libraries for almost six months now, after applying, interviewing, and formally accepting this advertised position. Prior to that I was a reference and instruction librarian at a liberal arts college in Maryland, which I then morphed into an informal role as instruction coordinator. My title and responsibilities shifted so that I was overseeing the library's instruction program, but not supervising people. It was a position born out of interest—I genuinely cared about teaching and learning—but also need. There were many administrative tasks that needed to be accomplished, and the teaching program needed a bit of direction. I was able to translate those experiences into my new position at the UH Libraries. This job is unique for an instruction coordinator in that it is a supervisory role. As previously mentioned in this chapter, I supervise three librarians within my department, but I oversee an information literacy education program that involves fifteen different liaison and functional specialist librarians. I think that working as a social science liaison librarian for ten years has informed my approach to instruction coordination in that I understand the pressures all librarians have on their time. I know what it's like to try to build partnerships with disciplinary faculty, and I want to help other liaison librarians translate information literacy education to their own faculty.

I would be hard-pressed to offer percentages of time spent teaching, coordinating, planning, mentoring, training, and so on, but I do know that because my Instruction Team is not fully staffed, my teaching responsibilities are far greater than what they would be under normal circumstances. As coordinator, I pick up the slack. It's something I am expected to do and something I feel is my responsibility. Ultimately, I'm responsible for the well-being of this instruction program. I know that as our team grows and new librarians are onboarded within our department, my responsibilities will likely shift more toward mentoring and training; however, I will always teach, plan, and coordinate. I get to create the spreadsheets with fifty library classes timed and organized and ready for volunteers to type in their names. I step in when an instructor outside the library is being problematic. It's my responsibility to understand the greater library and university landscape in which our program operates and find ways to advocate for information literacy education and the librarians who teach within our program.

What I Wish People Knew

I don't know if this is an infusion of personality, some kind of patriarchal legacy, or just a healthy dose of empathy, but I want all of the librarians in my department and especially on my team to have good teaching experiences. When someone has a negative interaction with a student or faculty member, feels upset after teaching a class that didn't go as planned, or expresses self-doubt about their own abilities in the classroom, I tend to take responsibility for those feelings. I know from teaching for over a decade that sometimes classes just don't go well. Sometimes it's something we did, sometimes it's the class context, and sometimes the semester is just wearing us all down, including the students and course instructor. Yet despite this firsthand experience and my own increased ability to reflect on less-than-stellar classes in a healthy way, I still tend to want to "fix" the bad teaching experiences of others. I'll think: Maybe if I'd been a better scheduler, trainer, supervisor, consultant, collaborator, intermediary, etc., that class would have gone better and that librarian wouldn't be feeling as down as they are now.

I am thinking about that "bad class" a colleague experienced long after they have stopped thinking about it because I see it as a reflection of the program I am actively working to create. I want my colleagues to feel well prepared and empowered to succeed in any and all educational contexts. I understand that I cannot over-function for my teaching team or my liaison colleagues. However, I am always thinking of individual teaching experiences in terms of the effectiveness of our overall teaching program. This is perhaps what continues to be so surprising to me: just how much caring and emotional labor goes into managing an instruction program. Teaching is deeply affective work. We put so much care into our work with students. It naturally follows that we put that same kind of care and concern into our work with our teaching colleagues. Part of that concern and care is for the individual librarian. I know what a post-class emotional low can feel like, and I don't wish that kind of self-doubt and shame on others. I am also concerned about the health and well-being of our teaching program. I want our teaching librarians to want to teach, and that is a difficult ask if all classroom experiences start to feel negative.

I don't think this kind of emotional labor is an instruction coordinator requirement, but the more I talk to fellow coordinators, the more I am aware of the strong affective component of our work. It's unreported, often unacknowledged, and frequently exhausting work that functions for the good of the instruction program, the library, and ultimately our university. I mention this not to solicit pity, but to call attention to the aspects of instruction program coordination that so frequently get dismissed as soft skills, when really this relational work is what makes our programs successful.

Notes

1. University of Houston Office of Institutional Research, "University of Houston Facts at a Glance," Fall 2018, http://www.uh.edu/ir/reports/facts-at-a-glance/facts-at-a-glance.pdf (2018 version removed from web page).
2. "UH Moment: UH Residential Living Designed for Student Success," *University of Houston News & Events* (blog), February 19, 2014, https://ssl.uh.edu/news-events/stories/2014/February/02192014UHMomentResidentialLife.
3. Renu Khator, "New Research Initiative—50 in 5," Communications from the President, University of Houston, June 18, 2018, https://www.uh.edu/president/communications/communicae/university-community/2018-06-18-new-research-initiative-50-in-5/index.
4. Laura Banfield and Jo-Anne Petropoulos, "Re-visioning a Library Liaison Program in Light of External Forces and Internal Pressures," *Journal of Library Administration* 57, no. 8 (2017): 836, https://doi.org/10.1080/01930826.2017.1367250.
5. Veronica Arellano Douglas and Joanna Gadsby, "Gendered Labor and Library Instruction Coordinators: The Undervaluing of Feminized Work," in *At the Helm: Leading Transformation: ACRL 2017 Conference Proceedings*, ed. Dawn M. Mueller (Chicago: Association of College and Research Libraries, 2017), 266–74, http://www.ala.org/acrl/sites/ala.org.acrl/files/content/conferences/confsandpreconfs/2017/GenderedLaborandLibraryInstructionCoordinators.pdf.
6. Christina Neigel, "LIS Leadership and Leadership Education: A Matter of Gender," *Journal of Library Administration* 55, no. 7 (2015): 521–34, https://doi.org/10.1080/01930826.2015.1076307.
7. Veronica Arellano Douglas, Joanna Gadsby, and Sian Evans, "Peers, Guest Lecturers, or Babysitters: Constructions of Power in the Library Classroom" (presentation, Critical Librarianship and Pedagogy Symposium, Tucso, AZ, November 15, 2018), https://repository.arizona.edu/handle/10150/631576.
8. Veronica Arellano Douglas, "Trust Me," *ACRLog* (blog), November 8, 2018, https://acrlog.org/2017/11/08/trust-me-2.
9. "About the TWC," Olin Library, Rollins College, accessed March 28, 2019, https://www.rollins.edu/library/twc/aboutus.html; Grace Kaletski-Maisel and Megan O'Neill, "From Launch Pad to Stratosphere: Following the Trajectory of Student Learning" (presentation, LOEX annual conference, Houston, TX, May 3, 2018).
10. Carrie Allen, *Alverno College: Lessons from an Assessment Pioneer* (National Institute for Learning Outcomes Assessment, July 2016), http://www.learningoutcomesassessment.org/documents/AlvernoCaseStudy.pdf.
11. See "Worksheets and Lesson Plans for Notes," https://goo.gl/3u7rh7, for lesson plans and student artifact examples.
12. Ebony Magnus, Jackie Belanger, and Maggie Faber, "Towards a Critical Assessment Practice," *In the Library with the Lead Pipe*, October 31, 2018, http://www.inthelibrarywiththeleadpipe.org/2018/towards-critical-assessment-practice.
13. Magnus, Belanger, and Faber, "Towards a Critical Assessment Practice."
14. Mary Ann Affleck, "Burnout among Bibliographic Instruction Librarians," *Library and Information Science Research* 18, no. 2 (Spring 1996): 165–83; Deborah F. Sheesley, "Burnout and the Academic Teaching Librarian: An Examination of the Problem and Suggested Solutions," *Journal of Academic Librarianship* 27, no. 6 (November 2001): 447–451.

Bibliography

Affleck, Mary Ann. "Burnout among Bibliographic Instruction Librarians." *Library and Information Science Research* 18, no. 2 (Spring 1996): 165–83.

Allen, Carrie. *Alverno College: Lessons from an Assessment Pioneer.* National Institute for Learning Outcomes Assessment, July 2016. http://www.learningoutcomesassessment.org/documents/Alverno-CaseStudy.pdf.

Arellano Douglas, Veronica. "Trust Me." *ACRLog* (blog), November 8, 2018. https://acrlog.org/2017/11/08/trust-me-2.

Arellano Douglas, Veronica, and Joanna Gadsby. "Gendered Labor and Library Instruction Coordinators: The Undervaluing of Feminized Work." In *At the Helm: Leading Transformation: ACRL 2017 Conference Proceedings.* Edited by Dawn M. Mueller, 266–74. Chicago: Association of College and Research Libraries, 2017. http://www.ala.org/acrl/sites/ala.org.acrl/files/content/conferences/confsandpreconfs/2017/GenderedLaborandLibraryInstructionCoordinators.pdf.

Arellano Douglas, Veronica, Joanna Gadsby, and Sian Evans. "Peers, Guest Lecturers, or Babysitters: Constructions of Power in the Library Classroom." Presentation, Critical Librarianship and Pedagogy Symposium, University of Arizona, Tucson, AZ, November 15, 2018. https://repository.arizona.edu/handle/10150/631576.

Banfield, Laura, and Jo-Anne Petropoulos. "Re-visioning a Library Liaison Program in Light of External Forces and Internal Pressures." *Journal of Library Administration* 57, no. 8 (2017): 827–45. https://doi.org/10.1080/01930826.2017.1367250.

Jordan, Judith V., Linda M. Hartling, and Maureen Walker. *The Complexity of Connection: Writings from the Stone Center's Jean Baker Miller Training Institute.* New York: Guilford, 2004.

Kaletski-Maisel, Grace, and Megan O'Neill. "From Launch Pad to Stratosphere: Following the Trajectory of Student Learning." Presentation, LOEX annual conference, Houston, TX, May 3, 2018.

Khator, Renu. "New Research Initiative—50 in 5." Communications from the President, University of Houston. June 18, 2018. https://www.uh.edu/president/communications/communicae/university-community/2018-06-18-new-research-initiative-50-in-5/index.

Magnus, Ebony, Jackie Belanger, and Maggie Faber. "Towards a Critical Assessment Practice." *In the Library with the Lead Pipe*, October 31, 2018. http://www.inthelibrarywiththeleadpipe.org/2018/towards-critical-assessment-practice.

Neigel, Christina. "LIS Leadership and Leadership Education: A Matter of Gender." *Journal of Library Administration* 55, no. 7 (2015): 521–34. https://doi.org/10.1080/01930826.2015.1076307.

Olin Library, Rollins College. "About the TWC." Accessed March 28, 2019. https://www.rollins.edu/library/twc/aboutus.html.

Sheesley, Deborah F. "Burnout and the Academic Teaching Librarian: An Examination of the Problem and Suggested Solutions." *Journal of Academic Librarianship* 27, no. 6 (November 2001): 447–51.

University of Houston. "UH Moment: UH Residential Living Designed for Student Success." *University of Houston News & Events* (blog), February 19, 2014. https://ssl.uh.edu/news-events/stories/2014/February/02192014UHMomentResidentialLife.

University of Houston Office of Institutional Research. "University of Houston Facts at a Glance." Fall 2018. http://www.uh.edu/ir/reports/facts-at-a-glance/facts-at-a-glance.pdf (2018 version removed from web page).

Chapter 28

University of Nevada, Las Vegas

Liaisons and Teaching Librarians—Navigating Overlapping Responsibilities and Identities

Chelsea Heinbach and Susan Wainscott

Population Served

University of Nevada, Las Vegas (UNLV) is a public, doctoral-granting research university that recently earned Carnegie Foundation R1 ranking.[1] Of our approximately 28,000 students, about 23,000 are undergraduates.[2] UNLV has sixteen degree-granting academic colleges and schools, including a law school and a medical school. It is a minority-serving institution; is among the most diverse college campuses in the United States; and is an Asian American and Native American Pacific Islander-Serving Institution and Hispanic-Serving Institution.[3] Many undergraduates are first-generation students, and more than 90 percent commute to campus.[4]

UNLV is a young and innovative university founded in 1957. As the university is unburdened by a legacy library collection or deeply seated traditions, librarians have the opportunity to pursue roles not traditionally afforded to them. For example, after nearly a decade without a teaching and learning center on campus, librarians at UNLV have been able to use their pedagogical expertise to lead teaching initiatives. Additionally, our librarians are tenure-eligible faculty with expectations for scholarship and service. This provides opportunities to meet and collaborate with colleagues outside the library by contributing to or leading campus-wide initiatives.

Program Scope

The instruction program at UNLV Libraries aims to create vertically aligned programmatic instruction that is embedded into the curriculum. We are involved in classes where students are required to do research. This includes first-year seminars, English Composition II, and milestone and culminating experience classes. We also work with various other undergraduate, graduate, and professional courses. We estimate that around 70 percent of our undergraduate students experience library instruction during their time at UNLV.

We contribute to learning in the classroom through course-integrated instruction, online learning objects, research consultations, assessment, research assignments cocreated with instructors, and various combinations of these methods. The assignment requirements of each class, desired learning outcomes, and expertise of both librarians and instructors influence what strategy is best in a given situation.

Our online tutorials and research guides are often created for specific courses, but they are available to all students through the learning management system and the library website. In addition to these strategies, UNLV Libraries offers cocurricular events and workshops that contribute significantly to student learning.[5]

We prioritize just-in-time, course-integrated instruction with direct assignment ties over just-in-case sessions. On occasion, we may decline a session if it is unlikely to be meaningful for students or sustainable across semesters. We might suggest using a collaboratively built research assignment or preexisting materials such as tutorials or course guides to ensure classes are informed by the librarians' expertise, even if they are not teaching a session.

Operations

There are various departments throughout UNLV Libraries that contribute to information literacy education. The Educational Initiatives department (EI), Liaison Librarian Program (LLP), Branch Libraries, Special Collections department, and Knowledge Production department all teach course-integrated information literacy. Based on the experiences of the authors and for the purposes of this chapter, we will focus exclusively on the programmatic, vertically aligned instruction conducted by two departments: EI and LLP (see figure 28.1).

EI is focused on general education and outreach and includes one department head, five teaching and learning librarians (TLLs), an outreach librarian, five to seven undergraduate peer research coaches, and a library technician (a skilled staff position that does not require an MLIS). This department also often temporarily hires students as information literacy fellows who contribute to teaching efforts. Meanwhile, the LLP is focused on subject-specific education and outreach and includes one department head, eleven liaison librarians (LLs), and a library technician.

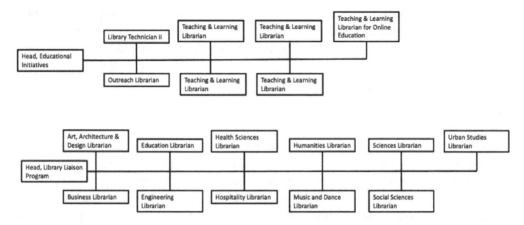

Figure 28.1
An organizational chart depicting the EI department and the LLP.

Roles and Responsibilities

Disclaimer: These are generalizations, and both TLL and LL roles allow for exploration and expertise in many areas. For example, LLs also contribute to the professional development of the library community and sometimes lead first-year classes. TLLs also help with upper-level courses in some cases.

Due to their focus on general education, EI has primary responsibility for English composition classes and most of the first-year seminars (FYSs). The English Composition II class focuses on research and scholarly writing and is UNLV's highest enrolled course, with around sixty sections of twenty-four students each in the fall semester and ninety sections in the spring. This totals around 3,600, or approximately 59 percent of first-year students. FYSs at UNLV are separated by college, and each TLL leads outreach and instruction for the FYSs in one or two colleges. Most FYS library partnerships are led by the TLL, though there are some exceptions.

The undergraduate peer research coaches help EI design the library instruction for English composition. They also teach part of the lesson in every English Composition II library session and are an integral part of the instruction program.[6] As mentioned previously, we sometimes have temporary student employees, and these students help us with instruction, outreach, and research projects as well.

Meanwhile, the LLP has primary responsibility for the remaining undergraduate and graduate courses. For example, the authors of this chapter share coordination for the College of Engineering. Chelsea, as the TLL, leads assignment design, teaching, and outreach initiatives with instructors for the FYS. She consults with Sue, the engineering librarian, on the unique needs of engineering students. Chelsea and Sue choose to teach the library session of the FYS together, though that is not required. Meanwhile, Sue leads the instruction and outreach for upper-level and graduate classes in the college, while sometimes inviting Chelsea to co-teach or consulting with her for teaching ideas.

The two departments coordinate on curriculum mapping and strive to scaffold learning outcomes across degree programs. In the event of vacancies or overwhelming workloads within the library, both TLLs and LLs might take on instruction outside their usual areas.

Administrative Support

Library administration has invested resources into building a curriculum-integrated library instruction program. For example, the Committee on Culture of Teaching and Learning, which developed a set of campus-wide undergraduate learning outcomes, was chaired by the libraries' dean for its first two years.[7] Because of this work, library values were represented in the revision of the general education program.

The libraries also invest financially in the instruction program in various ways. For example, they supply donor money for Faculty Institutes, a librarian-led professional development opportunity for faculty more fully described in the next section of this chapter.[8] EI also regularly receives one-time funding for the aforementioned part-time information literacy fellows, who work on research and teaching projects. Librarians are given additional financial support to seek out teaching-related professional development such as ACRL Immersion, a week-long intensive program focused on information literacy education.

Marketing

UNLV Libraries market information literacy instruction through a combination of efforts including traditional communications, relationship building, and professional development on campus.

Communications

The Director of Communications and the multimedia designer in the UNLV Libraries Development and Communications department create the majority of our traditional marketing materials, including a library newsletter for disciplinary faculty. They also communicate librarian initiatives and accomplishments to campus venues such as the daily campus newsletter and the research magazine *Innovation*.[9] These venues regularly feature librarian initiatives and research, many of which focus on instruction.

Additionally, LLs send periodic emails to disciplinary faculty and instructors, and EI maintains a web page that includes programmatic learning outcomes and ways we collaborate with faculty.[10] The website also has an online form that instructors can use to request a teaching session.

Building Relationships

Librarians in EI and the LLP seek to build long-term relationships with their respective disciplinary faculty. Relationships often grow steadily, and what begins as a request for a database demonstration may expand over time to include anything from assignment design partnerships to embedded librarianship. In time, a successful experience with one course can transfer to other teaching opportunities through word of mouth or shifting teaching assignments.

Professional Development for Faculty

UNLV Libraries offer many professional development opportunities for disciplinary faculty. These include workshops, consultations on emerging technologies, partnership in assignment design, and multiday institutes. These are all chances for librarians to demonstrate their expertise and expose disciplinary faculty to the ways they could work with librarians.

Perhaps the most unique professional development program the libraries offer is the two-day intensive workshop called the Faculty Institute. Offered and led by EI annually since 2010, these institutes assist faculty and instructors in integrating information literacy into their curriculum and assignments.[11] We advertise through our website, where we encourage faculty to apply to the latest institute. Faculty Institutes focus on various topics, including research assignments for first-year seminars, creative research assignments, and more. Participants receive a stipend of between $500 and $1,000 for attending and leave the institute with a completed syllabus and research assignment informed by the expertise of library workers from multiple departments. Around twenty participants attend each institute.

The first set of Faculty Institutes were scaffolded over several years to support the aforementioned revision of the core curriculum, including the FYS, second-year seminars, milestone, and capstone courses.[12] Current Faculty Institutes focus on creative assignment design and revamping the English composition curriculum.

In addition to the Faculty Institutes, librarians are engaged in other teaching and learning events on campus. For example, when the campus created a Teaching for Retention Workshop using the Transparency in Learning and Teaching (TILT) method, librarians were invited as experts in teaching and assignment design.[13]

Collaboration

Library workers collaborate with a large group of external partners. The Office of Online Education, the Office of Undergraduate Education, and the Office of Academic Assessment are some of the strongest allies of the instruction program. TLLs and LLs both partner with non-degree-granting departments such as the Academic Success Center, Career Services, The Intersection (a multicultural education center), the local public school district, and more.

As discussed earlier, both the TLLs and LLs work with faculty, administrators, and staff responsible for advising, tutoring, and program development to integrate information literacy education into the curriculum. LLs also collaborate with disciplinary faculty to develop collections that are relevant to students and course assignments. In addition, as described in several publications, librarians partner with instructors on scholarship of teaching and learning studies.[14]

This model also requires that librarians in both of these roles collaborate heavily with one another. Each pair assigned to a core undergraduate course must navigate differences in working styles to communicate with instructors, share lesson plans, and collect assessment data. LLs and TLLs may also act as backup instructors for one another. It is expected that each of us will make intentional efforts to share documentation for course session materials and build relationships with our library colleagues. Currently, the LL and TLL groups schedule periodic, informal, and supervisor-free meetups to share announcements and brainstorm solutions to collective challenges. These meetups are in addition to periodic joint staff meetings where the two departments work on strategic planning.

A unique collaboration in the EI department is the collective design of the library's Composition II class session. Every two years everyone in the department discusses limitations and strengths of the current lesson plan and decides how to proceed the next year. For example, in 2018 we changed the activities completely. The entire department met to identify learning outcomes and brainstorm ideas for how we could meet them. Then, a voluntary subgroup designed a draft lesson plan, tested it with students and librarians, gathered feedback from the department as a whole, and finalized the lesson.

While our departments share similar goals, our collaboration is not without tension. The model of two departments serving the same disciplines began in 2015, and in some ways is still in transition.[15] As we mentioned above, there are exceptions to the tidy splitting up of FYS and upper-division and graduate courses, so we do not yet have a simple division of labor. It is understandable that a new model might cause some uncertainty around roles. For example, some LLs are concerned that they will not have substantial time with students. As some programs don't have many research assignments between first and final years, students may not meet their LL in the classroom setting until late in their academic career. LLs may prefer more contact with students, faculty, instructors, and teaching assistants as it informs the rest of their work in collection development, upper-level instruction, and more.

Meanwhile, the TLLs' focus on first-year students may incorrectly be perceived as a "helper" role to the LL. It may seem that they are there to teach what the LL is not interested in, instead of being an equal partner with valuable expertise. This incorrect assessment of the role of the TLL may be made by disciplinary faculty, students, LLs, or library leadership. It diminishes the perceived value of the instruction provided by those who teach information literacy in early undergraduate courses.

Compounding this tension is a sense of territory around colleges and degree programs, including the core curriculum courses. Colleges design their FYS to provide academic success skills and an introduction to the discipline. There is an assumption that most students in an FYS will continue in that subject area; however, students' enrollment in an FYS is not a definitive indicator of the major they will continue through. About 30 percent of students take a general FYS, such as Exploring Majors, or one that doesn't align with their ultimate degree.[16] This data indicates that the emphasis of FYSs should be on general education.

The complexity of this model (see figure 28.2) can also cause confusion outside the library. Without understanding the differences between our roles, instructors may reach out to a librarian who isn't the right fit for their course. Students may experience discipline-specific needs throughout their academic careers through student organization projects, personal research interests, or career exploration and may not realize that the disciplines have an assigned LL. Meanwhile, instructors teaching FYSs may refer their students to an LL they know rather than seeking out the TLL most familiar with that course. A library culture that encourages referrals is key to ensuring that undergraduates are properly served as their information needs evolve.

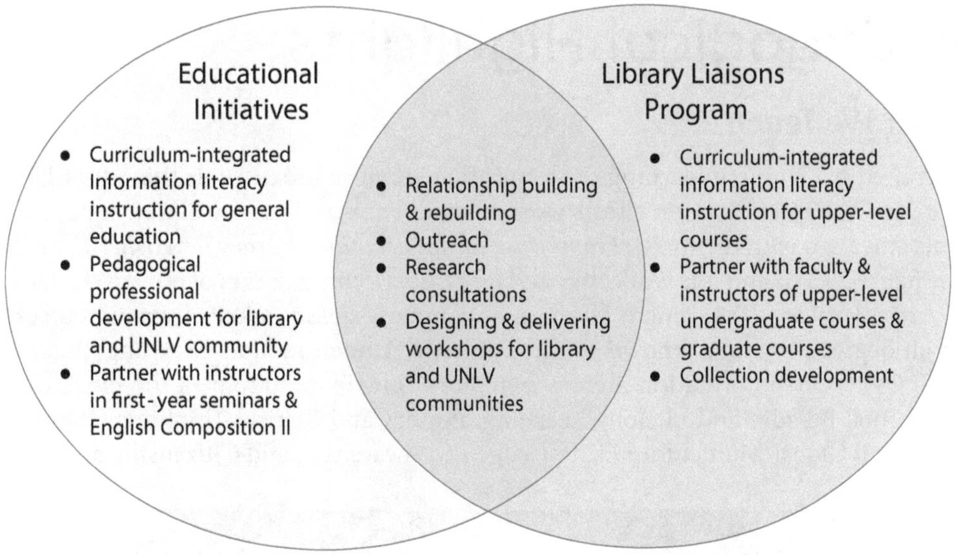

Educational Initiatives

- Curriculum-integrated Information literacy instruction for general education
- Pedagogical professional development for library and UNLV community
- Partner with instructors in first-year seminars & English Composition II

(Shared)
- Relationship building & rebuilding
- Outreach
- Research consultations
- Designing & delivering workshops for library and UNLV communities

Library Liaisons Program

- Curriculum-integrated information literacy instruction for upper-level courses
- Partner with faculty & instructors of upper-level undergraduate courses & graduate courses
- Collection development

Disclaimer that these are generalizations and both roles allow for exploration and expertise in many areas. It is not altogether uncommon for liaisons to also contribute to the professional development of the library community and assist with first-year classes or for the librarians in Educational Initiatives to help with upper-level courses.

Figure 28.2
This image depicts a Venn diagram of common duties shared and divided between the Educational Initiatives Department and Liaison Librarian Program.

Assessment

EI contributes to the three-year assessment cycle on campus.[17] This is coordinated by a TLL and the head of EI. The overall goal of this project changes every three years. For example, in the 2015–2018 cycle, we focused on students' ability to develop research questions. We did this by evaluating student work, including final papers and annotated bibliographies, using rubrics rating information literacy learning outcomes. In the 2019–2021 cycle, we will work to answer new questions about student learning at UNLV.

UNLV Libraries also reports out to a multi-institutional assessment project led by the Greater Western Library Alliance (GWLA) Student Learning Outcomes Task Force.[18] All library instructors report their course-related instruction data in Springshare's LibAnalytics. Librarians are also encouraged to use formative and summative assessment activities of their choosing in the classroom.

Pedagogical Highlights

What We Teach

EI crafted five guiding learning outcomes that serve as broad goals that all of UNLV Libraries' varied instruction efforts work toward. Four of these are aimed at curricular goals and align with the ACRL *Framework for Information Literacy for Higher Education* (see figure 28.3),[19] and one is affective and represents a combination of our curricular and cocurricular work. The campus has a set of common undergraduate learning outcomes for all degree programs, known as the University Undergraduate Learning Outcomes (UULOs).[20] Our information literacy outcomes contribute to four of the five UULOs: Intellectual Breadth and Lifelong Learning; Inquiry and Critical Thinking; Communication and Global/Multicultural Knowledge and Awareness; and Citizenship and Ethics.

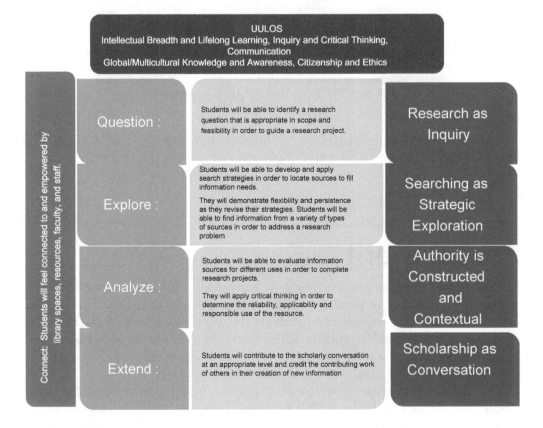

Figure 28.3
Map of programmatic learning outcomes to University Undergraduate Learning Outcomes and the ACRL Framework for Information Literacy in Higher Education

TLLs focus on transferable skills in English composition and FYSs. English composition library instruction currently focuses on keywords, evaluating the components of a scholarly article, and discovery layer searching. As every FYS is unique, the information literacy curriculum is approached by balancing the expertise and goals of the TLL, the LL, the instructor, and the coordinator from the college. Teaching at this level often includes discussing information needs and formats, exploring the information life cycle, writing research questions, and fostering a sense of belonging within the library. Alongside instructors, TLLs might design creative research assignments such as infographic creation, Wikipedia editing, and poster design to encourage student engagement and demystify the research process. Because most students will take both Composition II and an FYS, library instructors avoid duplicating content and focus on reinforcing and building upon skills and knowledge.

Meanwhile, LLs use their familiarity with disciplinary practices to create customized course guides, provide information literacy instruction, and collaborate with disciplinary faculty on course and assignment design. LLs use curriculum mapping and degree program goals to focus on key upper-level undergraduate and graduate courses and scaffold learning activities. They may collaborate with TLLs or not, depending on the needs of the class.

For example, Sue (LL) is embedded in a required culminating experience senior design engineering course. For this course she teaches two sessions, and Chelsea (TLL) collaborates with her on one of them. In the first session, Chelsea leads a brainstorming exercise for design-alternative development and search term exploration. The students then utilize this exercise to identify information needs, and Sue generates database and other resource suggestions based on needs identified. Sue runs the second class session without Chelsea. This class focuses on data literacy, and students follow a directed exploration of several databases with relevant data sets.

Community of Practice

Our model encourages a community of practice. The LLP and EI share learning outcomes and goals for the undergraduate core curriculum.[21] These collective goals, combined with regular opportunities to share best practices, new ideas, and lessons learned, keep the two departments aligned. The EI department collectively creates the curriculum for Composition II class sessions, and the FYS and Faculty Institutes call for partnerships between TLLs and LLs. In addition, EI hosts informal learning opportunities for the libraries, such as brown bags or lightning talk events where library workers from all departments can share educational theory, strategies, and activities. EI also facilitates more formal workshops, such as how to develop learning outcomes or strategies for active learning.

We are lucky to have collective expertise between our departments that informs our work, conversations, and teaching practice. Library workers from multiple departments are exploring the ACRL *Framework* in the classroom, and many are contributing to the literature.[22] In addition, the head of EI is an ACRL Immersion Program Facilitator and an LL is a presenter for the "Engaging with the ACRL Framework" ACRL RoadShow.[23]

Administrative Highlights

We are fortunate to have an experienced library technician who contributes to the instruction program greatly through teaching and through administrative tasks such as scheduling, classroom and technology management, and coordination. This position supports the partnership between TLLs and the English composition program by fielding over

150 instruction requests and teaching several classes. This position also coordinates and teaches for an FYS course and conducts outreach to the K–12 community in surrounding Clark County.

Our lead TLL for English composition and our library technician both contribute to scheduling English composition classes by adding course requests to a shared spreadsheet. They send this sheet to library instructors in EI, who sign up for the classes they are available to teach. Then, the library instructors reach out to the instructor of record to set up a meeting to discuss the library session and what they can expect from the library instructor that semester.

Information Literacy Coordinator Profile

The tasks of an information literacy coordinator are somewhat decentralized in our staffing model, but many core aspects of this role are undertaken by the head of EI. The head of EI has a middle management, tenured-faculty position and is able to avoid some of the pitfalls of a "coordinator" role.[24] The coordination of the English composition program is shared between the head of EI, the library technician in EI, and the TLL who is liaison to the English composition program. The TLLs that work with FYSs and LLs generally coordinate their own instruction with disciplinary faculty. For example, the authors of this chapter share coordination of the College of Engineering. As mentioned above, Chelsea leads instruction to the FYS in engineering and Sue leads upper-level and graduate courses.

What We Wish People Knew

Within this model, it is important to foster a collaborative culture with space for connection between the two departments. Opportunities for informal discussions to brainstorm new ideas, share information, solve problems, and air grievances can encourage trust and help ensure these groups stay informed. The preferred collaboration will differ from pair to pair and would likely be negatively impacted by standardization.

However, centralized communication and support from department heads are necessary. It is vital for department heads to clarify roles and responsibilities for new librarians as well as for those being assigned to new roles. The department heads also need to communicate closely with one another to ensure a common understanding of shared goals, milestones, and deadlines. This can help identify when the groups need to meet to address challenges.

This dual-department model is challenging at times, but also offers opportunities for fruitful collaboration, continued learning, and trust between colleagues. Libraries considering adoption of this model would benefit from surveying existing staff to identify needs in their current staffing model. Holistic appraisal of roles and a transition plan may also be valuable. This model offers a scalable approach that leverages the differing expertise of library workers. In academia, which is riddled by silos, it is powerful to have a consistent reminder that we all share the same goal of student success and to learn from each other as we work to achieve it.

Acknowledgement: Thank you to Melissa Bowles-Terry, Brittany Paloma Fiedler, Priscilla Finley, Lateka Grays, Rosan Mitola, and Amy Tureen for reviewing this chapter and informing our work throughout the process. It is difficult to capture all of the amazing work our colleagues do, and your insight is much appreciated!

Notes

1. "UNLV Attains Highest Status as Research University," News Center, University of Nevada, Las Vegas, December 19, 2018, https://www.unlv.edu/news/release/unlv-attains-highest-status-research-university.
2. "2182 Final Official Enrollment Report for UNLV," University of Nevada, Las Vegas, June 18, 2018, https://ir.unlv.edu/IAP/Files/Final+NSHE+Enrollment+Report+-+Spring+2018.aspx.
3. "Minority-Serving Institution," University of Nevada, Las Vegas, accessed March 18, 2019, https://www.unlv.edu/diversityinitiatives/msi.
4. Natalie Bruzda, "UNLV Looks to Shed Commuter Campus Label with New Housing," *Las Vegas Review-Journal*," August 3, 2018, https://www.reviewjournal.com/news/education/unlv-looks-to-shed-commuter-campus-label-with-new-housing.
5. Rosan Mitola, "University Libraries Co-curricular Outreach Plan July 2017–June 2019," University of Nevada, Las Vegas, accessed March 25, 2019, https://digitalscholarship.unlv.edu/lib_instr/3.
6. Erin Rinto, John Watts, and Rosan Mitola, "The Mason Undergraduate Peer Research Coach Program at the University of Nevada, Las Vegas Libraries" in *Peer-Assisted Learning in Academic Libraries*, ed. Erin Rinto, John Watts, and Rosan Mitola (Santa Barbara, CA: Libraries Unlimited, 2017), 64–79.
7. Jeanne M. Brown and Carrie Gaxiola, "Why Would They Try? Motivation and Motivating in Low-Stakes Information Skills Testing," *Journal of Information Literacy* 4, no. 2 (December 2010): 23–36; Patricia A. Iannuzzi, "Leveraging Library Strengths: Contributions to Undergraduate Education Reform" (presentation, Greater Western Library Alliance Spring 2011 Meeting, Las Vegas, NV, March 2011), online video, 39:30, timestamp 28:22–29:35, https://digitalscholarship.unlv.edu/libfacpresentation/131; Patricia A. Iannuzzi, "Changing Learning, Changing Roles: Collaboration at Every Angle" (presentation, Workshop for Instruction in Library Use, York, Ontario, Canada, May 2007). https://digitalscholarship.unlv.edu/libfacpresentation/54.
8. "Rpietrucha," "Faculty Institutes: Partnering with Faculty, Ensuring Student Success," eConnections, University Libraries, University of Nevada, Las Vegas, December 1, 2015, accessed March 18, 2019, https://www.library.unlv.edu/econnections/2015/12/faculty-institutes-partnering-faculty-ensuring-student-success.html.
9. "Accomplishments," University of Nevada, Las Vegas, accessed March 18, 2019, https://www.unlv.edu/news/accomplishments; "UNLV *Innovation*," University of Nevada, Las Vegas, accessed March 18, 2019, https://www.unlv.edu/research/innovation.
10. "Library Instruction," University Libraries, University of Nevada, Las Vegas, accessed March 18, 2019, https://www.library.unlv.edu/services/instruction.
11. Melissa Bowles-Terry et al., "Collaborating with Teaching Faculty on Transparent Assignment Design," in *Creative Instructional Design: Practical Applications for Librarians*, ed. Brandon K. West, Kimberly D. Hoffman, and Michelle Costello (Chicago: Association of College and Research Libraries, 2017), 291–311.
12. Bowles-Terry et al., "Collaborating with Teaching Faculty."
13. Celeste Calkins and Mary-Ann Winkelmes, "A Teaching Method That Boosts UNLV Student Retention" (poster presentation, UNLV Best Teaching Practices Expo, Las Vegas, NV, January 18, 2018), https://digitalscholarship.unlv.edu/btp_expo/3.
14. Xan Goodman et al., "Applying an Information Literacy Rubric to First-Year Health Sciences Student Research Posters," *Journal of the Medical Library Association* 106, no. 1 (2018): 108–12, https://doi.org/10.5195/jmla.2018.400; Susan Beth Wainscott and Joshua W. Bonde, "Mining for the Best

Information Value with Geoscience Students," in *Disciplinary Applications of Information Literacy Threshold Concepts*, ed. Samantha Godbey, Susan Beth Wainscott, and Xan Goodman (Chicago: Association of College and Research Libraries, 2017), 149–62, https://digitalscholarship.unlv.edu/lib_articles/539; Anna Smedley-López, Heidi Johnson, and Arléne Amarante, "SLICES: Critical Theory as Praxis and Research-Based Service Learning," *Humboldt Journal of Social Relations* 1, no. 39 (2017): 176–91; Erin Rinto, Melissa Bowles-Terry, and Ariel J. Santos, "Assessing the Scope and Feasibility of First-Year Students' Research Paper Topics," *College and Research Libraries* 77, no. 6 (2017): 749–64, https://doi.org/10.5860/crl.v77i6.16554.

15. Greg Carr, "'Rowing the Big Boat Together': Mixed Staffing Arrangements for Large Instruction Programs, a UNLV Case Study," in *User-Centered Design for First-Year Library Instruction Programs*, ed. Cinthya M. Ippoliti and Rachel W. Gammons (Santa Barbara, CA: Libraries Unlimited, 2017), 153–56.

16. Pete Rinto, unpublished data for UNLV undergraduate students completing a first year seminar course and an undergraduate degree who started in 2012, 2018.

17. "Assessment of Student Learning," University Libraries, University of Nevada, Las Vegas, accessed March 18, 2019, https://www.library.unlv.edu/assessment-student-learning (page discontinued).

18. "Student Learning Outcomes Task Force," Greater Western Library Alliance, accessed March 18, 2019, https://www.gwla.org/Committees/slo.

19. Association of College and Research Libraries, *Framework for Information Literacy for Higher Education* (Chicago: Association of College and Research Libraries, 2016), http://www.ala.org/acrl/sites/ala.org.acrl/files/content/issues/infolit/Framework_ILHE.pdf.

20. "University Undergraduate Learning Outcomes," University of Nevada, Las Vegas, accessed March 19, 2019, https://www.unlv.edu/sites/default/files/page_files/3/UNLV-Undergraduate-Learning-Outcomes.pdf.

21. "Library Instruction"; "General Education Core," University of Nevada, Las Vegas, accessed March 18, 2019, https://www.unlv.edu/provost/gen-ed/core.

22. Joshua J. Vossler and John Watts, "Educational Story as a Tool for Addressing the Framework for Information Literacy for Higher Education Background: The Framework," *portal: Libraries and the Academy* 17, no. 3 (July 2017): 529–42, https://doi.org/10.1353/pla.2017.0033; Krystyna K. Matusiak et al., "Visual Literacy in Practice: Use of Images in Students' Academic Work," *College and Research Libraries* 80, no. 1 (January 2019): 123–39, https://crl.acrl.org/index.php/crl/article/view/16950; Krystyna K. Matusiak and Chelsea Heinbach, "Methodological Approaches for Exploring Visual Literacy Practices" (presentation, International Federation of Library Associations and Institutions World Library and Information Congress 2018, Kuala Lumpur, Malaysia, August 26, 2018), http://library.ifla.org/2150; Samantha Godbey and Xan Goodman. "Co-design: Integrating Information Literacy into Your Disciplinary Course" (workshop presentation, AMICAL Consortium, Paris, France, March 31–April 1, 2017), https://www.amicalnet.org/events/co-design-integrating-information-literacy-into-your-disciplinary-course/about-the-workshop; Samantha Godbey, "Testing Future Teachers: A Quantitative Exploration of Factors Impacting the Information Literacy of Teacher Education Students," *College and Research Libraries* 79, no. 5 (2018): 611–23. https://doi.org/10.5860/crl.79.5.611; Samantha Godbey, Susan Beth Wainscott, and Xan Goodman, eds., *Disciplinary Applications of Information Literacy Threshold Concepts* (Chicago: Association of College and Research Libraries, 2017).

23. "Immersion Program Facilitators," Association of College and Research Libraries, accessed March 21, 2019, http://www.ala.org/acrl/immersion/faculty; "Engaging with the ACRL Framework," ACRL RoadShows, Association of College and Research Libraries, accessed March 21, 2019, http://www.ala.org/acrl/conferences/roadshows/frameworkroadshow.

24. Veronica Arellano Douglas and Joanna Gadsby, "Gendered Labor and Library Instruction Coordinators: The Undervaluing of Feminized Work," in *At the Helm: Leading Transformation: ACRL 2017 Conference Proceedings*, ed. Dawn M. Mueller (Chicago: Association of College and Research Libraries, 2017), 266–74, http://www.ala.org/acrl/conferences/acrl2017/papers.

Bibliography

Arellano Douglas, Veronica, and Joanna Gadsby. "Gendered Labor and Library Instruction Coordinators: The Undervaluing of Feminized Work." In *At the Helm: Leading Transformation: ACRL 2017 Conference Proceedings*. Edited by Dawn M. Mueller, 266–74. Chicago: Association of College and Research Libraries, 2017. http://www.ala.org/acrl/conferences/acrl2017/papers.

Association of College and Research Libraries. "Engaging with the ACRL Framework: A Catalyst for Exploring and Expanding Our Teaching Practices." ACRL RoadShows. Accessed March 21, 2019. http://www.ala.org/acrl/conferences/roadshows/frameworkroadshow.

———. *Framework for Information Literacy for Higher Education*. Chicago: Association of College and Research Libraries, 2016. http://www.ala.org/acrl/sites/ala.org.acrl/files/content/issues/infolit/Framework_ILHE.pdf.

———. "Immersion Program Facilitators." Accessed March 21, 2019. http://www.ala.org/acrl/immersion/faculty.

Bowles-Terry, Melissa, John C. Watts, Pat Hawthorne, and Patricia Iannuzzi. "Collaborating with Teaching Faculty on Transparent Assignment Design." In *Creative Instructional Design: Practical Applications for Librarians*. Edited by Brandon K. West, Kimberly D. Hoffman, and Michelle Costello, 291–311. Chicago: Association of College and Research Libraries, 2017.

Brown, Jeanne M., and Carrie Gaxiola. "Why Would They Try? Motivation and Motivating in Low-Stakes Information Skills Testing." *Journal of Information Literacy* 4, no. 2 (December 2010): 23–36.

Bruzda, Natalie. "UNLV Looks to Shed Commuter Campus Label with New Housing." *Las Vegas Review-Journal*, August 3, 2018. https://www.reviewjournal.com/news/education/unlv-looks-to-shed-commuter-campus-label-with-new-housing.

Calkins, Celeste, and Mary-Ann Winkelmes. "A Teaching Method That Boosts UNLV Student Retention." Poster presentation, UNLV Best Teaching Practices Expo, Las Vegas, NV, January 18, 2018. https://digitalscholarship.unlv.edu/btp_expo/3.

Carr, Greg. "'Rowing the Big Boat Together': Mixed Staffing Arrangements for Large Instruction Programs, a UNLV Case Study." In *User-Centered Design for First-Year Library Instruction Programs*. Edited by Cinthya M. Ippoliti and Rachel W. Gammons, 153–56. Santa Barbara, CA: Libraries Unlimited, 2016.

Godbey, Samantha. "Testing Future Teachers: A Quantitative Exploration of Factors Impacting the Information Literacy of Teacher Education Students." *College and Research Libraries* 79, no. 5 (2018): 611–23. https://doi.org/10.5860/crl.79.5.611.

Godbey, Samantha, and Xan Goodman. "Co-design: Integrating Information Literacy into Your Disciplinary Course." Workshop presentation, AMICAL Consortium, Paris, France, March 31–April 1, 2017. https://www.amicalnet.org/events/co-design-integrating-information-literacy-into-your-disciplinary-course/about-the-workshop.

Godbey, Samantha, Susan Beth Wainscott, and Xan Goodman, eds. *Disciplinary Applications of Information Literacy Threshold Concepts*. Chicago: Association of College and Research Libraries, 2017.

Goodman, Xan, John Watts, Rogelio Arenas, Rachelle Weigel, and Tony Terrel. "Applying an Information Literacy Rubric to First-Year Health Sciences Student Research Posters." *Journal of the Medical Library Association* 106, no. 1 (2018): 108–12. https://doi.org/10.5195/jmla.2018.400.

Greater Western Library Alliance. "Student Learning Outcomes Task Force." Accessed March 18, 2019. https://www.gwla.org/Committees/slo.

Iannuzzi, Patricia A. "Changing Learning, Changing Roles: Collaboration at Every Angle." Presentation, Workshop for Instruction in Library Use, York, Ontario, Canada, May 2007. https://digitalscholarship.unlv.edu/libfacpresentation/54.

———. "Leveraging Library Strengths: Contributions to Undergraduate Education Reform." Presentation, Greater Western Library Alliance Spring 2011 Meeting, Las Vegas, NV, March 2011. https://digitalscholarship.unlv.edu/libfacpresentation/131.

Matusiak, Krystyna K., and Chelsea Heinbach. "Methodological Approaches for Exploring Visual Literacy Practices." Presentation, International Federation of Library Associations and Institutions World Library and Information Congress 2018, Kuala Lumpur, Malaysia, August 26, 2018. http://library.ifla.org/2150.

Matusiak, Krystyna K., Chelsea Heinbach, Anna Harper, and Michael Bovee. "Visual Literacy in Practice: Use of Images in Students' Academic Work." *College and Research Libraries* 80, no. 1 (January 2019): 123–39. https://crl.acrl.org/index.php/crl/article/view/16950.

Mitola, Rosan. "University Libraries Co-curricular Outreach Plan July 2017–June 2019." University of Nevada, Las Vegas. Accessed March 25, 2019. https://digitalscholarship.unlv.edu/lib_instr/3.

Rinto, Erin, Melissa Bowles-Terry, and Ariel J. Santos. "Assessing the Scope and Feasibility of First-Year Students' Research Paper Topics." *College and Research Libraries* 77, no. 6 (2016): 749–64. https://doi.org/10.5860/crl.v77i6.16554.

Rinto, Erin, John Watts, and Rosan Mitola. "The Mason Undergraduate Peer Research Coach Program at the University of Nevada, Las Vegas Libraries." In *Peer-Assisted Learning in Academic Libraries*. Edited by Erin Rinto, John Watts, and Rosan Mitola, 64–79. Santa Barbara, CA: Libraries Unlimited, 2017.

Rinto, Pete. Unpublished data for UNLV students completing a first year seminar course and an undergraduate degree who started in 2012. 2018.

"Rpietrucha." "Faculty Institutes: Partnering with Faculty, Ensuring Student Success." eConnections, University of Nevada, Las Vegas, University Libraries. December 1. 2015. https://www.library.unlv.edu/econnections/2015/12/faculty-institutes-partnering-faculty-ensuring-student-success.html.

Smedley-López, Anna, Heidi Johnson, and Arléne Amarante. "SLICES: Critical Theory as Praxis and Research-Based Service Learning." *Humboldt Journal of Social Relations* 1, no. 39 (2017): 176–91.

University of Nevada, Las Vegas. "Accomplishments." Accessed March 18, 2019. https://www.unlv.edu/news/accomplishments.

———. "General Education Core." Accessed March 18, 2019. https://www.unlv.edu/provost/gen-ed/core.

———. "Minority-Serving Institution." Accessed March 18, 2019. https://www.unlv.edu/diversityinitiatives/msi.

———. "2182 Final Official Enrollment Report for UNLV." June 18, 2018. https://ir.unlv.edu/IAP/Files/Final+NSHE+Enrollment+Report+-+Spring+2018.aspx.

———. "University Undergraduate Learning Outcomes." Accessed March 19, 2019. https://www.unlv.edu/sites/default/files/page_files/3/UNLV-Undergraduate-Learning-Outcomes.pdf.

———. "UNLV Attains Highest Status as Research University." News Center. December 19, 2018. https://www.unlv.edu/news/release/unlv-attains-highest-status-research-university.

———. "UNLV *Innovation*." Accessed March 18, 2019. https://www.unlv.edu/research/innovation.

University of Nevada, Las Vegas, University Libraries. "Assessment of Student Learning." Accessed March 18, 2019. https://www.library.unlv.edu/assessment-student-learning (page discontinued).

———. "Library Instruction." Accessed March 18, 2019. https://www.library.unlv.edu/services/instruction.

Vossler, Joshua J., and John Watts. "Educational Story as a Tool for Addressing the Framework for Information Literacy for Higher Education Background: The Framework." *portal: Libraries and the Academy* 17, no. 3 (July 2017): 529–42. https://doi.org/10.1353/pla.2017.0033.

Wainscott, Susan Beth, and Joshua W. Bonde. "Mining for the Best Information Value with Geoscience Students." In *Disciplinary Applications of Information Literacy Threshold Concepts*. Edited by Samantha Godbey, Susan Beth Wainscott, and Xan Goodman, 149–62. Chicago: Association of College and Research Libraries, 2017. https://digitalscholarship.unlv.edu/lib_articles/539.

Chapter 29

University of Portland

Strong Relationships and a Respected Instruction Program

Stephanie Michel, Jane Scott, Heidi Senior, and Diane Sotak

Population Served

The University of Portland is a comprehensive, private, Catholic university located in an urban setting. The university is open to all faiths, with 46 percent of the students self-identifying as Catholic. It serves approximately 3,800 undergraduate students and 500 graduate students in the schools of business, education, engineering, and nursing; a College of Arts and Sciences; and a graduate school.[1] Transfer students constitute 6 percent of the student body. Because of the university's strong focus on traditional undergraduate education, the average age of entering students is 18.3 years.[2] The university's retention rate is high; around 88 percent of first-year students return the following fall.[3]

The University of Portland values residential education; the majority of first-year students live on campus, and 56 percent of the overall student body live in campus housing.[4] Within this environment, the Clark Library is central to campus life as a place to study, to receive research or technology support, to check out items, or to hang out between classes or meetings. Students take their studies seriously, and the library is usually full to capacity with students engaged in solo and collaborative work.

Program Scope

The instruction program covers all levels of the undergraduate curriculum and graduate programs, within all four of the professional schools and many of the departments comprising the College of Arts and Sciences. The majority of our sessions are opt-in and rely on teaching faculty awareness and interest, but some courses have standing requirements for librarian-taught research sessions. For example, undergraduate nursing students have one session in each of their four years, while some first- and second-year business courses automatically schedule sessions for all sections. Faculty value this instruction, and librarians collectively teach between 210 and 250 sessions per year.

Information literacy is included in the goals of the University of Portland's core curriculum.[5] Goal One is to "develop the foundational knowledge and skills necessary for informed inquiry, decision-making, and communication."[6] Among the outcomes for this goal are that students will be able to "find and use information to support the process of critical and analytical pursuits."[7] The information literacy outcome for the core curriculum is currently associated with lower-division science classes for non-majors as well as a fine arts course. The integration of the information literacy outcome into the core curriculum has evolved to equitably distribute the core elements across the undergraduate curriculum. In fact, the core curriculum is currently being reviewed and plans for restructuring are anticipated. An instruction librarian serves on the Core Curriculum Revitalization Committee and provides insight and input into this process.

Because most of our involvement is by faculty request, we do not necessarily meet with all sections of a course. Depending on a student's selection of core and major courses, the number of instruction sessions they attend varies. Therefore, we have identified separate learning outcomes for frequently taught courses to differentiate and scaffold instruction. To demonstrate this effort to faculty, we post the outcomes on our Curriculum Involvement and Outcomes guide,[8] which was inspired by curriculum mapping at Loyola Marymount University.[9]

In order to gain a better understanding of undergraduate students' exposure to information literacy, we partnered with an institutional intelligence analyst from the university's Information Services department and sought Institutional Review Board approval to obtain student course registration data. We matched the ID number of each student who graduated in 2017 with the ID number for each of the courses in which the graduate was registered and information literacy was taught. Our analysis of this data showed that 99 percent of students had at least one information literacy session during their course of study at the university. Eighty-six percent had a library session within their major. For students who did not receive information literacy instruction within their major (such as math), the data revealed that these students had two to five instruction sessions within the undergraduate core curriculum.

The University of Portland emphasizes face-to-face teaching even in our distance education programs. Currently, the university's School of Education offers distance education in Edmonton, Canada, and the School of Business offers courses in local off-site locations. Instruction librarians travel to these sites to meet with students, which provides them with a similar level of contact as with on-campus students.

Operations

The library has eight full-time librarians, including the dean; three of these are Reference/Instruction Librarians who report to the Head of Public Services. The Reference/Instruction Librarians, along with one part-time adjunct instruction librarian in the fall semester, deliver the library's information literacy instruction. One of these librarians also serves as the instruction coordinator. Instruction is one portion of our job responsibilities; we also provide research assistance, develop collections in our subject areas, and support other functional areas such as marketing, assessment, and website development.

Library administration has demonstrated support of the instruction program. As our program has grown, the Dean of the Library successfully advocated for the addition of an adjunct librarian position to assist with the teaching load. In addition, the dean actively sought input from the instruction librarians about our needs for the library classroom during a building renovation. The redesigned classroom has modular seating, thirty laptops for student use, and an instructor's station; this flexible space works well for many class sizes and instructional approaches (see figure 29.1). Although the information literacy program lacks a formal budget, the instruction librarians have successfully lobbied for additional funding for technology or other teaching resources when needed.

Figure 29.1
Clark Library instruction classroom (Photograph taken by José Velazco, 2016)

Marketing

Due to long-standing instructional relationships with teaching faculty, our instruction program is well known on campus. We take advantage of all available communication channels to proactively promote instruction in advance of each semester. We send out a call for library instruction scheduling via a weekly staff and faculty newsletter delivered by email. We also use the university's intranet announcements tool that sends an email digest to selected groups (e.g., all faculty) twice a week. One of the instruction librarians (who also chairs the Library Marketing Committee) disseminates the messaging that highlights how instruction librarians can help faculty and encourages them to schedule early to get their preferred time. This messaging seems to be effective; we see a concurrent increase in requests for instruction. We also benefit from a high referral rate by faculty to new colleagues.

In addition, a few weeks before the start of each semester, the instruction coordinator emails professors who have previously scheduled instruction to offer to plan a library session. We also obtain a list of new faculty from the provost's office before the start of fall semester. The librarian charged with marketing provides librarian liaisons with content for a "welcome" email to send to new faculty in their areas, which includes information about the library instruction program.

Collaboration

Overall, the university has a long history of support and appreciation for the library, its faculty librarians, and its staff. Librarians serve on the Academic Senate and are actively involved in university-wide conversations about campus governance, including revisions to the core curriculum. Librarians also have a standing appointment to the Curriculum and Academic Regulations committee, which approves changes and additions to the university's curriculum. This enables us to advocate for the inclusion of information literacy.

The library's strongest allies include the provost's office, Information Services (IS), and the Shepard Academic Resource Center (SARC). As the university's chief academic officer, the provost oversees all academic units, including the library. The library's strong relationship with the provost's office is evidenced by its support for new initiatives and budget requests. We reciprocate by participating in the provost's New Faculty Academy to orient new faculty to library services and resources and providing meeting space for their events.

IS provides, implements, and supports campus technologies, which are essential to our instruction program and for ongoing access to library resources and services. We work collegially with many IS staff, and they view us as partners who advocate for technology solutions. We have quarterly check-in meetings with IS directors that facilitate ongoing communication about technology needs and issues.

SARC provides student academic support services including learning assistance counseling, peer tutoring, accessible education services, and an early alert system for struggling students. Its staff view us as a campus partner, and we work with them to ensure that course reserves are fully accessible and to raise awareness of our complementary research assistance services. SARC also coordinates a first-year workshop program in which incoming students take a ten-week course led by an upper-level student in their major. The workshop includes a lesson covering essential information about using the library. The librarians provide content and support materials for the library activity and host a train-the-trainer session for the student workshop leaders to discuss goals and strategies they can use for the library lesson.

More recently, in the spirit of reaching students where they are, we have explored strengthening ties with Residence Life. An instruction librarian serves on a steering committee for Academic Resource Ambassadors, who are student volunteers seeking to foster a supportive academic environment in their residence halls. The librarian also meets with their companion leadership course to discuss library services and resources.

Relationships with student support staff are ad hoc since librarians do not have a formal liaison role with these units. At times we have to reestablish relationships when these units have staff turnover or new priorities. We invest the most time in relationships with teaching faculty, particularly in our liaison departments. Librarians consult with faculty to develop instruction for their courses, including scaffolded research assignments and research guides.

Assessment

We utilize multiple formative and summative approaches, and also work with faculty and the campus Office of Institutional Research (OIR), to assess student learning.

One method of formative assessment is polling. We have used various types of poll questions to check for student understanding:

- multiple-choice, in which students determine the correct definition of a research term or type of source
- interactive, in which students place markers on errors in citations
- open-ended, having students submit the search strategy they would use in a given situation

In-class activities are also an opportunity for formative assessment. Many instruction sessions incorporate activities where students explore and present library databases to the class. This gives us an idea of students' understanding of database interfaces and content and allows us to build on that foundation during the session.

Summative assessment helps us ascertain what students have learned. We have established a pattern of conducting pre- and posttests with students in an introductory business course. We obtain class rosters and email a link to a pretest two weeks prior to the instruction session. The pretest asks students to define research terms, select research starting points, choose appropriate search strategies, and prioritize website evaluation criteria. In our emails to students, we frame the pretest as a "survey" to reduce anxiety and encourage responses, and emphasize that the results will help the librarians modify session content to address student needs and to avoid covering content that the whole class knows. Two weeks after the session, students receive a posttest asking the same questions as the pretest. We compare results for students who attended the library session and completed both the pretest and posttest. The results demonstrate that the sessions impact student learning. In fall 2018, 20 percent of students selected an optimal search strategy from the pretest list, and 76 percent selected it on the posttest. Knowledge of scholarly information sources, peer review, and appropriate research starting points all increased by twenty percentage points or more from the pretest to the posttest.

Summative assessment also takes place for a public-speaking course. The librarian teaching those sessions attends one or two class periods when students are giving speeches to see what information students use to substantiate their claims and how they cite it. To document the resources, the librarian uses a modified rubric with two columns: Speech Topic and Cited Resources. The librarian records the resources as they are described by the students. Results show that students seem to have gained resource evaluation and citation strategies in the library session, as they generally use high-quality sources and cite them either by title or publisher to communicate the source's quality.

After each of these summative assessment activities, results are shared with classroom faculty and sometimes with department faculty responsible for program assessment. Faculty have expressed appreciation for the insights provided about their students' learning.

Additionally, faculty who have scheduled instruction are surveyed at the end of each fall semester to gather their feedback; this survey is described in more detail in the Administrative Highlights section below. This gives the instruction librarians assessment data from the faculty perspective.

Librarians collaborate with the campus OIR to include questions related to information literacy within their student surveys. Every three or four years, the University of Portland participates in the National Survey of Student Engagement (NSSE), administered by the OIR. During its 2017–18 administration of NSSE, OIR appended the NSSE Experiences with Information Literacy module.[10] Results from this module showed that students at the University of Portland engaged in a similar number of information literacy experiences as the other institutions participating in NSSE that year.

Role of the One-Shot

At the University of Portland, the one-shot session has been our bread-and-butter method for reaching students at point of need, and we work closely with faculty to tailor our instruction to the course and to the assignment that will be addressed in the session. In a few classes, faculty request two sessions, which usually takes one of two forms. In one case, the librarian meets briefly with a class early in the semester and in a longer session later. In the other, the librarian meets with the class on two consecutive days, with the first session devoted to research instruction and the second session a workshop with the librarian available to assist students with their research.

Being at ease with the one-shot approach does not mean that no tension exists. A library session's length and the number of learning outcomes it can reasonably include can be in opposition to a professor's expectations that students will learn everything they need to know in one session. At the University of Portland, class periods for the same course vary in length according to the number of weekly meetings. Monday-Wednesday-Friday classes are fifty-five minutes long, while Tuesday-Thursday classes last eighty-five minutes. Because the shorter session is more common, we prepare content to fit in this period length. To allow enough time for the active learning that defines our program, we identify two to three goals for a session. We also remind the faculty member that all aspects of information literacy can't be covered in a single session. We point them to the Curriculum

Involvement and Outcomes guide to illustrate how their session builds on content covered in other courses.[11] When a session is longer, we expand activity time or devote more of the session to consulting on individual student research, rather than adding session goals.

Pedagogical Highlights

We view information literacy as a suite of skills and dispositions that are essential to a student's development of knowledge in any discipline. We also recognize that the discovery and use of information is a reflective and iterative process. Therefore, students develop information literacy skills over time through coursework and with guidance from professors and librarians.

What we teach is guided by the ACRL *Framework for Information Literacy for Higher Education*, curricular outcomes, and requests from teaching faculty.[12] Instruction librarians frequently use Springshare's LibGuides to create course guides as a ready resource for students to use during and after the class. Online tutorials are often added to the guides, such as in the PSY/SOC/SW 214 course guide.[13]

We have experimented with polling technology (iClicker, LibGuide polls, and Poll Everywhere) to engage students and provide formative assessment. We are in the early stages of experimenting with untethered lecture capture using an iPad with wireless display technology that can record sessions and make them available to students afterward.[14] We were inspired to try this after it was piloted for a year by the School of Nursing and College of Arts and Sciences. The pilot was so successful that they are expanding it to more courses on a permanent basis.

As an example, we frequently teach sessions for Introduction to Fine Arts (FA 207), one of three classes that fulfill a fine arts credit (and an information literacy outcome) in the core curriculum. During the session, the librarian uses the course guide to lead students to online resources for researching topics related to art, music, and theater.[15] To achieve the course outcomes, students work in groups to discover and then present to the class about an assigned online resource related to the arts.[16] Additionally, the librarian leads a discussion about evaluating the credibility of sources and then uses Poll Everywhere questions to invite students to apply evaluation criteria to a library research scenario. Throughout the session, students are prompted to look for preformatted citations within research tools, and the session closes with reminders of how students can get more help after the class session.

Continuous learning and improvement underpin our work. We consult with teaching experts on campus, participate in learning circles with teaching faculty, and keep up with information literacy, pedagogical, and technology trends. Instruction-related topics are discussed at monthly meetings, with assigned readings to provide background. Past topics have included learning theories, incorporating the ACRL *Framework*, tools for assessing information literacy, web and digital literacy, and inclusive teaching.

Ongoing reflective practice occurs through an internal peer observation process. In fall semesters, the Head of Public Services observes instruction librarians teaching a class, and in spring semesters, we observe each other. Prior to teaching, the librarian notifies the observer about any areas about which they would like feedback. Observers use a form to take notes addressing organization, performance skills, use of active learning techniques, audience reactions, and other comments. The feedback is provided in conversation after a class and also written up and sent to the librarian, which is useful for future planning. It is up to the librarian to use the feedback as they choose, but it often provides insights on the organization and flow of content and ideas for adjusting activities or associated course guides. The librarians' annual review includes a self-reflection on their teaching practice and associated challenges and successes, as well as the observation by the Head of Public Services.

Administrative Highlights

For over a decade, the Information Literacy Coordinator, with input from the instruction librarians, has administered a Library Instruction Faculty Survey seeking feedback from faculty who teach classes that included a library instruction session. Throughout the duration of the survey, the questions have remained the same, offering comparative data about faculty perceptions of the relevance and impact of instruction on their classes. The accumulated data reveals that faculty consistently have positive perceptions about the benefit of library instruction for their students. The survey closes with open-ended questions about the most useful aspect of the instruction session as well as how the session could be improved; these questions often reveal opportunities for shaping future instruction sessions.

Another strength of our program is that each of the instruction librarians has served in our current positions for over fifteen years. As a result, we have developed deep, ongoing relationships with teaching faculty. This continuity provides opportunities to build on past collaborations and creates a foundation of trust, which facilitates openness to trying new ideas and technologies. Since we have collaborated (and even shared office space) for such a long time, we are able to depend on each other to expand and improve the information literacy program.

Information Literacy Coordinator Profile

One of the instruction librarians is the designated Information Literacy Coordinator. The job description indicates that this position "takes the lead role in coordinating the instruction program; scheduling, conducting outreach and conducting assessment."[17] In practice, while the coordinator takes the lead in information literacy outreach, scheduling interdisciplinary courses, and managing the Library Classroom calendar, all of the instruction librarians participate in promoting, scheduling, and communicating with faculty about classes in their liaison areas.

We collectively maintain statistics about our instruction sessions on a shared spreadsheet; this includes a running count of the number of classes taught by each librarian both by semester and annually. We try to balance the teaching workload across the instruction librarians, and also set a target number of sessions for the adjunct to teach. When scheduling classes that occur later in the semester, we don't assign an instruction librarian until we know who has the capacity to take on additional classes. Often, one librarian will end up teaching more classes during a semester due to requests from their liaison area; however, over the course of the year the numbers usually balance out.

The Information Literacy Coordinator also takes the lead in managing the technology in the Library Classroom. She investigates equipment or network issues reported by the instruction librarians and then coordinates with IS to report and resolve them. In addition, she coordinates annually with IS to update the software on the Library Classroom laptops. She also works closely with IS when equipment is due to be replaced to identify the best device, seek additional budget funds if needed, and then test the new devices to confirm they meet our needs.

For our Information Literacy Coordinator, there wasn't a formal path to this role. She was hired with the expectation of coordinating information literacy; although this was a new role for her, information literacy had been a key component of her prior positions. She had also sought opportunities to develop her skills by attending relevant workshops and conferences, including the Librarian as Teacher track of the ACRL Immersion Program in 1999. After appointment to this position, she obtained approval and funding to attend the Librarian as Program Developer track of the ACRL Immersion program in 2003. Knowledge gleaned through participation, service, and networking with colleagues in these roles has had a positive impact on her teaching and coordination of information literacy.

What We Wish People Knew

It is important to invest time in creating a framework of support for managing technology, coordinating schedules of librarians and teaching spaces, collecting data in a meaningful and usable format, and documenting procedures and teaching strategies. Regular communication, joint decision-making, and agreed-upon goals among teaching librarians are also key to the smooth operation of an instruction program. Meanwhile, remaining flexible, keeping a sense of humor, and being mindful of work-life balance are essential for maintaining a sustainable instruction program that is based on the one-shot. In our case, the instruction librarians share an office with a well-stocked candy jar and create little moments of delight by hiding stuffed animals in each other's cubicles. We also have each other's backs and encourage each other to take advantage of personal and professional growth opportunities.

Notes

1. "Total Enrollment," Office of Institutional Research, University of Portland, accessed December 12, 2018, https://www.up.edu/ir/institutional-data/2018-at-a-glance.html
2. "Common Data Set 2017–2018," Office of Institutional Research, University of Portland, accessed January 9, 2019, https://www.up.edu/ir/files/cds1718.pdf.
3. "Common Data Set 2017–2018."
4. "Common Data Set 2017–2018."
5. "Goals of the Core," Bulletin 2018-2019, University of Portland, accessed October 30, 2018, http://up.smartcatalogiq.com/en/2018-2019/bulletin/General-Information/Goals-of-the-Core.
6. "Goals of the Core."
7. "Goals of the Core."
8. "Curriculum Involvement and Outcomes: Introduction," Clark Library, University of Portland, last modified November 1, 2018, https://libguides.up.edu/curriculum.

9. Susan Gardner Archambault and Jennifer Masunaga, "Curriculum Mapping as a Strategic Planning Tool," *Journal of Library Administration* 55, no. 6 (2015): 512.
10. "NSSE Topical Modules," National Survey of Student Engagement, accessed October 30, 2018, http://nsse.indiana.edu/html/modules.cfm.
11. "Curriculum Involvement and Outcomes: Introduction."
12. Association of College and Research Libraries, *Framework for Information Literacy for Higher Education* (Chicago: Association of College and Research Libraries, 2016), http://www.ala.org/acrl/standards/ilframework.
13. "PSY/SOC/SW 214: Research Methods," Clark Library, University of Portland, last modified January 24, 2019, https://libguides.up.edu/psy214.
14. Lorretta Krautscheid et al., "Untethered Lecture Capture: A Qualitative Investigation of College Student Experiences," *Journal of Educational Technology Systems*, preprint, March 13, 2019, https://doi.org/10.1177/0047239519833690.
15. "FA 207: Introduction to Fine Arts: Ask Us," Clark Library, University of Portland, last modified January 15, 2019, https://libguides.up.edu/fa207.
16. "Curriculum Involvement and Outcomes: Performing and Fine Arts," Clark Library, University of Portland, last modified November 1, 2018, https://libguides.up.edu/curriculum/pfa.
17. "Reference/Instruction Librarian," unpublished job description, University of Portland, May 2, 2017, Microsoft Word file.

Bibliography

Archambault, Susan Gardner, and Jennifer Masunaga. "Curriculum Mapping as a Strategic Planning Tool." *Journal of Library Administration* 55, no. 6 (2015): 503–19.

Association of College and Research Libraries. *Framework for Information Literacy for Higher Education.* Chicago: Association of College and Research Libraries, 2016. http://www.ala.org/acrl/standards/ilframework.

Krautscheid, Lorretta, Samuel Williams, Benjamin Kahn, and Katherine Adams. "Untethered Lecture Capture: A Qualitative Investigation of College Student Experiences." *Journal of Educational Technology Systems.* Preprint, March 13, 2019. https://doi.org/10.1177/0047239519833690.

National Survey of Student Engagement. "NSSE Topical Modules." Accessed October 30, 2018. http://nsse.indiana.edu/html/modules.cfm.

University of Portland. "Common Data Set 2017–2018." Office of Institutional Research. Accessed January 9, 2019. https://www.up.edu/ir/files/cds1718.pdf.

———. "Curriculum Involvement and Outcomes: Introduction." Clark Library. Last modified November 1, 2018. https://libguides.up.edu/curriculum.

———. "Curriculum Involvement and Outcomes: Performing and Fine Arts." Clark Library. Last modified November 1, 2018. https://libguides.up.edu/curriculum/pfa.

———. "FA 207: Introduction to Fine Arts: Ask Us." Clark Library. Last modified January 15, 2019. https://libguides.up.edu/fa207.

———. "Goals of the Core." Bulletin 2018–2019. Accessed October 30, 2018. http://up.smartcatalogiq.com/en/2018-2019/bulletin/General-Information/Goals-of-the-Core.

———. "PSY/SOC/SW 214: Research Methods: Types of Sources." Clark Library. Last modified January 24, 2019. https://libguides.up.edu/psy214.

———. "Reference/Instruction Librarian." Unpublished job description. Last modified May 2, 2017. Microsoft Word file.

———. "Total Enrollment." Office of Institutional Research. Accessed December 12, 2018. https://www.up.edu/ir/institutional-data/2018-at-a-glance.html.

Chapter 30

University of Washington Bothell/Cascadia College

Scaffolded Curriculum Supported by a Community of Practice

Leslie Hurst, Dani Rowland, and Sarah Leadley

Population Served

The Campus Library is part of the University of Washington Libraries tri-campus system and is at the UW Bothell (UWB) campus that is colocated with Cascadia College. The library serves both institutions. The UW Bothell campus, founded in 1990, initially offered only upper-division courses. In 2000, UW Bothell moved to its current colocated campus site, and Cascadia College opened. A lower-division curriculum was added to UW Bothell in 2006, creating a four-year undergraduate experience for its students. The combined 2017–18 student headcount across campus was 9,865, comprised of 3,873 Cascadia students and 5,995 UWB students.[1]

Cascadia's students are primarily traditional-age undergraduates seeking academic transfer degrees (71%) but also include smaller proportions in precollege or English language programs or in two-year and four-year professional/technical degrees. Cascadia has the highest percentage of working students among the state's community and technical colleges, though its student population is also the youngest. It includes high school students taking college courses, but also returning adult students and a small number of international students.

UW Bothell's students are primarily undergraduates earning bachelor's degrees, though there are also a small number of graduate and professional degrees. Nearly half of UW Bothell students are the first in their families to earn a four-year degree. The majority of them are also traditional age, with a high rate of incoming transfer students (86% of whom come from Washington state community colleges). Sixty percent of students at UW Bothell are nonwhite. UWB also has a considerable population of students who speak a language other than English at home and a small international student population.[2]

Librarians remain mindful of these demographics and factor them into their pedagogy and instruction. With all types of students, we strive to honor and bring their experiences and ways of knowing into our teaching and learning spaces.

Program Scope

At both UW Bothell and Cascadia, librarians collaborate closely with faculty to integrate information literacy (IL) instruction into targeted courses across their curricula. We do not teach credit-bearing courses and instead have a structured IL curriculum strategically overlaid upon the undergraduate curricula and also in UW Bothell's graduate curricula. We teach in the classroom, online, and in any combination of those modes, and students can also set appointments with librarians for one-on-one or small-group consultations.

The greatest proportion of our instruction at both institutions occurs in required lower-division first-year seminars or college success courses and in 100-level research writing courses. Targeting these courses (which run multiple sections per quarter) makes sense due to their content and assignments and since it allows us to reach a large breadth of the student body to lay a foundation of introductory IL skills. In the lower-division research writing courses, our classroom instruction is robust and typically includes two 2-hour workshops, often complemented by online instruction or learning activities that further integrate the librarian and instruction into the course.

Librarians reinforce and extend IL skills established through our lower-division instruction when teaching in upper-division courses within the majors. They teach advanced research strategies or subject-specific resources and methods in targeted courses such as degree core courses, research methods or writing courses, and senior seminars or capstone courses. This approach is also taken with UW Bothell's graduate programs, though due to those programs' smaller size and graduate students' more specialized needs, individual student consultations are more common than course-integrated instruction.

Operations

The instruction program is the central occupation of the Campus Library and is independent from those at other UW campus libraries. Our fifteen subject liaison librarians engage in instruction as a core job responsibility, along with providing reference services and collection development. Liaison librarians with administrative duties typically have lighter subject and teaching loads. The instruction program does not have a designated budget and instead is supported by the library's central budget. When resource needs arise, the Head of Teaching and Learning brings them to the director, and they work together to identify possible solutions. The program has ardent support from the library director, who plays a key role in advocacy and making the program visible to high-level administrators such as the Cascadia's Vice President of Student Learning and UW Bothell's Vice Chancellor of Academic Affairs.

The Head of Teaching and Learning leads and manages the program and supervises the majority of the librarians (i.e., those without administrative duties), while the Assistant Head of Teaching and Learning assists with mentoring and program logistics like coordination of teaching meetings, instruction statistics reporting and analysis, and assessment. These two nonrotating roles are formalized through job titles and descriptions. The program also has five instruction coordinators, one for each of our targeted courses that run several sections per quarter. For example, English 102 at Cascadia has a coordinator who handles the scheduling for fifty to sixty sections of the course per year. Coordinators provide support for librarians who teach within the course through mentoring, consulting, or developing teaching tool kits. They attend faculty meetings centered on their courses and track, communicate, and respond to curricular shifts in the course impacting our instruction. Coordinators serve a two-to-four-year term, and while not formalized in job titles or descriptions, the roles are structured by documented scopes of responsibility.

One of the subject liaisons also serves as an eLearning liaison to offer support and resources for our online instruction and pedagogy and maintains relationships with eLearning staff at both Cascadia and UW Bothell. This role is acknowledged in their job description.

Teaching in the targeted lower-division courses (first-year seminars and 100-level research writing classes) is a shared responsibility across the group. Regardless of subject areas, all librarians teach in these courses, which comprise the largest part of the program. This allows us to sustain integrating instruction into each section, foster a sense of shared responsibility for teaching students foundational IL skills, and ensure librarians have an understanding of our lower-division instruction to build from when teaching in upper-division courses in their subject areas. It also protects First Year Experience and English Composition liaisons from bearing the brunt of the program's instructional load, which would likely to lead to burnout.

Coordinators work online and in person to schedule librarians for the shared lower-division courses. Teaching assignments are outlined in a document showing each librarian's teaching for the quarter, including in their subject liaison areas. During the scheduling process, the document is distributed to the whole group by the Assistant Head of Teaching and Learning, and current and former schedules are saved in a shared folder accessible to them at any time. This transparency can mitigate real or perceived equity issues regarding teaching loads or opportunities, facilitate individual librarians' understanding of the full extent of instruction across the group and campus, and help librarians see where colleagues are teaching in their subject areas.

The librarian group comprises a rich teaching community of practice that is supported by monthly teaching meetings librarians take turns leading, where we discuss pedagogy and workshop our teaching ideas, challenges, or "failures." Mentoring occurs in all directions within the group (i.e., not provided solely by senior librarians) and is facilitated by the teaching meetings as well as co-teaching and peer observations, which are common and contribute to building trust and community within the group. All librarians' teaching materials are open to everyone on a department server and in Canvas, further facilitating idea sharing. Additionally, we intentionally recruit and hire librarians who have a passion for teaching and learning and who are interested in joining a supportive and collaborative teaching and learning community.

Marketing

Marketing our instruction occurs through librarians' rich involvement with their schools and programs. This, along with our strategic and scaffolded IL curriculum structure where librarians proactively reach out to faculty teaching their targeted courses each term, means we do not need to engage in other marketing activities. Occasionally we receive unsolicited requests to teach in courses outside of our IL curriculum. In these cases, the librarian will take on the course if their teaching load allows or will offer to consult with the faculty member to identify alternative means for supporting their students, such as a customized online research guide or integration of resources into the course learning management system.

Collaboration

Librarians are highly integrated into their programs and attend faculty meetings, participate in email discussion lists, and often sit on curriculum or assessment committees. This facilitates the rich culture of librarian-faculty collaboration we have at both institutions. Librarians connect with instructors of our targeted courses to codesign IL instruction and activities supporting the course and assignment learning outcomes where students are developmentally and in their research process. Librarians also participate in faculty teaching circles centered on our targeted courses to enrich these collaborations and inform our teaching within the course.

Occasionally we offer faculty development workshops on IL topics, though the majority of our faculty development occurs via one-on-one consultations with instructors. We also partner with our colleagues in UW Bothell and Cascadia's Teaching and Learning and Writing Centers and with eLearning staff to provide faculty development. Particularly at UW Bothell, relationships with colleagues in these units are long-standing and valuable since we often share skill sets and goals for supporting our students and faculty. Partnerships with eLearning staff are especially important for supporting our online instructional efforts. They contribute to our e-learning professional development and facilitate our access to and presence in the campus learning management systems.

Other important collaborative relationships include faculty coordinators for courses we target for instruction, who help us stay informed, navigate curricular shifts, and communicate with instructors of the course. At Cascadia College, the two Deans of Student Learning are key partners for similar reasons and for bigger-picture conversations regarding program resource needs or constraints.

Assessment

Other than accreditation or program reviews, there are no campus-level assessment processes. Student learning assessment at both Cascadia and UW Bothell occurs within programs or schools. Some librarians are able to participate in their programs' student learning assessments, and faculty welcome and appreciate their involvement, while librarians value those opportunities to review student work they often don't get to see.

The library's assessment of teaching and student learning occurs in a variety of ways. Teaching observations are not required, nor a part of librarian evaluations; however, many participate in peer teaching observation circles or engage in co-teaching as a means for expanding or receiving feedback on their instruction. Librarians use specific assignment outcomes, workshop outcomes, or our overall IL outcomes to assess student learning.[3] Assessment methods may include librarian review of student work, observation of student performance during class, and classroom assessment techniques.

The library's most robust student learning assessment process is at the program level and typically spans an academic year. Usually centered on one of our targeted courses where we invest a lot of resources, this process involves identifying the outcomes we are teaching to and that we want to assess, collecting student work from several sections of the course, developing a rubric, and gathering as a group and with selected faculty and academic staff to assess and discuss the assignments and student work. This is followed with a report outlining our methods, rubric scores, qualitative observations, and practical recommendations for application, which are published online in summary form.[4] Lastly, we share and discuss within the group, and with key faculty, staff or administrators, any implications and next steps.

We have undertaken this process nearly annually since 2012, and it consistently results in shifts to our pedagogy and assignments, and often for the faculty members as well. By participating, the faculty gain an opportunity to deepen their understanding of IL and how students navigate learning it. Each librarian participates regardless of their subject areas, which helps them see how our students learn and to gain new pedagogical strategies and a broader understanding of how their instruction fits within the entire program.[5]

Role of the One-Shot

One-shots are prominent in the program; however, they are typically supplemented with pre- or post-session online instruction or learning activities. Providing one-shot workshops allows us to sustain our reach across the curriculum, though we experience the common challenges they present, such as limiting the volume and depth of IL learning outcomes we can address and our access to students and their work. However, we do have the luxury of two-hour course time blocks, and the majority of our one-shot sessions run for that duration.

Pedagogical Highlights

The program's teaching philosophy embraces critical pedagogy and teaching research as a creative and iterative process that is often shaped by students' analytical and technology skills.[6] Our instruction is conceptual and process-oriented, and while research tools (e.g., databases) are taught, they often are not front and center. Our pedagogy centers on delivering active learning experiences, both in the classroom and online, and assessment is an integral part of librarians' instructional design.

Librarians develop instruction in connection to a specific class assignment and moment of the students' research process. They are resistant to doing so without this context and may even decline a teaching request in cases where there isn't a relevant assignment. We most often teach the following, tailored to the students' assignment, research process, and subject areas:

- strategies for navigating the complex information environment, such as critical internet searching and the subjectivity of information organizations and systems (e.g., biased algorithms), and a variety of source formats and genres
- negotiating research processes, such as activities to help students develop and refine their research topics or questions
- evaluating and using sources, such as activities and discussions addressing the nuances of authority, and information production and distribution channels

Depending on the context and developmental level of the students, other instruction may include subject-specific research methods or resources, finding and using primary sources, and IL-related topics like data literacy or digital privacy.

Our online pedagogy is not centered on the production of video tutorials, though we have a few on library basics to orient students to our services and spaces and to our catalog. Instead, we develop customized learning objects to integrate into instruction or assignments. It may be an online class research guide (LibGuides), though the majority of our online instruction occurs through thoughtfully structured, active learning exercises delivered through the learning management system (Canvas). These are designed to both guide students through library resources and their research process and to engage students through question prompts they respond to that help them articulate their process and learning. Librarians work with faculty to get added to Canvas courses, including permissions to add content and view student work, allowing librarians to see how students perform and to offer feedback to them and the instructor. This access also means librarians can see how whether their learning activity design was effective and can make informed improvements for future classes. Librarians frequently experiment with other ways to connect with students online, such as creating brief videos introducing themselves to the class, facilitating or chiming in on discussion board conversations, and holding online office hours.

One highlight of the program includes a philosophy and practice centered on both critical information literacy and critical digital pedagogy. Considering our large proportion of first-generation and underrepresented student populations, we are invested in critical IL pedagogy that honors and brings students' prior experiences and ways of knowing into teaching research processes, methods, and tools. For example, Cascadia's College 101 IL curriculum contains a section on Critical Internet Searching, comparing a video of a Google representative explaining Google's search mechanism with a video of Safiya Umoja Noble highlighting her research that reveals how search results based on algorithms can perpetuate racism and sexism.[7] To highlight the effects of "filter bubbles," we ask students through pointed question prompts to compare Google results when signed in versus not signed in. Meanwhile, UW Bothell recruits underrepresented students who are also first-generation, low-income, or both for its first-year academic transition class. In that course, we incorporate critical IL by starting with students' personal stories related to vectors of intersectional identity and work with them to find connections between their lived experience and the work of academic researchers.

Another pedagogical highlight includes offering a series of sequential IL workshops in some courses. In select targeted courses we are able to sustain offering two or more workshops in the course as students move through their inquiry and research process. This does require faculty to relinquish valuable class time to librarians, though ideally the librarian and faculty member co-teach the workshops. The value of this model for the librarian includes the opportunity to build stronger relationships with the faculty and students, the chance to directly see and experience the students' progress and process unfolding over time, and the ability to follow up on students' specific needs. Students benefit by receiving ongoing, accessible, and tailored librarian support as they navigate their research.

The other notable highlight is the collaborative work our Head of Digital Scholarship and Collections, librarians, faculty, and students undertake to create content and build our digital collections, comprising oral histories, videos, documents, and more.[8] As part of a course, faculty prepare students to undertake the primary research methods of interviewing, conducting oral histories, or collecting other digital artifacts, while the librarian and Head of Digital Scholarship and Collections integrate and co-teach workshops instructing students on copyright and creating the metadata for their digital objects to be added to the library's digital collections. Librarians and faculty members have described in journal articles[9] how this part of the program supports students as researchers and knowledge producers and exemplifies the ways IL and scholarly communication can intersect.

Administrative Highlights

In addition to scaffolding the students' IL learning, the program's strategic, structured curriculum model (see Program Scope) also affords several administrative benefits, allowing us to

- Have a structure for undertaking student learning assessment. To engage in assessment that will deliver the highest impact or return on investment, efforts can be centered on targeted courses librarians are consistently teaching in and that a large proportion of the students take (see also the Assessment section).
- Predict instructional staffing needs based on the number of course sections offered during a quarter or a year. This also provides a useful framework for managing the expansion or contraction of the IL curriculum. For example, if additional sections of a targeted course are consistently being offered, we know how that impacts our staffing and then can explore whether we need to seek additional staff, pull back from that course or another part of the curriculum, or generate other solutions.
- Manage librarian teaching loads. We strive to keep each librarian's teaching load in the range of ten to fifteen sessions per quarter (or some equivalent when teaching in online courses). By also strategically targeting courses in their subject areas and by prioritizing among them, librarians can manage their commitments as needed should they see an increase or decrease in the number of sections of those courses or among our shared lower-division courses.
- Clearly communicate the program's mission and scope within the library and to campus stakeholders. A structured curriculum can be clearly described through IL plan documents at the IL program-, school- or degree-level that clarify for librarians and faculty where IL instruction takes place (see figures 30.1 and 30.2). The plans may also indicate which targeted courses take priority over others and describe specific IL outcomes addressed in the courses (see figure 30.2). These documents serve both as communication tools and policy documents that can help avoid "scope creep" and empower librarians to decline requests for instruction falling outside the designated courses.

Cascadia College Information Literacy Program 2018-19*

What is Information Literacy?

Information literacy is the set of integrated abilities encompassing the reflective discovery of information, the understanding of how information is produced and valued, and the use of information in creating new knowledge and participating ethically in communities of learning. These skills are best learned and retained when taught as part of the curriculum and in conjunction with the companion skills of critical thinking, reading, writing, and production. They are developmental and must be introduced, applied, reinforced, and extended throughout a student's educational career.

The ACRL *Framework for Information Literacy for Higher Education* offers educators a structure around which instruction sessions, assignments, courses, and even curricula may be designed. *The Framework* is organized into six frames articulating the concepts, knowledge practices, and dispositions central to information literacy: Authority Is Constructed and Contextual; Information Creation as a Process; Information Has Value; Research as Inquiry; Scholarship as Conversation; and Searching as Strategic Exploration.

Adapted from the Association of College and Research Libraries http://www.ala.org/acrl/ (ACRL) Framework for Information Literacy for Higher Education, accessed 30 June 2016. http://www.ala.org/acrl/standards/ilframework

1. Information Literacy Core Curriculum—Librarians partner with faculty to team teach hands-on information literacy workshops in these courses/areas:

ABE/ESL: Classes vary	2-3 workshops per quarter
BIO 320: Biodiversity (BAASP)	1 workshop per section
COLL 101: College Strategies	up to 1 workshop or online activity per section
ENGL 102: Composition II: Writing from Research	1-2 workshops per section
ETSP 101: Introduction to Environmental Technologies and Sustainable Practices	To be determined; in development
HUMAN 330: Design Research Methodologies (MOBAS)	1 workshop per section
SUPR 410: Research Design & Methods in Sustainable Practices (BAASP)	1 workshop per section

A limited number of hands-on workshops may be implemented in other courses, subject to review by the subject librarian and the Library's Head of Teaching and Learning. Our limited resources may not allow us to address all workshop requests, but we will do our best to honor additional requests when possible.

2. Information Literacy Across the Curriculum—Librarians as consultants to faculty:

All instruction librarians are available to consult with faculty on the availability of library resources and assignment design. Course specific online research guides can be created (with advance notice and feedback from faculty). Librarians are also available to meet with faculty individually for training in using our research databases or other library resources. To read more about these services, see: https://guides.lib.uw.edu/bothell/teaching

3. Other collaborations include:

Course Outcome Guide revisions, student learning assessment, and participation in discipline faculty meetings.

Find your subject librarian here: http://library.uwb.edu/selectors.html or contact Leslie Hurst, Head of Teaching and Learning at lhurst@uw.edu

*The structure and content of Cascadia's Information Literacy Program will be reviewed annually by faculty and librarians and revised as needed.

Figure 30.1
Information literacy plan for Cascadia College

The integration of information literacy into the curriculum directly supports the learning goals and outcomes of the School of Business as well as specific course and assignment outcomes.

The role of librarians in your teaching:

The Campus Library supports the UW Bothell School of Business students and faculty by integrating information literacy and library research instruction into the curriculum via the following courses:

1. Undergraduate Curriculum—Librarians partner with faculty to team teach hands-on information literacy workshops in these courses/areas:

BBUS 300: Management of Organizations	1 in-class workshop (2 hours of classroom instruction per section)
BBUS 320: Marketing Management	1 in-class workshop (45-60 minutes of classroom instruction per section)

BUS 300: Targeting BBUS 300 allows us to work with students early in the undergraduate program and scaffold research skills throughout the curriculum. Usually BBUS 300 instructors assign a company management/leadership research assignment where students need a basic understanding of how to do company and industry research. The information literacy session provides a foundation for students to understand the types of company and industry information produced and how to locate, use and appropriately credit these different resources. These basic company and industry research skills provide needed grounding for doing more intensive research projects in other business classes, such as BUS 320 and BUS 470 Business Policy and Strategic Management.

BUS 320: The advanced research strategies and resources covered in BUS 320 focus on the complexities of developing a marketing plan. Strategies also include an understanding of and the ability to apply required analysis, interpretation, extrapolation and utilization of raw data and information, plus the intricacies of personal studies/surveys. These advanced research skills are also needed for other marketing classes such as BUS 426 International Marketing, as well as for BUS 480 Global Business and entrepreneurship classes taught at both locations.

2. Graduate Curriculum—Librarians are available to consult with faculty on course or assignment design, and are available for online or in person appointments to help students with their research.

A limited number of hands-on workshops may be implemented in other courses within the School of Business undergraduate and graduate curricula, subject to review by Business Librarian liaisons and the Library's Head of Teaching and Learning. Our limited resources may not allow us to address all workshop requests, but we strive to honor additional requests when possible.

3. Information Literacy Across the entire School of Business curriculum—The Business librarians are available to consult with faculty on the availability of library resources and assignment design. Course specific web research guides can be created (with advance notice and feedback from faculty).

Figure 30.2
Excerpt of Information Literacy Plan for UW Bothell's School of Business

Information Literacy Coordinator Profile

The Head of Teaching and Learning (formerly Instruction) has always been a formalized role with considerable influence at the Campus Library, supervising most of the librarians on staff. Rapid campus growth over the past several years has been the primary force in creating additional leadership roles for the program. In 2005, the first two instruction coordinator roles were created, with three more added later. In 2008, the former Head of Instruction became the library director, and one of the first instruction coordinators became the Head of Teaching and Learning. Then the Assistant Head of Teaching and Learning role was established in 2013.

Over time we have tried different ways of dividing the labor and positioning coordinators in response to how the programs in which we target courses conceive of their curricula. Working alongside faculty as the campus grew and new curricula were designed and implemented, librarians in these roles got valuable exposure for how to do that work and gained insights into opportunities to leverage for building out the IL curriculum. Through our liaising closely with the faculty communities of our targeted courses, these opportunities continue for the coordinators and now center on curriculum revision or assessment.

The Head and Assistant Head of Teaching and Learning participate in teaching, though their administrative responsibilities are taken into consideration when determining their teaching commitments. The head is able to allot approximately one-quarter of their time to instruction, and we strive to keep the assistant head's at approximately three-quarters of their time. The other instruction coordinators' administrative workload is modest enough that they can sustain teaching loads in line with others in the group.

What We Wish People Knew

Challenges we have faced relate to adapting and building new portions of our program during a period of rapid campus growth over several years. In this context, we have had to contract our curriculum in some degree areas in order to build it into new ones, which necessitated developing skills in data analysis for undertaking evidence-based decision-making. It also required learning how to develop a vision for specific segments of our instruction program (and the program as a whole). In reviewing a school's or degree's curriculum through a strategic lens, we learned to identify courses suitable to target for instruction while also being mindful of what degree of integration would be sustainable. Additionally, it required furthering political, negotiation, and communication skills as we had conversations with both librarians and faculty about building up or scaling back instruction in their programs. Faculty degree or course coordinators serve as useful consultants and allies for having these conversations.

Some of the instruction coordinators' most critical work is hidden labor. They mentor and support librarians teaching in the courses for which they coordinate instruction, and provide faculty development individually and via their participation in faculty teaching circles. They engage in IL program management by developing, revising, and maintaining our IL outcomes, curriculum, and related documentation for their course. These roles offer a great opportunity for librarians to lead from within the unit, albeit without formal authority. As a result, coordinators develop and practice their ability to influence, negotiate, and build trust as they conduct their work within the group and navigate and communicate shifts in our instruction with key faculty or administrators.

Advice we would like to offer:

- Scaffold the IL curriculum by strategically targeting courses that reach a breadth of the student body and depth within a degree's or school's curricula to reap several benefits. It helps librarians make informed choices about activities to focus on in their targeted courses, helps inform faculty about the developmental level at which to aim research assignments, and may help minimize "library session burnout" for students who have multiple workshops while undergraduates.
- Engage in consistent communication with the academic programs to keep the library's curricular goals present in curriculum planning and student learning conversations.
- Manage and predict teaching loads individually and collectively to prevent burnout. Develop a rough metric to serve as a threshold (e.g., no more than ten to fifteen workshops per quarter, per librarian). This metric also aids in calculating the estimated teaching capacity of the group.
- Create and foster a teaching community of practice within the program, where librarians have space to gather regularly to discuss teaching and learning theory, trends, and their day-to-day instructional challenges and successes. This builds community and support for their teaching and helps them continue to develop their practice and big-picture understanding of what goes on across the program.

Notes

1. "Cascadia at a Glance," Cascadia College, accessed March 13, 2019, http://www.cascadia.edu/discover/about
2. "Fast Facts 2017–2018."
3. "Teaching and Learning at the Campus Library: Learning Outcomes," Campus Library, University of Washington Libraries, accessed October 25, 2018, http://guides.lib.uw.edu/bothell/teaching/outcomes.
4. "Campus Library Assessment: Student Learning Impact," Campus Library, University of Washington Libraries, accessed October 1, 2018, https://guides.lib.uw.edu/bothell/assessment/studentlearning.
5. Jackie Belanger and Leslie Hurst, "Implementing a Sustainable, Long-Term Student Learning Assessment Program," in *User-Centered Design for First-Year Library Instruction Programs*, ed. Rachel W. Gammons and Cinthya M. Ippoliti (Santa Barbara, CA: ABC-CLIO, 2017), 62–66.
6. "Teaching and Learning at the Campus Library: Teaching and Learning Philosophy," Campus Library, University of Washington Libraries, accessed October 1, 2018, http://guides.lib.uw.edu/bothell/teaching/philosophy.
7. USC Annenberg, "Algorithms of Oppression: Faculty Focus: Safiya Umoja Noble," YouTube video, 3:43, February 28, 2018, https://www.youtube.com/watch?v=6KLTpoTpkXo&t=144s.
8. "Digital Collections: Home," Campus Library, University of Washington Libraries, accessed October 9, 2018, https://guides.lib.uw.edu/bothell/dsc/digitalcollections.
9. Denise Hattwig, Nia Lam, and Jill Freidberg, "Student Participation in Scholarly Communication and Library Digital Collections: A Case Study from the University of Washington Bothell Library," *College and Undergraduate Libraries* 22, no. 2 (2015): 188–208, https://doi.org/10.1080/10691316.2014.9507 81; Julie Shayne et al., "Creating Counter Archives: The University of Washington Bothell's Feminist

Community Archive of Washington Project," *Feminist Teacher*, 27, no. 1 (2018): 47–65, https://doi.org/10.5406/femteacher.27.1.0047.

Bibliography

Belanger, Jackie, and Leslie Hurst. "Implementing a Sustainable, Long-Term Student Learning Assessment Program." In *User-Centered Design for First-Year Library Instruction Programs*. Edited by Rachel W. Gammons and Cinthya M. Ippoliti, 62–66. Santa Barbara, CA: ABC-CLIO, 2017.

Campus Library, University of Washington Libraries. "Campus Library Assessment: Student Learning Impact." Accessed October 1, 2018. https://guides.lib.uw.edu/bothell/assessment/studentlearning.

———. "Digital Collections: Home." Accessed October 9, 2018. https://guides.lib.uw.edu/bothell/dsc/digitalcollections.

———. "Teaching and Learning at the Campus Library: Learning Outcomes." Accessed October 25, 2018. http://guides.lib.uw.edu/bothell/teaching/outcomes.

———. "Teaching and Learning at the Campus Library: Teaching and Learning Philosophy." Accessed October 1, 2018. http://guides.lib.uw.edu/bothell/teaching/philosophy.

Cascadia College. "Cascadia at a Glance." Accessed March 13, 2019. http://www.cascadia.edu/discover/about.

Hattwig, Denise, Nia Lam, and Jill Freidberg. "Student Participation in Scholarly Communication and Library Digital Collections: A Case Study from the University of Washington Bothell Library." *College and Undergraduate Libraries* 22, no. 2 (2015): 188–208, https://doi.org/10.1080/10691316.2014.950781.

Shayne, Julie, Denise Hattwig, Dave Ellenwood, and Taylor Hiner. "Creating Counter Archives: The University of Washington Bothell's Feminist Community Archive of Washington Project." *Feminist Teacher* 27, no. 1 (2018): 47–65, https://doi.org/10.5406/femteacher.27.1.0047.

University of Washington Bothell. "Fast Facts 2017–2018." Office of Institutional Research. Accessed March 13, 2019. https://www.uwb.edu/about/facts/fast-facts-2017.

USC Annenberg. "Algorithms of Oppression: Faculty Focus: Safiya Umoja Noble." YouTube video, 3:43. February 28, 2018. https://www.youtube.com/watch?v=6KLTpoTpkXo&t=144s.

Chapter 31

Wheaton College
Equipping Lifelong Learners

Joshua M. Avery and Cathy Troupos

Population Served

Wheaton College is a Christian, liberal arts institution located in the western suburbs of Chicago with an undergraduate population of 2,400 students, 89 percent of whom live on campus. The college maintains a robust focus on undergraduate teaching with an undergraduate-faculty ratio of eleven to one. Undergraduates have a strong academic profile with an average SAT score 300+ points above the national mean and, nearly 5 percent are National Merit Scholars.[1] The college offers around forty undergraduate programs in the liberal arts and sciences, with a strong emphasis on the integration of faith and scholarship.

Program Scope

The current information literacy (IL) program at Wheaton College began in 2016 when the college initiated a new general education curriculum, moving toward a distribution model that would incorporate course-level, embedded information literacy instruction. Prior to this, information literacy had been a part of the undergraduate curriculum, although instruction did not reach all students equally. First-year writing students attended a one-shot session and took an online library skills test as part of their coursework; however, some students tested out of this course. Students completed another library assignment as part of a required Biblical studies and theology class, but instruction was specific to the assignment and did not focus on broader information literacy concepts. Subject liaison librarians visited classes by faculty request; some departments had more active engagement with the library than others.

When the college began planning for the new general education core, the library seized the opportunity and advocated strongly for the place of information literacy within the curriculum. Through persistent effort and strategic planning, information literacy changed from informal, disconnected activities to a fully embedded program based on the six threshold concepts of the ACRL *Framework for Information Literacy for Higher Education*.[2] The four components of the IL program were implemented over a student's four years of study and are

- *First-Year Seminar (FYS):* Students take an online, interactive tutorial within the FYS course in the learning management system (LMS), Schoology. This tutorial introduces students to the foundations of academic research, including the research cycle, types of information, the peer-review process, and citation basics, as well the library website, the catalog, and interlibrary loan. The grades are recorded in the LMS, and students must achieve at least 70 percent to pass. All first-year and transfer students take FYS during their first semesters at the college.
- *Advanced Integrative Seminar (AIS):* Students take an online, interactive tutorial within the AIS course in the LMS. This tutorial builds on the FYS tutorial and deepens understanding of the scholarly conversation, academic disciplines, database searching, synthesizing sources, and integrating faith into research. The grades are recorded in the LMS, and students must achieve at least 70 percent to pass. AIS is a required course under the new curriculum and is generally taken a student's sophomore or junior year.
- *Course in the Major (CIM):* Subject liaison librarians present discipline-specific research strategies and resources within a departmentally designated, research-based CIM. As part of the general education core, each CIM is identified in collaboration with the subject liaison librarian, the department chair, and the Dean of Library and Archives. The students apply what they learn to a research-based project for the course. Instruction for most courses takes place face-to-face.
- *Capstone:* Students attend a workshop focused on research beyond Wheaton College. There are two tracks: one for those entering the professional world and one for those continuing their academic careers. For profession-bound students, participants learn how to transfer their "research skills" to "information skills" that are necessary in the workplace. For those going on to graduate school, the discussion centers on academic publishing. All students take a capstone course within their majors; most take it during their senior year.

Operations

There are nine library faculty at Buswell Library at Wheaton College, all of whom report to the Dean of Library and Archives. In addition to working within a major group within the library (Special Collections, Operations, Teaching and Outreach, and Resource Description and Digital Initiatives), each member of the library faculty serves as a subject liaison librarian with responsibility for various duties, including instruction and collection development for their assigned subject area. The Teaching and Outreach Group is comprised of four library faculty and is responsible for leadership and oversight of all library assessment, instruction, outreach, and reference. The Teaching and Outreach Group also organizes a variety of workshops throughout the year, focusing on bibliographic technologies (e.g., reference management software) or specific research skills that would typically fall outside the scope of either a one-shot session or the formal IL curriculum. Marketing is done through campus email discussion lists and on social media, with details and reservations managed through the LibCal booking platform.

Within this group, the instruction librarian coordinates IL program. Additionally, the instruction librarian develops new elements (such as the capstone workshop), creates and maintains online tutorials for the FYS and AIS, tracks statistics, and serves as the formal liaison between the library and the Dean of Curriculum and Advising, who is responsible for the general education core.

The subject liaison librarians utilize a variety of tools for scheduling and recording instruction data. A LibGuide serves as a central point of information for librarians about their liaison responsibilities, including instruction. Teaching schedules are tracked through a shared Outlook calendar, which allows for communication of schedules and general oversight by the instruction librarian. After all instruction sessions, librarians enter session data (e.g., attendance, course number, department, etc.) into a Google Form; the instruction librarian maintains the form and uses this data to monitor and assess departmental compliance with the CIM portion of the IL program.

Assessment

Tutorial data is also important in capturing compliance with the plan and student progress. After several semesters of trial and error, the most effective method of inserting the tutorial into the courses and tracking the data has been to add the instruction librarian as an administrator of each FYS and AIS course in the LMS. This method ensures that the tutorials are loaded correctly and that the instruction librarian has easy access to student grades and rates of completion. In addition, student issues are filtered directly to the instruction librarian, who can then access the students' tutorial attempts. Since the tutorials have launched, compliance with the requirements has been very high, and the vast majority of students pass. Should the data indicate a change in compliance or completion rates, the tutorials will need to be revisited.

Because the IL program is part of the general education core curriculum for the college, the final responsibility for assessment of the plan resides in the Office of the Dean of Curriculum and Advising. Unfortunately, the Dean of Curriculum and Advising does not currently provide robust assessment of information literacy outcomes, and the library is not able to collect assessment data or feedback. However, the library does assess instruction informally. Subject liaison librarians voluntarily participate in a peer-teaching scheme that pairs up librarians for feedback throughout the academic year; many librarians distribute evaluation forms to students or use pre- and posttests during their instruction sessions. Additionally, course faculty have an opportunity to give feedback to subject liaison librarians after each instructional session.

Collaboration

We feel very fortunate to have a robust IL program embedded into the general education curriculum that is supported by the administration; however, because the program is a part of the curriculum, oversight by library faculty is limited and largely falls to the Office of the Dean of Curriculum and Advising. In practice this means that, on occasion, required components of the IL program are left out of course planning by general education teaching faculty. Teaching faculty are generally supportive of the library, yet in the midst of other requirements from their departments or the college, IL can fall between the cracks. As expected, there are constant and ongoing changes—new chairs of departments do not know the IL program; a major suddenly changes course requirements, and the designated CIM is eliminated; each semester, different faculty teach FYS and AIS courses, and most are unfamiliar with the format, content, and administration of the tutorials. Therefore, in the absence of oversight from the dean or department chair, there is a continual need for subject liaison librarians to monitor the IL program and educate teaching faculty about their need to participate and integrate these elements into their classes. While we could simply *inform* our teaching faculty colleagues that these elements are required, we strive to go beyond these types of interactions and *educate* faculty on the vision of the plan and the benefit to students. Our hope is that faculty then will help to educate students on its importance when incorporating the IL program into their curricular planning.

Changes within the library also affect the program. There are frequent changes to the website, resources, and processes at Buswell Library, any of which can cause the tutorials to fall out-of-date. Not a semester goes by where the instruction librarian does not need to make updates; sometimes, the changes are minor—a tweak to one slide or an additional set of instructions for students—but sometimes the changes are significant, such as when all interactive components needed to be updated to reflect a website redesign. Revising and testing tutorials, embedding them in the LMS courses, and communicating with faculty takes significant time for the instruction librarian.

In addition, since the tutorials are preloaded into the courses, they cannot be updated during the semester. Timing for website updates, then, is crucial, and changes that affect the tutorials can take place only during semester breaks. Communication between the library's website developer and the instruction librarian is important in maintaining the tutorials.

Many of these challenges are, in great measure, a result of the newness of the general education curriculum. As the curriculum (and the IL program) become more familiar to the teaching faculty, we expect greater understanding and compliance with the IL program. We are well aware that the ongoing success of this plan largely depends on the support we receive from both the Dean of Library and Archives and the Dean of Curriculum and Advising.

Role of the One-Shot

While not a formal component of our IL curriculum, one-shot instruction is an important dynamic in helping to inform students of what the library offers, especially as it relates to a particular course. One-shot instruction, like CIM instruction, is provided by subject liaison librarians in communication with departmental faculty. There is no formal oversight or assessment of one-shot instruction. One-shot instructional sessions tend to be tailored specifically to the courses or disciplines in which they are delivered, and the IL curriculum is largely related to developing information literacy skills that are not confined to disciplinary boundaries.

Marketing for one-shot sessions is largely the responsibility of individual subject librarians, with materials and resources provided by the librarian for outreach and promotion. Subject liaison librarians are encouraged to develop relationships with subject faculty, maintain awareness of faculty research priorities and interests, and regularly communicate with faculty. These efforts allow librarians to create opportunities for one-shot instruction session invitations.

Pedagogical Highlights

FYS and AIS Tutorials

Both the FYS and AIS tutorials are embedded in LMS courses. The tutorials were developed using Articulate Storyline, an interactive course-creation software, and take around one hour to complete.

The FYS tutorial gives an overview of the research process based on a scenario that students are likely to encounter at Wheaton College—a study-abroad opportunity (see figure 31.1). This is not an academic research topic though the tutorial does utilize library resources to address the research question. Students go through the research process (information need, search, evaluate and reflect, and refine) while interacting with the library website and tools. They learn about library-based resources, such as interlibrary loan and research guides. The tutorial covers search strategies, introduces basic citation practices, and discusses ways to prevent plagiarism.

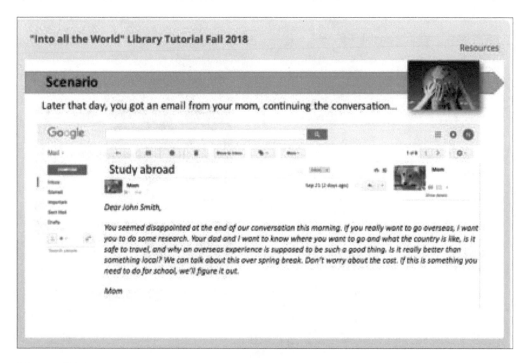

Figure 31.1
The scenario from the FYS tutorial (Nancy Falciani-White, "'Into All the World' Library Tutorial Fall 2018 | Schoology,")

Integration of the tutorials within the FYS courses varies. Anecdotal evidence from students and faculty suggests that, while some faculty simply present the tutorial as a required component of the course, others contextualize and discuss how information literacy is a crucial component of the students' intellectual lives. Our hope is that all faculty would engage with the content so students could understand its importance rather than see it simply as an assignment to check off the list.

For most students, the tutorial is their initial interaction with the library as they must take it within the first half of their first semester at the college. The seminar is perhaps not the best place in which to situate the tutorials since the course does not include a research project, but the timing is ideal in ensuring students receive accurate foundational information about the library soon after they arrive.

The AIS tutorial goes more deeply into the topic of the scholarly conversation; students learn the unique perspectives of different academic disciplines. Since the AIS courses are designed to examine topics from interdisciplinary perspectives, in the tutorial, students probe one particular research question—How does access to clean water impact education?—through multiple lenses. In addition to exploring the topic from standard disciplinary viewpoints, students also learn skills, strategies, and resources to develop an informed Christian perspective on a topic, namely by exploring resources relating to research of scripture, theological scholarship, and tradition (see figure 31.2). While taking the tutorial, students explore the ATLA Religion Database, which includes biblical and theological scholarship; in addition, the tutorial presents various types of commentaries, dictionaries, and encyclopedias that shed light on the cultural, textual, and historical issues present in scripture that can help students understand how, for instance, a biblical

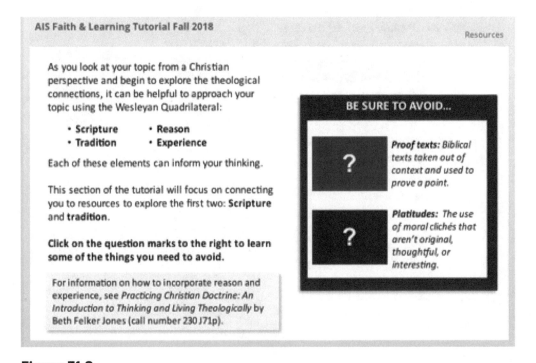

Figure 31.2
Introduction to the Faith and Learning portion of the AIS tutorial (Nancy Falciani-White, "'AIS Faith and Learning Tutorial Fall 2018 | Schoology,'")

concept of justice can relate to the global water crisis today. The tutorial also discusses how to organize and synthesize sources. Students apply the learning from this tutorial to a research project for the course that must integrate interdisciplinary research.

Course in the Major (CIM)

Each CIM was selected by the academic department offering that particular major in collaboration with the subject liaison librarian, the department chair, and the Dean of Library and Archives. Within each department, the designated course is one that is required for all majors and includes a major research component tied to the research methods of the discipline. Prior to the new curriculum, some departments, such as English, already included IL sessions at several points. For other departments, such as mathematics, the CIM broke new ground in including a required library element. Most departments were willing to work with the library in implementing this new component, but some that had little interaction prior with the library were resistant. Similarly, some departments could easily identify courses that are a good fit for collaboration with the library in that there is a required course that focused on discipline-specific research; for other departments, major requirements are more flexible, and at times, multiple courses are identified to ensure that all students were exposed to discipline-specific library instruction.

Knowing the students have taken the FYS tutorial and learned basic concepts and skills before entering the CIM frees the subject liaison librarian to focus on more advanced concepts and resources related to a particular discipline. While the CIM content and outcomes are developed by the subject liaison librarian in collaboration with the teaching faculty, librarians are encouraged to utilize the theme of the information landscape, which we define as the shared resources and tools that help people discover and use information in a particular context.[3] This theme exposes students to a wider context of information than they may need for the immediate project but gives a deeper understanding of what research is within the discipline. While the shared theme is encouraged, subject liaison librarians are free to tailor their CIM instruction to content most appropriate for the discipline and research project of the individual course. This results in a wide variety of approaches to CIM instruction; below are a few examples.

The instruction for English courses begins with a discussion about the information landscape of literary scholarship (see figure 31.3). Students encounter this course early in their major coursework; the theme of learning how to research like a literary scholar plays well with the overall purpose of the course, which the course catalog describes as an introduction "to terms and techniques of literary analysis, important questions within the discipline, and the research process."[4] As each feature of the landscape is explored, the class discusses the kind of sources found in that category and how a literary scholar may use those to inform their work. For example, students are encouraged to enlarge their view of primary texts to not just the novels, poems, plays, and stories they are studying, but also to include manuscripts, journals, maps, and any other sources that a literary scholar might use to illuminate those texts. While students most likely will not turn to an archive or special collection while researching their own topics for this introductory course, discussing the role that archival material plays in literary scholarship may help them better understand the scholarship that they encounter in their research.

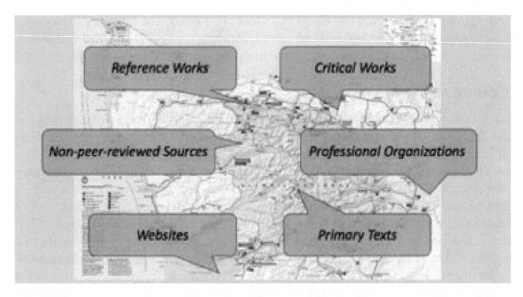

Figure 31.3
An overview of the English literature information landscape

Other CIMs use a presession online element. The CIM designed by the biology liaison librarian uses a Guide on the Side tutorial to teach students about research in the sciences as they explore the database Web of Science.[5] As they search the database, the tutorial prompts students to reflect on their experiences (see figure 31.4). Students answer

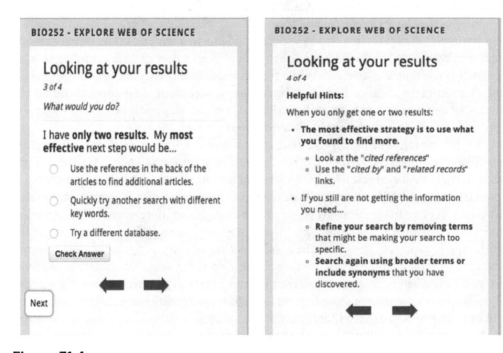

Figure 31.4
Guide on the Side tutorial for the biology CIM (Terry Huttenlock, "BIO252—Explore Web of Science".)

questions such as What worked? What didn't work? What would you do differently next time? The tutorial also instructs the students in how to download and use the reference management software Zotero in preparation for their group projects. The results of the tutorial are reviewed and graded by the subject liaison librarian. While the presession tutorial could stand alone as a learning tool, the librarian does a follow-up session in which the class has more time to focus on problem areas and questions revealed by the tutorial.

Another variation of instruction occurs within Survey of Twentieth Century Music, the CIM for students majoring in music. There is no in-class session for that course; rather, the music liaison librarian meets with the students individually for a reference/instruction session after the students have chosen their topics. This model is perhaps not sustainable for all CIMs, but it has created an inroad for instruction where there was none before; as music faculty increasingly see value, there will be more opportunities for formal instruction.

Capstone

The final component of the IL program is integrated within the capstone courses for each major. This was perhaps the biggest challenge in developing the program—How to create an engaging library session for seniors who have one foot out the door? The answer was to focus on that next step—research beyond Wheaton College. Two workshops were developed that are offered several times throughout the semester; students are required to attend one as part of their capstone course.

Since the majority of students head to the professional world upon graduation, the first workshop developed focused on information in the workplace. Wheaton College students largely prove themselves to be competent academic researchers by graduation; however, research shows that, in general, new graduates are not transferring these skills to their jobs, proving their research skills to be "inadequate."[6] The challenge was then to help students navigate this gap in a seventy-five-minute session. The concept of the information landscape proved helpful in addressing this need. The session is structured as follows:

- Students first discuss what they already know as the class develops the information landscape for college research.
- The instructor then discusses the skills that new graduates lack according to employers and how the concept of an information landscape could help address these skills.[7]
- Students then form small groups; each group watches an online interactive module based on interviews with recent alumni. At the end of the module, the group is presented with a scenario in which they must develop and present an information landscape that could help them address a workplace issue.

For those going onto graduate school, the workshop is designed to enlarge understanding of the world of scholarly communication and academic publishing. This workshop draws heavily on the concepts of critical information literacy. The session looks as follows:

- Students first discuss what they know as they sketch out and discuss the peer-review process.
- The instructor then shows how this process fits into the wider context of academic publishing.
- Students watch brief videos of Wheaton College faculty discussing how publishing and access affect research in their own fields.

- Students then work in groups on scenarios in which they must find appropriate venues to disseminate research.

These workshops are not intended to teach everything students need to know upon graduation in one session; rather, they seek to expose students to the idea of an information context and encourage them to think about their own participation in those settings.

What We Wish People Knew

Embedding an information literacy program within the general education curriculum is rewarding; however, it is not always straightforward. Developing and maintaining a program requires many skills and expertise, including the ability to design instruction and assessment, collaborate with and persuade key campus partners, and organize and administer the plan elements. Most of all, maintaining and improving the program requires flexibility. The program components are tied to many different courses and require the cooperation of many faculty; while there is general support for the plan, changes are constant, and the plan needs to be flexible in adapting the components to match the standards of the campus. Having college-wide support for the plan is encouraging; ensuring its success requires a committed, engaged, and flexible team.

Notes

1. Wheaton College, *Annual Academic Assessment 2017–2018* (Wheaton, IL: Wheaton College, 2018).
2. Association of College and Research Libraries, *Framework for Information Literacy for Higher Education* (Chicago: Association of College and Research Libraries, 2016).
3. The concept of information landscape was largely informed by Annemaree Lloyd, *Information Literacy Landscapes*, Chandos Information Professional Series (Oxford: Chandos, 2010).
4. "Course Catalog," Wheaton College, accessed March 14, 2019, https://www.wheaton.edu/academics/course-catalog.
5. Guide on the Side is an open source software developed at the University of Arizona Libraries. It allows users to create interactive tutorials. See "About," Guide on the Side, University of Arizona Libraries, accessed March 14, 2019, https://ualibraries.github.io/Guide-on-the-Side/about.html.
6. Alison J. Head et al., "What Information Competencies Matter in Today's Workplace?" *Library and Information Research* 37, no. 114 (2013): 74–104.
7. Dale Cyphert and Stanley P. Lyle, "Employer Expectations of Information Literacy: Identifying the Skills Gap," in *Information Literacy: Research and Collaboration across Disciplines*, ed. Barbara J. D'Angelo, Sandra Jamieson, Barry Maid, and Janice R. Walker (Fort Collins, CO: WAC Clearinghouse and Boulder: University Press of Colorado, 2016), https://wac.colostate.edu/books/infolit/chapter3.pdf; Head et al., "What Information Competencies Matter?"

Bibliography

Association of College and Research Libraries. *Framework for Information Literacy for Higher Education.* Chicago: Association of College and Research Libraries, 2016.

Cyphert, Dale, and Stanley P. Lyle. "Employer Expectations of Information Literacy: Identifying the Skills Gap." In *Information Literacy: Research and Collaboration across Disciplines.* Edited by Barbara J. D'Angelo, Sandra Jamieson, Barry Maid, and Janice R. Walker, 51–76. Fort Collins, CO: WAC Clearinghouse and Boulder: University Press of Colorado, 2016. https://wac.colostate.edu/books/infolit/chapter3.pdf.

Falciani-White, Nancy. "'AIS Faith and Learning Tutorial Fall 2018 | Schoology." Accessed October 19, 2018. https://lms.wheaton.edu/course/641721565/materials/package/1940920415/launch (requires sign-in).

———. "'Into All the World' Library Tutorial Fall 2018 | Schoology." Accessed October 19, 2018. https://lms.wheaton.edu/course/641721565/materials/package/1940920415/launch (requires sign-in).

Guide on the Side. "About." University of Arizona Libraries. Accessed March 14, 2019. https://ualibraries.github.io/Guide-on-the-Side/about.html.

Head, Alison J., Michele Van Hoeck, Jordan Eschler, and Sean Fullerton. "What Information Competencies Matter in Today's Workplace?" *Library and Information Research* 37, no. 114 (2013): 74–104.

Huttenlock, Terry. "BIO252—Explore Web of Science." Accessed December 19, 2019. https://wheaton.libwizard.com/f/BIO252.

Lloyd, Annemaree. *Information Literacy Landscapes: Information Literacy in Education, Workplace and Everyday Contexts*. Oxford: Chandos, 2010.

Wheaton College. *Annual Academic Assessment 2017–2018*. Wheaton, IL: Wheaton College, 2018.

———. "Course Catalog." Accessed March 14, 2019. https://www.wheaton.edu/academics/course-catalog.

Chapter 32

Worcester State University
All Hands on Deck

Vicki Gruzynski

Population Served

Worcester State University (WSU) in Massachusetts is a public liberal arts and sciences university that offers thirty-one undergraduate majors and thirty minors, twenty-nine master's degrees, and a handful of postbaccalaureate certificates. There are approximately 4,000 full- and 1,300 part-time students enrolled, with 25 percent of students coming from underrepresented groups and a gender ratio of sixty-forty female to male.

Approximately 50 percent of our students are transfer students, and 50 percent are first-generation college students. Sixty-five percent of our students are commuter students, though over 90 percent of our students, both commuter and residential, come from Worcester County, and most stay after graduation. The campus is considered an "urban" campus, though it is in a decidedly more residential-feeling part of Worcester. Our programs with the largest enrollments are health sciences (including nursing, public health, and occupational therapy), psychology, criminal justice, and biology, though the clear front-runner is the business administration program. Our campus has put a lot of emphasis on community outreach and civic engagement and has encouraged more global initiatives such as study abroad. Anecdotally, our students mostly choose Worcester State for the cost and location. Most hold part- or full-time jobs, and many are caregivers for parents, children, or members of their extended families.[1]

The makeup of the student body means several things for our instruction program. The large population of transfer and part-time students do not move through the curriculum in a sequence, which makes it challenging to reach all of our students through our library instruction program. Even in upper-division courses, students come to library sessions with widely varied information literacy skills. Students' exposure to school libraries also varies widely: many of our feeder secondary schools do not have libraries or have sparsely staffed and resourced libraries, so students often enter our university without an understanding of the role a librarian and the library can play in their educational success. Our students tend to have multiple responsibilities outside of class, so they have less time to focus on studies. Many students work full-time and have family obligations, which means that students want to know what they can do from home or from off-campus. Our students are mostly from Worcester County and sometimes have little experience outside of their lives in central Massachusetts, so I (and many of the non-library faculty on campus) feel that it is important to make global and national events locally relevant to our students during instruction and reference interactions.

Program Scope

WSU librarians try to be in as many of the First Year Seminar (FYS) classes as possible, usually around forty sections per fall semester. All first-time, first-year students and students transferring with fewer than fifteen credits will be enrolled in and must complete an FYS course. The FYS program is always in flux, as the program suffers from a constant push and pull between faculty and administration. The administration seeks to make the program an extended orientation, whereas many (but not all) faculty use the course as an opportunity to teach a special topic that they may not have an opportunity to teach in a standard department course. It is challenging to find faculty to teach the course, as we are severely understaffed as an institution and it can be difficult for faculty to find time in their departmental schedules to teach something that is not a required major or minor course in their department. Often the courses are filled by adjuncts and WSU staff. Despite these programmatic challenges to FYS, we strive to make our library sessions customized to the theme of the course and the needs of the students, and we try to hold a library session for each section of FYS.

In my role as the liaison to the program, I serve on the FYS Advisory Board and try to help shape the program to meet its objectives, the three core goals of the program being development of oral communication skills, written communication skills, and information literacy skills. We have decided that FYS courses are the best place to be able to reach all of our first-year students and introduce them to information literacy skills and library resources, as almost all non-transfer students are required to take this course. Beyond that, we teach in whatever setting is requested: undergraduate, graduate, capstone, and so on. So far, our instruction program is only face-to-face, though as our state pushes for more online education, that will undoubtedly compel changes in how we conduct instruction in the future. For example, the education department will be offering a fully online master's degree program starting in spring 2020.

Course-integrated instruction varies by department and liaison librarian. After the liaison model was introduced in 2013, requests for library instruction have been on the upswing. Since our hiring spurt in 2016, instruction requests have steadily increased overall, but the numbers vary by department. History has become a frequent flier in our library instruction program, as well as the health sciences (occupational therapy, nursing, public health, and nutrition). This speaks to not only the increase in outreach by our liaisons, but also the quality of instruction those liaisons provide to those departments. Slowly but surely, we are integrating ourselves into all of the departments on campus.

The main focus is course-integrated instruction, but in the fall 2018 semester, we began experimenting with drop-in workshops and online tutorial creation. Worcester State University does not have an established culture of drop-in workshops, but the Teaching and Learning Librarian who is also the liaison to the English department has started to offer workshops in conjunction with the Writing Center on campus.

The Teaching and Learning Librarians have their first graduate assistant (GA) this year (fall 2018–spring 2019), and one of the GA's assignments is to create tutorials for our students. I think our library instruction program would be much more effective if students could complete short, low-stakes learning modules before meeting as a class with their librarian, and I foresee offering Research 101–type tutorials on topics such as the information cycle, peer review, keyword searching, and other basic library skills so that time in class with the instructor and librarian could be more targeted to their particular assignments, in a flipped classroom model. These online tutorials will be able to help our online students and online course offerings, as well as our commuter students who are not able to come to the library in person for research help.

Operations

There are a total of fifteen full-time library employees at Worcester State University: six Massachusetts State College Association (MSCA) union librarians, one library director who holds an MLS, and nine staff. According to a recent report by the AFL-CIO Department for Professional Employees, 26 percent of librarians are union members, and 23 percent of library assistants are union members.[2] All full-time library employees, with the exception of the executive director, who is an at-will university employee, are union members. The MSCA union librarians are tenure-track and are represented in the faculty bargaining agreements with the state. We have the same timelines and very similar requirements for tenure and promotion as the non-library faculty. As part of our bargaining agreement, we are required to work thirty-seven-and-a-half hours per week and also receive two research days per year.

The six MSCA Librarians and the library director comprise the group within the library we refer to as RIL: Research and Instruction Librarians. The two Teaching and Learning Librarians do not have direct reports, but the Electronic Resources Librarian, Access Services Librarian, and Cataloging Librarian each have up to three direct reports. The six MSCA union librarians report to the Executive Director of the Library and are required to meet very similar guidelines for tenure and promotion as the teaching faculty. Two MSCA librarians have the title of Teaching and Learning Librarian and handle the bulk of the instruction, and those two positions split management of public services coordination: I serve as the de facto coordinator of instruction, while the other Teaching and Learning Librarian manages research help services. However, all librarians staff the research help desk and are department liaisons with instruction duties. For example, our archivist is also the liaison to urban studies and history. Our library director recently (fall 2018) relinquished his official liaison duties, though he continues to serve as a backup instruction librarian should the need arise.

Our program has no dedicated budget, though we have been using library funds to improve our instruction space. In the summer of 2018, we added multiple outlets to the space, added movable tables and chairs, and upgraded our computer monitor. In the long term, we would like to have walls and a door for our instruction space. In spring of 2019, there has been a discussion of using the library instruction space as a pilot space for whiteboard paint walls, an idea we enthusiastically support and that would bring even more flexibility and utility to the instruction space.

Marketing

Our outreach happens in many ways: email, campus news, word of mouth, department meetings, and new faculty orientation. Every semester, we send a general reminder about library services to all full- and part-time teaching faculty, with a link to our library instruction request form, a list of our librarians and their liaison areas, a link to our faculty services guide, and a link to optional syllabus language that faculty are welcome to use. Additionally, librarians are encouraged to attend one to two department meetings a year for their liaison departments to meet new faculty and to generally keep lines of communication open regarding all library services, including instruction.

Collaboration

The library is occasionally asked to present on information literacy to the faculty. A few places we have been asked to participate in the past have been through the First Year Seminar training workshops, the Center for Teaching and Learning, and at New Faculty Orientation. Our biggest allies tend to be specific faculty members, and programmatic alliances will often emerge from these personal connections. For example, the previous director of our First Year Seminar program was a library supporter and a heavy library user, but with the transition of leadership to a teaching faculty member who has never used the library in their courses, that connection has become more tenuous. Our librarians try to be involved and present on campus so that these connections do not break down when faculty leadership experiences turnover, but it is challenging.

Assessment

In the past, we have had no formal summative assessment system in place, which is a huge gap in our instruction program. As one of the Teaching and Learning Librarians and the de facto coordinator, I would like to solidify this as part of our library instruction program. We gather plenty of quantitative data on our program, such as number of courses, number of students, length of instruction session, course department, and faculty of record, but mostly this assessment data is gathered for our accrediting body, the New England Association of Schools and Colleges (NEASC). In fiscal year 2019, we revived the practice of sharing this data and other library data in the form of an annual library report. Moving forward, I want us to focus on qualitative data once we formalize our assessment program. This is a process we are piloting as a department in spring 2019 with a short optional survey we ask students to complete at the end of their library session. The survey requires three short answers from students: List something you learned in today's session. List something about which you still have questions. List something you wish we had covered but didn't. Our plan is to review this student feedback as a department at the conclusion of the semester and make adjustments to our instruction sessions based on student responses. Our history liaison will also be piloting a feedback form focused on history faculty in spring 2019; we hope to make this a campus-wide feedback form after the pilot semester. Faculty and students will have different feedback relating to our instruction sessions to share, and we think it will be useful to us as librarians to offer both groups the chance to give targeted feedback.

Role of the One-Shot

Our program mostly provides course-related one-shot instruction at the request of the instructor. The library has a longtime reputation of being an unfriendly, even hostile environment, but the librarians who contributed to that reputation have retired. The librarian previously in my position (now the director) ramped up our instruction program when he started about five years ago, so minus a semester before the two new Teaching and Learning Librarians were hired (when there were literally two librarians here), instruction requests have been steadily climbing. As we build goodwill on campus and become more integrated into the academic community, I want us to be more programmatic and targeted in our instruction offerings, but for now, we are focused on the one-shot.

Additional goals for building our instruction program include curriculum mapping and strategic scaffolding in order to align our instruction sessions with both course and programmatic goals. Our students do not typically move through their programs of study in a prescribed order, and we also have many transfer students, which means that when a librarian steps into almost any course level, they will find a range of beginning to expert-level researchers.

Pedagogical Highlights

The more I learn about critical librarianship, the more I move away from teaching the tools toward teaching concepts and skills that students will need to use the tools. I encourage other librarians to do the same. As teaching librarians, we meet once a semester to exchange activity ideas, read articles, solve problems, and work to improve upon our instruction program as a whole.

It has been challenging to establish a community of practice: four of our librarians have additional roles in our library's operations: archives, access services, electronic resources, and cataloging. We meet biweekly as a department, but that tends to be a catchall meeting for various ongoing projects, not only instruction. However, once or twice a year, we meet as instruction librarians to focus solely on instruction. In the past, we have read articles and discussed them, done a close read of and had an in-depth conversation about the ACRL *Framework for Information Literacy for Higher Education*, shared instruction activities, and tested out new ideas for instruction activities on each other.[3] When we met in spring 2018, we did a group activity that involved brainstorming what our ideal instruction program would look like and as a group came up with a list of qualities that our program would have in an ideal world: multi-format, data-driven, continual, scaffolded, scaled, integrated, flexible, customizable, assessable, and many others. Our spring 2019 topics included discussions about assessment; open access publishing, and open scholarship more broadly; and gender inclusivity work on the campus.

Administrative Highlights

Since attending ACRL Immersion in the summer of 2017, I have had retooling our instruction program constantly on my mind. This academic year (2018–19), my plan is to revamp the instruction program's mission statement so that it can serve as a road map for being more strategic in scaffolding our instruction work. I plan to incorporate more explicit language around critical information literacy and social justice. I think it is important to celebrate all the victories, no matter how small they seem. Two examples: in the spring 2017 semester, we introduced a library instruction sign-up form. I was frustrated by sending multiple emails back and forth in order to establish basic information about the library session (course name, meeting time, suggested dates, course location, etc.) and developed a form to streamline that process. In fall 2018, we updated the extremely out-of-date and collections-focused library syllabus paragraph, letting both faculty and students know that we are more than our collections.

Information Literacy Coordinator Profile

We have two Teaching and Learning Librarians who handle the bulk of the instruction. However, when it came time to divide the public service duties, we agreed that I would focus on the outreach and instruction coordination side of the house, while our other Teaching and Learning Librarian manages the research help desk and library subject guides. It was an easy decision to make when we both started in winter 2016, as it is a natural split based on our skills, interests, and personality types. These coordination duties are outlined in my job description, but they do not appear in my title. In graduate school, my assistantship was teaching beginning Spanish language courses, which I came to enjoy, and I naturally shifted into library instruction in my time at library school. I have held primarily instruction-focused positions ever since.

What I Wish People Knew

Being a known entity on campus is really important to the success of a library instruction program. People know me because they see me at various campus events and interact with me on campus working groups, advisory boards, and committees as a representative of the library. I would say that networking and outreach is a huge amount of hidden labor. If our liaison librarians and I were not active and involved on campus, the library's instruction program would not be so well known on campus.

I would also like to dispel the "myth of summer," as my director and I call it. So many tasks that I, in my role as de facto instruction coordinator, would like to accomplish require that I make time and space for research, reflection, and planning. I think that is why attending ACRL Immersion in summer 2017 was so useful: it was an entire week away from the office to focus on our instruction program.[4] However, being back at work does not allow those same opportunities for dedicated time to think about instruction planning. My tendency is to push off this time until summer, thinking that the lack of students and faculty will somehow provide me with a magically free schedule to dedicate to this work. This does not seem to ever happen: though the ebb and flow of students and teaching faculty is low, other projects and events take over the summer and make it almost as busy as the normal semester. After two summers (2017 and 2018) of not accomplishing my planning goals for our instruction program, I have realized that if anything is going to happen, I need to structure time for it throughout the semester. Thus, I am hopeful that in spring 2019, I will be able to work on some of the tasks associated with updating our library instruction program. The key will be breaking it into manageable pieces, versus looking at the overall long-term goal of redoing the program in its entirety, and we have already made progress with the implementation of an instruction form, as well as updating the library information template for syllabi. The next goal for spring 2019 is updating our instruction program mission statement, as it is based on the *Information Literacy Competency Standards for Higher Education* and needs to be updated to reflect the *Framework*.[5] Overall, our instruction program is doing well, but as with anything, we could be more integrated into the curriculum. As it stands, we are doing what we can with limited time and limited resources.

The further I get in my career and the more confident I become with my skill set, the more I am able to advocate for how an instruction session could and should look (versus meeting every demand, reasonable or unreasonable, from non-library faculty). I have learned to emphasize that my teaching in their classroom is a partnership, not just my being a guest speaker for the day. In spite of our campus presence, advocacy, and outreach, some of our teaching faculty are still receiving mixed messages about what it is we do in the library. For example, just this semester (fall 2018), a First Year Seminar instructor told me that she was told that there was a "standard library session" that we do for all First Year Seminars. So even if it seems repetitive, it is important to have consistent and scheduled messaging and to continually watch for gaps in communication and outreach so those miscommunications can be corrected. My advice for a coordinator is to view these brief interactions through the lens of a program coordinator and use this information in your messaging.

Notes

1. For more detailed information, see "University Data," Worcester State University, accessed March 29, 2019, page: https://www.worcester.edu/University-Data.
2. See "Library Workers: Facts and Figures," Fact Sheet 2018, Department for Professional Employees, AFL-CO, accessed March 29, 2019, https://dpeaflcio.org/programs-publications/issue-fact-sheets/library-workers-facts-figures (2018 version removed from web page). This report does not break down union membership by library type.
3. Association of College and Research Libraries, *Framework for Information Literacy for Higher Education* (Chicago: Association of College and Research Libraries, 2016). Two articles I can recommend that we have shared and discussed: Carrie Donovan, "Sense of Self: Embracing Your Teacher Identity," *In the Library with the Lead Pipe*, August 19, 2009, http://www.inthelibrarywiththeleadpipe.org/2009/sense-of-self-embracing-your-teacher-identity; Yvonne Nalani Meulemans and Allison Carr, "Not at Your Service: Building Genuine Faculty-Librarian Partnerships," *Reference Services Review* 41, no. 1 (February 2013): 80–90.

4. For more information, see "Immersion Program," Conferences and Events, Association of College and Research Libraries, accessed November 26, 2019, http://www.ala.org/acrl/conferences/immersion.
5. Association of College and Research Libraries, *Information Literacy Competency Standards for Higher Education* (Chicago: Association of College and Research Libraries, 2000); Association of College and Research Libraries, *Framework*.

Bibliography

Association of College and Research Libraries. *Framework for Information Literacy for Higher Education.* Chicago: Association of College and Research Libraries, 2016.

———. "Immersion Program." Conferences and Events. Accessed November 26, 2019. http://www.ala.org/acrl/conferences/immersion.

———. *Information Literacy Competency Standards for Higher Education.* Chicago: Association of College and Research Libraries, 2000.

Department for Professional Employees, AFL-CO. "Library Workers: Facts and Figures." Fact Sheet 2018. Accessed March 29, 2019. https://dpeaflcio.org/programs-publications/issue-fact-sheets/library-workers-facts-figures (2018 version removed from web page).

Donovan, Carrie. "Sense of Self: Embracing Your Teacher Identity." *In the Library with the Lead Pipe*, August 19, 2009. http://www.inthelibrarywiththeleadpipe.org/2009/sense-of-self-embracing-your-teacher-identity.

Meulemans, Yvonne Nalani, and Allison Carr. "Not at Your Service: Building Genuine Faculty-Librarian Partnerships." *Reference Services Review* 41, no. 1 (February 2013): 80–90.

Worcester State University. "University Data." Accessed March 29, 2019. https://www.worcester.edu/University-Data.

Chapter 33

Ozarks Technical Community College

Doing More by Doing Less—Radically Reinventing a Community College Instruction Program

Sarah H. Mabee and Sarah E. Fancher

Population Served

Ozarks Technical Community College (OTC) is an open-enrollment, two-year community college with three campuses and two education centers located in southwest Missouri. It enrolls approximately 13,000 students in a variety of general education, allied health, and technical programs and courses. Counties in the surrounding OTC service area have poverty rates between 15 and 28 percent.[1] Approximately 63 percent of the student population are first-generation college students, at least 66 percent receive federal financial aid, and 79 percent work while attending college. Although the college does serve many nontraditional students, the average student age is just twenty-one.[2] Like the surrounding geographic area, the student population is demographically quite homogeneous, but 14 percent of students are underrepresented minorities.[3] More than 40 percent of students take at least one online course per semester. According to OTC's Office of Research, Strategic Planning and Grant Development, 30 percent of full-time, first-time students eventually transfer to a four-year institution; 58 percent of students who complete an AA degree go on to transfer to a four-year school.

As an open-enrollment community college in a high-poverty area, we have some students who are academically underprepared. However, they also tend to be hardworking, motivated, and driven. Because the vast majority of our students also work, have caretaking responsibilities to their families, or both, we prioritize teaching the big ideas that are most important for creating enduring understanding and strive to transparently communicate the value and relevance of what we are teaching. We believe that our students are rational actors who make decisions about how to spend their time and energy; they rightfully won't spend it using library search tools if they don't understand how and why such tools offer advantages for college-level research.

Program Scope

Our current information literacy program is in its infancy, with a new library director in place since August 2016 and the sole instruction librarian hired in November 2017. The two of us have worked intensively together to refine our philosophy of library instruction, envision programmatic goals, and begin to implement a major overhaul of our instruction praxis. In past years, generic "library tours" disconnected from any specific assignment were offered, which largely left students bored and library staff frustrated. Though these tours were undoubtedly done with good intentions, library staff members would indiscriminately demonstrate various catalog and database searches, drone about Boolean operators, and navigate the library's website without inviting any student participation for fifty minutes or more. It should be noted that the library does not have an instruction classroom, so these sessions would take place elsewhere on campus—thwarting any attempt to practice even using a call number to actually locate a book. Additionally, library staff would consent to visit classes at inappropriate times of the semester (the first week or the final class session!). These sessions were truly treated as a "one-shot," in that a nursing course might be shown a history database "just in case." Although no formal or informal assessment was undertaken, we feel confident in saying that these old instruction practices were exactly as effective as riding a unicycle at the front of the classroom would have been.

With the bar previously set so low, we could hardly help but improve! Because of our limited librarian staffing, we began by focusing our instruction efforts on the first- and second-year English composition courses, which are required for all degree programs. Some sections of first-year composition courses (English 100) are five instead of three credit hours, allowing for embedded library instruction during these extra "support" hours. We mostly do in-person instruction and try to meet with a single class section on three to five occasions during the semester. In this series of sessions, we strive to acknowledge and build upon students' existing knowledge about the information ecosystem and go beyond the library-as-resource model. This leads to lively discussions about Wikipedia, perceived media bias, and critical understanding of scholarly sources. This succession of interactions allows us to cover the ideas of research as inquiry and the different contexts of authority in web versus library sources and to break down the anatomy of scholarly writing to identify its relative value to first-year research. However, while our collaborations with English composition instructors have been most fruitful, we've found we are open to collaborations in other departments as long as they are substantive and follow our best practices.

To address the growing role of online courses at OTC, we have created videos and accompanying assignments that cover the basics of accessing library resources as well as information literacy concepts. One of these online modules, "Research Is Asking Questions"—which introduces research as inquiry and the idea that college-level research involves asking questions and formulating, not just finding, answers—was built for OTC 101, the college-readiness course required for all new students. The module includes a short video modeling research question development and revision, as well as developing questions from a Wikipedia article (see figure 33.1). Here we also emphasize the relative value of Wikipedia, a source students are often familiar and comfortable with, as a jumping-off point to ask more complicated questions. While many instructors are resistant to even mentioning Wikipedia in the classroom, this is one small way we've begun to insist that instructors have realistic and thoughtful expectations about their students' research. The video is accompanied by a short assignment to brainstorm questions, intended to be used as a low-stakes assignment to generate questions without worrying about whether they're the "right" research topic or question. The assignment pushes students to ask questions they want to know the answers to and worry about the research later. At the heart of this assignment is the threshold concept of research as inquiry: if we can find a question a student genuinely wants to know the answer to, the research process becomes easier and, hopefully, more interesting. At present, this "Research Is Asking Questions" module is optional and incorporated into individual sections of OTC 101 or ENG 100 at instructor discretion.

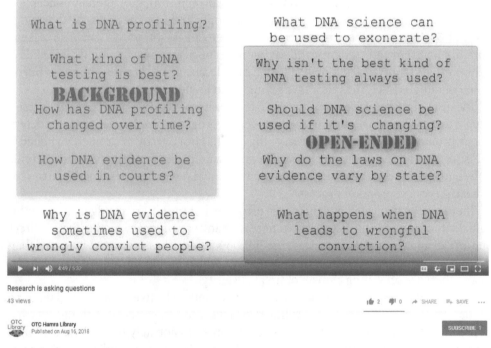

Figure 33.1
Screenshot from "Research Is Asking Questions" video. OTC Hamra Library, "Research Is Asking Questions," produced by Ozarks Technical Community College, posted August 16, 2018, YouTube video, 5:32, https://youtu.be/TpsVklONu84.

However, as the college's strategic plan explicitly identifies OTC 101 as a delivery mechanism for information literacy,[4] we hope to expand our role in this course. We are working on more paired video/assignment modules that can be deployed for online courses, and increasingly this content is also used by face-to-face instructors in the place of traditional one-shot instruction. We are also tiptoeing cautiously into the world of offering credit-bearing courses, developing both a three-credit media and information literacy elective course through the English department and an embedded library instruction component for English 102 in spring 2019. These forays into credit-bearing information literacy instruction are baby steps to formalizing our role in the curriculum, as well as defining and demonstrating our value as teachers.

Operations

Our program, based at OTC's largest campus in Springfield, only has one instruction librarian, with a library director and a collections librarian who will each step in in a pinch. There are no librarians at any other campus or center, and although our electronic resources and repository of tutorial videos are available to students and faculty throughout the system, our instruction program efforts are for now exclusive to the Springfield campus. Because of our significant staffing constraints, we are extremely selective about the requests we accept. We require instructors to commit to what we know to be best practices about library instruction using a collaborative model, including meeting with a librarian to discuss the assignment and possible learning objectives, declining database demonstrations in favor of holistic instruction that focuses on information literacy concepts and not tools, designing assignments with librarian input and in some cases collaborating on instructional design, tying in-person instruction to an assignment to establish stakes for both the librarian and students, and saying no to in-person instruction if we decide it is inappropriate (short instructional videos are made available). Avoiding librarian burnout is one of our guiding principles, as is saying no to ineffective collaborations.

The dean of academic services, to whom the library director reports, has been extremely supportive of our reinvention of the instruction program. She has consistently deferred to our professional expertise and reasoning and has not overtly or implicitly applied any pressure to continue doing one-shots. She understands our fundamental shift in philosophy and continues to help us advocate for additional resources and to navigate the credit-bearing course proposal process.

There is not a dedicated budget for the program, but the library's budget has so far been sufficient to support our instructional needs. Thanks to advocacy by the library director and the dean of academic services, the library's budget has increased by more than 8 percent in each of three consecutive fiscal years, which is a significant vote of confidence in an otherwise prevailing climate of fiscal austerity.

The library's paraprofessional staff have considerable collective longevity and remember the days of generic "library tours." While they have some awareness that the approach has changed and have heard the library director opine passionately that a "one-size-fits-all approach doesn't exist," they don't currently have a clear understanding of what is now actually being taught. Because we have a relatively small staff, we believe it would be positive for our overall team dynamic for those without teaching responsibilities to have some shared understanding of and appreciation for our philosophy of instruction. We are fortunate to get one day each semester in which the college is closed for regular business in order to pursue staff development activities, and we hope to use an upcoming staff development day to model some information literacy lesson plans in order to make our programmatic goals and content more transparent to all library staff.

We are optimistic that our efforts will continue to gather momentum because information literacy has been explicitly identified as an institutional priority in the college's new strategic plan. Missouri legislation has also codified "managing information" and "higher order thinking" as core competencies for graduates of all public institutions of higher education in the state.[5]

Collaboration

Our earliest and strongest allies on campus are the instructional designers in our Online and Faculty Development department. They have helped to connect us with individual instructors, to incorporate library resources and services (e.g., the Ask A Librarian chat widget) into the college's learning management system, and to intentionally integrate information literacy content and library resources into the course redesign and program development processes. We have co-facilitated a professional development session for instructors about the value of process-based research assignments (see figure 33.2), and we have a standing weekly collaboration meeting. Going forward, we intend to work with them in implementing our information literacy program through instructional design, working with faculty on developing assignments rather than having a librarian come in for a one-shot.

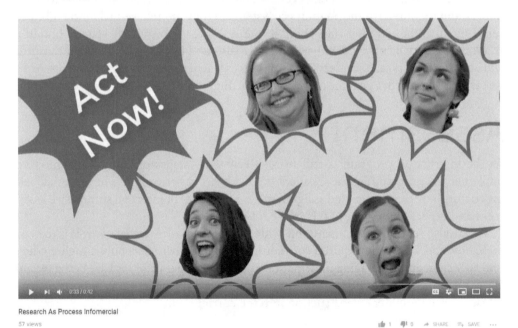

Figure 33.2
Marketing video for a workshop with librarians and instructional designers. Jacque Harris, "Research As Process Infomercial," posted June 1, 2018, YouTube video, 0:42, https://www.youtube.com/watch?v=kBfUfxvtjTc.

When we do in-person instruction, we model our collaborations with faculty on those of our fabulous instructional designer colleagues. When faculty request instruction, we try to get them to sit down and plan our lessons for the specific context of the course. It doesn't always work, but at the very least we try to make our collaborations with faculty sustained and focused on pedagogy, not on databases. One English 100 instructor came to us, referred by the instructional design team, and immediately was open to embedded instruction, with five instruction sessions tied to the course's most research-heavy essay. The essay topic was "problem-solution": students were to research a problem in their life or community and identify a practical solution. This instructor and this assignment lent themselves perfectly to building critically engaged instruction; examining the relative value of web sources, personal interviews, and academic articles; and then breaking down the different ways these sources need to be read and cited. The faculty member was so happy with the collaboration that it led to word-of-mouth marketing, and several more English instructors came to us looking for the same kind of engaged instruction.

Successful collaborations with several English faculty in spring and fall 2018 led to a positive relationship with the department as a whole, and the department chair in particular. As a result, the English department chair has become open to collaborative offerings such as the above-mentioned credit-bearing media and information literacy course and embedded instruction in one section of English 102 in the future. Select English faculty and the chair of that department have become strong allies, beginning to recognize the role of the library in their teaching in a new way. This relationship is built on meeting faculty on the instructional design level to teaching information literacy, but also showing them the value of a librarian-as-teacher. Several faculty have stated bluntly that they no longer understand the modern information ecosystem, so they are relieved when the librarian can come in and teach their class about it. We're still at the beginning stages of building relationships with faculty and with getting the main campus (let alone the other campuses and outlying centers) as a whole to see librarians as teachers. But as we get faculty to realize we can help them with a genuine need, we are starting to develop sustainable collaborations.

Assessment

As the instruction program is still in relatively early stages of being reinvented and implemented, programmatic assessment has not been our priority. We have worked with instructors to review completed assignments for purposes of informal summative assessment and expect to do more of this in the future.

We are also serving on an institution-wide assessment task force whose role is to determine how and where the required core competencies of a Missouri public higher education (which include managing information and higher order thinking) are being taught.[6] We expect that this institution-level participation will provide more opportunities to infuse information literacy instruction into the curriculum.

Role of the One-Shot

We are deliberately pivoting away from one-shots; in fact, we are regularly declining to perform them. Like others in our profession, we don't believe they are especially impactful, and we just don't have the staff resources to allocate in this way.[7] We have one devoted instruction librarian and more than 7,000 students on the Springfield campus. We began by nixing one-shots that were not located in computer classrooms and subsequently decided to phase them out altogether. And we've finally admitted that teaching how to use a database in isolation, without any context, is no longer an efficient use of our labor. Instead, we are building meaningful relationships with instructors via ongoing collaborations, as mentioned above. So we use videos in place of, not as a marketing tool for, one-shot instruction. We refer many instructors to our growing repository of brief tutorial videos (e.g., "Searching the Discovery System," "Understanding the Information Cycle") and paired assignments/quizzes. Instead, we are focusing our energy on marketing our instructional collaborations to faculty who are interested in active learning opportunities and meaningful instruction on information access and evaluation in a more holistic way.

Pedagogical Highlights

Our approach over the last two years has been to move away from one-shot sessions and toward collaborations with instructors teaching gateway courses (e.g., English composition) or those where scholarly communication is especially pertinent (e.g., research methods, intro to scientific research).

We strive to make our collaborations sustained (several classroom visits and librarian interactions), embedded (specific to the context of the assignment, course, and discipline), and active (engaging student knowledge in finding and analyzing information). We have adopted a constructivist teaching philosophy and aim to center and build upon students' existing knowledge and lived experiences of information consumption in approaching discussions of source evaluation and use for rhetorical purposes. We are also working directly with instructors to design process-based research assignments to address information literacy problems.

This student-centered approach can be seen in some of our developing course content as well as collaborative instruction, discussed above. The English 102 collaboration offers opportunities not just to engage with sources beyond the library, but also to encourage research outputs beyond the annotated bibliography: real-life applications for research output including blog entries, infographics, and executive summaries. And our media and information literacy course pilot will teach skills such Wikipedia editing and research analysis through video and graphic design and focus on ways for students to share their knowledge of media and information. The media and information literacy course has been temporarily put on hold, but we hope to pursue it in the future to develop pedagogical tools that can be deployed in our embedded instruction as well as any credit-bearing courses.

Administrative Highlights

The administration of our program has been a work in progress and, given the size of our staff, very limited. Our mission statement, broadly, is to prepare students to *create, find, analyze, and use information for professional and personal growth.* This is directly in support of the college's core values, institutional learning outcomes, and new strategic plan. We have mapped our mission statement broadly to the ACRL *Framework for Information Literacy for Higher Education* and the *Framework* to our instruction and lesson plans, although we are still working on a program plan, goals, and mapped learning outcomes.[8]

Our initial step to formalize our instruction was an instruction request form. Prior to 2016, this form was the way to receive any outreach or instruction request, including library tours. It included all OTC campuses, but we made changes to the Springfield campus form (other campuses are directed to the old form).We created an instruction menu with options ranging from concept-mapping research topics to the information cycle to the anatomy of a scholarly article. This menu was created in spring 2018, and modified for fall 2018 (see figure 33.3). But we found that the menu was often ignored, and very often the same requests for library tours and database demos came in despite it. We discovered it was best to work with faculty who were willing to sit down and meet with our instruction librarian to build a meaningful learning experience and decided the consultation model was the best way to ensure successful collaborations.

Menu Item	Time	Topics Covered	Concept(s)
Librarian Drop-In	5-10 minutes	• Know your librarian • Locate the library website and chat services	Searching as Strategic Exploration
Research is Asking Questions	50 minutes	• Develop research questions based on background information • Understand college research as a process rather than a search for the right answer	Research as Inquiry
Brainstorming Topics for Research	50 minutes	• Know a librarian • Create a concept map to explore a topic • Refine your topic through with initial research	Research as Inquiry
Evaluating Sources	50 minutes	• Know your librarian • Understand information production as a cycle • Communicate the relative value of a source	Authority Is Constructed and Contextual
Searching for Articles Workshop	50+ minutes	• One-on-one consultations with librarian • Access online resources through the library • Retrieve full text and citations • *Must be tied to a class assignment*	Information Has Value Searching as Strategic Exploration
How to Read a Scholarly Article	50 minutes	• Know your librarian • Identify the parts of a scholarly article. • Annotate a scholarly article for summary, authority, questions, and relevant methods or evidence.	Research as Inquiry Scholarship as Conversation
Instructional Design Collaboration	TBD	• Meet with a librarian to collaborate on a research assignment, from instructional design to librarian interventions customized for your course • *Requires at least one meeting with a librarian.*	

Figure 33.3
Our second attempt at an instruction menu (fall 2018).

As of spring 2019, we have done away with the instruction menu altogether and use a consultation model for administering our instruction program. Faculty need to meet one-on-one with a librarian if we are to provide library instruction (see figure 33.4). In some cases, this meeting may not result in instruction, but in collaborative instructional design. This has the added benefit of building relationships with thoughtful interactions, rather than reducing interactions by use of an online form. And realistically, with only one instruction librarian, often the best solution is not face-to-face instruction, but a collaboration on assignment or course design.

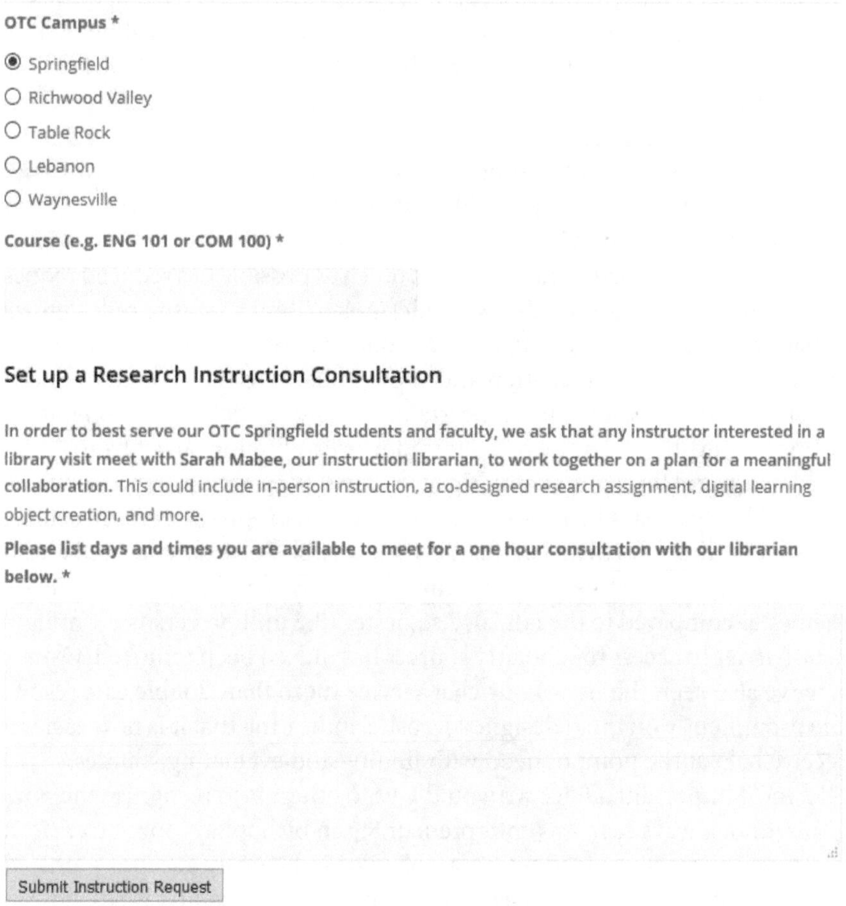

OTC Campus *

◉ Springfield

○ Richwood Valley

○ Table Rock

○ Lebanon

○ Waynesville

Course (e.g. ENG 101 or COM 100) *

Set up a Research Instruction Consultation

In order to best serve our OTC Springfield students and faculty, we ask that any instructor interested in a library visit meet with **Sarah Mabee**, our instruction librarian, to work together on a plan for a meaningful collaboration. This could include in-person instruction, a co-designed research assignment, digital learning object creation, and more.

Please list days and times you are available to meet for a one hour consultation with our librarian below. *

Submit Instruction Request

Figure 33.4
Our instruction request form as of spring 2019.

What We Wish People Knew

The most challenging thing about implementing an instruction program at OTC has been the pervasive and outdated expectations of a college library we've encountered in students, faculty, staff, and administrators. When the library director arrived in 2016, she was shocked and dismayed to find that in addition to being underfunded and underutilized, the library was a bit of a laughingstock among faculty and administrators. Librarians were certainly not viewed as instructional collaborators or experts in any sort of pedagogy. We have continued to encounter instructor requirements that are not necessarily reasonable; for example, some instructors require print books as sources, although we do not have appropriate sources in this format for all research projects (and our collection of more than 200,000 e-books is thereby dismissed). Likewise, some instructors misrepresent scholarly sources as "the gold standard" and insist that students rely on them even when it doesn't particularly make sense (for example, when examining current events in a political science course). We are working to educate our faculty colleagues about realistic expectations for research assignments, including the implications for cognitive load (and therefore learning) when novices are expected to decipher and interpret scholarly sources without support or contextualization.[9]

In order to make a move toward teaching more enduring concepts remotely feasible, we decided to implement a discovery layer. Although we did not anticipate that electronic resources management and troubleshooting would be central to an instruction program, taking efforts to streamline the searching process as much as possible has reduced requests for the most basic one-shots. Additionally, we undertook a library website redesign with the intention that by implementing intuitive, user-centered design we could remove some of the initial barriers to finding information and allow students to move on to evaluating and using information more easily. Though certainly a unique challenge of operating a small library, this behind-the-scenes work allowed us to shift effort away from "teaching" website navigation and toward teaching bigger-picture information literacy concepts. Although there will likely always be room for continued enhancements to user-centered design, we believe that this effort has been largely successful. For example, statistics for our discovery layer indicate that nearly three times as many searches were executed in the fall 2018 semester compared to the fall 2017 semester (3.2 million versus 1.1 million), indicating that a barrier to access to scholarly sources has indeed been removed. Over the same period, we've also seen the use of our chat service more than double as a result of placing it more prominently on the redesigned website, indicating that it is now easier for students to receive help at the point of need with finding and evaluating sources.

However, the most important advice we would give to others is to recognize the power of saying no. This is not always easy—as entrepreneur Susan Bishop says about transforming her once-struggling startup by adopting a policy of judiciously accepting only the right kind of opportunities, "saying no [seems] like uttering a profanity."[10] Nonetheless, we have found it to be imperative. Based on our past professional experiences, we are keenly aware of the dangers of mission creep and attempting to say yes to every request, which is usually a short road to burnout. We recognized immediately that in order to accomplish transformative change to our library's reputation and culture, we would need to make many strategic choices about which instruction requests to accept or deny and which other priorities and initiatives to pursue. While we recognize that we have been lucky to find ourselves in an institutional culture where our insistence on drawing firm boundaries is supported by administrators, we encourage others elsewhere to be brave, own their own power, and approach interactions with faculty as collaborations between peers. We have found inspiration in the work of Yvonne N. Meulemans and Allison Carr and wholeheartedly agree that "the 'customer is always right' attitude is not an effective teaching or collaborative philosophy."[11] We strive to stay true to our professional values as partners in the endeavor of teaching and learning and believe that in so doing we ultimately advance the best interests of students, even if a few instructors are disappointed in the short term.

Notes

1. "Missouri Poverty Facts," Missouri Community Action Network, accessed 21 Oct 2018. http://www. communityaction.org/missouri-poverty-facts.
2. "Fall 2017 Fact Sheet," Ozarks Technical Community College, p. 1, accessed 20 Oct 2018. https:// research.otc.edu/media/uploads/2017/11/2017-Fast-Facts_Web.pdf.
3. "Dreams Plan: 2018–2025 Strategic Plan," Ozarks Technical Community College, p. 14, accessed 20 Oct 2018..https://research.otc.edu/strategicplan.
4. "Dreams Plan," 16.
5. "Core Transfer Curriculum," Missouri Department of Higher Education, updated April 27, 2018, pp. 3–4, https://dhe.mo.gov/documents/CORE42April27.pdf
6. "Core Transfer Curriculum," 3–4.
7. Yvonne Mery, Jill Newby, and Ke Peng, "Why One-Shot Information Literacy Sessions Are Not the Future of Instruction: A Case for Online Credit Courses," *College and Research Libraries* 73, no. 4 (2012): 377.
8. Association of College and Research Libraries, *Framework for Information Literacy for Higher Education* (Chicago: Association of College and Research Libraries, 2016).
9. Mary Snyder Broussard, *Reading, Research, and Writing* (Chicago: Association of College and Research Libraries, 2017), 26–28.
10. Susan Bishop, "The Strategic Power of Saying No," *Harvard Business Review* 77, no. 6 (November– December, 1999): 52.
11. Meulemans and Carr, "Not at Your Service," 83.

Bibliography

Association of College and Research Libraries. *Framework for Information Literacy for Higher Education.* Chicago: Association of College and Research Libraries, 2016.

Bishop, Susan. "The Strategic Power of Saying No." *Harvard Business Review* 77, no. 6 (November–December 1999): 50–61.

Broussard, Mary Snyder. *Reading, Research, and Writing: Teaching Information Literacy with Process-Based Research Assignments.* Chicago: Association of College and Research Libraries, 2017.

Meulemans, Yvonne Nalani, and Allison Carr. "Not at Your Service: Building Genuine Faculty-Librarian Partnerships." *Reference Services Review* 41, no 1 (2013): 80–90.

Mery, Yvonne, Jill Newby, and Ke Peng. "Why One-Shot Information Literacy Sessions Are Not the Future of Instruction: A Case for Online Credit Courses." *College and Research Libraries* 73, no. 4 (2012): 366–77.

Missouri Community Action Network. "Missouri Poverty Facts." Accessed 20 Oct 2018. http://www. communityaction.org/missouri-poverty-facts.

Missouri Department of Higher Education. "Missouri Higher Education Core Transfer Curriculum." Updated April 27, 2018. https://dhe.mo.gov/documents/CORE42April27.pdf.

OTC Hamra Library, "Research Is Asking Questions," produced by Ozarks Technical Community College, posted August 16, 2018, YouTube video, 5:32, https://youtu.be/TpsVklONu84.

Ozarks Technical Community College. "Dreams Plan: 2018–2025 Strategic Plan." Accessed 20 Oct 2018. https://research.otc.edu/strategicplan.

———. "Fall 2017 Fact Sheet." Accessed 20 Oct 2018. https://research.otc.edu/media/ uploads/2017/11/2017-Fast-Facts_Web.pdf.

Chapter 34

Paul Smith's College

Engaging Student Workers through Student-Led Information Literacy

Amy Pajewski

Population Served

Paul Smith's College (PSC), known for its experiential, hands-on educational environment, is nestled within the rural Adirondack Mountains and is the only baccalaureate-granting institution within the boundary of the Adirondack Park, a 6.1-million-acre wilderness protected by the New York Forest Preserve. With roughly 700 students, over 60 percent of whom are male, the college boasts a self-reliant, creative spirit—one where students can design their own path and learn on the ground with their professors within the 14,000-acre property. While the college is extremely isolated, the entrepreneurial spirit is fierce, so our program hoped to allow students the opportunity to lead their own education.[1]

With the release of the college's strategic plan emphasizing "inspired learning," we knew our program would align with "ensuring academic excellence and career readiness" and fostering "authentic engagement."[2] We wanted to build a program that ignited the students' entrepreneurial spark while engaging them in meaningful workplace practice and inspiring learning.

Program Scope

The information literacy program at Paul Smith's College reaches all first-year English composition (ENG 101) and first-year experience classes (FYS) through required library instruction in the curriculum. Each ENG 101 course requires two face-to-face information literacy instruction sessions, and each FYS requires one, putting us at about sixty instruction sessions per semester. Since Paul Smith's employs only two librarians, this amount of face-to-face instruction can feel like a burden to our other job duties such as cataloging, outreach, and day-to-day operations. However, to mitigate the librarians' burden, ENG 101 faculty are able to choose only from a menu of instruction offerings that have been designed to offer the greatest amount of flexibility with the least amount of overlap between sessions. Currently, capstone-level information literacy isn't a curriculum requirement, but faculty are highly encouraged to include it by the Student Outreach Librarian as students' information literacy skills aren't scaffolded throughout their tenure at the institution. In order to cover the library's operations efficiently, three student workers were placed on each of three teams: Student Ambassadors, Outreach, and Peer-to-Peer Educators (PtP team). This chapter will focus on the student-led information literacy instruction program by the PtP team while providing context of the overall information literacy program at PSC.

Student workers involved in the instruction program are generally upper-division undergraduates conducting instruction in the form of peer-to-peer workshops, orientation sessions for Writing Center Coaches, resource development such as handouts or other tools, and in-classroom instruction in FYS courses, all of which are conducted face-to-face. Peer-to-peer workshops are designed by the library's PtP team, and students provide in-person and virtual reference services for the campus community, as well as in-person workshops for other student workers on campus. The PtP team delivers in-person instruction to teach all Writing Center Coaches when it's appropriate to direct a student to the library for research assistance. The PtP team also works directly with the Student Outreach Librarian to develop learning objectives and outcomes for required FYS and ENG 101 instruction sessions; upper-division undergraduate team members assist within the classroom.

At the beginning of the spring 2018 semester, Paul Smith's had just acquired the learning management system Canvas, and the library plans to move some of these workshops, trainings, and classes online.

Operations

The PSC library is staffed by one Cataloging and eResources Librarian, the Student Outreach Librarian, two technicians, ten student workers, and the library director. Each of the librarians and the director are expected to teach information literacy instruction courses for both ENG 101 and FYS as well as additional sessions for liaison departments. Because of our small student population, the library houses not only library operations, but also the Writing Center, peer tutoring, accommodative services, and the career center. By adapting the peer-to-peer education models already in place in those offices, we were better able to make a case for hiring additional student employees for the development and implementation of our student-led program.

The student worker program at PSC began from a source of need as my priorities for the library changed. In the spring of 2015, institutional staffing changes left me to restructure my position in collaboration with the director to also include coordinating the information literacy program. Since I was focusing more of my time on teaching, I pitched an opportunity that would help me and my work as well as giving student employees a more beneficial and marketable work experience—one that aligned with the current college priorities. Leadership experience is emphasized within the college experience at PSC and is valued by the National Association of Colleges and Employers (NACE).[3] Through training, students learn to develop interpersonal skills for the workforce and support success for both the library and institutional communities. The only way I saw to improve our services in the context of a staffing deficit was to give opportunities for our students to lead the way, while also showing our value by providing experiential learning opportunities and creating a high-impact practice and user experience that benefits both the library and the student employees.

Peer-to-Peer Educators: Responsibilities and Training Schedule

RESPONSIBILITIES

Peer-to-Peer Educators provide in-person and virtual reference services and information literacy instruction for the campus community, which allows for the fulfillment of patrons' and students' information needs, as well as providing a personal educational opportunity for educators.

REQUIRED TIERED TRAINING SCHEDULE

Year 1: Students are introduced to basic reference interviewing skills, including shadowing librarians at the desk, learning how to search the catalog for known items, and learning about keyword searching within library databases. Students are required to observe five information literacy instruction (IL) sessions taught by the Student Outreach Librarian and write a reflection describing key IL concepts covered in the sessions. The Student Outreach Librarian provides readings on Char Booth's USER model and introduces the concept of backward design in building lesson plans.[4]

Year 2: Students learn how to conduct a more advanced reference interview using role-playing with recorded reference questions from previous years. They develop advanced search strategies, differentiating subject-specific databases and choosing the proper resources for the question. The Student Outreach Librarian reinforces the concepts of Booth's USER model and backward design, and students begin building learning objectives and lesson plans to use in training Writing Center tutors and within the ENG 101 classroom. Students are expected to develop activities within their lesson plans and execute those plans by co-teaching some sections of ENG 101 with the Student Outreach Librarian.

Year 3+: The Student Outreach Librarian aids students in how to facilitate discussion in the classroom. Students are expected to continue to co-teach with the Student Outreach

Librarian, observe IL instruction sessions, and write reflections on their teaching. Students have the choice to step into leading solo sessions for ENG 101 when comfortable.

Professional Staff Roles

Student Outreach Librarian

- Schedules and conducts all trainings.
- Plans and executes all-staff meetings.
- Attends monthly meetings with PtP team.
- Manages student Office 365 workspace. This includes monitoring student meeting minutes, to-do lists, and calendar.
- Serves as mentor to student teams and student worker supervisor.
- Conducts student evaluations at the end of each semester and career exit interviews that focus on interview preparation for graduating seniors.

Library Technician

- Serves as direct student supervisor—the go-to person for time-clock errors, immediate student worker issues, and scheduling.
- Completes student payroll.
- Reaches out to students before timesheets are due. Ensures students are completing tasks within each student's building advocacy duties. These include things like hourly walk-throughs, shelving books, conducting inventory assignments, and cleaning up the library.
- Conducts student evaluations with Student Outreach Librarian at end of each semester.
- Posts vacant student worker positions as needed.

During summer and winter breaks, I worked on creating the fall/spring semester plan in collaboration with the library technician and uploaded that document into the Office 365 student worker group. For each item of the semester plan, I created a to-do bullet in the Office 365 workspace within the appropriate student worker team. This allowed me to assign these tasks to the particular students on the team responsible for that outcome. By doing this, I was able to assess progress on the full semester plan throughout the semester before performance evaluations.

Once all of the student tasks were added to the to-do list, I worked on scheduling the welcome meeting and trainings. Luckily, Paul Smith's has "Common Time," a one-hour period on Mondays, Wednesdays, and Fridays that students are not in class. Typically, I ran four trainings per semester in addition to two all-staff meetings at the beginning and end of the semester. I scheduled a welcome training within the first week of the semester to go over the semester plan, introduce the Office 365 workspace, and show students their office. As for the other trainings, they are team-specific (unless there is a universal issue that must be addressed).

Collaboration

The library leads information literacy workshops specifically tailored for student tutors in the Center for Academic and Career Success and for writing tutors in the Writing Center. For the Writing Center students, the Student Outreach Librarian teaches up to ten tutors how to identify when a writing question becomes a research question, how to cite using

MLA and APA, and when to refer to a librarian. Writing Center tutors are then paired with the Peer-to-Peer Educators and receive instruction on known-item searching within the library's databases and training materials with directions on searching. During finals week each semester, Writing Center tutors and the Peer-to-Peer Educators work together to provide writing and research help to students in the residence halls. These sessions are held in the evening hours to accommodate students' needs and have been successful in terms of attendance (fifteen or more students) for a small institution such as PSC.

Assessment

At the time I left, we were in the process of figuring out how to assess student learning in a one-shot model and did not currently have an assessment strategy in place. Instead, we focused on assessing the student workers' teaching through written librarian observations as well as using metrics like retention, internship/job rates of our student employees, and NACE competencies (see figure 34.1) during one-on-one evaluations.

PSC Student Worker Competencies Evaluation Form

Student Worker's Name: _____
Team Title: _____
Evaluation Period: _____ Todays' Date: _____

All characteristics may not apply to each student, therefore, if a category cannot be rated OBJECTIVELY, please write "N/A"
Please rate the student worker's performance in the areas listed, using the rating scale below.
NOTE: There is a section for both the employee and the supervisor to provide a rating.
1 -Exceeds Expectations   2- Meets Expectations   NI- Needs Improvement   N/A- Not Applicable

Competencies	Employee Rating	Supervisor Rating
CRITICAL THINKING/PROBLEM SOLVING: Exercises sound reasoning to analyze issues, makes decisions and overcomes problems. Able to obtain, interpret and use knowledge, facts and data.		
ORAL/WRITTEN COMMUNICATIONS: Expresses thoughts and ideas clearly and effectively in written and oral form to all constituents.		
TEAMWORK/COLLABORATION: Builds collaborative relationships with colleagues and customers with diverse backgrounds and viewpoints. Able to work in a team structure and manage conflict.		
INFORMATION TECHNOLOGY APPLICATION: Uses appropriate technology to accomplish a given task. Able to apply computing skills to solve problems.		
LEADERSHIP: Leverages the strengths of others to achieve common goals. Uses interpersonal skills to coach and develop others. Able to manage own emotions and those of others. Uses empathy to guide and motivate, organize, prioritize and delegate work.		
PROFESSIONALISM/WORK ETHIC: Demonstrates personal accountability and effective work habits, e.g., punctuality, productivity, workload management. Understands the impact of non-verbal communication. Demonstrates integrity and ethical behavior, acts responsibly with the interests of the larger community in mind. Able to learn from his/her mistakes.		
CAREER MANAGEMENT: Identifies and articulates skills, strengths, knowledge and experiences relevant to position. Understands how to appropriately self-advocate in the workplace.		
QUALITY AND QUANTITY OF WORK: Works effectively and efficiently. Able to meet deadlines and accomplish multiple tasks with accuracy and thoroughness.		
CUSTOMER SERVICE: Insures that department and university are accurately and positively portrayed. Requests are timely and accurate, and response is complete.		
KNOWLEDGE AND SKILLS: Demonstrates working level of skill/knowledge in area of expertise. Applies professional and technical expertise to best meet department/area needs.		

Adopted from NACE (National Association of Colleges and Employers) http://www.naceweb.org/knowledge/career-readiness-competencies.aspx

Figure 34.1
Student Worker Competencies Evaluation Form

Each semester, students are required to fill out a self-assessment rubric mapping their perceived performance relative to the NACE competencies and sit in with me and the library technician for a performance evaluation. As of spring 2018, we collected one year's worth of data, but we intend to continue to collect it to see how students grow within the program and give them the opportunity to reflect on their personal and professional goals.

Role of the One-Shot

One-shot instruction is the significant focus of the PSC information literacy program, which as a whole is unbalanced. We reach students in the first year and at the capstone level but struggle to reach those in the middle (who arguably need us the most). The great thing about our program is that our Peer-to-Peer Educators are upper-division undergraduates who have incredible relationships with their faculty, which opens up future areas for collaboration.

Annually in mid-August, I compiled a list of all faculty who have required library instruction. All FYS classes have one required session, and all ENG 101 classes have two required sessions, so I make it a point to contact them first to schedule with us, and include our instruction offerings.

For ENG 101, classroom faculty may choose one option for each session from the following menu:[5]

1. *Keywords:* This class covers taking a topic statement, turning it into effective keywords, and brainstorming other words that might also work. Students use databases and trial and error to learn how keywords matter. Year 2 Peer-to-Peer Educators are typically assigned as assistants for these sections; Year 3 and above can teach these sections solo.
2. *Resource identification:* This class features group work and active learning as students identify the strengths and weaknesses of six types of resources in order to better understand information publishing and make a research plan. Year 2 Peer-to-Peer Educators are typically assigned as assistants for these sections; Year 3 and above can teach these sections solo.
3. *Mind-mapping:* Our most popular ENG 101 class, this session helps students go from a general idea of what they might research to a more researchable topic focused on the connections between ideas rather than reporting out on a particular idea. Students have time to research in class, and we make sure to have a one-on-one consultation with each student in the class. Year 3 Peer-to-Peer Educators assist in facilitating discussion in these sessions.
4. *Bibliography peer review:* This is a new class that is meant to show students that research is iterative while allowing them to make adjustments to the sources they will use. Students come to class with partially completed bibliographies and spend some time with others' work to help each other come to the best possible resource list for their papers. Year 3 and 4 Peer-to-Peer Educators are assigned as facilitators in these sections.

I typically like to provide faculty with a couple of natural pairings, such as mind-mapping and bibliography peer review, with at least two weeks between sessions.

Pedagogical Highlights

Lave and Wenger defined a community of practice as "a set of relations among persons, activity, and world"[6] and Wenger, McDermott, and Snyder as "groups of people who share a concern, a set of problems, or a passion about a topic, and who deepen their knowledge and expertise in this area by interacting on an ongoing basis."[7] The Peer-to-Peer Educator model and PSC student worker program are in themselves a community of practice as students are learning together and with each other at the same time over a mutual concern: teaching and learning information literacy.

Administrative Highlights

We are a Microsoft campus, so students are used to logging in to Office 365 automatically. Because of this, and in an effort to get them to check their email more often, I used some of the other tools within that suite. Students use the planner tool, which functions as a project management space (one where I can assign students to certain areas) and the calendar (for their instruction schedules) and conduct their own meetings and keep meeting minutes in a designated OneNote space.

What I Wish People Knew

I didn't realize at first how time-intensive this program would be. Our first semester was rough because I thought giving students more creative freedom would be good—turns out I wasn't giving them enough direction. For example, when I was developing student worker responsibilities, I expected students to be able to take general program goals and develop them into projects, not realizing that for many, this was their first job. To adjust in the second semester, an upper-level student and I reconfigured the program, including more specific assignments and projects broken down into individual tasks so student workers could see exactly what was expected. I think the number one thing people should remember is that most things aren't a huge success right at the start—it takes time to figure it out, to learn to manage people, and to make meaningful connections on campus that can help support a program.

Notes

1. This chapter is written in retrospect. The author of this chapter hasn't worked at PSC since August 2018.
2. "Strategic Plan 2016–2020," Paul Smith's College, accessed October 10, 2018, https://www.paulsmiths.edu/about/strategic-plan.
3. "Career Readiness Defined," National Association of Colleges and Employers, accessed October 1, 2018, http://www.naceweb.org/career-readiness/competencies/career-readiness-defined.
4. Char Booth, *Reflective Teaching, Effective Learning* (Chicago: American Library Association , 2011), 93–102; Grant P. Wiggins and Jay McTighe, *Understanding by Design*, 2nd ed. (Alexandria, VA: Association for Supervision and Curriculum Development, 2005), 13–34.
5. Meggan Press, internal PSC Information Literacy program document, 2016.

6. Jean Lave and Etienne Wenger, *Situated Learning* (New York: Cambridge University Press, 1991), 98–100.

7. Etienne Wenger, Richard McDermott, and William Snyder, *Cultivating Communities of Practice* (Boston: Harvard Business Press, 2002), 4.

Bibliography

Booth, Char. *Reflective Teaching, Effective Learning: Instructional Literacy for Library Educators*. Chicago: American Library Association, 2011.

Lave, Jean, and Etienne Wenger. *Situated Learning: Legitimate Peripheral Participation*. New York: Cambridge University Press, 1991.

National Association of Colleges and Employers. "Career Readiness Defined." Accessed October 1, 2018. http://www.naceweb.org/career-readiness/competencies/career-readiness-defined.

Paul Smith's College. "Strategic Plan 2016–2020." Accessed October 10, 2018. https://www.paulsmiths.edu/about/strategic-plan.

Press, Meggan. Internal Paul Smith's College Information Literacy program document. 2016.

Wenger, Etienne, Richard McDermott, and William Snyder. *Cultivating Communities of Practice: A Guide to Managing Knowledge*. Boston: Harvard Business Press, 2002.

Wiggins, Grant P., and Jay McTighe. *Understanding by Design*, 2nd ed. Alexandria, VA: Association for Supervision and Curriculum Development, 2005.

Chapter 35

State University of New York College of Agriculture and Technology at Cobleskill

A One-Person Instruction Program

Don LaPlant

Population Served

State University of New York (SUNY) Cobleskill is a public agricultural and technical college serving approximately 1,400 students in bachelor's degree programs and another 900 in associate's degree and certificate programs. Our small, rural campus is distinguished from many others of its size by specialized facilities and lab spaces, including a 200-cow dairy farm, an equestrian center, fish hatcheries, greenhouses, arboreta, biotechnology labs, a child development center, and a student-run restaurant.[1] Our college prides itself on its commitment to integrating an applied learning component in every program; in addition to a range of required lab courses, most of our students must complete semester-long internships, practicum placements, capstone projects, or clinical rotations as a graduation requirement. The students we attract are deeply committed to their disciplines and relish the hands-on work required of them in departmental coursework, but they often arrive underprepared for—and sometimes surprised and intimidated by—the depth and rigor of the scholarship expected of them here. Our students may have been drawn to SUNY Cobleskill because they're passionate about the kind of practical work required in their therapeutic horsemanship, graphic design, or diesel technology classes, but they're also required to complete the sort of research-intensive papers and projects assigned at more traditional liberal arts colleges.

Our library instruction program is designed to help students—regardless of their major or career aspiration—develop the skills required to effectively identify their information needs, then access, evaluate, use, and cite appropriate, credible information sources. Often those essential principles and skills are introduced in information literacy sessions scheduled at the instructors' discretion as part of certain required general education courses. Ideally—yet again at the individual instructors' discretion—the basic principles and skills are expanded and given a more discipline-specific focus as students work on more complex research articles, presentations, or conference posters in upper-division major courses.

Program Scope

Our campus currently offers no credit-bearing information literacy courses, and no departments or programs have established information literacy instruction as a formal curricular requirement. Several faculty members have been receptive to making library instruction a regularly scheduled event in certain of their department's courses, but this isn't yet a widespread practice across campus. As a result, exposure to information literacy instruction might vary considerably from student to student, even among students in the same program. Some students have four or five library one-shot sessions during their time here, while others might conceivably graduate without any.

In the absence of formalized curriculum mapping for library instruction, we have endeavored to find creative ways to reach the broadest range of students. Our students' first introduction to library instruction often comes in the form of two asynchronous online tutorials delivered in a one-credit Foundations for College Success (FFCS) course required of all incoming first-year students. These interactive tutorials, created using Springshare's LibWizard, provide an introduction to library resources and services, an overview of the diverse range of information sources students may encounter in their academic careers, and a discussion of campus policies on academic integrity with a focus on avoiding plagiarism. These tutorials also introduce students to other optional forms of self-guided instruction such as LibGuides, a library FAQ, and a curated collection of online library tutorials. After finishing both tutorials, students are required to complete two quizzes that count for part of the final grade for the FFCS course. As my institution's Instructional Design Librarian, I am an administrator of our LibWizard platform and am responsible for collating students' quiz scores and sharing them with the appropriate instructors of FFCS sections. Data gathered from analysis of students' performance on these quizzes has enabled me to assess the effectiveness of the tutorials and inspired significant changes to both the tutorials and the wording of quiz questions over the course of several semesters.

Beyond these tutorials, most students encounter library instruction through one- or two-shot sessions scheduled as part of a class. Given that we have only one librarian accommodating all library instruction requests, we have had to think strategically about how to efficiently reach the most students. After reviewing curricula and enrollment numbers and talking with many faculty, we decided to target our marketing efforts on three categories of classes:

1. the lower-division general education classes that—based on an analysis of curricular prerequisites, enrollment statistics, and number of sections offered annually—are the most commonly required across various majors (e.g., English composition, intro. to psychology, Western civilization, public speaking),
2. the highest enrolled introductory courses within popular majors—often the 100-level courses that serve as prerequisites for the most other courses in a given department, and
3. the most research-intensive upper-division courses in a major—often 400-level capstone courses with a semester-long research project.

While these are the types of classes we devote the most marketing energy toward, we certainly strive to accommodate all requests we receive for instruction related to specific research-based assignments. The scheduling limitations inherent in having only one instruction librarian have enabled us to maintain a policy that there are two types of instruction requests we typically cannot accommodate:

1. library tours or general orientation sessions not directly connected to a specific research assignment, and
2. "cover my class" sessions when faculty members will not be attending with their students.

Responses to requests like these can inspire discussions about more effective ways to integrate information literacy instruction into a program and have more than once resulted in sessions being scheduled in later semesters or other courses.

We've tried to supplement our tutorials and one-shot sessions with other instructional approaches, but these have met with varying degrees of success so far. For instance, we have offered drop-in workshops for both students and faculty, but attendance has remained low. We have also offered students the opportunity to sign up for thirty-minute one-on-one research consultation appointments, which straddle the line between reference and instruction. These appointments have been most popular when offered as a follow-up to a class that has already attended a traditional one-shot session, especially when the course instructor encourages, requires, or offers extra credit for attendance. Unfortunately, this approach is rather time-intensive and difficult to scale up; one-shots can reach dozens of students in an hour, but consultations can reach only two students in the same time.

Operations

Our campus library is staffed by five full-time tenure-track faculty librarians and three paraprofessional staff. All of our librarians participate in reference, collection development, and liaison work in addition to one or more areas of specialization (e.g., serials, cataloging, interlibrary loan, circulation). I am the sole librarian tasked with instruction. My official title is Instructional Design Librarian, and I am responsible for the administration of the entire instruction program, which involves coordinating, teaching, and assessing all instruction sessions as well as developing and maintaining a full range of promotional and instructional materials.

Some of my librarian colleagues have voluntarily agreed to make themselves available for research consultation appointments on an as-needed basis. Students can sign up for an appointment with the librarian of their choice using a LibCal interface on the library's website. So far, however, the students who have signed up for consultation appointments have (in all but a few instances) scheduled appointments with me—most likely because I'm the person who taught their instruction session and told them about the appointment scheduler in the first place.

The relatively small size of our library and our professional staff simplifies coordination with other library initiatives. Instruction, reference, outreach, and liaison services all have some areas of overlap, and my librarian colleagues and I communicate directly about issues that might impact each others' areas and collaborate on programs and initiatives. We believe the library's instruction program is an important contributor to our campus-wide retention initiatives as we actively work to develop students' basic research skills, combat academic integrity violations, and provide targeted academic support to students enrolled in lower-division general education courses with traditionally high failure rates.

Marketing

Given our belief in the value of library instruction and the lack of any campus-wide information literacy instruction requirement beyond the aforementioned FFCS tutorials, our library has made it a goal to actively promote library instruction in hopes of expanding its reach. Our promotional efforts have allowed us to increase the number of students served in one-shots by 112 percent over the past four years. Word-of-mouth and face-to-face appeals have been essential to our marketing strategy. All our librarians make in-person appeals at division and department meetings at the beginning of each semester as well as adding reminders to their regular communications with their respective liaison areas. As coordinator of the program, I have reached out separately via email and in person to instructors of the courses that meet the three target categories described above.

We also refer faculty members to a "Faculty Resources" LibGuide reachable through a direct link on the library's home page.[2] In addition to introducing the full range of library services we provide, this LibGuide also offers details about the range of instructional options available and provides regularly updated summaries of student and faculty evaluations of past instruction sessions. Direct links to a separate Library Skills Tutorials page have also been helpful marketing tools as we've heard that the high quality of our locally produced tutorial content has inspired some previously reluctant faculty to "take a chance" on scheduling a class session in the library.

Collaboration

Information literacy skills are listed among the standards and competencies expected by the State University of New York system and our regional accrediting body, the Middle States Commission on Higher Education. Currently, however, our institution has no clearly articulated requirement or assessment system in place that might require librarian-led instruction as the means of meeting these expectations. Since there is currently no institutional mandate that students attend IL sessions with a librarian, we rely on faculty to voluntarily schedule sessions and administrators to strongly encourage faculty to do so. Deans, department chairs, and program directors are important collaborators when it comes to encouraging faculty engagement with the library's instructional efforts. We also benefit greatly from respected senior faculty members willing to promote our programs to new faculty and adjuncts in their programs. More than once I've had interactions with faculty members contacting me to see if they could arrange something similar to what I did for another faculty member's class.

Establishing relationships with individual faculty is essential to the continued success of our instruction program, but ultimately the instruction program would benefit much more from administrative influence resulting in curricular changes. A series of thoughtful conversations with the coordinator of the First Year Experience program resulted in the aforementioned online FFCS tutorials and quizzes now reaching a quarter of our total campus student population enrolled in over thirty sections of a single course. We are hopeful that ongoing efforts to promote the value and effectiveness of information literacy instruction to academic deans, the provost, department chairs, and faculty officers in shared governance committees might inspire more productive conversations about making informational literacy a curricular requirement for all students. Establishing and maintaining strong relationships with these highly influential people could strengthen our promotional efforts and make a tremendous difference in the continued expansion of the library's instructional program.

Assessment

Institutional assessment of the library's instruction program for external groups such as the Integrated Postsecondary Education Data System (IPEDS) and the annual Association of College and Research Libraries' (ACRL) Academic Library Trends and Statistics survey has focused on gathering basic statistics such as the number of sessions offered and the total number of students served. My internal program assessment goes beyond this sort of record keeping, however. Qualitative and quantitative evaluations of student satisfaction are administered at the end of most instruction sessions, and similar evaluations are distributed to faculty at the end of the semester asking them, among other things, to evaluate their perception of the impact of library instruction on students' performance on research papers and projects. I review feedback from student satisfaction surveys immediately after the session ends so that helpful suggestions may be implemented prior to the next session. At the end of each semester, I review feedback from the faculty surveys and analyze broader trends from both faculty and student evaluations by comparing data from previous semesters.

I also conduct formative and summative assessments during IL sessions by using LibWizard to administer a pretest at the start of many one-shots. This pretest allows me to assess students' comprehension of basic principles and their ability to apply essential information literacy skills. I'm able to quickly review the students' general level of success on the pretests and identify questions that seem to have given students the most trouble. This on-the-fly assessment serves a diagnostic purpose by allowing me to quickly determine which skills most need to be introduced or reinforced and which points in my lesson plan might be reviewed quickly or skipped over entirely. As an added benefit, the difficulty many lower-division students have with this pretest seems to inspire an increased degree of motivated attention during the remainder of the session, helping to moderate some students' tendency to overestimate their preexisting knowledge of how to find information effectively.

The pretest asks students to find specific sources, to identify strong search queries and keywords, to demonstrate the ability to navigate the library's website, and to effectively use limiters and filters. In addition to these practical questions, the pretest asks students to describe their level of prior library instruction experience and report whether they have previously attended other information literacy sessions or completed the tutorials required in our Foundations for College Success course. At the end of the semester, I get some helpful assessment data by comparing pretest performance by students who have attended previous instruction sessions to those without any prior instruction. Not only does it provide information about how effective my previous instruction sessions have been, it also suggests how well the information has been retained over time.

My examination of this aggregated data has helped identify which tasks students have the greatest difficulty with and which they typically succeed at even without prior instruction. For example, after my analysis of pretests showed that nearly all students were able to find the call number for a book and locate helpful links on the library's website (e.g., hours, our chat service, and LibGuides), I cut those topics from my standard lesson plan. Conversely, after seeing a considerable percentage of lower-division students using poorly focused natural language searches, I was inspired to devote additional class time to helping students construct more effective search queries and use subject terms from initial searches to help discover more effective keywords.

In some classes where research consultation appointments have been offered as an optional supplement to the regular classroom sessions, I've made arrangements with students and faculty to collect and review bibliographies from final research papers. Using a rubric, I've evaluated the sources listed to assess students' efficacy at finding an acceptable number and range of credible, relevant sources. By comparing the relative success of those students who attended a consultation appointment with those who didn't, I'm able to get a sense of the degree to which my instruction efforts have been effective. One particularly productive outcome of this sort of assessment was a research poster about the relative effectiveness of consultation appointments as a supplement to traditional one-shot instruction, which I copresented at a conference and subsequently shared with faculty as a marketing tool for the consultation program.[3]

Role of the One-Shot

Information literacy sessions reached just under 1,400 students during the 2017–18 academic year, which—given our total student enrollment of roughly 2,300—indicates one-shots are our instructional bread and butter. During the same period, however, we also recorded over 700 visits to our online library tutorials page and over 25,000 visits to our LibGuides, suggesting asynchronous learning opportunities are also valued by our students and faculty. In fact, I have had some success encouraging faculty to combine a one-shot with a secondary mode of instruction. Some have used a flipped classroom approach where students are required to complete an online tutorial or review the resources on a LibGuide before attending a one-shot. Others require students to complete a post-session quiz or assignment or to schedule a research consultation appointment after having attended a session with me.

In recent years, a number of faculty (particularly those teaching writing-intensive general education classes) have begun asking to schedule two sessions per class. The first is often focused on topic selection, research question formation, and the variety of information sources available, while the second is focused on finding, evaluating, and citing sources.

The applied nature of so many of our degree programs at SUNY Cobleskill inspires a large number of assignments focused on using a limited range of trusted sources to find a specific answer or to solve a narrow research problem rather than exploring a range of theoretical or interpretive perspectives on an issue. Sometimes faculty ask that my sessions provide detailed instruction on how to use a specific reference source or navigate a specific database. While I'm happy to meet that need, I recognize that such sessions address only a few of the many basic skills required of an information-literate student. Consequently, I work to convince these faculty of the benefits of expanding beyond tips on navigating a specific resource to a broader consideration of principles of query construction and the iterative nature of searching. Ultimately, however, my access to these classes depends on the invitation of instructors, so I do my best to meet the instructors' stated technical goals for the session while smuggling in as many higher-level principles and concepts as I can.

Pedagogical Highlights

As the sole librarian charged with teaching library instruction sessions, I'm fortunate enough to let my own teaching philosophy guide what and how I teach. My instruction program's mission statement and student learning objectives were largely inspired by the *Information Literacy Competency Standards for Higher Education* rescinded by ACRL in June 2016 and by the "Information Literacy VALUE Rubric" published by the American Association of Colleges and Universities.[4] Consequently, my instruction sessions typically focus on developing, expanding, and measuring students' practical ability to effectively identify their information needs, then access, evaluate, use, and cite appropriate, credible information sources.

SUNY Cobleskill faculty and students tend to privilege practical, technical instruction on navigating databases and subject-specific reference sources over discussions of the more abstract concepts addressed in the ACRL *Framework for Information Literacy for*

Higher Education.[5] I strive to customize my lesson plans to the research tasks the students will need to accomplish to successfully complete their assignments. While this approach admittedly neglects many of the bigger-picture philosophical issues that might be covered in a three-credit information literacy course, I've made peace with the fact that only so much can be covered in a single fifty-to-seventy-five-minute one-shot. I believe it would be foolhardy and counterproductive to try to squeeze a semester's worth of material into a single class session.

Given my time limitations, I feel it's most important to help students meet their immediate research needs. In the process of introducing the skills I believe students will need, I try to highlight transferable skills and principles they will be able to apply to other research tasks in the future. My practical, hands-on, problem-solving students appear to appreciate my practical, hands-on, problem-solving approach to instruction. This, I believe, greatly increases the likelihood that they will have positive feelings about the session and the library in general and, consequently, be more comfortable asking a librarian for research help if they need it in the future.

Administrative Highlights

From an administrative perspective, our instruction program is relatively simple and low-tech. My interactions with faculty to schedule and coordinate plans for instruction sessions are made via emails, phone calls, and face-to-face interactions. Though my library uses Springshare's LibCal system to handle sign-ups for research consultation appointments, I manually post scheduled IL sessions on the library's shared calendar in Moodle, our campus-wide LMS, so my library colleagues can see where and when I'm teaching in case students show up at the front desk looking for their class. I also record statistical details about instruction sessions on a shared spreadsheet on Google Drive. These details include course name, instructor's name, number of students, and location and duration of sessions. This not only proves useful when compiling my end-of-semester statistics, but also makes it easier for my colleagues to directly access this type of data when they're filling out reports or surveys asking for the number of classes or students served by our instruction program.

Information Literacy Coordinator Profile

My official title is Instructional Design Librarian, and the position is responsible for coordinating the information literacy instruction program and developing instructional content, with additional duties shared by all librarians at my institution. Instruction-related activities account for roughly 60 percent of my average workday, with reference, collection development, liaison responsibilities, and other administrative and service functions filling the rest of my time. Librarians at SUNY Cobleskill work on a twelve-month contract, which is fortunate in that it allows time in the summer and between semesters to focus on the development and assessment of instructional content that my extensive teaching, librarianship, and service responsibilities make difficult to complete while classes are in session.

As recently as eight years ago, one-shot instruction duties were split among multiple librarians as schedules allowed, though one librarian carried the bulk of the teaching load. The decision to switch to the current model where a designated instruction librarian does all the teaching was made before I took the position, three years and two instruction librarians ago. The motivation for making instruction the primary responsibility of a single instruction librarian was a shared sense that aptitude for and interest in teaching wasn't evenly shared among all librarians. The quality of instruction varied widely from session to session, and hiring someone specifically focused on instruction was intended to solve that problem.

What I Wish People Knew

I believe that librarians having tenure-track faculty status makes it easier to establish relationships and win faculty members' trust and support. Librarians at SUNY Cobleskill serve on governance committees with other faculty members and attend the same faculty meetings; we face similar expectations for scholarship and service and go through the same tenure review process. As the instructional librarian, I have my classroom performance evaluated using the same observation form used by any other member of the teaching faculty. I'm convinced these commonalities make it easier for faculty to consider me a teaching colleague rather than an administrative staff member, and consequently, they are more comfortable with the idea of letting me lead a class session for their students.

One final point I want people to know is that, though I have identified my program as a "one-person program," it would not be able to function effectively without the support of my fellow librarians, the library's paraprofessional staff, and the dean of libraries. My irregular and unpredictable teaching schedule means I frequently need to ask another librarian to cover a reference shift for me if I've got a class conflict. Likewise, I rely on other librarians to promote my services to the faculty in their liaison subject areas and keep me updated about new acquisitions and sources that might be worth introducing in my instruction sessions. I rely on my library's dean to initiate conversations with the administrators most likely to influence curriculum development or encourage broader implementation of information literacy across the campus. So while instruction is technically a one-person department in our library, its success depends on a tremendous amount of collaboration and cooperation from my colleagues. I would strongly encourage anyone just starting out as a library's sole instruction librarian to invest time establishing strong relationships both inside the library and across campus. This investment has been instrumental to the success of the instruction program at SUNY Cobleskill.

Notes

1. "About SUNY Cobleskill," SUNY Cobleskill, accessed March 31, 2019, https://www.cobleskill.edu/about/index.aspx.
2. Don LaPlant, "Information Literacy: Faculty Resources," Van Wagenen Library, SUNY Cobleskill, last modified December 18, 2018, http://libraryguides.cobleskill.edu/InfoLit/faculty.

3. Don LaPlant and Brendan Aucoin, "The Effectiveness of Individual Research Consultations as a Supplement to Traditional Library Instruction Approaches; or, 1:1 ≥ (25:1) 2" (poster presentation, Annual Conference of the SUNY Librarians Association, Canandaigua, NY, June 14, 2019), http://hdl.handle.net/1951/70313.

4. Association of College and Research Libraries, *Information Literacy Competency Standards for Higher Education* (Chicago: Association of College and Research Libraries, 2000), https://alair.ala.org/handle/11213/7668; "Information Literacy VALUE Rubric," Association of American Colleges and Universities, last updated July 2013, https://www.aacu.org/value/rubrics/information-literacy.

5. Association of College and Research Libraries, *Framework for Information Literacy for Higher Education* (Chicago: Association of College and Research Libraries, 2016), http://www.ala.org/acrl/standards/ilframework.

Bibliography

Association of American Colleges and Universities. "Information Literacy VALUE Rubric." Last updated July 2013. https://www.aacu.org/value/rubrics/information-literacy.

Association of College and Research Libraries. *Framework for Information Literacy for Higher Education.* Chicago: Association of College and Research Libraries, 2016. http://www.ala.org/acrl/standards/ilframework.

———. *Information Literacy Competency Standards for Higher Education.* Chicago: Association of College and Research Libraries, 2000. https://alair.ala.org/handle/11213/7668.

LaPlant, Don. "Information Literacy: Faculty Resources." Van Wagenen Library, SUNY Cobleskill. Last modified December 18, 2018. http://libraryguides.cobleskill.edu/InfoLit/faculty.

LaPlant, Don, and Brendan Aucoin. "The Effectiveness of Individual Research Consultations as a Supplement to Traditional Library Instruction Approaches; or, 1:1 ≥ (25:1) 2. Poster presentation, Annual Conference of the SUNY Librarians Association, Canandaigua, NY, June 14, 2019. http://hdl.handle.net/1951/70313.

SUNY Cobleskill. "About SUNY Cobleskill." Accessed March 31, 2019. https://www.cobleskill.edu/about/index.aspx.

Chapter 36

Mary Baldwin University

Student-Centered Information Literacy Instruction on a Shoestring Staff

Anaya Jones

Population Served

Martha Stackhouse Grafton Library serves Mary Baldwin University's (MBU) residential and commuter student population of young adults, a large online student population of nontraditional and returning students, and graduate programs in education, business, health sciences and the performing arts.

Mary Baldwin University is a small, private, coeducational institution in western Virginia with a rich history of women's education. According to the Carnegie Classification of Institutions of Higher Education, Mary Baldwin is a master's level university with a student full-time equivalent of 1,752 in 2016–17. Mary Baldwin has had a few challenging admissions years but welcomed our largest incoming class in the fall of 2018.

Mary Baldwin was founded in 1842 as the Augusta Female Seminary. While Mary Baldwin's residential college began accepting students of all genders in 2017 and existing graduate programs have accepted students of all genders since their respective introductions, our history as a single-sex institution influences our population. In the fall of 2018 the majority of students enrolled in all programs identified as female (see figure 36.1).

Program	% of student population who identified as female
College for Women	100%
University College	67%
All Residential	86%
Baldwin Online Undergraduate	86%
College of Education	86%
Professional Studies	87%
Shakespeare & Performance	73%
Murphy Deming College of Health Sciences	82%
Grand Total	85%

Figure 36.1
Percent of enrolled residential students who identified as female by program in 2018 (Mary Baldwin University Office of Institutional Research, 2018).

Mary Baldwin University has a high acceptance rate of students with varied scholastic achievement. Thirty percent of the incoming class in 2018 were first-generation students—a slight dip as this figure has been as high as 43 percent in the last ten years.[1] Mary Baldwin was named by *U.S. News and World Report*'s "Best Colleges" report as one of the most racially and ethnically diverse colleges or universities in the South.[2] Mary Baldwin is home to a larger percentage of black students (31% in 2018) than the general population of the United States (12.6% in 2010) and Virginia (19.2% in 2017).[3] In 2018, 14 percent of residential students identified as Hispanic, and a further 9 percent of residential students identified as another non-Caucasian ethnicity.[4] Mary Baldwin has long-standing relationships with universities in the United Kingdom, India, Japan, and South Korea. Students from these universities visit Mary Baldwin for one or two semesters.

As we plan information literacy sessions and programs, we consider the experiences and knowledge our students bring to Mary Baldwin and aim to make instruction accessible and interesting for all of our students, with care given to retention and cultural sensitivity. In class we discuss the limitations and biases of scholarly information production and, as discussed in the Pedagogical Highlights section, we work to incorporate and value student experiences. We are strong believers in the importance of information literacy to students' futures. We are constantly trying to design accessible instruction that allows us to reach students who have never learned about research before while giving students who are already familiar a chance to brush up on those skills and move on to their next challenge.

Program Scope

Mary Baldwin's information literacy program focuses on foundational skills for first-year undergraduate students through a one-credit required information literacy course offered both on campus and online and as-needed instruction for all undergraduate and graduate students. As-needed instruction includes face-to-face sessions and various forms of online instruction including learning objects within our learning management system, Blackboard, instruction offered over videoconferencing software, and instructional materials available on the library website.

Mary Baldwin faculty and administration have shown uncommon support of Grafton's information literacy initiatives. The university faculty approved adding the information literacy course, INT103: Information Literacy, to the general education requirements in 2011. Since then, librarians have worked successfully with the registrar and student advisors to register students for this course in their first year. The course is now predominantly taken by first-year students, though there is the occasional upper-class student who delayed taking or needs to retake the course. On average, we offer nine sections with fifteen seats each, adjusting offerings as needed for class size and staffing. We have engaged in similar efforts with our online programs, but many students transfer into the online programs as juniors or seniors, and thus this effort has proved challenging. Having students in the online classes in different years adds another layer of difficulty to delivering the right instruction at the right time. While the instructional focus has been on foundational skills for first-year students, we are in the process of increasing instruction throughout the curriculum. In particular, we would like to increase meaningful instruction to support students' work on their senior theses. Combined with existing efforts, instruction aimed at undergraduate students' senior projects would naturally bookend a student's time at Mary Baldwin University.

Reference and instruction are offered by the same librarians. Due to the small campus size, the reference interaction becomes an extension of in-class instruction. Reference interactions with current or former students begin with an established relationship that eases student anxiety about asking for help, builds new knowledge on established trust, and reinforces transferable skills.

The information literacy program does not have its own budget line. Over the years the library has purchased materials to support instruction and remodeled the library instruction space (see figure 36.2) to include whiteboard paint walls, flexible furniture, and Chromebooks for student searching.

Figure 36.2
Martha S. Grafton's library instruction classroom (Photograph by Anaya Jones, 2018).

Operations

Martha S. Grafton Library has a very small staff, and staffing is one of our bigger challenges. The library is led by the university librarian, who reports to the academic provost. Including the university librarian, there are three full-time librarians, one part-time librarian, and two library staff members in four departments. Grafton's reference and instruction department includes the information literacy librarian and the digital projects and academic engagement librarian. Grafton's circulation and student staff coordinator, interlibrary loan coordinator and part-time cataloger, the remainder of the staff, are wholly responsible for their departments and do not participate in information literacy instruction. The library also relies on our student staff of about thirty-five students to staff the circulation desk. The information literacy librarian designs and coordinates Grafton's information literacy instruction program. The information literacy librarian, the digital projects librarian and (to the limited extent allowed by administrative duties) the university librarian teach information literacy instruction. The information literacy and digital projects librarians liaise with educational departments to offer instruction and support collection development. Sections of the required one-credit information literacy course are divided based on scheduling, with the information literacy librarian taking slightly more than half of the sections offered. While faculty are instructed to contact their liaison librarian for as-needed instruction, the two librarians fill in for each other when scheduling issues interfere.

Collaboration

There are fertile, if underused, opportunities for collaboration with the writing center and other student services on campus. In the past, Grafton librarians have jointly hosted an event each semester with the writing center where students could get help from a writing center tutor or a librarian just in time for the crush of papers near the end of the term. Attendance for this event fell, and it was discontinued. We have had some staff turnover and lost some of the relationships with these departments that had proven collaborative and supportive in the past. Reinvigorating this type of project and partnership hasn't been our top priority.

On Mary Baldwin's small campus the relationships librarians build with faculty are very important. It is these relationships that keep faculty coming back for one-shot instruction and that allow us to try new projects with faculty support. One way we sustain these relationships is by reaching out to faculty departments, ideally once a semester, to update them on library resources and projects. In the past, this contact has taken the form of office visits or targeted newsletters. The library participates in faculty-led initiatives for Hispanic-Latino Heritage, African American History, and Women's History months with coordinating book displays and advertising related campus events, bolstering cross-campus connections.

Grafton librarians also participate in a regional group of librarian instructors who meet a few times a year to swap information and observe each other teaching called Libraries Exchange Observation, or LEO. This community, started by librarians at Radford University, Hollins University, and Virginia Tech, has been incredibly valuable to honing teaching skills and learning from local colleagues.

Assessment

Mary Baldwin's one-shot information literacy instruction is assessed in a variety of ways depending on the instructor, the course and session, and the material covered. Generally, efforts at assessment lean to the unobtrusive and informal. Instructors collect informal feedback with quick verbal checks during sessions, assessing student body language and attention, asking students for input on searches or topics, and monitoring student output from assignments. Instructors have also utilized the survey programs Google Forms and Poll Everywhere to gather information before a session begins, at the beginning of the class, or after the session has finished. Instructors collaborate with faculty to adjust planned material based on prior sessions.

For the required information literacy course, assessment has historically been more intentional and consistent. All students in the course are asked to complete an evaluation at the end of the term. This evaluation asks them about their experience with their instructor, with the material, and, when we've made significant changes, with the format of the class or new instructional materials. Some questions can be compared over time; others cannot. These evaluations differ from the standard course evaluations students are asked to complete in other courses at Mary Baldwin. We have the flexibility to add and remove questions as needed because librarians are staff and course evaluations are not submitted as part of a tenure review process. The information students provide is valuable and has helped us to adjust the course. In one memorable example, a student's feedback led to a greater emphasis on how to use and cite copyrighted material in addition to content about copyright restrictions.

The required course also includes a pretest. For many years, this pretest served as a way to gauge student attitudes on the first day of class and didn't attempt to measure the knowledge or skills students brought to the course. During a recent redesign, the pretest was reimagined to include a sample of questions that then appear in later quizzes. At the end of the term, instructors export and collate student scores and can compare how students answered those selected questions at the start of the term and right after completing each related module. Like any instrument, it has its limitations, but it is a way for instructors to gauge achievement while factoring in knowledge students brought with them into the classroom while saving students from taking another test.

Role of the One-Shot

Grafton librarians do a significant number of one-shots, but focus on the required information literacy course, limited staff and faculty member time, and faculty attitudes that assume the course is enough information literacy instruction create a tension around the role of the one-shot in the information literacy program. While the required course is our focal point, librarians know it isn't all the information literacy instruction students need.

The majority of one-shot instruction is provided in person to on-campus classes. Campus faculty are vocal supporters of the library and reach out for library instruction consistently. One-shot instruction for online classes has been underrepresented in our instruction statistics. Some faculty who teach on campus can and do teach online classes, but most instructors for Mary Baldwin's online programs are adjunct instructors and do not teach on Mary Baldwin's physical campus. However, despite good relationships with the Baldwin Online program administration, fewer online faculty request information literacy instruction in their courses.

This phenomenon could be due in part to lack of awareness or marketing of online library instruction, differences in how new faculty are oriented, differences in communication between programs, or some combination of those factors. Setting aside the very real issues of staff availability and workload, the library is able and willing to engage in a variety of instructional activities to support online classes. The next step is to better market information literacy instruction to online faculty.

During the 2017–18 school year, Grafton Library piloted an asynchronous one-shot program designed to leverage existing library instructional materials and strengthen support for online classes. Librarians offer online instructors a menu of videos from which they can select the skills students need to complete assignments. The selected videos are bookended by a video tour of the library's website, an introduction to a Grafton librarian, and an auto-graded quiz built for the included skills.

This project was sparked by the information literacy librarian's attendance at a 2017 Association of College and Research Libraries (ACRL) conference session where multiple presenters spoke about integrating information literacy into their learning management systems.[5] While Grafton's initiative has involved making a series of instructional videos that conform to updated pedagogical standards, the asynchronous one-shot program is really a remarketing of a service already offered. These same videos and others like them have been, and continue to be, available for students as needed on the library website and video channel.

Grafton librarians load these videos into a course's Blackboard course shell by instructor request. This requires instructors to add librarians as editors to their courses. Usually, this means adding a new folder to the main menu titled "Library Module." An accompanying quiz is built for each one-shot from a pool of questions mapped to the skill videos. This brings the librarian and library instruction into the learning environment for students, increasing student exposure to library resources.

As we head into the second year of this service, the focus is on expanding available skills and using the service as a reason to reach out to online instructors. As this program moves out of the initial pilot phase, we are also making videos available for instructors who feel comfortable building and editing in the LMS to install selected videos themselves. This method means instructors don't have to give librarians editor access to their courses or submit requests for each one-shot. We give instructors access to the library of videos and let them install what they want.

Librarians will have less access to usage data and less control over the inclusion of welcome videos and quizzes. There is value in including auto-graded quizzes and the ability to ensure faculty are using the most up-to-date version of instructional materials by personally installing material in learning management system classes, but allowing instructors to install selected videos themselves may ultimately serve faculty better and conserve librarian time. This program has been well received; faculty who use videos have continued to do so, and this service seems to suit instructors who have otherwise been infrequent library users.

Pedagogical Highlights

A course called Research Methodology first appeared on Mary Baldwin's course offering lists in the 1970s. Librarians taught one section of this course per term. The library redesigned and relaunched the course in 1999, and the economics, art history and communication majors required the course shortly after. When Mary Baldwin updated the general education requirements in 2011, the information literacy course became required for graduation and Grafton Library began offering more sections of the course.

When students leave our instruction, we want them to have a better understanding of what information they need and how to find it. In the current version of the required information literacy course, we teach learners about different types of information and how it is created, packaged, and assessed so that they can begin the process of finding and evaluating their sources, both in library resources and elsewhere. We touch on the ethical use of information, both in terms of citation and copyright. We introduce students to database searching and begin the conversations they can expect to continue throughout their academic careers about appropriate use and citation of sources.

While the content of this course has remained fairly constant over the years it has been required, we have frequently made changes to the format of both the on-campus and online sections, striving for curriculum that adequately and clearly instructs students in the abovementioned foundational skills, is engaging for students who have been exposed to similar material in the past, is respectful of librarian/instructor time investment, and is appropriate to the one-credit designation of the course. In the past, we've explored a variety of delivery options, including meeting once a week for the full semester, half-semester terms, traditional lectures, flipped classes, hybrid classes, and so on. The students' final exam has variously been a test, an annotated bibliography, and a presentation.

In the summer of 2018, expecting a particularly large incoming class and fewer instructors due to an open instructor position, and armed with knowledge gained from several previous variations of the course, we made some significant changes to the way the course is delivered. We broke the content of the course into four modules. Readings, videos, and quizzes for each module are available in Blackboard. An additional introductory module instructs students on how to navigate the modules and includes the required pretest. On-campus students meet with a librarian five times during the six-and-a-half-week term and participate in an activity related to each module. Online students complete a related activity online for each module and have the entire thirteen-week semester to complete all modules.

In lieu of a final exam, students apply what they learn during the term to a research-based project. At the start of the term, instructors ask students to write five hundred words about something they know or have experienced and a few sentences about how they know it. Students submit this artifact to a Blackboard discussion board. To give students more topics to choose from, we have set up the Blackboard course so that students from all sections of the course submit this assignment to the same discussion board. Then, students choose a peer's artifact to research and write about, using the skills they learn in class.

Some students are very excited about the topics they choose from their peers—but the hesitation of other students creates a great opportunity to talk with them about narrowing or broadening topics to choose a research direction that interests them and suits the requirements of the assignment. In this case, they need to find at least four sources, where one is the artifact they choose and two are scholarly books or articles.

In the modules where instructors cover searching techniques and database searching, students search for sources on their topics as homework. In the module where instructors cover citation and copyright, students choose a citation style, fully cite their sources, and consider both attribution and copyright when selecting required images for their project. When students work on the source evaluation module, the artifacts provide a great starting point for conversations about the value of different kinds of information and how both scholarly research and their peers' experiences fit into the landscape of information and can be useful, if not always for the same purposes.

Finally, students conclude the course by submitting their research projects, which have required them to find sources, synthesize information, and attribute the ideas of others, to their instructor for grading and to the peer whose artifact they choose. Students are encouraged to be creative when presenting their research. The emphasis is on information literacy skills rather than submitting a technically correct paper. Students have submitted very successful brochures, posters, and handouts. Students then participate in a peer review activity where as a class they consider how their participation in this assignment mirrors the process of collaborative scholarly information production and how they fit into that process. This assignment invites students into the scholarly process, asking them to see themselves are participants instead of observers.[6]

Information Literacy Coordinator Profile

It's the official, primary responsibility of the information literacy librarian to coordinate and teach the information literacy program (50% of working time), though the university librarian plays a hands-on role in guiding the direction of the program. Before Grafton Library had a librarian dedicated to coordinating instruction, the duties were shared less formally between the two librarians responsible for instruction. The digital projects librarian provides input and feedback on the overarching program, and has a good amount of autonomy over instruction in their subject liaison areas. The remainder of the information literacy librarian's time is spent providing reference services (20% of working time), on outreach efforts (15% of working time), collection development efforts (10% of working time), and professional development and reporting (5% of working time).

The information literacy librarian is expected to teach a little over half of the sections of the required information literacy course. The number of sections offered depends on the student demand and, to a lesser extent, on staffing. This position is also expected to teach one-shot instruction as requested from liaison faculty members and fill in for other liaison areas as needed.

What I Wish People Knew

Teaching a required term- or semester-long class is an envied teaching situation. It is certainly evidence of invaluable support from our administration and faculty and has many benefits. However, like any information literacy program, it is one of many valuable approaches and not the arrangement that is best for every library or school. It certainly comes with its own challenges.

Based on student evaluations and comments students have made in class, some students who learned similar content in high school are even less pleased to be registered for a term-long course than they are to sit through a single session they don't believe they need. While some of these same students indicate that they have learned something by the end of the course or session, initial resistance is a barrier to establishing a good environment for learning.

Grafton Library has the same number of instructor librarians that it did before the information literacy course was added to the general education requirements and the number of offered sections rose dramatically. The library saw a redistribution of instruction from one-shots to the required course, but overall the move to the required course saw librarians spending more time in the classroom. This necessarily means that those instructor librarians are less often around the public services spaces of the library, covering the reference desk or jumping in to help at the circulation desk.

Librarian instructors spend a significant amount of time grading, monitoring student engagement, and even pursuing honor code investigations in relation to the required term-long course. These activities have a psychological weight that we must work to balance with the benefits of a required course.

Instructors of our required course have what so many librarians would love: more time in the classroom. As instructors of both the required course and one-shots, we are constantly reminded how valuable our extended time with our students in the required course is. We are able to cover more and have meaningful conversations about research, information, and scholarly process that aren't stymied by the ending of a single period. We are able to address topics at a more specific level and engage in active learning around tough topics that make learning personal. We are able to build relationships with students over several consecutive sessions. Instructors find these relationships fulfilling, and numerous researchers as documented by O'Keeffe agree that positive relationships that foster feelings of connection are key to student retention and success.[7] We have the opportunity to choose what we teach and how we teach it, not as a guest in someone else's classroom, but as instructors outright.

Notes

1. Carrie Boyd, Mary Baldwin University Office of Institutional Research, email message to author, July 24, 2018.
2. Leighton Carruth, "U.S. News Recognizes MBU among the Best in the South for Its Vibrant Community, Affordable Costs," News, Mary Baldwin University, September 13, 2017, https://go.marybaldwin.edu/news/2017/09/13/us-news-recognizes-mbu.
3. United States Census Bureau, "DP05—ACS Demographic and Housing Estimates: 2017 United States," American FactFinder, December 2018, https://factfinder.census.gov/faces/tableservices/jsf/pages/productview.xhtml?pid=ACS_17_5YR_DP05&src=pt; United States Census Bureau, "DP05—ACS Demographic and Housing Estimates: 2017 Virginia," American FactFinder, December 2018, https://factfinder.census.gov/faces/tableservices/jsf/pages/productview.xhtml?src=CF.
4. Carrie Boyd, Mary Baldwin University Office of Institutional Research, email message to author, January 15, 2019.

5. Paul Glassman et al., "Taking a Different Tack: Adapting First-Year Information Literacy Instruction to the Online Environment" (presentation, ACRL Conference, Baltimore, MD, March 24, 2017).
6. Anaya Jones, "Cast Your Students as Scholars," ACRL Framework for Information Literacy Sandbox, March 19, 2019, http://sandbox.acrl.org/library-collection/cast-your-students-scholars.
7. Patrick O'Keeffe, "A Sense of Belonging: Improving Student Retention," *College Student Journal* 47, no. 4 (Winter 2013): 608, https://www.projectinnovation.com/college-student-journal.html.

Bibliography

Carruth, Leighton. "U.S. News Recognizes MBU among the Best in the South for Its Vibrant Community, Affordable Costs." News, Mary Baldwin University. September 13, 2017. https://go.marybaldwin.edu/news/2017/09/13/us-news-recognizes-mbu.

Glassman, Paul, Catherine Baird, Francesca Marineo, and Susan Engler. "Taking a Different Tack: Adapting First-Year Information Literacy Instruction to the Online Environment." Presentation, ACRL Conference, Baltimore, MD, March 24, 2017.

Jones, Anaya. "Cast Your Students as Scholars." ACRL Framework for Information Literacy Sandbox. March 19, 2019. http://sandbox.acrl.org/library-collection/cast-your-students-scholars.

O'Keeffe, Patrick. "A Sense of Belonging: Improving Student Retention." *College Student Journal* 47, no. 4 (Winter 2013): 605–13. https://www.projectinnovation.com/college-student-journal.html.

United States Census Bureau. "DP-05 - ACS Demographic and Housing Estimates: 2017 United States." American FactFinder, December 2018. https://factfinder.census.gov/faces/tableservices/jsf/pages/productview.xhtml?pid=ACS_17_5YR_DP05&src=pt.

———. "DP05—ACS Demographic and Housing Estimates: 2017 Virginia." American FactFinder, December 2018. https://factfinder.census.gov/faces/tableservices/jsf/pages/productview.xhtml?src=CF.

Chapter 37

State University of New York at Plattsburgh
Immersed in Teaching

Michelle Toth

Population Served

The State University of New York (SUNY) Plattsburgh is a public comprehensive college with between 5,000 and 6,000 students. We are located in the northeast corner of the state, adjacent to Vermont and the Canadian province of Quebec. We have Lake Champlain to the east of us and the six-million-acre New York State Adirondack Park to our west.

Because we are a state institution, most of our students (89%) are from New York State. Our largest concentrations are from our local tri-county area (22%) and the greater New York City and Long Island region (28%).[1] We also have about 350 international students. Our students graduate with degrees from our School of Arts and Sciences (53%), School of Business and Economics (24%), and School of Education, Health and Human Services (21%); the final 2% of students graduate in Individual Studies.[2] We are focused on undergraduate education with a few master's programs. We have a branch campus in Queensbury, New York, that offers BA and BS completion programs for students with two-year degrees, and we offer online completion programs for bachelor's degrees in nursing and accounting.

Feinberg Library is part of the division of Library and Information Technology Services. We serve our main campus, branch campus, and online populations from our centrally located building on the Plattsburgh campus. The library also houses the main computer lab, Learning Center, advising office, three computer classrooms, Center for Teaching Excellence, and our One-Button Studio, a dedicated video-recording space with green screen using Pennsylvania State University's One Button app to simplify video production for our faculty and students.

Our students come to us with a wide range of information literacy skills. This variability is likely related to if students had library media specialists in their schools or if they came to us as transfer students from other colleges. In the librarians' meetings where we talk about our teaching, we have anecdotally noted that since New York State implemented the Common Core State Standards for K–12, students are coming into college having had less research, writing, and citation experience than in the past.

Program Scope

The cornerstone of our library instruction program is a one-credit general education course, a requirement for students since 1979. The course has gone through several teaching format and student learning outcome revisions over the years. We are currently offering the LIB200: Critical Research Skills course in on-campus, hybrid, and online sections in a five-week format. In addition, we offer a couple of online sections in the summer and winter sessions. Class size is generally twenty-five seats per section. We teach over 1,000 students a year in our course (see Table 37.1).

While most of our LIB200 sections are general in nature, meaning the course content is appropriate for any major, over the years we have worked with different departments, groups, and individuals on campus to provide integrated or discipline-specific sections. Most recently we have been offering science and history sections for incoming students in the fall semesters who have declared these majors. We have a section tied to one of the Expeditionary Studies program courses so students are taking both courses together outside of our usual five-week schedule. Expeditionary Studies majors have an outdoor adventure sports curriculum of hiking, kayaking, and ice climbing and tend to need classes that can work around a schedule where they can be off-campus for weeks at a time. We have worked with the nursing program to have both its online and branch campus RN-to-BS students take our course as a program requirement via a dedicated online section. In the past, we have also worked with campus learning communities and our Educational Opportunity Program, a New York State–funded program providing support for students who, while having potential, might not have otherwise been admitted to college.

We provide a proficiency exam option so students who have already developed research skills can test out of the course. The exam initially was used when the library course first became a requirement because there were too many students for the number of seats that could be offered. Now, if a student passes the exam, they meet the requirement but do not earn the credit hour. The exam has the reputation of being difficult to pass, and over the years we have worked hard to develop it into a reliable instrument to ensure that those passing the exam do have the appropriate level of skill. The pass rate for the exam for the past couple of years has been around 50 percent. There is no penalty or letter grade that goes on a student's transcript if they do not pass, so we do get a number of students taking the exam as a bit of a gamble just to see if they can test out of the course. The exams are held the Sunday before each semester starts and again during the academic advising period when students are building or adjusting their course schedules.

Along with the course and exam, we offer one-shot course-related sessions as requested by faculty. While our credit course is a general introduction to doing college-level research, our one-shot library sessions allow us to work with students with particular discipline-specific research needs. We average between fifty and sixty sessions each semester. We work with everything from first-semester composition to senior capstone courses and a few graduate-level courses. The majority of requests come from faculty in the School of Arts and Sciences (64%), followed by the School of Education, Health and Human Services (31%). A majority (58%) of our one-shot sessions are for upper-level courses, and 13 percent of our requests are for teaching students to use Zotero, an online bibliographic collection and citation tool. We have also been branching out and doing live, real-time online sessions with our branch campus, using tools like Google Hangouts or Zoom, and creating videos for online courses. Occasionally, we accommodate visits from local high school classes with tours and research sessions during college breaks.

Table 37.1
Summary of Feinberg Library instruction program services for the 2017-18 academic year.

2017–18	Sections/Sessions	Number of Students
LIB200	46	1,131
One-Shots	106	2,300
LIB Exam	14	187

Operations

Our ten full-time librarians are tenured or tenure-track faculty with twelve-month appointments, with one exception—our Systems Librarian is on a professional line, which means he has a continuing appointment, but without the obligation of doing scholarship. All full-time librarians teach the credit course. The typical teaching obligation is two sections of the course per semester. We also employ adjunct librarians to teach a few sections. Our adjuncts are all librarians with MLS/MLIS degrees; most are library media specialists who work in local schools.

The LIB200 Course Coordinator position is assigned by the dean, is formally acknowledged with a three-year contract, and receives half of the Library Faculty Chair stipend for doing the academic work of the department: scheduling courses and working with the librarians, faculty, students, the registrar's office, and the advising office. The librarian elected as the Library Faculty Chair also gets a three-year contact, the other half of the stipend, and a one-course reduction. The chair position is responsible for holding departmental meetings and writing performance review letters. The chair position is seen as a shared service responsibility for senior members of the department, and many of us have served. In contrast the LIB200 Course Coordinator position is an individual workload responsibility.

Librarians are divided into two operational units: the Collection Development and Delivery (CD&D) unit with three full-time librarians (including the Systems Librarian) and one part-time librarian cataloger, and the Instruction and Reference Services (IRS) unit with seven full-time librarians. Only the IRS unit librarians teach one-shot sessions. While we have a library liaison program and we try to match the appropriate librarian to courses in their liaison areas, it is not always possible. The CD&D librarians who are liaisons do not teach one-shots. And of course sometimes IRS librarians' schedules do not line up with the course requests from their departments.

While we have a librarian designated as the one-shot coordinator who receives the requests sent through our online request form, many librarians are contacted directly by faculty and simply notify the coordinator, who keeps the statistics for one-shot instruction. All librarians have an individual workload document that is reviewed annually with our supervisor, the dean. In the workload document, the number of one-shot sessions is not uniform for librarians and generally ranges from five to ten sessions per semester, based in part on our other work obligations. We do have a history of agreeing to teach additional sessions, as we have developed good relationships with faculty and we don't want to decline offers to teach sessions for them.

The LIB200 course gets priority scheduling in one of the computer classrooms in the library. If there is space in the schedule after our course is entered, other classes get scheduled there by the registrar's office. In contrast, the one-shot sessions do not have a dedicated space. Occasionally the class is already in a computer classroom, but in many cases the one-shot coordinator needs to work with the registrar's office to see if a computer classroom of an appropriate size is available at the requested days and times. Our preference is to have computer classrooms so that we can provide students with hands-on learning. When computer classrooms are unavailable, we have tried to come up with ways to make the sessions as interactive as possible to keep students engaged.

Marketing

Marketing efforts for the credit course are minimal, as it is a requirement and we have support from faculty and staff advisors who value the course and know that students should take it sooner rather than later. Librarians teaching subject-specific sections typically work with the chairs in those departments to ensure the students get enrolled in the correct sections. In the past we had to promote our summer and winter session classes, but in recent years these have filled up very quickly so simply sending an email reminder to students has been sufficient.

The course proficiency exam is less well known and is offered only a few times during the semester. In the past we have posted signs in the library, the college center, the advising office, and the dorms to remind students of the exam and how to register for it. But we discovered that most students found it easier to use the registration links we provided in emails, so the paper signs have been discontinued.

For our one-shot sessions, we largely rely on librarians contacting their liaison departments and reminding them at the beginning of the semesters about scheduling library instruction sections. In addition, many of our sessions are recurring requests, where faculty contact us automatically every semester, so we typically don't do any additional promotion for this service.

Collaboration

As much as having a required stand-alone course indicates that information literacy is valued on our campus, it also can sometimes mean that other faculty don't have to think about it as often. Particularly when campus program revisions are being made, information literacy can sometimes be overlooked. Being and staying in the general education program is a priority for us, so we always have a librarian serving on the campus general education committee. I also serve on the Campus Assessment Advisory Committee. In 2018, I chaired the committee that revised our Campus Institutional Student Learning Outcomes, which I am happy to say continue to include information literacy. We generally try to have a librarian on all the major campus committees; it is a great way to stay informed about what is happening on campus, and it is another way to interact face-to-face with other faculty and staff outside the library. Most campus committees are open to any who want to volunteer to serve on them. The librarians generally have a discussion when the call for volunteers comes out each year to see who is serving on what committees and see if there are any gaps.

In other small ways, we try to integrate the library into other faculty or campus events. For example, during the new faculty campus orientation, the library hosts a wine and cheese reception so new faculty actually come to the library and can meet the librarians. We also host a Celebration of Scholarship event each year in the library, which celebrates and displays the faculty's scholarship from the previous year.

Assessment

Our credit course LIB200, as part of the campus general education program, is included in ongoing student learning outcomes assessment. We have data going back to 2003, although the methods and assessment instruments have changed significantly over time. The current method, started in fall 2017, involves librarians taking a random sample of five students per class and using a shared rubric to score an assignment whose outcomes have been mapped to the LIB200 course outcomes. The rubrics on campus all use the same scoring method: Mastery (3 points), Accomplished (2 points), Developing (1 point), and Beginning (0 points).

The assessment data we collect gets used in a couple of different ways. To meet the requirements for our general education assessment, we map our more specific LIB200 outcomes to the three broader outcomes provided by SUNY. The SUNY outcomes are "perform basic operations of computer use; understand and use basic research techniques; and locate, evaluate and synthesize information from a variety of sources."[3] Results for all general education categories are presented in an online dashboard that is available to the campus.

Currently the LIB200 course is the only course in the Information Management general education category. The dashboard (see figure 37.1) provides each semester's average scores for the three SUNY outcomes and the number of students with average scores in each of the rubric's four levels.

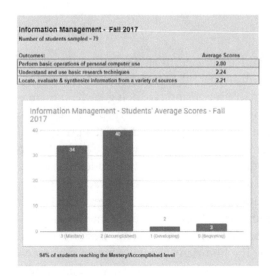
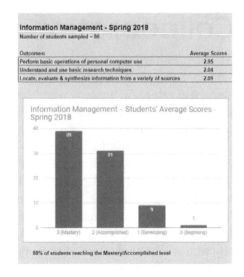

Figure 37.1
General education assessment dashboard for Information Management

To make the data more useful for librarians, as the course coordinator I set up a separate dashboard for our internal use (see figure 37.2) that provides the full list of course outcomes and the average scores for each. We can delve deeper into the data and scores for the specific skills and knowledge we are trying to teach.

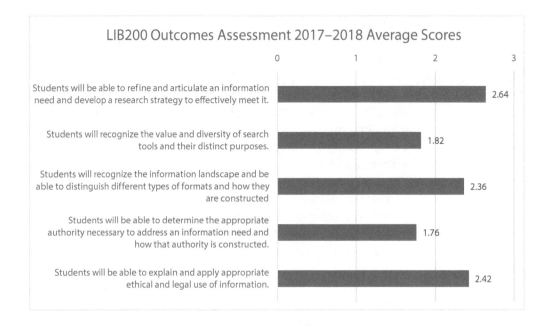

Figure 37.2
LIB200 outcomes assessment average scores for 2017–18

Our focus for the data we are collecting is to help us generate discussion about those areas that could use improvement. The librarians have at least one or two "talking about teaching" meetings a year to share what we are struggling with and discuss new ideas or pedagogical approaches that we have tried recently.

Along with outcomes assessment, we use our own customized student course evaluation survey for LIB200. This asks students about the content of the course, the instructor's effectiveness, and the teaching methods used. The data from this survey is included in our "effectiveness in teaching" section of our performance review files for contract renewals, promotions, and tenure. There is a general course opinion survey the campus makes available to all faculty, but all departments and instructors can work with their own instrument if they want to develop one. Given the skills-based and active learning pedagogy we work with, we have found we can get more relevant feedback from students using our own survey.

For our one-shot classes, we use a student evaluation survey at the end of the session. As the same survey is used for all sessions, the questions are pretty generic in wording and ask if students have an improved understanding of the content covered, if the librarian presented the information clearly, and if the librarian effectively addressed their questions. Three weeks after the one-shot, a follow-up survey is sent to faculty asking how the students made use of the information and skills covered the in session. For the 2017–18 year, 88 percent of faculty respondents indicated improved quality of student assignments, while the remaining 12 percent indicated it was too soon to tell.

Role of the One-Shot

Programmatically, one-shots are a good and needed complement to our credit course. In one-shot sessions we are able to address the subject- or assignment-specific needs of students. We can cover particular tools or resources within the context students will need them; for example, showing journalism students how to find data sources for newspaper stories or showing chemistry students how journals are ranked in their field. A one-credit course is simply not adequate to address all the various information needs our students have.

One-shot library sessions are also a valuable tool for connecting and working with faculty. While we try through our library liaison program to do outreach, one-shots are an opportunity to be face-to-face with faculty. During one-shots, faculty regularly ask us their own questions about research when we visit with their classes.

We have been branching out from our usual live, in-person library sessions. Last year, we experimented with creating an instruction video for an online anthropology course, with very favorable feedback from the instructor. We also held a few live, online one-shots using Google Hangouts and Zoom to work with business and nursing classes at our branch campus. And a new chemistry professor this year asked to record and post an audio file of our of our library session with her class on her course site.

There have been times when we have struggled with balancing our workload and meeting all the requests for one-shot sessions, but so far we have been able to keep up with demand. Perhaps one of the most taxing issues is that a majority of our one-shot requests come at the same time we are teaching our own course, typically the first few weeks in the semester. We have not come up with a particular strategy to address this, but when possible we try not to overcommit ourselves with service or committee work early in the semester.

Pedagogical Highlights

Given our library's long history with library instruction, it is not surprising that we have had ties to broader initiatives around information literacy. Our former Dean of Library and Information Technology Services was one of the founders and champions for the Association of College and Research Libraries' Information Literacy Immersion Program. In fact, SUNY Plattsburgh hosted the very first Immersion Program in July 1999. The result is that all of our full-time librarians have attended at least one Immersion Program, and a few of us have attended more than one. Because of this, we have a shared base of knowledge for both information literacy and pedagogy that enables us to have productive discussions about teaching and learning.

For the LIB200 course, we designed a single set of student learning outcomes, but we have the pedagogical freedom for each librarian to approach sections of the course in their own way. When we updated our course outcomes about four years ago, the librarians working on the revisions drafted course outlines that included sample resources and activities. These sample outlines were then shared with all teaching librarians as starting points that librarians could then adapt or revise.

This model provides flexibility that enables us to customize our sections, whether they are discipline-specific or general, with students still achieving the same outcomes. For example, whether a librarian is teaching a section for science majors or a general section that is exploring diversity issues in higher education, we know that all students in these sections will meet the course outcome "to select appropriate search tools in order to access the type of information sought."

Administrative Highlights

I am proud of the way we can accommodate opportunities for our librarians to work with other faculty through learning communities, cross-listed courses, or discipline-specific sections in our credit course. Some of these courses follow our current five-week format, but in some cases we have deviated from our course schedule to make the partnership work. For example, in some cases, the courses start at different times in the semester than our regular sections, while others have been scheduled to meet every few weeks the whole semester long. We successfully work with the registrar's office and department chairs to make these sessions happen.

It is challenging to keep librarians engaged and excited about teaching since we do so much of it. We have used a teaching rotation to allow librarians an occasional semester off from teaching the credit course. Librarians are encouraged to use that time to make revisions to their course or work on other library projects. Originally, our rotation happened every three semesters, but with a reduction in the number of librarians over the years, our current rotation is set so that a librarian is off once every six semesters.

Information Literacy Coordinator Profile

My professional focus, even before I got to graduate school, was on being an instruction librarian in an academic library, so taking on instruction coordination responsibilities was a natural progression for me. It likely helped that shortly before my arrival, Feinberg Library had moved to a flat reporting structure, meaning that rather than having a head or supervisor for an area, we had coordinators who were not permanently assigned. This allowed librarians to focus on chosen areas of service or expertise. I have now served as the course coordinator for over fifteen years and began coordinating our proficiency exam the first year I started at Feinberg Library.

What I Wish People Knew

As all our full-time librarians teach, everyone has strong opinions about anything to do with our instruction program. When issues come up or revisions are discussed, tensions can run pretty high as these changes can affect our daily work life in significant ways. I have discovered that in both our department and our campus culture, the least effective approach is to come up with a new plan or idea and present it to the group. It will get ripped to shreds, and all doubts, complaints, and cynicism will come out. It is times like these that it is good to take a step back and realize that (hopefully) this reaction is not out of spite, but because your coworkers also care a great deal about these issues.

Within the library, years ago, I recall a proposal that was put forward about changing our priorities and scheduling for our one-shot sessions. The plan seemed like a needed and logical change to those who came up with the idea, but they were instead shocked by the dissent it generated when brought to the library faculty. While it was eventually worked out, it generated some short-term tensions and brought up larger issues around what we view as our professional obligations.

I have found that any new idea or revision process really benefits from several preliminary individual conversations before presenting any new idea to a group. I know to start conversations with a few individuals to help gauge general support, identify concerns or questions, and perhaps most importantly let my colleagues know what I am thinking and get some understanding of their positions. In particular, I have found it helpful to seek out those who have voiced concerns or dissent on previous ideas.

This method for moving ideas forward was reinforced for me when I attended an assessment conference a few years ago, where some administrators were talking about trying to get something approved at the campus level. They explained that they went into that meeting knowing a vast majority would approve their plan because they took the time to have individual conversations and were able to address any concerns. Not all new ideas will succeed, or perhaps not move out of beta testing, but it is immensely important that the services, methods, and outcomes in instruction programs be reviewed, updated, and improved upon to stay relevant. Understanding the dynamics of your library, department, and culture can go a long way in moving things forward.

Notes

1. Bob Karp and Erin Campbell, "SUNY Plattsburgh Undergraduate and Graduate Student Demographic Handbook: Fall 2013–2017," internal report, Office of Institutional Effectiveness, SUNY Plattsburgh, 2017.
2. Bob Karp and Erin Campbell, "SUNY Plattsburgh Departmental Comparative Enrollment Statistics, Fall 2017," Office of Institutional Effectiveness, SUNY Plattsburgh, 2017.
3. "Guidelines for the Approval of State University General Education Requirement Courses," Office of Academic Affairs and the Provost, State University of New York, July 2017, https://system.suny.edu/media/suny/content-assets/documents/academic-affairs/general-education/GenEdCourseGuidelines_2017.pdf.

Bibliography

"Guidelines for the Approval of State University General Education Requirement Courses." Office of Academic Affairs and the Provost, State University of New York, July 2017. https://system.suny.edu/media/suny/content-assets/documents/academic-affairs/general-education/GenEdCourseGuidelines_2017.pdf.

Karp, Bob, and Erin Campbell. "SUNY Plattsburgh Departmental Comparative Enrollment Statistics, Fall 2017." SUNY Plattsburgh, Office of Institutional Effectiveness, 2017.

———. "SUNY Plattsburgh Undergraduate and Graduate Student Demographic Handbook: Fall 2013–2017." Internal report. SUNY Plattsburgh, Office of Institutional Effectiveness, 2017.

Chapter 38

University of Northern Colorado

Collaborate. Standardize. Grow.

Lyda Fontes McCartin

Population Served

The University of Northern Colorado (UNC) was founded in 1889 with a mission to train qualified teachers. Since its opening, UNC has become a renowned doctorate-granting research university (R2) with premier programs in education, health sciences, and the performing arts. The institution stresses teaching as a primary focus for faculty. UNC enrolls 13,000 students with 77 percent undergraduates, 37 percent of whom are first-generation students. We have a dedicated liaison to the various federal TRIO programs on campus, which support first generation-students as well as students with disabilities and low-income students.[1] One important characteristic of our undergraduate population is that 86 percent of undergraduates work while attending school; 56 percent of those work off campus. This particular characteristic influences how we create syllabi and activities for our credit courses and how we work with course-embedded instruction. For example, we are considerate of student time and availability when we design partner or group assignments. We offer one-shots and other workshops on nights and weekends to accommodate student schedules.

Program Scope

University Libraries includes the James A. Michener Library and the Howard M. Skinner Music Library. University Libraries operates with a liaison librarian model; library faculty are assigned to one or more programs. The Michener Library includes two public services departments, Information Literacy & Undergraduate Support (ILUS) and Library Research Services (LRS). Majority of liaisons work in LRS and ILUS. However, there are liaisons in Technical Services, Archives, and the Music Library. LRS consists of seven full-time library faculty; its main initiatives are scholarly communication, graduate student support, and faculty research support. ILUS, the focus of this chapter, consists of four full-time library faculty (including the head), one nine-month contract lecturer, and one full-time staff member. ILUS has four strategic initiatives that support undergraduate students—the Core Library Instruction Program, the Credit Course Program, the Undergraduate Research Tutorial, and Orientation.

Core Library Instruction Program

The Core Library Instruction Program (CLIP) is focused on first- and second-year students. Through CLIP we integrate information literacy into large-scale undergraduate programs using the one-shot model. Currently this includes English composition (ENG 122 and ENG 123) and first-year experience (UNIV 101). The CLIP consists of three distinct curricular components—CLIP 1 (UNIV 101), CLIP 2 (ENG 122), and CLIP 3 (ENG 123). CLIP 1 is only taught during fall semester; CLIP 2 and CLIP 3 are taught both semesters. Students are required to take ENG 122 and 123, so they come to the CLIP 1 and 2 sessions in that sequence. UNIV 101 is an elective; students are usually enrolled in UNIV 101 and ENG 122 simultaneously. Thus, they attend the CLIP 1 and 2 workshops in the same semester. Each CLIP session has a distinct set of learning outcomes, discussed in the Assessment section. In an academic year ILUS teaches approximately 150 CLIP one-shots and reaches approximately 3,900 students.[2]

Each component of CLIP is led by a different ILUS member. Leading a component involves developing and piloting curriculum and overseeing assessment. All lesson plans and assessments are discussed collaboratively and undergo extensive revision before being implemented in the classroom. The key to this successful, large-scale program is collaboratively designed, standardized lesson plans. The learning outcomes and assessment methods for CLIP are discussed in the Assessment section later in the chapter.

Credit Course Program

In 2006, University Libraries offered one one-credit course, LIB 150: Introduction to Undergraduate Research. It was required for students in the Center for Human Enrichment TRIO program and offered as an elective for other students. Over the past decade the Credit Course Program (CCP) has grown to include seven distinct credit courses, which are now all degree requirements for programs across campus:

- *LIB 123: Introduction to Library Research:* Undergraduate research course designed for Center for Human Enrichment students. Introduces effective library research techniques designed to increase the student's ability to identify, access, and evaluate information and to participate in scholarly discourse.

- *LIB 150: Introduction to Undergraduate Research:* Undergraduate research course designed for Athlete Academic Bridge. This is one of three courses in the Athlete Academic Bridge program, which is focused on preparing incoming student athletes for college through an intensive summer session.
- *LIB 151: Research Skills for Beginning Researchers:* Undergraduate research course designed for students in the UNC Honors Program. This course is the first of four courses in the Independent Project sequence—LIB 151, LIB 251, HON 351, and HON 451.
- *LIB 160: Criminal Justice Library Research:* Undergraduate research course designed for criminology and criminal justice majors. LIB 160 is a corequisite of CRJ 380: Justice Research & Statistics I.
- *LIB 170: Audiology & Speech Language Pathology Library Research:* Undergraduate research course designed for audiology and speech language sciences majors.
- *LIB 180: History Library Research:* Undergraduate research course designed for history majors. LIB 100 is a corequisite of HIST 280: Sophomore Seminar
- *LIB 251: Research as Inquiry: Exploration for Beginning Researchers:* Sophomore-level course designed for students in the UNC Honors Program. This course is the second of four courses in the Independent Project sequence. The course focuses on skills in critical reading and writing and developing a literature review.

We also offer directed study courses to provide internship experiences and a variable title special topics course to experiment with new course offerings. Through the CCP, we teach thirteen courses in an academic year, including summer. ILUS faculty are able to rotate teaching these courses, providing everyone with opportunities for new classroom experiences. The only exception is LIB 123, which is the course integrated into a UNC TRIO program and exclusively taught by the TRIO liaison. Enrollment in the courses depends on the program size. UNC's criminology and criminal justice program is one of the highest enrolled majors on campus. Thus, enrollment in LIB 160 is the highest of all our courses; we teach five sections each academic year with twenty-five students per section. Our lowest enrolled course is LIB 123, with fifteen to twenty students, as required by the TRIO federal funding.

For years, the single course we offered was an open-enrollment course that any student could take. As we shifted our focus to embedding into degree-granting programs, we developed new courses and restricted enrollment to majors only. This resulted in a low number of students in the open-enrollment section. Low enrollments are not fiscally sustainable, and cancelling courses causes stress in creating the course schedule and determining workload assignments. These enrollment concerns prompted a larger conversation about the procedures for developing library credit courses and the importance of campus partnerships. In 2017 the library Curriculum Committee determined that all credit courses taught in University Libraries would be embedded into a degree-granting program (e.g., Criminal Justice) or an academic program (e.g., Honors Program) or would be created through a campus partnership to ensure enrollment and scheduling efficiency. This change means that we no longer offer an elective LIB course.

All credit courses are taught in person. In 2016, after extensive assessment looking at grade comparisons and student and faculty perceptions of our online courses, we made the decision to stop teaching library credit courses online.[3] This decision was easily accepted by our campus partners because we had data to show why this decision was in the best interests of the students.

Undergraduate Research Tutorial

The Undergraduate Research Tutorial (URT) is a new initiative for ILUS. A team of four ILUS members began developing the URT in 2017 using newly developed content, freely available videos, and videos and tutorials from Credo Instruct, which University Libraries licensed in 2016. We debuted the tutorial for faculty in fall 2018. The URT is a series of five online modules that guide undergraduate students through the research process. Since the CLIP is mapped specifically to a set of first-year courses, the URT is meant to provide support both to faculty in undergraduate courses that are not part of the CLIP and also to graduate faculty. The URT helps integrate information literacy instruction into courses where faculty either do not opt for one-shot teaching or for situations where a librarian may not be able to offer in-person instruction, such as online courses. The motivation behind the creation of the URT was to provide faculty with a customizable tutorial that they can use to integrate information literacy into their courses regardless of discipline or academic focus. The URT was developed in the Canvas course management system and is available in Canvas Commons for any Canvas users. Faculty can use all five modules or select individual modules. Once the modules are imported into their own Canvas course, faculty can delete and add content to the modules as they see fit. A survey sent to faculty using the URT in spring 2019 indicates positive responses from both students and faculty.[4]

Orientations

ILUS represents University Libraries at new student, transfer student, and nontraditional student orientations as a way to support undergraduate students when they first arrive on campus. One ILUS faculty member leads our New Student Orientation initiative, which includes collaborating with the Director of Orientation, overseeing updates to our online orientation materials, developing content for each summer, and creating the orientation schedule. For most orientations we are, with other campus programs, meeting with large groups of students in an information fair–style event. We have participated in different formats, such as faculty panels, roundtables, and workshops. Orientations are important for connecting with undergraduate students when they arrive on campus.

Operations

ILUS faculty librarians are responsible for teaching and content development of CLIP, CCP, URT, and Orientations. Library faculty in other departments do participate in one-shot instruction related to their liaison areas, but that instruction is separate from ILUS's strategic initiatives. The only connection is in the scheduling of the library classrooms, which is under the purview of ILUS. There is collaboration with liaisons outside of the department who do instruction; ILUS faculty partner with other liaisons on peer observation of teaching and participate in professional development through a monthly library liaison meeting. In addition to our strategic initiatives, each library faculty member in ILUS is a subject liaison, which requires additional one-shot teaching to both undergraduate and graduate students as well as outreach and collection development. ILUS faculty teach 50 percent of all one-shot instruction sessions in University Libraries.

ILUS faculty are generally responsible for teaching all credit-bearing courses, although other library faculty may occasionally teach them. For example, the Health Sciences Librarian has taught LIB 170: Audiology and Speech Language Pathology Library Research. If a new subject-specific course is created, the head of ILUS will meet with stakeholders, including disciplinary faculty and the liaison librarian, for input into the curriculum.

The University Libraries' Curriculum Committee is a crucial component to the CCP. Its main responsibilities are assessment of the CCP and approval of new curriculum. The Curriculum Committee membership consists of all ILUS librarians and any other library faculty or adjuncts teaching a credit course.

Marketing

We don't really market for the programs discussed in this chapter. Individual liaisons will market in a sense by telling faculty in their areas about information literacy and coming in for one-shots. With the change from open enrollment to required courses, we don't have the need to market the credit courses. That said, as a member and now department head of ILUS, I've been building relationships at UNC for thirteen years, so in a passing conversation I can mention our work to faculty and take their temperature about creating a credit course for their major; this is how the partnership with history developed, leading to the creation of LIB 180.

Collaboration

Because everything we do is integrated into other programs, maintaining positive working relationships with department chairs and program coordinators is important. We work hard to develop partnerships, answering the call by Meulemans and Carr to work toward genuine partnerships in student learning with other faculty.[5] Our partners are invited into our classroom to see a lesson plan in action. We've worked with disciplinary faculty in a Critical Friends Group, a group peer-review method that helps improve teaching, to improve lesson plans and to ensure that our curriculum is preparing students for upper-division courses in a major.[6] ILUS has led focus groups with ENG 122 instructors to get input on the curriculum before making major changes.

The model for our credit courses helps us maintain relationships with our program partners. Our courses are integrated into programs as degree requirements, and in a few cases the courses are corequisites with a discipline research methods course. This means that the library and the program are integrated, making relationships easier to sustain. When a new department chair comes in, there is not usually a restructuring of the entire program, and when new faculty come in, they are just acculturated to the curriculum and the LIB course.

Relationships are more difficult to maintain with the CLIP if communication with stakeholders is not persistent. Surprisingly, this is especially true with long-term relationships. For example, we've been integrated into ENG 122 and ENG 123 for decades; every adjunct, TA, and faculty member knows that if they teach one of these courses, they are bringing students to the library. This is great, but because the integration is so well established to the point of being taken for granted, I am not always informed about changing leadership. I have to keep up with retirements, new jobs, and new faculty coming in to make sure that I know who is coordinating the composition program in any given year. The relationship I maintain with the Composition Coordinator is crucial to our sustained success.

Assessment

Assessment is foundational and essential since everything we do is integrated into other campus programs. The key to relationship building is to make sure that these stakeholders see the impact that information literacy has on their students' success. We have formal assessment processes for both the CLIP and the CCP.

Assessment of the Core Library Instruction Program

Each piece of the CLIP has a unique set of student learning outcomes:

CLIP 1 Student Learning Outcomes
- Students will be able to find a peer-reviewed article in Summon, the library's discovery layer.
- Students will be able to read a research study.
- Students will be able to identify appropriate evidence to support an argument.

CLIP 2 Student Learning Outcomes
- Students will be able to determine appropriate keywords for a topic.
- Students will be able to use Summon to find books and articles.

CLIP 3 Student Learning Outcomes
- Students will be able to determine if a source is relevant to a research topic.
- Student will be able to determine if a source is scholarly.
- Students will be able to discuss why it is important to use a bibliography during the research process.

Assessment of all CLIP sessions is integrated into the one-shot lesson plan. We collect data on each student learning outcome (SLO) during each session, although we do not analyze data for each SLO every semester. We select a SLO to focus on for an academic year, make improvements to the curriculum, and reassess. Assessment of CLIP is focused on improving the lesson plan and making adjustments to curriculum and outcomes. In addition to embedded assessment, we have used student surveys and focus groups to assess one-shot instruction indirectly.[7] We have also applied a rubric to CLIP 1 final papers as a direct method of assessing students.[8]

Assessment of the Credit Course Program

In 2014, we overhauled our credit course SLOs using the *Framework for Information Literacy for Higher Education* as our guide.[9] At that time we also decided that every 100-level course, regardless of population, would have the same core SLOs so that we could begin assessing learning across courses. These SLOs are
- Students will be able to develop a research process.
- Students will be able to demonstrate effective search strategies.

- Students will be able to evaluate information.
- Students will be able to develop an argument supported by evidence.

We assess our 100-level courses using signature assignments, which are collaboratively created assessments used to collect evidence for a specific learning outcome.[10] Faculty teaching the courses can use any kind of formative assessments, but they must use the signature assignments for summative assessment of each SLO. Each signature assignment is developed collaboratively, then piloted, improved, and finally implemented in each course. The Curriculum Committee analyzes the data and discusses needed improvements to the curriculum at a biannual assessment retreat held in May and December. See figure 38.1 for an example signature assignment.

The signature assignment for the SLO *Students will be able to develop a research process* is a concept map. Students map out a research process at the beginning of the semester and again at the end of the course. The purpose of the maps is to see change and growth in students' research process.

Pre-prompt:

Think about a time when you had to research something for school. How did you start your research process? Where did you go from there?

Map out the research process you personally follow from selecting a topic to turning in the final research project.

Post-prompt:

Take a few minutes to reflect on your research process. How has it changed based on the skills you've learned in this course? How has it stayed the same?

The signature assignment for the SLO Students will be able to develop a research process is a mind map. Students map out a research process at the beginning of the semester and again at the end of the course. The purpose of the maps is to see change and growth in students' research process .

Figure 38.1
Sample signature assignment for the SLO "Students will be able to develop a research process."

Role of the One-Shot

In terms of teaching hours, one-shots constitute less than 50 percent of the department's teaching time; 56 percent of our time is spent teaching credit courses. When looking at student numbers, we see the most students in one-shots. While we reach fewer students in credit courses, we have more time with them and cover more in-depth topics, so the impact may be larger. That said, one-shot instruction is important for our program and for the institution. One-shots taught in the CLIP are the first introduction to an academic library for most of these students. We take this very seriously and work carefully to develop lesson plans that will support students in writing their first college research papers.

Pedagogical Highlights

Collaboration is a key philosophy in ILUS. There is no lesson plan that has not been brainstormed with and reviewed by multiple department members. Seeking and giving critical feedback is part of the culture of ILUS that makes the department successful. In monthly development meetings, we focus on expanding our knowledge of theory and pedagogy through discussion and reflection. Each month we have an assigned reading selected by different department members. For our discussion we each bring main take-aways or questions to start the conversation. We then relate the reading to our practice, which leads to reflections of our practice and ultimately improvement. We also challenge each other's ideas and perspectives and learn from each other through these meetings.

Administrative Highlights

There are two specific aspects of ILUS's instructional offerings that have guided the department to sustained success. The first is that we offer only credit courses integrated into established programs, which means not worrying about course enrollment issues. The second is that we teach a standardized one-shot curriculum in the CLIP. When I speak with people at conferences about this program and I tell them to standardize their one-shot curriculum, they balk! They tell me that the librarians at their library want to do their own thing. I assure them that librarians in ILUS still maintain autonomy in the classroom. I also emphasize that standardizing curriculum helps to foster collaboration and effective pedagogy because we are working together to discuss assessment results and develop the curriculum. If your aim is to grow a successful, large-scale program that can continue to grow without causing librarian burnout, the biggest piece of advice I can give is to standardize curriculum and develop and assess that curriculum as a team.

Information Literacy Coordinator Profile

I began working at UNC in 2006 as an assistant professor and instruction librarian. When I arrived, the department consisted of three full-time faculty and one staff member. We offered library tours and taught CLIP 2 and 3. We had one open enrollment section of LIB 150 each semester, and each spring we taught LIB 150 for our TRIO program. Audiology and speech language pathology was the only major requiring an LIB course at that time, but there was not an audiology-specific course or section. Since 2007, I've been working with campus partners to build the credit program; expansion of the program began with the addition of LIB 160 and then LIB 151 and 251. In 2014 I was appointed interim head of the department, and in 2015 I was appointed permanently to the position.

The role of Head of Information Literacy & Undergraduate Support is a formal role that is parallel to the department chair role on our campus, except that the position does not rotate. In this role I coordinate all of the department's strategic initiatives, lead the department annual goal setting, evaluate faculty in the annual review process, supervise a full-time staff member, oversee the classroom scheduling, set the teaching schedule, oversee all assessment activities, and advocate for resources. Because this is a department head position and not a coordinator position, I also get to hire the faculty and staff in the department. While I do less one-shot teaching than other ILUS members, I have the same credit course load, which is typically three to four courses per person each academic year. The majority of my supervisory work is done through monthly department meetings, monthly one-on-one meetings, and teaching observations.

As the head of ILUS, I serve in two leadership positions in University Libraries. This position serves as chair of the Library Curriculum Committee overseeing curriculum development and assessment. I also serve on the Library Leadership Group along with seven other department heads and three deans. This group leads strategic planning for University Libraries.

What I Wish People Knew

An essential skill I had to develop quickly in this role is the ability to have difficult conversations. The major problem with learning this skill is that the only time you can practice is in the midst of a problem. I have a lot of difficult conversations, and they are all about different issues, such as instructor behavior in the classroom, position funding, perceived special treatment of other team members, and workload concerns. In each situation I've had to work with a different librarian, and I can say that there is not a one-way-fits-all approach to difficult conversations. You need to really know your team members as individuals to know how to approach a difficult topic. One way to build this knowledge about your team is to meet regularly. I've implemented bimonthly team meetings and monthly one-on-one meetings to make sure that I have face time with my team and that they have opportunities to meet as a group and also individually to discuss concerns. These meetings have provided each team member a candid forum to express their concerns. While addressing all their concerns may not be possible, it is important for the morale of the team that everyone's voice is heard.

I supervise faculty, which means along with helping new librarians do great work as liaisons and teachers, I also guide them as new faculty members through the annual faculty evaluation process and work with them to develop their service and scholarship. There is hidden labor in this work in terms of the amount of time I spend talking to new faculty about making choices related to service obligations and scholarship to ensure that they are successful in the evaluation, tenure, and promotion processes. This mentor role means that I must be open to anything from team members popping into my office to ask a quick question to engaged discussions regarding career decisions.

It may be surprising, but a significant amount of my time is spent on scheduling. I spend a lot of time working with our administrative staff member improving the scheduling system and regularly reviewing how requests come in and how people are using the request form in order to make the process as efficient as possible. Our most important relationships are with other campus schedulers who control the calendars for various labs on campus. Michener Library has two classrooms, and many times we need additional computer labs to meet instruction demands. It is important to have the right person in the role of library scheduler because this person will need to reach out to their colleagues throughout the academic year and work with them to ensure that we can do our work. If you and your scheduler do not work well together, it can mean disaster for your program and also disaster for relationships you've built across campus. The scheduler is sometimes the only person a faculty member will interact with during the scheduling process, so hire well.

Most importantly, a team mentality is crucial to success, and I've worked to build a culture of collaboration in this program. It's important to position yourself not just as team leader, but as a team member. While you may mandate some things as part of your position, in general it is best to let everyone bring ideas to the table. An example of this is through annual goal setting. Every summer, ILUS faculty and staff bring forth ideas; these are discussed and decided on as a team. This year I worked with the department chair of LRS to develop a video peer observation process for subject liaisons. I did mandate this as department goal because I know it's important for professional growth. Once we decide on the annual goals, each ILUS member, including our staff member, takes the lead on a goal and oversees the goal for the year, bringing on other department members to help as needed. This provides leadership experience for all department members and helps maintain a healthy workload for everyone. As a team member, I also take the lead on one or more annual goals. It is important that I'm doing the work of the department and not just overseeing the work of others.

Notes

1. See "Federal TRIO Programs—Home Page," Office of Postsecondary Education, US Department of Education, accessed November 26, 2019, https://www2.ed.gov/about/offices/list/ope/trio/index.html.
2. Note that this is just one-shot data for CLIP 1, 2, and 3. If subject-specific one-shots are included for all of University Libraries, the total number of one-shots in an academic year is approximately 340 sessions reaching approximately 8,300 students.
3. Lyda Fontes McCartin,, Brian Iannacchione, and Mary K. Evans "Student Perceptions of a Required Information Literacy Course on Their Success in Research and Writing Intensive Criminal Justice Courses," *Journal of Academic Librarianship* 43, no. 3 (2017): 242–47.
4. IRB approval was not sought for this internal assessment survey. Thus, direct quotes from the data are not shared.
5. Yvonne Nalani Meulemans and Allison Carr, "Not at Your Service: Building Genuine Faculty-Librarian Partnerships," *Reference Services Review* 41, no. 1 (2013): 80–90.
6. Lyda Fontes McCartin and Rachel Dineen, *Toward a Critical-Inclusive Assessment Practice for Library Instruction* (Sacramento: Library Juice Press, 2018), 37–38.
7. Lyda Fontes McCartin, Brianne Markowski, and Stephanie Evers, "Closing the Loop: Using Direct and Indirect Assessment of Student Learning to Inform Library Instruction" (presentation, Librarians' Information Literacy Annual Conference, Liverpool, UK, April 2018), https://www. lilacconference.com/events/2018/closing-the-loop-using-direct-and-indirect-assessment-of-student-learning-to-inform-library-instruction; McCartin and Dineen, *Toward a Critical-Inclusive Assessment Practice*, 66.
8. Brianne Markowski, Lyda Fontes McCartin, and Stephanie Evers, "Meeting Students Where They Are: Using Rubric-Based Assessment to Inform Information Literacy Curriculum," *Communications in Information Literacy* 12, no. 2 (2019):128–49.
9. Association of College and Research Libraries, *Framework for Information Literacy for Higher Education* (Chicago: Association of College and Research Libraries, 2016). For an overview of this process, see Andrea Falcone and Lyda McCartin, "Be Critical, but Be Flexible," *College and Research Libraries News* 79, no. 1 (2018), https://crln.acrl.org/index.php/crlnews/article/view/16859/18479
10. Ruth E. Cain, "Signature Assignments: Definitions and Characteristics," University of Missouri–Kansas City, last modified May 2019, https://online.umkc.edu/wp-content/uploads/2018/08/Signature-Assignments.pdf

Bibliography

Association of College and Research Libraries. *Framework for Information Literacy for Higher Education.* Chicago: Association of College and Research Libraries, 2016.

Cain, Ruth E. "Signature Assignments: Definitions and Characteristics." University of Missouri–Kansas City. Last modified May 2019. https://online.umkc.edu/wp-content/uploads/2018/08/Signature-Assignments.pdf

Falcone, Andrea, and Lyda McCartin. "Be Critical, but Be Flexible: Using the Framework to Facilitate Student Learning Outcome Development." *College and Research Libraries News* 79, no. 1 (2018). https://crln.acrl.org/index.php/crlnews/article/view/16859/18479.

Markowski, Brianne, Lyda Fontes McCartin, and Stephanie Evers. "Meeting Students Where They Are: Using Rubric-Based Assessment to Inform Information Literacy Curriculum." *Communications in Information Literacy* 12, no. 2 (2019): 128–49.

McCartin, Lyda Fontes, and Rachel Dineen. *Toward a Critical-Inclusive Assessment Practice for Library Instruction.* Sacramento: Library Juice Press, 2018.

McCartin, Lyda Fontes, Brian Iannacchione, and Mary K. Evans. "Student Perceptions of a Required Information Literacy Course on Their Success in Research and Writing Intensive Criminal Justice Courses." *Journal of Academic Librarianship* 43, no. 3 (2017): 242–47.

McCartin, Lyda Fontes, Brianne Markowski, and Stephanie Evers, "Closing the Loop: Using Direct and Indirect Assessment of Student Learning to Inform Library Instruction." Presentation, Librarians' Information Literacy Annual Conference, Liverpool, UK, April 2018. https://www.lilacconference.com/events/2018/closing-the-loop-using-direct-and-indirect-assessment-of-student-learning-to-inform-library-instruction.

Meulemans, Yvonne Nalani, and Allison Carr. "Not at Your Service: Building Genuine Faculty-Librarian Partnerships." *Reference Services Review* 41, no. 1 (2013): 80–90.

US Department of Education. "Federal TRIO Programs—Home Page." Office of Postsecondary Education. Accessed November 26, 2019. https://www2.ed.gov/about/offices/list/ope/trio/index.html.

Chapter 39

University of Maryland, Baltimore County

Building Relationships at a Public Research University

Joanna Gadsby and Katy Sullivan

Population Served

The University of Maryland, Baltimore County (UMBC), is a mid-sized public research university and is the third-largest institution in the twelve-member University System of Maryland. Fall 2018 enrollment included 11,260 undergraduate and 2,507 graduate students.[1] The campus is in a suburban location just outside of Baltimore, Maryland. UMBC serves a diverse student population, including a sizable number of international students (5% of undergraduate students and 24% of graduate students).[2] The first-year undergraduate population is nearly evenly split between freshmen and transfer students, with many of the transfer students coming from other Maryland universities or community colleges. Recognizing the diversity of student backgrounds and levels of experience using libraries, instruction librarians at UMBC work to design lesson plans and learning activities that provide opportunities for student learning and growth without requiring students to have previous experience with research. Within the classroom, librarians acknowledge that doing library research can be difficult and frustrating and encourage students to take an active and engaged role in their learning and development. At the UMBC library, we aspire to create a comfortable and inclusive environment that takes into account the varied backgrounds of our students and provides a place of learning for all of them.

Program Scope

Information Literacy Program

The instruction program is overseen by the library's Instruction Coordinator as well as the Head of Reference and Instruction. All of the librarians and staff in the Reference and Instruction department, including the Instruction Coordinator, report directly to the Head of Reference and Instruction. The Instruction Coordinator guides long-term planning and assessment projects, as well as professional development and mentoring for teaching librarians. In addition, the coordinator generally monitors instruction throughout the course of the semester and addresses any instruction-related issues that emerge.

In 2015, all teaching librarians worked collaboratively to develop a set of programmatic learning outcomes based on the ACRL *Framework for Information Literacy for Higher Education* to use as a guide for lesson planning.[3] We have been using these outcomes as a foundation for a curriculum map, which shows which learning goals are being taught in which departments at UMBC.

The library's instruction program provides instruction for both undergraduate and graduate courses, with a large majority of sessions scheduled for undergraduate classes. The program operates primarily on a liaison model, with each librarian taking responsibility for approximately six or seven academic departments. Within each department, the liaison librarian is aware of what is been taught across the information literacy curriculum, though we are at the beginning of the aforementioned curriculum mapping project to formalize this scaffolding process further. Across the different disciplines, there may be some content repetition related to basic library navigation skills, but this occurs less frequently in classes that are tailored to address a particular assignment.

Some academic departments require a heavier teaching load than others, and we try to regularly review the instruction statistics to ensure that each librarian has only one or two high-frequency departments. For some librarians and their liaison departments, this proves more problematic. Such is the case for our humanities librarian and the workload of English 100, the introductory composition course. English 100 is the main cornerstone class for the library's instruction program and represents our best opportunity to work with most undergraduate students. There is no required course that is common to every student. Many students test out of the English 100 course or transfer in credit, so it is also not a guaranteed contact point, but through it we still reach a significant number of students. Currently, the humanities librarian is responsible for the English department as well as five other academic departments. There are often between twenty-five and forty-five sections of English 100 taught each semester, though at this time, only twenty to twenty-five request instruction sessions. We are experimenting with different modes of library instruction that would make this a sustainable undertaking. For now, the humanities librarian teaches all of these classes, and we agreed to cap the number of sessions they would teach before asking other librarians to take some of these requests.

Liaison librarians usually do broad outreach to all instructors teaching courses during a given semester, with some emphasis on foundational or methods courses. Our established best practices ask teaching librarians to contact their departments each semester to encourage faculty to schedule library instruction sessions. Librarians send an email to departmental chairs or administrators and occasionally attend departmental meetings.

Currently, there is not a great demand for online sessions, but librarians will conduct virtual sessions upon request. When we do provide instruction online, it is typically through software available in Blackboard, the campus's learning management system. This is a potential area for growth, but since it is largely untested, librarians prefer to schedule in-person instruction when possible. In addition to in-class instruction, subject librarians provide support through research appointments, often scheduled through the library's website.

The library's instruction team also offers regular research-oriented workshops that are open to any UMBC student, staff member, or faculty member. These workshops focus on using citation management tools, designing research posters, conducting literature reviews, and other broad-based research topics. Additionally, our instruction program provides an extensive collection of video and text-based tutorials that can be used for asynchronous, point-of-need learning.

First Year Experience Program

The library instruction program is closely involved with the campus's first-year experience program, which includes smaller, discussion-based classes designed to orient new students to a university experience. New students are strongly encouraged by academic advisors to enroll in these one-to-three-credit courses, but they are not mandatory courses for any students. Librarians and administrators within the first-year experience program encourage instructors to schedule library instruction sessions for their classes, and in turn the library provides library orientation sessions, as described below, for many sections of these classes. There are several types of optional first-year experience classes offered on campus, and the library's orientation-style sessions are most commonly requested for Introduction to an Honors University, one-credit classes that are tied to a three-credit academic course. The goals of these one-credit courses focus on skills for academic success, campus resources, and career readiness. Separate sections of these classes are offered for both freshmen and transfer students.

The library's orientation sessions have different learning outcomes from the information literacy–focused instruction sessions. The learning outcomes are primarily centered on identifying different types of publications and how they might be used in research, as well as providing the students with an opportunity to navigate the library's layout. These sessions are currently taught by specialized staff and have a common lesson plan. Previously, they were divided up among the librarians according to liaison area.

First-Year Seminar

The first-year seminar is another type of course offered through the first-year experience program and is intended to provide a small class environment that focuses on a specific topic. When requested, we teach information literacy sessions focused on a particular assignment for these classes.

The authors proposed, designed, and now teach one of these first-year seminar courses, which are offered for three credits. These courses are not required for students but are among several types of small classes geared toward first-year students that are offered and encouraged during new student orientation. The enrollment is capped at twenty students, and there are usually five to ten first-year seminars offered each semester. The seminar we teach is titled The Information Diet, and it introduces students to many elements of information literacy, including the reflective discovery and critique of information and the ways information is produced and valued.

Operations

Reference and Instruction is its own department under the library's public services division, which also includes circulation and media as well as special collections. Teaching for the library's instruction program is primarily done by five reference librarians and one specialized reference staff person. Three to four additional librarians outside of the reference department provide instruction either as a subject librarian or as a special collections librarian. Subject assignments are sometimes tied directly to a position (a science librarian, for instance, is hired as a subject librarian for specific disciplines) and sometimes negotiated as staffing needs change. Overall, each subject librarian is responsible for providing service for approximately six to eight departments on campus. These responsibilities include providing all levels of library instruction (introductory classes through graduate classes), research consultations, and collection development.

The instruction program does not have a budget per se, but library administration has provided money from the overall budget for some increased staffing, as well as new furniture and technology for the library's classroom. The library's administration has supported small staffing increases as the number of instruction classes has increased. In one case, a part-time staff line was transferred from another department into the Reference and Instruction department to assist with desk and administrative work and to free up librarians to do more instruction. In another, when a nonteaching librarian left the library for another position, their position was converted to a teaching librarian position.

The goals of the library's instruction program mirror the language of the library's strategic plan, which includes a focus area for "Teaching and Learning." This section of the strategic plan has a specific goal to "Integrate information literacy into the UMBC curriculum" with supporting objectives that outline the need for robust staffing, library instructor development, and the promotion of course-integrated instruction.[4] Departmentally, Reference and Instruction chose to focus annual efforts on two components of the library's strategic plan, one of which is "Teaching and Learning." Together, we prioritized departmental projects that support the objectives outlined in the strategic plan. These projects range from creating greater partnerships (with the campus Writing Center, for example) to creating a library instruction best practices web page in order to create more timely and enriching instruction experiences.

Information literacy and library instruction are not specifically mentioned in the campus strategic plan, but information literacy is one of five functional competencies for the general education program on campus.

Marketing

At the start of each semester, subject librarians send emails to instructors in their disciplines encouraging them to incorporate library instruction sessions into their classes. These emails provide links to the instruction calendar and a form to submit an instruction request. These messages may go to all faculty teaching a course in that discipline at that time, as determined by the campus schedule of classes, or sometimes just faculty we have worked with in the past. Instruction librarians work hard to strike a balance between encouraging one-shot instruction sessions and ensuring that those sessions are scheduled in a way that the librarian can prepare meaningful material that is tied to the course content. In addition, subject librarians are heavily involved in campus service and shared governance committees and often use these relationships to network for the library and its instruction program. Librarians make a point of connecting with faculty at campus events and through requested participation in faculty meetings and retreats. Additionally, librarians give presentations at new faculty orientations in order to highlight the library instruction program.

Collaboration

Building relationships on campus is the most time-consuming, and also the most effective, method for librarians to help the instruction program grow. Staffing changes, within both the library's instruction program and academic departments, can greatly impact the program, as the close ties we develop with other departments are often based on strong relationships between one or two members within their staff. These relationships, built and strengthened over time, can't be quickly replaced. New librarians spend much of their first year meeting potential partners and cultivating relationships. This dependence on individual relationships is problematic for the program overall, and our librarians are always seeking new ways to form structural partnerships that won't fluctuate with staff turnover. One way we have found success has been to establish nonnegotiable curricular integration for information literacy workshops or instruction sessions that don't depend on staffing or relationships. In one department, the liaison librarian and a professor built a library session into a common syllabus for a new cornerstone course that was required for the major. Each semester, the class is taught by different professors, but they always schedule a library instruction session because the library's learning outcomes and content are included in the syllabus.

We aim to establish more partnerships that are structurally integrated within programs in order to maintain continuity despite staffing changes. Another example is a partnership with the Meyerhoff Scholars, a research-focused program that works to increase diversity in STEM fields.[5] Our science librarian meets with the first-year cohort as a whole to discuss foundational research skills and then scaffolds instruction for the second- and third-year cohorts by discipline. We also have a long-standing relationship with the McNair Scholars, another program that focuses on increasing research opportunities for first-generation college students and other underrepresented groups on campus.[6] For over ten years, librarians in our department have taught an eight-week course that is integrated into a research methods course required for each cohort of scholars. Due to recent changes in the program, we have been working with the McNair administrators on campus to move the library modules online so the scholars can complete them as prework for the research methods course instead.

The Humanities Librarian and a library services specialist in Reference and Instruction are working together to strengthen partnerships with the English Language Institute (ELI), the campus center for English as a Second Language, as well as the campus Writing Center, which is located in the library. They partner with ELI to provide library instruction for two levels of English language learning that the center offers. Each semester, they contact the instructors who are currently teaching and offer to work with students on website navigation and research skills. They are working with the Writing Center to provide training for writing tutors and to encourage referrals between the two campus units. This partnership has grown in recent months, and we are investigating whether this collaboration can be further integrated with the classes we teach for the first-year experience program and English 100.

For faculty and staff, instruction librarians have presented and conducted workshops about teaching and learning through the campus Faculty Development Center and the provost's Teaching and Learning Symposium. Primarily, we have discussed and demonstrated information literacy activities that can be customized for a variety of course content. Recent presentations at the symposium have included active demonstrations of teaching activities related to the ACRL *Framework for Information Literacy* and poster sessions that highlight our reflective teaching portfolios.

In 2018, the authors proposed and led a yearlong faculty learning community on campus that focused on cultivating critical thinking through course-integrated information literacy. This learning community investigated ways to introduce students to a reflective discovery and critique of information, an understanding of how information is produced and valued in our various disciplines, and an understanding of the use of information in creating new knowledge. Over the course of a year, the participants met to discuss issues related to information literacy in their classes. They worked to develop teaching activities or assessments that support students' abilities to critically evaluate information and in time will create workshops for other faculty on campus.

Assessment

For the most part, the library's instruction program has been left out of conversations surrounding assessment on our campus. Even though one of our university's functional competencies for general education is information literacy, there aren't many courses that choose this competency as a focus for their class. We have worked with the Academic Engagement and Transition Program on a smaller project to collect data from students participating in first-year experience courses. Students in these courses answer questions related to using the library on a pre- and posttest, and initial evaluation shows that students in these courses who have participated in library instruction are better prepared to answer these questions about the library. The questions focus on library services, building and website navigation, and basic source evaluation. The students' understanding of these answers helps us shape the way we teach these orientation sessions. We are also able to use this data to advocate for instructors to schedule a session for their students since we can point to evidence of student learning as compared to those who have not gone through the orientation.

Our instruction librarians are developing an assessment process that works for us. We can assume that we will eventually be asked to show the impact of our teaching and would like to develop strategies that make sense for our program. With that in mind, we are documenting our modes of assessment in an organized way so we may critically evaluate our teaching and how our students learn from it. In our classes, we often conduct formative assessment both to improve our teaching practices and to better understand how to help our students. We have hesitated to call this classroom assessment summative since we analyze only the learning done in our brief one-shot sessions and not how it is tied to a final project in the class. There may be opportunities in the future where we find this type of assessment appropriate, but currently, we think there are too many variables to untangle in order to directly tie library instruction to the outcomes of a particular project. We are focusing primarily on formative assessment to inform our reflective teaching practice.

We are also working to map our instruction sessions across the curriculum and align classes with the ACRL *Framework for Information Literacy*. We plan to focus each year on collecting a set of artifacts in the fall semester that show work toward a particular frame and analyzing those artifacts with a common rubric in the spring semester. Fall 2018 is the first semester for this project, which is based on the assessment plan used at University of Maryland, College Park.[7]

Role of the One-Shot

Currently, the one-shot is our main access point for students, and we haven't found a good way around this yet. There are some librarians who teach two-shots after negotiation with the course instructor. We recognize the limitations of this structure but maintain it primarily because we don't have the additional time and staffing needed to reimagine it.

Pedagogical Highlights

In 2015, our department wrote programmatic learning outcomes based on the ACRL *Framework for Information Literacy*, and we use these outcomes as a guide for structuring our teaching. As a group, we are moving toward more consistent use of active learning techniques and formative student assessment in the classroom. The program also has overarching instructional goals, and our classes focus primarily on helping students prepare for a particular research assignment (though we do see some classes for more generalized information literacy sessions). We compile general teaching activities that are tied to programmatic learning outcomes and use them to supplement assignment-driven sessions and provide content for those that aren't tied to an assignment. An example of a session that is not assignment-driven is taught for a 200-level psychology course that introduces students to the major. For that library session, the activities focus on reading magazine and newsletter articles that discuss psychological research. We analyze the language used to discuss the research in order to evaluate the findings and attempt to locate the original research study for comparison. These activities are designed to help students locate and evaluate psychological research, but also to think critically about sources they would be likely to encounter on social media or other news-related sites. In comparison, an example of instruction in a 400-level class in this major focuses on finding one particular journal article of high quality to use for a class presentation. The learning activities for this session focus on using specific tools and databases for evaluation metrics and ask students to draw on their own research experience to create criteria for determining quality.

Our community of practice takes the shape of the Information Literacy Working Group (ILWG), an optional committee for library workers involved with instruction, whose structure is modified based on ongoing projects. Recently, we restructured ILWG and formed task groups that focus on projects and report out at our general meetings. These task groups are periodically evaluated for need and will disband if a project has been completed. Our current task groups include Learning Objects, Instructor Development, Instruction Assessment, and Collaborative Outreach. Currently, the Instructor Development task group is focused on creating opportunities for learning and growth for librarians. In addition to teach-arounds and workshops, the instruction librarians have participated in a number of article discussion groups over the last few years and are currently developing a specific discussion series on topics related to critical librarianship.

The Instructor Development group also manages our fledgling peer coaching program, which is based on librarian and instruction coordinator Dale Vidmar's model.[8] We implemented peer coaching instead of having the coordinator conduct observations for all of the instruction librarians. Neither the coordinator nor the teaching librarians were particularly comfortable with conducting teaching observations, and they eventually decided this type of critique and feedback were also not very useful. We find that we learn more from one another using peer coaching. The instruction librarians are paired (or occasionally made into a trio if numbers are odd) and meet each semester to discuss a particular class in which they would like to implement a new strategy. After the pair discusses their goals and teaches the class, the pair meets again to reflect on how well they feel they met the goal. Our team has also used this structure when we do peer review for other learning objects, such as research guides. The pairs are rotated once a year to provide variety, and the librarians have given positive feedback for this model. We find it useful and enjoyable to work with a partner in a structured way, and it is helpful for people to focus on meeting their goals for the program in a low-stakes manner.

Administrative Highlights

Along with the learning outcomes, we have a departmental mission and goals that we revisit annually. We have started a reflective teaching portfolio program that houses teaching materials, student artifacts (for assessment and reflection), and instructor reflections for improvement. Ideally, the curriculum map, which lists the programmatic learning outcomes, will eventually link to all of the teaching portfolios for each class where those outcomes are taught and help us assess which concepts are being taught across the curriculum. The map also links to some general teaching activities that can be used for a class that is focusing on a particular frame.

Librarians schedule their own classes with a shared Google calendar that is assigned to the instruction room. Course instructors may email specific librarians to schedule an instruction session, but we encourage them to use the web-based form that was set up for that purpose. Once classes come in through the form, subject liaisons or designated library workers claim the classes and schedule them. In addition, we use LibCal for creating "office hours" during which students can schedule research appointments.

Our subject librarians teach classes in their assigned liaison departments. The exception to this rule are the classes from the first-year experience program, which aren't tied to a particular department. For these classes, we are fortunate to have a specialized staff position, and that person takes on the majority of these sessions. If there are classes they are unable to take, the instruction librarians divide up the responsibilities based on interest, availability, and how closely tied the class is to their liaison areas.

Information Literacy Coordinator Profile

As the current Instruction Coordinator, I (Joanna) was asked if I wanted to take on the associated responsibilities in addition to my regular job as a Reference and Instruction Librarian. Before this occurred, there was a long period of time when there wasn't any formal coordination outside of what the Head of Reference and Instruction did administratively. The department did not engage in a great deal of formal programmatic planning or pedagogical development. The role is official in both title and practice. However, there was no additional compensation or supervisory responsibilities with this role, only additional work responsibilities.

In my official position description, the coordination role is 40 percent of my job and is described as providing "leadership and vision for library instruction initiatives by planning, implementing, and assessing the library instruction program and services." The reference and instruction component is listed as 45 percent, and I still serve as a subject liaison for six academic departments. I also pick up classes that don't fall under a particular subject area. Before the department hired a specialized staff member for our first-year experience courses, I was teaching the bulk of those sessions as well.

What We Wish People Knew

Coordination is all about negotiating relationships with other people, often without any official supervisory authority or power. Relationship building is a necessary component of the work, not only with other teaching librarians, but also with library administration, academic faculty and staff, and campus administration. The coordinator position should be a leadership role with supervisory input since it is difficult to manage a program without also managing people. The hidden labor is often in the outreach, networking, and administrative housework that you constantly do to keep your program at the front of everyone's mind. Coordinators tend to exist as the face of their programs and are put in the position of advocating for structural integration of information literacy on campus.

Coordinators often get loaded up with additional teaching responsibilities because they are the people who are most comfortable or knowledgeable about teaching. This position also involves a lot of administrative work or housekeeping, as well as mentoring and helping your colleagues develop as teachers. This labor is difficult to quantify, and it takes a tremendous amount of time and emotional intelligence.

Notes

1. "Welcome to UMBC," University of Maryland, Baltimore County, accessed January 25, 2019, https://about.umbc.edu.
2. "Common Data Set." Institutional Research, Analysis and Decision Support, University of Maryland, Baltimore County, accessed January 25, 2019, https://oir.umbc.edu/university-data/common-data-set-cds; "Graduate School: At a Glance," University of Maryland, Baltimore County, accessed January 25, 2019, https://gradschool.umbc.edu/glance.
3. Association of College and Research Libraries, *Framework for Information Literacy for Higher Education* (Chicago: Association of College and Research Libraries, 2016).
4. "Strategic Plan: 2018–2023," Albin O. Kuhn Library and Gallery, University of Maryland, Baltimore County, accessed January 25, 2019, https://library.umbc.edu/admin/StrategicPlan2018.pdf.
5. "Meyerhoff Scholars Program," University of Maryland, Baltimore County, accessed January 25, 2019, https://meyerhoff.umbc.edu.
6. "McNair Scholars Program," University of Maryland, Baltimore County, accessed January 25, 2019, https://mcnair.umbc.edu.
7. Rachel Gammons and Lindsay Inge, "Using the ACRL Framework to Develop a Student-Centered Model for Program-Level Assessment," *Communications in Information Literacy* 11, no. 1 (2017): 168–84.
8. Dale J. Vidmar, "Reflective Peer Coaching: Crafting Collaborative Self-Assessment in Teaching," *Research Strategies* 20, no. 3 (2005): 135–48, https://doi.org/10.1016/j.resstr.2006.06.002.

Bibliography

Association of College and Research Libraries. *Framework for Information Literacy for Higher Education.* Chicago: Association of College and Research Libraries, 2016. Gammons, Rachel, and Lindsay Inge. "Using the ACRL Framework to Develop a Student-Centered Model for Program-Level Assessment." *Communications in Information Literacy* 11, no. 1 (2017): 168–84.

University of Maryland, Baltimore County. "Common Data Set." Institutional Research, Analysis and Decision Support. Accessed January 25, 2019. https://oir.umbc.edu/university-data/common-data-set-cds.

———. "Graduate School: At a Glance." Accessed January 25, 2019. https://gradschool.umbc.edu/glance.

———. "McNair Scholars Program." Accessed January 25, 2019. https://mcnair.umbc.edu.

———. "Meyerhoff Scholars Program." Accessed January 25, 2019. https://meyerhoff.umbc.edu.

———. "Strategic Plan: 2018–2023." Albin O. Kuhn Library and Gallery. Accessed January 25, 2019. https://library.umbc.edu/admin/StrategicPlan2018.pdf.

———. "Welcome to UMBC." Accessed January 25, 2019. https://about.umbc.edu.

Vidmar, Dale J. "Reflective Peer Coaching: Crafting Collaborative Self-Assessment in Teaching." *Research Strategies* 20, no. 3 (2005): 135–48. https://doi.org/10.1016/j.resstr.2006.06.002.

About the Authors

Amanda B. Albert is the Information Literacy Coordinator and director of the Instruction and Information Literacy Program at Washington University in St. Louis. She is also an adjunct instructor in the iSchool at Syracuse University. She holds an MSLIS from Syracuse University.

Amanda's current research interests include instructional design, assessment, and critical information literacy instruction. As a teacher, Amanda strives to reach the whole student, creating a safe space for students to explore challenging ideas and concepts. As a colleague, Amanda supports librarians as they enter into the classroom space, providing guidance in trying new teaching and assessment methods. She believes learning is best accomplished by doing, both as a student and as a teacher, and encourages reflective practice.

Veronica Arellano Douglas is the Instruction Coordinator at the University of Houston Libraries. She blogs at http://veronicaarellanodouglas.com and http://ACRLog.org and tweets as @arellanover.

Joshua M. Avery is the Group Leader for the Teaching and Outreach Group at Buswell Memorial Library, Wheaton College (IL). He holds degrees from the University of Cincinnati, Miami University, and the University at Albany, State University of New York.

Kathrine C. Aydelott is Information Literacy Librarian and Head of Research and Learning Services at Dimond Library at the University of New Hampshire. A loyal New Englander, she has a BA degree from Colby College in her native Maine, a doctorate in English from the University of Connecticut, and an MLIS from Simmons in Massachusetts. She has published and presented on information literacy, assessment, gamification, and genealogy. She and her husband enjoy hiking and their three small dogs.

Courtney Baron is an Assistant Professor and Director of the Bridwell Art Library at the University of Louisville. Previously, she was the Head of Library Teaching and Outreach Services at Emory University's Oxford College campus. In this role, she led the Research Practices and Events teams and coordinated the information literacy instruction program and outreach initiatives for the Oxford College Library. She received her Bachelor of Arts dual degree in Classical Archaeology and Latin from the University of Georgia and a Master of Library and Information Science degree from Valdosta State University. Baron's research interests include art librarianship, feminist pedagogy, visual literacy, and game-based learning.

Jennifer Beach is the Research and Instructional Services Librarian, and an Assistant Professor, at Longwood University (Farmville, VA). She holds a bachelor of arts degree in English from St. Mary's College of Maryland and a master of science in library science degree from the University of North Carolina, Chapel Hill. Her career spans service in public libraries, state libraries, and academia. Prior to her appointment at Longwood, Jennifer served as the Director of the Cumberland County Public Library (VA) from 2011 to 2016. Jennifer lives with her family in Farmville and spends her free time kayaking its beautiful waterways.

Stefanie R. Bluemle is research and instruction librarian; library liaison to the humanities division (departments of history, philosophy, and religion); and coordinator of the information literacy instruction program at Augustana College in Illinois. She has published and presented on performance-based assessment, collaborations between information literacy programs and special collections, and the intersection of information literacy with national politics.

Andrea Brooks is an assistant professor and information literacy coordinator at Northern Kentucky University. Her current research interests include examining dispositional characteristics related to information literacy and considering how information literacy is situated within the broad academic library structure. Andrea earned her MLIS from Kent State University and an MA in communication from NKU.

Rosalind Bucy is a research and instruction librarian at the University of Nevada, Reno, where she is the liaison librarian to the humanities. Rosalind teaches information literacy to students at all levels, with a special focus on information literacy in first-year composition.

Becky Canovan coordinates and is an active participant in both the information literacy and reference teams as the Assistant Director of Public Services at the University of Dubuque in Iowa. She coleads an annual statewide IL-focused professional development workshop. She also scratches her creative itch by designing and installing themed displays and doing reader's advisory at her library.

Allison Carr currently serves as the Director of the Faculty Center with a dual appointment as the Academic Transitions Librarian at California State University San Marcos. Her current area of research is centered around the sense of belonging of transfer students, but she has also published about the teacher identity of academic librarians and the student-scholar identity of undergraduate students. She has a master of library and information science from San José State University.

Dani Brecher Cook is the Director of Teaching and Learning at the University of California, Riverside, Library. She is the coauthor of *Learner-Centered Pedagogy: Principles and*

Practice (with Kevin Michael Klipfel). Dani holds an MSLS from the University of North Carolina, Chapel Hill, and an AB in English literature from the University of Chicago. She is currently completing a master's degree in research, evaluation, measurement, and statistics from UCR's Graduate School of Education. You can find her on Twitter as @ danibcook.

Jenny Dale is an associate professor and Information Literacy Coordinator at UNC Greensboro University Libraries in Greensboro, North Carolina. In addition to coordinating information literacy programs and supervising two first-year instruction librarians, she serves as a liaison to communication studies, English, media studies, and women's and gender studies. She has also taught both undergraduate and graduate courses in the library and information studies department at UNC Greensboro. She holds an MS in library science from UNC Chapel Hill.

Elsa De Jong is an adjunct faculty member in the University of Nevada, Reno, Department of English and a former library instructor at the Matthewson-IGT Knowledge Center. Her interests include designing active learning strategies for the classroom and creating online instruction modules using learning management systems.

Tim Dolan has worked at Greenfield Community College since 2015, and in addition to instruction he works in the areas of open access, open education, and scholarly communication issues. Tim holds an MA in ethnomusicology from Indiana University and an MSLIS from Simmons College. He is currently the vice president of the campus's faculty-staff union chapter, serves on the college's Curriculum and Academic Policy Committee, and is a member of ACRL's Research and Scholarly Environment Committee.

Karen Doster-Greenleaf is the student success librarian at Georgia State University and a liaison to the English department for Perimeter College. As the Librarian for Student Success, she leads GSU Libraries' instruction initiatives to support first- and second-year student success. Karen holds a master of science in library and information studies and a bachelor of arts in literature from Florida State University. Her current research interests focus on the impact of library services on undergraduate academic success and retention and the use of performative-based assessment in library instruction.

Andrea Falcone is the Dean of the Library at Northern Kentucky University and former Associate Director for Education and Public Services at the Auraria Library, a tri-institutional library serving the University of Colorado Denver, Metropolitan State University of Denver, and the Community College of Denver. She was responsible for envisioning and managing information services that enhance research within and across disciplines, including academic success in and beyond the classroom. Since 2013, she has been a presenter for the ACRL RoadShow Planning, Assessing and Communicating Library Impact: Putting the Standards for Libraries in Higher Education into Action. Andrea is also the editor of the Beta Phi Mu *Scholars Series* published by Rowman and Littlefield and is the column editor for "Perspectives on Public Services," which appears in *International Information and Library Review*.

Sarah E. Fancher is the Library Director at Ozarks Technical Community College; she holds an MS from the University of Illinois. Her research interests include leadership, organizational change, and information literacy. She can be reached at fanchers@otc.edu.

Joanna Gadsby is the Instruction Coordinator as well as a reference and instruction librarian at the Albin O. Kuhn Library and Gallery at the University of Maryland, Baltimore County (UMBC). With her coauthor, she teaches a first-year seminar related to information literacy and coleads a faculty learning community on the same topic. Her research interests include critical and constructivist pedagogies, librarian and teacher identity, and gendered labor in librarianship. She is currently coediting a book called *Deconstructing Service in Libraries*.

Elizabeth Galoozis is Head of Information Literacy at the University of Southern California Libraries, where she focuses on integrating information literacy throughout the curriculum. Her research interests include critical information literacy, feminist pedagogy, and identity in the library workplace. Her work has appeared in the *Library Quarterly*, *In the Library with the Lead Pipe*, Library Juice Press, and ACRL and LOEX conferences.

Carolyn Caffrey Gardner is the information literacy coordinator at California State University, Dominguez Hills. After completing her MLS from Indiana University Bloomington, Gardner worked as an instruction librarian at University of Wisconsin–Superior and then University of Southern California, where she focused on the intersections of first-year writing programs and information literacy instruction. Her research interests include critical pedagogy and assessment, peer-to-peer scholarly resource sharing through social media, and information literacy program structures.

Vicki Gruzynski is Teaching and Learning Librarian at Worcester State University, where she has worked since 2016. Her main liaison duties include the First-Year Seminar program, women's studies, world languages, education, and the Intensive English Language Institute. She served as vice president and president of the Association of College and Research Libraries New England Chapter from 2017 to 2019. From Fall 2019 through Spring 2022, she is serving as the Director of Women's, Gender, and Sexuality Studies for the campus, in addition to her librarian role. Her professional and research interests include critical information literacy, open educational resources, leadership, and gender in the profession. She holds a master of library science and a master of arts in Latin American and Caribbean Studies from Indiana University in Bloomington.

Rebecca Halpern is the Undergraduate Engagement Team Leader at The Claremont Colleges Library. After spending several years as a subject librarian at the University of Southern California, Rebecca wanted to use her facilitation, strategic planning, and teaching skills to coordinate an instruction program. At The Claremont Colleges, she supervises a team of teaching librarians and oversees the first-year instruction and outreach programs. Her research interests are in antiracist pedagogy and management, critical librarianship, and ethnographic methodologies.

Jane Hammons served as Instructional Services Librarian at Northern Kentucky University from 2014 to 2018. Her research is focused on the ways in which faculty programming can support the integration of information literacy into the curriculum. Jane has an MS in library and information science from the University of Illinois at Urbana-Champaign and an MS in instructional design from Western Kentucky University and is currently employed in the University Libraries at the Ohio State University.

Liza Harrington is the Coordinator of Library Services at Greenfield Community College, having been hired as a librarian in 2011. Her primary responsibilities are around reference and instruction, but she also coordinates the information literacy program and serves on a variety of college-wide committees and initiatives, including cochairing the college's 2020 accreditation self-study process. She has an MSLIS from Simmons College, participated in the ACRL Immersion Program Teacher Track in July 2012, and was in the first cohort of the ACRL Assessment in Action program in 2014. She also serves on a variety of ACRL committees.

Chelsea Heinbach works to create meaningful learning experiences for undergraduate students new to the University of Nevada, Las Vegas. Chelsea is a cofounder and editor of the Librarian Parlor (#libparlor), a community for librarians interested in conducting research. Her research interests include critical pedagogy, strengths-based approaches to students, and the intersection between civic engagement and information literacy education.

Leslie Hurst is the Head of Teaching and Learning and the literature and humanities liaison at the Campus Library, serving Cascadia College and the University of Washington Bothell. In addition to information literacy program design and management, Leslie's research interests include library and student learning assessment.

McKenzie Hyde is a library teaching assistant at Utah State University. McKenzie leads instruction for first- and second-year composition courses. Prior to working in the library, McKenzie was a graduate instructor for English composition at Utah State University. McKenzie received her MA in English from Utah State University and her BA in English from Brigham Young University-Idaho.

Anaya Jones was the Information Literacy Librarian at Mary Baldwin University in Staunton, Virginia, from January 2014 through November 2018. She has experience teaching information literacy in physical classrooms and online and is interested in teaching information literacy in innovative ways at scale. Anaya earned her MLIS from Drexel University and is currently an eLearning Librarian at Southern New Hampshire University. She can be reached at r.jones2@snhu.edu. Mary Baldwin librarians can be reached at ask@marybaldwin.edu.

Denise Kane is an instruction librarian at California State University San Marcos. She has a master of library and information science from San José State University and a master of arts in history from California State University San Marcos.

Don LaPlant has served as Instructional Design Librarian at SUNY Cobleskill's Van Wagenen Library since 2015. He earned his MS in information sciences from the University of Tennessee in Knoxville.

Michael LaMagna currently serves as the Information Literacy Program and Library Services Coordinator, associate professor, and reference librarian with liaison responsibilities to the Science, Technology, Engineering, and Mathematics (STEM) division at Delaware County Community College. Previously, Michael served as the Coordinator of Electronic Resources at Cabrini College (now University). Michael received his EdD in higher education administration from Northeastern University, master of library science from St. John's University, master of arts in history from Villanova University, and bachelor of arts in history from Susquehanna University. Michael publishes and presents on e-books, open educational resources, digital badges, information literacy, and synchronous online instruction.

Sarah Leadley is Director of the University of Washington Bothell and Cascadia College Campus Library and Associate Dean of University of Washington Libraries. Sarah's research interests include social justice work in academic libraries and leadership development.

Gina Kessler Lee is an associate librarian and the library's Instruction and Outreach Coordinator at Saint Mary's College of California in the San Francisco Bay area. She received her MLIS from the University of Washington.

Claire Lobdell is the Distance Education Librarian and Archivist at Greenfield Community College. Prior to coming to GCC in 2017, she worked as the Archivist and Museum Educator at Wood Memorial Library and Museum in South Windsor, Connecticut, for which she wrote a book, *South Windsor*, part of the Images of America series. She was part of the inaugural 2018 cohort of the Library Freedom Institute and frequently leads workshops and trainings about digital privacy issues. She cochairs the college's Student Development Committee, is a member of the ACRL Instruction Section Building Virtual Community Task Force, and has a MSLIS from Simmons College.

Sarah H. Mabee holds an MS from the University of Illinois and an MA from the University of Oregon. She is currently the Instruction Librarian at Ozarks Technical Community College in Springfield, Missouri. Her research interests include media literacy and patron privacy. She can be reached at mabees@otc.edu.

Talitha Matlin is the STEM Librarian at California State University San Marcos. She received her master of library and information science from San José State University, a bachelor of arts in linguistics and communication from UC San Diego, and is currently pursuing a master's degree in learning, design, and technology from San Diego State University. Her research interests focus on applying instructional design methodologies to nontraditional instructional settings.

Lyda Fontes McCartin served as the Head of Information Literacy and Undergraduate Support at the University of Northern Colorado from 2014-2019 where she led a team of innovative librarians who are recognized as an ACRL Information Literacy Best Practices Exemplary Program in Pedagogy. She is currently the Interim Director of The Center for the Enhancement of Teaching and Learning at the University of Northern Colorado where she oversees faculty development initiatives around pedagogy and assessment. Lyda earned her MA in history and her MLIS from the University of Alabama in Tuscaloosa.

She has presented on assessment of student learning at state, national, and international conferences. Her current research agenda includes academic librarian behavior, critical information literacy, inclusive pedagogies, and d assessment of student learning.

Kitty McNeill is the Dean of the Library at Oxford College of Emory University. McNeill received her bachelor of science from Winthrop College and a master of librarianship degree from Emory University. She attained a doctor of philosophy degree from Simmons College in May 2017. The title of her dissertation is "Leadership Influence to Transform Organizational Cultures." Kitty completed the ACRL/Harvard Leadership Institute in August 2000. She is a 2006 Peabody College Library Leadership Fellow and a 2007 Frye Institute Fellow. In September 2013, she received the Honorary Alumna Award from the Oxford College Alumni Board.

Tati Mesfin is a library instructor at the University of Nevada, Reno. Her interests include information literacy, peer-to-peer research assistance, and promoting library resources and instruction related to diversity, equity, and inclusion.

Yvonne Nalani Meulemans is the Head of Teaching and Learning at California State University San Marcos. She has done research on establishing librarian-faculty partnerships, teaching theories in reference, and learning activities that make use of threshold concept theory. Her current research focuses on threshold concept theory as a tool for student reflection and as an inclusive pedagogy. She earned tenure in 2008 and promotion to librarian in 2014. She has a master's of library and information science from University of Hawai'i.

Stephanie Michel has been a reference/instruction librarian and the Instruction Coordinator at the University of Portland Clark Library since 2002. She is interested in instructional pedagogies, web design, and user experience. She has a master of library science from Indiana University Bloomington. She can be reached at michel@up.edu.

Suchi Mohanty is the head of the R. B. House Undergraduate Library, part of the University Libraries at the University of North Carolina at Chapel Hill. She leads a dynamic team offering 24-hour service, student-centered learning spaces, information and digital literacy programs, and print and media collections. Suchi works closely with campus partners to offer programming to foster information literacy development through co-curricular programming, most recently piloting the popular Adulting 101 series.

Lalitha Nataraj is an instruction and reference librarian at California State University San Marcos. Her professional interests and research include feminist pedagogy, critical information literacy, South Asians in librarianship, first-year experience, and scholarly inquiry and the research cycle. She earned a master of library and information science from UCLA and a bachelor of arts in English literature and women's studies from UC Berkeley.

Ellen Neufeld is the Deputy Director of the Oxford College Library. She has been responsible for a variety of different teams and projects since joining the Oxford Library in 2005, including overseeing annual exhibits and events, systems, collection development, and research practices.

She received a BS in journalism from the University of Tennessee, and an MS in library science from the University of North Texas, where she was an Institute of Museum and Library Services/Emory University/University of North Texas/Atlanta University Center Librarians for the Digital Age Scholar and Grant Recipient (Laura Bush 21st Century Librarian IMLS Grant). Neufeld completed the ACRL/Harvard Leadership Institute in August 2015 and recently completed emotional intelligence, design thinking, and leading and inspiring change programs with Emory Executive Education at the Goizueta Business School.

Benjamin Oberdick is the Head of Teaching and Learning at the Michigan State University Libraries, where he leads a team responsible for teaching information literacy sessions for students in a first-year writing class. Ben earned an MLIS from UNC Greensboro, an MA in education from Michigan State University, and a BS in elementary education from Millersville University of Pennsylvania.

Judith Opdahl is an instruction and reference librarian at California State University San Marcos. Her current research interests include using visual indicators in learning management systems to improve motivation of first-year students and building business information literacy in business undergraduates. She has an master of library and information science from San José State University and a bachelor of arts in speech: interpersonal and organizational communication from California State University, Long Beach.

Amy Pajewski is the Student Success Librarian and assistant professor at West Chester University and former Student Outreach Librarian at Paul Smith's College. She received her MSLS from Clarion University of Pennsylvania, and her current research examines the intersections between campus partnerships, information literacy pedagogy, and high-impact practices that foster student success. She can be contacted at apajewski@wcupa.edu

Kim Pittman is Head of Research & Learning at the University of Minnesota Duluth. She is a cofounder and former cochair of the Minnesota Library Association Instruction Roundtable (IRT) and a presenter for the ACRL-licensed workshop Engaging with the ACRL Framework: A Catalyst for Exploring and Expanding Our Teaching Practices. With Amy Mars and Trent Brager, Kim helped develop https://23frameworkthings.wordpress. com, an online professional development program which was recognized with the 2018 ACRL Instruction Section Innovation Award. She holds a master's in library and information studies from the University of Wisconsin-Madison.

Jessica Robinson is the Director of Library Finance and Operations at Oxford College of Emory University. Jessica received a bachelor of business administration in marketing from Valdosta State University and a master of science in library science from the University of Alabama. She started working at the Oxford College Library in 2007, and her responsibilities include being Student Employee Team Leader, personal librarian to thirty-plus faculty members in various disciplines, and member of the leadership team. In 2018, she completed Emory University's Essentials of Leadership program.

Dory Rosenberg is a reference and instruction librarian at Utah State University. In addition to serving as the library liaison for the English and psychology departments, Dory is the USU Libraries' English Composition Library Instruction Program Coordinator. Dory received her MLIS at the University of Pittsburgh, an MA in English with a graduate certificate in women's studies at Kansas State University, and a BA in English and women's studies from University of Kansas.

Dani Rowland is the Assistant Head of Teaching and Learning, American and Ethnic Studies liaison, and First-Year Experience Coordinator at the University of Washington Bothell and Cascadia College Campus Library. Dani's research and organizing interests include critical pedagogy, anti-racist education, and prison abolition.

Jane Scott is the Head of Public Services at the University of Portland Clark Library. She is interested in student learning, undergraduate research, library ethics, and user services in academic libraries. She has a master of library science from Emporia State University. She can be reached at scottj@up.edu.

Carolyn Seaman is the instruction librarian at Saddleback College in Mission Viejo, California. She holds an MLIS from San José State University, a single subject teaching credential, and a BA in English literature from California State University, Long Beach. Carolyn's academic interests include equity and culturally responsive teaching. She teaches the online course, LIB2 Honors: Advanced Information Competency and Online Searching. Prior to becoming a librarian, she was a language arts middle school teacher and an online course developer for University of California, Irvine Extension.

Heidi Senior has been a reference/instruction librarian at the University of Portland Clark Library since 1997. Her research interests include assessment practices and research methodology design, as well as student research behavior and program development. She has a master of library and information science from University of Washington. She can be reached at senior@up.edu.

Diane Sotak has been a reference/instruction librarian at the University of Portland Clark Library since 2001. She is interested in student success, instructional pedagogies, and library marketing. She has a master of library science from Syracuse University. She can be reached at sotak@up.edu.

Kaitlin Springmier is the Instruction and Learning Assessment Librarian at Sonoma State University, where she has worked since 2017 coordinating and assessing the library's instruction program and serving as liaison to the Sonoma State's School of Business and Economics. Prior to Sonoma, she was the Resident Librarian for Online Learning at the University of Chicago. She has a master's of library and information science from the University of Wisconsin-Madison and a bachelor's in English literature from the University of Georgia. Her research interests include inclusive pedagogy, instructional design and assessment, and organizational climate and culture. She can be reached at kaitlin.springmier@sonoma.edu.

Katie Strand is the First-Year Experience Librarian at Utah State University, where she also previously served as a Composition Teaching Assistant for three years. Her primary role is coordinating the library's first-year programming efforts, including the face-to-face and online composition program, first-year orientation, and other first-year partnerships. Along with her first-year focus, Katie also serves as the library liaison to the Watershed Sciences and Wildland Resources departments. Katie received her MLS from Emporia State University and her BA in English from Idaho State University.

Katy Sullivan is Head of Reference and Instruction at the Albin O. Kuhn Library and Gallery at the University of Maryland, Baltimore County (UMBC). She also serves as a social sciences subject librarian providing library instruction, collection development, and faculty and student support. At UMBC, she co-teaches a first-year seminar that introduces students to the reflective discovery and critique of information and the understanding of how information is produced and valued. She and her co-instructor also facilitate a faculty learning community on the topic. She is a longtime member of the American Library Association, the Association of College and Research Libraries, and the Maryland Library Association.

Rayla E. Tokarz is the Information Literacy Librarian at the University of Nevada, Reno. Her current role includes supporting the library's efforts to integrate information literacy into the curriculum and developing and extending the library's e-learning initiatives.

Michelle Toth is an instruction librarian at SUNY Plattsburgh. Her professional focus is on active learning, student-centered and student-directed learning, and assessment. She has an MLS from Indiana University. She also received a Fulbright scholarship and attended the University of Toronto as part of her graduate work. She is an alumna of both the teacher track and assessment track of the ACRL Immersion program.

Cathy Troupos is the librarian for instruction at Buswell Memorial Library, Wheaton College (IL). She holds degrees from Cedarville University, the University of Cincinnati, and Drexel University.

David Vrooman is the information literacy librarian at Eastern Connecticut State University in Willimantic, Connecticut. He is currently the chair of the university's Liberal Arts Program Committee, which oversees the general education curriculum. He has presented at conferences on several of his academic interests, including evaluating online resources, predatory publications, fake news, and storytelling. David received his MLS from Southern Connecticut State University. He also holds an MA in education and a BA in English, both from the University of Connecticut.

Susan Wainscott is the engineering liaison librarian serving a college with 950 undergraduates, 160 graduate students and 155 faculty and staff. Her research interests include how librarians can use information literacy threshold concepts in reference and collections work, as well as the role of student affect on learning information literacy skills.

Elizabeth A. Webster is the librarian for education and children's and young adult literature at Michigan State University. She earned her MLIS at Wayne State University and an MA in teaching from the School of International Training in Brattleboro, Vermont.

Tessa Withorn is the online learning librarian and liaison for health sciences and nursing at California State University, Dominguez Hills. Tessa received a master of library science degree from Indiana University Bloomington (2017) and a bachelor of arts in English from the University of Louisville (2015).

Conrad M. Woxland is a Reference and Instruction Librarian and works with graduate students in the counseling, education, and leadership departments at Saint Mary's College of California in the San Francisco Bay area. He graduated with an MLIS from the University of Wisconsin–Madison.

Lijuan Xu (Ms.) is the Associate Director of Research and Instructional Services at Lafayette College in Easton, Pennsylvania. Prior to joining Lafayette, she was a user education librarian at SUNY Albany. At Lafayette, Xu leads the library's IL program by focusing on faculty-librarian IL partnerships, assignment design, and IL pedagogy, areas on which she has presented and published. Her coauthored book with Trudi Jacobson, *Motivating Students in Information Literacy Classes*, was the winner of the 2005 ACRL Instruction Section's Publication of the Year Award (now the Ilene F. Rockman Instruction Publication of the Year Award). The article she coauthored with Nestor Gil, "Librarians as Co-teachers and Curators: Integrating Information Literacy in a Studio Art Course at a Liberal Arts College," was selected by the ALA Library Instruction Round Table as one of the top twenty instruction articles in 2017.